The Washington Lobby

THIRD EDITION

**Timely Reports to Keep
Journalists, Scholars and the Public
Abreast of Developing Issues, Events and Trends**

October 1979

CONGRESSIONAL QUARTERLY
1414 22ND STREET, N.W., WASHINGTON, D.C. 2003

Congressional Quarterly Inc.

Congressional Quarterly Inc., an editorial research service and publishing company, serves clients in the fields of news, education, business and government. It combines specific coverage of Congress, government and politics by Congressional Quarterly with the more general subject range of an affiliated service, Editorial Research Reports.

Congressional Quarterly was founded in 1945 by Henrietta and Nelson Poynter. Its basic periodical publication was and still is the CQ *Weekly Report,* mailed to clients every Saturday. A cumulative index is published quarterly.

The CQ *Almanac,* a compendium of legislation for one session of Congress, is published every spring. *Congress and the Nation* is published every four years as a record of government for one presidential term.

Congressional Quarterly also publishes paperback books on public affairs. These include the twice-yearly *Guide to Current American Government* and such recent titles as *The Middle East: U.S. Policy, Israel, Oil and the Arabs, Fourth Edition; Energy Policy;* and *Inside Congress, Second Edition.*

CQ Direct Research is a consulting service that performs contract research and maintains a reference library and query desk for the convenience of clients.

Editorial Research Reports covers subjects beyond the specialized scope of Congressional Quarterly. It publishes reference material on foreign affairs, business, education, cultural affairs, national security, science and other topics of news interest. Service to clients includes a 6,000-word report four times a month bound and indexed semiannually. Editorial Research Reports publishes paperback books in its fields of coverage. Founded in 1923, the service merged with Congressional Quarterly in 1956.

Editor: John L. Moore.
Major Contributors: Robert E. Healy, Margaret Thompson.
Contributors: Irwin B. Arieff, Alan Berlow, Rhodes Cook, Harrison H. Donnelly, Alan Ehrenhalt, Edna Frazier, Al Gordon, Martha V. Gottron, Gail Gregg, Mark Gruenberg, Barry M. Hager, Sari Horwitz, Charles W. Hucker, Larry Light, Bob Livernash, David M. Maxfield, Lynda McNeil, Ann Pelham, David E. Rosenbaum, Judy Sarasohn, Pat Towell.
Index: Diane Huffman.
Art Director: Richard Pottern. **Staff Artist:** Gwendolyn Hammond.
Production Manager: I. D. Fuller. **Assistant Production Manager:** Maceo Mayo.
Book Department Editor: Patricia Ann O'Connor.

Copyright 1979 by Congressional Quarterly Inc.
1414 22nd Street, N.W., Washington, D.C. 20037

Cover Photo: Steven Karafyllakis.

Library of Congress Cataloging in Publication Data

Congressional Quarterly, inc.
   The Washington lobby.

   Bibliography: p.
   Includes index.
   1. Lobbying — Law and legislation — United States. 2. Lobbying. I. Title.
KF4948.Z9C6   1979   328.73'07'8   79-19957
ISBN 0-87187-178-5

Table of Contents

Editor's Note

The Washington Lobby, Third Edition, expands and updates Congressional Quarterly's comprehensive paperback on lobbying, which was first published in 1971 and revised in a second edition in 1974.

New introductory material in the Third Edition provides a compact history of lobbying and federal efforts to regulate it, including recent congressional action on proposals to tighten those laws and disclose more information about pressure group activities and spending.

This new edition also looks at the White House lobby staff, which gained in proficiency after being blamed for some of President Carter's difficulties with Congress in the early days of his administration. The presidential lobby section includes chapters on executive branch lobbying, the selling of the Panama Canal and SALT II treaties, and the White House campaign to win passage of the natural gas pricing bill.

The lobbying and politics section traces the explosive growth of corporate political action committees (PACs), showing how much they and their labor counterparts spent in the 1978 congressional elections. Also provided are chapters on lobby and campaign finance reform bills, and on pressure group ratings of members of Congress.

Major business and labor lobbies are profiled, as well as public interest lobbies, and lobbies at work on specific issues. With lobbying by foreign interests taking on more importance in Congress, a new chapter tells how the Foreign Agents Registration Act works and recounts the congressional investigations into illicit Korean lobbying. Other foreign interest groups examined are the Arab, Israel and Taiwan lobbies.

Introduction

The Washington Lobby: A Vital Part of the Legislative Process

Of all the pressures on Congress, none has received such widespread publicity and yet is so dimly understood as the role of Washington-based lobbyists and the groups they represent. The popular image of a rotund agent for special interests buying up members' votes is a vast over-simplification. The role of today's lobbyist is far more subtle, his or her techniques more refined.

Lobbyists and lobby groups have played an increasingly active part in the modern legislative process. The corps of Washington lobbyists has grown markedly since the 1930s, in line with the expansion of federal authority into new areas and with the huge increase in federal spending. The federal government has become a tremendous force in the life of the nation, and the number of fields in which changes in federal policy may spell success or failure for special interest groups has been greatly enlarged. Thus commercial and industrial interests, labor unions, ethnic and racial groups, professional organizations, citizen groups and representatives of foreign interests — all from time to time and some continuously — have sought by one method or another to exert pressure on Congress to attain their legislative goals.

The pressure usually has selfish aims — to assert rights or to win a special privilege or financial benefit for the group exerting it. But in other cases the objective may be disinterested — to achieve an ideological goal or to further a group's particular conception of the national interest.

Lobbying: Pros and Cons

It is widely recognized that pressure groups, whether operating through general campaigns designed to sway public opinion or through direct contacts with members of Congress, perform some important and indispensable functions. Such functions include helping to inform both Congress and the public about problems and issues, stimulating public debate, opening a path to Congress for the wronged and needy, and making known to Congress the practical aspects of proposed legislation — whom it would help, whom it would hurt, who is for it and who against it. The spinoff from this process is considerable technical information produced by research on legislative proposals.

Against benefits to the public that result from pressure activities, critics point to certain serious liabilities. The most important is that in pursuing their own objectives the pressure groups are apt to lead Congress into decisions that benefit the pressure group but that do not necessarily serve other parts of the public. A group's power to influence legislation often is based less on its arguments than on the size of its membership, the amount of financial and manpower resources it can commit to a legislative pressure campaign and the astuteness of its representatives.

Origins of Lobbying

Representatives of special interests haunted the environs of the First Continental Congress, but the word "lobby" was not recorded until 1808 when it appeared in the annals of the 10th Congress. By 1829 the term "lobby-agents" was applied to favor-seekers at the state capitol in Albany, N.Y. By 1832 it had been shortened to "lobbyist" and was in wide use at the U.S. Capitol. [1]

Although the term had not yet been coined, the right to "lobby" was made implicit by the First Amendment to the

Constitution, which provided that "Congress shall make no law . . . abridging the freedom of speech or of the press; or the right of the people peaceably to assemble and to petition the Government for redress of grievances." Among the Founding Fathers, only James Madison expressed concern over the dangers posed by pressure groups. In *The Federalist* (No. 10), Madison warned against the self-serving activities of the "factions."

"Among the numerous advantages promised by a well-constructed union," he wrote, "none deserves to be more accurately developed than its tendency to break and control the violence of faction. . . . By a faction, I understand a number of citizens, whether amounting to a majority or minority of the whole, who are united and actuated by some common impulse of passion, or of interest, adverse to the rights of other citizens, or to the permanent and aggregate interests of the community." A strong federal government, Madison concluded, was the only effective counterbalance to the influence of such "factions."[2]

Regulation of Lobbying

In the 19th and early 20th centuries, abundant evidence accumulated that venal, selfish or misguided methods used by pressure groups could often result in legislation designed to enrich the pressure group at the expense of the public or to impose the group's own standards on the nation.

Following a series of congressional investigations, which began in 1913 with a probe of lobbying activities by the National Association of Manufacturers, proposals were repeatedly made for some kind of congressional regulation of pressure groups and lobbyists in the nation's capital. Bills requiring lobbyists to register and report on their

activities were passed by one chamber or the other on several occasions, including 1928, 1935 and 1936, but were not enacted into law.

Laws were passed in 1935 and 1936 that required registration of utilities and shipping representatives who appeared before committees of Congress or specified federal agencies; and in 1938 Congress first enacted the Foreign Agents Registration Act, requiring persons in the United States acting for foreign governments or principals in any capacity to register with the Justice Department. It was not until 1946 that a general lobby registration law was put on the statute books.

As it turned out, the 1946 measure was full of loopholes, and it was further emasculated by a narrow Supreme Court interpretation. *(Details, pp. 19-24, 61-66)*

The problem in gaining the approval of Congress and the courts for federal legislation regulating lobbying was how to curb dishonest pressure activities without interfering with constitutional rights of free speech and petition. Equally significant was congressional reluctance to delve into activity that might result in a lowered public image of Congress.

Pressure Methods

A Washington lobby group is out to get results. It pursues them wherever results are likely to be found in the governmental process. Many organizations, directed by professionals in the art of government, focus major efforts at key points where decisions are made and policy interpreted into action. They use the methods they deem appropriate for the circumstances within the limits of their resources, group policies and ethical outlook.

If a group loses a round in Congress, it may continue the fight in the agency charged with execution or in the courts. A year or two later, it may resume the struggle in Congress. This process can continue indefinitely.

Groups' goals are as numerous and varied as the organizations themselves. Many are primarily bent on protecting or promoting their specialized interests. Some assert public benefit purposes.

One group might work, for example, for the reduction of a tax burden, the passage of a subsidy program or the defense of existing advantages against proposals to eliminate them. A competing organization might actively work against some or all of the other groups' main purposes. Even so, they might find themselves on the same side upon occasion.

On a long-range basis, both groups naturally might strive through the years to build up what they consider a sympathetic or at least neutral attitude in places of power where their particular interests are affected.

These and other factors can induce some organizations not only to attempt to influence the views of members of Congress on specific issues, but also to participate in the political activities that select the occupants of positions in which they are interested.

Background. Bribery of members of Congress was a well-documented occurrence in the 19th and early 20th centuries.

When Congress in the 1830s became embroiled in President Andrew Jackson's battle with the Bank of the United States, it was disclosed that Daniel Webster, then a senator from Massachusetts, enjoyed a retainer from the bank. On Dec. 21, 1833, Webster complained to bank president Nicholas Biddle: "My retainer has not been renewed or refreshed as usual. If it is wished that my relation to the Bank should be continued, it may be well to send me the usual retainers." Historian Arthur M. Schlesinger Jr. observed in *The Age of Jackson* that Henry Clay supported the bank "because it fitted in with his superb vision of America, but Webster was fighting for it in great part because it was a dependable source of private income." [3]

In the biggest scandal of the Grant administration, it was rumored that 12 members of Congress had received stock in the Crédit Mobilier, a joint stock company, in return for large congressional grants for construction of the transcontinental Union Pacific Railroad, which controlled the Crédit Mobilier. Following an investigation, two of the alleged participants were censured by the House.

Col. Martin M. Mulhall, a lobbyist for the National Association of Manufacturers, stated publicly in 1913 that he had bribed members of Congress for legislative favors, had paid the chief House page $50 a month for inside information from the cloakrooms, and had influenced House leaders to place members friendly to the NAM on House committees and subcommittees. In a subsequent congressional probe, six members were exonerated but one was censured and resigned.

After World War II, direct vote-buying by lobbyists was replaced by sophisticated techniques. Indirect, grass-roots pressures and political support became the predominant methods. However, bribery did not disappear altogether. In 1969, for example, Maryland Sen. Daniel Brewster, D, was indicted for accepting a bribe from a mail-order house to influence his vote on postal rate legislation. Brewster eventually pleaded no contest to the lesser charge of accepting an unlawful gratuity and was fined $10,000.

Campaign Support

While corporations have been barred since 1907, and labor unions since 1943, from making direct contributions to campaigns for federal office, it is widely acknowledged that contributors have found numerous ways to get around the restrictions. Although unions are prohibited from using dues money to assist political candidates in federal elections, it is legal for them to set up separate political arms, such as the AFL-CIO's Committee on Political Education (COPE), which collect voluntary contributions from union members and their families and use the funds for political expenditures calculated to benefit senators and representatives friendly to labor. It is also legal for unions to endorse political candidates.

Similarly, while corporations are prohibited from making direct campaign contributions, they can set up corporate political action committees (PACs) to seek contributions from stockholders and executive and administrative personnel and their families. (Twice a year both union and corporate political action committees may seek anonymous contributions by mail from all employees, not just those they are initially restricted to.)

The same general resources for political support and opposition are available to members of citizens' groups and, indeed, to a wide range of organizations seeking to exert political pressure on members of Congress.

In approaching the typical member, a pressure group has no need to tell the member outright that future political support or opposition, and perhaps future political expenditures and the voluntary campaign efforts of its members, depend on how the member votes on a particular bill or whether, over a long period, the member acts favorably toward the group. The member understands this without being told. The member understands that, in the nature of the political process, positions taken on legislation help to determine which groups will provide support. The member understands that when the vital interests of some group are at stake in legislation, a vote for it would normally win the group's friendship and future support, and a vote against it would mean the group's enmity and future opposition.

Journalist James Deakin pointed out in *The Lobbyists* that when lobbyists themselves are asked to assess the main value of campaign contributions, "they frequently reply with one word: access." The campaign donation helps them to gain access to the legislator to present their case. "The reasoning is that the other fellow is contributing to the campaign of Congressman Doe and therefore is likely to get a cordial reception when he visits Doe's office, so we had better do the same. This, according to many lobbyists, is all that is gained from a campaign donation — a chance to present facts, figures and arguments to the lawmaker in the privacy of his office." [4]

In 1971, 1974 and 1976 Congress enacted legislation dealing with campaign financing, which included detailed provisions on political contributions by pressure groups.

The House in 1979 considered legislation to severely restrict the amount of money PACs would be allowed to contribute to each candidate. The existing limit for most candidates of $5,000 per PAC per election (primary, runoff and general) would be cut in half. In addition, there were proposals to prohibit a candidate from accepting more than $50,000 of PAC money during a two-year House election cycle.

Grass-Roots Pressures

Except on obscure or highly specialized legislation, most lobby campaigns now are accompanied by massive propaganda or "educational" drives in which pressure groups seek to mobilize public opinion to support their aims. In most cases, citizens are urged to respond by contacting members of Congress in support of or opposition to a particular bill.

One of the most notable successes for this technique came in 1962, when the U.S. Savings and Loan League sought to defeat President Kennedy's proposal for withholding the taxes due on interest earned on savings deposits. Because the speedup in collections would have cut back the funds on deposit at the savings and loan institutions, it would have reduced the amount of S & L money available for housing loans.

After the plan had been approved by the House, the league launched a massive effort to generate pressures that would kill the proposal in the Senate. Some of the league's advertisements depicted the plan as a new tax on savings, not a mere speedup in the collection of existing levies on interest from the savings. "The result," James Deakin has said, "was an avalanche, a flood, a torrent of letters to members of the Senate. So many stacks of letters piled up that Senate staffs had to drop everything else to cope with the deluge. The Senate post office said there had been nothing to compare with it since Truman fired General MacArthur, or possibly the Army-McCarthy hearings." [5] The plan was summarily dropped by the Senate Finance Committee.

Another grass-roots effort acknowledged as highly successful came in the mid-1960s, when the National Rifle Association instigated an outpouring of mail against ad-

Lobbying Act Federal Court Cases Since 1946

The Justice Department in 1979 told Congressional Quarterly it knew of only five federal court cases involving the Federal Regulation of Lobbying Act of 1946. Only four of the cases were prosecuted. Following are summaries of the cases:

NAM Test Suit. The National Association of Manufacturers on Jan. 28, 1948, brought a test suit challenging the validity of the lobbying law. On March 17, 1952, a federal court in Washington, D.C., ruled that the law was unconstitutional. It held that definitions in the law were too "indefinite and vague to constitute an ascertainable standard of guilt." Eight months later, on Oct. 13, 1952, the U.S. Supreme Court on a technicality reversed the lower court, leaving the 1946 law in full force but open to further challenge. (*J. Howard McGrath v. National Association of Manufacturers of the U.S.*, 344 U.S. 804).

Harriss Case. The government on June 16, 1948, obtained indictments of several individuals and an organization for alleged violations of the registration or reporting sections of the 1946 lobbying law. It was charged that, without registering or reporting, New York cotton broker Robert M. Harriss had made payments to Ralph W. Moore, a Washington commodity trader and secretary of the National Farm Committee, for the purpose of pressuring Congress on legislation, and that Moore had made similar payments to James E. McDonald, the agricultural commissioner of Texas, and Tom Linder, the agricultural commissioner of Georgia. A lower court ruling, Jan. 30, 1953, by Judge Alexander Holtzoff held the lobbying law unconstitutional on grounds that it was too vague and indefinite to meet the requirements of due process, that the registration and reporting requirements violated the First Amendment (freedom of speech, assembly, etc.) and that certain of the penalty provisions violated the constitutional right to petition Congress. Holtzoff's ruling was appealed by the government to the Supreme Court. On June 7, 1954, in a 5-3 decision, the Supreme Court reversed Holtzoff and upheld the constitutionality of the 1946 lobbying law, though construing it narrowly (*United States v. Harriss*, 347 U.S. 612).

In upholding the validity of the lobbying law, the Supreme Court sent the cases of the individual defendants back to the lower court to decide whether the individuals involved were guilty. None of the defendants was found guilty. The case against Harriss was dismissed on the ground that the lobbying law, as construed by the Supreme Court, applied only to those who solicited or received money for the purpose of lobbying, whereas Harriss was charged merely with paying money to Moore. The case against Linder was dismissed because he was exempt from the lobbying law under a specific provision exempting public officials. The charge against McDonald was dropped because of his death earlier in the case. The lower court dismissed the charges against Moore and acquitted the National Farm Committee, Nov. 2, 1955.

The importance of the *Harriss* case lay not in the decisions on the individual defendants but in the ruling that the 1946 lobbying law was constitutional.

Savings & Loan League. A federal grand jury in Washington, D.C., March 30, 1948, indicted the U.S. Savings and Loan League for failure to comply with the 1946 lobbying law. The case was dismissed April 19, 1949, by a federal district court. (*United States v. U.S. Savings and Loan League*)

Slaughter Case. On Nov. 23, 1948, ex-Rep. Roger C. Slaughter, D-Mo. (1943-47), a bitter political foe of President Truman, was indicted on charges he had lobbied for the North American Grain Association without registering under the lobbying act. Slaughter's defense was that he had merely acted as an attorney and had helped prepare testimony for witnesses. On April 17, 1950, Slaughter was acquitted, with the judge holding that the specific provision of the lobbying act which exempted persons who merely testified before a congressional committee applied, also, to those who helped such persons prepare testimony (*United States v. Slaughter*, 89 F. Supp. 205).

Natural Gas Case. On Feb. 3, 1956, Sen. Francis Case, R-S.D. (1951-62), announced on the floor of the Senate that he would vote against the natural gas bill because an out-of-state lawyer who was interested in passage of the bill, and who had learned that Case was favorably inclined to the measure, had left a $2,500 campaign contribution for the senator. (Case had refused the contribution.) As a result of this incident, President Eisenhower on Feb. 17 vetoed the natural gas bill on the ground that agents of a natural gas producer had made an "arrogant" effort to influence legislation with a campaign contribution.

John M. Neff of Lexington, Neb., the man who had offered the contribution to Sen. Case, was indicted on charges of violating the Federal Regulation of Lobbying Act. Also indicted were Elmer Patman of Austin, Texas, and the Superior Oil Co. of California. Both Neff and Patman were attorneys for Superior Oil. In a Senate investigation and at court proceedings, Neff and Patman said the $2,500 offered to Case came from the personal funds of Superior Oil President Howard B. Keck. The money was given by Keck to Patman, who in turn gave it to Neff. Neff then offered it to Case. The accused denied any attempt at bribery and said the purpose of the offer was to aid senators they believed to be of the economic school of thought that would favor the natural gas bill, which would exempt producers from certain federal regulation.

On Dec. 14, 1956, both Neff and Patman pleaded guilty to charges of violating the lobbying act by failing to register although engaged in lobbying the natural gas bill. They were fined $2,500 each and given one-year suspended sentences by Judge Joseph C. McGarraghy in Washington, D.C. Superior Oil was fined $5,000 on each of two counts of aiding and abetting Neff and Patman to violate the lobbying law. Bribery charges arising from the case were dropped. The convictions of Neff, Patman and Superior Oil were the first (and through the late 1970s the only) convictions ever obtained under the 1946 lobbying law. There was never any suggestion that Sen. Case had sought the campaign contribution or had accepted it or had in any way acted improperly.

ministration proposals for tighter gun controls. Even after the assassinations of President Kennedy, the Rev. Martin Luther King Jr. and Sen. Robert F. Kennedy, D-N.Y. (1965-68), the gun lobby was able to bottle up proposals for tough controls, and all that was passed was watered-down legislation not vigorously opposed by the NRA.

Anti-Saloon League Drive. Sometimes lobbying efforts originate at the grass roots and then attract national attention. A classic campaign of this type was the drive by the Anti-Saloon League and associated organizations to prevent the sale of alcoholic beverages. After 15 years devoted to building up local support, particularly among Protestant denominations, the league met in Washington in 1911 to map strategy for its assault on Congress. To sway public opinion, the league launched an advertising campaign that blamed all the evils of society on the saloon.

Although the league's initial effort was not immediately productive, Congress deferred to this increasingly powerful lobby two years later by passing the Webb-Kenyon Act, which outlawed transportation of alcoholic beverages into states where their sale was illegal. Spurred by that victory, the league went on to push through nationwide prohibition.

Following substantial gains by "dry" candidates in the congressional election of 1916, Congress the next year submitted the Eighteenth Amendment, prohibiting the sale or consumption of alcoholic beverages, to the states for ratification. Ratification was completed early in 1919, and the amendment went into effect in January 1920 (it was repealed in 1933).

Disadvantages. Despite the frequent success of grass-roots lobbying, such an approach has several inherent limitations that make its use questionable unless it is carefully and cleverly managed. If a member's mail on an issue appears artificially generated, the member may feel that the response is not representative of the member's constituency. Such pressure mail is easily recognized because the letters all arrive at about the same time, are mimeographed or printed, or are identically or similarly worded. Political scientist David B. Truman has observed that "Filling up the legislator's mailbag is essentially a crude device, a shotgun technique which may only wound where a rifle would kill." While Truman concedes that there may be times when a member will add up the pros and cons and vote with the majority, he cautions that "one fact is clear" in such instances: "The usual channels of access to him are empty or silent." [6]

Occasionally, this method may boomerang and leave the lobbyist worse off than when he started. A noteworthy example was the utility fight of 1935, when lobbyists for private utilities sought unsuccessfully to defeat President Roosevelt's proposed curbs on utility holding companies. A congressional investigation brought out the fact that thousands of phony telegrams to Congress had been financed by utility interests. A resulting wave of adverse publicity helped assure passage of Roosevelt's proposals.

Direct Lobbying

Much lobbying still is conducted on a face-to-face basis. In a study of pressures on the Senate, Donald R. Matthews, a political scientist, observed that the vast majority of such lobbying was directed at members "who are already convinced." He added: "The services a lobby can provide a friendly senator are substantial. Few senators could survive without them. First, they can perform much of the research and speech-writing chores of the senator's office. This service is especially attractive to the more publicity-oriented senators. Members of the party that does not control the White House also find this service especially valuable, since they cannot draw upon the research services of the departments as much as can the other members. But most senators find this service at first a convenience and soon a necessity." [7]

Once established, Matthews has said, "Senator-lobbyist friendships also tend to reinforce the senator's commitment to a particular group and line of policy. . . . Relatively few senators are actually changed by lobbyists from a hostile or neutral position to a friendly one. Perhaps a few on every major issue are converted and this handful of votes may carry the day. But quantitatively, the conversion effect is relatively small." [8]

Ensuring continued access to members of Congress requires considerable tact on the part of the lobbyist. Lobbyists must be particularly wary of overstaying their welcome and appearing overly aggressive. Rep. Emanuel Celler, D-N.Y. (1923-73), wrote: "The man who keeps his appointment, presents his problem or proposal and lets the congressman get on with his other work comes to be liked and respected. His message has an excellent chance of being effective. The man who feels that it somehow adds to his usefulness and prestige to be seen constantly in the company of one legislator or another, or who seeks to ingratiate himself with congressional staffs, gets under foot and becomes a nuisance. He does his principal and cause no good." [9] Another member of Congress commented that "it doesn't take very long to figure out which lobbyists are straightforward, and which ones are trying to snow you. The good ones will give you the weak points as well as the strong points of their case. If anyone ever gives me false or misleading information, that's it—I'll never see him again."[10]

Above all, the lobbyist must be certain that the information he gives the member is accurate and complete. Former White House aide Douglass Cater has said: "The smart lobbyist . . . knows he can be most effective by being helpful, by being timely, and, not least, by being accurate. According to the testimony of lobbyists themselves, the cardinal sin is to supply faulty information which puts a trusting policy-maker in an exposed position." [11]

Most contemporary lobbyists carefully avoid approaches that the member may interpret as threatening or as constituting excessive pressure. An adverse reaction by a member may lead to unfavorable publicity or even a damaging congressional investigation. Matthews has described the lobbyist as a "sitting duck — their public reputation is so low that public attack is bound to be damaging. . . . To invite public attack, or even worse a congressional investigation, is, from the lobbyist's point of view, clearly undesirable." Matthews adds: "It is the threat of and use of these countermeasures which help explain why so little lobbying is aimed at conversion. A lobbyist minimizes the risk of his job, the cause which he serves, and his ego by staying away from those senators clearly against him and his program. For, of all types of lobbying, attempts at conversion are most likely to boomerang." [12]

Information-Gathering Function. Some lobbyists may be of more use to their employers as a conduit of information than as a source of direct pressure on Congress. Merriman Smith, longtime White House correspondent for United Press International, wrote in 1962: "[The typical lobbyist] arises when he feels like it, usually midmorning, in a spacious, comfortable, but definitely unflashy home in the Northwest residential section of town. Over breakfast,

Famous Lobbyists Reflect . . .

Most Washington lobbyists are known only to their clients and contacts; the public never hears about them. A few over the years have run counter to the pattern. They either have achieved fame as lobbyists, or have carried into a lobbying career fame earned elsewhere. Below are brief profiles of selected lobbyists who have achieved some measure of fame. Their working styles tend to reflect the changing styles of lobbying.

'King of the Lobby'

Samuel Ward. Most colorful of all the early Washington lobbyists was Samuel Ward, brother of Julia Ward Howe, author of "The Battle Hymn of the Republic." Ward, known widely as "King of the Lobby," reigned in Washington for 15 years in the period following the Civil War. His clients included the railroads and other financial interests concerned with federal legislation.

In his study of the House of Representatives, journalist Neil MacNeil described Ward as "a short, stout man with the imperial white beard of a French count . . . a man of refined education, who sported diamond studs in his shirts and never appeared without a rose in his coat lapel. . . . He entertained nightly the political leaders of Washington at a table groaning with choice viands and fine wines. Himself a wit and gentleman of culture, Ward lavished on his guests a plentiful bounty with never so much as an indelicate suggestion of his ulterior motives; he never asked a man for a favor at his table. That came later." Ward is reported to have bragged repeatedly that "The way to a man's 'Aye' is through his stomach."

The size of Ward's fees was not a matter of record. On one occasion, however, he wrote his friend Henry Wadsworth Longfellow: "When I see you again, I will tell you how a client, eager to prevent the arrival at a committee of a certain member before it should adjourn, offered me $5,000 to accomplish his purpose, which I did by having his (the congressman's) boots mislaid while I smoked a cigar and condoled with him until they would be found at 11:45. I had the satisfaction of a good laugh, a good fee in my pocket, and of having prevented a conspiracy." By "conspiracy," Ward is reported to have meant legislation in which he saw no merit.

On other occasions, Ward reportedly received $50,000 for influencing tariff legislation and $1 million for his work on a mail subsidy case. When a congressional committee asked him what he had done to earn his fee in the mail case, Ward denied that he had bribed anyone to influence the legislation. He supposed he had been retained, he said, because "I am called King of the Lobby, but I am not Treasurer of the Lobby, that is certain."

Vote Broker

Edward Pendleton. A lobbyist of the immediate pre-Civil War era who achieved a reputation almost equal to Ward's was Edward Pendleton, who operated a popular gambling house on Pennsylvania Avenue. Pendleton's establishment, known as the "Palace of Fortune" and "Hall of the Bleeding Heart," was elaborately furnished and equipped with a wine cellar in which Pendleton was said to have invested $10,000. Perley Poore, a contempo-

rary of Pendleton's, wrote: "The people who nightly assemble to see and to take part in the entertainments of the house consisted of candidates for the presidency, senators and representatives, members of the Cabinet, editors and journalists and the master workmen of the third house, the lobby. Pendleton's in its palmiest days might have been called the vestibule of the lobby."

It was reported that the transfer of bribes to members of Congress in the form of winnings at cards was another of the methods followed at Pendleton's. But lending money to members who went broke at his tables was Pendleton's main stock in trade. Neil MacNeil has observed that "This was the source of his power as a lobbyist, and he proved successful many times in having bills passed for his clients." Perley Poore said of Pendleton that "A broker in parliamentary notes is an inevitable retainer of broker votes."

'Tommy the Cork'

Thomas G. Corcoran. Among contemporary lobbyists, one of the best-known and most influential has been Thomas G. Corcoran, a powerful White House adviser in New Deal days who later became a highly paid lobbyist for Washington business interests.

During five years in the White House, Corcoran (dubbed "Tommy the Cork" by President Roosevelt) assisted in writing much of the major New Deal legislation, including the Securities and Exchange Act, the Public Utility Holding Company Act and the Fair Labor Standards Act. Corcoran also helped on Roosevelt's abortive plan to "pack" the Supreme Court with additional justices. He thus became one of the most controversial of the White House staff members, and when he sought the post of solicitor general in 1940, President Roosevelt declined to nominate him for fear the Senate would deny confirmation. Corcoran resigned his White House job and, almost overnight, reappeared as representative of the same business interests he had opposed as a New Deal crusader. Within a few months, he testified before a congressional committee that he had received $100,000 in legal fees and was turning away clients "by the hundreds."

Louis W. Koenig has described Corcoran as "an adventurer who . . . sought to introduce banana-growing on the island fortress of Taiwan and to establish across the length and breadth of Brazil a chain of restaurants under the auspices of the Union News Company." He added: "In reality, he belongs not to the twentieth century, but to another age. He is a medieval character who operated in the era of the New Deal with the fervor, bravado and finesse of a top-notch grand duke of an Italian principality. . . . 'The way to get ahead,' he would say, 'is to fish in troubled waters.' "

Journalist James Deakin has observed that when a 1960 House subcommittee investigating lobbyist contacts with members of the Federal Power Commission began probing the alleged activities of Corcoran, the panel "got out of its league." Deakin went on to say: "This was no plodding political hack caught cozying up to the industry, but a wily old pro who had forgotten more about the regulatory agencies and regulatory law than the subcom-

... Changing Styles of Lobbying

mittee members ever knew. . . . Corcoran ran rings around the subcommittee in some of the stormiest and funniest hearings ever held on Capitol Hill."

Strictly a Lawyer

Clark M. Clifford. Another highly paid representative for powerful business interests has been Clark M. Clifford, prominent Washington attorney and a former White House aide in the Truman administration, adviser to Presidents Kennedy and Johnson, and secretary of Defense (1968-69) for the last 11 months of the Johnson administration. Clifford has long been a senior partner in the Washington law firm of Clifford and Warnke (formerly Clifford, Warnke, Glass, McIlwain and Finney and before that Clifford and Miller), which has held retainers from some of the nation's largest corporations, including Du Pont, General Electric, Standard Oil of California, Phillips Petroleum, Hughes Tool and a number of mutual funds.

Clifford's firm declined for many years to register as a lobby group, contending that it did no actual lobbying. (Finally, in 1969, it did register for Hughes Tool, the Avco Corp. and several smaller clients.) Soon after setting up the firm, Clifford told reporters: "I have not and will not register as a lobbyist, for that is not the kind of work we do. We run a law office here, with a background of experience in the general practice of law, topped off by an intimate knowledge of how the government operates." Associates of Clifford's firm often said their role in the legislative process was to advise clients on positions to take on legislation and to suggest the tactics that they use in lobbying campaigns. The firm followed the legislation closely for the client, but if the situation called for active lobbying, it recommended someone else for that job.

It was widely rumored that Clifford's firm received a fee of $1 million from the Du Pont Co. for its assistance in a stock divestiture case. The firm claimed that the size of the fee was exaggerated and said it had received only its regular retainer as Du Pont's Washington counsel. The bulk of the fee, it said, went to the Washington law firm of Cleary, Gottlieb and Steen, which Clifford's firm recommended for the lobbying job.

Mr. Labor

Andrew J. Biemiller. For many years the most prominent labor lobbyist in Washington was Andrew J. Biemiller, a former Democratic U.S. representative from Wisconsin, who registered as a lobbyist for the AFL in 1953, became chief lobbyist for the AFL-CIO when the organizations merged in 1955, and remained in that position until his retirement at the end of 1978. James Deakin called Biemiller "one of the best-known men on Capitol Hill" and points out that he had "one of the toughest jobs in Washington" because he was caught in the occasional cross fire between the AFL and CIO and beset by the prickly personalities of some of labor's top

brass. Deakin quotes Biemiller as saying that the only labor lobbyists over which he had direct control were those directly employed by the AFL-CIO. There were many other labor lobbyists in Washington, Biemiller said, and with those all "I could use was suasion."

Biemiller had a reputation as a man who could influence legislative history with a mere phone call. His influence was such that Rep. John M. Ashbrook, R-Ohio, commented, "I've watched him call off bills that could pass."

Despite Biemiller's widely acclaimed skills in mobilizing a united labor front, Congress during his tenure as labor's top lobbyist passed relatively few of the major bills of direct interest to labor. However, Biemiller's overall effectiveness was not questioned. Many of the flood of labor-supported civil rights and welfare bills that won approval during that period were at the top of the AFL-CIO's priorities list, right after the bills of exclusive interest to labor.

'I Know Who to Call'

Charls E. Walker. Charls E. Walker, a 20-year veteran of Washington politics and banking interests, was deputy secretary of the Treasury during the first Nixon presidential term. In that post, Walker managed a wide range of legislative activities for the administration — tax measures, economic stabilization legislation, general revenue sharing. He also played a major role in wage and price control planning.

In leaving the Nixon administration early in 1973 to set up his own economic consulting firm (Charls E. Walker Associates Inc.), Walker followed the custom of other high-ranking officials who have put their government experience to work in private business.

Like them, he left with an intimate knowledge of government affairs and a reservoir of political connections throughout Washington and the world of finance. (Before serving as President Nixon's No. 2 man at the Treasury, Walker was executive vice president of the American Bankers Association (1961-69); during the second Eisenhower administration, he was special assistant to Treasury Secretary Robert B. Anderson.)

His experience — when something is needed "I know where to get it and who to call" — proved irresistible to many corporations. Walker himself recalled in a 1973 interview that when he told President Nixon of his plans at Camp David, Nixon observed: "You're going to be doing what you have been, but now making money at it."

Only six months after the Walker firm was incorporated, three of the four corporations (General Motors, Ford and General Electric) that headed *Fortune* magazine's ranking of the 500 largest manufacturers in the nation had hired Walker as a lobbyist. In all, 14 major corporations were Walker clients — 12 of them ranked in the top 90 on *Fortune's* list in 1973. Besides the two auto giants and General Electric, Walker represented Gulf Oil, Procter and Gamble, Bethlehem Steel, Allied Chemical and Time Inc.

Sources: Neil MacNeil, *Forge of Democracy* (David McKay Co., 1963); James Deakin, *The Lobbyists* (Public Affairs Press, 1966); Louis W. Koenig, *The Invisible Presidency* (Rinehart and Co. Inc., 1960); Congressional Quarterly, *Weekly Report*, Aug. 18, 1972, p. 2269.

he reads four or five major morning newspapers. If interested, he skims through the *Congressional Record* for the day before.... These are the golden hours of his day. He may earn his keep more from intelligent reading than from any other single activity. Years of experience have taught him to read between the lines and to search for indicative but seemingly small details....

"Once 'read' for the day, he may make it to town for luncheon with one or two key men in government at the Carlton or the Mayflower. Mostly, they talk about golf or fishing. Possibly in parting, he may ask casually, 'You fellows heard anything new on depreciation allowances?'... This man is more effective for his employer than a dozen more energetic fellows patrolling the halls of the Senate and House office buildings.... By being highly selective in his friendships, he manages to keep in touch with virtually any government move that might help or hinder his company.... Our man's effectiveness would be destroyed if he had to play the lobbyist's conventional role in attempting to push or halt specific bills before Congress." [13]

Strategic Contacts. In fights over a specific bill, most direct approaches by lobbyists are likely to center on a few strategic members instead of a large part of the membership of the House or Senate. In most lobby battles, approval of a measure by a congressional committee is tantamount to final passage. Except on highly controversial issues, committee decisions are almost always upheld by the full chamber. Lobby pressures may focus not only on key members of a committee but also on the committee's professional staff. Particularly on legislation involving highly technical matters, such staffs are extremely influential. Political scientist Lester W. Milbrath has noted that "failure to locate such key persons (members and staff) may result in the sending of many superfluous messages, and if the key persons cannot be persuaded, there is a high likelihood that the decision will go adversely." [14] Any inroads the lobbyist may have made outside the circle of strategic members are likely to be negated if these key members start pushing the other way.

Testimony at Hearings

Another useful technique for lobbyists is testimony at congressional hearings. The hearing provides the lobbyist with a propaganda forum that has few parallels in Washington. It also provides access to key members whom the lobbyist may not have been able to contact in any other way. On important legislation, lobbyists normally rehearse their statements before the hearing, seek to ensure a large turnout from their constituency on the hearing day, and may even hand friendly committee members leading questions for the group's witness to answer.

The degree of propaganda success for the hearing, however, is likely to depend on how well the committee's controlling factions are disposed to the group's position. In his book, *House Out of Order,* Rep. Richard Bolling, D-Mo., says that within congressional committees "proponents and opponents of legislation jockey for position — each complementing the activities of their alter egos in lobbies outside." He points out: "Adverse witnesses can be kept to a minimum, for example, or they can be sandwiched among friendly witnesses in scheduled appearances so that their testimony does not receive as much attention from the press as it deserves. Scant attention will be given, for example, to a knowledgeable opponent of the federal fallout shelter program if he is scheduled to testify on such legislation on the same day as are Dr. Edward Teller, an

assistant secretary of Defense and a three-star general. The opponent is neatly boxed in." [15]

Lobby Coalitions

Most major legislation is backed by alliances of interest groups on one side and opposed by alliances on the other. Such lobby coalitions, while having the advantage of bigger memberships and more financial resources for lobbying, are difficult to control because of the differences of viewpoint that are likely within the coalition. Despite these inner tensions, however, lobby coalitions have been instrumental in obtaining passage of much major legislation, such as Medicare, civil rights bills and housing legislation. Notable coalition efforts that failed have included a 1967 push for import restrictions, which ran into trouble when too many industries sought protective quotas, and a 1970 drive for cuts in military spending, which lost impact when liberal and conservative critics of Pentagon spending levels fell to quarreling over use of the prospective savings. Liberals sought to earmark the cuts for domestic programs, while the conservatives favored tax reductions.

In a broad sense, lobby coalitions have broken down into liberal and conservative camps, the former usually led by the labor unions and civil rights groups and the latter by business associations such as the Chamber of Commerce of the United States and the National Association of Manufacturers. Disparities within these groups usually lead to shifting of alliances among individual organizations as issues change and to formation of ad hoc coalitions to exert pressure on a particular issue. In 1979 some liberal and conservative groups formed an unusual coalition that tried unsuccessfully to block the creation of a new Department of Education.

Although there is considerable log-rolling, with organizations getting assistance on one issue by promising future support on another, the activity of many groups is limited mainly to matters of immediate concern to them. Thus, the American Medical Association, one of the most powerful pressure groups in the capital, is extremely active on questions of medical practice and health but normally shows little interest in such questions as agricultural policy, foreign trade or economic policy in general.

Defensive Lobby Alignments. While massive promotional campaigns by lobbyists have attracted wide public attention, a large share of lobby activity is defensive or preventive. Political scientist Lewis Dexter has observed that this is only natural because "it is much easier to get successful people — the kind who finance and initiate most lobbies — excited about having a favorable situation disturbed than to stir them up — at least in American society — about a contingent benefit." [16]

The bicameral structure of the legislative branch and the constitutional separation of powers also gives a considerable natural advantage to defensive lobbying efforts. David B. Truman has written that these structures "operate, as they were designed, to delay or obstruct action rather than to facilitate it." He adds: "Requirement of extensive majorities for particular kinds of measures and the absence of limits on the duration of debate have a like effect as do numerous technical details of the parliamentary rules. Finally, the diffuseness of leadership, and the power and independence of committees and their chairmen, not only provide a multiplicity of points of access ... but also furnish abundant activities for obstruction and delay, opportunities that buttress the position of defensive groups." [17]

Alliance Building: Major Strategy of Pressure Groups

Masses of unorganized individuals ordinarily exert little direct influence on the major activities of the federal government. As they organize in groups geared to specialized interests and goals, they build power bases from which their leaders and spokesmen can promote those interests.

Hence the formation of trade associations, labor and professional political action committees, self-styled citizens' groups and other organizations of many kinds that exert lobbying pressure.

As the nation has grown, and with it the crush of competing interests, individual interest groups even as large as the American Farm Bureau Federal, AFL-CIO or the Chamber of Commerce of the United States have found they sometimes lack sufficient impact to achieve their legislative purposes unassisted.

A major trend in the mid-20th century has been the pyramiding of pressure group on pressure group into combinations aimed at accumulating enough collective strength to compel power holders to heed them.

'Far From New'

While this movement toward coalitions accelerated after World War II, it was far from new. For example, Secretary-Treasurer Roger Fleming of the American Farm Bureau Federation in 1971 noted the emergence of an opposition farm coalition and said: "But the greatest farm coalition ever assembled was when the American Farm Bureau Federation was founded in 1919." He explained its basis as follows:

"Farm Bureau offered a means whereby producers of every commodity in every area of the country could get together, regardless of their political affiliations, to reconcile their differences, and thereby develop honest-to-goodness farm unity." As for intergroup alliances on the legislative front, Fleming said: "We, in fact, have allies on practically every issue in which we are involved."

Education is another of the many fields in which interest groups have formed alliances to pressure national policy. John Lumley, former director of the National Education Association's office of legislation, told Congressional Quarterly in 1970 while discussing proposals to merge the NEA and the AFL-CIO's American Federation of Teachers: "Legislatively, we've worked together through the years with the AFL-CIO."

By 1950 the House Select Committee on Lobbying Activities said in a report: "The lone-wolf pressure group, wanting nothing more from other groups than to be left unmolested, is largely a thing of the past."

Prof. Stephen K. Bailey went so far as to tell the House committee his conclusion was "that lobbying can be understood only as the reflection of interests shared by shifting coalitions made up by members of Congress, outside pressures, and executive agencies." He added: "If this is a correct assumption, then it seems to me that your problem is the enormously complicated one of analyzing the interrelationships among private group interests, members of Congress and agency personnel."

In the pursuit of power, the ways of coalition are many. Their workings are sometimes open, easily traced and readily acknowledged by all. At other times, the cooperation is concealed, perhaps detectable mainly through after-the-fact disclosure that participants with seemingly variant interests arrive at the same result by divergent routes or that the same individuals show up in different places wearing different hats.

'More Apparent Than Real'

Some coalitions may be more apparent than real. Rather than indicating strength, they can at times suggest weakness among the separate entities and a lack of unity within the organizations. A frequent practice is the selection of certain top officers of various organizations to head a cluster of groups under a separate name.

Such a coalition may in fact be composed of a comparative handful of individuals and may operate under its own internal governing structure and bylaws that may or may not conform with those of the cooperating groups. Their responsible posts put coalition leaders in a position to draw upon the financial and educational resources, prestige and pressure mechanisms of individual groups to exert pressure on public officials.

In the case of organizations with millions of members, real internal unity would suggest the strong possibility of remedies at the polls and less necessity for combined pressure activities. This aspect sometimes prompts opponents in Congress to refer to coalitions of leaders as "generals without troops." This naturally draws stout rebuttals, and there are strong incentives for alliances from the viewpoint of group leaders.

At times groups that are usually opponents will join to lobby on an issue, as when the Sierra Club joined the Chamber of Commerce to oppose legislation requiring disclosure of grass-roots lobbying expenses.

Two fairly lasting coalitions that have operated from time to time since the 1930s have been a coalition of northern liberals, civil rights and labor organizations opposed on some issues by a coalition of Republicans and southern conservatives. This has been demonstrated in pressure groups as in Congress. The clash between the two forces came into evidence in the battles over Senate confirmation of Supreme Court nominees Clement F. Haynsworth Jr. (1969) and G. Harrold Carswell (1970), both rejected.

'Mutual Interest'

Bayard Rustin, an anti-war activist and a leading strategist of the civil rights and anti-poverty movements, told an AFL-CIO convention that alliances of the kind formed during the 1969 battle over the nomination of Clement F. Haynsworth to the Supreme Court "are not made in the way in which one marries his wife. Alliances are not made out of affection. Alliances are made out of mutual interest, and although there will be difficult times for us, we must remember that this mutual interest does in fact exist and we must hold on to it. . . . Let us build upon that which unites us."

Sources of Pressure

Traditionally, pressure groups in the United States have been comprised of similar economic or social interests. Classic examples of such traditional groups were farmers, businessmen, workers, veterans. Their interests were few and usually drew the united support of a large majority of members.

As the federal government broadened its activities, a new type of pressure group developed — the coalition of diverse economic and social interests brought together by concern for a certain issue. A coalition of this type could include, for example, both business and labor interests. An example of the broad coalition was the protectionist bloc, which was effective in raising protective U.S. tariffs. A more modern example is the education lobby. *(Details p. 209)*

Foreign nations increasingly are concerned with American policies. Their representatives comprise a special group of lobbyists. *(The foreign interest lobby, see p. 127)*

Finally, there is a collection of groups with no single special interest to promote or protect. These self-styled citizens' or public interest lobbies are concerned with a vast array of issues, and usually have large numbers of individual members.

Selected examples are described briefly in the following section.

Executive Branch

Executive branch lobbying activities have been described as the most pervasive, influential and costly of any of the pressures converging on Capitol Hill.

Although every president since George Washington has sought to influence the content of legislation, it was not until the Eisenhower administration that a formal congressional liaison office in the White House was created. In addition, each executive department has a congressional liaison office charged with selling the department's legislative programs to Congress. *(Executive branch lobbying, p. 27)*

While senators and representatives sometimes criticize what they regard as excessive executive pressures, they tend on the other hand to complain of lack of leadership when executive influence is missing. The inter-branch pressure process also works in reverse. Members of Congress exert pressure on executive agencies, if only through inquiries that demonstrate an interest on the part of the body that must pass agency appropriations.

Veterans

In the period from World War I to World War II, the veterans' bloc, led by the American Legion, the Disabled American Veterans and the Veterans of Foreign Wars, exercised considerable influence over legislation within its purview. In legislation enacted in 1930, veterans' groups won extension of World War I veterans' disability compensation to veterans who had become disabled since the war, whether or not the disability was service-connected. In 1924 pressure from veterans' groups pushed Congress into overriding President Coolidge's veto of a bill calling for eventual payment of a World War I veterans' bonus. Similar pressure in 1934 caused Congress to override President Roosevelt's veto of a bill restoring certain veterans' benefits, which had been curtailed for economy reasons a year earlier. And in 1936, veterans' groups again persuaded Congress to override Roosevelt and pass a bill requiring immediate payment of the World War I bonus.

After World War II, veterans' groups (still dominated by the American Legion, Disabled American Veterans and Veterans of Foreign Wars) did not exhibit the same legislative potency. One reason was that they did not have to. An extremely generous program of veterans' benefits enacted by Congress for World War II and Korean War veterans undermined current and future claims that veterans had been mistreated or forgotten, which had been a major argument after earlier wars.

Veterans' groups remained active on Capitol Hill, nevertheless. One example of their success was the continued growth and expansion of the Veterans Administration, the largest non-Cabinet agency in the federal government. Veterans' groups lobbied actively each year for VA appropriations. Amid fluctuating congressional interest in national health insurance, veterans' groups worked carefully to retain their preferred free health care at VA hospitals and to assure VA hospitals of a continuing role under a national health insurance program.

Farmers

The farm lobby underwent a substantial change in character as the number of farmers declined, as family farms disappeared and as farming became big business. In effect, what had been a "people's lobby" slowly became an interest group, subject to much the same public suspicion and criticism as other special interests.

Three major organizations claimed to represent the majority of American farmers — the American Farm Bureau Federation, the National Grange and the National Farmers Union. Occasionally the groups were able to work together. More frequently they were divided and fought against each other. In 1973 some 20 farm groups formed a loose, working coalition to coordinate their efforts against a Nixon administration farm bill. Standing aloof from the coalition was the conservative American Farm Bureau Federation.

The coalition was the first effort by farm organizations to ban together for a joint purpose. National Farmers Union officials, who together with the National Grange had sponsored the coalition, explained that a number of the groups had worked together in the past, in shifting alliances, on different pieces of farm legislation, but that no major concerted effort previously had developed on a farm bill.

The late 1970s saw the emergence of the American Agriculture Movement (AAM), a much more militant organization than any of the older farm groups. This loosely organized coalition sponsored several tractorcades to Washington, D.C., and encouraged farmers to personally lobby members of Congress. These tactics generated substantial publicity for the group. *(Details, p. 211)*

Labor

Before World War II, labor union lobbying was a relatively negligible force in the nation's capital. There was a remarkable growth in union membership from 1935 to 1945. At the same time, many labor union officials "learned the ropes" in Washington when they came to the capital during the Second World War to serve on the War Labor Board's tripartite dispute settlement sections. These developments set the stage for the emergence of labor unions as an important pressure group in the nation's capital.

The unions carried on both grass-roots pressure campaigns designed to influence public opinion and active lobbying of Congress (and frequently of the president and other executive branch leaders). Their large membership,

Mass Pressure Demonstrations in Washington

Over the years, some pressure groups that lacked large financial resources have sought to make their pressure felt by staging demonstrations in the nation's capital. This method was particularly popular in the 1960s and early 1970s.

The first of these large demonstrations came in 1894, when an army of the unemployed was organized by Jacob S. Coxey to pressure Congress into authorizing a $500 million highway improvement program and interest-free loans to state and local governments to finance public improvements. Coxey's army set out from Massillon, Ohio; others were soon organized in many parts of the West. The total number of men involved has been estimated at 6,000 to 11,000.

Only about 500 men reached Washington. The District of Columbia police department was greatly enlarged for their arrival and government buildings were heavily guarded. When Coxey and his men arrived May 1 and started to march into the Capitol grounds the police assaulted the men with clubs. Coxey and two other leaders reached the Senate steps but were arrested and subsequently convicted of trampling the shrubbery and unlawfully displaying banners.

Coxey's army established camps at various places in and around Washington. They subsisted on donated food and by begging. By mid-July they had been abandoned by most of their leaders. The demonstration ended when the Virginia militia drove the men out of a large encampment on the Virginia side of the Potomac and burned down their camp. The District of Columbia government then offered to provide transportation to the West, which most accepted.

The Bonus Expeditionary Force. The Bonus Expeditionary Force which marched on Washington in 1932 was much larger than Coxey's army. An estimated 15,000 men participated.

The Bonus marchers, like Coxey's army, were the product of a depression era. The specific purpose of the Bonus Expeditionary Force was to pressure Congress into providing immediate payment to World War I veterans of bonus certificates that were scheduled to mature in 1945. Late in 1931 Rep. Wright Patman, D-Texas, had introduced a bill to that end.

The Bonus marchers, led by Walter W. Waters, started arriving in Washington at the end of May 1932, three weeks after Patman's bill had been reported out unfavorably by the Ways and Means Committee. Some of the men found shelter in partly razed buildings along Pennsylvania Avenue. The main camp of the Bonus marchers was on the Anacostia Flats and consisted of tents and shacks. Food, clothing and other supplies were donated by private individuals and charities.

The House passed the bonus bill June 15 by a 211-176 roll-call vote but it was rejected by the Senate June 17 on an 18-62 roll-call vote. A contemporary journalist described the Senate action as a "rebuke to what some senators regarded as practically physical intimidation by the bonus marchers."

The Bonus marchers remained in Washington hoping to pressure the Senate into reversing its vote. Congress adjourned on July 16 without reconsidering the bonus bill, but it authorized $100,000 in loans to veterans to enable them to return home. However, an estimated 11,000 people were still in camps a week after Congress had adjourned.

The Bonus Expeditionary Force finally was dispersed by federal troops on July 28. Troops were called to quell a riot that broke out when the police tried to evict marchers who were camping out in federally owned buildings. The federal troops were led by the Army chief of staff, General Douglas MacArthur; Major Dwight D. Eisenhower commanded a tank detachment. The marchers were driven toward Anacostia and the encampment there was burned that night. The following day President Hoover said of the marchers, "Government cannot be coerced by mob rule."

1963 March on Washington. On Aug. 28, 1963, about 200,000 persons descended on the capital for a "March on Washington for Jobs and Freedom." Goals of the massive demonstration included stronger civil rights laws and tougher enforcement of existing laws. A massive federal training program for the unemployed and a broadened minimum wage law also were demanded.

Lafayette Park Camp-in. A group of about 90 unemployed Mississippi blacks organized a camp-in in Lafayette Park, across from the White House, in April 1966. The campers were protesting delays in processing their application for poverty funds. Four tents were set up in Lafayette Park April 4-7. The demonstrators took turns living in them. They were given a permit by the Department of Interior.

Poor People's Campaign. Some 3,000 persons, most of them black, camped near the Lincoln Memorial from April 29 through June 23, 1968, in a demonstration for jobs and welfare legislation. Termed the "Poor People's Campaign," the demonstration was dispersed when federal officials refused to renew the demonstrators' camping permit.

Anti-War Demonstrations. Crowds estimated in the tens of thousands turned out on numerous occasions from 1966 into 1971 to demonstrate for American withdrawal from the war in Vietnam. Pro-war groups also demonstrated, but turnouts were much smaller.

Farmers' Protest. Farmers driving an estimated 2,000 tractors and trucks entered Washington Feb. 5, 1979, snarling the morning commuter traffic for hours. Police efforts to untangle the tie-up led to sporadic violence that resulted in about 20 arrests.

The attention-getting demonstration was organized by the American Agriculture Movement (AAM), which was more militant in its methods than the older farm lobby organizations.

The farmers remained in Washington for several weeks, lobbying on Capitol Hill to set the loan rate for wheat, corn and other commodities at 90 percent of parity.

Sources: *Encyclopedia of American History,* edited by Richard B. Morris (Harper & Row, 1965); Congressional Quarterly, *Congress and the Nation,* Vols. I-IV.

strength in urban centers, comparatively substantial financial resources, organizational know-how and, in many cases, the liberally oriented idealism of most of their spokesmen made them a formidable force in legislative pressure activities. An important aspect of their influence was that many unions, and notably the AFL-CIO, maintained research and publications staffs that contributed importantly to the development and popularization of many new policy proposals in the welfare and labor fields.

Also important, probably even more than research and propaganda activities, was the willingness of the unions to use political means to achieve their ends. Both the AFL and the CIO maintained political action arms (the AFL Labor's League for Political Education and the CIO Political Action Committee) which, when the two federations merged in 1955, were united to form the AFL-CIO Committee on Political Education (COPE).

Despite their usefulness as shorthand, terms such as "labor victory" and "labor defeat" imply a cohesiveness among unions that rarely exists. Even within the AFL-CIO, there are 103 unions ranging from teachers and government employees to craft-based building trades unions.

The affiliates vary almost as much in the intensity of their lobbying as they do in ideology. Sometimes individual unions not only refuse to help with the lobbying, but actually oppose an AFL-CIO position. The federation supported federal land use planning legislation, but the United Brotherhood of Carpenters fought it in 1974 and was instrumental in its defeat in the House.

Organized labor wins its share of arguments in Congress. Much of the civil rights and Great Society legislation of the 1960s was largely the product of its lobbying. But the irony that frustrates many union lobbyists is that labor has rarely won on the issues that affect it most directly.

The unions lost in 1948 when Congress overrode President Truman's veto of the Taft-Hartley Act. They lost in 1959, when they could not prevent passage of the restrictions in the Landrum-Griffin Act. They lost in 1966, when the House failed to pass legislation repealing Section 14B of Taft-Hartley, which permits states to enact "right-to-work" laws sanctioning a non-union shop.

In 1975-77 labor thought for a time it had achieved a long-sought success in encouraging Congress to enact a common-site picketing bill. Congress enacted the bill, but it was vetoed by President Ford. The measure would have allowed a local union with a grievance against one contractor to picket all other contractors or subcontractors at the same construction site. After President Carter took office, labor again thought common-site picketing had clear sailing. But the bill was defeated in the House, and the setback presaged another disappointment the following year when Congress refused to pass changes that labor wanted made in the National Labor Relations Act.

The reason labor fails to win on its own issues, members and lobbyists agree, is that it comes to be perceived as a special interest, rather than the public interest lobby it can portray itself as on behalf of social legislation. *(Details, p. 97)*

For many legislators, fear of union retaliation when the legislator did not vote as the unions wished was lessened by the recognition that union leaders, on many non-"bread and butter" issues, tended to be far more liberal than their members and that union leaders did not always control the vote of members on election day. Moreover, there was a general feeling that the strength of labor unions as a pressure group was greatest in the 1940s and early 1950s and had begun to decline in the later 1950s and 1960s — in part because unions were no longer expanding their membership very rapidly, in part because the experience of the preceding 15-20 years demonstrated that unions alone simply were not strong enough to dominate congressional elections in a way that once was feared.

Business

Modern business groups no longer wield the power over members of Congress that business magnates wielded during the 70 years between the Civil War and the New Deal. The groups, nevertheless, continue to exert considerable influence on legislative decisions.

Journalist James Deakin illustrated some of the past and current techniques of business influence. He described the Senate in the late years of the 19th century as a home for business barons who had paid their way in Congress. Quoting William Allen White, Deakin continued: "One Senator represented the Union Pacific Railway system, another the New York Central, still another the insurance interests. . . . Coal and iron owned a coterie. . . . Cotton had half a dozen Senators. The collar of any great financial interest was worn with pride." [18]

Deakin also told about a luncheon in the 1960s in the private Pentagon dining room of Secretary of Defense Robert S. McNamara. At the head of the table was McNamara. Arrayed around him were four top defense aides and five men from the U.S. Chamber of Commerce, including Theron J. "Terry" Rice, then the chamber's manager of the national defense committee and later its chief lobbyist. During the cordial luncheon, the 10 men discussed various defense issues likely to come up in the next session of Congress, including the military assistance part of the foreign aid program, civil defense and fallout shelters, the Renegotiation Act, government patent policy on inventions resulting from government-financed research, conflict of interest legislation and the Defense Production Act.[19]

The two best-known business groups have been the Chamber of Commerce of the United States and the National Association of Manufacturers (NAM). The two organizations have spoken for American business in the councils of government, usually with one voice, but not always.

Chamber Lobbying Methods. Of the two groups, the chamber has been the more active in attempting to influence Congress. In 1975 and 1979 interviews with Congressional Quarterly, R. Hilton "Dixie" Davis, general manager of the chamber's legislative action department, described some of the group's lobbying methods. *(Details, p. 113)*

Davis' principal objective was to get chamber members to write their senators or representatives on any given issue, and he had four techniques for doing this:

● What he called the "foundation" was the use of the legislative action operation's weekly newsletter, "Congressional Action."

● Much more sophisticated were "action calls," a direct-mail campaign to a selected audience "when issues start to reach the critical stage."

● Similar, but more specialized was the distribution of a memorandum from Davis, much the same in format as the "action call" but briefer and printed on a different letterhead intended to make it look even more urgent. These memos were mailed to a very small group of members.

● When time was extremely short and the issue deemed sufficiently vital, Davis sent out mailgrams. He said he tried to keep them to a minimum because "the cost builds up."

Ex-Members of Congress as Lobbyists

Among the most influential and active lobbyists in Washington have been former members of Congress.

Some ex-members become permanently associated with a single organization whose views they share. Others lobby for many different organizations, frequently changing or adding employers from year to year.

Because of their service in Congress, former members enjoy several advantages in lobbying activities. They have an excellent knowledge of the legislative process and frequently a good "feel" for when and what kind of pressure to exert on behalf of their clients. They often enjoy easy access to congressional staff members and members who are friends and former colleagues.

This enables them to see and speak with key legislative personnel, perhaps the chairman of a committee or subcommittee, at the proper time. The ordinary lobbyist might spend weeks trying to obtain an appointment. Former members also frequently have an expert knowledge of the subject matter of legislation through having dealt with it while in Congress. Thus it is not uncommon for the chairman or senior member of a congressional committee to appear as a lobbyist for the industry regulated by that committee after retiring from Congress.

Not all former members who try to influence legislation are personally registered as lobbyists. Some work for law firms or other organizations that are registered as lobbyists for their clients.

Floor Privileges

The privilege of being admitted to the floor and private lobbies of the House and Senate, which is granted in each chamber to former members of that chamber, is used relatively little by former members directly for lobbying purposes, although it is useful for maintaining contacts and old acquaintances. In the House, use of the floor by former members for lobbying purposes has been circumscribed by House Rule 32 and a chair ruling in 1945 by Speaker Sam Rayburn, D-Texas. Under the "Rayburn rule," a former member is forbidden the privilege of the floor at any time the House is debating or voting on legislation in which he is interested, either personally or as an employee of some other person or group.

In the Senate, no similar formal rule exists. But as a matter of custom, it is considered improper for a former senator, or any other non-member granted the privilege of the floor, to use the privilege to lobby for legislation in which he is interested either personally or as a representative or lobbyist for another person or organization.

Not All Go Home

After every congressional election, some retired or defeated members remain in Washington in law or other offices whose business depends on actions of the federal government. About 20 of the more than 70 men and women who left Congress after the 1978 elections found other jobs in the capital. A few became active lobbyists but others said they were not engaged in lobbying activities in their new lines of work. Among those who stayed in Washington were:

Senate. James Abourezk, D-S.D., lobbyist for Arab interest as partner in Abourezk, Shack & Mendenhall; Dick Clark, D-Iowa, ambassador-at-large for refugee affairs; Carl T. Curtis, R-Neb., practicing law, Nelson & Harding; William D. Hathaway, D-Maine, practicing law; Thomas J. McIntyre, D-N.H., practicing law, Sullivan & Worcester, and president of Americans for SALT, a group lobbying for Senate approval of the SALT II treaty; James B. Pearson, R-Kan., partner, Strook, Strook and Lavan (no lobbying activities); Bill Scott, R-Va., practicing law, Foldenaver, Madigan, Scott & Scott (no lobbying activities).

House. Garry Brown, R-Mich., practicing law, Hill, Christopher & Phillips, including lobbying activity for Michigan State Housing Authority on tax-exempt mortgage bill; Walter Flowers, D-Ala., practicing law, Collier, Shannon, Rill, Edwards & Scott, lobbying on energy issues; Louis J. Frey Jr., R-Fla., partner, Pepper, Hamilton & Scheetz, lobbying on varied subjects according to client interest; Robert L. Leggett, D-Calif., president, Joint Maritime Congress; Lloyd Meeds, D-Wash., counsel to Preston, Thorgrinson, Ellis, Holman & Fletcher, engaged in "legislative advocacy" for states of Alaska and Washington, among other clients; Paul G. Rogers, D-Fla., partner in Hogan & Hartson (no lobbying activities); Teno Roncalio, D-Wyo., partner, O'Neill, Forgotson & Roncalio, lobbyists for Parahoe Development Corp., Northwest Alaskan Pipeline Co., Westinghouse Electric Corp.; Philip E. Ruppe, R-Mich., Washington director for Amex Inc., mining company; Jim Guy Tucker Jr., D-Ark., practicing law, Lobel, Novins & Lamont (no lobbying activities); Charles W. Whalen Jr., R-Ohio, president, New Directions foreign policy lobby.

One reason the chamber was able to be selective was the computerization of its membership lists, which were broken down by congressional districts and states. Davis and his aides needed only to determine which legislators held the swing votes and the computer would churn out address labels for chamber members in those districts.

Foreign Trade

The high point of high-tariff sentiment in the United States was reached when the 1930 Smoot-Hawley Act imposed the highest tariff barriers in history. It was not long, however, before the Roosevelt administration began a move away from protectionism with passage of the Trade Agreements Act of 1934. Successive liberalizations of the Trade Agreements Act followed. It became clear in the post-1945 period that protectionist forces, led by the American Tariff League (renamed Trade Relations Council of the United States in 1958), though still powerful were not able to regain the strength and influence they had held before 1934. Despite the efforts of this group and some others, the nation never went back to a position of rigorous protectionism.

The reasons for this development were partly ideological, partly practical. The cold war and the national interest in the development of a Western alliance and Western community of nations led to internationalist attitudes and the need for closer ties with Western Europe and other non-communist areas — ends which would be served, many believed, by a low tariff policy. At the same time there was a development within the United States of economic interests that would benefit by liberal trade policies — corporations with large investments and subsidiaries overseas that sought access to the American market, and agricultural interests fearing exclusion from overseas markets if the United States pursued a protectionist policy. The upshot was that the business community in the post-war era was far less united than it had been on many occasions in the past in favor of protectionism.

Still, congressional consideration of a major foreign trade bill could produce intense lobbying by a variety of interests. Such lobbying occurred in 1970 over a bill imposing quotas on textile and footwear imports, and setting up machinery for imposing quotas on many other imports.

A new factor took on importance — the multinational corporation. The 1970 contest found some of the largest U.S.-based international business concerns, including a faction that contained three of the top five U.S. defense contractors and 10 of the top 25, throwing their substantial weight against tariffs, quotas and other trade barriers.

Major free trade and protectionist lobby coalition groups took active parts in the 1970 legislative action. The leading free trade groups were the Emergency Committee for American Trade and the Committee for a National Trade Policy. The leading protectionist groups were the Nation-Wide Committee on Import-Export Policy and the Trade Relations Council of the United States.

A major trade reform act in 1974 (PL 93-618) also was accompanied by heavy lobbying. The measure gave the president trade negotiating authority for five years. The bill had been actively supported by the Nixon and Ford administrations and by major multinational corporations and business groups interested in trade with the Soviet Union, working primarily through the Emergency Committee for American Trade. Also involved in lobbying on the bill's sections dealing with Soviet emigration and trade benefits were various Jewish groups, particularly the National Conference on Soviet Jewry, an umbrella organization. The major opponent of the bill was the AFL-CIO, which had favored more protectionist legislation.

1979 Agreement. Congress in July 1979 acted on major trade legislation to ratify agreements reached after five and one half years of negotiations in Geneva, Switzerland. The agreements focused on lowering tariffs, reducing or eliminating non-tariff trade barriers and generally promoting free trade.

There was considerable lobbying on the issue, almost all of it coming before the measure was formally introduced.

In the minds of many trade experts, the lobbying on the trade bill was less a matter of building a winning coalition than avoiding the formation of a losing one.

One leading trade consultant and former deputy trade representative, Harald B. Malmgren, noted that building a winning coalition was difficult because there was little clear-cut support for the trade package. Traditional supporters of trade liberalization, such as farm groups and much of the business community, had become increasingly concerned about rising competition from abroad.

Industries such as electronics, Malmgren said, were split right down the middle, with TV companies favoring protectionism and other segments of the industry willing to liberalize. Though the AFL-CIO traditionally opposed

trade liberalization measures, organized labor was also divided on the issue.

In particular, concessions had to be made to the textile and steel industries, which could have mustered enough strength to defeat the bill otherwise.

Other lobbying pressures came from the chemical industry, unhappy about cuts in tariffs on chemical products; the paper industry, displeased about the relatively minor advantages they gained, and the dairy industry, unhappy about expanded quotas for cheese.

The Chamber of Commerce of the United States and the National Association of Manufacturers supported the bill, citing the potential expansion of overseas trade opportunities for their members.

Education

The idea that the federal government should take some part in the support of education is an old one, dating from the post-Revolutionary years when certain land in every township in the Northwest Territory was set aside by Congress for support of public schools.

Not until 1862 did Congress act again to aid education, then establishing in each state land-grant colleges of agricultural and mechanical arts. In 1867 Congress approved a bill introduced by Rep. (later President) James A. Garfield, creating a non-Cabinet Department of Education. In 1917, Congress authorized federal aid to vocational education.

The federal government made its largest total financial contribution to education through the GI bill (Servicemen's Readjustment Act, 1944) and its successor laws.

In 1950, Congress authorized federal grants for schools in areas where federal activities were adding population while removing property from the tax rolls. But only after the Russians launched Sputnik did Congress pass the National Defense Education Act (NDEA) authorizing $1 billion in federal aid to education.

The decade of the 1960s, particularly the administration of former schoolteacher Lyndon B. Johnson brought the greatest extension of federal aid to education through the Higher Education Facilities Act of 1963, the Elementary and Secondary Education Act of 1965 and the Higher Education Act of 1965.

As Congress enlarged the federal role in aiding education, many education groups set up Washington offices.

The American Federation of Teachers (AFT) moved from Chicago — where it had been chartered by Samuel Gompers in 1916 — to Washington. The Association of American Universities (AAU) moved to Washington in 1962 at age 62. The National School Boards Association, founded in 1940, set up a Washington office in 1966.

By the 1970s, there were hundreds of such groups represented in Washington. Almost every type of institution and teacher was represented, as well as parents, libraries and educational administrators. School librarians and school secretaries each had their own group; as did college governing boards, college registrars and college business officers. In addition, dozens of the colleges and universities had their own Washington representatives.

Diversity. The education community covers a wide spectrum of groups and specific interests. Among the largest are the 446,000-member American Federation of Teachers, the 1.8-million-member National Education Association and the seven-million-member National Congress of Parents and Teachers. Among the smallest education groups are the 57-member Council of Chief State School Officers and the 50-member Association of American Universities.

Lobby Groups Rate Members

The number of organizations that rate members of Congress on their votes has increased steadily in recent years. Nearly 70 groups are now in the ratings business, compared with only a handful a few years ago.

Some of the newer raters are established organizations that have decided to adopt the ratings techniques successfully used for years by labor and political groups such as the Americans for Democratic Action, Americans for Constitutional Action and the AFL-CIO's COPE (Committee on Political Education).

Another reason for the increase is the proliferation of public interest groups, many of which issue congressional ratings. One of the leaders in this field is Ralph Nader's Public Citizen organization, which compiles consumer ratings of Congress.

Praise for and protests against group ratings of Congress are particularly intense during election years, when they provide handy weapons in the campaigns of members or their opponents.

The ratings provide a percentage or numerical label that can be used to characterize a member or a voting record, favorably or unfavorably, on an ideological scale or in a particular area of interest.

Voters may not believe a candidate's charge that a senator or representative is against consumers, particularly if the incumbent has some pro-consumer votes that can be pointed to in rebuttal. But the opponent's task is simplified if the incumbent appears on the Consumer Federation of America's list of "Consumer Zeroes," who have voted 100 percent "wrong" from the organization's standpoint on its selection of key votes. On the other hand, an incumbent "Consumer Hero" can turn that label to an advantage.

Democrats running for re-election in heavily Republican districts fear a 100 percent rating from the liberal Americans for Democratic Action (ADA). Republicans highly rated by the Americans for Constitutional Action (ACA) run a similar risk. They can be branded as conservatives, and risk losing Democratic votes in the general election.

Labels and numerical scores can be used by the opposition as a convenient "objective proof" of campaign charges and can force an incumbent onto the defensive. Since members of Congress win re-election largely because they are incumbents and often face under-financed and unpublicized opposition, unfavorable ratings from national interest groups can focus unwanted attention on a local campaign and pose a threat to these advantages.

Listed below are some of the major organizations that regularly compile congressional ratings:

Business. Chamber of Commerce of the United States, National Associated Businessmen, National Association of Manufacturers, National Federation of Independent Business.

Conservatives. American Conservative Union, Americans for Constitutional Action, Liberty Lobby.

Consumer Affairs. Consumer Federation of America, Public Citizen.

Defense/Foreign Policy. American Security Council, Coalition for a New Foreign and Military Policy, Friends Committee on National Legislation, SANE.

Education. American Federation of Teachers, National Education Association, National Student Lobby.

Environment. Environmental Action, League of Conservation Voters.

Labor. AFL-CIO Committee on Political Education; Amalgamated Clothing and Textile Workers Union; American Federation of Government Employees; American Federation of State, County and Municipal Employees; Communications Workers of America; International Association of Machinists; International Brotherhood of Teamsters; Public Employees Department, AFL-CIO; United Auto Workers; United Mine Workers.

Liberals. Americans for Democratic Action, Ripon Society.

Rural/Farm. American Farm Bureau Federation, National Farmers Organization, National Farmers Union.

Other. American Parents Committee, Common Cause, League of Women Voters, Leadership Conference on Civil Rights, National Council of Senior Citizens, National Taxpayers Union, Taxation With Representation, Women's Lobby.

(For 1978 ratings of members of Congress by four organizations — ACA, ADA, Chamber of Commerce and COPE — see p. 87.)

No umbrella is large enough to cover all education interest groups although for a brief period in 1970 it seemed that the emergency Committee for Full Funding of Education Programs might be able to.

The emergency committee — its creation and operations — cast into relief the difficulty of fusing these diverse groups into an effective cooperating community and the sensitivity of many of them to any suggestion that they were lobbies in the traditional meaning of the word.

Despite a basic common interest, many conflicts arose between groups, relating to the various sectors of education which each represented. Black colleges and community colleges often did not benefit from the same programs as did large universities. The all-teacher associations did not see the issues from the same perspective as groups composed primarily of administrators.

Because of these divisions, categorical aid programs—library services and school lunch—were enacted by Congress long before any type of general aid to schools. A proposal for general aid brought out all the contradictions in the educational community—church-state, public-private—while categorical grant programs won support from certain groups without incurring the opposition of others.

In 1971 external threats contributed to an unusual unity within the educational community. The financial crunch produced the cooperative effort of the emergency committee where the groups could hash out their differences and then arrive at a common strategy.

Its "package approach," developing one amendment increasing funding for a variety of education programs, was designed to overcome the fragmentation that often had beset the education community.

Early in 1971, most of the major higher education groups agreed upon one statement on institutional aid; later they agreed upon the best formula for allocating such aid. This unified pressure won an institutional aid proposal from the Nixon administration, which had said early in 1971 that it would not submit such a bill during the year.

A number of other prominent and often-disagreeing groups united to oppose a program of education vouchers, which was seen as a serious threat to the public school system. Yet the divisions remained, submerged only temporarily. One participant in the Government Relations Group, the congressional liaison representatives of the various associations, said that there often was more infighting than communication.

Department of Education. The National Education Association scored one of its biggest victories in 1979, when Congress approved President Carter's proposal to split off education from the Department of Health, Education and Welfare, where it had lodged since the 1950s, and create a separate Cabinet-level Department of Education.

But here again the education lobby was divided. The NEA's rival American Federation of Teachers and the AFL-CIO fought the proposal as part of an unusual coalition of liberals and conservatives who feared the department would lead to greater federal control over education. Black groups successfully fought to keep the Head Start program for underprivileged children in HEW, which was to become the Department of Health and Human Services. *(Details, p. 209)*

Foreign Interests

Since World War II, lobbying by foreign interests and by American groups with foreign members or interests has become an increasingly important factor in Washington's legislative and executive decision-making. Foreign-oriented lobbying is based on international politics, world trade and many American domestic issues, for any action by the U.S. government may have foreign or global implications.

Some examples of foreign interests that registered in 1979 included: The Chinese National Association of Industry and Commerce, interested in protecting commercial relations between the United States and Taiwan; the government of Morocco, interested in all legislation affecting Morocco; The Washington Office on Africa, a group with religious connections interested in legislation concerning southern Africa; Republic of the Philippines, interested in legislation concerning the right of foreign governments to bring suit under U.S. antitrust laws; the governments of El Salvador, Zaire, Somalia and Saudi Arabia, all interested in legislation that would affect their national interests. [20]

Arab and Israeli Interests. A new type of foreign lobbying developed in the 1970s. The 1973 Yom Kippur war in the Middle East resulted in new instability in the area, in growing doubts about Israel's security and in more aggressive control of oil production by the Arab states. In the aftermath of the war, Arab and Israeli interests in the United States, some of them longstanding groups, have taken on new roles.

On the one hand are various groups representing the interests of Israel: the American Israel Public Affairs Committee, the American Jewish Committee and B'nai B'rith's Anti-Defamation League. In the view both of people on Capitol Hill and of representatives of Jewish organizations, the Jewish lobby gains much of its power from citizen activism — both Jewish and non-Jewish — and widespread public backing for the longstanding U.S. policy of support for an independent Israel.

On the other hand are Arab interests in the United States, represented by a number of organizations. Two major groups are the National Association of Arab-Americans (NAAA) and the Arab Information Centers (AIC).

The NAAA presented position papers to the platform committees at the 1976 Democratic and Republican national conventions — the first time any Arab-American group had done so.

For years, according to Hatem I. Hussaini, former assistant director of the Arab Information Center in Washington, the Arab Information Center has worked with this set of facts: "The Congress is in general pro-Israel. The Congress in general is not interested in the Arab point of view." The 1973-74 oil crisis changed these attitudes only a bit, he said. Now the AIC gets a few more queries from individual members of Congress regarding the Arab side of the Israeli conflict, on oil policy or other Middle East matters. *(Details, Israel lobby, see p. 141; Arab lobby, see p. 148)*

Public Interest Groups

Public interest lobbies are a relatively new development in the long history of attempts to influence members of Congress. The League of Women Voters and Americans for Democratic Action are examples of public interest lobbies, and their activities helped to set the pattern for other groups. Two of the groups that followed have attracted wide public attention and have almost come to characterize public interest lobbies. The two groups are Common Cause, founded by John Gardner, and Public Citizen, developed by Ralph Nader.

While Common Cause and Public Citizen share the general goal of giving the average citizen more influence in political, economic and social matters, the two organizations have evolved their own areas of specialty.

Public Citizen groups pursue a broad agenda of substantive economic, consumer, environmental, legal and social policy issues while Common Cause has focused on issues of political structure and procedure. Skillful use of publicity, shrewd legislative and political tactics and recognized expertise on previously undeveloped issues were key ingredients in the groups' success.

Both groups can claim some notable successes. Common Cause, for example, is credited with a major role in the enactment of the 1974 campaign finance law (PL 93-443), with helping to develop public pressure for House and Senate reforms and with aiding pending "government in the sunshine" legislation.

Nader's groups have won lawsuits against corporations, professional organizations and the federal government. Nader lobbyists helped shape congressional energy and tax legislation, including repeal of the oil depletion allowance, and won approval for a fund to help consumers petition the Federal Trade Commission.

Both groups also have succeeded in involving the public in their work. Common Cause has approximately 220,000 members. Public Citizen, though not a membership organization, is supported by an estimated 196,000 contributors annually. By way of comparison, Consumers Union has in excess of 200,000 members, the League of Women Voters 123,000 and Americans for Democratic Action 55,000.

Common Cause and Public Citizen have adopted most of the normal pressure techniques used by interest groups with one major exception — neither group endorses candidates or makes campaign contributions. However, the groups do rate legislators' votes on selected issues.

Both Public Citizen and Common Cause have done organizational work at the grass-roots level — but in different ways and with different objectives.

Common Cause has attempted to develop an indirect lobbying operation capable of producing letters and constituent contacts in response to important issues. Approximately 10 percent of the organization's membership participates in the lobbying work, organized by congressional district and linked with Washington through an elaborate telephone "chain" and newsletter "action alerts."

The Nader operation's grass-roots objective, in contrast, is to stimulate local action on local problems. One of Nader's main themes in his speeches is to urge his audience to become actively involved in public affairs. *(For further discussion see pp. 169-176)*

Lobbying Investigations

Investigations of lobbying have stemmed from a wide range of motives and have sought to achieve nearly as broad a range of objectives. Lobbying investigations have been used to respond to intense public concern about lobbying, to gather information on the workings of existing regulatory legislation and to help prepare the way for, and to shape, proposed new regulatory legislation.

The first thorough investigation of lobbying was undertaken by the Senate in 1913 in reaction to President Wilson's charges of a massive grass-roots lobbying effort by the tariff lobby opposing the administration's tariff program. Since 1913, committees in 25 Congresses have investigated particular allegations of lobbying abuses or lobbying activities in general.

Following are summary accounts of selected major lobbying investigations.

Business Lobbying, 1913

Senate Investigation. In 1913 President Woodrow Wilson was enraged over alleged lobbying activity by the National Association of Manufacturers (NAM) and other protectionist groups on the Underwood tariff bill. On May 26, 1913, Wilson denounced the presence of an "insidious" lobby that sought to bring on a new tide of protectionism. "I think the public ought to know," he said, "that extraordinary exertions are being made by the lobby in Washington to gain recognition for certain alterations in the tariff bill.... Washington has seldom seen so numerous, so industrious, or so insidious a lobby.... There is every evidence that money without limit is being spent to sustain this lobby.... The government ought to be relieved from this intolerable burden and the constant interruption to the calm progress of debate." [21]

In the Senate hearings that followed, testimony disclosed that large amounts had been spent for entertainment and for other lobbying purposes both by the interests seeking high tariff duties and by those interested in low duties, such as the sugar refiners. Following the hearings, a bill for registration of lobbyists was introduced, but farm, labor and other special interests succeeded in warding off a vote on it.

House Investigation. Also in 1913, Col. Martin M. Mulhall, lobbyist for the NAM published a sensational account of his activities in a front-page article in the *New York World.* Among other disclosures, Mulhall said he had paid "between $1,500 and $2,000" to help Rep. James T. McDermott, D-Ill., for legislative favors.

A four-month inquiry by a select House panel chaired by Majority Leader Finis J. Garrett, D-Tenn. (1905-29), found that many of Mulhall's allegations were exaggerated. The panel established that Mulhall had set up his own office in the Capitol, had paid the chief House page $50 a month for inside information, had received advance information on pending legislation from McDermott and House Republican leader John Dwight of New York (1902-13) and had influenced the appointment of members to House committees and subcommittees. Six of seven House members implicated by Mulhall were exonerated, but the panel recommended that McDermott be "strongly censured." The House adopted the panel's recommendations. Although McDermott was not expelled from the House, he resigned the following year. [22]

Tax and Utilities Lobbying, 1927

Interest in lobbying activities was rekindled in the 1920s after the American Legion and other veterans' groups had succeeded in obtaining passage of a bonus bill over the veto of President Coolidge.

In 1927 an investigation committee under Sen. Thaddeus H. Caraway, D-Ark. (H 1913-21, S 1921-31), conducted extensive public hearings on lobbying efforts. One of the immediate reasons for the 1927 investigation was the pressure being brought to bear on the Ways and Means Committee for repeal of the federal estate tax. More than 200 witnesses, including one governor and many state legislators, had been brought to Washington by the American Taxpayers League to appear before the committee. All travel expenses were paid and some of the witnesses received additional compensation. The second activity to which Congress objected at the time was the establishment of Washington headquarters by the Joint Committee of National Utility Associations to block a proposed Senate investigation of utility financing. The joint committee succeeded in having the investigation transferred to the Federal Trade Commission, but that agency took its assignment seriously and gave the utility situation a thorough going-over.

At the end of the investigation, a sweeping registration bill was recommended. The bill defined lobbying as "...any effort in influencing Congress upon any matter coming before it, whether it be by distributing literature, appearing before committees of Congress, or seeking to interview members of either the House or Senate." A lobbyist was defined as "...one who shall engage, for pay, to attempt to influence legislation, or to prevent legislation by the national Congress." [23] The bill passed the Senate by a unanimous vote but was pigeonholed by a House committee.

Despite failure of the Caraway bill, the Senate Judiciary Committee's report on the measure contributed greatly to the public's knowledge of lobbying. The panel asserted that about 90 percent of the lobbying associations listed in the Washington telephone directory were "fakes" whose aim was to bilk unwary clients. These organizations, according to the committee report, included groups that purported to represent scientific, agricultural, religious, temperance, and anti-prohibition interests. "In fact," the panel said, "every activity of the human mind has been capitalized by some grafter." The committee estimated that $99 of every $100 paid to these groups "go into the pockets of the promoters." Caraway himself disclosed that one of the lobbyists had collected $60,000 in one year from business interests by simply writing them every time a bill

---

Tax Deductions for Lobbying

Under a 1919 regulation by the Internal Revenue Service interpreting federal tax laws, money spent by businesses or individuals for lobbying purposes was not deductible from taxable income. The application of the regulation led to protests by businesses and several attempts to upset the regulation.

Finally, in the omnibus tax bill of 1962 (HR 10650 — PL 87-834), Congress authorized federal income tax deductions for sums of money spent for lobbying purposes. The authorization permitted a business to deduct the cost of lobbying for legislation — whether federal, state or local legislatures were involved — if the legislation was of direct interest to the taxpayer concerned. The company's interest had to be truly direct (e.g., tax or labor legislation affecting it) and not remote and speculative.

Lobbying for a presidential disability amendment, for example, was considered remote and therefore not deductible. Deductions were made permissible for any otherwise legal type of direct contact with a legislative body designed to influence the public. Under the legislation, a business could also deduct any portion of the dues it paid to a trade organization or chamber of commerce allocable to lobbying, and an individual union member could deduct union dues allocable to lobbying purposes.

---

favorable to business was passed and claiming sole credit for its passage. [24]

Naval Armaments, 1929

The next congressional probe of lobbying came in 1929, when a Senate Naval Affairs Subcommittee looked into the activities of William B. Shearer, who represented shipping, electrical, metals, machinery and similar concerns interested in blocking limitation of naval armaments and in obtaining larger appropriations for Navy ships. The path to Shearer's exposure had been paved when he filed a suit in the New York courts to recover $257,655, which he said was owed to him by the New York Shipbuilding Co. Shearer claimed the money was due for lobbying services he had performed in Washington and at the Geneva naval limitation conference of 1927.

Testimony before the subcommittee showed that Shearer had been sent to Geneva by shipbuilding interests and had done everything he could to torpedo an agreement. Following the conference, at which no agreement was reached, Shearer had led industry lobbying efforts for bigger naval appropriations and for subsidies for the merchant marine. His other activities included preparing pro-Navy articles for the Hearst newspaper chain, writing articles for the 1938 Republican presidential campaign, in which he characterized peace advocates as traitors, and writing speeches for the American Legion and like-minded lobby groups.

Utility Lobbies, 1935

A decade of congressional concern over the influence exerted by private utilities led to a stormy probe of that industry's lobbying activities in 1935. Although Congress nine years earlier had instructed the Federal Trade Commission to investigate utility lobbying, a two-year probe by the FTC had been largely inconclusive.

After intensive lobbying by the utilities had threatened to emasculate an administration bill to regulate utility holding companies, President Roosevelt in a special message to Congress described the holding companies as "private empires within the nation" and denounced their lobbying techniques. Congressional supporters of the measure demanded an investigation to bring out the lengths to which the power interests' lobbying had gone. [25]

A special investigative panel was set up in the Senate under the chairmanship of Sen. Hugo L. Black, D-Ala. (1927-37), an administration stalwart who later was to become an associate justice of the Supreme Court. Following a sometimes raucous hearing, Black concluded that the utilities had spent about $4 million to defeat the utility bill and had engaged in massive propagandizing to convince the public that the bill was an iniquitous invasion of private rights and a sharp turn toward socialism. Among other findings, Black's panel stated that the utilities had financed thousands of phony telegrams to Congress, in which the names of the senders had been picked at random from telephone books. [26]

Amid a furor over the telegrams, Congress passed the Public Utilities Holding Company Act, which included provisions requiring reports to federal agencies on some utility lobbying activities.

The Senate and House also passed lobbyist registration bills. A conference agreement was reached but the House rejected the agreement and final adjournment came before a new agreement could be reached. The defeat of the measure was attributed to the combined efforts of hundreds of lobbyists.

Munitions Lobby, 1935

Another investigation during 1935 involved the munitions lobby and the Senate Special Committee Investigating the Munitions Industry, under Sen. Gerald P. Nye, R-N.D. (1925-45). Committee disclosures of bribery and arms deals brought sharp responses in Latin America and Great Britain, where the incidents had occurred.

Further Studies, 1938 and 1945

The Temporary National Economic Committee, set up by Congress at President Roosevelt's request, under the chairmanship of Sen. Joseph O'Mahoney, D-Wyo. (1934-53; 1954-61), included lobbying among its subjects of study in 1938.

The Joint Committee on the Organization of Congress, established in 1945, studied lobbying activities along with other matters pertaining to Congress. On the basis of the committee's recommendations, Congress in 1946 passed the Legislative Reorganization Act, which included the first general lobby registration law. *(Details, p. 19)*

Omnibus Lobbying Probe, 1950

A House Select Committee on Lobbying Activities headed by Rep. Frank M. Buchanan, D-Pa. (1946-51), investigated the lobbying and related activities of a wide range of organizations in 1950. The committee's probe had been prompted largely by the assertion of President Truman that the 80th Congress was "the most thoroughly surrounded ... with lobbies in the whole history of this great country of ours." Truman said: "There were more lobbyists in Washington, there was more money spent by lobbyists in Washington, than ever before in the history of the Congress of the United States. It's disgraceful. . . ." [27] Most of the publicity centered on the efforts of the Committee for Constitutional Government to distribute low-cost or free "right-wing" books and pamphlets designed to influence the public.

In an effort to determine more accurately the amount of money spent by organizations to influence legislation, the House investigating committee requested detailed information from 200 corporations, labor unions and farm groups. Replies from 152 corporations gave a total of $32 million spent for this purpose from Jan. 1, 1947, through May 21, 1950. More than 100 of these corporations had not filed reports under the 1946 Federal Regulation of Lobbying Act. Reports of the 37 that had done so showed expenditures of $776,000, which was less than 3 percent of the amount reported by respondents to the committee questionnaire. In releasing results of the questionnaire, Chairman Buchanan noted that the survey covered activities of only 152 of the country's 500,000 corporations. "I firmly believe," he said, "that the business of influencing legislation is a billion-dollar industry."[28]

The House committee made recommendations for strengthening the 1946 lobbying law but no action was taken.

Omnibus Lobbying Probe, 1956

In 1956 a major lobbying inquiry was conducted by the Senate Special Committee to Investigate Political Activities, Lobbying and Campaign Contributions. The inquiry was initiated against a background of an alleged campaign contribution to Sen. Francis Case, R-S.D. (H 1937-51; S 1951-62), in connection with voting on a natural gas bill. The panel was chaired by Sen. John L. McClellan, D-Ark. (1943-77).

Following a long investigation, McClellan on May 31, 1957, introduced a new lobbying registration bill designed to replace the 1946 act. The bill proposed to tighten the existing law by making the comptroller general responsible for enforcing it (there was no administrator under the 1946 act); by eliminating a loophole that required registration of only those lobbyists whose "principal purpose" was lobbying; by extending the coverage to anyone who spent $50,000 or more a year on grass-roots lobbying; and by eliminating an exemption that made the law inapplicable to persons who merely testified on proposed legislation.

The bill was vigorously opposed by the Chamber of Commerce of the United States and was criticized on certain points by the National Association of Manufacturers, the Association of American Railroads and the American Medical Association, although the latter endorsed the measure as a whole. The bill did not reach the floor and died with the close of the 85th Congress.

Retired Military Lobbyists, 1959

In 1959 the Special Investigations Subcommittee of the House Armed Services Committee held three months of hearings on the employment of former Army, Navy and Air Force officers by defense contractors, and the influence of the retired officers in obtaining government contracts for their new employers. The subcommittee found that more than 1,400 retired officers with the rank of major or higher — including 261 of general or flag rank — were employed by the top 100 defense contractors.

In its report in 1960, the subcommittee said that "The coincidence of contracts and personal contacts with firms represented by retired officers and retired civilian officials sometimes raises serious doubts as to the objectivity of these [contract] decisions."[29] Congress largely accepted subcommittee recommendations for tighter restrictions on sales to the government by retired personnel.

Foreign Lobbyists, 1962

Lobbying in connection with the Sugar Act of 1962 led the Senate Foreign Relations Committee to vote, July 6, 1962, to launch an investigation of foreign lobbies and the extent to which they attempted to influence United States policies. At the request of Foreign Relations Committee Chairman J. William Fulbright, D-Ark. (1945-74), and Sen. Paul H. Douglas, D-Ill. (1949-67), the Senate Finance Committee, which had jurisdiction over the sugar bill, had queried sugar lobbyists on their arrangements with their employers, mostly foreign countries. A compendium of the answers, made public June 26, 1962, showed that some payments to the sugar lobbyists were made on the basis of the size of the sugar quotas granted by Congress.

Hearings conducted some months later by the Foreign Relations Committee produced evidence that some lobbyists also lobbied their own clients. Fulbright disclosed, for example, that Michael B. Deane, a Washington public relations man who had been hired by the Dominican Sugar Commission to lobby for its interests before Congress, had apparently filed exaggerated, sometimes inaccurate reports to the commission regarding his effectiveness. Deane admitted that he had falsely reported to commission officials that he had been invited by the president to the White House and had talked with the secretary of Agriculture. Deane said he occasionally gave himself "too much credit," but "one tends to do that a little bit when they have a client who is outside of Washington."[30] Similar testimony was elicited from other sugar lobbyists.

The Fulbright probe continued well into 1963, and at its conclusion, Fulbright introduced a bill to tighten registration requirements under the Foreign Agents Registration Act of 1938 for persons in the United States representing foreign interests. The bill passed the Senate in 1964 but died in the House. It was revived in the 89th Congress and enacted in 1966. *(Details, p. 129)*

Regulation of Lobbying

In 1876 the House first passed a resolution requiring lobbyists to register during the 44th Congress with the Clerk of the House. Since the advent of the 62nd Congress in 1911, federal lobbying legislation has continued to be proposed in practically every Congress.[31] Yet only one comprehensive lobbying regulation law and only a handful of more specialized measures have been enacted.

Since 1975 Congress has been attempting to pass new lobby registration legislation.

The principal method of regulating lobbying has been disclosure rather than control. In four laws, lobbyists have been required to identify themselves, whom they represent and their legislative interests. In one law, lobbyists also have been required to report how much they and their employers spend on lobbying. But definitions have been unclear, and enforcement has been minimal. As a result, the few existing disclosure laws have produced only limited information, and its effects have been questionable.

One reason for the relative lack of restrictions on lobbies has been the difficulty of imposing meaningful restrictions without infringing on the constitutional rights of free speech, press, assembly and petition. Other reasons include a fear that restrictions would hamper legitimate lobbies without reaching more serious lobby abuses; the consolidated and highly effective opposition of lobbies; the desire of some members to keep open avenues to a possible lobbying career they may wish to pursue later.

The two major lobbying laws Congress has succeeded in enacting have dealt with lobbyists in general who meet certain definitions of lobbying. The Foreign Agents Registration Act was first enacted in 1938 amid reports of fascist and Nazi propaganda circulating in the United States in the period before World War II. It has been amended frequently since then, and its history is as much a part of this country's struggle with internal security as it is a part of efforts to regulate lobbying.

The one existing omnibus lobbying law, the Federal Regulation of Lobbying Act, was enacted in 1946 as part of the Legislative Reorganization Act. The act's vague language and subsequent court interpretations have combined to reduce seriously the effectiveness of the law's spending and lobbying disclosure provisions.

The following sections review controls on spending by lobbyists and lobby registration requirements.

Spending Controls

Lobbying Expenditures

Although lobby spending by private individuals or groups is not restricted by federal law, a federal statute, first passed in 1919, attempted to restrict pressure on Congress by the federal executive branch. This statute (18 USC 1913) forbade federal employees and officials from using appropriated funds to lobby Congress on legislation. The provision was not designed to prevent normal federal employee communications and contacts with Congress in connection with legislative requests by executive branch agencies. Rather, it was designed to prevent flagrant spending to manipulate public opinion or to bombard members of Congress with letters and telegrams from the executive branch. In practice the law did not block high officials from publicly advocating legislation and pressuring Congress.

Judicial Restraints. A Supreme Court decision in 1961 somewhat limited the financial resources upon which railway labor unions could draw for their lobbying and similar activities.

The decision was handed down by a five-member majority in a Railway Labor Act case *(International Assn. of Machinists v. Street, 367 U.S. 740)*. The case involved several employees of the Southern Railway System. They contended their rights were being interfered with because, under a union shop contract sanctioned by a 1951 amendment to the Railway Labor Act, they were required to join a union and pay dues, part of which were used to promote legislation and public policies they opposed.

The court majority held that the employees had a valid grievance. The court held that under the 1951 Railway Labor Act provision, the union could not use an employee's dues to support legislation and general public policies to which the employee objected. As a remedy, it suggested to the lower federal courts that they order the return to the complaining employees of that portion of their dues which had been used, not for collective bargaining activities, but for legislative and lobbying activities to which the employees objected.

Charitable Groups. Charitable organizations that engage in lobbying — and many of them do — face an uncertain test on limiting their lobbying expenditures. The problem arises out of the wording of a portion of section 501 (c)(3) of the Internal Revenue Code of 1954, under which the groups are granted tax-exempt status, and the way in which courts and the Internal Revenue Service have interpreted the wording.

As a condition of exemption, organizations are prohibited from engaging in "substantial" activities relating to lobbying. No statutory definition is provided for "substantial." One court has ruled that if less than 5 percent of an exempt group's expenditures were for influencing legislation, the political activity was not substantial *(Murray Seasongood v. Commissioner, 227 F. 2d 907 (6th Cir. 1955))*. Other judges and the IRS have listed an exempt group's legislative activities and non-legislative activities in parallel columns, and have used human judgment to determine whether the lobbying activity was substantial. [32]

In recent years there have been a number of legislative proposals to provide a statutory base for judging the extent of an exempt group's lobbying efforts. While specific approaches have varied, most have sought to apply some percentage limitation on the dollar amount of total organization spending that can be spent on legislative activity. In 1976 Congress passed legislation imposing such limits. *(See p. 177)*

Spending Reports. Under terms of the 1946 Federal Regulation of Lobbying Act, persons employed for the "principal purpose" of lobbying Congress were required to file financial reports with the Clerk of the House and the Secretary of the Senate. Because of loopholes in the act, however, the reports filed were scarcely an indication of the amounts spent on lobbying. *(1950 investigation, p. 18)*

One of the loopholes in the lobby law resulted from its vague language on who had to file, what information was to be included and who was to ensure enforcement. Some organizations, after filing reports for the first few years after 1946, stopped reporting on the ground that lobbying was not their "principal purpose." Others filed reports but did so under protest, contending that they were not covered under their interpretations of the act.

Many groups engaged primarily in grass-roots lobbying filed for a time but stopped after the Supreme Court ruled in *United States v. Harriss* (347 U.S. 612) in 1954 that grass-roots activities were not covered unless the organization, in effect, urged the public to contact Congress on legislation. Some groups that filed began subtracting the amounts they spent on their grass-roots work. The issue of grass-roots lobbying has been a key issue in recent congressional debate on lobby disclosure.

Another weakness was that the law left it up to each group or lobbyist to determine what portion of total expenditures were to be reported as spending for lobbying. As a result, some organizations whose budgets for their Washington, D.C., operation ran into the hundreds of thousands of dollars reported only very small amounts for spending on lobbying activities, contending that the remainder of their spending was for general public information purposes, research and other matters. Other organizations, interpreting the law quite differently, reported a much larger percentage of their total budgets as being for lobbying. The result was that some groups which year after year reported a large portion of their budgets gained reputations as "big lobby spenders" when, in fact, they simply were reporting more fully, at least under one view of the law, than other groups spending just as much.

Political Spending

The promise of electoral support or opposition has been perhaps the most effective device available to pressure groups in their attempts to influence Congress on legislation. Precisely for this reason, Congress attempted on several occasions to limit campaign contributions made by corporations, organizations and individuals in connection with federal elections. The limitations were intended to prevent those with great financial resources from using them to dominate the selection of members of Congress and thereby the legislative decisions of Congress.

Two major sets of federal laws long restricted campaign spending and contributions by pressure groups. The first, the Federal Corrupt Practices Act of 1925, strengthened a 1907 ban on campaign contributions by corporations in connection with federal elections. This prohibition was extended to labor unions temporarily by the 1943 wartime Smith-Connally (War Labor Disputes) Act and permanently by the 1947 Taft-Hartley Act. The Taft-Hartley Act also broadened the ban on both corporations and unions.

The second set of restrictions was contained in the second Hatch Act, passed in 1940, which (among other things) limited to $5,000 the amount an individual or group could contribute to any one candidate in a single calendar year in connection with any federal election campaign.

Had either of these restrictions been truly effective, they might well have sealed off unions, businesses and other pressure groups from any major influence over federal elections. But loopholes in these laws, coupled with lack of clarity about the applicability and constitutionality of the ban on contributions by unions and corporations, left labor, business and other pressure groups numerous ways to continue effective political activity in federal elections.

Taft-Hartley Restrictions. The Taft-Hartley Act prohibition actually consisted of two parts: the ban on campaign contributions and the ban on direct expenditures. With regard to the prohibition on campaign contributions, there was no question that such contributions were barred in connection with federal elections and primaries if proposed to be made from corporate funds or from general union revenue derived from member dues. The ban applied whether the contribution was made directly to a candidate or to some group which used it on the candidate's behalf. But there was nothing in the law stating that business executives or union members were barred from making voluntary contributions from their own personal funds to candidates for federal office.

Labor unions developed an additional technique that later was adopted by businesses. The unions set up separate political arms that technically were not labor unions and that received funds not from dues money but from voluntary contributions made by union members. These groups, the best known of which was the AFL-CIO's Committee on Political Education (COPE), were, in effect, simply voluntary political organizations and were not subject to the Taft-Hartley Act prohibition against political contributions by unions in federal elections. COPE and similar groups were free to make campaign contributions in connection with federal elections, primaries, conventions and caucuses. A major business political action committee was the Business-Industrial Political Action Committee (BIPAC), set up by the National Association of Manufacturers.

With regard to the second part of the Taft-Hartley prohibition, which barred direct expenditures by corporations and unions in connection with federal elections, "leakages" developed there too. The reason was, in part, that the ban on direct expenditures had to be construed narrowly lest it run afoul of the guarantees of freedom of

Antitrust Action Against Lobbying

An attempt to use federal antitrust laws to restrain lobbying activities failed in 1961 when the U.S. Supreme Court held the antitrust laws inapplicable to campaigns for or against legislation.

In the case of *Eastern Railroad v. Noerr*, the Supreme Court held unanimously, Feb. 20, 1961, that attempts by any group to obtain legislation harmful to a competitor could not be considered a conspiracy in restraint of trade or any other violation of the federal antitrust laws. The court, speaking through Justice Hugo L. Black, said that because of the importance of the right to petition in the U.S. constitutional system, the federal antitrust laws could not be construed as outlawing action that was genuinely aimed at securing legislation — even if the legislation would injure a competitor and reduce competition, even if the legislative campaign had the effect of injuring the competitor's reputation and business or even if the publicity used in the campaign was not wholly ethical.

The *Noerr* case arose in 1953 when 41 Pennsylvania truck operators and the Pennsylvania Motor Truck Association brought suit against 24 railroads associated in the Eastern Railroad Presidents' Conference. The truckers alleged that the railroads had engaged the Carl Byoir public relations firm to conduct a publicity campaign against truckers designed to foster adoption and retention of laws and law enforcement policies destructive of the trucking industry.

The real motive, it was alleged, was to destroy the trucking industry as a competitor of the railroads in the long-haul freight business. It was alleged that the Byoir agency had, among other things, "planted" anti-trucker editorials and articles in newspapers and magazines, helped to created supposedly spontaneous grass-roots citizens' groups, which called for anti-trucker legislation, conducted public opinion polls with questions loaded against the industry and publicized the results as if they were unbiased findings.

These tactics, it was asserted, resulted in a number of state actions injurious to the trucking industry, including the 1951 veto by Gov. John S. Fine, R, of a state "fair-truck" bill that would have permitted heavier loads on Pennsylvania highways. The truckers contended that this campaign violated the federal antitrust laws.

A lower court decision on Oct. 10, 1957, by federal Judge Thomas J. Clary upheld the truckers' position. Judge Clary conceded that legitimate lobbying activities and efforts to influence public opinion were not actionable under the antitrust laws, but he held that in this case the antitrust laws did apply because the objective of the railroad campaign was to destroy competition in the long-haul freight industry, the methods used to secure legislation were deceitful and the result had been to destroy the trucking industry's good will with the public. When the case reached the Supreme Court in 1961, however, it reversed the lower court, holding that the antitrust laws could not be construed as intended to permit injunctions or damage suits in a campaign involving a genuine attempt to obtain legislation, even when the legislation sought would be injurious to a particular group.

speech contained in the First Amendment to the U.S. Constitution. In the years following the Taft-Hartley Act, a long list of expenditures in federal elections came to be accepted as permissible for corporations and unions.

Hatch Act Restrictions. The $5,000 limitation on campaign contributions in the Hatch Act did help to prevent massive spending in small areas by political and pressure organizations. But it was vitiated by several glaring loopholes. The $5,000 limitation did not prevent an individual, the individual's spouse, their children and other relatives from giving $5,000 each to the same candidate. Nor did it prevent a single individual from making contributions of $5,000 each to many different candidates and political committees. The limit was lowered to $1,000 by the Federal Election Campaign Act Amendments of 1974.

Campaign Finance Act Restrictions. In 1971, 1974 and 1976 Congress enacted campaign finance legislation that included provisions affecting political expenditures by pressure groups.

The Federal Election Campaign Act of 1971 (PL 92-225), which repealed the Federal Corrupt Practices Act of 1925, included a series of provisions that more strictly defined the roles unions and corporations could play in political campaigns.

The Federal Election Campaign Amendments of 1974 (PL 93-443) included provisions that set contribution limits for individuals and organizations.

The 1976 act (PL 94-283) tightened the contribution limits established in the 1974 campaign law for individuals and political committees and limited the ability of corporate and union political action committees to proliferate to circumvent the statute's contribution ceilings. The law also restricted the fund-raising ability of union and corporate political action committees.

In 1979 Congress considered proposals that would further limit campaign contributions by political action committees. *(Campaign finance law revision, p. 67; political action committees spending, p. 73)*

Lobby Registration Laws

Utilities Holding Company Act

Section 12(i) of the Public Utilities Holding Company Act of 1935 required anyone employed or retained by a registered holding company or a subsidiary to file certain information with the Securities and Exchange Commission before attempting to influence Congress, the Federal Power Commission or the Securities and Exchange Commission on any legislative or administrative matter affecting any registered companies. Information required to be filed included a statement of the subject matter in which the individual was interested, the nature of the individual's employment and the nature of the individual's compensation.

Merchant Marine Act

Section 807 of the Merchant Marine Act of 1936 required any persons employed by or representing firms affected by various federal shipping laws to file certain information with the secretary of Commerce before attempting to influence Congress, the Commerce Department and certain federal shipping agencies on shipping legislation or administrative decisions. The information included a statement of the subject matter in which the person was interested, the nature of the person's employment and the amount of the person's compensation.

Foreign Agents Registration Act

The Foreign Agents Registration Act of 1938, as amended, required registration with the Justice Department of anyone in the United States representing a foreign government or principal. Exceptions from the registration requirement were allowed for purely commercial groups and certain other categories. The act brought to public view many groups, individuals and associations that, while not necessarily engaged in lobbying Congress directly, carried on propaganda activities which might ultimately affect congressional legislation and national policy.

The Foreign Agents Registration Act was amended frequently following its passage in 1938 — for example, in 1939, 1942, 1946, 1950, 1956, 1961 and 1966 — without changing its broad purposes. From 1950 on, the Justice Department followed the practice of reporting annually to Congress, in the form of a booklet listing registrants under the act and their receipts and the names of the foreign principals of registrants.

The 1966 amendments sought to clarify and strengthen the act by imposing stricter disclosure requirements for foreign lobbyists, by adding to the scope of activities for which individuals must register under the act, by requiring foreign agents to disclose their status as agents when contacting members of Congress and other government officials, and by prohibiting contingent fees for contracts (where the fee was based upon the success of political activities) and campaign contributions on behalf of foreign interests.

In 1976 the Justice Department, acting under the 1966 amendments, filed a civil suit in federal district court in Washington, D.C., against two trade organizations, the United States-Japan Trade Council Inc. and the Japan Trade Promotion Office, charging the groups with filing misleading statements with the department under the Foreign Agents Registration Act. The suit alleged that the council claimed it was a non-profit trade association with U.S. members interested in promoting trade between the United States and Japan, when it actually was an organization using a trade association facade to conceal its foreign agent activities in representing Japanese governmental interests.

The 1976 action marked the first time a suit had been filed under the act alleging fraudulent reporting. The suit reflected a move by the Justice Department to tighten its enforcement of the Foreign Agents Registration Act. *(Enforcement policy, p. 129)*

Federal Regulation of Lobbying Act

The Federal Regulation of Lobbying Act actually was passed as part of the Legislative Reorganization Act of 1946 (S 2177 — PL 79-601). The lobbying provisions prompted little debate at the time. The Federal Regulation of Lobbying Act was never subsequently amended, and, as of late 1979, there had been only five federal court cases involving the act, of which four were prosecuted. *(Box, p. 4)*

The 1946 act did not in any way directly restrict the activities of lobbyists. It simply required any person who was hired by someone else for the principal purpose of lobbying Congress to register with the Secretary of the Senate and Clerk of the House and to file certain quarterly financial reports so that the lobbyist's activities would be known to Congress and the public. Organizations that solicited or received money for the principal purpose of lobbying Congress did not necessarily have to register, but they did have to file quarterly spending reports with the clerk detailing how much they spent to influence legislation. In 1954 the Supreme Court upheld the constitutionality of the 1946 lobbyist law (*United States v. Harriss*, 347 U.S. 612).

Loopholes. The court said that the law applied only to groups and individuals who collected or received money for the principal purpose of influencing legislation through direct contacts with members of Congress. This interpretation, based upon the court's reading of the legislative history, contained several major loopholes or vague areas permitting various organizations and individuals to avoid registering and/or reporting on spending.

One loophole involved collection or receipt of money. Under the language of the law as interpreted by the court, groups or individuals that merely spent money out of their own funds to finance activities designed to influence legislation apparently were not covered by the law unless they also solicited, collected or received money for that purpose.

Another loophole involved the term "principal purpose." A number of organizations argued that since influencing Congress was not the principal purpose for which they collected or received money, they were not covered by the law regardless of what kind of activities they carried on. This argument was used by the National Association of Manufacturers and the Chamber of Commerce of the United States, but both organizations filed spending reports nevertheless. *(Chamber of Commerce lobbying, p. 113)*

The court held, in addition, that an organization or individual was not covered unless the method used to influence Congress contemplated some direct contact with members. The significance of this interpretation was that individuals or groups whose activities were confined to influencing the public on legislation or issues (so-called "grass-roots" lobbying) were not subject to the 1946 law.

The law left vague precisely what kind of contacts with Congress constituted lobbying subject to the law's reporting and registration requirements. The language of the law itself specifically exempted testimony before a congressional committee, and in 1950, in *United States v. Slaughter* (89 F. Supp. 205), a lower federal court held that this exemption applied also to those helping to prepare the testimony. Other direct contacts presumably were covered, but a gray area soon emerged, with some groups contending that their contacts with members of Congress were informational and could not be considered subject to the law.

Another weakness in the lobbying law was that it applied only to attempts to influence Congress, not administrative agencies or the executive branch where a considerable amount of legislation was generated that was later enacted by Congress, and where many decisions and regulations similar to legislation were put into effect under administrative rule-making and quasi-judicial powers.

Finally, reinforcing all the other weaknesses was the fact that the 1946 law did not designate anyone to investigate the truthfulness of lobbying registrations and reports and to seek enforcement. The Clerk of the House and Secretary of the Senate were to receive registrations and reports but were not directed or empowered to investigate reports or to compel anyone to register. Since violation of the law was made a crime, the Justice Department had power to prosecute violators but no mandate was given the department to investigate reports. In fact, the Justice Department eventually adopted a policy of investigating only when it received complaints and initiated only five prosecutions (some involving several individuals) from 1946 to 1979.

1970s Legislative Proposals

Congress renewed its interest in lobbying legislation in the 1970s. A proposed Legislative Activities Disclosure Act, drafted as a possible replacement for the Federal Regulation of Lobbying Act of 1946, was the subject of hearings in 1971 by the House Committee on Standards of Official Conduct. The bill stemmed from exploratory committee hearings in 1970 and was patterned after a bill with the same title recommended by the Special Committee to Investigate Political Activities, Lobbying, and Campaign Contributions in 1957. The 1971 proposal was broader, however.

The bill declared as its purpose "to provide for the disclosure to the Congress, to the President, and to the public, of the activities, and the origin, amounts and utilization of funds and other resources, of and by persons who seek to influence the legislative process." The proposal transferred administration to the comptroller general, avoided such words as "regulation" in favor of disclosure, and eliminated the controversial "principal purpose" test of the 1946 act.

It required registration of persons defined as falling within the measure's provisions and required detailed reports of receipts and expenditures every six months.

1976 Proposal

In 1976 there was action in both the Senate and the House on major lobbying legislation.

Senate Action. The Senate June 15 overrode the objections of an unusual coalition of lobby groups to pass, 82-9, the Lobbying Disclosure Act of 1976 (S 2477). The bill would repeal the 30-year-old Federal Regulation of Lobbying Act and replace it with tighter regulation of organizations that seek to influence legislation before Congress directly and through "grass-roots" efforts.

Although there appeared to be unanimous agreement on the need for a new lobby law, as it came to the floor, the bill was opposed by virtually every major lobby group in Washington, with the exception of Common Cause. Among the groups critical of the measure were the AFL-CIO, Ralph Nader's Congress Watch, the National Association of Manufacturers, the Sierra Club, the American Civil Liberties Union, the Chamber of Commerce of the United States, the League of Women Voters and the U.S. Catholic Conference. Their reasons for opposition varied: Some felt the disclosure requirements would unduly burden smaller organizations, some felt that the First Amendment freedoms of expression and association were abridged by the various disclosure requirements.

Groups meeting the bill's definition of lobbyists were required to register with the General Accounting Office and to provide information on the organization, its contributors, legislative interests, and on the persons lobbying on its behalf. Each quarter a lobbying group was to file a report on issues on which the organization had lobbied, and on gifts, loans or honoraria above a certain amount to a member or an employee of Congress. Also, in certain cases, it was to provide samples of its lobbying materials. The bill provided for both civil and criminal action against violators.

House Action. The House Judiciary Committee Aug. 25 ordered reported a bill (HR 15) regarded as less stringent than the measure passed by the Senate. Among the more important differences from the Senate bill were HR 15's exemption from coverage of small citizens' groups and voluntary associations; less voluminous record-keeping and reporting requirements and a less inclusive definition of a lobbyist than under the Senate bill.

Efforts to resolve the differences between the House and Senate versions failed and the legislation expired when Congress adjourned in 1976.

Action in the 95th Congress

The House made more progress than the Senate in pushing lobbying disclosure legislation forward in the 95th Congress. The House Judiciary Subcommittee on Administrative Law and Governmental Relations, after extensive markup sessions, reported a clean bill, HR 8494, on July 22, 1977. But the bill underwent intense scrutiny and considerable alteration when it came up for full Judiciary Committee consideration in 1978.

The major debate in the Judiciary Committee was over the "threshold" for determining which organizations should be covered by the lobbying law. Debate focused on the amount of expenditures and the number and kinds of communications that should trigger registration.

House Floor Action. The House passed HR 8494 April 26, 1978, by a vote of 259-140, after three days of debate and after turning back nearly 20 efforts to weaken the bill. Two major amendments that significantly expanded the bill's disclosure requirements were adopted.

The two amendments that expanded the bill's coverage to require disclosure of 1) grass-roots lobbying efforts and 2) the names of major organizations contributing to lobby groups led major business, civil liberties, church and environmental groups to charge that the bill interfered with privacy and with citizens' rights to petition public officials.

Senate Committee Action. The Senate Governmental Affairs Committee began marking up its lobby bill (S 2971) on May 10 and 11, but the bill was shelved in late July as key senators were unable to reach agreement on how to get a bill to the floor.

The bill as introduced by the committee's chairman, Abraham Ribicoff, D-Conn., was considered far more rigorous than the House-passed bill. But the final Senate committee proposal was in some ways more lenient than the House-passed threshold. It applied only to oral communications, where the House version included written lobbying communications. And a Senate amendment specifically exempted small groups that lobby on six or fewer consecutive working days a year and non-Washington-based groups that are "locally oriented" and have a total annual budget of less than $75,000.

1979 Action

In May 1979 a House Judiciary subcommittee began markup of a lobby reform measure (HR 81) with at least one important controversial issue resolved. All parties agreed that any House-approved lobby bill would provide civil rather than criminal penalties for registration and reporting violations.

That change might not have seemed like a major step forward in the tortuous four-year odyssey of lobby reform. But the compromise, fostered by the White House, plus the nature of amendments offered in subcommittee suggested a serious effort was being made to write a lobby bill that would stand a chance of enactment.

In mid-1979 the Administrative Law Subcommittee voted 5-0 to report HR 81 to the full House Judiciary Committee. The subcommittee bill was supported by both the American Civil Liberties Union (ACLU) and Common Cause, and thus was considered the likely vehicle for any lobby law revision to emerge from the 96th Congress. *(Lobby law reform, p. 61)* ∎

Footnotes

¹ Douglass Cater, *Power in Washington* (New York: Random House, 1964), p. 206.

² *The Federalist Papers* (New York: Mentor, 1961), No. 10, pp. 77-78.

³ Arthur M. Schlesinger Jr., *The Age of Jackson* (Boston: Little, Brown and Co., 1946), p. 84.

⁴ James Deakin, *The Lobbyists* (Washington, D.C.: Public Affairs Press, 1966), p. 101.

⁵ Ibid., pp. 197-99.

⁶ David B. Truman, *The Governmental Process* 10th ed. (New York: Alfred A. Knopf, 1964), p. 389.

⁷ Donald R. Matthews, "Senators and Lobbyists," *Congressional Reform,* ed. Joseph Clark (New York: Thomas Y. Crowell Co., 1965), pp. 182-83.

⁸ Ibid., 191-93.

⁹ Emanuel Celler, "Pressure Groups in Congress," *Annals of the American Academy of Political and Social Science,* September 1958, p. 241.

¹⁰ Norman J. Ornstein and Shirley Elder, *Interest Groups, Lobbying and Policymaking* (Washington: Congressional Quarterly Press, 1978), p. 77.

¹¹ Cater, *Power in Washington,* p. 209.

¹² Matthews, "Senators and Lobbyists," pp. 194-96.

¹³ Merriman Smith, *The Good New Days* (Indianapolis: Bobbs-Merrill, 1962), pp. 198-200.

¹⁴ Lester W. Milbrath, *The Washington Lobbyists* (Chicago: Rand McNally Co., 1963), pp. 216-17.

¹⁵ Richard Bolling, *House Out of Order* (New York: E. P. Dutton Co., 1965), p. 141.

¹⁶ Lewis Anthony Dexter, *How Organizations Are Represented in Washington* (Indianapolis: Bobbs-Merrill, 1969), p. 62.

¹⁷ Truman, *The Governmental Process,* p. 354.

¹⁸ Deakin, *The Lobbyists,* p. 107.

¹⁹ Ibid., pp. 103-104.

²⁰ Congressional Quarterly *Weekly Report,* Aug. 18, 1979, pp. 1720-1735.

²¹ Kenneth G. Crawford, *The Pressure Boys* (New York: Julian Messner Inc., 1939), pp. 46-52.

²² Deakin, *The Lobbyists,* pp. 74-75.

²³ George H. Haynes, *The Senate of the United States: Its History and Practice,* 2 vols. (Boston: Houghton Mifflin Co., 1938), vol. 1, pp. 499-500.

²⁴ Karl Schriftgiesser, *The Lobbyists* (Boston: Little, Brown & Co., 1951), pp. 52-53, 155.

²⁵ Ibid., p. 68.

²⁶ Crawford, *The Pressure Boys,* p.56.

²⁷ *Public Papers of the Presidents of the United States: Harry S Truman, 1948* (Washington, D.C.: Government Printing Office, 1964), p. 916.

²⁸ Frank M. Buchanan, press statement, Oct. 18, 1950.

²⁹ U.S. Congress, House, Committee on Armed Services, *Report on Employment of Retired Commissioned Officers by Defense Department Contractors,* H Res 19, 86th Cong., 1st sess., 1960, p. 11.

³⁰ U.S. Congress, Senate, Committee on Foreign Relations, *Activities of Nondiplomatic Representatives of Foreign Principals in the United States, Hearings,* 86th Cong., 1st sess., 1963, pt. 5, p. 553.

³¹ U.S. Congress, Senate, Committee on Government Operations, *Lobbying Disclosure Act of 1976,* S Rept 94-763 to accompany S 2477, 94th Cong., 2nd sess., 1976, pp. 3-4.

³² Stuart D. Halpert, *Participation in the Development of Legislative Policy: Some Guidelines for 501(c)(3) Tax-Exempt Organizations* (National Health Council Inc., 1975), p. 12.

The Presidential Lobby

CQ

White House Lobby Gets Its Act Together

Early in the Carter presidency, stories about the administration's congressional lobbying efforts often drew snickers and groans. But less talk of White House clumsiness and naivete was being heard on Capitol Hill in 1979.

Jimmy Carter's liaison operation was coming of age, according to members, staffers and other observers questioned by Congressional Quarterly. And it was a timely maturation. The White House lobbyists faced immense challenges at the midpoint in Carter's term.

The inflation-wary administration was trying to push through the 96th Congress a budget that was austere on social programs and generous on defense spending. Opposition from liberal, labor and urban and minority groups was strong. At the same time, Carter was seeking ratification of a Strategic Arms Limitation Treaty (SALT II) in the teeth of intense conservative resistance.

The burden of selling Carter's program to Congress fell mainly on Frank B. Moore, assistant to the president for congressional liaison.

Soft-spoken, even-tempered, with a paunch and a slightly rumpled look, Moore hardly fit the glib and suave stereotype of a lobbyist. The sole counterpoint to his unassuming style lay next to his desk: a bright red University of Georgia throw rug bearing the picture of a pugnacious bulldog and the rallying cry, "Go you hairy dogs."

A loyalist who had been with Carter since he was an obscure southern governor, Moore was new to Washington when the administration took office. It quickly became apparent that he was ill prepared to steer a complex legislative agenda through Congress.

Moore's lobbying operation had significant problems for a year and a half as the White House's relationship with Congress and especially the Democratic leadership went through a series of rough spots, near-disasters and unpleasant episodes.

Problems ranged from Moore's frequent failure to return members' telephone calls to complete communications breakdowns between the White House and Democratic leaders. In mid-1978, relations with House Speaker Thomas P. O'Neill Jr., D-Mass., were nearly destroyed because of a lack of consultation when Carter fired an O'Neill crony from the General Services Administration. For a time, O'Neill had Moore banned from his office.

Not unexpectedly, there were a number of early predictions Moore would not last. But he confounded those pessimistic forecasts, and Moore's Capitol Hill lobbying efforts markedly improved, demonstrating both Carter's confidence in his head lobbyist and the administration's ability to learn from its mistakes.

Lessons Heeded

All those painful lessons that Moore and his lobbyists learned in their long struggle to enact an energy package and the Panama Canal treaties in the 95th Congress prompted some fundamental changes in the staff's operation: Phone calls were returned promptly, power centers were consulted regularly and pressure was applied more deftly. The results were demonstrable: Carter was able to get a number of his major proposals through Congress.

The improvements may generally be traced to a late-1977 review of Moore's lobbying operation by Vice President Mondale, a 12-year Senate veteran, and an April 1978 conference at Camp David with Carter and senior advisers.

Staff Enlarged

The size of the lobbying staff was increased from four to eight. Several Washington veterans were added, and the clerical and support staff was doubled. Tighter controls were put on lobbyists from the various government departments. Computers were used to analyze congressional voting and help pinpoint "swing" voters on big issues. (Box, p. 34)

A mid-1978 alteration in White House policy proved particularly helpful for Moore's work with Congress: The number of presidential priority bills was slashed in half, from about 60 to 30, allowing more resources to be concentrated on issues such as civil service reform and airline deregulation. The White House focused its legislative sights on an even smaller shopping list in 1979.

"We had too much on our platter," recalled Leslie C. Francis, who at the time coordinated the different elements in Moore's office and looked after relations with depart-

> *"What began as a comedy of errors has definitely matured. Now people on the Hill are more willing to work with Frank Moore."*
>
> —Professor Robert L. Peabody,
> Johns Hopkins University

mental lobbyists. (After Carter in mid-1979 gave Hamilton Jordan the title of White House chief of staff and a more visible role in dealing with Congress, Francis moved to Jordan's staff with duties similar to those he had been carrying out for Moore.)

In the smaller 1978-79 agenda, several bills were targeted for what Moore's people called "task force treatment." The task force concept first was used by the administration in early 1978 when it persuaded Congress not to continue the B-1 bomber, which the president found unnecessary and overly expensive. Energy, SALT II, the Panama Canal accords, Mideast arm sales, civil service reform and sustaining the public works veto were among issues for which task forces were mobilized. (*White House lobbying on SALT II, p. 39; on B-1, box, p. 32*)

Senior staff members directed the task forces, which were charged with seeing that all the White House's resources were utilized. Hubert L. Harris Jr., assistant director of the Office of Management and Budget, headed the

White House Liaison History

Presidents have had their own lobbyists on the Hill only since 1953. Before, congressional relations were handled on an ad hoc basis, with administration officials or allies in Congress tapped to guide bills into law.

The first formal liaison office appeared under President Eisenhower and was headed by a retired general, Wilton B. Persons, and later by Bryce N. Harlow, once staff director of the House Armed Services Committee.

Compared to the liaison operation under the Kennedy and Johnson administrations, however, the Eisenhower lobbying office was a somnambulistic affair. The reason: The go-slow Eisenhower legislative agenda was smaller than that of his successors. Also, the opposition Democrats controlled Congress for most of Eisenhower's tenure.

Under Kennedy, the liaison office took the form that persists to this day. The chief Kennedy lobbyist, former congressional staffer Lawrence F. O'Brien (currently commissioner of the National Basketball Association), expanded the staff to push through a number of far-reaching government programs. O'Brien maintained a close relationship with the Democratic leadership and tightly controlled the departmental lobbyists.

Even though O'Brien stayed on as office chief after Kennedy's death, the lobbying staff acquired a new head, President Johnson. Because of his many years in Congress, Johnson oversaw his liaison office on an almost-daily basis. During important votes, he kept in close phone contact with his lobbyists, directing strategy.

When O'Brien moved on to become postmaster general in 1965, he kept his congressional relations post, too, but the day-to-day White House lobbying was conducted in the Senate by Mike Manatos, a former Hill aide, and in the House by Harold Barefoot Sanders Jr., a Texas lawyer and politician.

President Nixon brought back Harlow, who had become a lobbyist for Procter and Gamble, for a short stint as liaison head. Harlow briefly tried to cut the office back to its size under Eisenhower, but found that to be unrealistic because Congress had since become used to relying on it for services.

With Harlow's return to P&G, William E. Timmons, who had been administrative assistant to then-Sen. Bill Brock, R-Tenn., took over and found himself in the middle of a growing conflict between the Democratic Congress and the Republican White House.

Provoked by the passions of the Vietnam War, the animosity was sharpened by the disdain that key presidential advisers H. R. Haldeman and John Ehrlichman felt for Capitol Hill.

When President Ford took over, Timmons left to start his own Washington lobbying firm, Timmons and Co., and Max L. Friedersdorf became top lobbyist. A 25-year veteran of the House, Ford initially promised a harmonious partnership with Congress. But these intentions foundered on partisan difference over economic policy. Ford ended up vetoing 66 bills, leaving his lobbyists the unhappy task of rounding up the votes to sustain.

budget task force in 1979 and Hamilton Jordan led the one for SALT.

Francis and his successor, James M. Copeland Jr., coordinated lobbyists enlisted from Moore's office and from the departments. Lobbying procedures used by the task forces conformed to those employed by past administrations: The lobbyists identified the undecided members, who were then divided up for personal contacts. The most difficult to convince were brought in for a talk with the president.

"Task forces serve as a clearinghouse," said Francis. "They minimize mixed signals. They're a forum to check things, like rumors, and to follow up and see that assignments are carried out."

Other improvements included the hiring of Atlanta public relations man Gerald Rafshoon and Connecticut political activist Anne Wexler, even though they were not part of Moore's office.

Rafshoon's assignment was to improve Carter's image of weakness, which had diminished the president's clout with Congress. Wexler's task was to mobilize behind the president's programs special interest groups, which in turn put pressure on Congress.

Another Camp David-inspired change beneficial to Moore was the shift of Tim Kraft from handling the president's appointments to dispensing patronage — a role that had been performed haphazardly by Jordan. After Kraft left the White House to head Carter's 1980 campaign, the patronage job was turned over to Sarah Weddington.

To overcome the setbacks experienced in the early part of the administration, Moore reshuffled his organization and modeled it after the most successful presidential lobbying effort of all time, that of Lawrence F. O'Brien, who handled congressional liaison for Presidents Kennedy and Johnson.

The task force concept had been a hallmark of the O'Brien liaison office. Other O'Brien techniques adopted by Moore included dividing coverage of the House by his lobbyists on a geographical basis, servicing of lawmakers' needs, closely coordinating departmental lobbyists and having the president personally intervene when rounding up votes on crucial issues.

Changed Committee Lineups

At first, Moore's office was too busy getting itself organized to worry much about the shape of the new 95th Congress. But in 1979 he and his staff spent a lot of time consulting with the Democratic leadership over committee assignment changes resulting from the 1978 election.

"We had 18 or 19 votes on Ways and Means last time and there [were] five vacancies this time," said William H. Cable, Moore's principal lobbyist in the House. "We want[ed] these vacancies to be filled with pro-Jimmy Carter people. Committee assignments are important. We lost hospital cost containment in 1978 in the Commerce Committee by one vote."

The administration's reaction to the outcome of the committee selection process was that the overall situation did not change much in the 96th Congress.

Evidencing the seriousness with which Moore looked upon the task ahead were his plans to have his own troops lobby on the subcommittee level, especially on the Appropriations Committee — something White House liaison staffers seldom did.

He also beefed up his staff by temporarily detailing additional lobbyists to the White House for help with the

The White House Lobbying Team

Frank B. Moore, 43, is a Georgia native who served as Carter's executive secretary during 1972-74 when Carter was governor. He also was the governor's liaison to the state legislature and to municipal governments. In the presidential campaign, Moore was first finance director and, later, southern states coordinator. He is a graduate of the University of Georgia with a bachelor's degree in business administration. A community development specialist, he was executive director of one of the first regional planning commissions in Georgia.

Robert Thomson, 35, Moore's deputy, comes from Washington state. A graduate of the University of Washington and Georgetown University Law Center, he specialized in campaign finance laws and was a counsel to the Democratic Senatorial Campaign Committee. He assisted Danny C. Tate as a Senate lobbyist in 1978-79. In August 1979 he received his current assignment, which he said was "outside the chain of command" and involved "transmitting messages in Frank's absence," as well as "making sure the congressional impact on administration decisions occurs at an earlier stage than in the past."

SENATE

Danny C. Tate, 35, the chief Senate lobbyist, is another Georgia native. Tate was legislative assistant to Sen. Herman E. Talmadge, D-Ga., for seven years. He holds a bachelor's degree from Emory University and a law degree from the University of Georgia.

HOUSE

William H. Cable, 34, the head House lobbyist and an Illinois native, was a congressional staffer for almost a dozen years before joining Moore's team. He received a law degree from George Washington University in 1970, and later served as staff counsel for the House Education and Labor Committee and staff director of the Committee on House Administration. He also served on the staffs of the commissions that drafted House reforms for the last two Congresses.

James C. Free, 32, was campaign chairman for Carter in the 1976 Tennessee primary and handled Alabama, Mississippi and Tennessee in the general election. A Tennessean, he served as chief clerk of that state's House of Representatives for four years, and previously held college administrative jobs for three years. Free holds a bachelor's degree from Middle Tennessee State University and a master's in public administration from the University of Tennessee.

Valerie Pinson, 50, joined Carter's transition staff in December 1976. Before that she was a lobbyist for the National Association of Counties, worked on the staff of Sen. Thomas J. Dodd, D-Conn. (1953-71), and in the Johnson White House on equal employment opportunities. She held several positions with the Office of Economic Opportunity and served as Rep. Yvonne Brathwaite Burke's, D-Calif. (1973-78), administrative assistant. Born in upstate New York, she earned her bachelor's degree at Howard University.

Terrence D. Straub, 33, was congressional affairs director at the Office of Management and Budget before shifting to Moore's staff in June 1978. He directed Carter's Indiana primary effort and helped organize 16 states in the November election. He was born in Indiana, graduated from Indiana University, and was legislative assistant to Indiana's secretary of state from 1970-72. He ran unsuccessfully for Congress in 1970.

Robert W. Maher, 41, was director of research and planning for the House Interstate and Foreign Commerce Subcommittee on Health and the Environment before joining the White House budget task force in January 1979. He transferred to Cable's staff late the following month. A native of Fort Lauderdale, Fla., he studied journalism at the University of Florida, from which he was graduated in 1961. He was sports editor of a newspaper in Hollywood, Fla., and assistant sports editor of the *Fort Lauderdale News* before going to work in June 1966 for Rep. Paul G. Rogers, D-Fla. (1955-79). Maher moved to the staff of the health subcommittee, which Rogers headed, in 1976.

FOREIGN AFFAIRS

Robert G. Beckel, 30, served on the State Department's lobbying staff before his transfer to the White House in January 1978. A New Yorker who graduated from Wagner College, he once had his own political consulting firm and was director of the liberal National Committee for an Effective Congress. Technically, Beckel is a House lobbyist, but he specializes in foreign affairs and he swings over to the Senate for votes on those issues.

ADMINISTRATIVE SUPPORT

James M. Copeland Jr., 36, is Moore's assistant in charge of coordinating the office's internal operations and its relations with the departmental lobbyists. A New Jersey native, he was administrative assistant to Rep. Fortney H. "Pete" Stark, D-Calif., for four years before directing the Carter-Mondale campaign in northern California in 1976. Returning to Washington in 1977, Copeland directed congressional liaison for the Federal Home Loan Bank Board before joining Moore's staff in May 1978. In August 1979 he succeeded Leslie C. Francis as coordinator, when Francis moved to the office of Hamilton Jordan, White House chief of staff.

Ronna Freiberg, 31, special assistant for congressional liaison (legislative coordinator), worked for Rep. Peter W. Rodino Jr., D-N.J., for three years before joining the Carter presidential campaign in 1976. A former French teacher and Ph.D. candidate at the University of Chicago, she received her A.B. degree from the University of Michigan and a master's in French from Ohio State University. She joined the White House staff in 1977.

Robert K. Russell Jr., 33, Moore's administrative assistant, is a graduate of Michigan State University. He worked at the Democratic National Committee in 1973-76.

White House Lobbyists' 'Typical Day' on the Hill

To hear Carter administration lobbyists tell it, their job often resembles an episode from the Keystone Cops.

A typical day is composed of frenetic racing from vital meeting to vital meeting while stacks of unanswered phone messages grow by the minute.

While styles and emphases differ between administrations, the rat race pace of a White House lobbyist remains the same.

"It's an impossible job," said a one-time Nixon administration lobbyist. "The phone never stops. Everyone wants 15 minutes, but there aren't 15 minutes in a day for each of 535 people. The problem is that the Hill doesn't want to fool around with the departments. They want to go straight to the top, the White House."

"On the Hill, I'm flying by the seat of my pants," said Danny C. Tate, Carter's chief lobbyist for the Senate. "I wish I had more time to go by and visit [senators and staff] when I didn't have business. But I never have the time."

Eight Lobbyists

In addition to its chief, Frank B. Moore, the Carter congressional liaison office fields a force of seven full-time lobbyists — most of them assigned to the House rather than the smaller Senate — an increase from the four-person staff that the administration started out with.

Tate and his assistants for the Senate do not stake out jurisdictions in that chamber. Tate instead apportions responsibility for legislation on "an ad hoc basis."

Until the fall of 1979 when he became Moore's deputy, Robert Thomson worked full time with Tate in the Senate. Besides Thomson's part-time help, Tate also has assistance when needed from Robert G. Beckel, a House lobbyist who swings over to the Senate on foreign policy issues.

Presidential lobbyists for the much larger House, captained by William H. Cable, have more defined territories. In keeping with the practice of past administrations, each lobbyist is given about 90 representatives to keep tabs on. "We do it on a geographic basis but don't make them from contiguous states," said Cable. "I don't want to find myself the lobbyist for the Northeast or the Southwest. This way makes us more responsible to Congress as a whole."

Originally, Carter's House lobbyists were split along departmental lines. Valerie Pinson, for example, oversaw bills relating to the Veterans Administration and the Departments of Health, Education and Welfare; Housing and Urban Development; Labor; and Justice. "We changed that because none of us will ever know as much as a departmental lobbyist on a lot of these issues," Cable said. "We felt we should go for individual members or otherwise things would slip past us."

Lobbyists for the 32 Cabinet and major non-Cabinet agencies — 675 people are doing Hill liaison work for the departments, the Office of Management and Budget estimates — carry the bulk of the legislative load. Moore's people become involved only on legislation of great importance to the administration or when agency lobbyists run into problems on one of their bills.

Moore's office directs the activities of the departmental lobbyists. Every Monday, Moore — or, if he is busy, his assistant, James M. Copeland Jr. — presides over an informal conference in the White House's Roosevelt Room for presidential liaison staff and their agency counterparts. The top lobbyists or their stand-ins for the largest agencies are present every week.

The chief lobbyists for smaller organizations like the Environmental Protection Agency join in only on alternate Mondays.

At the meetings, each liaison office reviews recent developments and presents the next week's outlook. Moore relates the president's upcoming schedule with them and focuses on key bills that require coordination among the executive branch's lobbyists.

Although departmental lobbyists answer to the heads of their agencies, the White House has tightened its rein on their activities to prevent the crossed signals that helped give Moore's office its early reputation on the Hill for bumbling.

Day Begins Early

The "average" day of a White House lobbyist — if, indeed, there is such a thing — begins with an 8 a.m. staff meeting. After other morning conferences at the White House, he goes to Capitol Hill about 10 a.m. where he sets off on a zig-zag course that takes him through congressional offices, hearings and his special headquarters outside the house he covers.

In the House, Carter lobbyists operate out of Speaker Thomas P. O'Neill Jr.'s, D-Mass., office, which is right off the floor. They can use a phone on a windowsill in one corner of the large room where O'Neill's staff works. If they want to get away from the hurly-burly of the Speaker's place, they go to the quieter office of Majority Leader Jim Wright, D-Texas.

In the Senate, presidential lobbyists employ the quarters of Vice President Mondale, which also are just off the floor since Mondale is the presiding officer of the upper house. Mondale's assistant for congressional relations, William C. Smith, has phones on either side of his office couch for Tate and his assistants. Because lobbyists are not allowed on the Senate floor, Smith acts as the go-between for Moore's people and senators during debates and votes.

Members and senators looking for White House lobbyists know they can be reached in O'Neill's or Mondale's offices. The lobbyists themselves carry paging devices to contact one another.

At the center of Moore's communications network is Copeland, who coordinates the staff's internal operations as well as the activities of the departmental lobbyists. In addition to ensuring that everyone is up to date and working together, he is responsible for seeing that the weekly legislative report for the president is prepared.

Moore is located in the West Wing, close to the Oval Office, which he visits at least once a day, and the offices of other top Carter aides. Copeland, Moore's eyes and ears, is in a room near his boss. The rest of the staff cannot be fitted into the crowded West Wing.

budget struggle. Among them were Christopher L. Davis and Robert M. Meyer from the Office of Management and Budget, Gael Sullivan from the Commerce Department, Sargent Carlton from the Interior Department, and Susan Elfving from the Housing and Urban Development Department.

Centralization

In an effort to revitalize his presidency, which according to public opinion polls was not providing enough leadership, Carter in mid-1979 shook up his Cabinet and adopted a tougher stance that demanded more loyalty from department heads and signaled a stronger White House role in enforcing policy decisions. The move to give Jordan more power to oversee executive branch relations with Congress was part of the shakeup.

Johnson and Ford

Carter's move toward a more centralized operation was in line with the pattern in some past administrations, particularly that of Lyndon B. Johnson. In Johnson's administration, according to a number of observers who were involved in the process then, it was very clear that all congressional liaison activities were directed from the White House.

Johnson's congressional liaison team met each Monday, and usually received specific assignments for the work that needed to be done that week. Those assignments regularly carried the department-level people outside their own legislative issues.

As Walter Hasty, one of Johnson's liaison people at HUD and later a Procter & Gamble Co. lobbyist, recalled: "We knew the members on our committees and we knew their districts. So we would even help draft the arguments they would need to explain a potentially unpopular vote to their people back home."

By contrast, the Ford team, headed by Max L. Friedersdorf, currently a member of the Federal Election Commission, seldom called on the departmental liaison people to lobby on issues outside their own jurisdiction.

Friedersdorf said, "The theory was that each agency could lobby the committee it knew best on a broad range of issues. That theory we found fallacious. The agency people only have credibility if they are lobbying in the area they know; if they lobbied where they didn't know what they were talking about as well, it was perceived as heavy-handed."

Workload

One reason that Carter was unlikely to go as far as Johnson in directing congressional relations from the White House was the growth in the number of contacts between the departmental lobbyists on one hand and members of Congress and their aides on the other. The job of answering congressional inquiries and demands for information was itself an immense task.

The State Department office headed by J. Brian Atwood recorded more than 1,500 letters a month from Congress in 1979. Jack L. Stempler's Department of Defense operation, admittedly the giant of the liaison teams, receives yearly more than 110,000 written inquiries and 220,000 telephone queries from Congress.

Perhaps half or more of such inquiries are of the "casework" variety, concerning a particular problem of a constituent or a specific program.

A HUD staffer said. "You can't appreciate until you've gone through it the importance of answering irate members." Treasury liaison Gene E. Godley said, "I take it as a given that the casework, responding to letters and phone calls, absolutely must be done properly, otherwise we're just not doing our job."

Carter's Role

A fundamental problem for the liaison teams concerned Carter's personal standing with members of Congress.

As one liaison aide stated, "When you go up to the Hill and the latest polls show Carter isn't doing well, there isn't much reason for a member to go along with him. There's little we can do if the member isn't persuaded on the issue."

In defense of Carter, some liaison officers emphasized that members of Congress no longer vote simply to please a president, whether Carter or another. One said that "it used to be that a central piece of information on a vote was the president's position. Now the central information is the issue.... With the breakdown of party discipline, it is clear that voters expect members to exercise independent judgment. That means voting on the issue, not just to agree with the president."

Experienced Predecessors

As veterans of Congress, Presidents Johnson and Ford personally immersed themselves in the legislative process to a greater degree than Carter did early in his presidency. As Walter Hasty recalled, "Every other week Johnson himself would come into the Monday meetings with Barefoot Sanders [Johnson's top liaison aide]."

"Johnson was right on top of it . . . totally involved," Hasty said. "And some days he would say to us, 'I want you to go up there today and find out what the members need. What do they need in the district? Do they need the little wife invited down to the White House, or can we help with a constituent?' Then we would go up to the Hill and say, 'The president asked me to come see you and ask if you need anything.' That was impressive. People felt warmly toward LBJ."

Friedersdorf, who headed Ford's liaison team from early 1975 through 1976, said that Ford frequently took part in the "headcount" sessions that preceded major votes and followed up by calling many members himself.

Above all to Friedersdorf, "the beauty of working for Ford was that he had just come off the Hill after 25 years. He had a personal rapport with these people. His first instinct was to ask, 'What will the Hill think?' He was always receptive to having meetings with congressmen at the White House. If there was a problem he would say, 'Get them over here.' "

Ford also took other steps to ensure the prestige of his congressional liaison aides. Nine of the liaison people, including five Friedersdorf aides, sat in on the weekly meetings with the Hill leadership.

"People up here saw us in a high visibility position in an important meeting," Friedersdorf said. "If you're not really included in major meetings, you can't pass along information about what's going on. You are perceived as a messenger boy rather than as the president's man."

Robert Thomson, Frank Moore's deputy, said the Carter administration was taking similar steps to include the congressional liaison team in policy meetings.

The B-1: First Victim of New White House Strategy

White House lobbying of rare intensity helped kill the B-1 bomber project in an early 1978 battle that marked the Carter administration's first use of a "task force" approach to lobbying.

The task force system drew departmental congressional relations officers into closer formation with those from the office of Frank B. Moore, chief presidential assistant for congressional liaison. Until then, Moore's office had been reining the departmental lobbyists loosely, in keeping with Carter's commitment to "Cabinet government."

Problems in the B-1's early development and its cost — estimated at $101 million a copy shortly before the project was killed — made it an easy target for critics of Pentagon spending. But the project had been supported by Presidents Nixon and Ford, and opponents were stymied by Congress' traditional reluctance to challenge the White House on major weapons decisions. Eventually, B-1 opponents hit on a tactical ploy that capitalized on this tendency. In 1976 a rider was attached to the annual defense funding bill, stipulating that full-scale production of the B-1 would be subject to approval by the winner of the 1976 presidential election.

Carter's opposition to the B-1 appeared to waver once in office. But by June 30, 1977, the former engineer had become convinced the strategic wave of the future was the cruise missile. He cancelled the B-1.

Although deeply disappointed, the Air Force quickly accepted his decision. To override Carter would have required the approval of both chambers, and the Senate long had been skeptical of the plane.

Gradually, leading congressional defense experts began to support Carter's position. By the fall of 1977 Appropriations Committee Chairman George Mahon, D-Texas, was leading the administration's fight in the House. Eventually, he was joined by Jack Edwards of Alabama, the senior Republican on the Defense Appropriations Subcommittee. And finally Carter was supported by several usually hawkish Democrats on the Armed Services Committee, including Chairman Melvin Price of Illinois, Mendel J. Davis of South Carolina and Harold Runnels of New Mexico.

Carter secured congressional cancellation of fiscal 1978 B-1 money by Sept. 8. But B-1 supporters were able to keep the fiscal 1977 program alive because of members' concern over the possibility that a new strategic arms limitation treaty with Moscow (SALT II) might impose severe limitations on the cruise missile.

The SALT argument and high absenteeism among Democrats beat a move in the House Dec. 6 to rescind the B-1 funds. But Carter was determined to kill the project, and he worked closely with the House Democratic leadership in preparing for a rematch.

B-1 Blitz

At a White House meeting Feb. 17, 1978, congressional relations officials from several Cabinet departments were given four or five names from a list of 55 House members thought to be doubtful on the B-1 issue. They were instructed to call the members and press the case for rescinding the B-1 funds to free the money in the supplemental appropriation bill to which the rescission was attached.

By the morning of the vote, Feb. 22, most of the calls had been made and reported back to Moore and William H. Cable, his top aide for the House. In a typical case, the liaison person had talked to a member who was still undecided. Cable told him to go back and have the head of the department call the undecided member and ask, "What do you want?"

Cable said the morning of the vote, "We want to win on the B-1, and we're willing to spend some chips, some capital, to win. There's a risk in doing this, but we don't want to lose."

The Pentagon's case was pressed by Defense Secretary Harold Brown in phone calls to some members and in a briefing arranged by Mahon for several members the day before the vote. Mahon also circulated a letter from Air Force Chief of Staff Gen. David C. Jones urging the rescission, and he personally lobbied several members vigorously on behalf of Carter.

Carter phoned several members personally — including Price. And in meetings with some members about other subjects he brought up the B-1, stressing his determination not to spend the fiscal 1977 money. He also sent a letter to each Democratic member of the Appropriations Committee soliciting support.

On the House floor, John Buchanan, R-Ala., an apparent target of the White House lobbying campaign, denounced a phone call to his office by the Environmental Protection Agency's second-ranking congressional liaison official, Larry Snowhite. Snowhite had urged Buchanan to vote for the rescission with the argument that $57 million in sewage treatment money for Alabama was tied up in the supplemental. "Can anyone explain to me the connection between this and the B-1 bomber?" Buchanan demanded.

But Carter's supporters, led by Mahon and Joseph P. Addabbo, D-N.Y., noted that the Senate had shown no tendency to give in on its rescission language.

In the end, the aggressive, well-coordinated administration lobbying paid off. Thirty-one votes were turned around and the House voted, 234-182, to kill the B-1.

White House lobbyists William H. Cable, left, and Frank B. Moore, right, confer with House Speaker Thomas P. O'Neill Jr., D-Mass.

Carter's Involvement

As time went on, Carter too became more involved in the legislative process, personally phoning scores of congressmen and senators on issues he considered crucial.

It already had been his practice to meet early each morning with Moore, to talk with him at various times during the day and to read the weekly digest prepared for him by Moore and the departmental liaisons. He also dropped by occasionally at the weekly meetings of liaison officers. (At first held on Fridays, these meetings took place on Mondays — the same as during the Johnson years — beginning in 1979.)

Carter also began seeing a steady stream of members individually, and taking other steps to improve his personal congressional ties.

Signs of Maturity

One sign that Carter's congressional relations operation was maturing was that it developed a fairly consistent style — in contrast to 1977 when Hill people complained they never knew what would come out of the White House next.

These characteristics were apparent:

● The administration showed a willingness to engage in political horsetrading — despite its expressed disdain for the practice — if a major bill were involved.

By all accounts, the White House blitzed fence-sitting House members with patronage enticements and other blandishments to gain their votes during the fight over sustaining Carter's veto of the public works bill in 1978.

Rep. Samuel L. Devine of Ohio was one of several Republicans who said the president had offered to cease campaigning for Democrats in their home districts in return for a vote upholding the veto.

● The White House continued to work through the Democratic leadership.

Cable contacted the office of House Speaker O'Neill at least once a day. "And four times or more when they have a bill they're interested in," said Gary Hymel, the Speaker's executive assistant. In the House, administration lobbyists used the Speaker's office as their base of operations.

The White House's lobbying team also consulted frequently with Democratic leaders of the Senate, and Carter met on Tuesdays with leaders of both chambers. The president had O'Neill and his wife over socially on several occasions — unlike the early days of the administration, when the Speaker and his family were assigned obscure seats at the inaugural ball.

The leadership is a superb source of intelligence, Moore's lobbyists found. Its vote counts often are the most reliable. When the administration early on tried to count votes itself, it had difficulty spotting which supporters were shaky.

Demonstrating the value he placed on his ties with O'Neill and Senate Majority Leader Robert C. Byrd, D-W.Va., Carter took pains to make up with both men after he went against the leadership in 1978 on the public works bill. "Don't gloat," Carter reportedly told Moore after the House upheld his veto of the water projects.

GOP Support

● Republicans were largely ignored unless their votes were needed on major issues.

Under both Presidents Nixon and Ford, the leadership of both parties had been invited to regular meetings. This obviously was because the GOP presidents had more need to call upon the majority held by the opposition party. Carter seldom had to go outside his own party.

"Nobody ever walked through this door and asked what the minority on Ways and Means wanted," commented Rep. Barber B. Conable of New York, ranking Republican on that important House committee. "And it isn't as though I were bitterly hostile toward the president," he noted. "I supported him on [the B-1 bomber] and civil service."

Although Moore denied that he used the Republicans only on "the tough things," he and his lobbyists admitted that the GOP got far less attention than the Democrats.

"Sure we spend more time with Democrats," said Cable. "You tend to go to people who do things for you. If you strike out 90 percent of the time with some people, it's not worth it."

To the extent that Republicans were consulted by the White House, the Senate minority leader fared far better than his House counterpart. That, said Moore, was because the administration got more backing from Senate Republicans than from those in the House. According to a Congressional Quarterly study, House Republicans backed Carter on only 36 percent of all roll-call votes in 1978, while Senate Republicans were behind him 41 percent of the time. House Democrats supported the president at a level of 60 percent and Senate Democrats 66 percent.

An aide to House Minority Leader John J. Rhodes, R-Ariz., said White House "consultation with us has been almost nil." But the White House kept in touch with Senate Minority Leader Howard H. Baker Jr., R-Tenn., "once every three weeks," said a Baker staffer.

"It's different with the Senate," said Moore. "Their rules tend to make them more of a bipartisan body. On domestic issues in the House, we're lucky to get 10 or 12 Republican votes."

Also, he acknowledged, the personalities of Baker and Rhodes were a factor in the treatment they received from the administration. The more outgoing, politically ambitious Baker was flexible on some issues, while the dour, ideologically conservative Rhodes seldom departed from traditional GOP doctrine, observers noted.

In 1978 the bulk of the support the administration received from Republicans came on issues affecting foreign policy (Panama, Mideast warplane sales, ending the Turkish arms embargo) and economy in government (civil service reform, public works veto). The reason for the pro-Carter foreign policy votes, students of Congress say, was that the Republicans have an internationalist element that habitually backs a president on such matters. And guarding the public till has long been a Republican tenet.

● The White House stayed away from internal issues in Congress and other emotional questions that were not likely to pay political dividends.

The government ethics bill, which affected the executive as well as the legislative branch, got virtually no administration lobbying, although Carter favored it and signed it. Ethics is a sensitive topic in Congress — one the administration believed was best avoided. During the two years the measure was being considered, several lawmakers were accused of improprieties, three were reprimanded by the House, two were indicted and another convicted.

Although Carter was on the record as favoring public financing of congressional campaigns — a controversial proposal on the Hill — his lobbyists did not push the issue in 1979. *(Background, p. 67)*

Computers Help White House Lobbyists . . .

Computers are giving a little extra torque to traditional White House arm twisting on Capitol Hill.

President Carter's lobbying team, headed by Frank B. Moore, turned to computer systems to strengthen and speed its analysis of congressional voting. The move was one of several steps credited with helping Moore's team to shed its initial reputation as inept and unprofessional.

The White House congressional liaison office put together a simple computerized file containing basic information about every senator and representative, including party, committee assignments, seniority, margin of victory in his most recent election, and ratings by interest groups.

Also punched in were major votes from current and past Congresses. By asking the computer to cross-reference past voting with political indices such as interest group ratings, Moore's team became quickly able to spot swing votes on issues crucial to the White House.

Consumer Agency Fight

For example, the White House used a computer analysis in its unsuccessful 1978 efforts to counter heavy lobbying against the proposed consumer protection agency.

Leslie C. Francis, then a Moore aide charged with coordinating use of the computer, said the White House asked the computer to compare a list of "undecideds" against their past record on consumer issues. Included in the past record were the two key consumer votes of 1977 — support for cooperative banks and controls on debt collection practices — along with ratings by the Consumer Federation of America and by COPE, the political arm of the AFL-CIO.

The result was a quickly readable list of House members who had been pro-consumer in the past, but who were not yet committed to the consumer agency proposal. Those members were the most fertile lobbying field for the White House. "It's just a matter of effective targeting," Francis explained. "We're trying to pick out the members who are 'gettable.'"

But such targeting does not tell the White House how to lobby a given member, and it doesn't guarantee success. The defeat of the consumer bill showed House members were not persuaded by the administration lobbying.

Francis and William H. Cable, chief White House lobbyist for the House, said they were pleased with the accuracy of the vote analyses. Operational since mid-1977, the computer system first produced such analyses during House floor action on the national energy bill. In preparation, liaison had produced a computer study of 17 major energy votes in the 94th Congress. Based on those votes and on a survey performed by representatives friendly to the White House position, an "energy profile" for each House member was created. That way the administration "saw where we were likely to have problems," Francis said.

Only Public Data

While the administration did not publicize the computer use in analyzing congressional votes, it did not try to hide it either, since "we are sensitive to how computers are viewed generally," Francis said. "But it's important to note that there is no sensitive information about anyone on the computer; it's all public information. Most of it comes from the *Congressional Directory,* and the voting records come from Congressional Quarterly."

Francis added that "even if we didn't have ethical standards to restrict us — which we do — the potential political controversy if we were to even think of putting sensitive stuff on there would stop it."

There was some congressional grumbling about use of the computer in September 1979 after the House at first rejected legislation needed to implement the Panama Canal treaties. Before the House reversed itself a few days later, an angry President Carter reportedly told a group of House Democrats that he keeps a computer list of members' voting records in his Oval Office desk drawer, and that it would be used in deciding which members to reward with invitations to the White House and other presidential favors. The remark reportedly annoyed members who heard it.

Management Techniques

The use of computers for congressional vote analysis was part of a larger effort within the Carter White House to bring more sophisticated and efficient management techniques to the executive branch. Leading that effort was the Office of Administration, headed by Richard M. Harden, an accountant who was a top administrator in Carter's Georgia government.

Harden's office was a major result of the first Carter reorganization plan. The office, in operation since the beginning of 1978, was set up to provide administrative support to the Executive Office of the President, made up of some 1,700 persons. Harden viewed his role as that of riding herd on the administration's hopes to cut staff size, reduce expenditures and still make decisions flow out of the White House in a smooth, politically astute process.

It was largely Harden's idea that computer time be employed to do the vote analyses and to help congressional liaison.

Similarly, Moore's team stayed clear of the 1977 battle over common-site picketing, a pro-labor bill that Carter at least had said he supported, but that the administration sensed was not popular with the public. The bill was defeated in a key loss for organized labor. *(Common-site picketing bill, p. 101)*

Abortion, regarded as a no-win issue in the White House, was another subject on which the administration was neutral. Despite the opposition Carter expressed toward abortion in his 1976 campaign, his lobbyists kept their distance when amendments cropped up aimed at curbing federally financed abortions.

"When abortion would come up, they'd find us in the House restaurant," said Moore.

Reassessment

Those surveyed agreed that the White House Office for Congressional Liaison in two years came a long way in learning how to navigate the treacherous shoals in Congress.

... To Function More Effectively on Hill

Moore's staff can retrieve two of the major computerized information products of Congress. Both the LEGIS system, which tracks legislation and gives a full record of the legislative background of a given proposal, and the Library of Congress' SCORPIO system, which produces issue briefs on a multitude of specific topics, are available to Moore's team and to Stuart Eizenstat's domestic policy staff.

Thus rather than tracking down a set of paper documents such as committee hearings and calendars or calling people to obtain information on an issue or legislative proposal, White House aides can get the needed information rapidly from a computer terminal screen.

Harden foresaw prospects for further use of computer systems to streamline — and most of all speed — many White House-Congress communications. In meetings and talks with those responsible for computer systems in the House and Senate, Harden discussed the future use of "electronic mail" to shuttle important, time-squeezed messages back and forth on Pennsylvania Avenue.

"Right now," Harden said, "if Frank needed to get a draft letter or a proposed policy statement over to the Hill to 20 congressmen, say everybody on a particular committee, for their opinions, he could have somebody messenger over individual copies to each one or have people call them on the phone.

"In situations where we need a quick turnaround, say within a few hours, you need to have their response to something a little complicated, the message could pop up on a terminal in those people's offices all at once, with no bureaucratic hitches in the paper flow."

Routine communications where speed of response is not so critical probably would not, in Harden's view, ever need to be handled electronically.

Logging the Mail

The Carter White House also implemented a computerized system of handling the large volume of mail it receives from the Hill. The "Congressional Correspondence Summary and Retrieval System" logs this mail, noting the date and the subject of the letter, and permits the administration to make sure the letters are promptly answered by the right person in the administration.

Robert Thomson, Moore's deputy, said the main purpose of the computer was "to help us better serve members of Congress who write us asking for information. The analysis of votes is secondary to the correspondence function."

The computer prints out a daily summary of the congressional letters received and prepares reports on correspondence that still needs Cabinet or White House follow-up. Also, the summaries provide a quick, readily retrievable analysis of congressional sentiment on various topics, since the computer can break out the letters on a particular issue and show how members of Congress feel about the issue.

Computers in Congress

White House aides involved in the project note that what they are doing is quite similar to Congress' own ongoing pursuit of ways to use computers to do its job better.

Harden discussed his project with Rep. Charlie Rose, D-N.C., the principal exponent of computer uses in Congress, and with the top computer staff people on the Hill: Boyd Alexander of the House Information System and John Swearingen of the Senate Information Service.

Alexander's office found a few ways to share information between the House computer system and the White House. For example, the House produces magnetic tapes each day with the votes as recorded by electronic voting machines. That tape is used to print up the votes each day in the *Congressional Record*.

Alexander's shop began sending a copy of the vote tape directly to the White House. "They would get the votes anyway from the *Record*," Alexander notes. "This way the taxpayer saves money by not having to punch the same information into a computer twice."

As a reciprocal move, the White House began supplying the House Information System with computer tapes of the president's budget, making it possible for an individual member to punch in a request and get the information about a particular program without scouring through the complicated budget document.

Alexander sounded a note of pragmatism in looking to future uses of computers and electronic communications between the branches.

"What we're talking about is mostly pushing messages around from office to office," he said. "For that you need terminals. Only about half the House members have terminals in their office now, and there won't be many more for the next while."

Whatever the future holds, the Carter aides expressed an awareness that the computer can only help, not substitute for, human efforts.

As Francis stated it, "There's no substitute for experience on the Hill and 'street savvy,' but the computer can add to your tools. If you've got no experience, then the fanciest computer system in the world is not going to help you, but if you have someone who knows politics and legislation and you help him to get information faster, it will help."

The bloopers committed at the outset of the administration stemmed partly from the inexperience of Moore, who had been Carter's lobbyist in the Georgia legislature, and of many other administration people.

Another cause of the early errors was that "we were undermanned," said Danny C. Tate, Moore's lieutenant in the Senate. Owing to Carter's initial desire to pare the size of the presidential staff, which he felt had grown too large under his predecessors, the White House liaison office began with only four lobbyists aside from Moore. Eventu-

ally it was able to double its size.

Foul-ups will occur in the chaotic start-up of any administration, regardless of who is in power. "You always get a lot of [complaining] in the beginning," said Tom C. Korologos, a lobbyist with the Ford administration. "Everybody's calling at once."

Early Errors

Democratic representatives and senators, eager to make points on pet legislative projects and to receive

Legal Limitations on Executive Branch Lobbying

When the executive branch tries to influence legislation, it must keep in mind limits that Congress has placed on such activity.

Taken literally, the legal restraints are severe. One criminal statute and a standard rider on most executive branch appropriations appear to prohibit the use of any appropriated monies for any effort by the president and his aides to influence the course of legislation, except in response to congressional inquiry.

However, those restrictions consistently have been interpreted as being less severe than they appear. No one has ever been prosecuted under the statutes, and only two court cases, both in recent years, prompted significant discussion of the statutes.

Inhibiting Force

Nevertheless, said White House Senior Associate Counsel Michael H. Cardozo V, "There are adversaries of certain initiatives of the government who use the statute to object to our doing certain things."

The specter of an opponent complaining that the White House or the Cabinet has violated the statutory limits is a restraint on congressional liaison and other administration officials. Cardozo and Michael S. Berman, counsel to the vice president, are regularly called upon to advise White House officials on the statutes.

The precise language of the pertinent criminal statute is contained in Title 18 U.S. Code, sec. 1913:

"No part of the money appropriated by any enactment of Congress shall, in the absence of express authorization by Congress, be used directly or indirectly to pay for any personal service, advertisement, telegram, telephone, letter, printed or written matter, or other device, intended or designed to influence in any manner a Member of Congress, to favor or oppose, by vote or otherwise, any legislation or appropriation by Congress, whether before or after the introduction of any bill or resolution proposing such legislation or appropriation..."

The exception is that executive branch officials may answer congressional queries and forward to Congress "requests for legislation or appropriations which they deem necessary...."

The appropriations riders, such as the one included in the Carter budget for the Executive Office of the President, have a slightly different focus: "No part of any appropriation contained in this or any other Act... shall be used for publicity or propaganda purposes designed to support or defeat legislation pending before Congress."

The penalty for violation of sec. 1913 is not more than $500 or up to one year imprisonment. The penalty for violation of the non-criminal appropriations riders is not stated, but presumably could entail personal financial liability of an official for any sums found to have been spent in violation of the provision.

The legislative and enforcement history of these statutes shows that they were intended to be less sweeping than they sound. The criminal statute, enacted in 1919, came in response to allegedly extensive use of telegrams by government agencies urging citizens to lobby members of Congress on appropriations. An attorney in the legal counsel's office at the Justice Department said, "There was a concern that members of Congress might think there was a groundswell of public opinion without knowing people were being solicited by the executive."

The appropriations riders, first placed on the books in 1951, arose from congressional concern over extensive government use of public relations personnel and publications to mold public opinion and in turn to influence legislation. Again, there was an objection to being lobbied with federal monies, for fear that "the executive branch might become self-perpetuating, using its vast resources...," according to Justice.

Most congressional liaison offices interpret the statutes to mean that they must be very cautious in indirect or "grass-roots" lobbying—soliciting or encouraging lobbying by private individuals or groups. In contrast, direct contact with members of Congress and their staffs is unanimously viewed as legitimate.

In fact, there is a constitutional requirement, in Article II, that the president "...from time to time give to the Congress information on the State of the Union and recommend to their consideration such measures as he shall judge necessary and expedient." That mandate frequently is cited in the arguing that the president and his aides have a duty to lobby Congress directly.

Freedom of Speech

Even in the touchier area of indirect lobbying, executive branch lawyers argue that the statutes are not meant to abridge First Amendment rights of free speech. Strictly oral communications intended to stir public interest in legislation and spur public lobbying therefore remain permissible. Thus public statements by administration officials urging passage of the president's legislative proposals are protected.

In the view of the White House, even explicit oral encouragement to "write your congressman" would be protected by the First Amendment. Some congressional liaison officers shy away from oral solicitations to lobby, however, particularly where they are done on a large scale. For example, some liaison people will not use a "telephone tree" to set in motion a network of calls intended to alert people around the country to the need for lobbying on a given measure.

As for written materials, most liaison officers say that explicit solicitations to others to contact members of Congress are taboo, but that "information" intended to tell private groups about pending legislation is permissible and can be disseminated.

Beyond those basic rules of thumb, there is no precise outline of the boundaries of executive lobbying. While a literal reading of the statutes indicates that the executive branch can do nothing to influence legislation, Congress has recognized the role of executive lobbying in key regulatory statutes such as the Hatch Act, which limits political activity by federal employees, and the 1946 Federal Regulation of Lobbying Act, which requires registration of lobbyists. And history has reserved a clear place for executive lobbying efforts.

patronage they had missed during eight years of Republican rule, besieged Moore with phone calls almost as soon as Carter was elected. Many calls were not returned, earning Moore a bad reputation among some Hill Democrats even before the inauguration.

Carter's disdain for the "wheeling and dealing" of Washington scored him points during the campaign. But it caused him problems once he moved into the White House. Many observers said that one of the reasons the energy package took nearly two years to be enacted was because it was drafted in secret by the administration with no Hill consultation.

Carter's relations with Congress, and especially with the Democratic leadership, were rocky for almost a year and a half. The incidents followed a predictable sequence: First came a usually uncalculated rebuff by Carter or his staff, then a public outcry from the damaged person, the administration's scurrying to make amends and, finally, a grudging acceptance of an apology.

Ill-tutored in the mechanics of working with Congress, the administration found itself often upsetting such potent figures in Congress as House Ways and Means Committee Chairman Al Ullman, D-Ore., and Senate Budget Committee Chairman Edmund S. Muskie, D-Maine. These two — stalwart backers of Carter's 1977 plan to offer a $50 tax rebate — were never even consulted when the White House decided suddenly to withdraw the idea.

O'Neill, although assiduously courted by the administration, was for a time the chronic recipient of unintended White House slights. Two prominent Republicans from O'Neill's home state were elevated to important positions by Carter in 1977 without checking with the Speaker — former Pittsfield, Mass., Mayor Evan S. Dobelle was made chief of protocol, and former Cabinet member Elliot L. Richardson was named ambassador to the Law of the Sea Conference. (Dobelle subsequently switched parties and became treasurer first of the Democratic National Committee and then the Carter 1980 campaign.)

Carter's ouster of Robert T. Griffin, an O'Neill protégé, from the No. 2 spot at the troubled General Services Administration caused the Speaker to ban Moore from his office. The breach was healed only after yet another quickly called conciliation meeting. Griffin was given a White House job to appease O'Neill.

Remedial Action

"Those horror stories of the early days had some merit," said Rep. Morris K. Udall, D-Ariz. "But the Carter staff proved in 1978 that they had learned the Hill."

By the end of its first year, the administration realized it had problems. A review of the Hill liaison effort, headed by the vice president was begun in November 1977, result-

Carter's congressional liaison got off to an inauspicious start because "we were undermanned."

—Danny C. Tate, chief White House lobbyist for the Senate

ing in the decision to enlarge the lobbying staff. Within two years Moore had seven assistant lobbyists, all experienced at working on Capitol Hill, plus a deputy and an administrative support staff. *(White House lobbying team, box, p. 29)*

Perhaps the most important personnel action in Moore's office occurred before the Mondale review, in June 1977, when Cable, a highly respected House staffer, was named to direct the House lobbying. He replaced Frederick T. Merrill Jr., a one-time aide for the reform-oriented House Democratic Study Group who had raised the hackles of some old-guard representatives. Merrill was shifted to the Department of Energy's lobbying staff.

Cable drew widespread praise from House members and aides. Typical was the assessment of Hymel, O'Neill's influential aide: "Bill Cable is known for his impeccable trustworthiness."

Moore's task also was helped when Carter chose to invite more members of Congress to the White House for personal meetings and entertainment. The president himself grew bolder in his approach to members during meetings.

"In the last six or eight months [of the 95th Congress], he became his own finest congressional liaison person," remarked Rep. Richard Bolling, D-Mo. "He moved from proposing and letting Congress dispose to knowing his priorities and how to get them through."

"The more you saw [Carter], the more you came to appreciate him," said former Rep. Paul G. Rogers, D-Fla.

The changes have impressed not only members of Congress who must work with the White House, but also those who study the workings of Capitol Hill.

"What began as a comedy of errors has definitely matured," said Robert L. Peabody, a Johns Hopkins University scholar who studies Congress. "Now people on the Hill are more willing to work with Frank Moore." ∎

SALT II: Emotional, High-Priced Lobbying

A State Department official trying to sell the new Strategic Arms Limitation Treaty asks an audience to consider the effects of a hypothetical one-megaton bomb dropped above the hotel in which they are sitting. He describes the grisly results at ground zero and at one, three, four, six and 10 miles from the blast.

The same audience later hears former Army Lt. Gen. Daniel O. Graham accuse the State Department speaker, James L. Montgomery, of using "mass terror tactics" to win public support for the treaty. Then Graham goes on to warn that approval of SALT II would "risk the very existence of this country and our entire Western value system to an aggressive entity determined to destroy us."

If there was a lesson to be learned from what the Carter administration had billed as the "debate of the decade," it was that SALT II was serious business — deadly serious. But separating fact from fiction was not easy. Throughout the long lobbying campaign that followed Carter's signing of the proposed treaty with the Soviet Union, experts on both sides of the U.S. debate made doomsday predictions based on mutually exclusive views of how to avoid nuclear war. But both sides agreed that limits the treaty placed on the arms race were modest at best.

The public also saw the Carter administration selling what it acknowledged were limited gains in arms control, while at the same time leading the fight for a new M-X missile system with a $20 billion plus price tag. Explaining the treaty proved to be a multimillion-dollar sales job, including television ads and half-hour films designed by each side to convince the public that the wrong vote on SALT II would guarantee Armageddon. *(Films, p. 42)*

Role for Public Opinion?

Ironically, all of the lobbying and public relations may have had less effect dollar for dollar than any major lobbying effort in recent memory. In the final analysis, the outcome was likely to depend on about a dozen undecided senators. But if the grass-roots appeals accomplished anything, they reinforced the widely accepted view among senators that the SALT votes would be among the most important of their careers.

"You have to come back to the uniqueness or transcendent nature of the issue — whether there will be a nuclear war. And that has an impact on everyone who thinks about it, his children and grandchildren," said Townsend Hoopes, former Air Force under secretary and co-chairman of Americans for SALT.

The fact that many senators placed SALT in a category distinct from most of their other concerns was evident in exhortations by Senate Majority Leader Robert C. Byrd, D-W.Va., that his colleagues avoid quick decisions and study the treaty thoroughly. There was further evidence in the fact that senators formed at least three SALT study groups, which met frequently without staff aides to be briefed directly by military and intelligence experts.

Sen. William V. Roth Jr., R-Del., the organizer of a 15-member group, said that he would not let public opinion influence his decision on an issue so complex as SALT. Many other senators made similar commitments.

In a debate that some observers expected to last six months, senators were likely to have plenty of time for contemplation. "The debate hasn't reached the emotional and rhetorical level that Panama did," said a State Department official. "One factor is it's so complex that relatively few people are able to talk about it. And most [senators] realize this is a lot more serious than Panama — you can't deal too recklessly with this one."

Head Counts and Players

Less than a week after the text of the treaty was released, most observers were discounting the value of head counts, with some insisting that as much as half of the Senate was undecided. But senators are not totally unpredictable, and there were several working estimates available on how close President Carter was to the 67 votes he needed to win.

These estimates — by lobby groups such as Americans for SALT and senators such as Alan Cranston, D-Calif., the majority whip — suggested a solid 25 to 30 votes likely to go against the treaty and a block of 20 undecided.

About 50 senators were considered likely to vote for the treaty.

Assuming the best — from the administration's point of view — Carter had to sway 12 of the 20 hard undecideds. Assuming the worst, he needed to bring around 17. Some of those undecided were more important than others, however. Among the senators likely to sway some votes were:

- Majority Leader Byrd. Without him, the treaty was likely to lose. Even more than Byrd's own vote, which

Principal Players in the Debate Over SALT

Among the principal interest groups working for and against the SALT II treaty were:

Pro-Treaty Groups

● **Americans for SALT.** A clearinghouse for liberal and moderate groups interested in SALT II. Funded by large donations from some of its founders, this lobby group was set up to build grass-roots support for the treaty. Co-chairmen included Clark Clifford, former secretary of Defense, and Henry Cabot Lodge, former U.N. ambassador.

● **New Directions.** A 14,000-member lobby group that began working on SALT II in 1977.

● **Council for a Livable World.** Formed in 1962 to lobby for arms reduction and control, the council's 12,000 supporters also have been active in financing candidates who support arms reductions.

● **Religious Committee on SALT.** A coalition of 25 church groups established to encourage grass-roots support for SALT.

● **American Committee for East-West Accord.** Founded in 1974, this educational group was set up to improve U.S.-Soviet relations. Funded largely by corporations with a direct interest in trade with the Soviets, the group's 200 members included former Ambassador to the Soviet Union George F. Kennan, economist John Kenneth Galbraith and United Auto Workers President Douglas A. Fraser. The group produced a pro-SALT movie and several books.

● **Center for Defense Information.** A tax-exempt educational group funded by several large foundations.

The center, directed by former Navy Rear Adm. Gene R. LaRocque, produced "War Without Winners," a film supporting the treaty.

Anti-SALT Forces

● **Committee on the Present Danger.** A non-profit educational group designed to encourage a national debate on increased defense spending to meet what it views as a threat of Soviet domination. The committee published strategic weapons analyses and conducted public opinion polls in connection with SALT II. The group's principal spokesman, former Deputy Defense Secretary Paul H. Nitze, was a member of the SALT negotiating delegation until 1974.

● **Coalition for Peace Through Strength.** Established by the American Security Council, a hawkish 200,000-member pro-defense lobby, the coalition included 194 members of Congress who signed the group's statement of purpose favoring military superiority over the Soviet Union. The coalition served as an umbrella lobby organization for anti-SALT groups nationwide.

● **American Conservative Union.** A 100,000-member grass-roots lobby organization headed by Rep. Robert E. Bauman, R-Md. The group used mass mail appeals to generate opposition to SALT and planned to release an anti-SALT movie.

● **Conservative Caucus.** A major conservative grass-roots lobby claiming 400,000 members, the caucus planned a 50-state speaking tour in opposition to the SALT treaty.

Carter was likely to receive, he needed Byrd's skills in bringing Democrats in line.

● Minority Leader Howard H. Baker Jr., R-Tenn. Baker was leaning against the treaty and early on said he thought SALT should be linked to the total military and foreign policy relationship between the United States and the Soviet Union. Conventional wisdom held that a Republican could not support SALT and win the presidential nomination, which Baker was seeking in 1980. But Baker had supported the administration on the Panama Canal treaties, an issue that struck a deeper emotional chord than SALT among conservatives, and he said he would not offer "killer" amendments to the SALT treaty. As a member of the Foreign Relations Committee, Baker had an inside track in offering reservations to the treaty that could make it acceptable to Republicans.

● Sam Nunn, D-Ga. Nunn made clear that the price Carter might have to pay for his support was approval of some expensive new weapons systems. A member of the Armed Services Committee and a a leading student of the strategic balance, Nunn wielded great influence with conservatives and southern Democrats. His support was also seen as crucial to countering Sen. Henry M. Jackson, D-Wash., who had labeled the treaty "appeasement."

● John C. Stennis, D-Miss. The chairman of the Armed Services Committee, Stennis was considered likely to support the administration and was another important voice among conservatives and southern Democrats. Nunn and Jackson were likely to help Stennis make up his mind.

The Kissinger Connection

Outside the Senate a number of other voices were likely to influence how senators voted on SALT II. The White House was particularly concerned about getting endorsements from former Secretary of State Henry A. Kissinger and former Presidents Ford and Nixon. Carter was selling the treaty as an extension of a foreign policy laid down in large measure by these three men.

In summer 1979 testimony, Kissinger expressed strong reservations about the treaty, insisting it had to be linked to the Soviets' showing restraint in actions that upset the balance of power. However, he avoided urging a flat approval or rejection, and both sides continued to hope for a more explicit statement from the former secretary.

One pro-SALT lobbyist, John Isaacs of the Council for a Livable World, said, "If Kissinger comes out against the treaty he could sink it on his own. He'll provide cover for a lot of Republicans" one way or the other.

White House officials said they did not underestimate Kissinger's influence, but thought he would come around. Political adviser Anne Wexler said an endorsement by the former secretary of State "would be useful and kind of logical under the circumstances. He was certainly a party to starting the [SALT] process and it doesn't make a hell of a lot of sense to interrupt it right now."

Hoopes of Americans for SALT offered a similar view. "I can't conceive of his coming out against it. It would nullify everything he's done. . . . It's his past. He's tied to SALT I with an umbilical cord made of piano wire."

The treaty, Carter told Congress June 19, "is more than a single arms control agreement. It is part of a long historical process of gradually reducing the danger of nuclear war — a process that we must not undermine." And White House lobbyists were trying to make senators keenly aware that rejection of the treaty would imply a drastic change in course for U.S. foreign policy.

The consequences of rejection were being compared with those that followed Woodrow Wilson's failure to win approval for the Treaty of Versailles after World War I, a move that kept the United States out of the League of Nations. But Carter's most difficult challenge was to convince senators that rejection would threaten U.S. strategic security.

In his first three years in office Carter did well in the Senate in winning support for his foreign policy initiatives. But Panama, the sale of jet fighters to Saudi Arabia, lifting the Turkish arms embargo and cutting ties with Taiwan were not on a par with SALT in its far-reaching implications for NATO allies. The administration argued that rejection would delay any future treaty for years, leading to a rapidly escalating arms race and proliferation of nuclear weapons in the Third World.

But Carter and the Senate also realized what rejection could mean for Carter's political future. It would diminish his clout among U.S. allies, making foreign policy initiatives in a second term difficult or impossible. Those political implications were difficult for senators to ignore.

Administration Lobby

The Carter administration lobby effort, directed at both the Senate and the grass roots, was easily one of the most elaborate and sophisticated ever put together. Its grass-roots effort was mobilized in the belief that the SALT II issue was of such fundamental importance that the administration had a responsibility to make sure the people knew what their leaders were getting them into.

But there were other pressures at work. The public relations effort was in part a response to the Panama Canal debate, in which the Senate demonstrated that the days of unamended treaties were long gone. The administration also was responding to a vocal, well-financed and highly visible opposition, led by several well-known defense experts, which set the tone for the debate long before the treaty was signed.

Criticism of the administration for cancelling the B-1 bomber and the neutron bomb forced it into a defensive posture of attempting to restore public confidence in U.S. defenses.

"Decisions are no longer made just from Washington," said a State Department SALT-seller. "You don't have a bipartisan approach to foreign policy with Congress just rubber stamping the executive. The American community, its leadership, has to be convinced the treaty is good or bad."

Supporters of the treaty also had been critical, charging the White House with dragging its feet. John Isaacs of the pro-SALT Council for a Livable World charged that the anti-SALT groups had "dominated the public relations field for the last year or two and helped set the negative tone for this debate. The administration has been too silent."

Townsend Hoopes of Americans for SALT said the administration missed opportunities "to educate the public on the generic benefits of arms control .... The adminis-

tration allowed the opposition to dominate the media with scare stories."

But if the administration did not seem so visible as its opponents, it was hardly asleep. "Our effort is much more extensive than what we did on Panama," said a White House lobbyist. "It's the most extensive undertaking I've seen here."

Just how many people the administration had working on selling SALT was difficult to estimate. But there were enough people involved that a White House computer was used to keep track of individuals and their assignments.

A General Accounting Office report on the administration's 1978 pro-SALT efforts concluded that more than $600,000 was spent by the State Department and the Arms Control and Disarmament Agency (ACDA), the agency with overall responsiblity for negotiating the treaty. GAO said State and ACDA had printed 10 SALT-related documents in 1978 and made about 400,000 copies available.

Capitol Hill Push

To get the treaty ratified by the requisite 67 senators, the administration came up with a two-part plan.

The White House recognized that it would be counterproductive to seek endorsements from senators before the text of the treaty was available. So the first phase, conducted over nine months late in 1978 and early in 1979, consisted of making sure each of the 100 senators was kept up-to-date on the negotiations and got all the briefings by all the experts they wanted. It was intended to lead to the second phase — getting the votes.

At the same time it was making its presence felt in the Senate, the White House undertook a massive effort to win support of community leaders throughout the country.

The SALT Task Force, which determined overall strategy and incorporated both the Hill and public outreach efforts, fell under the direction of Hamilton Jordan, Carter's top aide. Day-to-day operations were handled by Landon Butler, deputy assistant to the president. The congressional end of the operation was headed by Frank B. Moore, the administration's chief lobbyist, and by a congressional relations coordinating group chaired by White House lobbyist Robert Beckel. The outreach effort was overseen by political adviser Anne Wexler.

The task force meetings were held on Mondays. Attending were Jordan, Butler, Moore, Beckel, Wexler, press secretary Jody Powell, communications assistant Gerald Rafshoon, and vice presidential chief of staff Richard Moe. Also attending were agency representatives Warren Christopher, deputy secretary of State; Charles W. Duncan Jr., deputy Defense secretary; Gen. George M. Seignious II, director of ACDA; Frederick P. Hitz, CIA congressional liaison; David L. Aaron, deputy national security assistant, and Roger C. Molander, a staff member of the National Security Council. (Duncan later became Energy secretary.)

The task force divided itself into three subgroups. A SALT working group chaired by Molander cleared all official statements and testimony on SALT. A working group chaired by Butler met Thursdays to discuss press and the public outreach operation directed by Wexler. And immediately following those meetings Beckel's congressional liaison group would meet with the agency representatives.

It was this group that coordinated all contacts on Capitol Hill — briefings of senators and staff and all testimony. Each agency in the congressional relations group committed two representatives to do those briefings.

Dr. Strangelove Returns to Television. . .

"Quick cuts of rows of tanks coming from different locations. Artillery guns fire. Migs fire. Tanks fire. . . ; Ships fire guns. Planes fire guns. Explosions."

These descriptions of Soviet armaments in action are from the script of a film, "The Price of Peace and Freedom," opponents were showing across the nation as part of their effort to kill the SALT II treaty.

The half-hour documentary, which cost about $75,000, provided a weapon-by-weapon comparison of NATO and Warsaw Pact armaments. It was produced by the American Security Council (ASC), one of the largest conservative, pro-defense membership groups in the country and a leading opponent of SALT II.

The message: The United States was in imminent danger of annihilation by the Russians.

Also making its way around the country was "Survival. . . or Suicide," a $70,000 film put out by the American Committee on East-West Accord, an arms control group supporting the treaty.

It depicted victims of the Hiroshima bomb drop while a narrator explained the consequences of atomic weapons.

"A person who has received fatal amounts of radiation from direct exposure to the bombs, or from fallout, will appear relatively normal the first few weeks," the narrator said. "Then small hemorrhages will appear in the skin, and there's spontaneous bleeding from the mouth and intestinal tract. The hair will begin to fall out. Eventually the cells that normally control bleeding and fight infection are destroyed, resulting in hemorrhage, overwhelming infection and death."

The message: Controlling nuclear weapons is a life or death matter.

Living Room Wars

Those films were only two of at least six expensive SALT-related pieces that were to be flashed into the living rooms of millions of Americans while the Senate was considering the SALT treaty. (Description of sponsoring groups, box, p. 40)

Among the others:

● "Soviet Might, American Myth: The United States in Retreat," produced by the American Conservative Union (ACU), another major conservative group. It argued the case for increased U.S. weapons spending. The ACU spent more than $400,000 to produce the film and have it aired on more than 370 stations in 1978-79.

● "War Without Winners," by the Center for Defense Information (CDI), a liberal research group that favored arms reductions. To produce the $175,000 film, the Center teamed up with Academy Award winning cinematographer Haskell Wexler, who also did "American Graffiti" and "One Flew Over the Cuckoo's Nest."

● Two other films also were planned by conservative groups to specifically attack the SALT treaty.

By late 1979 the pro-SALT films had received limited exposure since supporters were relying entirely on the good graces of station managers to air their productions. About 125 stations had requested "War Without Winners" and "several dozen" had aired it, according to CDI staffer Arthur L. Kanegis.

NEA Endorsement

The National Education Association endorsed the other pro-SALT film, "Survival. . . or Suicide," and this was expected to help boost its ratings.

The anti-SALT films were a different story. While production costs were similar, opponents planned to buy airtime to get their message across. John M. Fisher, chairman of the American Security Council, said "Peace and Freedom" had been shown 852 times on television, most of the showings at no cost. The film was released in 1976, well before agreement on SALT II.

Fisher said ASC planned to spend about $300,000 to get its new film, tentatively titled "The SALT Syndrome," shown in the 100 major markets.

The anti-SALT groups also planned to use their film showings to help finance their anti-treaty efforts. "Soviet Might, American Myth" asked viewers four times in less than a half hour to call a toll-free number and pledge money to the ACU, a pitch an ACU spokesman said had nearly paid for the costs of the film.

Scenes from 'The Price of Peace and Freedom,' an anti-SALT film produced by the American Security Council.

... In Summer Nuclear Horror Movie Fare

Mushroom Cloud Images

The films produced by each side reached diametrically opposed conclusions — increased military spending versus greater arms reductions — but had several elements in common.

Each sought to frighten. The all-or-nothing choice asked of the viewer was repeatedly punctuated by images of atomic bombs exploding.

Each offered reasoned arguments to strategic arms questions while appealing to the viewer's most deeply rooted instincts, emotions and prejudices. The information was presented as factual, although the Center for Defense Information, in a 60-page rebuttal to "The Price of Peace and Freedom," charged the producers with numerous inaccuracies and distortions.

Each provided graphic evidence that the provisions of the SALT treaty would have little to do with how the treaty was sold to the public.

But despite the similarities in style, the messages were vastly different.

The anti-SALT films operated on the premise that more weapons would provide greater security and that Americans stood to lose the most in a nuclear confrontation. Military experts and well-known politicians were relied on heavily to make the case for Soviet superiority.

In the pro-SALT pieces the message was that more weapons provide greater instability and a better chance for a war in which the costs to each side would be unthinkable. "War Without Winners," trying to portray the insanity of a nuclear war, informed viewers that the United States has a facility to inform the public of the expected arrival time of a Soviet missile.

These films quoted defense experts, too, although CDI relied heavily on more mundane man-in-the-street interviews in the United States and in the Soviet Union. Those interviewed expressed their concerns about basic human survival in the event of nuclear war.

The pro-SALT films argued that both sides were well equipped to destroy the other and made a case for fearing atomic weapons. Negotiated arms reduction was viewed not only as a possibility, but as a necessity.

The anti-SALT films, on the other hand, built a case for fearing the Soviet Union, implicitly rejecting any possibility of successful negotiation for arms reduction.

A Winnable War?

In "Soviet Might, American Myth," Rep. Philip M. Crane, R-Ill., arguing along Cold War lines, warned viewers of the "threat of world communism." He charged the president and the State and Defense Departments with "weaving a web of self-deception" and failing "to recognize and act upon the unmistakable threats to our freedom and survival as a nation." Against what he viewed as a spineless and befuddled U.S. government, Crane described a determined Soviet Union that regarded nuclear war as "both feasible and winnable."

The anti-SALT films also portrayed the Soviets as imperialist monsters bent on world domination. Alexander Solzhenitsyn was quoted frequently.

"A concentration of world evil, of hatred for humanity is taking place, and it is fully determined to destroy your society," Solzhenitsyn said in "The Price of Peace and Freedom." "Must you wait until it comes with a crowbar to break through your borders — until the young men of America have to fall defending the borders of their continent?"

The pro-SALT "Survival. . . or Suicide," on the other hand, gave the viewer a different impression of the Soviets. The film argued that not one of 14 nuclear weapons agreements with the Soviet Union had been broken and quoted Soviet party leader Leonid Brezhnev as calling for an end to the arms race.

Cold warriors were criticized in one film by former Deputy CIA Director Herbert Scoville. "[T]he myth of U.S. inferiority is being spread to try and panic the public. . .," Scoville said in "War Without Winners." "The taxpayer is being raked off on this deal for the benefit of a very few corporations and individuals and in the meantime he's increasing the risk that he is going to be wiped off the face of the earth."

Bombed Back to 1925?

Neither side made a great effort to present opposing views. But the pro-SALT "War Without Winners," quoted Lt. Gen. Daniel O. Graham, one of the leading advocates of the winnable nuclear war theory, in an attempt to discredit arms race advocates.

'[I]f you count how many casualties would occur on both sides. . . it should cut the United States, in terms of its population, agriculture, industry and so forth, back to about somewhere around 1925 to 1935. . . . But that is not the end of the world. . .," Graham said.

Finally, the two sides reached back in history to find different mentors to preach their respective gospels. In the anti-SALT films, President John F. Kennedy, the spirit of liberalism, addressed the need for nuclear superiority. In the pro-SALT pieces, President Dwight D. Eisenhower, the embodiment of military strength, discussed food for the world's hungry.

Administration Goes on the Road to Promote SALT

Winning support for SALT from the nation's opinion leaders was a major component of the Carter administration's grass-roots campaign for the treaty.

By mid-1979 a traveling contingent of State Department officials had appeared in 19 major cities to brief selected groups. The guest list was designed to include people who represented a broad cross-section of public opinion but who had made no commitment for or against the treaty.

A typical briefing, held June 12 in Richmond, Va., was sponsored at the State Department's request by the local and state chambers of commerce and the Richmond newspapers.

Participants were selected by the sponsors and included leading academics, the state lieutenant governor, church and union leaders and representatives of Virginia's largest businesses and one public interest group — the League of Women Voters. The participants were white and largely middle and upper class.

Most of the participants interviewed before the conference began had no opinion on SALT II. They had come to hear the arguments. After three hours of briefings most remained uncommitted.

At the briefings, the administration made no effort to see that opposing arguments were presented. But at the Richmond session and others, organizers and opponents insisted that anti-treaty spokesmen be heard. A State Department official later acknowledged that the opposition's presence lent greater credibility to the administration because it allowed the department to respond to its critics.

Administration briefings were geared to appeal to a broad spectrum of liberal and conservative interests, to address the interests of those concerned with arms control as well as those concerned about being "number one" in military muscle. To make its case in Richmond the State Department sent Sherrod McCall, one of its experts on U.S.-Soviet relations, and James L. Montgomery, director of State's office of international security policy.

McCall's mission was to convince the audience that the United States had been tough with the Soviets in negotiating SALT II.

'Cold Eye of Pragmatism'

"The history of our attitude to the Soviets has been subject to broad swings of emotion," McCall told his listeners. Then he assured them that the Carter administration would be guided only by "the cold eye of pragmatism to secure our national interests."

But McCall also had to convince the audience that SALT II would not damage U.S. security. "No treaty will be worth the paper it's printed on if we haven't got a military strength second to none," he said.

Montgomery's job was to communicate some of the basic assumptions on which SALT II is founded, including:

● That neither side can seriously consider nuclear war.

● That "nuclear superiority" is an obsolete concept.

● That there is "essential equivalence" in U.S. and Soviet armaments.

Using a set of charts, Montgomery detailed provisions of the SALT treaty, comparing the respective armaments of the United States and the Soviet Union.

He also provided an additional perspective — a description of the effect of an atomic bomb dropped on the hotel where the conference was meeting. There was no apparent reaction from the audience.

Montgomery concluded by comparing the tension of U.S.-Soviet strategic negotiations to a football game where players are told that 350,000 tons of TNT under the stadium will explode if either side scores.

The argument was not subtle. But it got across one of the administration's key arguments — that the SALT dialogue is part of a process that must continue.

Following the administration talks, the opposition was given an opportunity to have its spokesman — Daniel O. Graham, a retired Army lieutenant general — make his case. In a question-and-answer period Graham declared that Carter's SALT policy embodied a "philosophy of despair."

Graham later gave a speech laying out what he considered the weaknesses of SALT:

● It did not limit nuclear arms.

● It gave the Soviets a "war winning" capability that would sap the United States of its will to fight.

● It could not be verified.

Samuel Vaughan Wilson, another former Army Lieutenant general, supported the treaty with "some trepidation," but was pro-SALT because in the long run, he said, it was better to continue the dialogue with the Russians.

"We could retaliate with such force that the living would envy the dead."

—Lt. Gen. George M. Seignious II, director, Arms Control and Disarmament Agency

After lunch came the keynote speaker — Lt. Gen. George M. Seignious II, director of the Arms Control and Disarmament Agency. Seignious insisted that United States arms be equal to the Soviets and that a treaty both enhance national security and be verifiable.

He further sought to dispel critics' assertions that a Soviet first strike could paralyze the nation. "[W]e could retaliate with such force that the living would envy the dead, and a nation — once a superpower — would lapse into some sort of 20th century feudal age," he said.

Vice President Mondale also devoted a major portion of his time to winning Senate votes for SALT, an effort that was strongly encouraged by Frank Church, D-Idaho, chairman of the Senate Foreign Relations Committee.

The Public Effort

The public campaign also was well organized. The White House had a limited "A" briefing list of key senators and national leaders who were to meet personally with the president and a "B" list of about 700 "notable" Americans who were to be invited to briefings by foreign policy adviser Zbigniew Brzezinski, Secretary of State Cyrus R. Vance or Defense Secretary Harold Brown.

Special briefings also were provided for former Presidents Ford and Nixon, former Secretary of State Henry A. Kissinger and other national leaders whose support was considered crucial to final Senate approval.

"A major dividend of [our] briefings is to develop national leaders who are knowledgeable about SALT even if they are not convinced of our position," said presidential adviser Anne Wexler, who was responsible for convincing the public that SALT would benefit the United States and the cause of world peace.

About 30 high level military retirees were invited to briefings at the White House. But in large part the administration effort was aimed at people who normally take no special interest in defense or foreign policy matters. They were described by administration lobbyists as "the great American middle."

This target group was composed largely of prominent businessmen and corporate executive officers. But it also included newspaper publishers, academics, religious and labor leaders and the leaders of various ethnic and special interest groups.

"If we can reach enough of those kinds of people, we'll get a trickle-down sense of confidence in the broader community," said Peter Johnson, head of the State Department SALT working group. Johnson's group sponsored 19 conferences in major cities to brief 100 to 200 leaders each. The sessions focused on U.S.-Soviet relations and on a comparison of the weapons available to both sides. *(Briefings, box, p. 44)*

The conferences were among more than 760 SALT-related speeches, briefings, media interviews and other events in 400 cities in which the administration participated during the first five months of 1979. More than 150 additional events had been scheduled.

State Department, ACDA and White House officials also made during this period 59 television appearances, conducted 137 briefings for newspaper executives and participated in 58 "direct line" radio interviews. State also produced television interviews at the request of four local stations.

State Department officials denied that these "events" were targeted at states where senators were undecided. But they acknowledged that areas where there was greater public doubt about the treaty received higher priority, specifically the South, Southwest and Midwest.

Participants at State's briefing conferences were sent follow-up letters asking them if they wanted further information on SALT II. A State Department speakers bureau consisted of about 60 employees working part-time on SALT. Each went through a two-day training session to learn how to sell the treaty. With the assistance of a department psychiatrist, speakers were trained to address the groups for which they were best suited. As one depart-

ment official explained, a 25-year-old female would not be sent to convince a gathering of retired military men that the treaty was a great idea.

But the administration sales effort was more than speeches or conferences. Names of conference participants were given to Wexler's SALT team, which then set up additional briefings at the White House. Seven major briefings, each attended by 60 to 80 opinion leaders, were held with the president in the weeks following his signing of the treaty. Twelve others for groups of about 30 were held at the White House for business, environmental and other groups. The White House was expected to be host to more than 1,000 opinion leaders before the treaty was voted on.

The impact of these briefings was hard to measure. One person who attended a presidential briefing — the Rev. Jesse Jackson, head of the Chicago-based Operation PUSH — subsequently sent out a mass mailing encouraging treaty support and made at least one speech endorsing it.

Wexler's operation actively sought endorsements from individuals and groups briefed by the White House. Lists of endorsement were sent to senators as they became available. The public outreach program was largely a State Department and White House effort, but the Defense Department also became involved.

A Defense Department SALT working group was headed by Walter Slocombe, deputy assistant secretary for international security. Slocombe's staff of five professionals worked largely on the substance of the treaty but also briefed groups of senators who had set up SALT study groups. The working group planned to hold briefings for about 30 top retired generals and admirals.

The Opponents

Opposition to the treaty was spearheaded by two groups — the Committee on the Present Danger (CPD) and the Coalition for Peace Through Strength (CPTS). Of the two, the committee could be called the brains behind the opposition. While it did not lobby, it kindled the fire of those who did lobby with its detailed analyses of issues.

The committee also conducted a poll that it said showed the vast majority of Americans would reject the treaty if they knew what was in it. The poll was conducted because the committee questioned the validity of national

Retired Army Lt. Gen. Daniel O. Graham, left, argues about the SALT II treaty with James H. Smylie of the Union Theological Seminary in Richmond, Va.

High-Powered Campaign to Sell SALT II Treaty...

Controversy over Carter administration efforts to sell the SALT II treaty underscored the absence of clear legal limitations on executive branch lobbying activities.

Opponents of SALT II charged that the administration was illegally lobbying for approval of the treaty and using public funds improperly. They commissioned two General Accounting Office (GAO) audits of the administration's SALT activities. The first, released March 16, 1979, led Rep. Jack F. Kemp, R-N.Y., to charge that "current activities go far beyond congressional intent for use of appropriated funds...."

The administration defended itself against such attacks, insisting that its pro-SALT efforts were merely a public education campaign, which it had a right and responsibility to pursue because of the importance of the treaty. But the semantics obscured the issue.

By any textbook definition, the administration was clearly engaged in a massive lobbying effort on behalf of the treaty. The real issue, then, was not whether the administration could lobby, but how it could lobby. Existing law suggested there were few clear limitations on what an administration could do to make its positions known. *(Related box, p. 36)*

1919 Law

SALT critics were not the first opponents of an administration policy to dredge up an ambiguous federal criminal statute that ostensibly prohibited any executive branch lobbying with public funds. The statute (18 U.S.C. 1913) was enacted in 1919 after virtually no debate in Congress, and has never provided the basis of any indictment or prosecution.

The statute states in part: "No part of the money appropriated by an enactment of Congress, shall in the absence of express authorization by Congress, be used directly or indirectly to pay for any personal service, advertisement, telegram, telephone, letter, printed or written matter ... intended or designed to influence in any manner a member of Congress, to favor or oppose ... any legislation or appropriation...."

That rather sweeping language would appear to be fairly straightforward as to the statute's applicability to legislation and spending measures. But it was not clear whether the prohibition was applicable to a treaty.

The prohibition was further complicated by an ambiguous caveat: "...this [prohibition] shall not prevent officers or employes of the United States or of its departments or agencies from communicating to members of Congress on the request of any member or to Congress, through the proper channels, requests for legislation or appropriations which they deem necessary for the efficient conduct of the public business."

The "proper channels" language has, over the years, served as a sort of catchall loophole through which administration lobbying troops periodically march. While critics have resurrected the statute from time to time to undercut or embarrass one administration initiative or another, there have been only a few instances where administrations have placed limitations on their lobbying efforts because of issues raised by the statute.

Neither the legislative history of the statute nor the few court cases in which it has been raised has clearly delineated executive lobbying authority. But these precedents provide some limited guidance as to what kind of executive branch lobbying is legally permissible and what is not.

Good's Intentions

When Rep. James William Good, R-Iowa (1909-21), brought up the lobbying provision amendment to a deficiency appropriation bill on May 29, 1919, he made clear that he did not intend to prevent government officials from communicating directly with congressmen. It was grass-roots lobbying Good had on his mind.

Good said the provision would "prohibit a practice that has been indulged in so often ... the practice of a bureau chief or the head of a department writing letters ... sending telegrams throughout the country, for this organization, for this man, for that company to write his congressman, to wire his congressman, in behalf of this or that legislation."

Good cited a specific case in which, he said, "thousands upon thousands of telegrams" emanating from Washington had been sent to one member's constituents urging them to wire the congressman on appropriations matters. Good's remarks were applauded.

While there is no record of debate on this provision in the House hearing record or bill report, the full House approved the measure after only minimal discussion.

---

newspaper and network polls showing that a majority of Americans favored SALT II.

'Present Danger'

The group's principal spokesman, former Deputy Defense Secretary Paul H. Nitze, was a member of the SALT negotiating delegation until 1974. Nitze and Yale law professor Eugene V. Rostow founded the group in 1976. They took its name from Justice Oliver Wendell Holmes' statement that freedom of speech does not give one the right to yell "fire" in a crowded theater unless there is "a clear and present danger."

The committee's stated mission was to "facilitate a national discussion of the foreign and national security policies of the United States directed toward a secure peace with freedom."

A policy statement said, "The principal threat to our nation, to world peace and to the cause of human freedom is the Soviet drive for dominance based upon an unparalleled military buildup."

While the committee spoke in terms of a "balance" of power between the United States and the Soviet Union, its ally, the Coalition for Peace Through Strength, insisted on U.S. military superiority.

Peace Through Strength

The coalition was founded and supported financially by the hawkish American Security Council (ASC), one of

...Points Up Few Limits on White House Lobbying

According to a Library of Congress study prepared by Richard Sachs, Good sought "to discourage lobbying of a 'grassroots' nature, that is, attempts to influence legislation by individuals not directly involved in the governmental process."

A 1973 court case, cited by Sachs, stated that the intention of the 1919 statute was to "prevent corruption of the legislative processes through government financial support of . . . a publicly funded special interest group." In other words, the statute proscribed use of taxpayer funds by private interest groups to influence public policy.

Related Statute

While there are several court cases and GAO investigations that address the 1919 statute, none provides a clear statement of the limits on executive branch lobbying.

A similar, but non-criminal, statute enacted in 1977 (PL 95-81), specifically prohibits the use of appropriated funds for "publicity or propaganda purposes designed to support or defeat legislation pending before Congress."

A GAO report interpreted this statute in connection with administration lobbying on a consumer protection bill: "An interpretation of [the statute] which strictly prohibits expenditures of public funds for dissemination of views on pending legislation would consequently preclude virtually any comment by officials on administration or agency policy, a result we do not believe was intended."

GAO did find, however, that the statute applied to "expenditures involving direct appeals addressed to members of the public suggesting that they contact their elected representatives and indicate their support of or opposition to pending legislation, or to urge their representatives to vote in a particular manner."

The GAO report also suggested several specific lobbying tactics that would have been illegal had they been employed by the administration including: 1) development of information at the request of groups lobbying on behalf of an administration position; 2) clearing administration actions with outside interest groups; 3) development of "canned editorial materials and sample letters to the editor" for use in a lobby campaign, and 4) other

actions "which would be equivalent to direct assignment of manpower paid for by government appropriations [to outside groups]."

Aside from becoming an agent or operative of an outside interest group, however, the statute appears to place few limits on White House lobbying.

SALT Debate

An examination of administration lobbying efforts on behalf of the SALT treaty suggests that the White House tried to avoid the kinds of legal pitfalls the GAO report suggested. For the most part, the White House was careful in its public pronouncements not to directly ask citizens to lobby their congressmen on behalf of SALT.

At a State Department SALT briefing in Richmond, Va., however, Arms Control and Disarmament Agency Director George M. Seignious II concluded an address to more than 100 business and community leaders with an appeal to "persuade your senators" that the risks involved in the SALT treaty were much less than the risks involved in delaying ratification.

While the administration worked closely with Americans for SALT and other outside groups pushing for the treaty, it did not appear to have directed or helped organize these outside efforts.

The administration did, however, provide these groups with brochures and pamphlets to use in selling the SALT treaty. And the White House put together a 16,000-name mailing list of people who regularly received information on the SALT treaty. Some of these people were on the list as a result of requests to the administration for information, but others, including persons invited to various administration SALT briefings, may not have requested the literature.

A 1939 statute prohibits the administration from mailing books, pamphlets, and similar materials free of postage, unless it has received a request for them. However, that statute would appear to have a large loophole: It provides that the administration may send "enclosures reasonably related to the subject matter of official correspondence."

Since "official correspondence" is not defined in the statute, it may be broadly interpreted and did not provide much of a handle for SALT critics.

---

the leading interest groups advocating increased defense spending. Like the committee, the coalition was interested in strategic issues beyond SALT II. The coalition consisted of about 50 small, medium and large conservative groups, most of which operated their own anti-SALT campaigns but were members of the coalition to present a united front.

The most active members included the American Conservative Union (ACU) and the Conservative Caucus, two of the nation's largest conservative membership organizations.

While a principal complaint of SALT opponents concerned administration spending on behalf of the treaty, the opposition was hardly strapped for funds. John M. Fisher, president of the ASC and co-chairman of the coalition, said

in an interview that of the $10 million the ASC hoped to raise in 1979, $3 million or more would be spent on SALT.

Larry A. Woldt, communications director for the Conservative Caucus, said his group had $1 million budgeted for its SALT campaign. But he noted that the group spent more than $1.3 million on the Panama campaign in 1978 and could top that figure on SALT. (Panama Canal treaties lobbying, p. 51)

Fran Griffin, communications director for the ACU, said her group spent about $1.8 million on its Panama effort and expected spending on SALT to be "around the same." Each of these anti-SALT groups planned to use a mass mail campaign both to stir up opposition to the treaty and to raise funds for their organizations. Fisher said he hoped to send out 10 million letters through ASC's Boston, Va., direct mail operation. "I'd like to send out 20 million, but I think 10 million is more realistic," Fisher said.

Woldt of the Conservative Caucus said his organization already had sent out 950,000 anti-SALT mailings and hoped to send out a total of five million. The ACU set a more modest goal of at least 500,000 letters. Neither the ASC nor the Conservative Caucus expected to include pre-printed anti-SALT postcards in their mailings. During the Panama debate millions of these cards flooded Senate offices with many senators complaining that they were nothing more than an irritant. Those groups instead planned to urge people to send personalized letters to their congressmen and senators. But the ACU planned a post-card drive.

Lecture Circuit

One sure indicator that SALT opponents were worried about the effectiveness of the Carter administration's nationwide briefings was their complaint that the administration seldom included opposition spokesmen.

"That's the infinite power of the presidency," said Lyle Ryter, a lobbyist for the Coalition for Peace Through Strength. "It's an abuse of power. It's a put up job where no opposition is allowed." But Ryter acknowledged that if he had it in his power, "I wouldn't do it any differently."

The administration sometimes included opposition speakers, but one official said, "It's not our responsibility to bring in opponents any more than when we present briefings on Capitol Hill." He noted that SALT opponents had made no effort to include SALT supporters at their presentations.

To counter the administration's public speaking, the Conservative Caucus organized a 50-state anti-SALT petition drive and speaking tour. Military leaders were to address conservative groups in large U.S. cities and urge local groups to organize against the treaty.

The Coalition for Peace Through Strength also put together a bureau, consisting of about 150 speakers, most of them retired military officers, according to Assistant Director Gina Mondres. Four paid coalition co-chairmen were included in this roster: Lt. Gen. Daniel O. Graham, former director of the Defense Intelligence Agency; Maj. Gen. George Keegan, former chief of Air Force Intelligence; Maj. Gen. John K. Singlaub (Ret.) and Brig. Gen. Robert C. Richarson III (Ret.). Richard N. Perle, a leading congressional defense analyst and aide to Sen. Henry M. Jackson, D-Wash., also was to speak against the treaty for the coalition.

Opponents also planned to buy radio, television, billboard and newspaper advertising to urge citizen opposition to the treaty. And the Conservative Caucus planned to set up a phone bank to urge about 25,000 conservatives to telephone their senators and representatives. Woldt said he hoped to generate at least 15,000 calls to the Hill.

The Supporters

In the summer of 1978 the leaders of three activist liberal disarmament lobbies agreed that liberals might not make the best salesmen for an arms control treaty. Leaders of New Directions, the Federation of American Scientists and the Council for a Livable World decided to call together more moderate opinion leaders who might be concerned about controlling the spread of nuclear weapons. In the fall of 1978 Americans for SALT (AFS) was created.

According to one of its founders, New Directions Co-ordinator Sanford Gottlieb, "The people who have signed on are liberals and moderates. There was a conscious effort to mobilize toward the center."

Americans for SALT organized under the leadership of six co-chairmen: Clark Clifford, former secretary of Defense; Townsend Hoopes, former under secretary of the Air Force; former United Nations Ambassadors Henry Cabot Lodge and Charles Yost; Marjorie Benton, former U.N. delegate, and the Rev. Theodore M. Hesburgh, president of Notre Dame University.

The organization's principal mission was to build a grass-roots constituency that AFS lobbyist Holmes Brown said would "demonstrate to senators that their constituency supports SALT." But with its limited staff and funding — an anticipated budget of $750,000 — the group had a long way to go before it could compete with the well-organized opposition. AFS funding was principally from individual contributions from the major participants in the organization. A spokesman said gifts ranged from $1,000 to $25,000. The strength of Americans for SALT appeared to lie with the groups on its executive committee that had larger memberships and resources.

AFS planned to work with the established local affiliates of these groups to build pro-SALT organizations in 21 of 34 states where it had identified at least one undecided senator. The executive committee included representatives of such organizations as the Union of Concerned Scientists, Members of Congress for Peace Through Law, New Directions, the Center for National Security Studies, the Federation of American Scientists, Americans for Democratic Action, the Friends Committee on National Legislation, the United Auto Workers, the International Association of

Don't Worry About Being Number Two — YOU CAN TRUST ME!

Anti-Salt newspaper advertisement

Machinists, the National Council of Churches and the U.S. Catholic Conference.

The meat-and-potatoes issues of many of these organizations were far removed from arms control, and it was not clear that the groups were ready to make a substantial commitment to push the treaty through the Senate. But several of them had begun organizing grass-roots efforts to win support of the treaty.

For example, the Religious Committee on SALT, formed by the National Council of Churches, brought together 25 national religious groups to organize their people in support of the treaty. Other groups, such as the Center for Defense Information and Institute for Policy Studies, provided information and analysis of the treaty. At the same time, AFS helped distribute the pro-SALT films of the Center for Defense Information and the American Committee on East-West Accord. *(Films, box, p. 42)*

AFS organized a speakers bureau with representatives of many of the groups on its executive committee as well as several congressmen, academics and retired military and intelligence experts. Among them were former CIA Director William Colby and Rep. Les Aspin, D-Wis.

While AFS operated without government financial support, it coordinated its activities closely with the State Department. State provided much of the SALT information that AFS sent out to its 20,000-name mailing list. According to Ed Savage, AFS press director, "We know what they're doing and vice versa."

AFS also planned to develop more permanent pro-treaty grass-roots organizations in areas where the State Department gave briefings for community leaders. In interviews, several administration officials were privately critical of what they perceived as AFS's failure to put together an effective grass-roots organization. And the White House clearly did not wait to see if AFS would succeed before launching its own campaign.

Case for Disarmament?

There was a possibility that AFS could run into another problem in rallying its troops. The group's executive committee included some of the nation's leading disarmament groups, some of which were not convinced that the SALT treaty was a serious step toward disarmament. Listed among AFS supporters were four members of the board of the Arms Control Association, a non-profit group whose principal mission was broadening public interest in arms control.

At least one of the groups on the executive committee — the American Federation of Scientists — was divided over SALT. Some of its leaders argued that the treaty reaffirmed the arms race, made no substantive reductions in armaments and that the two sides might have been better off going back to the drawing board.

Other organizations in the coalition questioned Carter's decision to move ahead with the M-X missile, suggesting that there might be further defections on the treaty. But it appeared likely most of the groups would continue to support the treaty and would fight Carter's M-X missile decision another day. Where the stronger arms control groups could prove decisive was in convincing Senate arms control advocates such as William Proxmire, D-Wis., George McGovern, D-S.D., and Mark O. Hatfield, R-Ore., that SALT II was better than the alternative. ∎

Canal Treaties Spurred Major Lobby Effort

In the fall of 1977, as Senate Minority Leader Howard H. Baker Jr. of Tennessee, then uncommitted on the Panama Canal treaties, took his seat at the University of Tennessee/Memphis State football game in Knoxville, even he must have been surprised. Above the stadium a light plane towed a banner calling upon the fans to "Save Our Canal."

Sponsored by the American Conservative Union (ACU), the streamer symbolized the variety of direct and indirect pressures placed on senators in the fight over ratification of the Panama Canal treaties.

Aside from presidential election campaigns and the anti-Vietnam War effort, there had been few political battles in the preceding 30 years to match the national emotion roused by President Carter's efforts to win approval of the treaties — a goal his immediate predecessors had approved but had not pushed to completion.

Although the terms of the agreements alone rubbed many raw nerves, those feelings were cultivated and channeled into a massive lobby campaign by a conservative coalition that tried unsuccessfully to obtain the 34 Senate votes needed to reject the pacts.

After the signing of the treaties in September 1977, the opposition fought Senate ratification with mail campaigns, radio spots, a TV documentary and "truth squads" of Senate and House members sent around the country to apply pressure on those senators still uncommitted. Many groups were involved, ranging from the American Legion and other veterans' groups, to conservative political organizations, to ad hoc committees set up to fight only this issue.

To counter the conservatives' effort, the Carter administration mounted a massive lobbying campaign that enlisted the help of private groups and the services of virtually every high administration official, from the president on down. *(Box, next page)*

The Panama Canal treaties presented Carter with the most difficult treaty ratification task since President Woodrow Wilson championed the ill-fated Treaty of Versailles. And they posed a particular challenge to the White House lobbying staff, which in Carter's first year in office had been widely criticized as inexperienced and bungling.

Narrow Victory

In the end, the administration's campaign paid off and supporters could claim a significant, albeit narrow, victory. By a 68-32 vote — one more than the required two-thirds majority — the Senate on March 16, 1978, approved the treaty declaring the canal's permanent neutrality. By the same margin the following April 18, the Senate approved the basic treaty, which turned over control of the canal to the Republic of Panama effective Dec. 31, 1999, with interim supervision placed in the hands of a joint Panamanian-U.S. commission.

But treaty opponents were successful in forcing the administration to accept at least part of a Senate-approved reservation that had threatened to scuttle the treaties. The compromise stated that any action the United States might take to keep the canal open did not give the United States the right to intervene in Panama's internal affairs.

All told, the Senate debate lasted 38 days, and the efforts on both sides to influence the vote amounted to a classic case study of high-pressure lobbying.

Treaty Support

Admittedly playing catch-up ball for public opinion on the treaties, private groups aiding the White House in early 1978 began crisscrossing the country for support. They also organized at the grass-roots level to show crucial members of the Senate that considerable but untapped support existed for the agreements. At first, the administration and supporters had focused chiefly on Capitol Hill lobbying, leaving the anti-treaty side free to cultivate local opposition.

The State Department reported that its officials had participated in 617 "forums," such as TV shows and speaking engagements, between September 1977 and January 1978, when Secretary of State Cyrus R. Vance took his first trip outside Washington on behalf of the treaties. Other State Department officials were booked for another 116 forums in the ensuing six weeks before the issue came to a head in the Senate. President Carter Feb. 1 gave a "fireside chat" on the merits of the treaties.

"At a minimum our purpose is to get mail to the Senate offices," said a spokesman for the Committee of Americans for the Canal Treaties Inc., which was established in October by prominent treaty backers. "When a senator — take [John C.] Danforth [R-Mo.], for example — gets 12,000 pieces of mail against the treaties, and only 200 for, he can't help but be concerned, although he may be planning to vote for the treaties. We're trying to ease that pressure."

Committee for the Treaties Inc.

Established to mount a "national program of education" about the treaties, the Committee of Americans for the Canal Treaties Inc. sported a roster of well-known members — former President Ford, Mrs. Lyndon B. Johnson and George Meany, among others enlisted for their opinion-molding abilities. The committee maintained a "loose cooperation" with the White House, although it was "totally independent" of its operations, according to a committee spokesman.

Unlike many of the conservative groups opposing the treaties, the committee planned to disband after the final Senate vote. Because it had no connection with federal election campaigns, the group could accept contributions from corporations.

Two other activities rounded out the group's efforts: the organization of state committees to drum up local treaty support and a speaker's bureau, whose most active members included former Sen. Hugh Scott, R-Pa. (1949-77), and former Ambassador Averell Harriman.

Carter Sent the Heavy Artillery to Lobby for Treaty

President Carter threw virtually every high official of his administration and the nation's defense and foreign policy establishment into the fray in the final days before the vote on the Panama Canal neutrality treaty.

The president courted reluctant senators from the White House with a heavy schedule of phone calls and Oval Office visits.

Among those personally lobbying senators were Vice President Walter F. Mondale, Secretary of State Cyrus R. Vance, Secretary of Defense Harold Brown, national security adviser Zbigniew Brzezinski, Ambassador Ellsworth Bunker, Deputy Secretary of State Warren M. Christopher, top White House aide Hamilton Jordan and a large team of congressional liaison aides headed by Frank B. Moore.

The administration was so intent on presenting its arguments personally to wavering senators that any senator could see anyone in the administration upon request, a far cry from past complaints about administration aloofness. At least one senator, at his request, saw all four of the Joint Chiefs of Staff. The top military brass and Brown were consulted by many senators, reflecting concern about the impact of the canal transfer on national security.

But Mondale, as the only Senate veteran in the Carter administration and as the constitutional head of the Senate, was perhaps Carter's most important advocate. An administration lobbyist referred to Mondale as "a living symbol of the administration's concern over this issue," adding that his "personal clout" and his own interest in the canal debate were vital assets.

The late-hour strategy of high-level persuasion reflected a shift in the White House lobbying approach on the treaties.

For months the administration had focused on shaping public opinion as an indirect way of influencing the Senate vote. The administration invited hundreds of "opinion leaders" to the White House for briefings, in hopes that those leaders would in turn help mold public opinion in favor of the treaties.

Administration officials claimed that public opinion had indeed shifted dramatically toward support for the treaties. But some senators, including Edward W. Brooke, R-Mass. (1957-79), complained that the expected groundswell had not occurred.

Nevertheless, it was clear in the final two days of debate that the White House did not have the needed 67 votes. Thus a strategy of personal lobbying and a new flexibility in accepting substantive reservations to the treaties was adopted.

The final flurry of administration efforts to sell the treaties also produced a raft of rumors and press stories that the White House was offering non-treaty-related "deals" to senators.

These stories were hotly denied by administration lobbyists.

The revised strategy was widely credited with helping to provide the votes that gave the treaties the necessary margin of victory.

Committee for Ratification

The administration's treaty fight also was aided by the Committee for Ratification of the Panama Canal Treaties. This group was initiated by New Directions, a liberal-leaning foreign policy organization founded in 1976 somewhat on the model of the well-known public affairs lobby Common Cause. Members of the committee included the AFL-CIO, Democratic National Committee, United Auto Workers, Americans for Democratic Action and the Washington Office on Latin America.

Focused on winning treaty support at the state and local levels, the organization was set up because treaty supporters felt, in the words of one organizer, that "nothing had happened" on lobbying for the agreements after the signing ceremonies in Washington Sept. 7, 1977.

The committee's operating budget amounted to only $19,000 for printing costs of a booklet about the treaties and travel expenses of field organizers dispatched by member organizations to rally support for the agreements. States targeted for special attention were Texas, Delaware, Florida, Pennsylvania, Kentucky and Tennessee.

New Directions itself, however, sent out a 1.1 million-piece mailing to liberal cause backers, such as Common Cause members, asking that they send letters to senators supporting the treaties. Signed by New Directions Chairperson Margaret Mead, the mailing cost $137,500, with $50,000 coming directly from New Directions and the remainder from the Democratic National Committee, United Steelworkers, Occidental Petroleum and the Communications Workers of America among other organizations.

Like the conservatives battling the treaties, New Directions was not blind to the possibility that the issue could be helpful for its organization building, much as the Watergate scandal helped to substantially boost the membership ranks of Common Cause.

Opponents

Opposition to the canal treaties came mainly from conservative organizations and members of Congress, many with political ties to former California Gov. Ronald Reagan, who sparked the canal debate during the 1976 Republican presidential primaries.

Reagan backer Sen. Paul Laxalt, R-Nev., for example, and Rep. Philip M. Crane, R-Ill., were responsible for organizing the "truth squad" of 20 members of Congress who left Washington Jan. 17, 1978, on a nationwide, week-long campaign "to focus renewed public interest in the treaties."

The campaign was initially planned in September 1977 at a strategy meeting held at the Virginia home of Richard Viguerie, a publicist for conservative causes. The "truth squad" was financed by $100,000 in individual donations and contributions from eight conservative groups operating under the Committee to Save the Panama Canal. This was a "short-term" organization set up to avoid restrictions placed on member groups under election, lobby and tax laws.

The eight organizations — the most active opponents on the canal fight — were American Conservative Union, Conservative Caucus, Committee for the Survival of a Free Congress, Citizens for the Republic, American Security Council, Young Republicans, National Conservative Political Action Committee and Council for National Defense.

Besides cooperating on the "truth squad" tour, a number of these conservative organizations plus such others as STOP ERA belonged to the Emergency Coalition to Save the Panama Canal. Organized by the ACU shortly after the treaties were signed, the coalition met in Washington to plan strategy for the Senate battle.

Although conservatives often pooled their efforts and resources, individual organizations continued their own activities. Representative of these groups were the ACU and the Conservative Caucus.

American Conservative Union

The ACU sent out at least 1.8 million pieces of mail aimed at raising funds to continue the anti-treaty campaign and urging recipients to write postcards and letters to Capitol Hill. Mailing lists included the ACU's own in addition to those of *The National Review, Human Events* and other conservative publications.

The organization also sponsored a 30-minute television program shown in 150 cities, anti-treaty newspaper ads that appeared in about 30 cities, a petition drive, and a trip by ACU Chairman Crane to Denver in October after President Carter appeared there.

Conservative Caucus

In addition to its work in the anti-treaty umbrella groups, the Conservative Caucus, which was "organized at the local level" to support conservative causes, sent out 2 million pieces of mail urging letters be sent to Senate and House members. This mailing was handled by Viguerie's company.

The group launched a radio-TV campaign in November 1977, sending to 500 stations messages based on excerpts of Reagan's testimony before a Senate subcommittee in September. The caucus said it hoped to "stem any erosion of anti-surrender sentiment among the general public. . . ."

The White House Lobby

White House marketing of the Panama Canal treaties was aimed largely at the same target pursued by opponents: public opinion.

But there were some differences in approach. Opponents worked directly at grass-roots lobbying, while the administration aimed its pitch at opinion-makers. Secondly, the administration had an asset opponents didn't — invitations to the White House.

Between August 1977 and mid-January 1978, "opinion leaders" from 25 states were invited to high-level White House treaty briefings, some lasting as long as two and a half hours. They were conducted variously by the president, his national security adviser Zbigniew Brzezinski, and Joint Chiefs of Staff Chairman George S. Brown. At each briefing, one of the two treaty negotiators, Ellsworth Bunker or Sol Linowitz, presented the administration viewpoint.

A White House spokesman said the list of those invited was compiled to influence larger segments of public opinion back home. Participants included local elected officials, educators, editorial writers, heads of organizations such as local League of Women Voters, labor leaders and political activists.

In addition to those "opinion leader" briefings, the White House conducted meetings with editors from around the country. And both the State and Defense departments sent speakers to reach local groups. Secretary of State Vance and Secretary of Defense Harold Brown went on speaking tours of their own.

After the campaign proved successful, and both treaties had been approved by the Senate, President Carter issued a statement saying that "this is a day of which Americans can feel proud: for now we have reminded the world and ourselves of the things that we stand for as a nation."

Fight Over Implementation

The canal controversy erupted again in 1979 during congressional consideration of legislation required to set up the Panama Canal Commission and otherwise carry out the transition phase of the treaties, effective Oct. 1.

Conservative members of the House, which had no role in the ratification of the treaties, used the opportunity to display their opposition to the "giveaway" of the canal and to try to impose conditions on the transfer that were not contained in the pacts themselves.

In a surprise vote Sept. 20, the House rejected, 192-203, a compromise with the Senate on the implementation bill (HR 111). Meeting with House Democrats at a dinner following the vote, President Carter called it "the biggest disappointment this year." He immediately began calling House members seeking support for a reversal of the vote.

Another compromise was announced a few days later and the bill cleared Congress Sept. 26. However, the White House again was forced to make concessions to the conservative opponents of the treaties as the price of their allowing the implementation legislation to go through. ∎

White House Lobbyists Employ the Hard Sell

On the afternoon of Aug. 28, 1978, two dozen executives from major paper, textile and glass companies crowded into the Roosevelt Room in the White House to hear the hard sell for the natural gas pricing bill. The measure gradually ends controls on the price of newly discovered gas until the price ceiling is lifted in 1985.

Some of the executives were dead set against the bill. Others were ambivalent. Not one could be counted on as a solid supporter. The session, aimed at winning them over, demonstrated how the White House marshaled its forces behind the bill, using James R. Schlesinger, then Energy secretary; G. William Miller, then chairman of the Federal Reserve Board, and other top administration officials and advisers.

First, according to the notes taken by one man who was there, Schlesinger, using multicolored charts and figures on gas production developed by his department, described the substance of the legislation (HR 5289).

Next, Miller, who as Federal Reserve chairman ostensibly was independent and not bound to press the administration's case, argued that passage of the bill was essential to stabilization of the dollar.

Finally, an hour or so into the meeting, the Carter administration's super salesman took the floor. It was a "time for candor," Robert S. Strauss, the president's all purpose adviser, told the businessmen, and he was not about to pretend that the compromise bill was first-rate legislation. But, he went on, "it no longer makes a difference whether the bill is a C-minus or an A-plus. Certainly, it is better than a zero, and it must pass."

Then, in the same folksy style he used to raise money for George McGovern in 1972 and to win votes for Jimmy Carter in 1976, in the same Texas drawl with which he spoke to the Japanese negotiators on trade policy and labor leaders on inflation, Strauss made his pitch.

"This is close enough," he asserted, "so a half-dozen bankers I had in this morning and the people in this room could pass or defeat the bill."

At least some of the executives must have been impressed. Those from the glass and paper companies remained opposed to the bill, but their opposition seemed somewhat muted after the session at the White House. Some of those from the textile industry switched to active support for the administration's position.

That meeting was one of a dozen held in the White House with key industrial consumers of natural gas in the three weeks before the bill was brought up on the Senate floor Sept. 11. The meetings were a cornerstone of the White House effort to win passage of the bill.

There were similar sessions, for instance, with representatives of the insurance, steel, automobile, construction and aerospace industries. A group of bankers had lunch with President Carter in the family dining room. One hundred thirty of the most ardent industrial opponents were called to the East Room on Sept. 6.

By all accounts, the lobbying was effective. In late August only a handful of important businessmen could be counted on to support the legislation. On Sept. 11, the Department of Energy supplied all senators with a list of 55 major industrial and financial corporations and 20 trade associations that were backing the bill.

Administration Strategy

The administration's basic problem was that the bill that came out of conference committee was the product of so many compromises that it had a wealth of natural opponents and no strong supporters. Therefore, according to administration officials, the strategy, designed primarily by Schlesinger, Strauss and Vice President Walter F. Mondale, was to mount a campaign to neutralize the opposition, while pleading for support on the grounds of national prestige and loyalty to the president.

The day-to-day tactics were planned by a group of ranking aides from the White House and the Department of Energy, who had met every weekday morning since mid-August in the White House office of Frank B. Moore, assistant to the president for congressional liaison.

The regulars at the 8:30 a.m. meetings were Hamilton Jordan, the president's chief political adviser; Anne Wexler, special assistant for political matters; Stuart E. Eizenstat, head of the domestic policy staff; Gerald Rafshoon, the president's media adviser; three top officials from the Department of Energy; one of Strauss's assistants, and two of Mondale's aides, William C. Smith and Gail L. Harrison. Danny C. Tate, the White House's chief Senate lobbyist, usually presided over the meetings and William H. Cable, the lobbyist assigned to the House, normally attended.

Participants at the meetings said that most of the time was spent deciding which senators should be approached by Strauss, which by Schlesinger, which by Mondale and which by the president himself.

Many uncommitted senators reported receiving repeated calls from each of them. "It's been Carter, Schlesinger, Strauss, Mondale and then they start all over again," said an aide to Sen. Patrick J. Leahy, D-Vt.

Sen. John C. Culver, D-Iowa, visited Alaska over Labor Day weekend and reportedly received a call from Carter on the natural gas issue at 5 a.m. Alaska time.

All told, a White House spokesman said, the president telephoned 26 senators that weekend. The following weekend, during breaks in the Middle East summit talks, he called several more from Camp David.

Once the bill hit the Senate floor, Mondale began to spend most of his time in the Capitol, buttonholing senators on the floor and calling them into his private office just off the Senate chamber. Mondale was given much of the credit for swinging Sen. Edmund S. Muskie, D-Maine, the influential chairman of the Budget Committee, to the administration's point of view.

"They don't talk about the merits of the bill," one senator said. "They tell you that the president needs a bill to pass to save face politically and that the country needs it for international prestige."

But, most of all, the administration's strategy was to seek support from special interest groups that could, in turn, pressure senators to back the bill. Wexler was in charge of finding out from senators the interest groups that were leaning most heavily on them, and it was representatives from those groups who were invited to the White House.

Entire industries were split. Some important oil companies, like the Atlantic-Richfield Corp., agreed to support the bill, and others, like Exxon, were persuaded to remain neutral. Some oil companies, like Amoco, continued to oppose the bill.

The steel industry and the automobile manufacturers were also divided, and many important financial institutions, including the Manufacturers Hanover Trust Co. and the Bank of America, came out for the president. The farm lobby was also split, with the American Farm Bureau Federation, for instance, opposing the bill, and the National Grange supporting it.

The divide-and-conquer tactics showed results. A ranking congressional staff member noted, for example, that Sen. Robert P. Griffin, R-Mich., could not support the bill as long as all the major automobile makers were in opposition, but once the Chrysler Corp. announced its support, Griffin, too, felt free to do so.

Opposition Strategy

Opponents of the bill were an unusual coalition of senators and interest groups. Some of them believed that the compromise bill would not lift price regulations on natural gas fast enough while others felt it would allow gas prices to rise too fast.

For example, Sen. Russell B. Long, D-La., one of the most ardent supporters of deregulation of gas prices, met regularly to plot strategy with Sens. James Abourezk, D-S.D., and Howard M. Metzenbaum, D-Ohio, who led a filibuster in 1977 against deregulation legislation.

Other senators who worked to round up votes against the bill included Edward M. Kennedy, D-Mass.; Howard H. Baker Jr., R-Tenn., the minority leader; John G. Tower, R-Texas, and Clifford P. Hansen, R-Wyo.

The interest groups working against the bill were equally unlikely bedfellows. Amoco officials, for instance, were working hand-in-glove with James Flug, director of Energy Action, an organization devoted to representing consumer interests against those of the oil companies. Lobbyists for the Chamber of Commerce of the United States consulted regularly on tactics with representatives of the AFL-CIO and the United Auto Workers. George Meany, president of the AFL-CIO, and Douglas A. Fraser, president of the UAW, wrote all senators urging defeat of the bill, primarily on the ground that it would be too costly to consumers.

For the most part, those against the bill concentrated on maintaining their strength against administration forays. Republicans were urged not to extricate the president from his political dilemma, and efforts were made to persuade Democrats that the compromise measure was such bad legislation that they could not afford blind loyalty to the administration.

Trade-off Controversy

Throughout the late summer, reports surfaced that the administration had made improper political trade-offs to win the votes of crucial senators. All the reports were denied by administration officials.

On Aug. 23, Sen. James A. McClure, R-Idaho, said he had agreed to support the bill and left the impression that he had done so in exchange for administration support for a $417 million energy research project in his state. Carter denied any deal.

On Sept. 2, *The Detroit News* reported that Sen. Paul Hatfield, D-Mont., had been offered a federal judgeship if he would vote for the natural gas bill. Hatfield and Jody Powell, the White House press secretary, said there was no truth to the report.

On Sept. 7, *The Washington Post* reported that the administration had promised tax relief, protection against imports and other aid to steel and textile manufacturers in order to obtain their support for the bill. The next day, the *Post* printed a letter from Strauss in which he called the allegation "so far from the truth as to do disservice not only to me but to the nation."

Rep. Clarence J. Brown, R-Ohio, ranking Republican on the House Subcommittee on Energy and Power, took note of alleged "threats, promises and warnings" in a letter he sent to more than 100 corporate officials. He urged the businessmen "not to be cajoled into silence or coerced into support by misinformation, threats of retaliation or untoward offers of reward."

Brown then charged in his letter that Schlesinger had warned industrial users of natural gas that they would lose their right to make emergency gas purchases from the intrastate market, which must be approved by the independent Federal Energy Regulatory Commission, if the bill were defeated. Schlesinger said that he had not made such a threat.

Single-Vote Question

The months of bargaining and high-level lobbying started to pay off Sept. 27 when the Senate, by a vote of 57-42, approved the compromise on natural gas pricing.

But the battle still wasn't over. On the House side, opponents of the compromise attempted to defeat it by pushing for a separate vote on gas, rather than a single vote on Carter's five-part energy package. But the House Oct. 13 voted, 207-206, to keep the energy package intact, linking the controversial gas measure with the more popular parts of the program.

The other sections included government aid for insulating homes and businesses, penalties for gas guzzling cars, reform of utility rate-making and requirements that industries switch from oil and gas use to coal.

Opponents, a coalition of liberals and conservatives, complained that the single vote provided a "sugar coating to avoid tasting the bitter pill," as Phillip Burton, D-Calif., put it.

But supporters said the bill had come to Congress as a package and should be sent back to Carter in a package.

The victory for the president came only after several members voted late or switched their votes. When Millicent Fenwick, R-N.J., went to the well of the House to change her vote, the tally was 207-206. But Fenwick picked up an orange card, changing her vote to "present." That tied the vote, 206-206.

Then Thomas B. Evans Jr., R-Del., voted "aye," and Speaker Thomas P. O'Neill Jr., D-Mass., banged his gavel. The single vote on energy was agreed to.

The vote actually was on a procedural motion, which opponents of the gas bill hoped to defeat. That would have given them a chance to try to force a separate vote on gas.

The motion to actually adopt the rule providing for a single energy vote was passed by voice vote.

Opponents of the gas bill had won a dramatic but short-lived victory Oct. 12 when the House Rules Committee refused, 8-8, to grant a rule allowing the single vote. But the panel reversed itself Oct. 13 and voted 9-5 to approve the rule permitting only one vote. The committee is responsible for determining which bills go to the floor and how they will be considered.

B. F. Sisk, D-Calif., one of three Rules Committee Democrats who voted with Republicans against the rule Oct. 12, was lobbied heavily by the House Democratic leadership and the Carter administration. He voted for the rule on Oct. 13.

Two other Democrats, Shirley Chisholm, D-N.Y., and Gillis W. Long, D-La., who voted against the rule on Oct. 12, softened their position Oct. 13 and voted "present."

Later, Brown of Ohio, a leading Republican opponent of the bill, blamed Sisk's reversal on "probably the most pressurized arm twisting we have seen since President Carter took office."

The Filibuster

But as the House cleared one obstacle to final passage, another skirmish was developing. A group of House members — Reps. Christopher J. Dodd, D-Conn., James M. Jeffords, R-Vt., Richard L. Ottinger, D-N.Y., and others — preferred a tax credit bill (HR 112) already passed by the Senate to the one reported by the energy tax conferees and included in the final energy package. HR 112 had no credits for business and provided bigger credits for homeowners. Dodd and company wanted the House to approve that bill and drop the conference version.

They found an ally in Abourezk. As long as he delayed the Senate vote on the tax conference report — the only portion of the energy package still before the Senate — the House could not vote on a five-part package. The House group hoped the House leadership would get impatient, agree to take up HR 112 and then vote on a four-part energy package.

Abourezk began to filibuster in mid-morning Oct. 14 — after the Senate voted 71-13 for cloture. He and a few other senators continued to tie up the proceedings by demanding quorum calls and employing other stalling tactics.

By late afternoon, Dodd was shuttling back and forth, carrying the message to House Speaker Thomas P. O'Neill Jr., D-Mass., that Abourezk would end the filibuster as soon as O'Neill agreed to take up HR 112. But the Speaker, who had worked for months to keep the package together, wouldn't give in.

But neither would Abourezk. As evening wore on, House members clustered near the Senate floor to watch.

A couple of hours later, about 12:30 a.m. Oct. 15, Abourezk finally gave up and the energy tax conference report was passed, 60-17.

House Floor Debate

The House finally began to debate the energy bill about 2:45 a.m. Rep. Thomas L. Ashley, D-Ohio, chairman of the Ad Hoc Energy Committee, led off. Only about two dozen members were on the floor. Most of them were sleeping elsewhere, having heard the arguments on the energy bill many times before.

"Millions of words have been exchanged. Millions of words have been printed.... Now is the time to declare," Ashley said, aware there was little left to say. "We have an energy bill which can be translated into a comprehensive national energy policy," he said. Later, he called it "an initial foundation for a national energy policy." "This is the best thing we could come up with," said Rep. Harley O. Staggers, D-W.Va.

Opponents were harsh in their criticism of the natural gas section. The gas bill, charged John B. Anderson, R-Ill., became "merely a convenient vehicle for the president to prove his supposed new dynamism, macho and legislative competence....

"The bill is, indeed, a marvel of tangled regulations and bureaucracy at its worse."

Brown of Ohio accused the White House of unfair lobbying tactics. "In mid-August, the smart money was betting that Congress would vote down the natural gas legislation. But that was before the White House invited the chief executive officers of major U.S. corporations to Washington for a little straight talk about the realities of doing business in a federally regulated environment," he said. Brown charged that business leaders were "threatened, promised and cajoled into passive opposition, silence or grudging support of this legislation."

The arguments continued through the scheduled four hours of debate. When the time for a vote came, the leadership asked for a quorum call first, giving the scattered members an extra 15 minutes to get to the floor. Finally, about 7:30 a.m., with Energy Secretary Schlesinger looking on from the gallery, the House voted 231-168 for the five-part energy bill. ∎

The Politics of Lobbying

CQ

Lobby Reform Efforts Make Steady Headway

Proposals to let the public know more about which special interests influence legislation in Congress have been circulating since lobby reform fever hit Washington in the aftermath of Watergate. But lobbyists representing virtually every interest group — from one-man church-run operations to the U.S. Chamber of Commerce — repeatedly have been able to kill reform proposals.

Following the Watergate scandals, the Senate in June 1976 passed a Lobbying Disclosure Act that made substantial changes in the 32-year-old Federal Regulation of Lobbying Act. Meanwhile, the House considered two variations of its own lobby legislation, passing one version in September. However, the two chambers could not reconcile the extensive differences in their bills before adjournment.

Persistent congressional attempts to tighten the 1946 lobby law produced results in 1978, with House passage of lobby disclosure legislation; however, the Senate Government Operations Committee was unable to report a bill.

Prospects for favorable action on a lobby disclosure bill appeared to brighten in the 96th Congress. On June 4, 1979, the House Judiciary Subcommittee on Administrative Law reported a bill that was supported by both the American Civil Liberties Union (ACLU) and Common Cause, the two principal adversaries in the lobby debate. The subcommittee bill appeared to be a better vehicle than any proposed in the previous two Congresses to pave the way for a new lobby law, because some of the controversies of past years had been resolved.

However, in October members of the full Judiciary Committee voted not to require lobby groups to disclose expenditures for grass-roots lobbying or the names of major organizational contributors.

Rejection of the two most controversial lobby disclosure amendments — which had been contained in the subcommittee version — left the committee with a bill (HR 4395) that was considerably weaker than lobby disclosure legislation passed by the House in 1978.

Before completing its work on the legislation Oct. 16, the Judiciary Committee approved an amendment to exempt tax-exempt church organizations from coverage by the bill. And the panel rejected an amendment that would have undermined the attorney general's ability to investigate violations of the act.

As in 1978, the decisive battle was expected to be waged on the House floor, where efforts probably would be made to restore provisions rejected by the Judiciary Committee that would have broadened the bill.

A major controversy in previous lobby debates — criminal penalties for registration and reporting violations of a lobby law — was resolved before markups began in favor of civil sanctions.

Background

Advocates of a new lobby law, including President Carter, have said the existing federal lobbying act (PL 79-601), passed in 1946, was less a law than a loophole that failed to cover numerous major lobbying groups.

The 1946 law was directed at individuals and organizations whose "principal purpose" was to influence the defeat or passage of legislation. It required such lobbyists to register and file reports with the Secretary of the Senate and the Clerk of the House.

However, large loopholes in the law allowed many interests to avoid registering. The law required registration only by persons paid to lobby for someone else.

Organizations not employed as lobbyists for someone else had to file financial reports but did not have to register.

Section 307 of the act required registration by any person "who by himself, or through any agent, or employee or other persons in any manner . . . solicits, collects or receives money or any other thing of value to be used principally to aid . . . the passage or defeat of any legislation by the Congress."

The act did not seriously limit the activities of lobbyists, especially the large number of interest groups whose lobbying activities did not fall under the narrow definitions of the law. For example:

● Many large organizations did not register as lobbyists because they contended that lobbying is not the principal purpose for which they collect or receive funds.

● Courts have interpreted the 1946 act to mean that lobbying efforts were not covered unless a lobbyist contacts members of Congress directly. Thus lobbyists who generate grass-roots pressure on Congress were not covered.

● Testifying before Congress or preparing such testimony did not fall under lobbying activities, according to the act.

● Some lobbyists contended that their contacts with members of Congress were designed to inform — not influence — and thus did not constitute lobbying.

● Groups or individuals who spend their own funds on lobbying did not have to register.

● Individuals and groups decide entirely for themselves what percentage of their budgets to attribute to lobbying activities.

● The act did not require the Clerk of the House and the Secretary of the Senate to investigate lobby registrations and financial reports for their truthfulness. Nor could they require individuals or groups to register as lobbyists. The Justice Department could prosecute lobby act violators but did not investigate reports and acted only when it received a complaint. There have been only four prosecutions and a test case since 1946.

1978 House Action

Throughout the years of debate over lobbying reform, the major difficulty had been to fashion a bill that would ensure disclosure of essential information by major lobbying organizations while ensuring that the requirements did not discourage groups from making their views known to public officials.

As approved by the House Judiciary Committee in March 1978, HR 8494 seemed to have accomplished the delicate balancing of constitutional rights with the need for information that all parties to the legislation agreed was essential.

The bill required annual registration and quarterly reporting with the comptroller general by major paid lobbying groups that make oral or written lobbying communications on legislative matters with representatives, senators and about 100,000 top level executive branch officials.

Individual communications were exempted as were communications with a House member by organizations located in a member's district or with a senator by organizations located in the senator's state. And the committee had set a threshold high enough to satisfy most groups that small lobby organizations would not be covered.

As a result, when the bill came out of the Judiciary Committee it had the support of a diverse group of lobbying interests, including Common Cause and Ralph Nader's Congress Watch, the ACLU and various environmental and church groups, as well as major business organizations, including the Chamber of Commerce of the United States.

Floor Debate

When debate began April 19, the bill's floor manager, George E. Danielson, D-Calif., told the House that "we have labored carefully to try to bring about an adequate disclosure of lobbying activities without at any time treading on the constitutionally protected rights of the people to petition their government for redress of grievances."

Nevertheless, the bill's principal opponent, Charles E. Wiggins, R-Calif., acknowledged that he was going to "tilt at windmills" and try to have the bill sent back to committee. Rejecting Wiggins' constitutional arguments, the House overwhelmingly defeated an attempt to kill the bill.

In three days of floor debate the House turned back nearly 20 efforts to weaken the bill. Two controversial amendments that significantly expanded the bill's disclosure requirements were adopted:

● The first, sponsored by Walter Flowers, D-Ala., required lobby organizations to report expenditures for grass-roots lobbying activities, such as computerized mass mailings designed to bring constituent pressure on congressmen.
● The second, sponsored by Tom Railsback, R-Ill., required any lobbying organization that spent more than 1 percent of its total budget on lobbying to report the names of organizations from which it received more than $3,000 a year in dues or contributions.

House Passage

The House passed HR 8494 on April 26 by a 259-140 vote.

Immediately upon passage of the Public Disclosure of Lobbying Act, the White House issued a statement from President Carter praising the vote and urging prompt Senate action. "This bill will enable the American people to understand and see more clearly how the legislative process is being affected by organizations that engage in significant lobbying activities," said Carter, who had pledged during his presidential campaign to push for lobby reform.

Common Cause, a public advocacy lobby that for years advocated a disclosure bill, also hailed the House action.

But the two amendments that expanded the bill's coverage led major business, civil liberties, church and environmental groups to charge that the bill interfered with privacy and with citizens' rights to petition public officials. The American Civil Liberties Union said the bill set up

"unprecedented surveillance of political activities" by the government.

House Provisions

As passed by the House April 26, 1978, HR 8494 contained the following major provisions:

Who Can Be Lobbied?

Lobbying activities covered by HR 8494 were limited to those communications made to a "federal officer or employee." The definition included a member of the House or Senate, a delegate or resident commissioner, an officer or employee of Congress, the comptroller general and certain high-level employees of the General Accounting Office, as well as officers of the executive branch from the Cabinet level down to assistant secretaries (executive schedule levels I through V).

What Is a Lobbying Organization?

The bill provided a twofold test for determining which organizations had to register and report on their lobbying activities on legislative matters. Organizations that qualified under either test were required to register. The "applicability" section of the bill:

● Required registration and reporting by any organization that spends more than $2,500 in any quarterly filing period to retain an individual or another organization to make "lobby communications" or "for the express purpose of drafting such communications."
● Required registration and reporting by an organization that spends $2,500 a quarter on oral or written lobbying communications and

1) employs one individual who spends all or part of 13 days in any quarter lobbying or,

2) employs at least two individuals who spend all or part of seven days a quarter lobbying (the $2,500 threshold in this provision was an aggregate expenditure test, so that an organization spending $1,000 for one lobbying communication and $1,600 for 12 others would meet the threshold.).

"Organizations" were defined as groups of individuals, corporations, foundations, associations, labor organizations, societies, joint stock companies, some organizations of state or local elected officials that engage in lobbying (such as national associations of state or local elected or appointed officials, including the National Governors' Association and the U.S. Conference of Mayors), "foreign agents" covered by the Foreign Agents Registration Act, and colleges and universities, including certain state colleges and universities. Corporations owned or controlled by the United States government were exempted from the definition.

"Affiliate" organizations were defined to include any organization formally associated by agreement or ownership with another organization, so that one organization maintains actual control or has the right of potential control over all or part of the activities of the other. Included in this definition were:

● Certain units of religious denominations or conventions or associations of churches.
● State and local units of national membership organizations.

● Organizations that are members of national trade associations, business leagues and labor organizations or federations that otherwise qualify under the definition.

What Is Lobbying?

The section defining "lobbying communications" included:

● An oral or written communication directed to any member or employee of the House or Senate to influence the content or disposition of a bill, resolution, treaty, nomination, hearing, report or investigation.

● Oral or written communications to certain officers or employees of the executive branch, the comptroller or deputy comptroller general and certain officers or employees of the General Accounting Office, concerning bills, resolutions, treaties and other measures that have been transmitted to or introduced in the House or Senate.

Exempt Communications. The following were excluded from the definition of "lobbying communications."

● Communications to a federal officer or employee that do not concern the above legislative matters but have to do with other government matters such as regulations, executive orders, contracts and so forth.

● Communications made at the request of a federal officer or employee, such as testimony before a committee or information submitted for inclusion in a public hearing or record.

● Nonpaid communications made through a speech or address, through a newspaper, book, periodical or magazine published for distribution to the general public, through a radio or television transmission, or through a regular publication of an organization published in substantial part for purposes unrelated to influencing legislation.

● Any communication by an individual for redress of grievances or to express a personal opinion.

● Communications on any subject directly affecting an organization to a senator or his staff — if the organization's principal place of business is located in the state represented by that senator.

● Communications with a member of the House or his staff — if the organization's principal place of business is located in a county within which all or part of a member's congressional district is located.

● Communications with representatives, senators or their staffs that deal only with the "existence or status" of any issue, or which seek only to determine the "subject matter of an issue."

● An individual who is a member or an officer, director or employee of an organization should not be presumed to be speaking on behalf of his organization in every instance but is entitled to express his views as an individual so that such expression is not necessarily a lobbying communication. (According to the committee report on HR 8494, "the general test would be whether the communication is made for the organization pursuant to the employee's general or specific responsibilities as an employee.")

Registration and Record-Keeping

HR 8494 required that lobbying organizations register annually and that they keep certain records of their lobbying activities. The bill required:

● Registration with the comptroller general no later than 30 days after engaging in lobbying activities (such registration would be effective until Jan. 15 of the following year).

● Reregistration by Jan. 30 of the following year if the quarterly filing threshold is met.

● Identification of the organization, including its name and address, principal place of business, the general nature of its business and the names of the organization's executive officers and directors (even if they were not paid).

● Identification of employees or retained individuals who qualify as lobbyists.

● Notification of the comptroller general if an organization terminates lobbying activities.

● Retention by the organization or retained lobbyist of "such records as are necessary" to file registrations and reports required under the act. (The bill prohibited the comptroller from requiring records beyond those normally maintained by the organization.)

● Preservation of such records for at least five years after the close of the quarterly filing period they cover.

Reports

Lobbying organizations were required to file quarterly reports with the comptroller within 30 days of the end of the quarter. Lobbying organizations that did not meet a threshold had to file a statement to that effect. Those meeting a threshold were required to report:

● An identification of the organization filing (similar to that provided under the registration provision).

● Total expenditures made by the organization or a retainee for lobbying communications during the period (including costs for mailing, printing, advertising, telephones, consultant fees, gifts or other expenditures made to or for the benefit of a federal officer or employee).

● An itemized listing of each expenditure of $35 or more made to or for the benefit of any federal officer or employee (including members of Congress) and the name of the recipient.

● Expenditures for receptions, dinners or other similar events held for a federal officer or employee if the cost to the reporting organization exceeded $500.

● The name and address of organizations contributing $3,000 or more during the calendar year to a lobbying group and the amount given if the contribution was spent in whole or in part for lobbying and the lobbying group spends at least 1 percent of its budget on lobbying activities.

● A description of the issues on which the organization expends a significant amount of lobbying effort, and the name of any retainee or employee as well as the chief executive officer of the lobby group, whether paid or unpaid, who engaged in lobbying on one of those issues on behalf of the organization.

● The name of any lobbyist retained by an organization and the name of any employee who meets the lobbying threshold, the amount of money spent to employ the employee or retained lobbyist, and expenditures made in connection with lobbying by such individuals.

● A statement that lobbying communications were made on the floor of the House of Representatives or Senate or in adjoining rooms if such communications were made by an employee or retainee of a reporting organization.

● Disclosure of each known "direct business relationship" between the reporting organization and a federal officer or employee the organization sought to influence in the quarterly reporting period.

● Lobbying activities (such as those listed above) engaged in by an affiliate organization meeting a threshold if such activities are not reported by the affiliate itself.

Congress Eases Rules on Ex- Officials Who Lobby

Congress in 1979 softened year-old revolving door restrictions designed to prevent former federal officials from influencing their old agencies as lobbyists or as other representatives of their new employers.

Passage of S 869 (PL 96-28) was prompted by fears that high-level federal officials would quit in droves to accept private-sector jobs before the new conflict-of-interest restrictions became effective. President Carter, whose administration requested the eased rules, signed S 869 into law into law June 22, nine days before the revolving door curbs took effect as part of the Ethics in Government Act of 1978 (PL 95-521). Critics had said that unless they were modified they would deter talented people from going to work for the government.

The 1979 revision exempted from the restrictions former federal officials who go to work for state and local governments or non-profit institutions. It also gave ex-officials freedom to advise a new private employer on how to deal with their former agencies.

Concerns

Causing concern were provisions of the new ethics law:

● Preventing ex-officials (GS-17 and above) from contacting their former agencies about any matter, regardless of whether they had had direct responsibility for it in government, for one year after resigning.

● Prohibiting these officials for two years after leaving from "assisting in representing" another person before their previous agency on matters they dealt with as federal employees. Thus, a former Securities and Exchange Commission lawyer could not for two years advise colleagues in his new law firm on a case pending before the SEC if he once had jurisdiction over the matter.

Objections arose from some in the House that S 869 went too far and that concern about an exodus was overblown. But these objections were ignored.

Rep. Bob Eckhardt, D-Texas, argued that softening the assisting-in-representing ban — as S 869 did — invited abuses and made the conflict-of-interest restrictions largely meaningless. An amendment by Eckhardt to toughen the assisting-in-representing bar failed.

But Rep. Thomas N. Kindness, R-Ohio, one of S 869's backers, argued that "the last Congress adopted [the restrictions] in a panic. They are far too broad."

Provisions

As signed into law, S 869:

● Clarified language in the ethics law on the two-year bar on assisting in representing. The bar would apply only to those matters that a person participated in "personally and substantially."

● Permitted a former official to advise lawyers, colleagues and others representing his new employer before his former agency. The assisting-in-representing restriction would apply solely to personal appearances of the ex-official before his former agency.

● Exempted from the one-year ban on contact with former agencies those former federal officials who go to work for colleges and universities, medical research and treatment facilities or state and local government.

● Limited automatic coverage under the post-employment curbs to executive-level civilian employees and military officers in grades O-9 and above. Decisions on which positions to cover at the GS-17 and GS-18 level, in the federal Senior Executive Service and in military grades O-7 and O-8 would be up to the Office of Government Ethics.

● Disclosure of each known "direct business relationship" between the reporting organization and a federal officer or employee the organization sought to influence in the quarterly reporting period. Under the provision, designed to prevent conflicts of interest, "direct business relationship" meant a relationship between the organization and any federal officer or employee in which:

1) the federal officer or employee was a partner in such organization or,

2) the federal officer or employee was an employee of the lobbying organization or a member of its board of directors or similar governing body or,

3) the organization and the federal officer or employee held a legal or beneficial interest in excess of $1,000 in the same business or joint venture (excluding stock holdings in publicly traded corporations, insurance policies and leases made in the ordinary course of business that are provided on terms that would be available to the general public).

Grass-Roots Lobbying. The reports section of the bill also required disclosure of grass-roots lobbying solicitations — requests an organization makes to other individuals or organizations to lobby on an issue. Organizations would report solicitations made through advertisements if such solicitations reached or could be reasonably expected to reach 500 or more persons, 100 or more employees of an or-

ganization, 25 or more officers or directors or 12 or more affiliates. Reports on grass-roots lobbying required disclosure of:

● The issue with which the solicitation was concerned.

● The means employed to make the solicitation and an indication of whether the recipients were in turn asked to solicit others.

● An identification of any persons retained to make the solicitation.

● The approximate number of persons solicited, if the solicitation is made through the mails or by telegram.

● An identification of the publication or radio or television station where the solicitation appeared and the total amount expended on such advertisements if the amount expended exceeded $5,000.

"Solicitation" under this provision included communications directly urging, requesting, or requiring another person to advocate a specific position on a particular issue and seeking to influence a member of Congress, but did not include communications between registered lobbying organizations.

Public Records

Public record-keeping provisions in the bill required that the comptroller general:

● Establish filing and indexing systems to make the registrations and reports publicly accessible.

● Make copies of registrations available by five days after the date a registration is filed.

● Compile and summarize the information contained in registrations and reports in each quarterly filing period and make that information available to the public within 60 days after the close of such period.

● Submit an annual report to the president and Congress detailing the comptroller's activities.

● Refer all apparent violations of the act to the attorney general.

Enforcement

The attorney general was given responsibility for enforcing the lobby disclosure act. The bill provided that:

● Alleged violators be notified of possible violations, except when it might interfere with enforcement of the act.

● The attorney general use "informal methods of conference and conciliation" as the first line of enforcement.

● If informal methods fail the attorney general may institute a civil action in the judicial district in which the organization is based or transacts business.

● The attorney general may institute criminal proceedings if a violation of the law is found.

● In civil actions brought under the act, a court may award attorneys' fees and expenses to the prevailing party (other than the government) if the court determines the action was brought "without foundation, vexatiously, frivolously, or in bad faith."

● Organizations or individuals knowingly violating the registration, record-keeping or reporting sections of the law or rules or regulations are subject to civil penalties of not more than $10,000 for each violation.

● Individuals or organizations willfully and knowingly making false statements or failing to provide information required under those sections may be fined up to $10,000 or imprisoned for up to two years or both for each violation.

● Any individual who sells or uses information retained under the public record-keeping sections for soliciting contributions or business may be fined up to $10,000.

1978 Senate Bill

Lobby disclosure legislation remained stalled in the Senate Governmental Affairs Committee from early May 1978 until Congress adjourned in October because key committee members couldn't agree on how to get a bill to the floor.

Despite intensive White House efforts to salvage a lobby bill in virtually any form, no committee member was ready to manage the legislation in the Senate.

Ribicoff Bill

Committee Chairman Abraham Ribicoff, D-Conn., had introduced his own bill (S 2971) which was considered far more rigorous than the House-passed bill. Besides requiring more groups to file reports, Ribicoff's bill contained more comprehensive grass-roots lobbying and contributor disclosure provisions than the House-passed bill, and more extensive coverage of lobbying of executive branch officials.

But when markup sessions began in May, the Governmental Affairs committee appeared to be moving toward a more moderate approach than that incorporated in S 2971. In its first vote on the bill, the panel drastically revised the "threshold" determining which and how many organizations would have to file reports with the federal government. The change would have made it easier for small groups to escape the bill's reporting requirements.

And more changes appeared to be in the offing. Sens. Charles McC. Mathias Jr., R-Md., and Edmund S. Muskie, D-Maine, had the votes to win committee approval for five or six major amendments they planned to propose. The amendments would have eliminated requirements for disclosure of grass-roots lobbying efforts and the names of major contributors to lobby groups, exempted organizations of state or local elected officials from the reporting requirements and eliminated the bill's criminal sanctions.

Seeking a Manager

Ribicoff said he would not manage his bill on the Senate floor if it were "emasculated" by the Mathias-Muskie amendments. "I couldn't manage a bill I didn't believe in," he told CQ. "I would prefer someone else manage it so I could offer strengthening amendments on the floor."

But Muskie wasn't interested in managing such a bill and Ribicoff couldn't find anyone who was.

Ribicoff said he'd "rather have no bill than a bad bill." But faced with the prospect of having no bill reported, Ribicoff offered to mark up any measure. He believed that a weak bill could be strengthened on the floor.

His offer challenged Mathias and Muskie. They had a lobby bill of their own (S 2026), a bill supported by civil libertarians but consistently opposed by Ribicoff. But Mathias said he feared that once his bill went to the floor or to conference it would be scuttled in favor of something closer to Ribicoff's proposal. Asked if he thought he could hold the Mathias-Muskie bill together on the floor, Mathias said he couldn't be "certain," and wanted "assurances" of support from the White House.

But the White House, allied with Ribicoff and Common Cause in pushing a far stronger bill, wouldn't make such a commitment. Like Ribicoff, White House strategists hoped to strengthen a weak bill by floor amendments.

Common Cause: Mathias 'Obstructionist'

Common Cause Vice President Fred Wertheimer charged Mathias with being "obstructionist" in refusing to agree on any compromise to get a bill to the floor. "He's not willing to face the consequences of the democratic process, of seeing his own bill go to the floor even in a situation where every major lobbyist in town is supporting him. He's trying to kill it."

As for Muskie, Wertheimer said, "If the same tactics were used on Muskie on his sunset legislation, he'd be on the Senate floor screaming bloody murder."

In the Mathias-Muskie camp, aides insisted they were only trying to ensure that whatever bill was reported "reflects our concerns." They objected to a Ribicoff proposal that their six amendments to S 2971 be voted on all at once. Said one aide, "We've worked successfully to amend it [the Ribicoff bill] and now he wants to send it to the floor without the benefit of developing a committee record on each amendment. That simply weakens our case for the amendments on the Senate floor."

The White House had made lobby disclosure legislation a top priority. President Carter called Muskie to ask that Muskie leave the door open to compromise and help get a bill through committee. Vice President Mondale was involved in talks with Ribicoff and at least one other committee member. But Ribicoff said White House lobbying on the bill had been ineffective compared with that of opponents.

Under White House prodding, Ribicoff and others continued to seek a compromise, although prospects appeared dim. As one aide summarized the situation, "This bill has had a four year history of divisiveness.... It's really in the hands of the senators." Said another, "It appears almost impossible to break this logjam."

No compromise was reached before the 95th Congress adjourned.

1979 House Bill

The House Judiciary Subcommittee on Administrative Law May 2 began marking up a lobby bill (HR 81) identical to one approved by the full committee in 1978. The subcommittee reported the measure after six meetings. The full committee began markup on a renumbered bill (HR 4395) July 10 and reported it Oct. 16 by a 26-2 vote.

During its markup, the full committee made substantial revisions in the subcommittee version of the bill, most of which weakened the legislation. As the 26-2 vote to report the bill suggested, a series of weakening amendments was the price backers of lobby disclosure paid to get support from a broad range of interest groups. Nevertheless, many observers saw the bill reported as a step in the right direction.

The subcommittee bill had contained a provision sponsored by Rep. Romano L. Mazzoli, D-Ky., that would have required registered lobby groups to disclose the names of organizations from which they receive $3,000 or more a year. On a 16-11 vote, the full committee voted Oct. 10 to eliminate the provision.

Rep. Don Edwards, D-Calif., author of the amendment to delete the contributor disclosure requirement, argued it would be unconstitutional. "Organizations, no less than individuals, have rights of privacy and anonymous political speech," Edwards said. The provision he succeeded in deleting was the weakest contributor disclosure requirement attached to any lobby bill in recent years.

The subcommittee had rejected another Mazzoli amendment that would have required organizations that had to register under the bill to report expenditures of $25,000 or more per calendar quarter on so-called grass-roots lobbying, such as paid advertisements and mass mailing campaigns designed to influence legislation.

When Mazzoli offered it again in the full committee, it was rejected on a voice vote.

Mazzoli's grass-roots amendment, offered in the full committee Oct. 11, was far less stringent than one approved by the full House in 1978. Mazzoli's amendment would have covered only major expenditures.

Under the amendment, an organization would not have had to report expenditures on grass-roots lobbying if it did not already have to register under the bill. Mazzoli's amendment contained no requirement to identify those persons solicited by grass-roots efforts, as did the 1978 bill. Opponents insisted that the amendment would create difficult record-keeping problems for organizations and would discourage the participation of citizens in government.

Provisions

HR 4395 would require organizations that spent $5,000 or more per calendar quarter making "lobbying communications" to register and file quarterly reports with the clerk of the House.

However, organizations meeting this spending threshold that did not hire outside lobbyists and used only their own employees would be covered by the act only if they spent significant time during a calendar quarter making lobbying communications.

An organization with one in-house lobbyist would be covered if the employee made lobbying contacts 13 or more days per calendar quarter. Organizations with two or more in-house lobbyists would be covered if lobbying communications were made seven or more days during a calendar quarter.

The bill would require organizations meeting the $5,000 per quarter spending threshold to disclose gifts worth more than $35 made to members or employees. Receptions or dinners costing more than $500 for the benefit of members or employees also would have to be reported. In addition, an organization covered by the bill would have to detail the 15 major issues upon which it lobbied.

HR 4395 would apply only to lobbying of Congress. It would not cover lobbying by individuals acting in their own capacity.

HR 4395 would require fewer organizations to register and report expenditures than bills passed by the House in the 94th and 95th Congresses.

The full committee raised to $5,000 from the $2,500 recommended by the subcommittee the required spending on lobbying per calendar quarter needed to bring an organization under the bill's registration and reporting provisions.

Judiciary Committee members agreed that the higher spending threshold would cover only major lobbying organizations. Groups expending small amounts of money or making only limited direct contacts with legislators would not be covered by the bill.

In addition to the higher spending threshold, the Judiciary Committee approved several other provisions that further narrowed the applicability of the bill.

Mortgage, rental and utility payments were exempted from the expenditure definition, thereby allowing greater spending by lobby groups before they would be covered.

In addition, inquiries as to the status, existence or subject matter of a bill were exempted from the definition of lobbying contacts.

A broad geographic exemption also was approved for groups without outside retained lobbyists. The exemption would not count lobbying communications made with home state representatives and senators in determining the number of days in a calendar quarter that the group had made lobbying contacts.

The provision would allow lobby groups in states with large congressional delegations to engage in much more extensive lobbying activity — without having to register and report under the bill — than organizations in less populous states.

Outlook

Although the bill as reported appeared acceptable to a broad spectrum of interests, inclusion of provisions to require disclosure of expenditures for grass-roots lobbying and the names of organizations contributing more than $3,000 a year to lobby groups — provisions that were likely to be offered by proponents of increased disclosure on the House floor — would make it unacceptable to many organizations. However, as of mid-November 1979, no floor action had been scheduled, and it appeared that consideration by the full House could be delayed until 1980. ▌

Support Wanes for Public Financing Bill

After six years of sporadic and unsuccessful efforts to enact public financing legislation, the death knell for public financing legislation may have been sounded by the House Administration Committee May 24, 1979, when it decisively voted 8-17 not to report a bill (HR 1) to provide federal funding for House general election campaigns.

While a congressional public financing measure had never been approved by the committee, the size of the defeat was a surprise. HR 1 had been heavily promoted by the White House, the Democratic congressional leadership, the Democratic Study Group (DSG) and a host of outside organizations, including the public affairs lobby Common Cause.

Backers of HR 1 indicated that they would continue the fight for public financing by seeking a ruling from the Rules Committee that would permit the measure to be brought to the floor. This type of "end run" has been the way proponents have proceeded in the past.

But defeat in the Administration Committee damaged the prospects for the controversial proposal. Administration Committee Chairman Frank Thompson Jr., D-N.J., observed that HR 1 was "probably dead" for the 96th Congress.

Democratic Defections

The bill was defeated by a coalition of Republicans and disaffected Democrats that had blunted earlier public financing efforts. Eight of the 16 Democrats defected to join all nine Republicans in opposing the bill.

The anti-public-financing coalition included the committee's three southern Democrats — Mendel J. Davis of South Carolina, Ed Jones of Tennessee and Charlie Rose of North Carolina — plus five veteran northern Democrats — Frank Annunzio of Illinois, Joseph M. Gaydos of Pennsylvania, Joseph G. Minish of New Jersey, Robert H. Mollohan of West Virginia and Lucien N. Nedzi of Michigan. Thompson indicated that part of the problem was that many of the bill's Democratic opponents represented safe, one-party districts and did not want to encourage potential challenges to their seats.

Yet proponents claimed that at least three of the Democrats were prepared to vote for public financing if their support made a difference. But with proponents unable to construct a majority, Thompson made no effort to sway them. "All three were reluctant dragons anyway," declared Common Cause's legislative director, Mike Cole.

Support within the committee for HR 1 was concentrated among the Democratic leadership — Thompson and House Majority Whip John Brademas — and the newest Democratic members. Augustus F. Hawkins and Lionel Van Deerlin, both of California, also supported the bill.

"It would have been a coup to get the bill out of committee," contended Cole. "It's a legacy of the Wayne Hays era — a group of people who have resisted reform."

Public financing hearings in March had produced unexpected criticism of HR 1, with adverse testimony focusing on the bill's certification process and an initially high cost estimate from the Federal Election Commission (FEC).

In an effort to simplify the bill and attract wider Democratic support, two major changes were made in HR 1 before markup: 1) an increase in the eligibility threshold for participating candidates from $1,000 to $10,000 (designed to keep fringe candidates out of the system); and 2) a transfer in major control of the certification process from the frequently criticized FEC to state secretaries of state.

'FEC Bypass'

Supporters were especially hopeful that the latter change, known as "the FEC bypass," would win enough Democratic converts to report out the bill. Thompson gambled that the secretaries of state would draw more approval than an earlier proposal that transferred major control of certification to state parties.

In a revision of HR 1 unveiled May 9, certification was given to the state parties. They would have been permitted to keep surplus funds for party-building activities such as get-out-the-vote drives. But when some Democratic members complained that they did not have good relations with their state chairmen, the major certification role was shifted to the secretaries of state.

Public financing proponents contended that the revisions in HR 1 helped to bring them within one or two votes of the necessary majority. But, according to DSG Staff Director Richard P. Conlon, further changes to win more votes "all had a price."

Minish wanted a limit on political action committee contributions of $1,000. Davis wanted to extend the bill to cover primaries. Republican Dave Stockman of Michigan proposed removal of the bill's spending ceiling. Nedzi might have given his support if certification responsibility was returned to the state parties. But if more changes were made to pick up individual votes, Conlon explained, "the bill would have gone to the floor with a hole in its bottom."

Lobbying Effort

Backers of HR 1 also felt that they were undercut by some effective lobbying by Democratic congressional opponents. While House Speaker Thomas P. O'Neill Jr., D-Mass., was urging wavering Democrats to report out the bill, proponents contended that John P. Murtha of Pennsylvania and Dan Rostenkowski of Illinois were forcefully telling their colleagues to vote against it. They augmented an outside lobbying effort that included the Chamber of Commerce of the United States and related business groups. *(Lobbying, box p. 70)*

The Republican National Committee and Republican Congressional Campaign Committee lobbied its party's members, but there were few GOP public financing sympathizers on the committee to begin with. Only two of the younger Republicans — Stockman, a second termer, and freshman Newt Gingrich of Georgia — had expressed interest in the concept. During the markup they both voiced their opposition to HR 1.

Stockman had helped draft the original House public financing bill in the early 1970s as an aide to Republican Rep. John B. Anderson of Illinois, and he had signed on as one of about 20 Republican co-sponsors of HR 1. But after his amendment to remove the spending ceiling was defeated, he announced that he could not support the bill.

Gingrich, the lone Republican in the Georgia congressional delegation and a House winner on his third try, showed interest in a public financing bill that would help challengers. He offered amendments that would have lowered the eligibility threshold and permitted several mass mailings.

After the overwhelming 8-17 vote not to report HR 1, Brademas sought approval for a motion to report the bill to the floor without a recommendation. It was defeated by an identical 8-17 vote. "This would do by indirection what the committee wouldn't do by direction," argued ranking Republican member William L. Dickinson of Alabama.

Following the vote, John Burton of California offered his own solution — a motion that HR 1 be sent to the floor with the recommendation "do not pass." The motion was not seconded.

Backers of HR 1 claimed their measure was far from dead, pointing to the nearly 160 House sponsors as indication that it would draw considerable support on the floor.

Provisions of Committee Bill

Under the version of the public financing legislation marked up by the House Administration Committee in May 1979, HR 1 was a voluntary plan. Candidates who participated in the program would have a spending ceiling of $150,000, plus $30,000 for fundraising expenses, and an automatic cost-of-living escalator using 1978 as the base year. Adding together all the ingredients, the total spending ceiling for a candidate in the 1980 general election would be about $220,000.

To receive federal money, candidates would first have to raise $10,000 on their own in contributions of $150 or less, with at least 80 percent of the total from residents in their own state. Contributions received between January 1 of the election year and election day could be submitted for matching payments. Funds would be matched in $10,000 increments up to 40 percent of the spending limit, or about $60,000.

All candidates who had early primaries (before the end of July) would have to indicate their intention to seek public funds by July 31. Candidates with later primaries would have until 15 days after the primary to indicate their participation in the system. In each case, candidates would have to meet the $10,000 eligibility threshold at the same time they indicated their participation.

Candidates accepting public financing would have to agree not to spend more than $25,000 out of their own pockets. The bill provided for removal of the spending ceiling only under certain conditions. The plan would be financed by money in the voluntary income tax check-off fund, which at the time financed only presidential campaigns. The FEC had estimated before the markup that it would cost between $22.2 million and $29.7 million to fund House candidates under HR 1. About $100 million was in the check-off fund in January 1979.

But lack of time could be a serious problem in implementing the bill for 1980. Thompson stated that a bill would have to be passed in 1979, warning that if action was postponed until the election year, the slim chance for success would have evaporated.

Background

Spurred by the Watergate revelations, the 93rd Congress passed a comprehensive campaign financing bill that included a provision for the public financing of presidential races. During the same Congress, the Senate twice approved public financing of congressional races, but each time the House rejected it, in large part because of the opposition of Wayne L. Hays, D-Ohio, chairman of the House Administration Committee, and the seeming indifference of House Democratic leaders.

1973 Action

The Senate first passed congressional public financing on Nov. 27, 1973, as part of a broad campaign reform rider to a bill raising the temporary debt ceiling. Nine senators, led by Edward M. Kennedy, D-Mass., fought successfully for the rider, which included a provision providing for complete federal financing of House and Senate general election campaigns, coupled with a ceiling on contributions and expenditures. The provision was approved 52-40, with the support of 42 of the 54 Democrats who voted and 10 of the 38 Republicans.

Congressional critics claimed that it was blackmail for public financing proponents to attach their measure to the debt ceiling bill; the House returned the bill to the Senate without the campaign reform rider. House leaders agreed, however, to schedule a vote on the rider if the Senate limited its coverage to presidential campaigns, eliminating the provision for the public financing of congressional races. The Senate, though, was unable to gain approval of the more limited measure, as a filibuster led by James B. Allen, D-Ala., forced Democratic leaders to drop the entire public financing rider to gain passage of the debt ceiling bill.

1974 Action

In 1974 the Senate again approved public financing of congressional races, but the section was deleted in conference with the House and the landmark campaign reform bill that was enacted (PL 93-443) provided for the public financing of presidential campaigns only.

Before passage of the Senate bill on April 11, there were repeated attempts to scuttle public financing and substitute a more closely supervised system of private financing. The final hurdle was cleared when proponents of public financing invoked cloture to break up a filibuster by southern Democrats and conservative Republicans who opposed the measure.

The bill reported by the House Administration Committee in July did not include congressional public financing. On the House floor, Wayne Hays dominated debate and fended off all major challenges to his committee's bill. Reps. John B. Anderson, R-Ill., and Morris K. Udall, D-Ariz., tried unsuccessfully to win approval of an amendment that would publicly fund congressional races through a system of matching federal grants.

By a vote of 187-228, the House on Aug. 8 defeated the Anderson-Udall amendment. Republicans rejected it by a 73-110 vote, while Democrats broke nearly even, 114-118 against. Southern Democrats, however, overwhelmingly disapproved of congressional public financing, voting against the amendment, 18-60.

In conference, Senate conferees, led by Kennedy and Dick Clark, D-Iowa, pressed for inclusion of some form of public financing for House and Senate races, but they finally dropped their fight in return for higher spending limits for congressional candidates.

The need to pass a bill quickly re-establishing the Federal Election Commission (FEC), though, preempted any move for congressional public financing. As a result, the issue was left for the 95th Congress to decide.

In 1976, the Supreme Court had ruled in *Buckley v. Valeo* that the FEC was improperly constituted and that the campaign spending limits and the amount of money candidates spent on their own campaigns were unconstitutional restrictions, unless the candidates accepted public funds (which in 1976 applied only to presidential candidates).

1977 Action

A successful filibuster in the Senate and a solid block of opposition in a House committee killed public financing legislation in 1977.

The defeats were a blow to public financing supporters who began the year with high hopes for success. They had thought times had changed since Congress last considered the issue in 1974. Then, leading officials, from the White House on down, were either opposed or seemingly indifferent to its passage.

In early 1977, the climate in Washington appeared to have been almost completely reversed. President Carter made the public financing of congressional races part of his election reform package, and House Speaker O'Neill, Senate Majority Leader Robert C. Byrd, D-W.Va., and Hays' successor as House Administration Committee chairman, Thompson, were in support. Prospects for public financing were brightened further by the overwhelming Democratic advantage in the House, far larger than during the 93rd Congress when the House rejected congressional public financing after it had been approved by the Senate.

But when a Senate financing bill came to the floor in late July, Republicans aided by southern Democrats blocked three cloture motions and then removed the public financing section from the bill (S 926). That left only relatively non-controversial amendments to the 1971 Federal Elections Campaign Act which the Senate approved Aug. 3.

The issue was considered dead for the session. But in October the House leadership asked the House Administration Committee to consider a public financing bill after 155 Democratic members signed a letter asking for prompt action. The committee took up an unnumbered bill, but put it aside after committee Republicans and veteran northern Democrats succeeded in attaching two crippling amendments.

1978: Another Defeat

Support from some of the biggest names in Washington — including President Carter and House Speaker O'Neill — was not sufficient to move legislation calling for public financing of congressional elections in 1978.

House backers of public financing failed in two parliamentary maneuvers to attach a public financing proposal to campaign finance bills. One of those bills, HR 11315, contained another controversial feature that would lower limits on contributions and expenditures by parties and multicandidate political action committees (PACs). The bill was reported March 16 by the House Administration Committee over the strong criticism of Republicans who had expected a bill similar to the 1977 Senate-passed version (S 926), which made basically non-controversial changes in the Federal Election Campaign Act (last amended in 1976) concerning campaign reporting and disclosure requirements. *(Political action groups, p. 73)*

The vote to report the bill was 16-9, with South Carolina's Mendel J. Davis the only Democrat to join the Republicans in opposition.

Angry Republicans, viewing the lower limits as a direct threat to their ability to challenge entrenched Democratic incumbents, were particularly upset with the limits on party spending, which would reduce from $30,000 to $10,000 the amount national, congressional and state party committees combined could contribute directly to a federal candidate in an election year. The bill also would lower from $20,000 to $5,000 the total amount the same party committees could spend on behalf of a federal candidate in a general election for services such as polling and staff assistance. Transfers between party committees, allowed by existing law, would be prohibited if they were made as a contribution or expenditure for a candidate. National and congressional committees, which currently operated under separate contribution limits, would be combined under one limit.

Republicans gained an unusual ally when Common Cause announced it opposed the bill. Common Cause feared that the Democrats' proposal would polarize the House on the campaign finance issue, dimming the chances for winning needed Republican votes for a public financing provision they sought to be added to the bill on the House floor. "It's over-partisan," remarked Common Cause Vice President Fred Wertheimer. "They played into the hands of the opponents of public financing."

After the measure was reported by the committee, a coalition of Republicans and disgruntled Democrats combined to defeat the rule to allow consideration of the leadership-backed measure.

The 198-209 March 21 vote to defeat the rule on HR 11315 had two practical effects. First, it blocked consideration of the bill's provision to lower the limits on spending by parties and political action committees. Second, it killed any hopes of adding to the bill an amendment allowing public financing of House general election campaigns.

Two major changes were made in the proposal after the March setback: The effective date was pushed back from 1978 to 1980, and the candidate spending limits were raised from $125,000 plus $25,000 for additional fundraising costs to $150,000 plus $30,000 for fund raising.

The rest of the proposal remained the same. It applied only to House general elections and was voluntary. Candidates would have 10 days after their nomination to decide whether to accept public financing.

Those who did would first have to raise $10,000 on their own in contributions of $100 or less, with 80 percent of the total in contributions from residents of their own state. Funds would then be matched up to the spending ceiling.

Candidates accepting public financing also would have to agree not to spend more than $25,000 out of their own pockets. In 1976 there were 68 House candidates who loaned or directly contributed more than $25,000 to their own campaigns, including 10 candidates who gave at least $100,000. Freshman Rep. Cecil Heftel, D-Hawaii, paced the list with $507,000 in personal loans.

Public Financing Bill Draws Heavy Lobbying

Proponents of the legislation to extend public financing to House general election campaigns (HR 1) were trying to sell the bill in a climate that had become increasingly partisan. At their national headquarters less than a block from the House office buildings, the Republican National Committee (RNC) and the National Republican Congressional Committee (NRCC) began to mount intensive drives to defeat HR 1. Their lobbying efforts were aimed primarily at reducing GOP support for the measure, which included 20 Republican co-sponsors (out of 155 House members who co-sponsored HR 1).

At a January 1979 meeting, the RNC voted to oppose HR 1. After that National Chairman Bill Brock worked actively to defeat the measure, writing articles of opposition in party journals and lobbying GOP House members to vote against the bill. He even threatened a legal challenge if HR 1 were to pass.

In a March 9 letter to House Republicans, Brock warned that passage of HR 1, with its low spending ceilings, would threaten the survival of the GOP. HR 1 is "the most blatantly pro-incumbent, anti-challenger bill that Congress has seen," Brock wrote. "HR 1 is a power play by the Democratic majority which seeks to control and stifle Republican challengers' access to the voters. Republicans do not favor suicide. They should not vote for HR 1."

"This is the type of 'reform,'" concluded Brock in colorful tones, "that Attila the Hun might have offered the hapless peasants who were unfortunate enough to lie in the path of his marauding band."

The NRCC sent a similar message to newspapers across the country. The committee mailed out editorial packages in opposition to HR 1 and responded to all pro-public financing editorials that they saw. "We don't have the votes alone to defeat the bill," NRCC Executive Director Steven Stockmeyer said in explaining the committee's strategy. "We must go public to bring pressure on the Democrats."

The Republicans were joined in their public lobbying effort by a variety of conservative and business groups that included the National Conservative Political Action Committee (NCPAC) and the Chamber of Commerce of the United States. NCPAC mounted the most visible effort. Starting in February with an anti-HR 1 letter written over the signature of Republican Rep. Robert K. Dornan of California, NCPAC sent out nearly 1.5 million pieces of mail with enclosed postcards to be returned to members of the House.

NCPAC did some targeted media advertising, spending about $12,000 on anti-HR 1 radio and newspaper ads in Democratic Rep. Thomas S. Foley's district in eastern Washington. In addition, the organization printed buttons and bumper stickers with the slogan, "Stop Welfare for Politicians."

The Chamber of Commerce adopted a lower profile in its campaign of personal lobbying and letter writing, but was just as committed as NCPAC to the bill's defeat. The demise of HR 1 was the Chamber's number-one priority in 1979.

Supporters of HR 1 doubted that a mass mailing campaign alone would sway many votes, but they began letter-writing efforts of their own to show there was grass-roots support for the measure.

Common Cause, which had long advocated congressional public financing, assumed the lead role in mobilizing outside support. It claimed that a diverse coalition of more than two dozen national organizations, ranging from the AFL-CIO to the United Methodist Church, were supporting HR 1. Like the NRCC, Common Cause sent editorial packages to newspapers across the country, and helped to coordinate the local lobbying efforts of the various proponents.

Perhaps the most unique lobbying effort was conducted by Ralph Nader's Public Citizens Congress Watch. The organization encouraged local chapters in about 25 districts to send one-dollar bills with strings attached to their congressmen. The "string campaign," as it was called, was designed to show that under the existing system large campaign contributors gave with the expectation of having influence with the House member.

Internal lobbying of House members was handled by the Democratic majority on the House Administration Committee, the Democratic Study Group (DSG) and the leadership. Of this triumvirate, the DSG was the nerve center, combating negative accounts of HR 1 with a flow of positive information to House members.

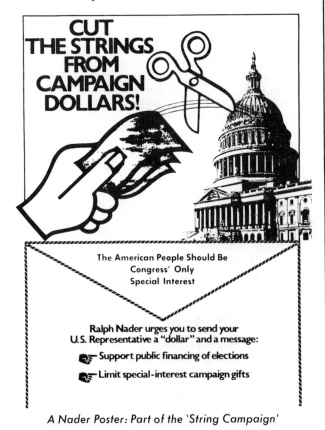

A Nader Poster: Part of the 'String Campaign'

The public financing plan called for removal of the spending ceiling where a candidate who did not accept public money spent more than $25,000 in personal funds or raised or spent in excess of $75,000. In such cases, candidates who signed up for public financing could receive up to $50,000 more in federal money.

Second Try

In a second attempt to secure a public financing measure, supporters of the concept turned to a generally non-controversial Federal Election Commission authorization bill (HR 11983) as a vehicle for the public financing amendment. But the House July 19 refused to approve a parliamentary maneuver that would have allowed floor consideration of the amendment. By a 213-196 vote on a procedural motion (H Res 1172), the House blocked consideration of public financing as an amendment to HR 11983.

Proponents of public financing had made no effort to win a favorable rule in the House Rules Committee, where they lacked majority support. Instead, they developed a complex alternative strategy, which hinged on defeating the rule for HR 11983 on the floor and then winning approval of a substitute that would have permitted their amendment.

The vote on H Res 1172 was billed as a clear indication of the strength of public financing forces in the House. "A vote on this rule," House Administration Committee Chairman Thompson told his colleagues, "is tantamount to your position on public financing."

Proponents of public financing promised to renew the fight in 1979. They hoped that with 60 to 80 new members and an increasing public awareness of the impact of special interest spending on congressional races, their chances would be improved. "It's an idea that is far from dead," said Anderson.

Yet it was also far from adoption. There was no public clamor for congressional public financing, and while the proposal drew some vocal support in Congress as a "good government" issue, resistance remained formidable.

"Support for public financing has always been very tentative," observed Rep. Edward W. Pattison, D-N.Y. "People make statements for it who are not really in favor of it."

1979 Committee Markup

Pattison's observation seemed to be borne out a year later, when the House Administration Committee again shelved a public financing bill. However, the atmosphere during the committee's markup of HR 1 May 15-24 was far more congenial than it had been in 1978.

In 1979 Thompson was more accommodating to the Republicans, offering a series of 18 amendments to HR 1 instead of a new, substitute bill that would have forced the minority to seek a delay in markup. House Minority Leader John J. Rhodes of Arizona anticipated that a new draft would be revealed at the last minute and wrote Thompson urging a one-month postponement.

But with Thompson's decision to submit amendments rather than a substitute, Republicans were pacified. "We are both well positioned this year," Frenzel commented on the opening of markup. "We know what your amendments are and you know what our amendments are."

Thompson won approval of all but one of his 18 amendments, but found on roll-call votes he had little margin for error. With Republicans voting as a unanimous bloc on all key votes, Thompson had to rely on some southern and veteran northern Democrats for his margin of victory.

The public financing coalition failed on one key roll call, when the committee rejected a Thompson amendment that would have funded "the FEC bypass." The amendment would have provided state secretaries of state with at least $5,000 per congressional district to pay certified public accountants and to administer other aspects of HR 1.

The vote against the amendment was 10-11, with Democrats Mollohan and Davis joining the nine Republicans in opposition. Four other Democrats — Annunzio, Gaydos, Minish and Rose — did not vote or provide proxies. At the end of the markup, Thompson submitted a new amendment that provided the secretaries of state $6,000 per district. It passed by voice vote.

Mollohan and Davis also joined the Republicans on the first key vote of the markup, a Davis motion on May 15 to extend HR 1 to cover primary elections. Davis had succeeded in gutting the 1977 public financing bill by winning approval of a similar amendment.

But Thompson was prepared this time with a ruling from the House parliamentarian that any amendment relating to primaries, Senate elections or PAC contribution limits was not germane to HR 1. Davis argued that his amendment was in order, pointing to a similar amendment that was added to the 1974 campaign finance act covering presidential primaries.

Thompson responded that in 1974 the committee had received a special waiver from the Rules Committee permitting such an amendment. The chairman offered to seek a similar waiver after the bill was reported if a majority of the committee wanted it.

Davis argued for more immediate action, moving to overturn the chairman's ruling. Davis contended that since a large minority of the House came from one-party districts where the election was decided in the primaries, there would be "a great inequity" if HR 1 were to apply only to general elections. This would also mean, noted Davis, that the PACs would simply buy influence in the primaries.

Speaking for the Republicans, Bill Frenzel of Minnesota voiced support for the Davis challenge, declaring that without it HR 1 was inconsistent and cut "close to the bone." Frenzel termed it the most important amendment facing the GOP.

Democrat John Burton of California countered that few one-party districts remained anywhere, even in the South, and that it would be wise to test public financing first in House general elections before extending it to primaries.

But it was Democrat Lucien N. Nedzi of Michigan who probably made the most significant argument. He contended that since the basic issue was maintaining orderly procedure, the chair's ruling should be upheld. He supported Thompson in urging that any vote to seek a waiver from the Rules Committee should be taken after HR 1 was reported.

By a one-vote margin, 11-12, the committee rejected Davis' motion. Three veteran northern Democrats who helped gut the 1977 public financing bill by voting to extend it to primaries, voted to sustain Thompson's ruling. All three — Annunzio, Hawkins and Minish — were subcommittee chairmen.

Helping Challengers

Noting the top-heavy Democratic House majority in recent years, Republican committee members tried unsuccessfully throughout the markup to amend the bill to aid challengers. Their first effort came with a series of amendments presented May 15 and 17 to lower the eligibility threshold for participation in the public financing system.

HR 1 originally required candidates to raise only $1,000 to become eligible for matching funds. To eliminate fringe candidates, Thompson raised the threshold to $10,000, although Republicans argued that the new figure was too high and discriminated against challengers who had limited fund-raising sources.

Gingrich suggested a dual threshold, with $10,000 for incumbents and $5,000 for challengers. Anticipating the reaction from Democratic incumbents, Thompson facetiously noted that "the chair registers a quake of about nine on the Richter scale." The Gingrich amendment and several others designed to lower the threshold were defeated.

Gingrich was more successful, though, in fashioning a compromise with Thompson that raised the amount of individual contributions that could be matched from $100 to $150. Gingrich initially had sought a $250 match, noting that it would be easier for challengers since it would require fewer contributors.

The $100 matching figure, he argued, was far too low and would simply drive candidates into the arms of direct-mail specialists. "In its passion for small contributors," Gingrich observed, "it should be called the Richard Viguerie memorial amendment."

The Republicans' second major effort came on May 21, when Stockman led the drive to remove the bill's spending ceiling. Although a co-sponsor of HR 1, Stockman argued in colorful language that a spending lid was "inherently reactionary," favoring incumbents and the status quo.

He contended that a spending lid in a public financing bill was like "blending oil and water." The only reason the two were combined, he claimed, was because the 1976 *Buckley v. Valeo* Supreme Court ruling struck down spending ceilings in all federal elections except the publicly financed presidential campaign.

Stockman noted that by tying spending limits to public financing, Democrats were using the only method they could to curb challengers' expenditures. HR 1, he concluded, "is a Trojan horse to breach the walls of *Buckley v. Valeo*."

Freshman Democratic Rep. William R. Ratchford of Connecticut responded that the current system, without any spending limits, was "like a reactor gone wild." Nearly all incumbents were winning re-election and access for newcomers was limited by personal or PAC wealth. The Stockman amendment, Ratchford declared, seems to be based on the assumption that "the most expensive campaign is the most representative campaign."

On the only party-line vote of the markup, nine Republicans voted to remove the spending limit, 12 Democrats voted to keep it.

Outlook: Waning Interest

Less than two weeks after HR 1 was defeated in the House Administration Committee, Democratic leaders decided against reviving the measure. They had been considering several alternative ways to bring the bill to the floor, but they were dissuaded by an unfavorable whip count that showed only a narrow majority of House Democrats would vote for HR 1. In the face of substantial Republican opposition, Democratic leaders decided the bill's prospects were bleak and dropped the fight.

According to Administration Committee counsel Bob Moss, HR 1 "is not dead; it's comatose." However, some proponents of revising campaign spending laws were considering a new battleground — political action committee spending limits. *(See p. 79)*

With public financing stopped in the House, interest in the issue also seemed to be flagging in the Senate. Hearings on a Senate version (S 623), scheduled to be held in the Rules Committee in early June, were indefinitely postponed. ∎

PACs: Major New Weapon for Lobbies

Whether they are praised as a healthy, new method of maximizing campaign contributions or denounced as an insidious outgrowth of post-Watergate legislation, political action committees (PACs) are assuming an increasingly important place in American politics.

According to the first Federal Election Commission (FEC) compilation of their spending, PACS contributed $35.1 million to federal candidates during the 1978 election cycle — the period between Jan. 1, 1977, and Dec. 31, 1978. That was nearly triple the $12.5 million in PAC contributions in 1974 and more than 50 percent above the 1976 level of $22.6 million. The 1974 and 1976 figures were based on Common Cause studies.

The FEC report on the 1978 elections indicated that more than two-thirds of the PAC money — $24.92 million — went to House candidates. Nearly all the rest of the money — $10.13 million — went to Senate candidates. Presidential contenders received the remaining $50,000 in PAC money.

The FEC advised that the 1978 figures could be altered by individual PACs filing late amendments, but a commission spokesman doubted there would be any large revision in the totals.

Spurred by the 1974 campaign finance law that limited individual contributions and favorable FEC rulings since then, the number of PACs more than tripled between December 1974 and June 1979. There were 1,938 PACs in operation during the 1978 campaign, with about three-quarters of them (1,459) making contributions to federal candidates. The FEC divided them into six categories, with three of them — trade, membership and health; labor; and corporate PACs — accounting for 90 percent ($31.6 million) of all PAC contributions. *(Chart, p. 76)*

The top three categories were closely grouped in their amount of contributions. A total of 399 trade, membership and health PACs gave $11.5 million to federal candidates; 211 labor committees gave $10.3 million, while 697 corporate PACs contributed $9.8 million. The remaining $3.5 million was given by what the FEC described as "no-connected" organizations (such as conservative and liberal ideological groups), cooperatives and corporations without stock.

The majority of PAC money — nearly $20 million — went to incumbents, with the remainder divided nearly evenly between challengers and candidates for open seats. This pro-incumbent bias was evident among all categories of PACs except the no-connected organizations, which gave their largest contributions to challengers. *(PAC contributions, box, p. 75)*

Thanks to a heavy Democratic tilt among labor committees, Democratic candidates enjoyed a modest advantage ($19.7 million to $15.3 million) over their Republican rivals in the battle for PAC funds. Labor contributed $9.7 million of its $10.3 million to Democratic candidates, offsetting less lopsided Republican biases among corporate, trade, membership and health, and no-connected organizations.

Democratic candidates actually were receiving a larger share of all PAC funds earlier in the fall campaign, but a late surge of non-labor money to Republican candidates in the closing weeks of the campaign reduced the Democrats' advantage.

Altogether, candidate contributions composed less than half of the $77.8 million disbursed by PACs in 1977-78. Of the six categories of PACs, only corporate and labor committees earmarked more than half their expenditures for candidate coffers.

'No-Connected' PACs

Committees in the group of no-connected organizations were most penurious, sending barely one-seventh of their money to federal candidates. The largest of the no-connected PACs, Ronald Reagan's Citizens for the Republic, contributed even a smaller share. Of $4.5 million in disbursements in 1977-78, the Reagan PAC made only $433,486 (9.6 percent) in candidate contributions. Much of the rest of the money went to pay a large staff, put out a newsletter and finance seminars and a large direct-mail operation.

The story was similar for other leading no-connected PACs. The National Conservative Political Action Committee (NCPAC) spent $3 million in the 1978 election cycle, $219,874 for federal candidates. The Committee for the Survival of a Free Congress (CSFC) had disbursements of $2 million, $241,233 to candidates, and the National Committee for an Effective Congress (NCEC) made candidate

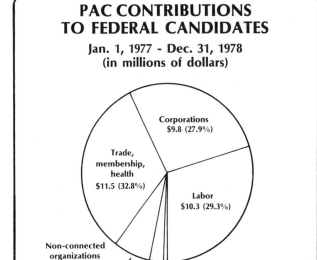

PAC CONTRIBUTIONS TO FEDERAL CANDIDATES

Jan. 1, 1977 - Dec. 31, 1978
(in millions of dollars)

Corporations
$9.8 (27.9%)

Trade, membership, health
$11.5 (32.8%)

Labor
$10.3 (29.3%)

Non-connected organizations
$2.5 (7.1%)

Cooperatives
$0.9 (2.6%)

Corporations without stock
$0.1 (0.3%)

Total contributions = $35.1 million.

NOTE: Each category's percentage of total PAC contributors to federal candidates during the 1977-78 election cycle is listed in parentheses.

SOURCE: Federal Election Commission.

contributions of $203,545 out of total expenditures of $1.1 million.

Citizens for the Republic, NCPAC and CSFC led all PACs in gross receipts and disbursements in 1977-78. The group that ranked fourth in disbursements, the American Medical Association PAC (AMPAC), directed nearly all its funds to federal candidates and ended up ranking number one in contributions. Of $1.9 million AMPAC spent during the 1978 campaign, $1,644,795 went to federal candidates.

AMPAC was joined by two other committees from the trade, membership and health category — the National Association of Realtors PAC and the National Automobile Dealers Association PAC — to comprise the top three in total contributions. But six of the other seven PACs in the overall top 10 were labor-related, led by the United Auto Workers committee.

Although as a group corporate PACs contributed nearly $10 million to federal candidates during the 1978 campaign, no single corporate committee made more than $175,000 in candidate contributions or came close to making the overall top 10. Corporate PACs exerted influence by sheer dint of numbers. There were nearly twice as many corporate committees active during the 1978 campaign as any other type, and the corporate category had shown the largest growth in recent years.

As a group, cooperatives contributed only $900,000 to federal candidates, but the category included three large dairy PACs that gave nearly the entire amount. The largest, the Associated Milk Producers PAC, contributed $446,161 to candidates and finished the campaign with more than $1.1 million cash on hand, the largest surplus of any PAC.

Contributions to Freshmen

On the eve of the House Administration Committee markup of legislation to provide for public financing of congressional elections (HR 1) in May 1979, Common Cause released a study indicating that nearly one-tenth of PAC contributions in 1977-78 ($3.3 million) went into the campaigns of the 77 candidates who entered the House as freshmen in 1979. On the average, the study disclosed, each freshman received $43,000 from PACs, just $2,000 below the average amount received by House committee chairmen.

According to Common Cause, the leading freshman recipient of PAC money was Democrat Phil Gramm of Texas, who received $119,387. He won the seat vacated by veteran Democrat Olin E. Teague. Two other freshmen collected more than $100,000 from PACs, Democrat Martin Frost of Texas and Republican Larry J. Hopkins of Kentucky.

Twenty-eight freshmen received between $50,000 and $100,000 in PAC money. More than three-quarters of the candidates receiving at least $50,000 from PACs were running for open seats, or seats where the incumbent was beaten in the primary. Of the seven general election challengers, six were Republicans. For most freshmen (43), PAC contributions represented at least 20 percent of their total receipts. Less than one-fifth (15) were elected with PAC money filling under 10 percent of their treasury.

Background: Growth of PACs

Because corporations and labor unions were prohibited by federal law from using corporate and union treasury funds for political contributions, PACs became a tightly regulated vehicle for political involvement by business and unions. Campaign contributions by political action committees must come from voluntary gifts to the PACs. But corporate and union funds may be used to establish and administer PACs and solicit money for them.

The emergence of corporate and labor PACs followed a long period when their activity was limited severely. In 1907 the Tillman Act banned corporate gifts of money to candidates for federal elective offices or to committees supporting the candidates. The ban was incorporated in the Federal Corrupt Practices Act of 1925, which extended the prohibition to cover contributions of "anything of value."

The Smith-Connally Act of 1943 and the Taft-Hartley Act of 1947 banned political contributions to federal candidates by unions from their members' dues. The Federal Election Campaign Act of 1971 modified that ban on corporations and unions specifically to allow the use of corporate funds and union treasury money for "the establishment, administration and solicitation of contributions to a separate, segregated fund to be utilized for a political purpose." Those funds became known commonly as PACs.

But the 1971 act did not make that modification to the ban on political contributions by government contractors. The result was that many corporations held back from forming PACs. Organized labor, which held government manpower contracts, became concerned it would be affected and led a move to have the law changed to permit government contractors to establish and administer PACs. That change was incorporated in the 1974 amendments to the federal election campaign law. The easing of that prohibition opened the way for the formation of corporate PACs. As one campaign finance expert said, "Labor pulled business' chestnuts out of the fire."

Corporations remained skittish about what they were permitted to do until November 1975, when the FEC released an opinion concerning Sun Oil Company's political committee, SunPAC, reaffirming that corporations could establish and administer PACs. But the six-member, bi-partisan commission was split on how wide an audience Sun would be allowed to solicit for its PAC. The majority held that Sun could solicit all employees, in addition to stockholders. The two dissenting commissioners argued that Sun could solicit only stockholders. Under federal law unions were permitted to solicit only their members.

The 1976 amendments to the Federal Election Campaign Act restricted the range of corporate solicitation to a company's management personnel and its stockholders. However, corporations and unions were given the right to solicit the other's group twice a year by mail. That authority has been little used.

The 1976 amendments also established restrictions on one company or one labor organization setting up a number of PACs to evade the ceiling of $5,000 on contributions by a PAC to a candidate in each election.

Under existing federal law, an individual could give up to $5,000 a year to a PAC. An individual also could give up to $1,000 to a candidate in each election. For the average union member, those limits were well above what he was likely to contribute politically. But for an affluent executive the limits provided several channels for large political contributions. Total political contributions by an individual in one year were not allowed to exceed $25,000.

The evolution of the federal law through 1976 made PACs more inviting to corporations. No better sign of that was the formation of PACs in 1977 by two business giants — General Motors and American Telephone & Telegraph.

Leading PACs in 1978 Elections

(Contributions made in 1977 and 1978)

ALL PACs

Contributions to Federal Candidates

1. American Medical Political
   Action Committee $1,644,795
   (American Medical Association)
2. Realtors Political Action Committee   1,122,378
   (National Association of Realtors)
3. Automobile and Truck Dealers
   Election Action Committee   975,675
   *(National Automobile Dealers
   Association)*
4. UAW Voluntary Community
   Action Program   964,465
   (United Auto Workers)
5. AFL-CIO COPE Political
   Contributions Committee   920,841
   (AFL-CIO)
6. United Steelworkers of America
   Political Action Fund   594,930
   (United Steelworkers of America)
7. Transportation Political
   Education League   557,603
   (United Transportation Union)
8. Machinists Non-Partisan
   Political League   536,538
   (Machinists and Aerospace Workers)
9. American Dental Political
   Action Committee   510,050
   (American Dental Association)
10. CWA-COPE Political
    Contributions Committee   474,633
    (Communications Workers of America)

Trade, Membership, Health

1. American Medical Political
   Action Committee   1,644,795
   (American Medical Association)
2. Realtors Political
   Action Committee   1,122,378
   (National Association of Realtors)
3. Automobile and Truck Dealers
   Election Action Committee   975,675
   *(National Automobile Dealers
   Association)*
4. American Dental Political
   Action Committee   510,050
   (American Dental Association)
5. Life Underwriters Political
   Action Committee   380,638
   *(National Association of
   Life Underwriters)*
6. NRA Political Victory Fund   369,412
   *(National Rifle Association of
   America)*
7. Attorneys Congressional
   Campaign Trust   350,350
   *(Association of Trial
   Lawyers of America)*

8. Conservative Victory Fund   273,104
   (American Conservative Union)
9. BANK PAC   232,180
   (American Bankers Association)
10. Commodity Futures Political Fund   217,675
    (Chicago Mercantile Exchange)

Labor

1. UAW Voluntary Community Action
   Program *(United Auto Workers)*   964,465
2. AFL-CIO COPE Political
   Contributions Committee   920,841
   (AFL-CIO)
3. United Steelworkers of America
   Political Action Fund   594,930
   (United Steelworkers of America)
4. Transportation Political
   Education League   557,603
   (United Transportation Union)
5. Machinists Non-Partisan
   Political League   536,538
   (Machinists and Aerospace Workers)
6. CWA-COPE Political
   Contributions Committee   474,633
   (Communications Workers of America)
7. MEBA Political Action Fund   409,180
   (Marine Engineers Beneficial Association)
8. Seafarers Political Activity Donation   390,552
   *(Seafarers International Union of
   North America)*
9. National Education Association
   Political Action Committee   335,347
   (National Education Association)
10. Railway Clerks Political League   322,058
    (Railway, Airline and Steamship Clerks)

Corporations

1. Voluntary Contributors for
   Better Government   173,056
   (International Paper Company)
2. Amoco Political Action Committee   154,800
   (Standard Oil of Indiana)
3. DARTPAC *(Dart Industries, Inc.)*   119,300
4. American Family Political
   Action Committee   113,650
   (American Family Corporation)
5. Sunbelt Good Government Committee   112,942
   (Winn-Dixie Stores, Inc.)
6. Non-Partisan Political Action Committee   112,020
   (General Electric Company)
7. Union Camp Political Action Committee   107,250
   (Union Camp Corporation)
8. Eaton Public Policy Association   101,000
   (Eaton Corporation)
9. Civic Involvement Program   99,725
   (General Motors Corporation)
10. United Technologies Corporation
    Political Action Committee   98,725
    (United Technologies Corporation)

Source: Federal Election Commission

Indeed, between 1975 and 1978 the number of corporate PACs more than quintupled, while the number of labor committees barely grew. Contributions by corporate and business-related trade PACs to all congressional candidates nearly tripled from 1974 to 1976, while labor PAC contributions increased by about 30 percent. In 1976 corporate and business-related trade PACs gave more than $6.9 million to congressional candidates in general elections, while labor PACs, including teacher associations, gave nearly $8.1 million.

How PACs Operate

Although the law permits corporate PACs to solicit stockholders, very few do. A U.S. Chamber of Commerce survey in April 1977 found that only 2 percent of the corporate PACs asked stockholders for contributions. "Stockholders are a broad and very diverse group," commented Frank S. Farrell, chairman of the Burlington Northern Employees Good Government Fund. "Many of them have differing political complexions and points of view. It's a question of whether it's worth the time and effort."

Management personnel are the main target for the corporate PACs, but corporations have varied widely in how far down into the management ranks they reached to solicit. The frequency of solicitation also has differed greatly among corporations.

Many of the larger corporations have used payroll withholding plans for their executives to make contributions. Some corporations have permitted a PAC contributor to designate which party was to receive his money or to allow the PAC to use it at its discretion. Decisions about which candidates would receive PAC contributions have been made by special committees of the PAC in many cases. But in some instances a PAC has not used a formal committee and has left the decisions up to the PAC chairman, who would consult informally with colleagues.

There has been less variation in solicitation practices among labor unions. Generally a union business agent or steward will solicit union members in person or in a group on an annual basis.

According to Al Zack, an AFL-CIO spokesman in Washington, few unions used payroll withholding for voluntary political contributions. If a company used payroll withholding to collect contributions from its executives, federal law required that payroll withholding be made available for a union to collect the political contributions of its members who work for the company. For the AFL-CIO Committee on Political Education (COPE) in each state to make a contribution, Zack said, a candidate must receive a two-thirds vote at a state labor convention or from a body designated by the convention.

Although corporate funds and union treasury money could not be used for political contributions, federal law allowed those funds to be used for non-partisan activities such as voter registration and get-out-the-vote drives. Labor unions have become skilled in these techniques, and those non-partisan efforts often have been designed to be of particular help to one candidate, as in get-out-the-vote drives in areas where pro-labor voters are known to predominate.

"Business is 20 years behind labor unions," commented Fred Radewagen, director of governmental and political participation programs for the U.S. Chamber of Commerce, about non-partisan methods. Part of the reason for that lag was that union memberships generally have been more cohesive and more easily mobilized through phone banks and targeting techniques than a company's executives and its stockholders, who are scattered throughout the country.

In the view of at least one union official, however, corporations have been catching up. Corporations "have made more effective use of trade union techniques than unions themselves," said William Dodds, national political director for the United Auto Workers.

Interviews with corporate PAC officials revealed no surge of interest in the use of non-partisan political programs as labor unions have employed them. But Stevenson Walker, a PAC specialist for the Public Affairs Council, a Washington-based association that had 325 corporate members in 1978, noted that there has been a gradual rise in sophistication in this area.

One of the least used political techniques by corporations has been partisan internal communications. Under federal law, corporations may spend company funds to send communications to their executives and their stockholders advocating the election or defeat of a candidate. If the costs of those communications exceed $2,000 in one election they must be reported to the FEC. Non-partisan political expen-

1977-78 PAC Contributions to Federal Candidates
(in millions of dollars)

| | Total Contributions | Party Affiliation | | Candidate Status | | |
		Dems.	Reps.	Incumbent	Challenger	Open
Trade, membership, health	$11.5	$ 5.0	$ 6.5	$ 6.7	$2.3	$2.5
Labor	10.3	9.7	0.6	6.1	2.2	2.0
Corporations	9.8	3.6	6.1	5.8	2.0	2.0
No-connected organizations	2.5	0.7	1.9	0.7	1.1	0.7
Cooperatives	0.9	0.6	0.2	0.6	0.1	0.2
Corporations without stock	0.1	0.1	0.0	0.1	0.0	0.0
Total	$35.1	$19.7	$15.3	$19.9	$7.7	$7.4

Note: Figures within the party affiliation and candidate status columns do not always equal the total contributions figure because of rounding.   *Source: Federal Election Commission.*

ditures by corporations and unions, as well as the cost of administering PACs, do not have to be reported.

Labor unions have a similar right to use members' dues to send partisan communications to their members. And they have used it much more than corporations. A study by the FEC showed that in 1976, 66 labor groups spent $2,014,326 for internal partisan communications, while four corporations spent $31,045. One membership group — the National Rifle Association — spent about $100,000. Most of the money was spent in the presidential contest, rather than for congressional races. President Carter was the overwhelming beneficiary. Expenditures in behalf of Carter totaled $1,160,432, while $44,249 was spent advocating the election of former President Ford. None of the funds was spent advocating Carter's defeat, but $43,958 was expended calling for Ford's defeat.

Most of the partisan communication money — 87.1 percent — went for direct mailings. Other uses included brochures, phone banks, posters, car stickers and peanuts, according to the FEC.

There has been considerable wariness in corporate circles about making partisan communications. "I question whether it is our business to educate people [stockholders and executives] on behalf of one candidate with stockholder money," commented Stephen K. Galpin, secretary of General Electric's Nonpartisan Political Support Committee. "That is a legitimacy question. But there is a credibility problem. Would it do any good?"

1978 Efforts to Control PACs

A move by Democratic congressional leaders early in 1978 to add controversial provisions placing limits on PAC spending were largely responsible for the defeat of a bill that would extend public financing to congressional elections. The attempt brought united Republican opposition and criticism from public financing backers, who claimed that it "poisoned the well" for their proposal. As a result, by a vote of 198-209, the House March 19 defeated the rule to allow consideration of the public financing/PAC bill (HR 11315). After the vote the bill was placed on a back burner and not brought up the rest of the session. *(Details, public financing chapter, p. 67)*

An analysis of party contributions to House candidates in 1976 and a compilation of party finances for most of 1977 by the FEC showed how seriously the Republicans could be crippled by the proposed changes.

In 1976, 39 percent of the Republican House candidates received more than $10,000 from party committees. Only 11 percent of the Democratic candidates, in contrast, received at least $10,000 from party sources.

In 1977, while affiliated Democratic committees raised $8 million through most of the year, Republican committees raised more than three times as much, $24.3 million. The cash-on-hand disparity was even greater, with Republican committees enjoying a nearly 10-1 advantage over their Democratic counterparts, $8.2 million to $867,000.

In 1978 last-minute injections of cash by corporate and trade association PACs boosted the campaigns of Republican congressional candidates. The business PACs — some participating in their first campaigns — apparently set aside at least a third of their budgets for contributions to many Republicans and some moderate Democrats in the final weeks before the Nov. 7 elections.

Labor unions, which had run PAC-type committees for years, followed tradition in giving almost all their money to

Top 1978 PAC Money Recipients

There were 176 House candidates who received at least $50,000 in contributions from political action committees (PACs) in the 1978 election cycle. The chart lists the top 50 recipients of PAC contributions. An "I" indicates an incumbent, a "C" a challenger, and an "O" an open seat. An asterisk (*) appears next to the names of winners.

	PAC Contributions	% of Total Receipts
John E. Porter, R-Ill. (C)	$171,906	31.4
Bob Gammage, D-Texas (I)	153,403	32.1
John M. Murphy, D-N.Y.* (I)	145,701	70.7
Mark W. Hannaford, D-Calif. (I)	143,791	44.0
Garry Brown, R-Mich. (I)	137,204	60.7
Thomas S. Foley, D-Wash.* (I)	127,450	41.5
John J. McFall, D-Calif. (I)	124,775	57.9
Phil Gramm, D-Texas* (O)	124,487	22.5
Larry J. Hopkins, R-Ky.* (C)	124,426	42.2
John Nance Garner, R-Wash. (O)	124,101	37.8
John E. Cunningham, R-Wash. (I)	113,844	22.1
Martin Frost, D-Texas* (I)	113,795	32.6
John J. Rhodes, R-Ariz.* (I)	112,661	56.2
Thomas A. Luken, D-Ohio* (I)	110,758	47.8
Dan Rostenkowski, D-Ill.* (I)	110,709	59.6
Dan Marriott, R-Utah* (I)	110,228	32.0
David W. Evans, D-Ind.* (I)	108,142	50.8
Daniel B. Crane, R-Ill.* (O)	107,034	24.4
Les AuCoin, D-Ore.* (I)	105,411	41.7
Charles J. Carney, D-Ohio (I)	101,362	71.2
Ed Scott, R-Colo. (C)	100,255	17.9
Timothy E. Wirth, D-Colo.* (I)	99,447	23.9
Jim Wright, D-Texas* (I)	95,979	35.3
Vic Fazio, D-Calif.* (O)	95,949	40.7
Jerry Huckaby, D-La.* (I)	95,168	24.9
James R. Jones, D-Okla.* (I)	95,070	40.3
Bob Eckhardt, D-Texas* (I)	94,658	33.1
Elford A. Cederberg, R-Mich. (I)	92,780	62.5
Samuel L. Devine, R-Ohio* (I)	92,579	58.5
Marty Russo, D-Ill.* (I)	89,815	41.3
Jim Jeffries, R-Kan.* (C)	88,187	26.4
E. Thomas Coleman, R-Mo.* (I)	84,374	29.4
Leo K. Thorsness, R-S.D. (O)	83,905	31.0
Robert A. Young, D-Mo.* (I)	83,565	46.9
Howard Wolpe, D-Mich.* (C)	83,423	37.7
John J. Duncan, R-Tenn.* (I)	83,229	48.7
Tony P. Hall, D-Ohio* (O)	83,218	38.4
Fred B. Rooney, D-Pa.* (I)	82,126	67.4
Tom Tauke, R-Iowa* (C)	81,843	32.6
Thomas A. Daschle, D-S.D.* (O)	81,216	36.0
James G. Martin, R-N.C.* (I)	81,005	31.7
Claude Pepper, D-Fla.* (I)	80,600	33.3
David G. Crane, R-Ind. (C)	80,467	19.0
Dan Lungren, R-Calif.* (C)	79,741	29.4
Doug Walgren, D-Pa.* (I)	79,689	45.1
Guy Vander Jagt, R-Mich.* (I)	79,681	39.0
Abner J. Mikva, D-Ill.* (I)	79,191	19.4
Floyd Fithian, D-Ind.* (I)	79,095	38.4
Frank Wolf, R-Va. (C)	78,883	33.7
Jim Mattox, D-Texas* (I)	78,462	27.8

SOURCE: Compiled by Congressional Quarterly from a Federal Election Commission study.

Democrats. The two biggest union funds, sponsored by the AFL-CIO and the United Auto Workers, virtually ignored Democrats who deserted labor on the key issues of labor law revision and common site picketing during the 95th Congress.

Although they had eagerly dispensed hundreds of contributions, some officials of political committees began to worry about the publicity that had resulted from their attempts to influence elections.

"We're in a fishbowl," said an executive for the Voluntary Contributors for Better Government, sponsored by the International Paper Co. "Everybody sees everything we do." Another trade association executive, who asked not to be identified, said huge contributions by special interest groups "could be self-defeating in the long run. It gets to be an easy target for people to shoot at."

Publicity about corporate, trade association and labor contributions "is just the kind of thing that will lead to a cry for public financing of elections," he said.

Apparent Spending Trends

Congressional Quarterly examined the 1977-78 contributions, through Oct. 23, 1978 (when the final pre-election FEC reports were filed) of 10 major PACs sponsored by labor unions, businesses, trade associations and other interest groups. Contributions by the 10 PACs appeared to follow definite trends.

Business. CQ examined six political action committees sponsored by businesses, trade associations and professional groups. Among them, the American Medical Political Action Committee contributed nearly $1.6 million through Oct. 23, and the realtors group contributed nearly $1.2 million. Both were among the largest of all PACs.

The other business and trade groups examined by CQ, and the total amount of contributions were: the Amoco Political Action Committee, sponsored by the Standard Oil Co. of Indiana ($144,600); the Automobile and Truck Dealers Election Action Committee ($950,275); the Business-Industry Political Action Committee, an independent group ($178,000); and the Voluntary Contributors for Better Government, sponsored by the International Paper Co. ($162,852).

These groups jumped into the campaign late in 1977 and early in 1978, making big pre-primary contributions of $1,000-to-$5,000 each to selected Republicans.

The groups also scattered dozens of smaller pre-primary and early summer contributions to conservative and moderate incumbent Democrats. Most of these contributions to Democrats were less than $1,000 each.

The PACs used several standards for making their contributions. Ralph W. Kittle, chairman of the International Paper Co. political committee, said his group's contributions were based on an incumbent's voting record and on the "general qualities" of a non-incumbent.

The Auto Dealers group, on the other hand, selected its candidates largely on the basis of how helpful they would be in congressional committees, according to a spokesman. "We're looking especially for members who serve on key committees, and people who help us on the floor," the spokesman said.

The business groups were not reluctant to contribute the maximum $10,000 each to Republican challengers of liberal Democrats. (Under existing law, PACs could give $5,000 each for primary and general elections.)

Even though PACs may have been growing bolder in their opposition to incumbents, however, they found it prudent to spread smaller contributions among a variety of Democrats seeking re-election, liberals as well as conservatives.

However, the business and trade groups became somewhat more partisan as election day approached. Prior to September, those groups gave an average of 60 to 65 percent of their contributions to Republicans, with the rest going to Democrats. But during September and the first three weeks of October, 70 to 75 percent of their contributions went to Republicans.

Labor. Labor unions' experience in the PAC business has shown them that it is best to stick with their friends, and they did just that in 1977-78 campaign contributions.

CQ examined all contributions made by the two biggest union PACs: the Committee on Political Education (COPE) sponsored by the AFL-CIO, and the United Auto Workers' Voluntary Community Action Program.

COPE contributed $833,200 to congressional candidates through Oct. 23; all but $27,600 went to Democrats. The UAW committee contributed $888,625, with all but $32,550 going to Democrats. Two liberal senators got most of the limited COPE and UAW money given to Republicans; Sen. Edward W. Brooke, R-Mass. ($20,000 combined), and Sen. Charles H. Percy, R-Ill. ($12,500 combined). (Brooke did not win re-election.)

The bulk of the money from the two groups went to moderate-to-liberal Democrats from northern states. Labor contributions often have not been welcomed by Democratic candidates in the South, where union membership was low and Republican candidates sometimes sought to portray liberal Democrats as labor lackeys.

After the defeat of the common-site picketing bill in 1977 and the labor law revision bill in 1978, some union officials said labor groups might boycott or even try to defeat Democrats who had deserted them on those two issues.

Instead, the two biggest groups simply concentrated their money on Democrats who supported the key labor issues. The AFL-CIO and COPE virtually ignored most Democrats who voted against one or both of the labor bills, but half of those Democrats were southerners who might not have received direct labor support in any event. Both the UAW and AFL-CIO concentrated some of their biggest contributions on incumbent Democrats who faced trouble in the general election.

Conservatives. Conservative political groups had plenty to rejoice about on election night 1978; many of their candidates did better than expected in House and Senate races.

CQ examined the complete contributions through Oct. 23 for the National Conservative Political Action Committee (NCPAC) and the Gun Owners of America Campaign Committee. Both groups gave most of their money to Republicans: 79 percent for NCPAC and 93 percent for the Gun Owners.

The two conservative groups concentrated more on open seats and on challenging incumbents than the other PACs examined. *(Boxscore on pressure groups' support of congressional candidates, p. 81)*

House Curbs Sought in 1979

If supporters of overhauling federal campaign finance law had their way, many House members would have to develop new fund-raising sources for their 1980 campaigns.

Joined by 130 co-sponsors, Democrat David R. Obey of Wisconsin and Republican Tom Railsback of Illinois in

Major PAC Contributions to 1978 House Candidates

The chart shows the number of Democratic and Republican House candidates who received at least $50,000 from political action committees (PACs) during the 1978 election cycle. The recipients are classified by winners and losers and by whether candidates were incumbents, challengers or running for open seats. An open seat is one in which an incumbent did not seek re-election in either the primary or general election. The numbers were tabulated by Congressional Quarterly from Federal Election Commission figures.

Party	Winners				Losers				All Candidates			
	Incum-bents	Chal-lengers	Open	Total	Incum-bents	Chal-lengers	Open	Total	Incum-bents	Chal-lengers	Open	Total
Democrats	65	4	12	81	9	3	4	16	74	7	16	97
Republicans	29	13	15	57	3	13	6	22	32	26	21	79
Amount of contribution:												
$100,000 +	8	2	2	12	6	2	1	9	14	4	3	21
$75,000-$99,999	21	6	4	31	2	2	2	6	23	8	6	37
$50,000-$74,999	65	9	21	95	4	12	7	23	69	21	28	118
Total	94	17	27	138	12	16	10	38	106	33	37	176

1979 introduced legislation in the House to curb contributions by PACs to House candidates.

As originally introduced HR 4970 cut in half the maximum a PAC could contribute to a candidate to $2,500 per primary, runoff or general election. The bill also would limit the total amount a candidate could accept from all PACs to $50,000 during an election cycle.

In an effort to gain more support, the sponsors revised the plan to raise the contribution limit to $3,000 per election for each PAC and to increase the total a candidate could receive from all PACs to $70,000. Candidates with runoffs could receive up to $85,000.

For House contests, HR 4970 also would place a 30-day limit on any extension of credit above $1,000 by PACs, political consultants and other vendors of media advertising or direct mail. The provision was aimed particularly at curtailing the role of large campaign specialists such as Richard Viguerie and Gerald Rafshoon.

But the heart of the bill was the PAC limitations, and both sides agreed that passage of HR 4970 could bring major changes in fund raising for House contests. No part of the bill would apply to Senate campaigns.

Nearly one-third of the House was elected in 1978 with the help of PAC contributions that exceeded the $50,000 cutoff proposed in the Obey-Railsback bill. According to a Congressional Quarterly tabulation of Federal Election Commission figures, there were 176 candidates in 1978 who received at least $50,000 in PAC contributions. A total of 138 of them won. *(Major PAC contributions, box, above)*

More than three-quarters of the leading Democratic beneficiaries of PAC money were incumbents. Among Republicans, though, the PAC contributions were more evenly distributed among incumbents, challengers and candidates for open seats.

While most of the candidates receiving more than $50,000 in PAC donations won, there were some notable exceptions, particularly among the largest recipients of PAC largess.

Of the 21 candidates who collected more than $100,000 from PACs, nine lost, including six incumbents.

PAC contributions represented 25 percent of the total receipts of House candidates in 1978 — up from 14 percent in 1972 and 23 percent in 1976.

But for most of the leading recipients, PAC money represented a much larger share of their total treasury. PAC contributions comprised more than 25 percent of the war chests of all but eight of the top recipients. *(Leading PAC money recipients, p. 77)*

Supporters of the Obey-Railsback bill claimed that the growth in PAC contributions was undermining the effectiveness and the integrity of Congress. PAC donations, they said, were designed to win influence on legislation of interest to the donors.

Backers of HR 4970 warned that action must be taken quickly if expanding PAC influence was to be curbed. "Unless there are some new controls on the PAC movement," contended Common Cause Vice President Fred Wertheimer, "we will see no controls for some time, if at all."

Opponents of the Obey-Railsback bill countered that rather than being curbed, PACs should be encouraged. They said that PACs raise money through voluntary donations from thousands of their members and that contributions to candidates are a legitimate exercise of their constitutional rights. "We're talking about voluntary contributions," said former Rep. Clark MacGregor, R-Miss. (1961-71), chairman of the United Technologies Corporation Political Action Committee, "not windfall profits by some insensitive corporation."

Critics doubted that enactment of HR 4970 would bring a new emphasis on small contributors. Instead, they saw a rise in wealthy candidates who finance their own campaigns, a movement by many PACs into independent expenditures to avoid the limits on contributions and more burdensome paperwork and bureaucracy.

Besides, opponents said, more money is needed in politics, not less. "More dollars were spent on fireworks last year than all congressional elections combined," claimed Guy Vander Jagt of Michigan, chairman of the National Republican Congressional Committee.

Most of the backers of the Obey-Railsback plan also supported public financing for House general election campaigns (HR 1), a measure that was defeated in the House Administration Committee in May. The Obey-Railsback plan was proposed in the wake of the defeat of the public financing bill. *(Public financing, p. 67)*

One of the major goals of HR 1 — curbing the influence of PACs — would be accomplished by the Obey-Railsback bill. Opponents were fearful that passage of HR 4970 could renew interest in public financing.

On Sept. 19, 1979, the House Rules Committee cleared the way for floor action on the Obey-Railsback plan. By a 5-10 vote the committee rejected a move that would have prohibited floor consideration of the PAC limitation proposal as part of the FEC authorization bill (S 832), which had passed the Senate in April.

Even though the Obey-Railsback plan was not germane, the Rules Committee permitted its consideration during floor debate on S 832.

House Passes Bill

Although opponents of the plan succeeded in delaying floor action for a time, the House Oct. 17, by a vote of 217-198, passed the compromise measure — despite heavy lobbying by business and conservative groups. The bill would reduce to $6,000 from the existing $10,000 the amount a House candidate could receive from a single PAC during each two-year election cycle, and it would place a $70,000 limit on the total amount he or she could receive from all PACs.

"The House needs to be taken off the auction block before the 1980 elections," said Rep. Frank Thompson Jr., D-N.J., arguing for passage of the legislation. Also speaking in favor of the bill was Speaker Thomas P. O'Neill Jr., D-Mass., who said that the "grab of special interests is staggering. It will destroy the legislative process. This is a matter of decency for the future of Congress."

Opponents — primarily Republicans (124 Republicans voted against the bill and 29 voted for passage) — countered that the legislation was an "incumbent protection bill." "There is nothing inherently evil about PACs," said Rep. Robert K. Dornan, R-Calif., who described the growth of PACs as "healthy" for the political process because it spurred citizens to become involved in the political process.

Following the House action, the bill, which also authorized funds for the FEC, went to House-Senate conference, where the outlook appeared uncertain in mid-October. Although the Senate usually refrains from interfering in rules applying only to House members, some Senate Republicans mentioned the possibility of staging a filibuster against the bill. ∎

Winners and Losers

How They Fared in 1978

Conservative pressure groups were generally pleased with the results of the 1978 elections, with labor and liberal groups licking their wounds and savoring their few triumphs. On the following pages, Congressional Quarterly offers a boxscore reporting how candidates backed by any of seven national pressure groups did in Senate and House contests. An asterisk denotes an incumbent member of Congress. (*Names of the seven groups, p. 82*)

Senate

	COPE[1]	NCEC[2]	UAW[3]	ACA[4]	BIPAC[5]	CSFC[6]	NCPAC[7]
ALABAMA							
Heflin (D)	W						
Martin (R)				L	L		L
Stewart (D)	W	W					
ALASKA							
Hobbs (D)							L
Stevens (R)*	W						W
ARKANSAS							
Pryor (D)							W
Kelly (R)				L			
COLORADO							
Haskell (D)*	L	L	L				
Armstrong (R)				W	W	W	W
DELAWARE							
Biden (D)*	W						
Baxter Jr. (R)						L	L
GEORGIA							
Nunn (D)*				W			W
IDAHO							
Jensen (D)	L						
McClure (R)*				W			W
ILLINOIS							
Percy (R)*	W		W				
IOWA							
Clark (D)*	L	L	L				
Jepsen (R)					W		W
KANSAS							
Roy (D)	L	L	L				
Kassebaum (R)				W			
KENTUCKY							
Huddleston (D)*	W		W				
Guenthner (R)							L
MAINE							
Hathaway (D)*	L	L					
Cohen (R)				W			
Gahagan (I)							L
MASSACHUSETTS							
Brooke (R)*	L		L				
MICHIGAN							
Levin (D)	W	W	W				
Griffin (R)*					L		L
MINNESOTA							
Six-year term							
Anderson (DFL)*	L	L	L				
Boschwitz (I-R)				W	W	W	W
Four-year term							
Short (DFL)	L						
Durenberger (I-R)				W	W		
MISSISSIPPI							
Dantin (D)	L						
Cochran (R)			W				W
MONTANA							
Baucus (D)	W	W					
Williams (R)							L
NEBRASKA							
Exon (D)	W		W				W
Shasteen (R)				L			L
NEW HAMPSHIRE							
McIntyre (D)*	L		L				
Humphrey (R)						W	W
NEW JERSEY							
Bradley (D)	W	W	W				
Bell (R)				L	L	L	L
NEW MEXICO							
Anaya (D)	L		L				
Domenici (R)*				W			W
NORTH CAROLINA							
Ingram (D)	L	L	L				
Helms (R)*				W	W		W
OKLAHOMA							
Boren (D)							W
Kamm (R)				L			L
OREGON							
Cook (D)							L
RHODE ISLAND							
Pell (D)*	W	W	W				
SOUTH CAROLINA							
Ravenel (D)	L	L					
Thurmond (R)*				W	W		W
SOUTH DAKOTA							
Barnett (D)	L						
TENNESSEE							
Eskind (D)	L						
Baker Jr. (R)*				W			
TEXAS							
Krueger (D)	L		L				
Tower (R)				W	W		W
VIRGINIA							
Miller (D)	L	L	L				
Warner (R)				W	W	W	W
WEST VIRGINIA							
Randolph (D)*	W		W				
Moore Jr. (R)				L		L	L
WYOMING							
Whitaker (D)	L						
Simpson (R)				W		W	W

House

	COPE[1]	NCEC[2]	UAW[3]	ACA[4]	BIPAC[5]	CSFC[6]	NCPAC[7]
ALABAMA							
1 Edwards (R)*				W			W
2 Mitchell (D)	L						L
Dickinson (R)*				W			W
3 Nichols (D)*							W
4 Bevill (D)*	W						W
5 Flippo (D)*	W						
6 Buchanan (R)*				W			
7 Shelby (D)	W						
ALASKA							
AL Rodey (D)	L						
Young (R)*			W				W
ARIZONA							
1 Rhodes (R)*				W			W
2 Udall (D)*	W						
Richey (R)				L		L	L
3 Stump (D)*				W			W
4 Rudd (R)*				W			W

Seven Groups

1. **American Federation of Labor — Congress of Industrial Organizations, Committee on Political Education.** Candidates endorsed locally by state. List completed Oct. 21, 1978.
2. **National Committee for an Effective Congress.** Endorsed candidates compiled from data provided by national committee Oct. 10, 1978.
3. **United Automobile, Aerospace and Agricultural Implement Workers of America (UAW).** Local endorsements as compiled by regional Voluntary Community Action Program offices week of Oct. 20, 1978.
4. **Americans for Constitutional Action.** Endorsements released Oct. 31, 1978.
5. **Business-Industry Political Action Committee.** Candidates endorsed as of Oct. 18, 1978.
6. **Committee for the Survival of a Free Congress.** Endorsed candidates as of Sept. 25, 1978.
7. **National Conservative Political Action Committee.** Endorsements obtained from national committee Nov. 1, 1978.

	COPE[1]	NCEC[2]	UAW[3]	ACA[4]	BIPAC[5]	CSFC[6]	NCPAC[7]
ARKANSAS							
2 Brandon (D)	L		L				
Bethune (R)					W		W
3 Hammerschmidt (R)*							W
4 Anthony (D)							W
CALIFORNIA							
1 Johnson (D)*	W		W				
Taylor (R)							L
2 Bork (D)		L	L				
Clausen (R)*				W			W
3 Matsui (D)	W		W				
4 Fazio (D)	W	W	W				
Hime (R)				L		L	L
5 Burton, J (D)*	W		W				
6 Burton, P (D)*	W		W				
7 Miller (D)*	W		W				
8 Dellums (D)*	W		W				
9 Stark (D)*	W		W				
10 Edwards (D)*	W		W				
11 Ryan (D)*	W		W				
12 Olsen (D)	L						
McCloskey Jr. (R)*			W				
13 Mineta (D)*	W		W				
14 McFall (D)*	L		L				
Shumway (R)				W	W	W	W
15 Coelho (D)	W		W				
16 Panetta (D)*	W	W	W				
Seastrand (R)					L	L	L
17 Krebs (D)*			L				
Pashayan Jr. (R)				W			
18 Sogge (D)	L	L	L				
Thomas (R)					W		W
19 Lagomarsino (R)*							W
20 Lear (D)			L				
Goldwater Jr. (R)*				W			W

	COPE[1]	NCEC[2]	UAW[3]	ACA[4]	BIPAC[5]	CSFC[6]	NCPAC[7]
21 Corman (D)*	W		W				
Walsh (R)							L
22 Henry (D)	L		L				
Moorhead (R)*				W	•		W
23 Beilenson (D)*	W		W				
24 Waxman (D)*	W		W				
25 Roybal (D)*	W		W				
26 Rousselot (R)*				W			W
27 Peck (D)	L	L	L				
Dornan (R)*				W	W		W
28 Dixon (D)	W		W				
29 Hawkins (D)*	W		W				
30 Danielson (D)*	W		W				
31 Wilson (D)*	W		W				
32 Anderson (D)*	W		W				
33 Kazarian (D)	L	L	L				
Grisham (R)					W		W
34 Hannaford (D)*	L	L	L				
Lungren (R)				W	W	W	W
35 Lloyd (D)*	W		W				
Dreier (R)							L
36 Brown Jr. (D)*	W		W				
37 Corcoran (D)	L						
Lewis (R)							W
38 Patterson (D)*	W		W				
Goedeke (R)					L		
39 Farris (D)	L		L				
Dannemeyer (R)				W		W	W
40 McGuy (D)	L						
Badham (R)*				W			W
41 Golden Jr. (D)	L		L				
Wilson (R)*				W			W
42 Van Deerlin (D)*	W		W				
43 Brooks (D)			L				
Burgener (R)*				W			W
COLORADO							
1 Schroeder (D)*	W	W	W				
Hutcheson (R)					L		L
2 Wirth (D)*	W	W	W				
Scott (R)					L	L	L
3 Kogovsek (D)	W	W					
McCormick (R)							L
4 Smith (D)	L						
5 Frank (D)	L						
Kramer (R)				W	W	W	W
CONNECTICUT							
1 Cotter (D)*	W		W				
2 Dodd (D)*	W		W				
3 Giaimo (D)*	W		W				
Pucciano (R)					L		L
4 Morgan (D)	L						
5 Ratchford (D)	W	W	W				
Guidera (R)					L		
6 Moffett (D)*	W	W	W				
MacKinnon (R)					L		
DELAWARE							
AL Hindes (D)	L						
Evans Jr. (R)*					W		W
FLORIDA							
1 Hutto (D)	W						W
Briggs (R)						L	L
3 Bennett (D)*	W						
4 Chappell Jr. (D)*				W			
5 Best (D)	L						
Kelly (R)*					W	W	W
6 Christison (D)	L						
Young (R)*					W		W

	COPE[1]	NCEC[2]	UAW[3]	ACA[4]	BIPAC[5]	CSFC[6]	NCPAC[7]
8 Ireland (D)*							W
9 Nelson (D)	W	W					W
Gurney (R)				L			L
10 Bafalis (R)*				W			W
11 Mica (D)							W
James (R)			L	L			L
12 Stack (D)	W						W
Burke (R)*				L			L
13 Lehman (D)*	W						
14 Pepper (D)*	W						
Cardenas (R)							L
15 Fascell (D)*	W						
GEORGIA							
1 Ginn (D)*							W
2 Mathis (D)*							W
3 Brinkley (D)*				W			W
6 Shapard (D)		L					
Gingrich (R)				W	W		W
7 McDonald (D)*				W			W
8 Evans (D)*							W
9 Jenkins (D)*				W			W
10 Barnard (D)*				W			W
HAWAII							
1 Heftel (D)*	W						
2 Akaka (D)*	W						
IDAHO							
1 Truby (D)	L	L					
Symms (R)*				W	W		W
2 Kress (D)	L	L					
Hansen (R)*				W	W		W
ILLINOIS							
1 Stewart (D)	W						
2 Murphy (D)*	W						
3 Russo (D)*	W		W				
Dunne (R)				L	L	L	L
4 Thomas (D)	L						
Derwinski (R)*				W			W
5 Fary (D)*	W						
6 Quinn (D)	L						
Hyde (R)*	W						W
7 Collins (D)*	W						
8 Rostenkowski (D)*	W						
9 Yates (D)*	W						
10 Mikva (D)*	W	W	W				
Porter (R)				L	L		L
11 Annunzio (D)*	W						
12 Bogen (D)	L						
Crane (R)*				W			W
13 Steffen (D)	L						
McClory (R)*				W			
14 Romanyak (D)	L						
Erlenborn (R)*							W
15 Hall (D)	L						
Corcoran (R)*				W	W		W
17 Sinclair (D)	L						
O'Brien (R)*							W
18 Michel (R)*				W			W
20 Roberts (D)	L						
Findley (R)*				W			
21 Madigan (R)*							W
22 Bruce (D)	L	L	L				
Crane (R)				W	W		W
23 Price (D)*	W						
24 Simon (D)*	W						
INDIANA							
1 Benjamin Jr. (D)*	W		W				
2 Fithian (D)*	W	W	W				

	COPE[1]	NCEC[2]	UAW[3]	ACA[4]	BIPAC[5]	CSFC[6]	NCPAC[7]
Oppenheim (R)				L		L	L
3 Brademas (D)*	W		W				
Thorsen (R)						L	L
4 Walda (D)	L		L				
Quayle (R)*							W
5 Hillis (R)*	W		W				
6 Evans (D)*	W	W	W				
Crane (R)				L		L	L
7 Zietlow (D)	L	L	L				
Myers (R)*				W	W		W
8 Cornwell (D)*	L	L	L				
Deckard (R)					W	W	W
9 Hamilton (D)*	W		W				
10 Sharp (D)*	W	W	W				
Frazier (R)				L		L	L
11 Jacobs Jr. (D)*	W						
IOWA							
1 Myers (D)	L		L				
Leach (R)*							W
2 Blouin (D)*	L	L	L				
Tauke (R)				W	W		W
3 Knudson (D)	L						
Grassley (R)*			W				W
4 Smith (D)*	W		W				
5 Harkin (D)*	W	W	W				
6 Bedell (D)*	W	W	W				
Junker (R)				L			
KANSAS							
1 Sebelius (R)*			W				W
2 Keys (D)*	L	L	L				
Jeffries (R)				W	W	W	W
3 Winn Jr. (R)*			W				W
4 Glickman (D)*	W		W				
Litsey (R)							L
5 Allegrucci (D)	L	L					
Whittaker (R)				W	W		W
KENTUCKY							
1 Hubbard Jr. (D)*			W				
2 Natcher (D)*	W		W				
3 Mazzoli (D)*	W		W				
4 Martin (D)			L				
Snyder (R)*				W			W
5 Carter (R)*							W
6 Easterly (D)	L		L				
Hopkins (R)				W	W		W
7 Perkins (D)*	W		W				
LOUISIANA							
2 Boggs (D)*	W		W				
3 Treen (R)*							W
4 Leach (D)			W				W
Wilson (R)						L	L
5 Huckaby (D)*							W
6 Moore (R)*							W
7 Breaux (D)*	W						W
8 Long (D)*	W		W				
MAINE							
1 Quinn (D)	L						
2 Gartley (D)	L						L
Snowe (R)							W
MARYLAND							
1 Quinn (D)			L				
Bauman (R)*				W			W
2 Long (D)*			W				
3 Mikulski (D)*	W		W				
4 Ward (D)	L		L				
Holt (R)*				W			W
5 Spellman (D)*	W	W	W				

	COPE[1]	NCEC[2]	UAW[3]	ACA[4]	BIPAC[5]	CSFC[6]	NCPAC[7]
6 Byron (D)			W				W
7 Mitchell (D)*	W		W				
8 Barnes (D)	W						
Steers Jr. (R)*	L		L				
MASSACHUSETTS							
1 Conte (R)*	W		W				
1 Boland (D)*	W		W				
3 Early (D)*	W		W				
4 Drinan (D)*	W		W				
5 Shannon (D)	W	W					
Buckley (R)					L		
6 Mavroules (D)	W	W					
Bronson (R)				L	L		L
7 Markey (D)*	W		W				
8 O'Neill Jr. (D)*	W		W				
9 Moakley (D)*	W		W				
10 Heckler (R)*	W		W				
11 Donnelly (D)	W						W
12 Studds (D)*	W		W				
MICHIGAN							
1 Conyers Jr. (D)*	W		W				
2 Pursell (R)*	W						
3 Wolpe (D)	W	W	W				
Brown (R)*				L	L		L
4 Hager Jr. (D)	L		L				
Stockman (R)*				W			W
5 Sprik (D)	L		L				
Sawyer (R)*				W			W
6 Carr (D)*	W	W	W				
Conlin (R)					L		L
7 Kildee (D)*	W		W				
8 Traxler (D)*	W		W				
9 Leroux (D)	L		L				
Vander Jagt (R)*				W			W
10 Albosta (D)	W		W				
Cederberg (R)*				L	L		L
11 McLeod (D)	L	L	L				L
Davis (R)					W		W
12 Bonior (D)*	W		W				
Holmes (R)						L	L
13 Diggs Jr. (D)*	W						
14 Nedzi (D)*	W		W				
15 Ford (D)*	W		W				
16 Dingell (D)*	W		W				
17 Brodhead (D)*	W		W				
18 Blanchard (D)*	W		W				
19 Collier (D)	L		L				
Broomfield (R)*				W			W
MINNESOTA							
1 Sikorski (DFL)	L	L	L				
Erdahl (I-R)				W	W		W
2 Considine (DFL)	L		L				
Hagedorn (I-R)*				W			W
3 Freeman (DFL)	L		L				
4 Vento (DFL)*	W		W				
5 Sabo (DFL)	W		W				
Till (I-R)					L		
6 Nolan (DFL)*	W	W	W				
Bjorhus (I-R)					L		
7 Wenstrom (DFL)	L	L	L				
Stangeland (I-R)*				W	W		W
8 Oberstar (DFL)*	W		W				
MISSISSIPPI							
1 Whitten (D)*					W		
2 Bowen (D)*					W		
Byrd (R)						L	L
3 Montgomery (D)*					W		W
4 Stennis (D)	L						
Hinson (R)							W
5 Lott (R)*			W				W
MISSOURI							
1 Clay (D)*	W		W				
2 Young (D)*	W		W				
Chase (R)					L		L
3 Gephardt (D)*	W		W				
5 Bolling (D)*	W		W				
6 Snowden (D)	L		L				
Coleman (R)*				W	W		W
7 Taylor (R)*				W			W
8 Ichord (D)*				W			W
9 Volkmer (D)*	W		W				
10 Burlison (D)*	W		W				
MONTANA							
1 Williams (D)	W	W					
Waltermire (R)						L	L
2 Monahan (D)	L						
Marlenee (R)*							W
NEBRASKA							
1 Dyas (D)	L	L	L				
Bereuter (R)					W		W
2 Cavanaugh (D)*	W	W	W				
Daub Jr. (R)				L		L	L
3 Fowler (D)	L						
Smith (R)*				W			W
NEW HAMPSHIRE							
1 D'Amours (D)*	W		W				
2 Helms (D)	L		L				
Cleveland (R)*							W
NEW JERSEY							
1 Florio (D)*	W	W	W				
2 Hughes (D)*	W		W				
3 Howard (D)*	W		W				
Coe (R)							L
4 Thompson Jr. (D)*	W		W				
5 Fahy (D)	L						
Fenwick (R)*			W				
6 McGann (D)	L		L				
7 Maguire (D)*	W		W				
Roukema (R)					L		
8 Roe (D)*	W		W				
9 Mastorelli (D)	L						
Hollenbeck (R)*			W		W		
10 Rodino Jr. (D)*	W		W				
11 Minish (D)*	W		W				
12 McCormack (D)	L						
Rinaldo (R)*			W				
13 Meyner (D)*	L	L	L				
Courter (R)					W		W
14 Guarini (D)	W		W				W
15 Patten (D)*	W		W				
Wiley (R)						L	L
NEW MEXICO							
1 Hawk (D)	L		L				
Lujan Jr. (R)*				W			W
2 Runnels (D)*				W			W
NEW YORK							
1 Randolph (D)	L	L					
Carney (R, C)					W	W	W
2 Downey (D)*	W	W					
3 Ambro (D)*	W	W					
Carman (R, C)				L	L	L	L
4 Rosenblum (D)	L						
Lent (R, C)*				W			W
5 Matthews (D, L)	L						

	COPE[1]	NCEC[2]	UAW[3]	ACA[4]	BIPAC[5]	CSFC[6]	NCPAC[7]
Wydler (R, C)*				W			W
6 Wolff (D, L)*	W						
7 Addabbo (D, R, L)*	W						
8 Rosenthal (D, L)*	W						
9 Ferraro (D)		W					
DelliBovi (R, C)				L	L		L
10 Biaggi (D, R, L)*	W						
11 Scheuer (D, L)*	W						
12 Chisholm (D, L)*	W						
13 Solarz (D, L)*	W						
14 Richmond (D, L)*	W						
15 Zeferetti (D, C)*	W						
16 Holtzman (D, L)*	W						
17 Murphy (D)*	W						
Peters (R, C)						L	
18 Burden (D, L)	L						
19 Rangel (D, R, L)*	W						
20 Weiss (D, L)*	W						
21 Garcia (D, R, L)*	W						
22 Bingham (D, L)*	W						
23 Peyser (D)	W	W					
Martinelli (R, C)				L	L	L	L
24 Ottinger (D)*	W						
26 Gilman (R)*	W		W				
27 McHugh (D)*	W		W				
Wallace (R, C)				L			
28 Stratton (D)*	W						W
29 Pattison (D, L)*	L	L					
Solomon (R, C)				W	W		W
30 Bartle (D, L)	L	L	L				
McEwen (R, C)*				W			W
31 Mitchell (R, C)*	W						W
32 Hanley (D)*	W		W				
33 Bernardi (D)		L	L				
Lee (R)				W	W		W
34 Horton (R)*	W		W				
35 Repicci (D)	L		L				
Conable Jr. (R)*				W			
36 LaFalce (D, L)*	W		W				
37 Nowak (D, L)*	W		W				
38 Kemp (R, C)*				W			W
Peck (L)	L						
39 Lundine (D)*	W	W	W				
NORTH CAROLINA							
1 Jones (D)*				W			
2 Fountain (D)*				W			W
3 Whitley (D)*				W			W
5 Neal (D)*		W					
Horton Jr. (R)						L	
6 Bemus (R)				L			
8 Austin (R)						L	
9 Martin (R)*				W			W
10 Broyhill (R)*							W
11 Gudger (D)*				W			
Ratcliff (R)							L
NORTH DAKOTA							
AL Hagen (D)	L						
OHIO							
1 Burke (D)*	L		L				
Gradison (R)*				W			W
2 Luken (D)*	W	W	W				
Aronoff (R)				L	L	L	L
3 Hall (D)	W	W	W				
Kircher (R)					L		L
4 Griffin (D)	L						
Guyer (R)*				W			W
5 Sherck (D)	L		L				
Latta (R)*				W			W
6 Strickland (D)	L		L				W
Harsha (R)*				W			W
7 Brown (R)*				W			W
8 Schroeder (D)	L						W
Kindness (R)*				W			W
9 Ashley (D)*	W		W				
10 Plummer (D)	L		L				
Miller (R)*				W			W
11 Donlin (D)	L		L				
Stanton (R)*							W
12 Baumann (D)	L	L	L				
Devine (R)*				W	W		W
13 Pease (D)*	W		W				
Whitfield (R)				L			
14 Seiberling (D)*	W		W				
15 Eckhart (D)	L		L				
Wylie (R)*				W			W
16 Hand Jr. (D)			L				
Regula (R)*							W
17 Grier (D)	L						
Ashbrook (R)*				W			W
18 Applegate (D)*	W		W				
Ress (R)				L			
19 Carney (D)*	L		L				
Williams (R)					W	W	W
20 Oakar (D)*	W		W				
21 Stokes (D)*	W		W				
22 Vanik (D)*	W		W				
23 Mottl (D)*	W		W				
OKLAHOMA							
1 Jones (D)*	W		W	W			W
Unruh (R)							L
2 Synar (D)	W		W				W
Richardson (R)					L	L	L
3 Watkins (D)*							W
4 Steed (D)*	W		W				W
Robb (R)					L		L
5 Edwards (R)*					W		W
6 English (D)*				W	W		W
OREGON							
1 AuCoin (D)*	W	W					
Bunick (R)							L
2 Ullman (D)*	W						
3 Duncan (D)*	W						
4 Weaver (D)*	W	W					
Lausmann (R)					L	L	L
PENNSYLVANIA							
1 Myers (D)*	W		W				
2 Gray III (D)	W	W	W				
3 Lederer (D)*	W		W				
4 Eilberg (D)*	L		L				
Dougherty (R)					W		W
5 Zealor (D)	L						
Schulze (R)*				W			W
6 Yatron (D)*	W		W				
7 Edgar (D)*	W	W	W				
Kane (R)						L	L
8 Kostmayer (D)*	W	W	W				
Bowers (R)							L
9 Havice Jr. (D)	L						
Shuster (R)*				W			W
10 McDade (R)*	W		W				
11 Flood (D)*	W						
Hudock (R)					L		
12 Murtha (D)*	W		W				
13 Rubenstein (D)	L		L				

	COPE[1]	NCEC[2]	UAW[3]	ACA[4]	BIPAC[5]	CSFC[6]	NCPAC[7]
14 Moorhead (D)*	W		W				
Thomas (R)					L	L	
15 Rooney (D)*	L		L				
16 Boohar (D)	L						
Walker (R)*				W			W
17 Ertel (D)*	W	W	W				
Rippon (R)				L	L		L
18 Walgren (D)*	W	W	W				
19 Goodling (R)*				W			W
20 Gaydos (D)*	W		W				
21 Bailey (D)	W		W				
Miller (R)						L	L
22 Murphy (D)*	W		W				
23 Ammerman (D)*	L	L	L				
Clinger Jr. (R)				W	W	W	W
24 Marks (R)*			W				
25 Atkinson (D)			W				
RHODE ISLAND							
1 St Germain (D)*	W		W				
2 Beard (D)*	W		W				
SOUTH CAROLINA							
1 Davis (D)*	W						
2 Bass (D)	L	L					
Spence (R)*				W	W		W
4 Campbell (R)				W			W
SOUTH DAKOTA							
1 Daschle (D)	L	L					
Thorsness (R)				W	W	W	
2 Abdnor (R)*				W			
Samuelson (D)	L						
TENNESSEE							
1 Ball (D)	L						
Quillen (R)*				W			W
2 Duncan (R)*							W
3 Lloyd (D)*	W						
4 Gore Jr. (D)*	W						
5 Boner (D)				W			W
Goodwin (R)				L			
6 Arline (D)	L						
Beard Jr. (R)*				W			W
7 Jones (D)*	W						
Cook (R)				L			
8 Ford (D)*	W						
Ragsdale (R)				L			
TEXAS							
1 Hall Jr. (D)*	W						W
2 Wilson (D)*	W		W				
3 Collins (R)*				W			W
4 Roberts (D)*	W			W			W
Glenn (R)							L
5 Mattox (D)*	W	W	W				
Pauken (R)						L	L
6 Gramm (D)	W					W	W
7 Hutchings (D)	L						
Archer (R)*				W			W
8 Eckhardt (D)*	W	W	W				
Gearhart (R)							L
9 Brooks (D)*	W		W				
10 Pickle (D)*	W						
11 Leath (D)	W						
Burgess (R)				L		L	L
12 Wright (D)*	W		W				
13 Hightower (D)*	W						
14 Wyatt (D)	W						W
15 de la Garza (D)*	W						
16 White (D)*	W						
17 Stenholm (D)	W						W
Fisher (R)						L	L

	COPE[1]	NCEC[2]	UAW[3]	ACA[4]	BIPAC[5]	CSFC[6]	NCPAC[7]
18 Leland (D)	W		W				
19 Hance (D)	W		W				W
Bush (R)							L
20 Gonzalez (D)*	W						
21 Wolff (D)	L						
Loeffler (R)						W	W
22 Gammage (D)*	L		L	L			
Paul (R)						W	W
23 Kazen Jr. (D)*	W						
24 Frost (D)	W	W	W				
Berman (R)					L	L	L
UTAH							
1 McKay (D)*	W						
Richardson (R)							L
2 Firmage (D)	L						
Marriott (R)*				W	W		W
VERMONT							
AL Dietz (D)							L
Jeffords (R)*	W						
VIRGINIA							
1 Puller (D)	L		L				
Trible Jr. (R)*				W	W		W
2 Whitehurst (R)*				W			W
3 Satterfield III (D)*				W			W
4 Daniel, R (R)*				W			W
5 Daniel, D (D)*				W			W
6 Butler (R)*				W			W
7 Fickett (D)	L		L				
Robinson (R)*				W			W
8 Harris II (D)*	W	W	W				
Herrity (R)						L	L
9 Clark (D)	L						
Wampler (R)*				W			W
10 Fisher (D)*	W		W				
Wolf (R)					L	L	
WASHINGTON							
1 Niemi (D)	L						
2 Swift (D)	W						
Garner (R)					L	L	L
3 Bonker (D)*	W						
4 McCormack (D)*	W						
5 Foley (D)*	W	W					
Alton (R)						L	L
6 Dicks (D)*	W						
7 Lowry (D)	W	W					
Cunningham (R)*					L	L	L
WEST VIRGINIA							
1 Mollohan (D)*	W		W				
2 Staggers (D)*	W		W				
3 Slack (D)*	W		W				
4 Rahall (D)*	W		W				
WISCONSIN							
1 Aspin (D)*	W		W				
Petrie (R)					L		
2 Kastenmeier (D)*	W		W				
Wright (R)						L	
3 Baldus (D)*	W		W				
4 Zablocki (D)*	W		W				
5 Reuss (D)*	W		W				
7 Obey (D)*	W		W				
8 Cornell (D)*	L	L	L				
Roth (R)					W	W	W
9 Flynn (D)	L		L				
Sensenbrenner Jr. (R)					W	W	W
WYOMING							
AL Bagley (D)	L						
Cheney (R)					W	W	W

Group Ratings Show Conservative Trend

Democratic members of Congress who faced tough re-election fights in 1978 reduced their support for liberal-backed positions during the election year, according to an analysis of key races by Congressional Quarterly.

The move to the right had mixed results for 17 House Democratic incumbents surveyed: just 11 won their re-election bids. But for Democratic Senate incumbents, a rightward shift yielded even less at the polls. Of the half dozen Democratic incumbents surveyed, five of whom received lower marks from the liberal Americans for Democratic Action (ADA), only one won re-election. *(Chart, p. 88)*

Those are the major findings of a 1978 study of key election races, based on Congressional Quarterly's annual review of pressure group ratings of members of Congress. *(Individual ratings, pp. 92-94)*

A survey of a half dozen hotly contested Senate races showed that the incumbents' average rating from the ADA fell by some 22 points from 1977 to 1978, from an average score of 72 to 50. For 17 House Democratic incumbents running against strong challengers, the falloff in average ADA support was also substantial. Scores dropped to an average of 53 in 1978 from a 1977 average of 65.

It should be noted that because the ADA counts absences and dead pairs as votes against its position, members who missed large numbers of votes — for example while campaigning — may register particularly low ADA scores. Several members surveyed were absent on a number of votes the ADA used in compiling its ratings.

At the same time, Democratic incumbents who ran in traditionally Republican districts, or who were locked in tight races with Republican challengers, increased their support in 1978 for positions backed by the conservative Americans for Constitutional Action (ACA). The House Democrats surveyed increased their average ACA support to 24 in 1978 from a 1977 average score of 19. The incumbent senators studied increased their support for conservative positions only slightly, to an average ACA score of 16 in 1978, from 15 in 1977.

To analyze whether incumbents moderated their voting records to stave off stiff election challenges, Congressional Quarterly picked 17 House and 6 Senate races where Democratic incumbents faced uphill re-election fights. In addition to these races, two House contests pitting Republican incumbents against strong challengers were also studied. Voting scores compiled by ADA and ACA were chosen because the two groups represent opposing ideological positions on the political spectrum.

Rightward Drift

The election analysis is part of CQ's annual review of pressure group ratings of members. The voting scores, which are based on selected 1978 roll call votes, are tabulated for the ADA and ACA, the AFL-CIO's Committee on Political Education (COPE) and the Chamber of Commerce of the United States (CCUS). Each group selected its own "key votes" for computing ratings.

Voting records compiled by the four groups suggest that House members have maintained their steady movement rightward. The percentage of House members who scored above 80 percent in the ADA ratings dropped from 113 in 1975 to 46 in 1978. On the other side of the political spectrum, the percentage of members scoring above 80 on the ACA's conservative "Consistency Index" stayed close to 90 in 1976 and 1977 but leaped to 110 in 1978. *(Chart, this page)*

Like ADA, labor's COPE also suffered a decline in the number of representatives scoring high on their ratings scale. The number of members scoring above 80 percent on COPE's scale has moved downward, from 192 in 1975 to 123 in 1978.

		1975	1976	1977	1978
ADA	80% or more	113	78	70	46
	20% or less	137	164	162	161
COPE	80% or more	192	155	159	123
	20% or less	102	85	101	113
CCUS	80% or more	100	85	131	76
	20% or less	160	152	126	56
ACA	80% or more	97	90	89	110
	20% or less	154	178	84	117

Members' support for business positions, as shown by the number of members who scored 80 percent or above, or 20 percent or below on the Chamber of Commerce's index, has become more moderate. In 1978, 76 members voted for the Chamber's positions at least 80 percent of the time and 56 members received scores of 20 percent or below. In 1977, many more members were strongly opposed or strongly in favor of the business group's positions: 131 received scores of 80 percent or above, and 126 had marks of 20 percent or below.

The 1978 scores continued a trend evident in 1977 voting studies compiled by CQ. The 1977 voting scores of these interest groups seemed to support the conclusion of many political observers that the 95th Congress — at least in the House — had not given as strong support to programs backed by liberal groups as had been forecast.

House Elections

Of the 17 Democratic incumbents surveyed in 1978 for the election study, a dozen decreased their 1977 support for ADA's position, another three stayed the same, and only two — Mark W. Hannaford (Calif.) and John Brademas (Ind.) — increased their ADA support in 1978.

Hannaford, who lost his re-election bid to Republican Dan Lungren, tried to stave off charges during the campaign that he had presented a conservative image in the district, while voting with the liberals in Washington. Lungren won the contest with 54 percent of the vote.

Twelve Democrats, led by New York's Jerome A. Ambro, registered decreases from their 1977 level of support

Congressional Quarterly Election Study

Senate

Senator	Party	1978 result	ADA ratings 1977	1978	change	ACA ratings 1977	1978	change
Haskell	D-Colo.	Lost	85	50	- 35	8	15	+ 7
Clark	D-Iowa	Lost	90	90	none	4	13	+ 9
Hathaway	D-Maine	Lost	85	55	- 30	9	0	- 9
Anderson	D-Minn.	Lost	80	35	- 45	4	8	+ 4
McIntyre	D-N.H.	Lost	55	40	- 15	22	23	+ 1
Randolph	D-W.Va.	Won	40	30	- 10	43	38	- 5

House

Representative	Party	1978 result	ADA ratings 1977	1978	change	ACA ratings 1977	1978	change
McFall	D-Calif.	Lost	65	45	- 20	8	23	+15
Hannaford	D-Calif.	Lost	50	60	+10	32	33	+ 1
Wirth	D-Colo.	Won	70	50	- 20	12	23	+11
Mikva	D-Ill.	Won	85	70	- 15	17	9	- 8
Brademas	D-Ind.	Won	75	80	+ 5	4	7	+ 3
Evans	D-Ind.	Won	40	25	- 15	56	63	+ 7
Blouin	D-Iowa	Lost	85	70	- 15	19	19	none
Patten	D-N.J.	Won	55	50	- 5	11	12	+ 1
Ambro	D-N.Y.	Won	70	20	- 50	27	35	+ 8
Pattison	D-N.Y.	Lost	80	65	- 15	12	15	+ 3
Hanley	D-N.Y.	Won	40	40	none	27	32	+ 5
Carney	D-Ohio	Lost	55	55	none	11	9	- 2
Edgar	D-Pa.	Won	100	80	- 20	11	11	none
McKay	D-Utah	Won	25	15	- 10	41	60	+19
Harris	D-Va.	Won	70	70	none	15	7	- 8
Foley	D-Wash.	Won	45	30	- 15	15	22	+ 7
Cornell	D-Wis.	Lost	95	80	- 15	7	22	+15
Brown	R-Mich.	Lost	25	25	none	65	59	- 6
Cederberg	R-Mich.	Lost	10	10	none	80	80	none

for ADA-backed issues. Ambro scored a dramatic 50 point drop in his ADA support score, falling to a 20 in 1978 from a moderately liberal 70 in 1977. His ACA score increased to 35 from a 1977 score of 27.

Ambro, whose district straddles Long Island's Nassau and Suffolk counties, faced a candidate backed by the strong Nassau County Republican machine. The New York representative's dramatic move rightward may have helped contribute to his 52 percent win over the Republican challenger, Gregory W. Carman.

But Ambro debunked the notion that the election caused him to moderate his earlier, more liberal voting record.

"I don't think I'm [voting] very much differently than before," asserted Ambro, who nevertheless conceded that "liberal is a dirty word where I come from."

The New York Democrat also took issue with ADA's vote selection process. Ambro charged that the liberal group picked votes that did not accurately gauge members' liberal leanings.

For example, Ambro objected to ADA's contention that a vote in favor of voting rights for the District of Columbia was a pro-liberal vote.

Ambro defended his vote against the D.C. voting rights constitutional amendment saying, "I don't think [D.C.] should have two senators any more than I should have a hole in the head."

Three other incumbents locked in tight re-election races — John J. McFall of California, Timothy E. Wirth of Colorado and Robert W. Edgar of Pennsylvania — registered 20 point drops in their 1978 ADA scores.

McFall's defeat at the hands of a strong Republican contender, Norman D. Shumway, undoubtedly sprang from his involvement in the Korean bribery scandals. The 21-year Democratic veteran's move rightward seemed to do little to improve his re-election chances.

Wirth nearly went down in defeat in 1976 against Republican challenger Ed Scott. In 1978, Wirth hammered away at conservative themes designed to please suburban voters in his district and won the election with 53 percent of the vote. The appeal to conservative voters is reflected in Wirth's 1978 ADA rating of 50, a drop of 20 points from the previous year. His ACA rating in 1978 nearly doubled, rising to 23 in 1978 from a 12 in 1977.

Edgar, who faced difficult election challenges in 1974 and 1976, faced a third tough race in 1978. In earlier elections, he had refused to temper his liberal beliefs to conform to the district's conservative leanings. Edgar's ADA scores for his first three years in the House were 100, 95, and 100, respectively. But Edgar's 1978 challenger, Eugene D. Kane, gave him a particularly strong fight. And Edgar, who supported the Republican demand for sharp cuts in federal taxes, showed a 20 point drop, to 80, from his perfect 100 percent 1977 ADA rating. Edgar eked out a win, with 51 percent of the vote.

Commenting on the 20-point drop in his ADA score, Edgar conceded that "before an election you watch your votes. You don't just throw away your vote where 10 people are voting in favor but 400 are voting against" an issue, he said.

Nevertheless, Edgar said that he "didn't look at [which interest group] is supporting which votes," before he made up his mind on an issue. "It's just a judgment call on my part" based on an individual assessment of each vote, Edgar said.

Congressional Quarterly also looked at two races in which Republican incumbents faced stiff re-election fights. Garry Brown and Elford A. Cederberg, both of Michigan, were both defeated by Democratic challengers. But unlike Democratic incumbents facing strong contenders, neither Republican significantly moderated his voting record to stave off his opponent's challenge.

Brown was defeated by Howard Wolpe, who received strong backing from labor and environmental interests. Brown's support for ACA-backed issues dropped slightly, to 59 in 1978 from 65 in 1977, but his ADA score remained at its 1977 level of 25. Like Brown, Cederberg's ADA score remained at its 1977 mark of 10. His 1977 ACA score of 80 remained the same in 1978.

Senate Elections

Of the half-dozen incumbent Democratic senators surveyed, all but Jennings Randolph of West Virginia were liberals facing stiff re-election bouts. Randolph himself faced a substantial challenge. All but one showed substantial drops in their 1978 ADA scores. However, as Floyd Haskell remarked in talking about the 35-point decline in his score, "the scores are skewed since absences are counted as no's."

Indeed, if Haskell's score was computed solely on the basis of votes he actually cast — 10 out of the 20 selected by ADA — his 1978 score jumps to 100. In another instance, Maine's William D. Hathaway, who was absent for five votes, registered a 30 point decline in his ADA score between 1977 and 1978. But if Hathaway's score was compiled in terms of the number of votes cast, his mark rises to a 73.

Using ADA's compilation method, Dick Clark of Iowa was the only one of the senators surveyed whose score remained constant. Some observers have explained Clark's consistently high showing — he registered no change in his ADA rating of 90 from the previous year — by pointing out that pre-election polls had shown him 10 or more points ahead of his Republican opponent, Roger W. Jepsen.

When asked if the ADA ratings played a role in his defeat, Clark said: "Those in opposition [to me] constantly referred to me as 'the most liberal senator in America'. When asked for the evidence, my ADA rating was cited. It helped substantiate a very liberal image at a time when liberalism is very unpopular," Clark said.

Asked if he would have moderated his liberal position were he able to "re-run" his race against Jepsen, Clark said

no, since he was unaware of ADA's position on votes before he cast them.

"If I had been aware of it, it wouldn't have been an important factor," he added.

For the five remaining senators who did moderate their liberal voting records to woo conservative voters, the strategy in most cases failed. Only Randolph, who despite his generally moderate views had cast himself as a New Dealer, won re-election. Moreover, Randolph's drop in ADA support, already low, was modest. The West Virginia Democrat's score fell to 30 in 1978 from a 1977 mark of 40.

For the four other Democrats facing tough re-election fights surveyed, the drop in ADA scores was more substantial. Hathaway of Maine, facing a formidable contender in moderate Republican Rep. William S. Cohen, reduced his support of ADA-backed positions in 1978 by 30 points. His opponent, Cohen, also trimmed his support for liberal issues, registering a 30 ADA score in 1978 as opposed to his 1977 rating of 65.

Wendell R. Anderson, of Minnesota, and Haskell also showed dramatic drops of 45 and 35 points respectively in their ADA scores. However, much of the falloff can be explained by the fact that both men were frequently absent during key roll-call votes.

Scoring and Selection

The ADA based its ratings on the percentage of times a representative or senator voted in agreement with the ADA position in 1978 on 20 selected issues in each house.

It chose for its ratings study a wide range of controversial issues, including tuition tax credits for private and parochial school students, ratification of the Panama Canal treaty and deregulation of natural gas.

The ADA included in its ratings "live pairs," which it defined as those cases in which a member is present but withdraws his or her vote and becomes part of a pair. The member's percentage of support is his ADA "liberal quotient," and, as noted above, failure to vote lowered a member's score.

Failure to vote does not affect the scores of the other three groups surveyed. A member, therefore, can get a 100 percent score from a group even if he votes only once, so long as the member agrees with the group on that one issue.

Labor's COPE used 20 House and 19 Senate votes for its study. The group selected 10 "key votes" in each house dealing with important employment and economic issues, such as labor law reform and job safety. COPE also judged members on such non-labor issues as ratification of the Panama Canal treaty and the sale of fighter planes to Israel, Saudi Arabia and Egypt.

The Chamber of Commerce of the United States (CCUS) rated members on 18 votes in each house. The Chamber's votes were based on a broad sweep of issues of interest to business, including extension of the Comprehensive Employment and Training Act, deregulation of natural gas and designation of wilderness lands in Alaska.

The issues ACA selected for its "ACA Consistency Index" were similarly wide-ranging. The index shows the percentage of times a member voted in favor of ACA's position on 24 votes in the Senate and 27 votes in the House. The group chose votes on such issues as gun control, aid to New York City, extension of the ratification deadline for the Equal Rights Amendment and rescission of B-1 bomber funds.

The ADA, ACA and Chamber compiled their own scores. The COPE scores were computed by Congressional Quarterly.

Americans for Democratic Action

The Americans for Democratic Action (ADA) was founded in 1947 by a group of liberal Democrats, including the late Sen. Hubert H. Humphrey, D-Minn., and Eleanor Roosevelt. The current national president, former Rep. Patsy T. Mink, D-Hawaii (1965-77), received a 1976 rating of 70 from the group she now heads.

ADA STUDY FINDINGS

Senate

High scorers — Four senators, all northern Democrats, scored 90 percent or better. Sen. Howard M. Metzenbaum, D-Ohio, had the Senate's only perfect ADA score. The other Democrats scoring above 90 percent were Kennedy (Mass.) with a 95, and Sarbanes (Md.) and Clark (Iowa) each with 90.

The highest scoring southern Democrat was Jim Sasser (Tenn.), who had a score of 55. Southern Democrat Kaneaster L. Hodges Jr. (Ark.) had a 50 percent score, and three other southern Democrats had 45 scores, Sparkman (Ala.), Bumpers (Ark.) and Ford (Ky.). The GOP leader was Jacob K. Javits, R-N.Y., with a 75. Four Republicans scored between 60 and 75 percent: Brooke (Mass.) 70, Case (N.J.) 65, Heinz (Pa.) 60, and Weicker (Conn.) 60.

Low scorers — Sen. James A. McClure, R-Idaho, and Sen. Maryon P. Allen, D-Ala. were the only senators to receive zero scores from the ADA. Five Republicans: Garn and Hatch (Utah), Helms (N.C.), Laxalt (Nev.) and Young (N.D.) each received a score of five. Three southern Democrats — Stennis and Eastland (both of Miss.) and Byrd (Va.) — each had an ADA rating of 10. The lowest scoring northern Democrat was Edward Zorinsky, D-Neb., with a score of 25. Four other northern Democrats had ADA scores below 40.

House

High scorers — Five northern Democrats received perfect ADA scores in 1978. They were Sidney R. Yates (Ill.), Robert F. Drinan (Mass.) and Shirley Chisholm, Elizabeth Holtzman and Ted Weiss, all of New York.

In addition, eight northern Democrats received scores of 95 from the ADA, and six northern Democrats joined by Republican Newton I. Steers (Md.) had ADA scores of 90. Of the 197 northern Democrats listed in the ADA ratings, 130 had ADA scores of 50 percent or better.

Six southern Democrats in the House obtained ADA scores between 70 and 80 percent. Reps. Barbara Jordan (Texas) and William Lehman (Fla.) had ADA scores of 80. Eckhardt (Texas) had a 75, and Harris (Va.), Gonzalez (Texas) and Ford (Tenn.), each had 70 percent scores.

Low scorers — Republicans Eldon Rudd (Ariz.), Louis Frey Jr. (Fla.) and Thad Cochran (Miss.) joined southern Democrat Dan Daniel (Va.) in receiving zero scores from the ADA in 1978. Some 43 other southern Democrats scored between five and 20 in the study. Of the 147 Republicans in the ADA study, a total of 104 had ADA scores of 20 or less.

Three northern Democrats received scores of five in the 1978 ADA study: Stump (Ariz.), Santini (Nev.) and Run-

nels (N.M). Another 10 received marks of between 5 and 20 from ADA in 1978.

COPE

COPE (The Committee on Political Education) was formed when the old American Federation of Labor merged with the Congress of Industrial Organizations on Dec. 5, 1955. COPE is the AFL-CIO political education arm, and prepares and distributes the voting records and its ratings of members of Congress. Alexander E. Barkan is the COPE national director, and AFL-CIO president George Meany serves as COPE's chairman.

COPE STUDY FINDINGS

Senate

High scorers — No senator achieved a perfect COPE score in 1978. Three northern Democrats and one Republican, Jacob K. Javits, R-N.Y., received scores of 95. The Democrats were Kennedy (Mass.), Sarbanes (Md.) and Durkin (N.H.). Two senators from each party had COPE scores between 90 and 95. They were Democrats Bayh (Ind.) 94, and Anderson (Minn.) 92, and Republicans Case (N.J.) and Brooke (Mass.), who had scores of 94 and 93 respectively.

Only four southern Democrats received scores of 50 percent or better from COPE in 1978: Sasser (Tenn.) 74, Ford (Ky.) 68, Huddleston (Ky.) 67 and Stone (Fla.) 50.

Low scorers — Jake Garn, R-Utah, had the lowest COPE score in the Senate, voting with COPE's position five percent of the time. Republicans McClure (Idaho), Curtis (Neb.), Tower (Texas) and Hansen (Wyo.) each received a six score from COPE, as did southern Democrat Stennis (Miss.). Stennis' Mississippi colleague, James O. Eastland, was the second-lowest southern Democrat, with a score of nine. The two lowest northern Democratic COPE scores belonged to Zorinsky (Nebr.) 16 and Cannon (Nev.) 33.

More than two-thirds (26 of 38) of the Senate's GOP members and 15 of the 19 southern Democrats received COPE ratings below 50 percent.

House

High scorers — Seven northern Democrats were the only members of the House to receive perfect scores from COPE in 1978. They were John Burton (Calif.), Metcalfe (Ill.), Ford and Brodhead (both of Mich.), Nolan (Minn.), Downey (N.Y.) and Stokes (Ohio).

Four southern Democrats joined 41 northern Democrats in receiving 1978 COPE scores of between 90 and 99 percent. Henry B. Gonzalez (Texas) led the southerners with a COPE score of 95, while Reps. Herbert E. Harris II (Va.), Harold E. Ford (Tenn.) and Claude Pepper (Fla.) received 90 percent marks. Charles W. Whalen Jr., R-Ohio, led all GOP members with a score of 89, but only four other Republicans scored above 75.

Low scorers — Rep. Joe D. Waggonner Jr., D-La., joined a dozen Republicans as zero scorers on the 1978 COPE chart. The Republicans were: Rudd (Ariz.), Goldwater, Moorhead and Clawson (Calif.), Kelly (Fla.), Sebelius (Kansas), Moore (La.), Hagedorn and Stangeland (Minn.), Beard (Tenn.), Archer (Texas) and Butler (Va.).

Thirty-two other House members — all but seven of them Republicans — scored between one and 10 percent on the 1978 COPE rating scale. Of the seven Democrats, only one, Rep. Harold M. Runnels (N.M.), was a non-southerner. He received a COPE score of six. Six southern Democrats received a score of five: Flynt, McDonald and Barnard (Ga.), Breaux (La.) and Satterfield and Dan Daniel (Va.).

Chamber of Commerce

The Chamber of Commerce of the United States (CCUS) represents local, regional and state chambers of commerce, along with trade and professional organizations. It was founded in 1912 to be "a voice for organized business in Washington." President of the Chamber is Richard Lesher.

CHAMBER STUDY FINDINGS

Senate

High scorers — Two Republicans, Dewey F. Bartlett, R-Okla., and Barry M. Goldwater, R-Ariz., received perfect 100 percent scores from the Chamber in 1978. They were joined by four other Republicans who scored between 90 and 99 percent: Garn and Hatch (Utah) and Scott (Va.) with 94, and Senate Minority Leader Howard H. Baker Jr. (Tenn.), with 93.

The only Democrats above 80 percent on the Chamber's list were from the South: Byrd (Va.), Eastland (Miss.) and Bentsen (Texas) with 83 scores, and Maryon Allen (Ala.) with an 82. Zorinsky (72) and Cannon (60) were the only northern Democrats who scored above 50 percent on the Chamber's ratings.

Low scorers — Sen. William D. Hathaway, D-Maine, was the only senator to receive a zero from the Chamber in 1978. His Maine colleague, Democrat Edmund S. Muskie, received a rating of six, followed by three other Democrats: Montana's Melcher (8), and Iowa's Clark and Culver (11).

Senators James B. Pearson, R-Kan., and Charles McC. Mathias Jr., R-Md., were the lowest scorers among the GOP, each with a rating of 25. Jacob K. Javits, R-N.Y., had a 29 and two other Republicans had 38 scores, Case (N.J.) and Hatfield (Ore.). Dale Bumpers (Ark.) and Ford (Ky.) were the lowest scoring southern Democrats, each with a 44 score.

House

High scorers — Seven Republicans received perfect scores from the Chamber: Goldwater, Clawson, Wiggins and Badham (all of California), Philip M. Crane (Ill.), Collins (Tex.) and Butler (Va.). Eight other Republicans scored above 90 percent: Ruppe (Mich.), Ashbrook and Brown (both of Ohio), Rousselot (Calif.), Hyde and Erlenborn (both of Ill.), Forsythe (N.J.) and Marriott (Utah). All but nine of 146 counted Republicans scored 50 percent or better on the Chamber's chart.

Other than New Mexico's Runnels, who scored 93, only two other Democrats, both from the party's southern wing, registered above-90 scores: Waggonner (La.), who scored 94, and McDonald (Ga.), who scored 91. Stump (Ariz.), who registered a perfect score in 1977, dropped to 82 in 1978.

Low Scorers — In addition to zero scores given to Reps. Richard Nolan (Minn.) and Peter W. Rodino Jr.(N.J.), nine other northern Democrats scored less than 10 on the 1978 Chamber rating: John Burton (Calif.), Harrington (Mass.), Brodhead (Mich.), Oberstar (Minn.),

D'Amours (N.H.), Weaver (Ore.), Roncalio (Wyo.), Spellman (Md.) and Howard (N.J.).

The GOP low scorer was Harold C. Hollenbeck (N.J.) with a 29. He was followed by Steers (Md.) and Rinaldo (N.J.), both with a score of 35. Two southern Democrats scored below 20 in 1978: Eckhardt (Tex.), who scored a 6, and Ford (Tenn.) who registered 19 on the Chamber ratings scale.

Americans for Constitutional Action

The ACA was formed in 1958 at the request of a group of conservative senators to elect more "constitutional conservatives" to Congress. Chairman is J. Charlene Baker.

ACA STUDY FINDINGS

Senate

High scorers — The Virginia delegation led the entire Senate in the 1978 ACA ratings. Both Independent Harry F. Byrd Jr. and Republican William Scott received perfect scores from the group in 1978.

Eight Republicans received ACA scores of between 90 and 99 percent: Helms (N.C.), Bartlett (Okla.), and Hatch (Utah) each with 96 scores; Goldwater (Ariz.), Curtis (Neb.) and Garn (Utah) with 95; Lugar (Ind.) 92, and McClure (Idaho) with a 91. Twenty-five of the 38 GOP senators scored 50 percent 'right' or better in the 1978 ACA ratings.

Sen. Edward Zorinsky, D-Neb., with a score of 74, was the only northern Democrat who scored more than 50 percent in the ACA ratings. Three southern Democrats scored ACA ratings in the 70s: Maryon Allen (Ala.) 77; Stennis (Miss.) 73 and Eastland (Miss.) 70.

Low scorers — Sens. William D. Hathaway, D-Maine and Donald W. Riegle Jr., D-Mich., voted with the ACA position zero percent of the time in 1978. Twelve northern Democrats and two Republicans received ACA marks of between one and 10 percent. The GOP low scorers were Sens. Clifford P. Case, R-N.J., with a 4 percent score, and Jacob K. Javits, R-N.Y, who received a 5 percent rating.

House

High Scorers — Joining 11 perfect GOP scorers were three Democrats, Stump (Ariz.), Satterfield (Va.) and McDonald (Ga.). Republicans receiving a 100 from ACA were: Marriott (Utah), Archer (Texas), Ashbrook (Ohio), Crane (Ill.), Bafalis and Kelly (both of Florida), and Badham, Clawson, Rousselot, Moorhead, and Goldwater (all of California). Scores between 90 and 99 went to 35 Republicans and 6 southern Democrats. Northern Democrats Runnels (N.M.) and Ichord (Mo.) scored 93 and 92 respectively. Of 146 Republican House members rated, 128 received ACA ratings of 50 percent or better.

Low Scorers — Two northern Democrats received a zero ACA rating: Lionel Van Deerlin (Calif.) and Peter W. Rodino Jr. (N.J.). Another 48 received ACA marks of between one and 10, joined by three southern Democrats: Eckhardt (Tex.), with a score of 4 percent, and Tucker (Ark.) and Harris (Va.), both with scores of 7 percent. The only three Republicans to score below 20 on the ACA scale were: Maryland's Steers with an 11 percent rating, New York's Green with 12 percent and Ohio's Whalen with a score of 13 percent.

How Special-Interest Groups Rate Representatives

ADA (Americans for Democratic Action) — The percentage of time each representative voted in accordance with or entered a live pair for the ADA position on 20 selected votes of 1978. The percentages were compiled by ADA. Failure to vote lowers the scores.

COPE (AFL-CIO Committee on Political Education) — The percentage of time each representative voted or was paired in favor of the COPE position on 20 selected votes of 1978. Failure to vote does not lower the scores, which were compiled by CQ.

CCUS (Chamber of Commerce of the United States) — The percentage of time each representative voted with the chamber's position on 18 selected votes in 1978. Failure to vote does not lower the scores, which were compiled by the chamber.

ACA (Americans for Constitutional Action) — The percentage of time each representative voted in accordance with the ACA position on 27 votes in 1978. Failure to vote does not lower the scores, which were compiled by ACA.

Rep. Clifford Allen, D-Tenn., who died June 18, 1978, was not rated by COPE, CCUS or the ACA.

Rep. William M. Ketchum, R-Calif., who died June 24, 1978, was not rated by COPE, CCUS or the ACA.

Rep. Ralph H. Metcalfe, D-Ill., who died Oct. 10, 1978, was not rated by the Chamber of Commerce.

Rep. Goodloe D. Byron, D-Md., who died Oct. 11, 1978, was not rated by the Chamber of Commerce.

* House Speaker Thomas P. O'Neill Jr., D-Mass., was not rated by any of the groups.

‡ Scores were compiled by Congressional Quarterly from the votes selected by the organization.

KEY

ADA —Americans for Democratic Action
COPE —AFL-CIO Committee on Political Education
CCUS —Chamber of Commerce of the United States
ACA —Americans for Constitutional Action

	ADA	COPE‡	CCUS	ACA
ALABAMA				
1 Edwards	20	11	78	89
2 *Dickinson*	5	16	81	96
3 Nichols	5	25	67	83
4 Bevill	15	35	44	67
5 Flippo	10	42	56	74
6 *Buchanan*	30	44	63	67
7 Flowers	20	58	42	62
ALASKA				
AL *Young*	5	53	54	73
ARIZONA				
1 *Rhodes*	15	13	80	70
2 Udall	70	83	25	13
3 *Stump*	5	10	82	100
4 *Rudd*	0	0	87	96
ARKANSAS				
1 Alexander	25	59	44	41
2 Tucker	30	75	36	7
3 *Hammerschmidt*	10	11	78	88
4 Thornton	15	36	38	25
CALIFORNIA				
1 Johnson	45	85	22	15
2 *Clausen*	10	24	82	89
3 Moss	60	87	23	5
4 Leggett	65	89	27	27
5 Burton, J.	80	100	6	13
6 Burton, P.	95	94	18	4
7 Miller	85	94	30	6
8 Dellums	95	95	19	8
9 Stark	95	95	19	17
10 Edwards	80	84	22	4
11 Ryan	55	68	44	16
12 *McCloskey*	65	58	59	32
13 Mineta	80	84	22	4
14 McFall	45	80	41	23
15 Sisk	15	54	73	65
16 Panetta	50	63	33	50
17 Krebs	60	80	39	30
18 *Ketchum##*	9			
19 *Lagomarsino*	5	5	89	96
20 *Goldwater*	5	0	100	100
21 Corman	70	80	22	4
22 *Moorhead*	5	0	88	100
23 Beilenson	80	79	31	8
24 Waxman	90	90	29	13
25 Roybal	85	79	24	15
26 *Rousselot*	5	5	94	100
27 *Dornan*	5	5	81	92
28 Burke	40	94	11	8
29 Hawkins	75	82	18	16
30 Danielson	60	85	18	4
31 Wilson, C.H.	30	60	43	40
32 Anderson	60	80	11	41
33 *Clawson*	5	0	100	100
34 Hannaford	60	89	28	33
35 Lloyd	45	75	18	38
36 Brown	70	79	13	8
37 *Pettis*	10	11	75	65
38 Patterson	60	94	11	24
39 *Wiggins*	20	11	100	87
40 *Badham*	10	21	100	100
41 *Wilson, B.*	15	26	82	73
42 Van Deerlin	60	77	24	0
43 *Burgener*	10	11	88	88
COLORADO				
1 Schroeder	85	85	33	37
2 Wirth	50	65	33	23
3 Evans	60	58	41	10
4 *Johnson*	25	15	88	67
5 *Armstrong*	5	6	81	92
CONNECTICUT				
1 Cotter	50	63	33	28
2 Dodd	80	90	29	8
3 Giaimo	50	55	47	33
4 *McKinney*	55	55	65	26
5 *Sarasin*	15	39	77	58
6 Moffett	95	89	22	16
DELAWARE				
AL *Evans*	15	21	82	76
FLORIDA				
1 Sikes	10	28	50	83
2 Fuqua	20	30	56	58
3 Bennett	30	25	61	85
4 Chappell	5	25	76	84
5 *Kelly*	5	0	88	100
6 *Young*	10	15	78	93
7 Gibbons	10	26	67	67
8 Ireland	20	21	67	78
9 *Frey*	0	15	83	92
10 *Bafalis*	10	10	78	100
11 Rogers	30	55	24	24
12 *Burke*	10	11	76	80
13 Lehman	80	85	31	12
14 Pepper	50	90	28	12
15 Fascell	65	85	29	17
GEORGIA				
1 Ginn	20	55	56	63
2 Mathis	5	29	60	82
3 Brinkley	15	35	56	70
4 Levitas	20	60	39	65
5 Fowler	45	58	33	36
6 Flynt	5	5	79	95
7 McDonald	15	5	91	100
8 Evans	15	32	56	65
9 Jenkins	5	18	43	73
10 Barnard	10	5	67	75
HAWAII				
1 Heftel	35	53	35	15
2 Akaka	55	80	25	7
IDAHO				
1 *Symms*	10	5	88	96
2 *Hansen*	5	6	79	96
ILLINOIS				
1 Metcalfe ###	89	100		10
2 Murphy	55	70	39	23
3 Russo	35	63	39	50
4 *Derwinski*	20	20	78	58
5 Fary	40	80	31	22
6 *Hyde*	10	5	94	70
7 Collins	65	85	29	14
8 Rostenkowski	50	63	33	21
9 Yates	100	85	22	7
10 Mikva	70	89	19	9
11 Annunzio	40	79	33	22
12 *Crane, P.*	5	6	100	100
13 *McClory*	45	21	88	73
14 *Erlenborn*	30	10	94	69
15 *Corcoran*	25	10	81	88
16 *Anderson*	55	39	69	44
17 *O'Brien*	25	10	76	77
18 *Michel*	15	5	89	75
19 *Railsback*	20	25	72	56
20 *Findley*	35	15	71	79
21 *Madigan*	30	25	75	80
22 Shipley	20	75	43	31
23 Price	45	85	22	23
24 Simon	65	84	22	10
INDIANA				
1 Benjamin	65	80	22	22
2 Fithian	25	50	33	58
3 Brademas	80	84	22	7
4 *Quayle*	15	11	76	81
5 *Hillis*	10	35	56	69
6 Evans	25	55	24	63
7 *Myers*	10	10	72	81
8 Cornwell	40	45	44	40
9 Hamilton	35	50	35	31
10 Sharp	50	70	22	26
11 Jacobs	50	50	39	59
IOWA				
1 *Leach*	35	25	78	63
2 Blouin	70	79	22	19
3 *Grassley*	5	10	78	93
4 Smith	60	70	39	11
5 Harkin	60	70	22	26
6 Bedell	70	53	35	22

Democrats   **Republicans**

	ADA	COPE‡	CCUS	ACA
KANSAS				
1 *Sebelius*	5	0	83	76
2 Keys	70	65	22	26
3 *Winn*	10	17	82	88
4 Glickman	50	50	39	48
5 *Skubitz*	10	22	73	65
KENTUCKY				
1 Hubbard	10	63	50	68
2 Natcher	35	60	33	26
3 Mazzoli	40	47	56	31
4 *Snyder*	15	20	72	96
5 *Carter*	20	40	69	65
6 Breckinridge	35	65	41	18
7 Perkins	45	67	33	23
LOUISIANA				
1 *Livingston*	10	15	82	92
2 Boggs	45	65	44	31
3 *Treen*	5	11	83	92
4 Waggonner	5	0	94	88
5 Huckaby	25	35	63	88
6 *Moore*	.5	0	78	96
7 Breaux	5	5	71	86
8 Long	50	63	38	21
MAINE				
1 *Emery*	25	35	59	69
2 *Cohen*	30	21	63	58
MARYLAND				
1 *Bauman*	10	15	78	93
2 Long	40	47	39	37
3 Mikulski	85	85	17	7
4 *Holt*	5	20	72	85
5 Spellman	70	89	7	4
6 Byron ####	21	33		70
7 Mitchell	90	95	24	8
8 *Steers*	90	75	35	11
MASSACHUSETTS				
1 *Conte*	50	55	50	26
2 Boland	50	75	29	15
3 Early	70	68	24	23
4 Drinan	100	95	17	11
5 Tsongas	50	88	36	18
6 Harrington	60	84	6	6
7 Markey	90	85	22	7
8 O'Neill*				
9 Moakley	75	90	17	4
10 *Heckler*	55	70	41	22
11 Burke	35	85	43	12
12 Studds	95	90	22	7
MICHIGAN				
1 Conyers	45	94	21	11
2 *Pursell*	60	56	65	31
3 Brown	25	16	75	59
4 *Stockman*	20	12	83	80
5 *Sawyer*	25	11	86	79
6 Carr	80	75	17	26
7 Kildee	80	95	11	7
8 Traxler	45	80	18	20
9 *Vander Jagt*	10	5	75	79
10 *Cederberg*	10	21	83	80
11 *Ruppe*	20	22	93	59
12 Bonior	90	90	18	11
13 Diggs	60	88	20	10
14 Nedzi	40	72	28	13
15 Ford	60	100	12	14
16 Dingell	50	90	24	25
17 Brodhead	85	100	6	7
18 Blanchard	65	95	17	15
19 *Broomfield*	10	5	82	76
MINNESOTA				
1 *Quie*	10	6	77	53
2 *Hagedorn*	5	0	82	92
3 *Frenzel*	35	20	82	64
4 Vento	65	95	17	7
5 Fraser	75	94	20	6
6 Nolan	80	100	0	4
7 *Stangeland*	5	0	83	91
8 Oberstar	70	85	6	7
MISSISSIPPI				
1 Whitten	20	39	43	55
2 Bowen	15	20	89	88
3 Montgomery	5	15	78	85
4 *Cochran*	0	7	71	83
5 *Lott*	10	25	78	93
MISSOURI				
1 Clay	85	95	24	12
2 Young	25	75	44	48
3 Gephardt	35	75	22	48

	ADA	COPE‡	CCUS	ACA
4 Skelton	20	61	28	68
5 Bolling	65	94	19	9
6 *Coleman*	20	11	61	93
7 *Taylor*	10	20	83	96
8 Ichord	20	30	61	92
9 Volkmer	45	65	29	54
10 Burlison	45	75	17	22
MONTANA				
1 Baucus	40	79	33	35
2 *Marlenee*	25	26	76	85
NEBRASKA				
1 *Thone*	15	6	78	86
2 Cavanaugh	60	65	28	27
3 *Smith*	10	5	76	78
NEVADA				
AL Santini	5	35	56	65
NEW HAMPSHIRE				
1 D'Amours	45	80	6	42
2 *Cleveland*	10	10	65	80
NEW JERSEY				
1 Florio	55	75	33	22
2 Hughes	55	68	17	35
3 Howard	60	84	7	9
4 Thompson	75	95	24	4
5 *Fenwick*	55	35	59	33
6 *Forsythe*	40	16	94	70
7 Maguire	90	84	18	12
8 Roe	35	85	22	19
9 *Hollenbeck*	50	75	29	22
10 Rodino	35	83	0	0
11 Minish	35	85	28	21
12 *Rinaldo*	50	80	35	33
13 Meyner	75	94	22	12
14 LeFante	20	94	22	25
15 Patten	50	90	29	12
NEW MEXICO				
1 *Lujan*	5	24	67	86
2 Runnels	5	6	93	93
NEW YORK				
1 Pike	35	30	50	52
2 Downey	60	100	18	7
3 Ambro	20	53	35	35
4 *Lent*	20	20	76	75
5 *Wydler*	10	30	81	69
6 Wolff	65	75	22	28
7 Addabbo	70	95	20	12
8 Rosenthal	90	94	28	8
9 Delaney	40	68	47	31
10 Biaggi	55	75	44	40
11 Scheuer	70	85	25	12
12 Chisholm	100	90	29	7
13 Solarz	80	85	18	13
14 Richmond	95	95	25	5
15 Zeferetti	35	80	25	36
16 Holtzman	100	90	22	7
17 Murphy	35	68	33	30
18 Green	58	61	44	12
19 Rangel	80	90	18	8
20 Weiss	100	90	29	8
21 Garcia	79	83	20	5
22 Bingham	80	83	20	4
23 *Caputo*	25	50	44	56
24 Ottinger	80	89	22	4
25 *Fish*	30	35	82	58
26 *Gilman*	55	75	39	38
27 McHugh	75	80	28	15
28 Stratton	15	50	47	44
29 Pattison	65	75	35	15
30 *McEwen*	15	5	82	72
31 *Mitchell*	25	45	50	70
32 Hanley	40	70	39	32
33 *Walsh*	15	30	78	79
34 *Horton*	55	55	53	33
35 *Conable*	30	25	76	56
36 LaFalce	40	60	33	37
37 Nowak	70	95	17	15
38 *Kemp*	15	15	88	96
39 Lundine	70	85	33	26
NORTH CAROLINA				
1 Jones	25	25	83	78
2 Fountain	15	10	71	88
3 Whitley	25	16	64	95
4 Andrews	25	37	56	59
5 Neal	25	25	67	67
6 Preyer	55	60	41	35
7 Rose	50	53	35	43
8 Hefner	25	20	67	63

	ADA	COPE‡	CCUS	ACA
9 *Martin*	15	5	71	88
10 *Broyhill*	20	5	83	88
11 Gudger	25	30	50	92
NORTH DAKOTA				
AL *Andrews*	5	5	65	73
OHIO				
1 *Gradison*	20	15	83	70
2 Luken	25	65	47	60
3 *Whalen*	65	89	38	13
4 *Guyer*	10	15	82	78
5 *Latta*	5	5	65	89
6 *Harsha*	15	26	59	85
7 *Brown*	15	5	94	80
8 *Kindness*	5	5	83	93
9 Ashley	65	74	25	20
10 *Miller*	20	15	67	92
11 Stanton	15	15	72	52
12 *Devine*	5	5	82	93
13 Pease	65	80	22	15
14 Seiberling	95	84	28	4
15 *Wylie*	25	30	72	65
16 *Regula*	20	25	72	63
17 *Ashbrook*	5	11	93	100
18 Applegate	20	55	50	46
19 Carney	55	85	24	9
20 Oakar	60	95	17	20
21 Stokes	85	100	19	10
22 Vanik	70	82	29	12
23 Mottl	30	60	28	58
OKLAHOMA				
1 Jones	25	25	67	92
2 Risenhoover	10	29	60	84
3 Watkins	20	37	59	84
4 Steed	20	45	61	41
5 *Edwards*	10	5	83	92
6 English	15	16	67	88
OREGON				
1 AuCoin	40	60	42	40
2 Ullman	30	35	50	25
3 Duncan	35	42	67	41
4 Weaver	75	89	6	32
PENNSYLVANIA				
1 Myers	50	78	24	24
2 Nix	40	75	21	17
3 Lederer	50	80	18	15
4 Eilberg	60	95	18	13
5 *Schulze*	10	16	75	88
6 Yatron	40	60	39	44
7 Edgar	80	89	22	11
8 Kostmayer	70	79	22	26
9 *Shuster*	5	16	78	96
10 *McDade*	30	45	61	54
11 Flood	40	74	21	21
12 Murtha	25	65	33	30
13 *Coughlin*	25	21	78	66
14 Moorhead	65	85	33	11
15 Rooney	50	90	24	7
16 *Walker*	15	20	83	96
17 Ertel	30	56	47	50
18 Walgren	55	80	22	26
19 *Goodling*	20	21	82	87
20 Gaydos	35	75	28	26
21 Dent	20	64	45	67
22 Murphy	40	72	22	40
23 Ammerman	50	80	13	31
24 *Marks*	50	55	44	38
25 *Myers G.*	35	30	72	65
RHODE ISLAND				
1 St Germain	65	85	18	15
2 Beard	45	95	13	12
SOUTH CAROLINA				
1 Davis	45	55	50	58
2 *Spence*	15	20	72	89
3 Derrick	45	68	24	44
4 Mann	30	18	63	62
5 Holland	35	61	39	46
6 Jenrette	40	74	33	43
SOUTH DAKOTA				
1 *Pressler*	25	44	56	37
2 *Abdnor*	20	22	75	91
TENNESSEE				
1 *Quillen*	15	25	83	85
2 *Duncan*	20	20	78	85
3 Lloyd	15	53	50	68
4 Gore	65	70	22	15
5 Allen #	27			
6 *Beard*	5	0	89	96

	ADA	COPE‡	CCUS	ACA
7 Jones	20	42	44	56
8 Ford	70	90	19	12
TEXAS				
1 Hall	20	15	83	92
2 Wilson, C.	35	68	65	50
3 *Collins*	10	5	100	96
4 Roberts	15	20	80	79
5 Mattox	40	79	33	50
6 Teague	5	19	75	60
7 *Archer*	10	0	89	100
8 Eckhardt	75	89	6	4
9 Brooks	30	45	50	40
10 Pickle	45	50	50	65
11 Poage	20	32	71	89
12 Wright	35	83	33	29
13 Hightower	30	35	81	67
14 Young	15	73	36	23
15 de la Garza	10	39	72	83
16 White	25	20	71	80
17 Burleson	10	10	88	89
18 Jordan	80	80	33	15
19 Mahon	25	21	67	56
20 Gonzalez	70	95	24	26
21 Krueger	30	38	73	64
22 Gammage	15	35	76	87
23 Kazen	10	33	71	64
24 Milford	15	12	88	81
UTAH				
1 McKay	15	37	50	60
2 *Marriott*	5	15	94	100
VERMONT				
AL *Jeffords*	40	30	56	25
VIRGINIA				
1 *Trible*	20	21	67	88
2 *Whitehurst*	15	25	78	89
3 Satterfield	10	5	89	100
4 *Daniel, R.W.*	10	11	89	93
5 Daniel, D.	0	5	89	96
6 *Butler*	10	0	100	96
7 *Robinson*	10	10	82	93
8 Harris	70	90	22	7
9 *Wampler*	10	20	78	85
10 Fisher	60	65	22	22
WASHINGTON				
1 *Pritchard*	40	32	78	39
2 Meeds	65	89	19	13
3 Bonker	65	89	22	21
4 McCormack	30	70	28	30
5 Foley	30	65	33	22
6 Dicks	45	90	33	19
7 *Cunningham*	5	20	89	92
WEST VIRGINIA				
1 Mollohan	30	55	50	48
2 Staggers	50	85	24	30
3 Slack	25	42	44	67
4 Rahall	60	79	31	29
WISCONSIN				
1 Aspin	60	85	28	12
2 Kastenmeier	95	95	22	4
3 Baldus	60	85	11	8
4 Zablocki	40	65	39	33
5 Reuss	80	90	22	8
6 *Steiger*	35	16	76	56
7 Obey	60	80	22	22
8 Cornell	80	90	22	22
9 *Kasten*	15	19	80	90
WYOMING				
AL Roncalio	60	78	6	16

Democrats   *Republicans*

	ADA	COPE‡	CCUS	ACA
ALABAMA				
Allen, M.	0	31	82	77
Sparkman	45	47	54	35
ALASKA				
Gravel	70	81	36	12
Stevens	10	33	65	61
ARIZONA				
DeConcini	35	58	47	39
Goldwater	10	12	100	95
ARKANSAS				
Bumpers	45	26	44	35
Hodges	50	21	50	48
CALIFORNIA				
Cranston	85	89	28	8
Hayakawa	15	24	82	68
COLORADO				
Hart	65	78	22	17
Haskell	50	75	20	15
CONNECTICUT				
Ribicoff	55	78	39	14
Weicker	60	87	53	20
DELAWARE				
Biden	50	61	44	27
Roth	15	11	89	83
FLORIDA				
Chiles	35	32	72	36
Stone	25	50	72	38
GEORGIA				
Nunn	25	26	78	67
Talmadge	40	42	53	39
HAWAII				
Inouye	60	80	41	19
Matsunaga	70	89	29	5
IDAHO				
Church	70	74	12	26
McClure	0	6	64	91
ILLINOIS				
Stevenson	65	74	19	13
Percy	50	47	59	18
INDIANA				
Bayh	85	94	22	5
Lugar	10	11	89	92
IOWA				
Culver	85	89	11	13
Clark	90	89	11	13
KANSAS				
Dole	20	22	83	58
Pearson	30	56	25	24
KENTUCKY				
Ford	45	68	44	42
Huddleston	30	67	50	27
LOUISIANA				
Johnston	15	13	77	60
Long	25	29	72	47
MAINE				
Muskie	75	67	6	8
Hathaway	55	84	0	0
MARYLAND				
Sarbanes	90	95	24	8
Mathias	50	76	25	22
MASSACHUSETTS				
Kennedy	95	95	20	4
Brooke	70	93	50	18
MICHIGAN				
Griffin	10	22	65	75
Riegle	85	89	29	0
MINNESOTA				
Anderson	35	92	27	8
Humphrey, M.	68	85	27	21
MISSISSIPPI				
Stennis	10	6	73	73
Eastland	10	9	83	70
MISSOURI				
Eagleton	50	79	35	9
Danforth	25	32	71	38
MONTANA				
Hatfield, P.	50	76	31	33
Melcher	45	63	8	39
NEBRASKA				
Curtis	10	6	82	95
Zorinsky	25	16	72	74
NEVADA				
Cannon	30	33	60	43
Laxalt	5	18	88	81
NEW HAMPSHIRE				
Durkin	65	95	33	21
McIntyre	40	59	41	23
NEW JERSEY				
Case	65	94	38	4
Williams	80	89	35	9
NEW MEXICO				
Domenici	15	40	56	65
Schmitt	20	24	87	75
NEW YORK				
Moynihan	60	89	35	4
Javits	75	95	29	5
NORTH CAROLINA				
Morgan	25	35	53	27
Helms	5	11	87	96
NORTH DAKOTA				
Burdick	55	74	18	23
Young	5	18	81	73
OHIO				
Glenn	65	74	28	25
Metzenbaum	100	84	22	13
OKLAHOMA				
Bartlett	10	11	100	96
Bellmon	25	21	89	52
OREGON				
Hatfield, M.	50	86	38	22
Packwood	45	69	44	41
PENNSYLVANIA				
Heinz	60	78	50	18
Schweiker	20	63	59	59
RHODE ISLAND				
Pell	75	89	19	4
Chafee	55	63	47	26
SOUTH CAROLINA				
Hollings	30	39	59	52
Thurmond	10	21	83	87
SOUTH DAKOTA				
McGovern	75	86	33	19
Abourezk	60	82	17	12
TENNESSEE				
Sasser	55	74	47	57
Baker	25	37	93	79
TEXAS				
Bentsen	35	26	83	57
Tower	10	6	89	86
UTAH				
Garn	5	5	94	95
Hatch	5	11	94	96
VERMONT				
Leahy	65	79	24	21
Stafford	55	58	59	29
VIRGINIA				
Byrd, H.*	10	11	83	100
Scott	10	22	94	100
WASHINGTON				
Jackson	55	84	17	8
Magnuson	45	75	38	13
WEST VIRGINIA				
Byrd, R.	45	78	28	29
Randolph	30	68	24	38
WISCONSIN				
Nelson	70	89	39	13
Proxmire	60	63	44	46
WYOMING				
Hansen	15	6	88	88
Wallop	10	11	80	78

- KEY -

ADA	—Americans for Democratic Action
COPE	—AFL-CIO Committee on Political Education
CCUS	—Chamber of Commerce of the United States
ACA	—Americans for Constitutional Action

Democrats   *Republicans*

* Harry F. Byrd Jr., Ind-Va., is counted for purposes of this study with the Democrats.

‡ Scores were compiled by Congressional Quarterly from the votes selected by the organization.

How Special-Interest Groups Rate Senators

ADA (Americans for Democratic Action) — The percentage of the time each senator voted in accordance with or entered a live pair for the ADA position on 20 selected votes of 1978. The percentages were compiled by ADA. Failure to vote lowers the scores.

COPE (AFL-CIO Committee on Political Education) — The percentage of time each senator voted or was paired in favor of the COPE position on 19 selected votes in 1978. Failure to vote does not lower the scores, which were compiled by CQ.

CCUS (Chamber of Commerce of the United States) — The perentage of time each senator voted with the chamber's position on 18 selected votes in 1978. Failure to vote does not lower the scores, which were compiled by the chamber.

ACA (Americans for Constitutional Action) — The percentage of the time each senator voted in accordance with the ACA position on 24 votes in 1978. Failure to vote does not lower the scores, which were compiled by ACA.

Business and Labor Lobbying

The Labor Lobby: Adapting to a New Climate

For years conservatives have portrayed organized labor as a monolithic force in Washington. During the 1974 elections President Ford and other Republicans warned that heavy Democratic voting in the November elections would result in a Congress under the domination of organized labor. Elect enough Democrats, they insisted, and the AFL-CIO president might just as well be Speaker of the House. The Democrats did very well in the 1974 elections, and repeated their success in 1976 and 1978. But labor has never even come close to controlling Congress, as the conservatives claimed they would.

The reasons for this perceived lack of influence are many and complex, but few think it means labor has lost its

clout. Labor lobbyists stress that the image of the all-powerful labor organization that could determine the fate of legislation was a myth from the very beginning, and they point out that the record shows a string of defeats on key issues.

However, no one would dispute that organized labor wins its share of arguments in

Congress. Much of the civil rights and Great Society legislation of the 1960s was largely the product of its lobbying. But the irony that frustrates many union lobbyists, and that they point to as proof that they don't control Congress, is that labor rarely has won on the issues that affect it most directly.

The unions lost in 1948 when Congress overrode President Truman's veto of the Taft-Hartley Act. They lost in 1959, when they could not prevent passage of the restrictions in the Landrum-Griffin Labor-Management Reporting Act. They lost in 1966, when the House failed to pass legislation repealing Section 14(b) of Taft-Hartley, which permits states to enact "right-to-work" laws sanctioning a non-union shop. They lost in 1977 on common-site picketing and in 1978 on labor law revision.

The reason labor fails to win on its own issues, members and lobbyists agree, is that it comes to be perceived as a special interest, not a public interest lobby, as it can portray itself on behalf of social legislation.

On the other side of labor's frustrations, however, is the fact that its opponents have been equally unsuccessful at persuading Congress to pass further restrictions on union activity. On labor-management issues, there have been no major labor victories in Congress since World War II, but since Landrum-Griffin in 1959, there have been no major reverses either. Labor has stood its ground.

To some labor antagonists, that very fact is evidence of a Congress under thorough labor domination. The National Right to Work Committee, which exists to promote a federal law permitting the non-union shop, says labor lobbyists have made sure right-to-work bills never even get a hearing.

"Union friends in Congress control the committee system," complained Reed Larson, president of the Right to Work Committee, "and the committee system has a powerful impact on what is considered. They're able to stop any legislation that would restrict or curtail their activities. There isn't any meaningful reform possible given their clout."

To a labor lobbyist, speaking in the wake of defeats on jobs, housing and labor law reform, such images of labor clout sound like sheer fantasy. "I'm still looking for the first piece of pure labor legislation to be enacted into law," said a senior member of the AFL-CIO legislative department. "If we've got that kind of power, we must be terrible lobbyists."

Changing Relationships

Relations between labor and Congress have changed greatly in recent years, and part of that is due to a change in the type of people being elected to Congress.

Labor lobbyists are concerned that some Democrats in both chambers who have been elected since 1974 are not so responsive to working-class concerns as liberal Democrats of years past. In the 1974 Colorado Senate campaign, Democrat Gary Hart made news by saying of his generation of liberals, "We are not a bunch of little Hubert Humphreys." To some on labor's side, that meant that new members like Hart were skeptical of the social programs that labor has long fought for.

"The freshman Democrat today is likely to be an upper-income type," said Kenneth Young, director of the AFL-CIO legislative department, "and that causes some problems with economic issues. It's not that they don't vote what they perceive to be working-class concerns, but I think a lot of them are more concerned with inflation than with unemployment. They aren't emotionally involved in unemployment. It's a political issue, and they come down on the side that unemployment is bad, but inflation is more important to their constituents."

Another labor lobbyist said there is a whole new generation of people serving in Congress, all of whom grew up since World War II. These younger members don't understand the labor movement, he said, and they have no feel whatsoever for the kinds of issues that affect labor.

However, one of the most active union lobbyists, Arnold Mayer of the United Food and Commercial Workers, feels that the new breed of Democrats may be more effective on behalf of labor and liberal causes, even if his loyalty is less automatic. "The party hack may be closer to the local union guys than the young independent lawyer is," he said, "but does that mean he's more effective? Is he more likely to understand complex legislation that we favor? ... The hack of 20 years ago manipulated the labor movement as much as labor manipulated him."

A reflection of the greater independence of newer members of Congress is the decline in the power of leadership and a breakdown in party responsibility. Being loyal to the party is no longer paramount to members who vote more to satisfy constituent pressures than to support party positions. This makes it more difficult for leadership to control members' votes. As a result the number of votes that can be counted on to support what are traditionally thought of as labor or Democratic positions has shrunk in the past few years.

Another problem that labor lobbyists feel has hindered their success in recent years is an ineffective White House lobbying organization. One labor lobbyist said that the Carter administration consistently fails to develop legislative programs and that its relations with Congress could be described as poor at best.

He also said that the White House was not adept at using the resources available to it. He cited as an example the legislation authorizing implementation of the Panama Canal treaties that Congress considered in September 1979. When that issue came before the House the administration asked for and received labor help in getting it through. However, during Senate consideration of the legislation labor was not approached. There, in committee, the administration allowed two amendments dealing with minimum wage in the Canal Zone to be dropped, even though they knew labor strongly supported them. That sort of thing makes some labor lobbyists feel that the White House does not understand — or does not care about — labor concerns.

But in spite of these problems labor continues to be an important force on Capitol Hill.

Power of Corridors

If there is one trademark of AFL-CIO and union lobbyists, it is their physical presence at the Capitol. Members of Congress sympathetic to labor goals never need to guess what the AFL-CIO lobbyists want them to do. There are almost always one or more of them around to make sure members know.

Labor opponents express a grudging respect for this patience and willingness to stand around for hours on end. "They're alert, and they're always there," admitted Andrew Hare, a Right to Work Committee lobbyist. "There's so damn many of them there's always bound to be somebody on the scene. And they've got the resources to provide information on any subject."

Mayer of the Food and Commercial Workers agreed that this was one of the most important parts of his job. "The most important difference between union lobbyists and company lobbyists," he said, "is that we stand there outside the House floor. It's an enormous time-saver. I can see 30 or 40 guys in an afternoon. We're not embarrassed to be there, plying our trade, and I think they are."

"I end up with a lot of respect for labor lobbyists.... They're participants, and business is a spectator most of the time."

—Rep. John Ashbrook
R-Ohio

Rep. John M. Ashbrook, R-Ohio, one of the most important business allies on the Education and Labor Committee, conceded that this is so. "I wish my allies were half as tough and half as dedicated as my adversaries. They're participants, and business is a spectator most of the time."

All the members of Congress who were interviewed said the AFL-CIO lobbyists are reluctant to use too strong an approach, even to those members who owe them the most politically. "I don't think there's any improper influence," said Ashbrook. "They have a friends-and-enemies approach that business doesn't have, and they reward their friends. I don't think they buy anyone."

Abner J. Mikva, D-Ill. (1969-73; 1975-79), then a member of the House Ways and Means Committee, said most AFL-CIO lobbyists try to develop the kind of personal contacts with members that allow for relaxed, casual discussions. "It's very informal," he explained. "Ray Denison handles the Ways and Means Committee for them, and we chat. He'll ask me if I've seen a certain section of the bill, and that they're for it, or against it. It's the same kind of contact most oil spokesmen have with me." That kind of casual relationship can be very important to lobbyists.

There are differences in the way unions lobby the Senate and the way they lobby the House. "In the Senate, it's mainly lobbying the staff," said the veteran committee aide. "It's only on the really crucial votes that they call the senator. If the senator is on the fence and they figure he might change his mind, they might call him. Otherwise not."

Playing Down Politics

Young stressed that the AFL-CIO legislative department uses the same tools of persuasion available to any lobbyist. "I can get a member's ear because I'm AFL-CIO," he said. "But that doesn't mean I get his vote. I'd better know what I'm talking about or I can't think of a single member — whether he's supposed to be in our pocket or not — that won't tell me to go to hell."

Mayer believes the soft-sell is a reflection of the professionalization and increased stability of labor lobbying in recent years. "Twenty or 30 years ago," he said, "most labor lobbyists were defeated union business agents or people defeated for some other union post. They looked at the short run, not at establishing long-term relationships. They equated lobbying with bargaining."

A Senate Labor Committee aide agreed that Young and his associates are careful not to overstep their bounds. "The AFL-CIO legislative department is marked by professionalism," he said, "and by a desire to do it soft-sell if possible, hard-sell only if necessary."

"They rarely come in heavy-handed," he continued. "That's not true of individual unions. You get the legislative directors of the unions calling up and saying they will withdraw their money in the next election."

The aide gave the example of a lobbyist for an AFL-CIO affiliate who threatened not to support a midwestern Democratic senator for re-election if he fought reform of the Hatch Act. The senator's opponent in the election was a former House member noted for his anti-union sentiments, but the threat was made anyway.

"Nobody in the legislative department would ever do that," the aide said. "They've got to come back and see you the next week. If somebody gets ticked off, they might not even get in the next time."

One union lobbyist said that the need to maintain long-term contacts with members makes the use of strong-arm tactics counterproductive. "I will not use a threat," he declared. "To save his own face, a member is going to turn around and say, 'to hell with you!' Even if he's scared, he's likely to do that.... If I say something is awfully damn important, and important for the following reasons, I don't have to mention a contribution. I may need the member's help on a major bill next month."

The relationship between politics and lobbying is always a sensitive one, because the enormous sums the unions spend at election time imply to many people that members of Congress are simply being bought. (Estimates are that labor spent more than $10 million in the 1978 congressional elections.) For that reason AFL-CIO lobbyists stress the separation between their legislative department and the Committee on Political Education (COPE), headed by Alexander Barkan. COPE is the federation's political unit, which decides who will receive its campaign contributions.

"COPE people don't lobby on the Hill," Young said resolutely, "and we don't get involved in political contributions.... When I go to see a member, I think he may be worried about the impact of a bill on local labor in his district. But I don't think his mind is on the contributions. I don't get asked for contributions.... If we got involved in politics, every time I went to see a member he'd be talking about funds. And I'd never get anything done."

A former legislative department lobbyist said the separation had been maintained rigorously. He cited cases in which a lobbyist asked for a member's help on an issue, only to find out that the individual had just been denied campaign funds and refused even to talk.

In Mayer's opinion, the legislative department would function better if it kept in better touch with COPE. "The relationship should be closer," he said. "I understand that contributions are made without too much legislative department input, and that's impossible. In my union, we get together on that."

"The legislative end and the political end have a great separation," said an aide to one Senate Democrat, "an ideological separation. I don't think the political disputes spill over into legislation...."

Richard Bolling, D-Mo., a longtime House member, remembers few occasions when AFL-CIO lobbyists used COPE as a legislative weapon. The time he recalls most vividly was the debate over Landrum-Griffin, in the late 1950s. "In '59 it got very blatant," he said. "it was made very clear to the people representing the House in conference that there was an intimate connection between COPE and the legislative department. But they're smart enough to keep it separate most of the time."

The most consistent labor allies in the House, such as Frank Thompson Jr., D-N.J., of the Education and Labor Committee, insist that politics does not enter into the lobbying.

"It happens that I'm philosophically in agreement with labor," Thompson said. "When I'm not, I vote the other way. I have a remarkably good understanding with them.... They'll squawk — I'm against the B-1 bomber. The whole labor movement could be for it, and I'd be against it."

"It really has no direct relationship at all with campaign contributions," Thompson contended, "although I'm one of their chief beneficiaries. No one from there has ever brought it up. They know better than that."

"I don't know why labor should be more pure than anyone else."

—Rep. Abner J. Mikva
D-Ill. (1969-73; 1975-79)

A Few Good Friends

By any definition, Thompson is one of the key labor allies in Congress, the chairman of the subcommittee that deals most directly with labor needs. He is the perennial nemesis of those who oppose labor's interests in Congress.

"Thompson sponsors a bill," complained Andrew Hare of the Right to Work Committee, "and Thompson's subcommittee calls hearings on it. Legislation opposed by labor is ignored by the committee." Hare said Thompson ought to bring right-to-work legislation up for debate, regardless of sentiments on the subcommittee against it.

Hare also charged that Thompson rigs the hearing schedule so that conservative witnesses get the least favorable time. "With the control of the committee the way it is," Hare said, "they're always the first witnesses, and we're always last, after the press is gone."

Losing Reputation

In recent years the full Education and Labor Committee, chaired by Rep. Carl D. Perkins, D-Ky., has developed a reputation for losing its bills on the floor, having them weakened by a House unwilling to accept its liberal legislative product.

Frequently Perkins has brought bills to the floor without a bipartisan committee majority in favor, and committee Republicans such as Ashbrook and John N. Erlenborn, R-Ill., have led the arguments against them.

When a House reorganization headed by Bolling discussed splitting Education and Labor in 1973, Perkins came under much criticism for what some members saw as the liberal and pro-labor biases of his committee.

"We are accused of being partisan and fractious," he responded at the time, "...almost always embroiled in nasty floor fights because of our inability to compose our differences.... We are accused of having a lopsided liberal majority which does not reflect the posture of the House."

"The fact is," Perkins added, "that these criticisms, which occasionally do apply, far overstate the case and the problem."

To labor lobbyists, the committee's divisiveness is in itself evidence that it is not under labor's control. "If we pulled the strings on Education and Labor, why didn't we just win on minimum wage? Nobody on that committee wants to lose on the floor. Nobody wants a reputation as labor's patsy," said one.

A look at the committee's makeup over the years indicates growing polarization, with the Democratic side moving left and the Republicans moving right. "When I came on the committee," said Ashbrook, "you had a few conservative southern Democrats, but now you don't have anything but liberals. They take a hard line against amendments in committee, which is the traditional labor bargaining position. Strategically, that's the best thing that has happened to our side, because the bills have a hard time making it on the floor."

"It's not fair to say labor runs the committee," Ashbrook concluded, "but it has the first leg up in influence."

Below Thompson and Perkins on Education and Labor, the AFL-CIO has among its allies some of the shrewdest and most effective liberal Democrats in the House, such as John Brademas of Indiana and Phillip Burton of California.

Stable Ally

In some ways, the Senate Labor and Public Welfare Committee is a more stable ally for the AFL-CIO than is the Education and Labor Committee in the House. Its chairman, Sen. Harrison A. Williams Jr., D-N.J., is as much a labor loyalist as Thompson or Perkins, and its senior Republicans are much more sympathetic to labor goals.

A look at the record of recent Congresses shows how labor has adjusted its tactics and goals in response to the changing climate on Capitol Hill.

94th Congress

The first legislative priority for 1975 for most unions was an immediate tax cut of more than $20 billion, keyed to lower- and middle-income taxpayers. They got that, but only after concessions that strained labor's credibility among some of its traditional allies in the House.

Oil Depletion Allowance

In negotiating with the White House, George Meany, then AFL-CIO president, and other labor leaders agreed not to press for an amendment ending the oil depletion allowance so that the tax cut bill would move through Congress faster. A strong anti-depletion amendment passed the House anyway, without AFL-CIO help. The federation ended up not only on the losing side, but on what seemed to many to be the anti-reform side.

"We got a lot of advice from labor to cool it on the depletion allowance," recalled Mikva, a leader in the anti-depletion fight. "Fortunately we ignored that advice, and the depletion allowance is gone."

"Labor got co-opted on some of those tax cut issues, such as oil depletion," Mikva added. "But I don't know

"I can get a member's ear because I'm AFL-CIO. But that doesn't mean I get his vote"
—Kenneth Young
AFL-CIO legislative director

why labor should be more pure than anyone else. While I criticize labor's parochialism, they're no more parochial than Common Cause is on some of its issues."

The AFL-CIO held back from supporting repeal of the depletion allowance in the legitimate belief that a repeal provision might jeopardize the entire tax cut. "At the point where it started in the House," said Kenneth Young, then assistant director of the legislative department, "we really were concerned that it might screw things up. Using hindsight, we may have misjudged it. But we damn well didn't do anything to hurt it."

When the House debated energy legislation in June 1975, the AFL-CIO was in a similarly delicate position. The federation had taken a formal position in favor of a gasoline tax and restrictions on gas-guzzling automobiles. But at the strong urging of the United Auto Workers, the AFL-CIO eventually fought a gas-guzzlers tax on the House floor and gave its support to a milder system of civil fines for those firms who fail to meet a fuel efficiency standard.

The UAW is not an AFL-CIO affiliate; it parted company with the federation in 1968. But in this case, it was able to persuade the AFL-CIO that too stringent a tax would create an unmanageable job shortage.

Some lobbyists for AFL-CIO affiliates ended up working for the UAW position. "The UAW has a hell of an employment problem," said one of them. "I felt I owed them one."

Rep. Mikva, who supported a gasoline tax, said it was understandable that the AFL-CIO would soften its position at the UAW's request, given the ties the two unions still maintain on many legislative issues. "If the AFL-CIO can't help the UAW on an issue like that," he said, "how can they expect UAW help on an issue like common-site picketing, which auto workers have no interest in?"

Were the tax cut and the energy bill victories or defeats for the AFL-CIO? A careful look at the evidence indicates that it would be simplistic to place them in either category.

Economic Recovery

There was less ambiguity about the defeat the AFL-CIO suffered April 30, when the Senate voted 29-64 against an amendment by then-Sen. Walter F. Mondale, D-Minn., to add $9 billion to the fiscal 1976 budget for economic recovery programs.

An aide to one liberal midwestern senator said he was struck by the amount of work AFL-CIO lobbyists put into the fight. "It's unusual for them to be that persistent or to spend that much time on it," he said. "They came very hard, very serious. But a lot of people that are normally thought of as pro-labor were on the other side."

Some observers think the AFL-CIO lost points with freshmen in the 94th Congress by refusing to favor depletion repeal during the tax cut debate. Many of the freshmen committed themselves to repeal of the allowance during their 1974 campaigns.

David Cohen, president of Common Cause and a former lobbyist for the AFL-CIO's industrial unions department, argued that labor's concentration on what was immediately practical would hinder its relations with some of the new members in the long run.

"They have problems with some of the newer, younger members, who often want to make their mark on things and want help," he said. "Labor's tendency is to tell you why it can't be done, instead of figuring out a way to do it." Young denied that vigorously, citing the budget amendments as evidence of a willingness to work even in a losing cause.

Common Site: Labor Lost to 'Intense' Lobby Effort

Lobbyists on both sides of the common site-picketing issue agreed that an intensive, well-orchestrated lobbying effort by the business groups opposing HR 4250, coupled with an inadequate labor push, caused the surprise defeat of the bill on March 23, 1977.

Two factors distinguished the successful lobbying effort against the common-site bill. The first was its sheer intensity. The second was what the business lobbyists proudly referred to as the "rifle," as opposed to "shotgun" strategy, in which they had carefully targeted those members of Congress they thought could be swayed to alter the outcome.

The intensity of the lobbying was apparent. Labor-Management Subcommittee Chairman Frank Thompson Jr., D-N.J., the bill's floor manager, referred to it as "massive" in blaming the lobbying effort for the defeat of the bill. House Speaker Thomas P. O'Neill Jr., D-Mass., warned just before debate began on the bill that it was in trouble, explaining that he had "never seen an organization function" like the Associated General Contractors, the home builders, and the other groups opposed to common-site picketing.

Role of Freshmen

The precise targeting of the opponents had centered on the freshmen members of Congress. A National Association of Manufacturers lobbyist stated that NAM had targeted 91 congressional districts for their campaign, of which 68 were represented by freshmen. A representative of the Chamber of Commerce of the United States said that the chamber "went after slightly more than 91; we also tried to reinforce those who were 'no' all the way."

The attention paid to the freshmen was based on the business groups' assessment that many of the new members were "truly open-minded, not committed on this issue," explained a chamber lobbyist. A spokesman for the contractors association broke the numbers down more specifically, saying that "after the last election, it was apparent that we were pretty strong on the Hill; 25 freshmen were committed to us on this issue, and only 4 to labor."

By Monday, March 21, the chamber estimated, the freshmen were one-third for, one-third against, and one-third undecided, with the business groups confident they could still get the votes of some of the uncommitted third.

The freshman-targeted lobbying effort apparently paid business dividends. A majority of the freshmen voting, 37 of 68, voted against HR 4250, including seven northern Democrats and 13 freshmen who were supported in their 1976 campaigns by the AFL-CIO's Committee on Political Education (COPE). Spokesmen from the offices of several freshmen supported by COPE confirmed that the flow of mail and the personal lobbying had been the most intensive yet seen by the new members and that it had played a role in determining their votes.

The office of Tony C. Beilenson, D-Calif., received 248 pieces of mail against the measure, and a single pro-bill letter. A spokesperson there characterized the lobbying as "extremely intense" against the bill. John J.

Cavanaugh, D-Neb., received 700 messages opposed, but "very, very little in favor of the bill." Jim Guy Tucker, D-Ark., received "a tremendous volume of mail, three times that on any other issue, and 95 percent or more was against," according to an aide.

The chief lobbyist for the Laborers' International Union of North America, said on March 25 that "many of the freshmen did not understand the issue, they took the scare stuff of the opposition, and believed it." But if the freshmen were ill-informed, many observers would blame an inadequate lobbying effort by labor. In addition to the chiding O'Neill gave labor March 23 for its laxity, Rep. Thompson made the same point indirectly: "I don't mean to be critical of anyone . . . they've worked awfully hard these last few days, but they may have started a few days late."

Business Effort

The business lobbying strategy was anything but late. The effort began in October 1976 when an umbrella group, the National Action Committee on Secondary Boycotts, was formed. The group included, according to an associated contractors lobbyist, "virtually the entire business community except bankers." Over 100 business associations and corporations were involved, including the Business Roundtable and the National Federation of Independent Business.

Regular meetings were held throughout the fall, and on a weekly basis in February, to plan strategy. "We divided up into teams for Hill heat," or personal lobbying of members, said one lobbyist.

The Chamber of Commerce produced a slide show for showing at local civic group meetings. The contractors association bought 119 of the shows to distribute to members around the country. An elaborate color brochure was published and 10,000 copies distributed. The aim of such publicity campaigns was to stir the "grassroots" lobbying that shows up as letters to Congress from local constituents rather than visits from national headquarters lobbyists.

Several of the groups, particularly the Chamber of Commerce and the contractors, insisted, however, that they were not responsible for the thousands of prewritten postcards that were the bulk of the mail received by Congress on the issue.

Warren S. Richardson, chief lobbyist for the associated contractors, said his group "never to his knowledge" advocated the use of prepared postcards that called only for the sender's signature without any personal expression on the issue. "They're useless," he explained. "Congressmen throw them in the trash and we know that." Richardson conceded, however, that local chapters might have advocated the packaged postcard approach, and at least one chapter did so.

Labor lobbyists were bitter about some of the techniques employed by the business lobbyists, including the postcards. One top labor official cited the approach of one business group that sent out pre-printed postcards as payroll inserts. The employer was asked by the group "to put his own 9¢ stamp on the postcard and mail it for the employee . . . if you have too many, sign them yourself and mail them."

Labor played very little part in one of the most significant freshman actions of the 94th Congress — the seniority revolt in which three committee chairmen were deposed in 1975. For the most part, labor's reluctance to get involved was a reaction to what happened in 1971, when it backed Rep. James G. O'Hara, D-Mich. (1959-77), for House majority leader.

"When Jim O'Hara ran for majority leader," Mayer recalled, "he had the very strong support of the labor unions. And that's probably one reason he did so poorly. That taught us that it's politically a mistake to get involved in internal matters. And we haven't since. When all the chairmanships came up this year [1977], we didn't get involved. It's painful to get embarrassed like that."

Broad Range of Issues

Whatever the frustrations for organized labor, however, few observers saw any decline in its congressional role — or in its influence. The AFL-CIO's official list of priorities for the 94th Congress started with economic relief, but also included health insurance, tax reform, housing assistance, and full funding for education programs, to mention a few. In all of these decisions, there was a lot of input from the AFL-CIO and its unions.

When the House Ways and Means Committee began to mark up tax reform legislation late in 1975, the AFL-CIO's legislative department had its own lobbyist, Ray Denison, working full time with the committee, as he did on energy and on the tax cut bill earlier in the year. "They've done a lot of work on tax reform," said a Senate aide. "They're probably the most effective public interest lobby on that."

The last contention might produce an argument from Common Cause and the Ralph Nader organization, but all "public interest" tax groups would concede that the AFL-CIO has the resources to document its case on complex economic questions. Backing the legislative department's lobbying team are economic research, social security, education and other divisions capable of turning out fact sheets and position papers to supplement what the lobbyists are saying in person.

"We work on a broader range of issues than any group in Washington," Young insisted. "In fact, we probably hurt ourselves by being so broad." Young said he believes members of Congress sometimes justify their decisions to vote against a labor position by reciting a litany of other times they have been on labor's side.

It works both ways, however. Some members who care more about liberal causes than labor issues feel more kindly to unions that take an interest in broader questions.

To some labor lobbyists on the left side of the AFL-CIO's political spectrum, the involvement in social con-

cerns is not just a supplement to constituent interests. It is the basis of the lobbying. "We are a social movement," Mayer argued. "We have a commitment to take care of our constituents, but taking care of our constituents involves some basic economic and social reforms. Some of the union lobbyists, like me, believe that. Others don't."

On a lot of issues, social concerns and constituent protection mix well. Better schools mean more jobs for teachers. Expanded housing opportunities mean more jobs in construction. In the past few years, however, there have been some conflicts, particularly on environmental issues.

The AFL-CIO supported the Alaska pipeline, the supersonic transport plane, and the anti-ballistic missile system, in part because jobs were involved. The UAW, conspicuously dovish on most war and defense issues, supported construction of the Air Force's B-1 bomber. Its members would have built the B-1 bomber. *(Lobbying on B-1 issue, see p. 32)*

With unemployment near 9 percent in 1975, many observers thought labor was becoming more vulnerable to those conflicts than in previous years. Opponents of a consumer protection agency worked hard on AFL-CIO affiliate unions to convince them that tougher consumer laws would put companies out of business.

Reform Disputes

To some liberal lobbyists outside the unions, including Cohen of Common Cause, the potential strains of social activism have made labor lobbyists too timid. Cohen said the AFL-CIO has become reluctant to stage a floor fight, or to campaign in the public media, for fear of offending a member union with specific constituent needs. He said the union lobbyists no longer think as far ahead as they should.

"Their whole style," he said, "is to figure out where the trends are going, and either to accept it or modify it at some marginal points. It's sort of a limited approach. They are limited by the immediacy of the legislative process."

Mikva, a labor lawyer in private life, agreed with Cohen in theory. But he expressed sympathy with the problems of the lobbyist for a union whose members worry more about bread-and-butter than about social goals. "That's a tough role for a group that has to deliver," Mikva said. "They have constituents who need help today and tomorrow. They have to win once in a while."

The AFL-CIO alienated Common Cause and other liberal groups in 1974 by working to kill the House committee reorganization proposal drawn up by Bolling's select committee.

The federation ended up opposing Bolling's proposal to split the Education and Labor Committee because of fears that a separate Labor Committee would become painfully polarized between pro-labor Democrats and anti-labor Republicans. In addition, the Seafarers union and other AFL-CIO affiliates could not accept the proposed abolition of the Merchant Marine and Fisheries Committee, which had been consistently friendly to the union.

Bolling said it was labor opposition that led to the defeat of his plan in the House Democratic Caucus by 16 votes. "We could have beaten everybody else," he said, "but labor put the muscle in that beat us. They support so many Democrats for re-election that it was very destructive in the caucus."

Prior to the committee reform dispute, Bolling had been a labor ally for more than two decades in the House, working in partnership on civil rights and other important legislation. They are not close any longer. "I was so

"If members of Congress sense that the labor movement is split, they figure they've got a free ride."

—Rep. Richard Bolling
D-Mo.

disappointed with some of them that I don't even talk to them," he said. "I still vote with them on some labor issues, but I don't waste my time on people who are so far out of touch with what Congress needs."

95th Congress

In the wake of a few surprise setbacks to its legislative agenda, organized labor revised its strategies for pushing its programs on Capitol Hill during 1977.

Labor's early defeats that year, particularly the common-site picketing bill, cast doubt on labor's power to get what it wanted from the strongly Democratic 95th Congress. Despite labor's belief that it contributed heavily to the election successes of many of the members of Congress, labor found it was being out-hustled and out-argued in some early votes of the 95th Congress. The impressive success of business and anti-labor groups in utilizing indirect, or "grass-roots," lobbying techniques spread concern among some labor supporters about its prospects with the 95th. *(Business lobbying, pp. 113-125)*

Besides scaling down its agenda to priority items such as labor law revision and an increase in the minimum wage, labor was forced to redouble its efforts to gain support for its legislative aspirations. Led by the AFL-CIO, organized labor began an intensive new grass-roots lobbying effort of its own. And labor negotiated hard for the needed backing of the new Democratic administration, which it also helped elect but whose support it found could not be taken for granted.

Organized labor and its congressional friends were forced to concede that their relationship with the 95th Congress was not what they might have predicted after the November 1976 elections. The heavy Democratic majorities in Congress and the new Democratic administration — both attributable in part to labor efforts — augured well for labor then.

The recognized need to revamp the labor agenda and to strengthen its lobbying and political efforts sprang in part from the impressive ability of labor's opponents to utilize techniques of indirect lobbying — the generation of grass-roots pressure from home-state constituents in the form of personal letters or pre-printed postcards to their representatives in Washington.

A related reason resulted from the tremendous turnover in Congress in the six previous years. Both House Speaker Thomas P. O'Neill Jr., D-Mass., and Majority Whip John Brademas, D-Ind., commented on the independence, hence unpredictability, of the new members of Congress, Democrats and Republicans alike.

Organized labor also suffered from its portrayal by opponents as a monolithic, boss-led force that was not democratic and was no longer responsive to its own rank and file, much less sensitive to the needs of non-union people. But labor began to address those image problems in 1977. As a part of a rejuvenated lobbying effort, labor and its friends worked to convey to people their own view of organized labor: the traditional "best friend" of working people everywhere in the nation.

Defeat on Common-Site Picketing

Predictions that labor would do poorly with the 95th Congress stemmed largely from the defeat of the common-site picketing bill. That bill, which would have broadened picketing rights at construction sites, had been passed by the 94th Congress but vetoed by President Ford. Many

"It happens that I'm philosophically in agreement with labor."
—Rep. Frank Thompson Jr., D-N.J.

considered it a sure winner in the new Congress. Its defeat in the House on March 23, 1977, by a narrow margin, stung labor badly.

Labor supporters such as Rep. William D. Ford, D-Mich., explained that loss by noting the intensive and sophisticated lobbying effort mounted by business interests against the bill. *(Box, p. 101)*

"It was the best-organized, best-financed effort to create the impression that you have grass-roots support for your position that I've ever seen," Ford said. "They used all the new developments in fund-raising and targeting. They targeted the vulnerable members. They blanketed newspaper ads and direct mail, and they picked members' districts where they thought they could create the most heat."

Frank Thompson, chairman of the House Education and Labor Subcommittee on Labor-Management Relations and floor manager of the common-site bill, concurred. "The Associated General Contractors in particular launched a fantastic mail drive. They even sent employers packets of postcards for employees to send in to members of Congress. I think the business groups surprised themselves by coalescing so successfully and defeating situs picketing."

While the business opponents of the picketing bill were credited with a well-orchestrated lobbying effort, labor's own lobbyists conceded that some laxity in their effort was also a cause of the bill's defeat. Victor Kamber, who headed the AFL-CIO task force on labor law reform, explained the failure to generate adequate pressure by saying, "We took for granted that the Congress understood our position, and knew that our people around the country cared. I do not believe on situs that the opposition won; we lost."

Kamber added that labor had focused on the Senate where it believed the more difficult fight would occur. "In the Senate, where we did target offices, mail was 100 to 1 our way, for example the offices of [Richard G.] Lugar [R-Ind.] and [Charles H.] Percy [R-Ill.]."

The defeat on common-site picketing was not the only indicator that labor had congressional troubles, but it was a primary one. Also widely mentioned as a labor embarrassment was the failure to gain passage of the Hatch Act bill (HR 10), which would have eased restrictions on political activity by the nation's 2.8 million federal employees.

Accomplishments

Though forced to make some concessions, labor groups took pride in a number of legislative accomplishments. To prod economic recovery along, Congress in May 1977 approved stimulus legislation designed to pump funds into the economy over a two-year period. Labor initially had wanted a much larger one-shot stimulus, but decided to

Kirkland: 'The Challenge Is to Maintain Progress'

The year 1979 will be remembered as a landmark in U. S. labor history. It was in 1979 that George Meany, for more than 40 years undisputed leader of the labor movement in America, announced that he would step down as president of the AFL-CIO. The man most observers expected to take his place was Lane Kirkland, for years federation secretary-treasurer.

Although it seemed unlikely Kirkland would win the top spot unopposed, few expected any potential challengers to be able to muster enough support to seriously impair his chances of becoming the second president in the AFL-CIO's history.

Kirkland expressed some of his views on the labor movement in an interview that took place shortly before the AFL-CIO's November 1979 convention.

Lane Kirkland   **George Meany**

Membership Drop

Asked about the dramatic drop in membership that organized labor had experienced in the 1970s, Kirkland said that repressive labor laws, "class warfare" and a metamorphosis of the American job market were primary reasons for the decline.

"If we had the legal climate that prevails in most of Western Europe," he said, "I'm sure we would be able to organize several million new members in fairly short order."

Speaking in his top-floor office overlooking the White House, the 57-year-old labor leader disputed charges by many union leaders that the AFL-CIO had lost interest in organizing. "I think we've been emphasizing organizing," he said. "We've added organizers to our field staff. And I think we've had some success."

Kirkland also countered criticism that the AFL-CIO had been slow to recognize the importance of service and public employee unions. "We do not focus on the craft unions particularly," he said, noting that the federation had responded to the "one broad area of expansion in this country" by establishing three new divisions: for professional employees, food and beverage workers and public employees.

While stressing that union membership, in real numbers, had increased since 1960, Kirkland acknowledged that organized labor's share of the work force had dropped (from 34 percent to 25 percent). An increase in hard-to-organize professional and technical workers, the flight of industry to right-to-work states and overseas and the Taft-Hartley Act on labor relations accounted for that membership drop, Kirkland claimed.

"Since 1947, we've been operating under a law [the Taft-Hartley Act] that places great handicaps on organizing. The effort to change that law is the great responsibility of the AFL-CIO." Particularly troublesome to unions, Kirkland said, is the act's ban on secondary boycotts — preventing one union from striking on behalf of another. That provision forces unions to use "ineffective" consumer boycotts to support strikers, he said, or drives them "to legal remedies, which take forever and yield little."

Also undermining the union movement is a section of the act that "invites states to campaign for new industry on the basis of anti-unionism," Kirkland said.

And lax enforcement of labor's organizing rights, he added, has encouraged business to "indulge in systematic and careful flouting of the law with the surest knowledge that the penalties for doing so are meaningless and long in coming."

Business Success

The chain-smoking labor career man said that business always has been anti-labor, but conceded that "their techniques have become a little more refined and sophisticated."

Kirkland accused the business community of having been "governed by principles of pure class solidarity" during the 1978 labor law reform battle in Congress. Although corporate executives often profess they want to maintain a strong union system, he added, "The best test is that business presented an unbroken phalanx — big, medium and small — in the Senate fight. If they feel so kindly about us, they should give us some legislation that would put some teeth" in the relationship.

But Kirkland said he does not believe that labor needs to match such business offensives as the right-to-work campaign with initiatives of its own. "I don't feel particularly on the defensive," he said. "We didn't lose anything, even in the labor law reform fight. We failed to get something we wanted but didn't have before. I would hate like hell to follow the practices of those groups. They're in the business of frightening people into giving them money."

He also questioned how successful such a campaign could be. "You can engage in all sorts of efforts to polish up your public image, and finally you're faced with a time when you have to do your responsibility to your members."

What kind of future does Kirkland envision for organized labor? "The challenge will be how to maintain increasing social and political progress in what appears to be a conservative, or even a reactionary, mythology of today," he said. "I am convinced that the public sector is going to have to play an increasing role to make life tolerable in this country." But he added, "There's great opportunity there — when things that need to be done become fairly clear."

push for Carter's package — especially the parts calling for expanded public jobs programs.

New youth employment programs, also strongly advocated by labor organizations, won congressional approval and, in the area of worker health and safety, mine safety legislation survived attempts in both houses to weaken it.

On occasion, unions have teamed up with their employers on legislation with potentially adverse employment implications. The United Auto Workers and the automobile companies, for example, pushed together for a relaxation of scheduled auto emission standards, while unions representing workers in import-threatened industries have joined with their employers in pressing for more stringent tariffs.

Seeking Broad-Based Support

At its February 1977 meeting, the AFL-CIO Executive Council decided to set up a special unit to shepherd key pieces of legislation through the 95th Congress. In anticipation of tough, potentially divisive fights over many of the issues within its charter, the new unit — known as the Task Force on Labor Law Reform — was specifically given the job of forming coalitions and marshaling the necessary grass-roots support for its proposals.

The task force had jurisdiction over the following matters:

● Revisions in the National Labor Relations Act, intended to streamline administration of the law and cut down on collective bargaining abuses by employers.
● Minimum wage increases.
● Collective bargaining rights for public employees and farm workers.
● Common-site picketing.
● Hatch Act revisions.
● Strip mining controls.
● "Cargo preference" legislation requiring that a proportion of imported oil be transported in American ships.

Legislation on each of the last four issues had been vetoed by former President Ford.

To finance the task force's work, the AFL-CIO charged its 14.2 million members an additional 1 cent apiece per month.

Kamber, the task force director, previously had served as director of research for the AFL-CIO building trades department. Having accepted the job March 20, 1977, Kamber was just starting to assemble his operation when the House acted on common-site picketing. "Our first task was to have been common-site picketing in the Senate," said Kamber in an interview, "but obviously the script changed. We didn't really get off the ground for another three weeks after that, because there was really nothing to get off the ground with."

Hatch Act Coalition

According to Kamber, the House defeat of common-site picketing legislation starkly dramatized the need to demonstrate that other task force issues had broad support outside the labor movement as well. The first chance came with the Hatch Act bill (HR 10), which reached the House floor in May.

To counter attacks on the bill as a "power grab by labor bosses," the task force put together a coalition of more than two dozen groups — including the American Civil Liberties Union, the Americans for Democratic Action, the National Association for the Advancement of Colored People, and a variety of civil rights organizations.

Statements and ads by this coalition stressed that HR 10 simply relaxed restrictions on certain kinds of political activity by federal employees — without changing the Civil Service merit system in any way. Noting that the bill retained existing curbs on partisan activities by employees in sensitive jobs such as law enforcement, intelligence and government contracting, the task force focused on its meaning for "ordinary" people.

One newspaper ad Kamber was especially proud of showed a secretary for the Veterans Administration in Fort Meade, S.D. "Charlotte Wilson wants to help elect her next senator, but the law won't let her," the ad read. "She'd like to get politically active . . . give a coffee hour for the candidate of her choice, distribute literature, address envelopes, speak at political meetings, play a citizen's normal role in politics."

Supporters of HR 10 won solidly in the House, passing the bill by an 80-vote margin June 7 after essentially nullifying an anti-union amendment that had been added earlier.

Labor groups attributed their earlier defeat on the amendment — which put restrictions on union activities that might coerce federal employees and forbade the use of union dues for political purposes — to fatigue and confusion. To save time the floor manager had sharply limited debate on amendments, and many members did not initially realize the "chilling" effect such an amendment could have.

The bill was strongly supported by the public employee unions, such as the American Federation of Government Employees and the American Postal Workers Union. Opponents were Common Cause and the anti-union Public Service Research Council. There was a sizable advertising and editorial campaign against the bill.

However, in spite of the success in the House, the bill did not go far in the Senate. It was opposed by Sen. Abraham Ribicoff, D-Conn., chairman of the Senate Governmental Affairs Committee which had jurisdiction over the legislation. It also faced a possible filibuster from the Senate Republicans. These factors contributed to a decision by supporters not to try to bring the bill to the floor for a vote.

Minimum Wage

With the minimum wage issue, Kamber's operation used the same coalition concept as in the Hatch Act effort — on a much larger scale. The Coalition for a Fair Minimum Wage, formed in April 1977, claimed 150 groups as members — including labor unions and a variety of civil rights, religious and social service organizations.

Noting that two-thirds of the workers earning the minimum of $2.30 an hour were women, the coalition actively sought participation by women's groups. A special coalition of youth groups was also formed, to help rebut arguments that higher minimum wages would worsen job prospects for young workers.

To mobilize grass-roots activity, the coalition made considerable use of pre-printed postcards — a technique used in the Hatch Act effort as well. Kamber said that 2.5 million green and white cards urging support for "a fair minimum wage that will provide a decent living" were distributed for mailings to Congress and the White House.

Though the aim of the cards was volume rather than a substantive message, Kamber added that the approach conveyed some personal feelings nonetheless. "It's difficult for our people to sit down and write thoughtful letters to their congressmen" after a hard day's work, he said, remarking that the opposition had greater access to dictaphones, secretaries and other help.

Labor credited the minimum wage campaign with helping to change President Carter's position on the issue. Instead of the $3.00 hourly wage floor labor wanted, the administration originally proposed $2.50 — an increase of only 20 cents an hour. Labor and the administration also initially disagreed on the pace of future increases, though both supported a form of "indexing" the minimum to average manufacturing wage levels.

The eventual compromise proposed an increase of $2.65 an hour starting Jan. 1, 1978. Under the indexing system, the minimum would rise automatically to 52 percent of the average manufacturing wage on Jan. 1, 1979, and to 53 percent of this average in 1980. After 1980, these automatic adjustments would proceed at the rate of 53 percent.

Though pleased with these developments, the coalition recognized plenty of pitfalls ahead. The wage and indexing provisions of HR 3744 were highly unpopular with business, and the coalition had to combat charges that the combination would be excessively costly and inflationary.

On indexing, many small, labor-intensive enterprises — such as restaurants, motels and convenience stores — protested bitterly to Congress about the prospect of being linked in any way with wage levels in manufacturing. "We do not belong in the manufacturing industry," said a lodging industry spokesman. "We are a service industry and our wages should be related to our industry and our problems."

In the House there was substantial support for some form of "subminimum" wage for youth — an idea labor groups detested. Though unsuccessful, proposals for youth wage differentials received significant bipartisan support in the Education and Labor Committee as members worried that the new higher minimum would price young workers out of the job market.

While they expected such a move from committee Republicans, labor groups were surprised that several Democrats — led by Robert J. Cornell, Wis., and Paul Simon, Ill. — proposed a lower youth minimum as well. In the wake of the House committee votes, the coalition stepped up its efforts to mobilize opposition to the differentials.

When the bill reached the House floor Cornell introduced an amendment to allow the youth subminimum wage. In a close vote of 210 to 211, the amendment was defeated, with Speaker O'Neill casting the tie-breaking vote. Indexing was rejected by a much wider margin — 223-193.

When the bill cleared the House, labor had won an increase in the minimum wage, but had lost on three other provisions. One was indexing. The others were an attempt to eliminate the "tip credit" that allowed employers of tipped workers to pay them up to 50 percent less than the minimum wage and an attempt to prevent doubling of the small business exemption from minimum wage coverage from $250,000 to $500,000 in annual sales.

It took intensive work on the part of labor strategists to obtain more favorable results in the Senate. There indexing still lost, but the Senate version of the bill carried a reduced tip credit of 30 percent and called for a smaller increase in the small business exemption.

The compromise between the two versions that finally became law called for a four-stage increase in the minimum

wage over a four-year period, achieving much the same goal as indexing. The tip credit was reduced to 40 percent in two stages and the small business exemption was increased by 50 percent rather than doubled. The compromise was supported by the minimum wage coalition, which had worked hard to see that the more favorable Senate provisions prevailed in conference.

Labor Law Revision

Labor's campaign for major revisions in the National Labor Relations Act began with months of negotiations in Washington, to put together a package that the administration could actively support. The result, a White House proposal announced July 18, 1977, was more moderate than the task force's original plans, but it still clearly aimed to help unions organize and deal with resistant employers.

Key parts of the plan sought to streamline federal regulatory procedures. The National Labor Relations Board (NLRB) was required to adhere to deadlines for holding union representation elections, settling challenges afterwards if necessary. Stronger enforcement powers for the NLRB were also recommended, to discourage employers from engaging in dilatory tactics and protracted court challenges to board decisions. And, to raise the costs of noncompliance, the package included stiff penalties. Employers could be ordered to pay double back wages to workers illegally fired for union activities, and could lose government contracts if found guilty of blatant or repeated labor law violations.

The plan did not include one long-sought labor goal — repeal of Section 14(b) of the Taft-Hartley Act, which permitted states to pass their own so-called "right-to-work" laws forbidding union shop contracts. Though they have not launched a major repeal drive in more than a decade, unions still consider 14(b) a significant obstacle to organizing. Twenty states — mainly in the South and West — currently have right-to-work laws.

After some preliminary vote counts, the labor task force decided to forgo a repeal attempt rather than risk sinking the entire labor law package with 14(b).

Severing 14(b) from the package also improved the likelihood of active support from the administration. Carter had said he would sign repeal legislation if it reached his desk, but would not work for it.

Legislation incorporating the White House labor law proposals was quickly introduced in both houses. Though different in detail, the bills (HR 8410, S 1883) covered the same areas as a set of proposals introduced by Thompson at the start of the session. That bill, HR 77, had catalyzed business opposition almost instantly. "It's more dangerous than situs picketing because it affects everyone — not just the construction industry," explained Rep. Erlenborn.

With the opposition focused on the possibilities for union coercion and unfair bargaining advantages, proponents argued that the changes were needed to give workers a free choice. "People are harassed and intimidated, and employers refuse to bargain with unions even after they win an election," said Nik B. Edes, deputy under secretary of labor for legislation, explaining that employers have found numerous ways to thwart the intent of the act and take advantage of the overworked NLRB. "If people want to join a union, they should be able to do so."

Supporters further maintained that companies with good records on labor relations had nothing to fear from the proposed revisions. Rep. Ford, a leading proponent on the Education and Labor Committee, held out hope that large, unionized employers would lend their support to the effort — or at least stay neutral. Thompson said further that the labor law changes — by aiding unionization in areas like the South — could help slow the migration of industry from the cities of the North and East to the Sun Belt states of the South and West.

Even with the president's backing, the revisions encounterd much controversy and resistance in both chambers.

Grass-Roots Opposition. "The fight against the labor law revision package will be grass roots, just like the situs fight; grass roots is the chamber's stock in trade."

That statement came from Argyll Campbell, then a top lobbyist for the Chamber of Commerce of the United States, on July 19 when the labor-supported labor law revision legislation was introduced. Other business lobbyists engaged in similar grass-roots emphasis. Their actions reflected one of the dominant lobbying developments of the 95th Congress — the use by lobbyists of sophisticated computer and direct-mail techniques to generate large volumes of precisely targeted constituent mail to members of Congress.

This intensive and well-managed indirect lobbying increasingly is displacing the traditional door-to-door Washington lobbyist as the mainstay in some influence groups' lobbying arsenal.

The Chamber of Commerce itself now utilizes a computer to target lobbying solicitation communications to the thousands of businesses and business people associated with the national and local chambers. By sending out what the chamber calls "action" letters, many of these individuals in the districts of swing members of Congress are informed of pending legislation like the labor law proposals and spurred to write their representatives to express their views. *(Chamber of Commerce lobbying, see p. 113)*

Other groups have refined the direct-mail and lobbying solicitation techniques to new levels of sophistication and effectiveness. One such group is the National Right to Work Committee, established in 1955 as a non-profit "single-purpose citizens' organization." Its single purpose is to oppose the spread of unionization by the closed shop, or what the committee believes to be "compulsory unionization." Its central legislative objective is the protection of the 14(b) provision and the passage of affirmative "right-to-work" federal legislation that would outlaw closed shops nationally. *(Box, this page)*

The Right to Work Committee's facility with direct-mail campaigns was widely credited with a crucial role in the opposition to the common-site picketing bill. Interviews with labor lobbyists and members of Congress friendly to labor consistently indicate that the current indirect lobbying skill of business, the Right to Work Committee and other groups opposing labor-supported legislation weighs on their minds.

Kamber noted that his task force intended to emulate the successful letter-campaign tactics of those groups. "We want to try to copy some of the tactics of our opponents . . . we want to try not to have just the Washington people go forward, but to try to demonstrate what the rank and file want."

Thompson applauded that idea, saying he expected business groups to continue to employ the mail-generation techniques. He continued that labor should and will do likewise in order to compete for the votes of members — particularly the younger members. Thompson observed that they were "overly sensitive to mail campaigns, not

Fighting 'Forced Unionism'

The volume of mail to and from the National Right to Work Committee's headquarters in the Virginia suburbs of Washington is so great that the Postal Service has assigned the committee its own zip code (22038).

During a major lobbying campaign such as labor law reform the committee receives as many as 40,000 letter a week. But this pales by comparison with the amount of mail the committee sends out — upwards of 60,000 pieces each working day. The group sends 15-18 million letters a year to all parts of the country. During the fight against labor law reform an additional 12 million pieces of mail specifically dealing with that issue were sent out.

As the numbers suggest, the Right to Work Committee is a believer in grass-roots lobbying — using the mails to win followers and exhort them, in turn, to bring pressure on members of Congress. While it usually operates independently, the committee's "antiunion-bosses" campaign has been in harmony with much of the grass-roots business lobbying that has plagued organized labor during recent Congresses.

The committee also uses direct mail for fund raising. It generated $6.8 million for its operations through mail solicitations in 1978.

Mailings from the Right to Work Committee are carefully targeted and analyzed. As Andrew Hare, the committee's chief lobbyist puts it, with that volume of mail "you can't simply dump it on the street."

The organization has analyzed the response rate by almost every conceivable index: congressional district, economic status, ethnic group and, improbable as it may sound, altitude. Hare noted with some humor that people who live at higher altitudes respond to the committee better than those at lower altitudes.

That is true within a given state, so it is not a question of, say, the higher-elevation West reacting differently from the lower East. "I don't know why," Hare said, "but it seems our people just took the higher ground."

The group's main target is what it calls "compulsory unionism." It protects Section 14(b) of the 1947 Taft-Hartley Act, which allows states to ban the closed shop. Twenty states, mostly in the South, have such laws.

The committee contends it is not interested in the broad range of labor-related legislation. Minimum wage, for example, is not an issue of great concern, according to Reed Larson, president. Larson, a 54-year-old electrical engineer from Kansas, has headed the committee since 1959.

only to letters but also to postcards, to obviously inspired mail."

Business groups also used another lobbying technique with great success in the 95th Congress — that of putting together ad hoc coalitions of business and other groups to spearhead a particular legislative effort. The "working group" typically brought together various traditional representatives of business interests, including the Chamber of Commerce, the National Association of Manufacturers (NAM), the Business Roundtable, the National Federation of Independent Business (NFIB), and the Washington

"Our position was not going to be controlled by whatever the AFL-CIO position was."

—Jack Sheehan, United Steelworkers

representatives of various corporations and trade associations.

One business lobbyist noted that the ad hoc coalition approach allows the groups to present what seems to be a fresh voice, and one with a lot of united clout behind it, to Congress. It avoids the tendency of some in Congress to brush off the statements of the separate groups as just "more of the same" position they already have heard.

Business groups moved quickly to form such an ad hoc working group to combat labor law revision proposals. Building on the core group that came together to defeat the picketing bill, the Associated General Contractors, the chamber and NAM teamed with the Associated Builders and Contractors, NFIB, some hospital groups and the Investor-Owned Utilities to form the group that orchestrated opposition to the labor-backed proposals to revise labor-management relations.

Randy Hale, of NAM, explained that the National Action Committee Against the Secondary Boycott, as it was called during the common-site debate, had been a somewhat narrower group than the National Committee on Labor and Management Relations. That was the case since the potential impact of the picketing bill was more limited than that of the labor law proposals.

Sen. Jacob K. Javits, R-N.Y., a longtime labor ally, felt that the business community was emboldened by its common-site success. Javits thought they were "trying to exploit an advantage coming out of the common situs fight, and the president's position on minimum wages. This [was] all tactical maneuvering . . . building up a fire in advance to head off what they see as a prairie fire with labor trying to get a wholesale revision of the Taft-Hartley Act, including Section 14(b)," Javits commented.

Tactical maneuvering is a crucial element of victorious lobbying. One well-connected business lobbyist echoed the Javits assessment by surmising that the introduction of HR 77, Thompson's original labor law revision proposal, hurt labor "because it got our people all riled up. I've never seen Washington representatives for companies that lobby the Hill so hot to do something."

The easy House passage of the labor law revision bill late in 1977 had seemed to augur well for the bill in the Senate, raising labor hopes that it could make up in 1978 for its 1977 disappointments. But backers of the bill were unable to translate their momentary advantage into quick action in the Senate. The bill was not reported by the Human Resources Committee until late January, and then lay idle for almost four months while the Senate debated the Panama Canal treaties.

When it finally came to the floor May 16, the bill was filibustered for five weeks. Unable to break their opposition

after six cloture votes, sponsors June 22 finally had to recommit the bill to committee. It never returned, although Chairman Harrison Williams made a last-minute unsuccessful attempt to bring back a stripped-down version of the bill.

Causes of Defeat. Among the factors causing labor's defeat on HR 8410 were some permanent problems likely to cause difficulties in the future. Others were temporary conditions, crucial in 1978 but not likely to be obstacles to the unions, or help to business, in subsequent Congresses.

Analysis of the cloture votes shows labor's long-term national weakness caused by its inability to exert much economic or political influence in an entire region of the country — the South. The solid southern opposition to the bill, grounded in generations of regional antipathy to unionism, was, in the eyes of many, the biggest single cause of the bill's defeat.

Southern Democrats voted against the key cloture motion, which failed 58-41, by a 3-15 margin. Of the three who supported it, two, Wendell H. Ford and Walter "Dee" Huddleston, were from Kentucky, a border state. Among senators from states of the old Confederacy, only one, Jim Sasser, D-Tenn., voted with labor — at considerable political cost to himself.

By contrast, only two Democrats from the rest of the country opposed all the cloture votes. Further highlighting the regional split was the unanimous support for cloture by members of both parties from the Northeast.

Stephen J. Paradise, staff director of the Human Resources Committee, said the bill finally lost because "it was made into a North-South issue. The historical attitude towards labor in the South hasn't changed."

Senate rules were another factor in the labor law rejection that will continue to plague labor's legislative efforts. Unless the rules are changed, labor's opponents could continue to use the Senate tradition of unlimited debate to block future efforts at labor law reform.

"The biggest thing working against us was an undemocratic system," said Howard Paster, UAW legislative director. Bill supporters won 58 votes for cloture — more than enough to pass the legislation. Comparison with the 257-163 House vote for passage shows that labor gained about the same percentage of support in both chambers; yet the House vote was a solid victory, the Senate vote a crushing defeat.

Finally, the continuing image problems of labor officials worked against the bill. Business opponents successfully drew a distinction between union members and union leaders, maintaining that the bill would help only the latter. One new member, Orrin G. Hatch, R-Utah, frequently proclaiming his sympathy for unionism and union members, concentrated his attacks on "the Washingtonian labor establishment," which he said would alone benefit from the bill.

"The unions picked the wrong fight," said Harold P. Coxson of the Chamber of Commerce. "The bill was perceived as legislation that would help the unions as institutions and not their members."

Short-Term Problems. Still, many key factors in the defeat of the labor law bill were not permanent conditions. To a great extent, the final result could be put down to chance, mistakes and personalities.

Above all, timing told the story. The coincidence that it was brought up in the same year as the Panama Canal treaties helped kill the bill. The extended delay for consideration of the treaties dissipated the momentum that labor had acquired from the easy House passage, and gave opponents time to marshal their forces.

Moreover, the labor and administration forces supporting the bill had already expended some of their legislative support in going all-out for the treaties. Several senators who had put their necks on the line for the treaties, were unwilling to further infuriate their conservative constituents by another controversial vote. One lobbyist described the attitude of some members as "I already bought one, I can't buy the other."

But, in labor's view, the real reason for the defeat was the fact that four senators who had promised to vote for cloture did not do so. According to Kamber, the entire labor strategy was based on what he thought were clear commitments from 62 senators to vote for cloture at some point. When that turned out not to be the case, everything fell apart.

"I don't think it's anything other than the fact that we designed our campaign based on an incorrect premise. We had 62 senators who told us they were with us. If we had had 57 votes, the strategy would have been different than if we had 62 votes," Kamber said.

The confidence that they had 62 votes for the House-passed bill determined the course of the unions' campaign. Most importantly, it convinced labor leaders to shun any early compromise efforts. Philip N. Pulizzi Jr. of the National Association of Manufacturers said, "They were so confident there was no reason to come to the business community to try to work out a bill." Labor's grass-roots pressure campaign was aimed not at switching any votes, just holding on to what it already had.

The determined lobbying efforts by business and conservative groups may have had an important effect on only a few senators — but that was enough to win. "It was one of the most intensive lobbying campaigns that has ever been put on," Edes said.

The estimated $5 million campaign was particularly successful in bringing out small business opposition to the bill. Key votes against cloture cast by five senators — Lawton Chiles, D-Fla.; Russell B. Long, D-La.; John Sparkman, D-Ala.; Edward Zorinsky, D-Neb., and Dale Bumpers, D-Ark. — were, according to Pulizzi, "almost totally attributed to grass-roots pressure."

Personal conflicts also affected the outcome.

The measure got off to a bad start in 1978 when its chief backers, Williams and Javits, had a temporary falling out over press coverage of their staffs. As the year wore on, relations between labor officials and the committee staff deteriorated, leaving labor feeling the bill had been sabotaged by staff delays. Paradise denied there were serious conflicts, however, and called suggestions that the bill could have come up earlier than it did "ridiculous."

Then too, labor and its allies made some mistakes. Perhaps most important was the inclusion in the bill of some provisions that served as "red flags" inciting business opposition. "Equal access clearly hurt us," Paster admitted, referring to a provision allowing union organizers to go on company premises — anathema to employers. And while it is impossible to say for sure, some observers speculated that a differently timed or worded compromise proposal might have carried the day. "A little more compromise in the eleventh hour, and they would have won," argued one lobbyist.

Administration Lobbying. The fact that the administration was busy lobbying for other bills didn't help either. Although Carter personally helped draft the House version,

"You can't go to the well too often. You have to pick the issues where you have the clout."
—Evelyn Dubrow, Ladies Garment Workers

and strongly supported it, the White House did not lend much active assistance in the Senate until the bill was on the floor. "At the time we were pushing for cloture, the administration put forth a major effort. But there's a difference between what you do for people you'd like to help, and what you do for yourself," according to a labor official.

Even after the bill was recommitted to the Human Resources Committee, sponsors had hopes that they would be able to design a new bill that could pick up enough support to overcome the filibuster. With the promise of floor time for a new bill, it seemed plausible that sponsors would find a package acceptable to one more senator, since Long by this time had agreed to go along.

But, as Kamber asked, "Who wants to be number 60?" After all the controversy, no one was willing to take responsibility for putting the bill over the top, no matter what the concessions. Potential vote switches "didn't want to stand out like a sore thumb," Paradise said.

In addition, labor lobbyists held off from pushing for the bill during the summer, at the request of the Senate leadership, which was preoccupied with other bills. "We were working with them too closely to ignore their advice. We knew the rules of the game too well. Had we been a bull in a china shop, we could have won," Kamber said.

A Bad Year

Addressing a convention of the Seafarers' Union in October 1978, after the defeat of the labor law revision bill, AFL-CIO President Meany said, "It hasn't been a very good year for labor on Capitol Hill. It may have been very good for the well-to-do, but not for the workers. We had a few victories, but some very severe disappointments."

There were some successes. Congress approved the Humphrey-Hawkins bill committing the nation to reducing unemployment to 4 percent of the work force by 1983, and public service jobs were reauthorized. New protections for older and pregnant workers were enacted.

But some of the victories were bought at the price of substantial concessions. The Humphrey-Hawkins bill was so weakened by the Senate that many backers considered it an empty shell. Public service jobs legislation had to be sharply cut back before it could pass the House.

Labor's record in the 95th Congress seemed even worse in light of its great expectations following the 1976 elections. After helping elect a new president, and many members of Congress, labor had looked forward to the new session with high hopes. To their dismay, the unions found that they couldn't count on support from all those they had helped to put in office.

The poor legislative showing appeared all the more ominous in light of labor's declining economic strength. Representing a steadily smaller share of the work force, and saddled with a deteriorating public image, unions had been losing more representation elections than they won. After the 95th Congress, labor faced increasingly aggressive business forces without the help that the labor law revision bill would have given them.

Still, with all its troubles, labor remains an extremely potent lobbying force, deeply entrenched in positions of power, and thoroughly skilled in the legislative process.

No Monolith

Despite their usefulness as shorthand, terms such as "labor victory" and "labor defeat" imply a cohesiveness among unions that rarely exists. Even within the AFL-CIO, there are 103 unions ranging ideologically from teachers and government employees on the left to traditional craft-based building trades unions on the right. The affiliates vary almost as much in the intensity of their lobbying as they do in ideology.

The only lobbyists who work specifically for the AFL-CIO are the members of its legislative department. The department implements policy made by the federation's executive council, headed by the federation president and composed of presidents of affiliated unions.

Lobbyists for individual affiliates wear two hats. When they are not lobbying directly for their unions, they often are working on assignment for the legislative department.

"There are certain areas where my union should lead," said Mayer of the United Food and Commercial Workers. "There are many more areas where we expect to follow leadership from others, and especially the AFL-CIO." Mayer considers food stamp and meat inspection to be legislative areas where his union must act independently, and hope to bring the federation along.

It was the Steelworkers who took the lead on pension reform, working toward passage of the comprehensive pension bill that became law in 1974. The same union went out on its own in lobbying for a strong occupational health and safety law.

"We considered these major objectives," said Jack Sheehan, the Steelworkers legislative director, "regardless of what anybody else was doing. . . . Our position was not going to be controlled by whatever the AFL-CIO position was."

An aide to a Democratic senator confirmed that much of the labor lobbying he receives is from affiliates acting apparently on their own. "I hear as much from individual unions as I do from the AFL-CIO itself," he said. "I don't think they sit down and wait for a unanimous decision before they take action on it. They leave a lot of decisions to the individual unions."

In most cases, a union that does not want to lobby strongly on an issue simply will limit itself to a formal gesture in accordance with the federation's position. "In some cases, it's just a matter of sending a letter up," said Evelyn Dubrow, veteran lobbyist for the International Ladies' Garment Workers. "You can't go to the well too often. You have to pick the issues where you have the clout."

Sometimes, however, individual unions not only refuse to help with the lobbying, but actually oppose an AFL-CIO position. The federation supported federal land use planning legislation, but the United Brotherhood of Carpenters fought it in 1974 and was instrumental in its defeat in the House.

The Garment Workers' and Clothing Workers' unions, which administer their own multi-employer pension plans, opposed the pension bill promoted by the steelworkers, who were still dependent on pension plans run by single employers. The American Federation of State, County and Municipal Employees, which represents day care workers, has fought over the issue of day care centers with the American Federation of Teachers, which wants day care to be handled by schools. The dispute has limited AFL-CIO efforts to lobby on the issue.

While the federation rarely conducts its internal disputes in public, the evidence that does leak out tends to undermine the image of the legislative department staff as the field generals who can force affiliates to fall in line.

Bolling feels, for example, that it was some of the affiliates, not the legislative department itself, that turned the federation against his House committee reforms. "I think [they were] more acted upon than acting," he said.

Young concedes that inter-union differences do make lobbying a difficult job. "If members of Congress sense that the labor movement is split," he said, "they figure they've got a free ride. They say, 'Maybe the AFL-CIO is for it, but X, Y and Z unions are against it.' It's unavoidable."

The Battle of Images

The continuing lobbying battle being waged between labor and its business and other opponents is heavily dependent upon sloganeering. Each side is working to project an image of labor that suits its purposes, and the two images of labor being sketched to the public are epically different.

Labor leaders and congressional allies of organized labor are occasionally bitter over the frequently effective opinion-molding against organized labor. Rep. Ford deplored the fact that some members of Congress, particularly the newer members, were "responding to pockets of the population that are being turned on by the mythology that has been sold regarding 'labor leaders.' Labor opponents paint a picture of monolithic, lockstep labor leadership which is patently ridiculous." Ford went on to complain of the anti-labor leaders' rhetoric by maintaining that "they speak of the leaders as if they materialized and formed a union behind them."

Kamber echoed that complaint, arguing that "our opponents are painting all issues as labor 'boss' issues." Particularly on such issues as the Hatch Act easing and universal voter registration, Kamber argued that labor leaders do not really gain, yet their power has been made the focus of the debate on those and other issues. He pointed with exasperation to a dramatic bumper sticker that was distributed around Capitol Hill reading, "Support Instant Election Day Registration — Help Labor Bosses Keep Control of Congress."

Attacking labor "bosses" has become so fruitful in indirect lobbying and public opinion molding that even issues with only remote connections to the goals of organized labor are cast as anti-labor-boss issues. In 1977 Rep. George E. Danielson, D-Calif., complained on the floor that a barrage of computer-prepared mail he had been receiving had been generated by "a complete misrepresentation" of the meaning of certain bills. Danielson cited lobbying solicitation letters from the "Gun Owners of America" attacking Hatch Act revision, universal voter registration and public financing of campaigns as designed to give "big city union bosses" control of Congress in order to pass "strong gun confiscation laws."

Labor defenders also take umbrage at the many semantic efforts to imply that labor is the opponent of individual freedoms. They object to the Right to Work Committee's phraseology, including both the "right-to-work" language and the "compulsory unionization" that is its partner phrase. One friend of labor joked with respect to the "organized labor" label that he couldn't understand why nobody ever called it "organized business."

For its part, organized labor is working to project a vastly different image: that of being the main guardian of the needs of working class people, whether or not they are unionized. Kamber stated that the labor agenda was not a selfish one relating only to the needs of unions as unions. Rather, "they're people issues, social justice issues, that affect the most downtrodden."

Rep. Thompson hit the same theme, citing as an example labor's work for the Elementary and Secondary Education Act: "Their real interest is in the education of their kids and the kids of other hourly wage-earners." Likewise, Sen. Williams argued that "the meaning of unions is not understood. The beneficial effect on everyone's standard of living is not widely appreciated. People don't understand how organized labor lifts everyone's standards."

This struggle to mold the popular stereotype of labor is being carried out through expensive newspaper and magazine ads and through the sophisticated direct-mail campaigns now widely available. Its outcome is far from certain. Nor will it necessarily ever end, but even the temporary swings in public opinion regarding unions could be crucial to labor's congressional prospects and how successful they will be in achieving their legislative goals.

Rep. Ford described labor's problem: "When you get the selfish label on you, you're in trouble. . . . Labor is at its best when its people are supporting causes that are broader than its own membership, so that it's not susceptible to this stereotype." ∎

U.S. Chamber: Emphasis on Grass Roots

The Chamber of Commerce of the United States believes that "the voice of business" can be heard best in Washington by making noise in lawmakers' districts.

So-called "grass-roots" or "indirect" lobbying is the principal tool of the national chamber in dealing with Congress, and the technique is playing a growing role in all business lobbying efforts.

For a while back in 1975 the chamber was afraid it would not be heard at all. The business community was  worried by the results of the 1974 congressional elections. The Democratic landslide, spurred by Watergate, brought a large number of young, liberal representatives to Washington who were generally regarded as anti-business. Predictions were made that there would be a flood of legislation to which business was opposed, a sharp increase in organized labor's influence on Capitol Hill and a great decrease in business' access to Congress.

By and large these predictions did not come true, but the business community was galvanized into action by the expectations of what might have happened. The momentum that was built up then had not yet spent itself by the 96th Congress. The business community has greatly increased its lobbying activities and runs a much more sophisticated operation than it did 10 years ago.

The Chamber of Commerce has been one of the leaders of this increased effort and has expanded its grass-roots lobbying effort since 1974. R. Hilton "Dixie" Davis, the chamber's chief lobbyist, observed that the 1974 election "was a blessing in disguise. . . . The business community is doing a better job of grass-roots lobbying than it has in years." Business has scored some impressive victories since 1974. Lobbying by the business community was credited with the surprise defeat of Common-Site Picketing legislation in 1977 and the Senate rejection of legislation to liberalize labor laws the following year. Labor remains a strong opponent however, as demonstrated by the refusal of Congress to adopt a subminimum wage and postpone the effective date of wage increases, both issues strongly supported by business.

Structure

The Chamber of Commerce of the United States — the national chamber — was founded in 1912 as a federation of businesses and business organizations.

In 1979 approximately 83,000 firms, corporations and individuals were classified as "business and professional members," nearly double the number of four years earlier. Classified as "organizational members" were 2,650 local, state and regional chambers of commerce and American chambers of commerce abroad, plus about 1,300 trade and professional associations.

Besides its headquarters in Washington, the organization maintains regional offices in New York, Atlanta, Minneapolis, Dallas, Burlingame, Calif., and Oakbrook, Ill. The annual meeting is held each April in Washington.

More than 400 employees operate out of the chamber's Lafayette Square headquarters, approximately 75 of whom comprise the professional staff. There is also a computer center in suburban Rockville, Md., employing approximately 100 people.

The major administrative divisions report directly to the senior vice president, William G. Van Meter, who in turn reports to chamber President Richard L. Lesher.

Below the administrative level are the operating departments—program and federation development, legislative and political affairs, economic policy, and communications.

Legislative Action

Vice president for legislative and political affairs is Hilton Davis, a one-time newspaper editor in Tarboro, N.C., and a former FBI agent, who has been with the chamber since 1954. He has eight legislative assistants, four of whom are designated as legislative counsel and work primarily on Capitol Hill. The bulk of the chamber's legislative work, particularly stimulating grass-roots pressure, is done at the headquarters building, but the legislative counsel spend considerable time making contact with congressional and committee staff and members.

The four legislative counsel plus Davis are registered lobbyists. The department's other staff members are not registered.

Chamber Headquarters in Washington

Davis' department is responsible for gathering "information and intelligence" on Capitol Hill and for mobilizing the chamber's membership. However, about 45 staff members from other departments (primarily program development) are the chamber's experts on specific issues and are responsible for developing detailed information on matters of interest to the chamber.

For example, the staff of the government and regulatory affairs section supplies the chamber's expertise on subjects such as lobby law revision and regulatory reform.

The legislative action department handles its own mailings, using an extensive list that can be broken down to target mailings to those members most affected by an issue. In addition the regional offices are sometimes asked to work on legislative projects, particularly if several key members of Congress are from the region covered by an office.

Testimony Team

Another operation that cuts across the organization chart is the "testimony team.' John L. K. Thomas, a member of the legislative action department staff, is chairman of the group, which reviews the organization's formal presentations to Congress. The staff specialist on an issue will prepare draft testimony but the team is responsible for working out the final form. The team is drawn from several sections of the chamber, including the general counsel's office, the economic policy department and the program development department.

In the mid 1970s the testimony team made 40 to 50 appearances a year before Congress. By 1978 that schedule had doubled, with 228 appearances during the two years of the 95th Congress. Davis and Thomas anticipated that the team would go before Congress about the same number of times during the 96th Congress. Part of the reason for the increased workload of the testimony team is the growing number of issues on which the chamber takes a position and part stems from the ever-increasing workload of Congress itself, particularly several of the reform efforts of recent Congresses. "So-called reforms get more people into the act," Thomas said.

Decision Making

Davis said that for the national chamber to take up an issue, the matter must be "national in scope, general in application to business and industry and timely." He said the chamber does not want to become involved in matters that would be of interest to only one segment of membershp, and tries to respond to the concerns of its smaller members as well as the larger corporations and trade associations. In fact the chamber has established a center to focus on the particular problems of small business and its relation to the federal government.

There are approximately 30 standing committees, special committees and councils, and panels and special subcommittees that generally initiate chamber policy positions. The groups are composed largely of professional and corporate executives, although members sometimes are drawn from college and univeristy faculties.

According to Davis, the executives are from big, medium and small companies and are from all sections of the country. However, he acknowledged that "it is not as easy for someone from a small company to get the time to participate."

Issues

The committees are organized around areas of interest to the chamber—antitrust and corporate policy, consumer affairs, environment, government and regulatory affairs, labor relations, taxation and so forth. The committees work with the chamber staff in those areas to develop suggested projects. The committees then study the selected issues and make recommendations.

The committees' recommendations are taken up at the quarterly meetings of the chamber's board of directors. The 65-member board, again primarily high-ranking corporate executives, normally has the final say on any issue.

However, the directors have held membership referendums on a small number of issues. In such a referendum only the chamber's organizational members (trade associations and local and state chambers of commerce) vote; corporate and professional members do not. Each organization is assigned one to 10 votes, depending on its size.

According to Lawrence B. Kraus, the chamber's vice president for finance and general counsel, four referendums were held between 1966 and 1970. A referendum has not been held since 1970 mainly because of the length of time it takes conduct one. Most issues move so quickly now, Kraus said, that they have been decided before a referendum can be completed. Much more frequent are informal surveys of membership opinion which the chamber conducts on a continuing basis. Members also are polled at the chamber's annual meeting. The polls are purely advisory, however, Kraus pointed out.

A chamber publication, "Congressional Issues '79," lists 82 items of interest to the organization for the year. Among the issues supported by the chamber were:

● Legislation giving Congress a veto over rules and regulation promulgated by federal agencies.

● Bills designed to ease the economic burdens of compliance with OSHA and provide more even-handed enforcement.

● Proposals to reduce federal paperwork and the burden it places on business.

● Changes in the tax laws to encourage capital formation.

Legislation opposed by the chamber included:

● Proposals to ban timbering, mining and exploration for oil and gas in the Alaskan wilderness

● Federal financing of congressional campaigns.

● Requirements for mandatory gasoline rationing and mandatory allocation of energy products.

● Any form of wage and price controls.

The number of issues the chamber is involved in has been increasing. In 1975 "Congressional Issues" included 49 items. The 82 issues in the 1979 edition probably will be topped in 1980. Davis and Thomas said a preliminary list for the second session of the 96th Congress contained 106 items. The chamber is not carrying out lobbying campaigns on every issue at all times. Usually 15 to 20 bills of concern to the chamber are moving forward at any given time and that is where the effort is concentrated.

Davis noted that inflation and issues related to the economy have been by far major area of interest in the first session of the 96th Congress. Reduction of the regulatory burdens imposed by the federal government is another area of great interest to the chamber.

Not Registered

Although much of the chamber's annual budget is devoted to legislative action, the chamber itself does not register as a lobby. Nor does it file any financial reports with the clerk of the House or the secretary of the Senate.

Stanley T. Kaleczyc, associate general counsel, said the chamber does not regard lobbying as its "principal purpose" and therefore does not feel obligated to register under existing laws. The chamber defines lobbying as direct contacts with members of congress and their staff. This is a slight modification of the chamber's position of a few years earlier, when only direct contacts with members, not staff, were considered lobbying.

The chamber's legislative counsels file as lobbyists individually, and report their expenses. During the early 1970s the chamber was criticized because the spending reports filed by its lobbyists showed very low expenses. In 1972-73 Davis reported spending only $14.25 and receiving $35 for lobbying. The very low figures were due to the chamber's policy at that time of reporting only on direct contacts with members. While the chamber still feels that is all that the law requires, it now reports all expenses having to do with contact with congressional staff as well as members, thus the spending reports are larger than in the past. But the major part of the chamber's lobbying effort still involves generation of grass-roots pressure. Spending on campaigns to generate grass-roots pressure is not disclosed in the reports.

There have been proposals in Congress to require that indirect lobbying expenses, such as efforts to create grass-roots pressure, should be disclosed. Such a bill, supported by Common Cause, was introduced in the 1975 session, but failed to pass. Similar legislation has been introduced in subsequent years, but by late 1979 none had yet cleared Congress.

Davis and Kaleczyc oppose such legislation. They say the chamber principally is an information service to its members. They challenge the constitutionality of regulating grass-roots lobbying and say there is no accurate way to distinguish between informational activities and indirect lobbying. "There is just no way to figure out how much of a staff member's salary, for instance, should be attributed to lobbying," Kaleczyc said.

Grass-roots Lobbying

"Most of our effort is designed to inform our members," Davis said. "We try to keep them informed and to keep them motivated to register their views."

'Grass-roots' Lobbying: Tighter Law Needed?

"Indirect" or "grass-roots" lobbying of the type practiced by the Chamber of Commerce of the United States has been one of the main areas of controversy in congressional deliberations on revision of federal lobby registration laws.

Indirect lobbying means urging others to contact Congress or the executive branch. Such activities are exempt from the reporting and registration requirements of the existing Federal Regulation of Lobbying Act, but they could come under the provisions of a lobbying bill being considered in Congress in 1979.

In fact, since 1975 Congress has been debating legislation to require registration and reporting by major lobbying organizations, a debate that has been dominated by the conflict between disclosure and the constitutional rights of privacy and free speech. Under existing law very few organizations are required to register.

These conflicts have been most pronounced in the debate over disclosure of indirect lobbying. Legislation passed by the House in 1978 would have required lobby groups to keep records of mass letter-writing campaigns and efforts to encourage others to lobby.

Opponents of indirect lobby expense reporting say the record-keeping requirements would be too burdensome and costly and could force small lobby groups out of business. As a result, they charge, there would be an infringement of free speech rights. In addition, they maintain that the Supreme Court has construed lobbying to mean 'direct' lobbying and legislation requiring reporting of indirect expenditures could be unconstitutional.

Proponents argue that the lack of reporting for indirect lobbying is one of the major loopholes in the existing lobby law. They say it is possible for an organization to launch an expensive campaign on an issue without the general public or Congress ever knowing who is behind it.

The Carter administration has supported a bill that attempts to reconcile the views of various groups with valid concerns about the First Amendment implications of a lobby reform bill as well as its paperwork burdens.

A broad alliance, including organizations with widely varying philosophical viewpoints, developed to oppose the legislation. Included were such groups as the Chamber of Commerce, the American Civil Liberties Union (ACLU), the Sierra Club and the United Church of Christ.

Groups that have supported reporting of grass-roots lobbying expenses include Common Cause, a citizen's lobby group; Ralph Nader's Congress Watch, the AFL-CIO and the Consumer Federation of America.

Congressional Action

In 1975 Sen. Abraham Ribicoff, D-Conn., introduced a lobby disclosure bill that represented a compromise among six earlier bills. After working on the bill for more than a year the Senate passed it, 82-9. A much milder version passed the House during chaotic debate in the last days of the session. However, the bill never went to conference to reconcile the House and Senate versions and died with the adjournment of the 94th Congress. *(Lobby disclosure bill, p. 61)*

Advocates of reform tried again in the 95th Congress. Legislation imposing strict new registration and reporting requirements passed the House in April 1978 but never came to the Senate floor.

Not giving up, supporters of lobby law revision tried again the the 96th Congress. In June 1979 a disclosure bill favored by the ACLU and Common Cause was reported by a House Judiciary subcommittee. It resolved what had been a major controversy in previous debate—imposing civil rather than criminal penalties for violations of the law. But the issue of reporting expenditures for grass-roots lobbying, although not included in the reported version, was expected to be a key point of floor debate in the House. Common Cause indicated that it would continue to press for such provisions, while the Chamber of Commerce continued to oppose the idea.

Grass-roots lobbying is by far the best way the chamber can get through to senators and representatives, Davis observed. "No one in this building votes for them [the lawmakers] but their constituents do."

Davis' principal objective is to get chamber members to write their senators or representatives on any given issue and he has several techniques for doing so.

What he calls the "foundation" of the chamber's lobbying effort is the legislative action department's weekly newsletter, "Congressional Action," which is distributed to all organizational members of the chamber, all local chamber congressional action committees and any business member requesting the service. There were plans to add all business members to the distribution list in early 1980. The circulation of "Congressional Action" has increased about 25,000 a year since 1976. Thomas estimated that by the spring of 1980 the circulation would be over 200,000. Sent as priority mail, the newsletter is used to provide general information and to generate letters when there are no time pressures.

Much more precise are the "action calls," a direct-mail campaign to a selected audience "when issues start to reach the critical stage." The action calls deal exclusively with one issue and usually are sent when the matter is in committee or on the floor. An action call memorandum provides the information a letter-writer would need to send a detailed message to his lawmaker. However, Davis emphasizes that the chamber avoids suggesting the wording of letters and never distributes form letters. During 1978 there were 54 action calls distributed. The normal action call mailing goes to between 25,000 and 30,000 chamber members, with different groups contacted on different issues. It is unlikely that any member would receive all the action calls; most get between eight and 10 a year. However some might get twice that number. *(Box, next page)*

Similar to an action call but of somewhat greater urgency is the distribution of a memorandum from Davis. The format is about the same as that of the action calls but the memorandums are briefer and printed on a different letterhead intended to make them look more urgent. These memos are mailed to a very small group of members, primarily those whose lawmakers' votes are critical to the outcome of the issue at hand.

When time is extremely short and the issue deemed sufficiently vital, Davis will send out Mailgrams. He said he tries to keep them to a minimum because "the cost builds up." He also added that space limitations in Mailgrams make it difficult to include all the necessary information. Mailgrams are used only for a very select audience that is already familiar with the issue.

"When the chamber wants to crank it up, it can generate quite a bit of mail from back home."
—Rep. John J. Rhodes
R-Ariz.

". . .Businessmen are stupid about politics. They talk too much about facts and figures."
—Rep. Barber B. Conable
Jr., R-N.Y.

Selectivity

The national chamber does relatively little telephone campaigning. Occasionally, the Washington office may try to contact a few influential chamber members by phone, but more often telephone operation is delegated to the regional offices.

In line with this policy, the chamber emphasizes letter writing on the part of its members, telling them to send a telegram or to telephone only when time is very short. The chamber does not organize trips to Washington for businessmen to lobby Congress personally, but it does provide a briefing service for member groups who visit Washington on their own. What the chamber does do is emphasize the importance of keeping in contact with senators and represenatives. Meetings with members of Congress visiting their districts during recesses are encouraged, as are appointments with their field office staffs.

The action call mailings are carefully targeted, and usually are distributed according to congressional district rather than industry. Thus if an issue involved pesticides the mailings would go the chamber members in the areas represented by members of the House Agriculture Committee, rather than to all chamber members that manufacture and use pesticides. This technique is in line with the chamber philosophy that the most effective lobbying can be carried out by constituents of a particular senator or representative at the grass-roots level.

One reason the chamber is able to be selective is the computerization of its membership lists, which are broken down by congressional districts and states. Davis and his aides need only determine which legislators hold the swing votes and the computer will churn out address labels for chamber members in those districts.

Other Activities

While the legislative action department is the most visible of the chamber's lobbying efforts, several other activities are designed to encourage members to become involved with Congress and contact their representatives.

Briefing Center

The National Chamber Briefing Center is operated to help members become better informed on issues affecting business. Briefings are set up for groups visiting Washington such as corporation executives or state chambers of commerce; up to 200 can be accommodated. The briefing center provides a list of issues such as labor law, government and regulatory affairs, taxes, economic policy and

'Action Call' on Congressional Veto of FTC Rules

One of the chamber's main techniques for mobilizing its membership on an issue is the distribution of what the chamber calls an "action call."

Essentially a memorandum outlining the chamber's position on an issue and urging members to contact their lawmakers, "action calls" typically are sent to selected districts and states where the representative or senator is thought to hold a key vote on the pending legislation.

Here is the chamber's June 12, 1979 "action call" on the issue of congressional veto of Federal Trade Commission (FTC) rules. *(Background, p. 199)*

ISSUE: CURBING GOVERNMENT REGULATION

ACTION NEEDED:

Letters, wires, phone calls to representatives and senators urging support for these amendments when the Federal Trade Commission authorization bills, HR 2313 and S 1020, reach floor action. Amendments are needed to *restrict FTC's growing legislative power.*

BACKGROUND

The Federal Trade Commission Act grants the FTC broad authority to write rules to prohibit certain "unfair or deceptive acts," rules which can apply to an entire industry or profession.

The problem is that, from the FTC's standpoint, "unfairness" has no bounds. It lies in the eyes of the beholder, in this case the FTC staff and commissioners. Consequently, its numerous rule-making proceedings to eliminate practices it deems "unfair" have brought the Commission into areas stretching from one end of society to another. Consider just these two examples:

• *Children's Advertising:* The Commission is trying to ban TV ads for products on programs designed for children aged eight and under. This raises Constitutional questions of freedom of speech, questions regarding the appropriate role of government, and questions regarding FTC's statutory limitations.

• *Voluntary Standards:* The Commission is trying to rigidify the voluntary product standards systems into a strict, costly, and burdensome system by which product standards are developed and products tested. The 400 diverse standards-setting organizations would have to struggle to conform to single set of stiff federal rules.

It has become obvious to those who are contesting FTC actions that the *FTC has become the second most powerful legislative body in Washington.*

But it is *Congress,* not the FTC, which *has its ear closest to the ground* and, therefore, hears the *rumblings in the grass roots.* Congress, particularly the House, has received the public's message loud and clear: *The FTC has gone too far.*

As a result, efforts will be made soon in both House and Senate *to restrain the FTC.* Specifically, there will be attempts to add three amendments to the FTC authorization bills (HR 2313 and S 1020).

THE THREE AMENDMENTS

1. The *Congressional veto amendment* would empower Congress, for the next three years, to review and veto FTC regulations which Congress deems excessive. The veto would force the FTC to conduct careful cost/benefit analyses *before* embarking on some costly and unnecessary crusade. Moreover, although limited to three years and applying only to the FTC, the veto could pave the way for broader curbs on federal rule-making by other agencies. When added to other tools at Congressional disposal — more effective oversight, stricter standards of appointment for agency heads, and greater attention to the authorization and appropriation process — *the veto amendment would help provide a deterrent to "regulatory overkill," and would stop the damage before it occurs.*

2. The *public interest group amendment* places a $75,000 limit on the amount a single public interest group can receive annually from the FTC for costs it incurs in providing information during the course of an FTC proceeding.

Any federal expenditure which is distributed unfairly or with gross partiality should be opposed. *The $75,000 ceiling would modify the FTC's loose standards for financial eligibility and would help ensure fairness and impartiality in the funding program.*

3. The *voluntary standards amendment* would bar FTC expenditures on a rule to regulate the voluntary standards and certification system. Such a rule would be detrimental to small business and large business alike. The rule-making proceeding now underway would be stopped in its tracks, and the *FTC would be precluded from issuing a regulation that could adversely affect every manufacturer and marketer in the country.*

THE LEGISLATIVE SITUATION

House: HR 2313 includes the Congressional veto and the public interest group subsidy amendments. An effort to add the voluntary standards amendment is expected on the floor. The fight in the House, then, will be to *hold the two amendments and add the third....*

Senate: S 1020 must be amended on the floor since it contains none of the three provisions essential to controlling the FTC. Sens. Nunn, D-Ga., and Schmitt, R-N Mex., have introduced a congressional veto amendment. Other senators are expected to offer the public interest groups subsidy and the voluntary standards amendments. *The fight in the Senate, then, will be harder than in the House.* Floor action is possible the week of June 25.

YOUR ROLE

Your opinion should be made known to your two senators and your representative — whether by *letter, phone call,* or *telegram.* Senators should be contacted before June 25.

Members of Congress are hearing a great deal from constituents who are unhappy with big government — but the comments are mostly generalities.

Here is a chance to be specific. These three amendments go to the heart of big government. They give you a chance to be specific.

We hope you'll take advantage of this opportunity to help curb *oppressive government regulation.*

similar topics and the group selects those it wishes to hear about.

The briefings are conducted at the headquarters by chamber professional staff, with the legislative action department's Thomas frequently participating. The sessions usually cover background, a description of the problems involved and a review of the current status of the issue. About 60 percent of the briefing time is devoted to the issue itself; 40 percent to answering questions. The sessions last about two hours. According to Thomas, groups frequently schedule briefings in the morning to get some background on an issue, then go on to previously arranged appointments with members of Congress.

Communications

The chamber's communications division, under the directon of Carl Grant, vice president for communications, has become more active since 1975. In particular the chamber has expanded its broadcast and audio-visual operation, which for years produced a half-hour radio show, "What's the Issue?" carried by about 300 stations. This has been joined by a chamber-produced show called "Enterprise" that is carried by many cable television systems.

In August 1979 the chamber announced plans to produce a nationally syndicated television talk show and to build a multimillion-dollar broadcasting studio equipped with satellite transmission equipment. The new program, "Its' Your Business," was patterned after the Sunday afternoon question and answer format of the major network shows such as "Meet the Press" and "Face the Nation."

The chamber budgeted $1.7 million for the first year's shows, which are produced by Bob Mead, a former television adviser to Gerald Ford. The first show aired Sept. 9 on 84 stations.

The chamber also planned to build a $2.5 million addition to its headquarters in Washington to house radio and television production facilities.

Chamber president Lesher said the show was the latest attempt to spread the organization's "pro-business, pro-free enterprise" message. The program was intended to bring the chamber's message to the greatest possible audience.

The communications division also produces "Washington Update" six times yearly. A 20-minute program featuring an interview with a member of Congress, it is distributed to the field staff and is used in meetings with members.

The chamber will arrange telephone hookups between the Washington professional staff and meetings of state and local chambers of commerce to discuss important legislative issues. These hookups range from 15 minutes to one hour in length.

Breakfast Meetings

Davis tries to maintain a rapport with other business lobbyists in Washington. He holds a breakfast meeting for corporate lobbyists the first and third Thursdays of each month when Congress is in session, and a similar meeting on the first and third Wednesdays for trade association lobbyists. The group, informally known as the "breakfast bunch," had more than 350 enrolled paid-up members in 1979; members may bring guests and there have been as many as 400 people at some meetings.

A member of Congress is usually invited to speak, and the status of legislation is discussed.

Effectiveness

Few on Capitol Hill question the potential effectiveness of indirect lobbying, but the specific performance of the chamber's operation has received mixed reviews.

Charls E. Walker, a top industrial lobbyist who was under secretary of Treasury during the Nixon administration, is an advocate of grass-roots lobbying. He said he urges his clients to employ this technique because "congressmen ought to know what the corporation is doing for their districts."

An aide to a moderate Republican senator gave an emphatic "yes" when asked if grass-roots lobbying is effective. "If the president of General Motors. . . well, maybe the president of GM might get in to see the senator," he said. "But the senator isn't going to pay much attention to any GM vice president. On the other hand, let him hear from a half-dozen GM dealers from his state and he'll pay a lot of attention."

An aide to a liberal midwestern Democratic representative suggested that "about the only way business groups are going to have access to a liberal Democrat is through the business people in the representative's district."

Assessment

Rep. Barber B. Conable Jr., R-N. Y., said that business groups such as the chamber are not very effective "because businessmen are stupid about politics. . . . They talk too much about facts and figures and don't spend enough time on politics."

He said lawmakers "get some letters from business but nowhere near the volume that organized labor generates."

Rep. Gerry E. Studds, D-Mass., said he deals with local chambers only on local issues. "I go to their functions but I don't hear from them much."

And an aide to a liberal Democratic senator said that the chamber is not "worth a damn." He said that the senator "never hears from local chambers except at their parties or for an occasional telegram."

On the other hand, House Minority Leader John J. Rhodes, R-Ariz., said: "When the chamber wants to crank it up, it can generate quite a bit of mail from back home."

Rep. Bill Frenzel, R-Minn., agreed that the chamber is "good at generating mail from back home on some issues." He added that "sometimes they can be doing work and I don't know it. . . . I'm not always aware whether the chamber was responsible for some letter or not."

Rep. John B. Anderson, R-Ill., said he felt the organization's "primary impact was through the local chambers." He cited the local chamber congressional affairs committees and contacts with chamber members back home as being possibly more important than mail.

"The chamber generates a lot of mail, but it's often obvious that the letters are not entirely spontaneous," he said. Anderson felt that indirect lobbying alone was inadequate.

Comparison With Labor

As did other lawmakers, Anderson drew comparison with the AFL-CIO. He noted that on a key vote "the lobbyists by the door are always from labor, never from business. Labor makes sure it gets the last lick in."

Davis agreed that the labor lobbyists may be more visible on the Hill, but pointed out that that did not mean business lobbyists weren't there. "Our people are up there day after day," but he added that they spend most of their

Chamber of Commerce Honoraria

In an attempt to write "a new agenda for human progress" in three days in the spring of 1978, the U.S. Chamber of Commerce was able to call on 10 members of Congress to give it a hand.

The members' attendance at the Chamber's annual meeting in Washington April 30-May 2 cost the group $7,000 in honoraria, according to financial disclosure forms filed by the members who attended.

The Chamber paid honoraria to more members of Congress than any other group for a single meeting that year, the disclosure records revealed.

Here is what a Chamber publication, the *Washington Report*, said the members did at the meeting and what they were paid for their appearances:

Baker. Sen. Howard H. Baker Jr., R-Tenn., delivered the opening address of the 1978 meeting. He warned an audience of more than 2,500 of "the possibility that the U.S., like her ally Great Britain, might slip into state socialism," the *Washington Report* said. Baker was paid an honorarium of $2,000 for the speech.

Heckler and Allen. Rep. Margaret M. Heckler, R-Mass., and Sen. James B. Allen, D-Ala. (1969-78), spoke during a program entitled "America's Religious Principles." Heckler was paid $500. Allen, now deceased, did not file a financial disclosure form.

Goldwater. Rep. Barry M. Goldwater Jr., R-Calif., provided "an update on the status of privacy legislation" in Congress, according to the *Report*. He was paid an honorarium of $1,000.

Muskie. Sen. Edmund S. Muskie, D-Maine, told a meeting that congressional spending estimates for new federal programs ran as high as $416 billion over the next five years while estimates of new funds amounted to only about $90 billion. Muskie did not report an honorarium for his participation.

Shuster. Rep. Bud Shuster, R-Pa., was a panelist in a discussion of "Congress, business and elections '78." The *Washington Report* did not report Shuster's remarks. He was paid a $500 honorarium.

McCormack. Rep. Mike McCormack, D-Wash., told an energy panel that the administration was partially to blame for the nation's energy problems because of its weak leadership, "based on opinion polls rather than scientific facts and the realities of life." McCormack received no honorarium for his participation, according to his financial disclosure form.

Hatch and Williams. Sens. Orrin G. Hatch, R-Utah, and Harrison A. Williams Jr., D-N.J., participated in a panel discussion on labor "reform" legislation. Hatch argued that the "reform" bill would harm small businesses while Williams said the legislation would not. Each was paid $1,000.

McClure. Sen. James A. McClure, R-Idaho, in a speech on "organization leadership," called on business to "realize that a permanent solution to its problems requires the election of a congressional majority that believes in the workings of the free enterprise system." He added that business can affect the way even "entrenched liberals" vote on many issues by "supporting a strong conservative opponent" against them. He was paid $1,000 for his speech.

time working with committees and staff members. "It's the labor lobbyists, not business representatives, that you see standing around with thumbs up or thumbs down to indicate how members should vote."

Davis went on to say that it is never possible to change a lot of votes because of physical presence. "It is votes back home that will change votes—that's the name of the game; we are visible and we will be more so, but grass-roots action is the key." *(Labor lobby, p. 97)*

Members of Congress and staff aides identified three basic elements for an effective lobby:

● A grass-roots effort to demonstrate support for the group's position in the lawmaker's district.

● A Washington operation that can count heads, supply information and contact the lawmakers and their staffs.

● A proven ability to deliver support (or opposition) in an election.

Election Assistance

Until the 1978 elections the chamber was at a disadvantage on the last point, for although it was active in the legislative area it had no political action committee (PAC) and was not directly involved in any congressional races. That changed in 1977 when the chamber established the National Chamber Alliance for Politics, a political action committee that supports candidates for Congress who can be expected to have views in line with those of the business community.

Unlike many PACs, the alliance does not make any direct cash contributions. Instead, it uses voluntary contributions from individuals to pay for campaign services and materials. Alliance support might include identifying business leaders who would help a candidate, scheduling plant tours, assisting in fund raising, distributing voting records and organizing political rallies.

The alliance has established three criteria to determine whether it will assist a candidate:

1. There is a clear philosophical difference between candidates.

2. The race is expected to be very close.

3. The broad support of the business community can affect the outcome.

Candidates supported are Republicans as well as Democrats, incumbents as well as challengers. In the 1978 elections 61 percent of the 83 candidates supported by the alliance won.

Perennial Foes

Any discussion about the Chamber of Commerce must deal with the AFL-CIO. Andrew J. Biemiller, formerly chief lobbyist for the AFL-CIO, once said that the chamber of commerce and organized labor could be characterized as perennial foes. The chamber and the AFL-CIO are "rarely on the same side of any question," he said.

During the 1970s both business and labor could claim their legislative victories, but neither could be said to have dominated Congress during the decade.

One of business' greatest successes, and a stunning defeat for labor, was congressional rejection of common-site picketing legislation. The measure had passed the 94th Congress but was vetoed by President Ford. Labor, apparently expecting that the new Democratic administration headed by Jimmy Carter would make passage of the bill much easier, did not lobby as hard as it had the previous year. A massive grass-roots effort by contractors and business paid off and the House rejected the bill in March 1977.

Prior to the debate, Speaker Thomas P. O'Neill Jr., D-Mass., criticized organized labor for insufficient efforts on behalf of the bill. While opposition lobbyists were flooding members with mail from their districts, he maintained, labor groups let things slide until the last minute.

Later in 1977 labor bounced back with a victory when minimum-wage legislation was enacted that was far closer to the version backed by the AFL-CIO than to that preferred by the Chamber of Commerce.

The chamber lobbied hard on the issue, stimulating letters to members and encouraging affected industries to contact their representatives and senators during the August recess, before House consideration of the bill was completed. These efforts were capped by a mailing to each member estimating how many jobs would be lost in his or her district if the measure passed without change.

The efforts of business lobbyists were effective in the House and labor had to work hard in the Senate to counter them. But in the end the House-Senate conference committee accepted the labor-backed version.

However, since passage of the bill the Chamber of Commerce has been lobbying to defer the effective date of the minimum wage increases it called for.

In 1978 Davis said that the chamber's biggest victory was the Senate rejection of a measure that would have speeded up the decision-making processes of the National Labor Relations Board (NLRB) and made it easier for unions to organize workers and negotiate collective bargaining agreements. It was one of the most intense grass-roots lobbying campaigns in recent history and saw a direct head-to-head confrontation between business and labor.

Philosophy

The chamber is usually considered to be wedded to a very conservative viewpoint.

Rep. Anderson, a Republican moderate, said that the chamber is unrealistically conservative: "All too often they seem to display a reflexive dislike for anything which involves the creation of another government agency."

Rep. Conable, however, said he believed the chamber is "more realistic [about what it can hope to accomplish] than most groups. . . . It lives in the real world to a considerable extent."

Rep. Rhodes said the chamber "is a lot better than it was a few years ago."

Spokesmen for the chamber are the first to admit that they have a rather conservative point of view, and in some respects they see that as the trend of the future. The legislative priorities of the chamber for the first session of the 96th Congress focus on the goal of reducing inflation and include what would be expected of a business organization:

- Restraint of federal spending.
- Reduction of taxes.
- Increased energy and resource development.
- Reduction of government-imposed costs.
- Increased foreign trade opportunities.
- Opposition to new forms of government controls and regulation.

Obstacles

Although the anti-business attitude that the chamber feared during the 94th Congress in 1975 did not cause as many problems as it could have, Hilton Davis pointed out that the chamber is still usually forced to take a defensive position, seeking to "delay, reduce and oppose" bills. On the other hand he cited labor law reform, minimum wage deferral, capital formation and spending reduction as areas where the chamber had begun to be on the offensive.

"Someone once observed that you never win the minimum wage issue," Davis said. "You just keep putting it off." He added, "Business is resilient. It can adjust to regulations, some of which are pretty oppressive. . . . But I think the nation has had less economic growth as a result."

John Thomas agreed with Davis' assessment of the chamber's position. He pointed out that the number of members that were sympathetic to organized labor outnumbered the conservative, business oriented members. Basically, he said, "the numbers are not right—and as long as they are not right we will take the defensive side. We will oppose more than we will support, but the scales are not as unbalanced as they were."

Thomas went on to say that the philosophical makeup of Congress was beginning to change, which would allow the chamber to take the offensive on issues such as the Davis-Bacon Act, which requires federal contractors to pay the highest prevailing wage.

Thomas and Davis agreed that the climate for business in Congress had improved. Not greatly, but somewhat. They pointed out that the 94th Congress had gotten businessmen aroused to the point where they began to work together better from the standpoint of coordination, and that trend has continued. The chamber's lobbyists also felt that congressional reforms that limited the role of committee chairman and opened the way for newer members to become subcommittee chairman have offered increased opportunities for business lobbyists.

According to Davis the elections of 1978 brought in a group that was more conservative, he calculated a net conservative gain of four in the Senate and 16 in the House. It is the feeling of the chamber, he added, that there is something of a conservative trend developing nationwide, and that Congress is more favorable to the conservative viewpoint than in the past. ∎

Business Roundtable: New Lobbying Force

Corporate executives, working through the Business Roundtable, are wielding new persuasive power in Congress by direct personal involvement in lobbying.

The comparatively young Roundtable, formally organized in 1974, has emerged as a potent pressure group largely because of its unique mobilization of the talent and prestige of the nation's top corporate heads.

The Roundtable has figured in several lobbying battles since it was established and has been credited with some significant victories.

A steady effort to become acquainted with more members of Congress and to voice business opinions on legislation has marked the Roundtable's efforts. The Roundtable's main strategy for participation in legislative deliberations is an articulate advocacy of a limited agenda by top business leaders.

Priority areas for the Roundtable have included energy, tax, inflation, government regulatory policy, conglomerate merger and antitrust policy and consumer legislation.

'It's Impressive'

A House aide who has attended meetings with Roundtable leaders said: "These guys knew their stuff. They had done their preparation; they had the figures. Even though you might argue with them, it's impressive — it just is. There are enough gladhanders and lightweights around here that you dismiss them rather easily. But these corporate presidents are different."

The group's increasing prominence as a lobbying force has stirred some controversy. Its backers see it as an appropriate, politically healthy response to the rising level of governmental intervention in business; its detractors see it as an unwholesome intervention by powerful private figures in the affairs of government.

Labor leaders view the Roundtable's emergence as bad news for workers and consumers. Robert A. Georgine, president of the AFL-CIO building and construction trades department, said: "It is apparent that the real purpose of the Roundtable is to destroy local unions and take away the gains they have made through the collective bargaining process."

The defeat of the common-site picketing bill in 1977, labor's difficulties in attaining passage of a new minimum wage and its inability to obtain revision of labor-management law in 1978 have been attributed mainly to aggressive lobbying by the Roundtable and other business groups.

Methods

The Roundtable brings together 190 chief executive officers (CEOs) of major corporations, including General Motors, General Electric, duPont, IBM and AT&T.

Despite the inherent clout possessed by these Roundtable members — who collectively direct billions of dollars of the gross national product and millions of American employees — the Roundtable has succeeded in keeping a low profile.

The group has not sought publicity and seldom takes officially announced positions on issues. It does not go in for major ad campaigns or mass mailings. Instead, the Roundtable works to influence legislation primarily through direct contact between its members or their corporate representatives on the one hand and Congress and the executive branch on the other.

This low profile too has provoked controversy. Some public interest and union lobbyists, as well as certain members of Congress, say that the Roundtable too often wields its substantial power behind the scenes, away from public scrutiny, because it has ready access to members of Congress and the executive branch.

Roundtable representatives and others on Capitol Hill insist that the group is a well-informed, articulate lobbying entity that aids in properly shaping legislation without seeking media attention or posturing before other interest groups.

Role of the CEOs

John "Jack" Post, a former New York and Houston lawyer and businessman who is the Roundtable's executive director in Washington, says that the idea of prominent corporate heads regularly plying congressional corridors has been "glamorized."

He said that most of the Roundtable's work on Capitol Hill continues to be done by the Washington "reps," the lobbyists who represent corporations typically headquartered in New York and elsewhere.

Nonetheless, the principal image connected with the Roundtable name in congressional minds is that of an executive of one of the "Fortune 500" calling personally to plump for or against a piece of legislation.

"The conventional wisdom is that they're extremely effective, for the very reason that they put themselves together," said a top House aide. "When they come in here, it's not some vice president for public relations, but *the* president of GM, duPont or another corporation, coming in themselves. That has a hell of a lot more impact than some lobbyist."

A former congressional aide who has worked with the Roundtable notes that it pulls together the men who "are in many ways the senior statesmen of the industrial community. Some have been advisers to presidents. They don't dirty their hands with the smaller issues." He added that "you can be sure that there would be very few members of Congress who would *not* meet with the president of a Business Roundtable corporation, even if there were no district connection."

Rep. Richardson Preyer, D-N.C., is a member of Congress who has found himself both allied with the Roundtable (on amendments to the Federal Trade Commission statute) and opposed to it (on the Agency for Consumer Protection proposal). "I have generally been very impressed with the quality of their research," Preyer said. "Certainly they are good, hard lobbyists, but that's what free speech is all about. For years, businessmen didn't participate in the legislative process; now they are, and that's a positive development."

But not everyone sees this development as benign. Mark Green, a longtime Ralph Nader aide who now heads the Nader-generated Congress Watch, compliments the executives' skill while at the same time criticizing their impact on Congress.

"The Business Roundtable is the most effective invisible lobby on Capitol Hill," Green said. "They are the quintessential big business lobby, because of the way they can push a button and get scores of Fortune 500 CEOs to descend on impressionable legislators.

"The U.S. Chamber of Commerce is visible and hamhanded — witness [Chamber President Richard] Lesher's personal attack on [White House consumer adviser] Esther Peterson as a 'woman scorned.' The Business Roundtable is low-profile and effective far beyond their announced budget."

Post denies that corporate presidents are easily and frequently called upon for Hill lobbying. He pointed out that Roundtable members are not among those who frequently testify before congressional committees. "The view that you have an avalanche of these characters coming down here on every issue is mistaken," said Post.

Complex Organization

Membership in the Roundtable requires a heavy commitment of many business executives' time, even if they rarely get to Capitol Hill. The real work of the Roundtable is done by its policy committee. This group, currently composed of 47 members, meets once every two months near the Roundtable's New York office on Park Avenue. *(Committee membership, box, this page)*

No Substitutes

Attendance at these meetings is high, given the time constraints on these business leaders. Some 35 of the 47 attend each meeting. To preserve the top-drawer character of the organization, the internal rules are that assistants may not be sent in one's stead, so that only business peers are meeting together on each occasion.

At this bimonthly meeting, the positions of the Roundtable and its legislative priorities are decided. The principal raw material before the executives as they work through issues and arrive at a consensus is the work-product of more than a dozen task forces, each one chaired by a member of the policy committee.

The group moves briskly to implement its positions. The day after the policy committee meeting, there is a second meeting, in Washington, of the Washington steering committee. This committee is composed of the Washington representatives of the same corporations whose chief executives comprise the policy committee.

At this steering committee meeting, the chairman of the Business Roundtable, during 1979 Thomas A. Murphy of General Motors, briefs the Washington reps on the results of the previous day's New York meeting. The gears thus are meshed for these Washington-based lobbyists and for the CEOs to pursue Roundtable policy.

The full contingent of 190 Roundtable members gets together only once a year. Hence, membership on the backbone policy committee is rotated annually in the interests of full participation. According to Post, some 20 percent of the committee is rotated off each year. These eight to 10 slots are then filled with an eye both to full

Roundtable Leaders

Chief executives of 47 companies, plus two senior members, make up the Business Roundtable's policy committee. Task forces headed by the members are shown after the company names in the following list:

Ray C. Adam, NL Industries
Robert A. Beck, Prudential Insurance, social security
John F. Bookout, Shell Oil
Theodore F. Brophy, GTE, taxation
Charles L. Brown, AT&T
Fletcher L. Byrom, Koppers Co.
Frank T. Cary, IBM, government regulation
Silas S. Cathcart, Illinois Tool Works
Alden W. Clausen, Bank of America, corporate organization policy
Justin Dart, Dart Industries
Robert F. Dee, SmithKline
James H. Evans, Union Pacific, environment
James L. Ferguson, General Foods, consumer interests
Lewis F. Foy, Bethlehem Steel, national planning and employment
Clifton C. Garvin Jr., Exxon, (Roundtable co-chairman)
Richard L. Gelb, Bristol-Myers
W. H. Krome George, ALCOA, energy users
John W. Hanley, Monsanto
John P. Harbin, Halliburton
Shearon Harris, Carolina Power & Light
Robert S. Hatfield, Continental Group, economic organization, field support
Jack K. Horton, Southern California Edison
Reginald H. Jones, General Electric (Roundtable co-chairman)
E. Robert Kinney, General Mills
William A. Klopman, Burlington Industries
Ralph Lazarus, Federated Department Stores
Ruben F. Mettler, TRW
Lee L. Morgan, Caterpillar Tractor
Thomas A. Murphy, General Motors, accounting principles (Roundtable chairman)
Charles J. Pilliod Jr., Goodyear, (Roundtable co-chairman)
Edmund T. Pratt Jr., Pfizer
Donald T. Regan, Merrill Lynch
David Rockefeller, Chase Manhattan Bank
Donald V. Seibert, J. C. Penney, inflation
Irving S. Shapiro, duPont
Richard R. Shinn, Metropolitan Life, welfare
George P. Shultz, Bechtel
Andrew C. Sigler, Champion International
William S. Sneath, Union Carbide, international trade
George A. Stinson, National Steel, antitrust
Edward R. Telling, Sears, Roebuck
Rawleigh Warner Jr., Mobil Oil, corporate constituencies
William L. Wearly, Ingersoll-Rand
Richard D. Wood, Eli Lilly
Walter B. Wriston, Citibank, national health
John D. Harper, ALCOA (senior member)
David Packard, Hewlett-Packard (senior member)

rotation and to getting a solid cross-section, by geography and industrial sector, of American industry.

An occasional death or retirement also results in change. In keeping with the strict rule of only allowing chief executive officers in the organization, a merger of one Roundtable company with another means the dropping of the new subsidiary's CEO.

Post and a small support staff run the Roundtable's modest, functionally designed Washington office at 1801 K Street N.W. In the New York office are G. Wallace Bates, the Roundtable president; James Keogh, former head of the U.S. Information Agency, now the Roundtable executive director for public information; and Richard F. Kibben, the executive director for construction.

Finally, the Roundtable superstructure includes several committees made up of counterparts from the member corporations: a public information committee composed of the public relations officers of the corporations, an economic research committee composed of economists from the corporations, and a labor-management committee of industrial relations vice presidents.

Post said that the CEOs "are very sophisticated. And when they get involved in something, they are really committed. They like to succeed. So this is not the care and feeding of unsophisticated people."

The Roundtable's budget is about $2.5 million a year, according to Post. That sum supports the two offices and pays for publications, outside research and legal work. Costs such as those associated with attendance by CEOs at Roundtable meetings are borne by the executives and their corporations, not by the Roundtable.

The budget money comes from assessments on the member corporations. A sliding scale, based on the company's annual revenues and its stockholders' equities, determines what each member must pay, ranging from as little as $2,600 a year to $40,000. Companies in the highest bracket have revenues and equities in the $6.5 billion range.

In addition the chairmen of the various task forces frequently draw on their own corporate resources when necessary to carry out special projects.

Relations With Labor

One of the architects of the Roundtable was Roger Blough, former head of United States Steel who became famous for his 1962 horn-locking with President Kennedy over price increases in the steel industry.

Blough in the spring of 1973 suggested rolling together two groups that had emerged in the late 1960s: a labor-management committee that had been formed in 1965 to resist labor's first major attempt to repeal Section 14(b) of the Taft-Hartley Act, and a "Construction Users Anti-Inflation Roundtable" that Blough had organized in 1969. The purpose of that Roundtable was to combat growing construction costs, particularly labor costs.

This anti-labor cast to the Business Roundtable's origins caused concern among labor unions. Jack Curran, legislative director for the Laborers' International Union, recalled that "we saw them emerging as a force to thwart the aims of the labor movement and to turn the clock back, to take away the gains that had been won at the collective bargaining table and in legislation, and to create an atmosphere of fear regarding unions."

Curran and other labor leaders agree that the Roundtable, along with other groups in an extensive coalition, "hurt us badly" with the defeat of the common-site picketing proposal early in the 95th Congress.

The business community's new aggressiveness has forced the unions to retool their own lobbying efforts to combat the negative image of labor that was having some impact on popular and congressional opinion.

In particular, labor was forced to fight hard for its labor law revision package, which the Roundtable opposed as part of a coalition even more extensive than the one that defeated the common situs proposal.

Labor was able to claim a significant victory when the House Oct. 6, 1977, passed the labor law revision bill without the weakening amendments supported by business. However a massive lobbying campaign supported by almost every business group in Washington led to the Senate's refusal to invoke cloture (cutoff of debate) and end a filibuster that had blocked consideration of the bill in that chamber. After six cloture votes failed supporters of the bill finally gave up and the legislation died. *(Labor lobby, p. 97)*

But the Roundtable has at times worked with labor unions, notably in the intensive fight over automobile exhaust emissions standards and non-degradation requirements for stationary pollution sources such as smokestacks contained in the Clean Air Act Amendments.

On that hotly lobbied issue, the linkage between production slowdowns and feared job losses had the chief executives of the major auto companies knocking on congressional doors side-by-side with former United Auto Workers head Leonard Woodcock. *(Clean air lobbying, p. 184)*

Legislative Priorities

The Roundtable's major interest include: 1) President Carter's energy package, 2) tax proposals, focusing primarily on changes that would provide capital-formation incentives, 3) lobbying disclosure changes, 4) inflation 5) consumer and antitrust legislation and 6) government regulations and their impact on business.

Consumer Bills

The Roundtable role in opposing a consumer protection agency has been particularly controversial. It consistently has fought the proposal, having made the agency a top priority as early as 1974.

In 1977 the fight against the agency was led by an "ad hoc" business lobbying group. But the Roundtable's role became prominent when the group provided money — some $5,000, according to Post — to pay former Watergate special prosecutor Leon A. Jaworski for preparing testimony opposing the agency.

The Business Roundtable was also the main opponent of 1978 amendments to Federal Trade Commission authorization legislation that would have had the effect of broadening the availability of class actions for aggrieved consumers. According to some members of Congress, including Paul Simon, D-Ill., the business community was slow in recognizing the significance of the proposed amendments since it was too riveted on the consumer agency. Once galvanized, however, the Roundtable and its allies fought hard to weaken the class-action provisions in the bill.

The opponents' primary strategem, according to congressional staffers, was to try to kill the measure in the Rules Committee. While Rules was once a common bottleneck for legislation, the committee only infrequently plays such a role since reforms have diluted its power in the last decade.

Tactics Criticized

The fight to kill the bill in the Rules Committee surprised some supporters of the proposal, and struck others as downright undemocratic.

Rep. Bob Eckhardt, D-Texas, chairman of the Consumer Protection and Finance Subcommittee and principal sponsor of the legislation, said that "the Roundtable activities on the consumer class action provisions personify the negative public image of lobbyists. . . . Rather than playing a constructive role by testifying at the [consumer subcommittee] hearing and openly discussing their objections, they instead insist on using the discredited technique of influence-peddling behind closed doors and relying on the good ol' boy network to get votes."

Largely due to the intervention of House Speaker Thomas P. O'Neill Jr., D-Mass., business opponents of the legislation were unable to kill the bill in Rules and settled for delay. By piling on witnesses before the Rules Committee at its final meetings in July, the opponents succeeded in keeping the FTC amendments, as well as the business-opposed minimum wage legislation, off the floor until after Congress returned from its August recess. The Roundtable and other business groups successfully worked to knock out the class-action provisions on the floor. The legislation was finally killed by the House Sept. 28.

The Eckhardt lament about the behind-closed-doors nature of Roundtable advocacy is frequently voiced on Capitol Hill, particularly by staffers and other lobbyists who have opposed the Roundtable on one issue or another.

One aide complained that "the purpose of hearings is to allow people to state their reasons for their position on a bill, and to have them scrutinized and questioned. The Roundtable doesn't do that." Another lobbyist for a "public interest" group echoed that criticism, saying that "it's difficult to assess how effective or active they are because their presence never really surfaces *qua* Business Roundtable."

Responding to such criticism, a Roundtable lobbyist pointed out that it is hard to get a consensus among diverse industrial giants. "We can't always get everyone to agree," he said, "so we can't go testify as 'the Roundtable.'" Instead, individual chief executives, having been alerted to issues through the Roundtable activities, may testify or work the Hill as corporate representatives.

Lobby Disclosure

One legislative proposal that may throw greater light on the Roundtable's and other groups' lobbying activities is the proposed bolstering of the lobbying disclosure law.

Roundtable representatives were an integral part of the months-long private negotiations among lobby groups seeking workable compromises among the various disclosure proposals.

Robert S. Hatfield, chairman of the Roundtable's economic organization task force, testified before the House subcommittee considering the legislation. He said the Roundtable feels that greater disclosure is appropriate, so long as "burdensome" record-keeping and reporting requirements are avoided.

The Roundtable has favored the coverage of indirect lobbying, that is the solicitation of "grass-roots" lobbying by local constituents.

That is consistent with the Roundtable's desire to avoid excessive record-keeping. "We're willing to file copies of our lobbying solicitations with the GAO [General Accounting Office] so a congressman can see, if he gets a lot of letters coming in, just who has been sending what to his constituents," said a Roundtable spokesman. "But we don't want to have to itemize the dollars we've spent" because that would entail extra accounting burdens.

After the House subcommittee approved a disclosure bill (HR 1180) in 1977, Hatfield wrote to his fellow Roundtable members: "The bill is certainly not perfect and further improvements are needed. It is burdensome in its reporting requirements. However, under the circumstances I believe it is a reasonable piece of legislation and could easily have been much worse."

Walter Hasty, Post's former assistant, said that the Roundtable role in the lobbying disclosure area was indicative of the "pragmatic" approach that the Roundtable tries to follow.

"It's not enough to say you don't want what's being proposed," he said. "You have to say, 'Okay, what do you want?' and come up with workable alternatives."

Arab Boycott

The Roundtable took an activist approach to the legislation barring U.S. firms from complying with the Arab boycott of Israel.

An aide to Rep. Benjamin S. Rosenthal, D-N.Y., noted that much of the Roundtable's lobbying on the boycott bill was with the administration, where "they feel more comfortable. They are on more intimate terms with Blumenthal [then Treasury Secretary W. Michael Blumenthal]" than with members of Congress. Blumenthal, formerly head of the Bendix Corp., was not himself a member of the Roundtable before joining the Carter administration, but was generally viewed as the administration's principal emissary to big business during his tenure as Treasury secretary.

Former Roundtable Chairman Irving S. Shapiro of duPont was the lead actor in the negotiations among business interests, Jewish groups active in supporting anti-boycott proposals, the Carter administration and Congress.

Shapiro was widely credited with having shaped the compromise outcome. From the Roundtable standpoint, Shapiro's involvement was an example of the Roundtable's technique of matching the CEO with the right expertise and contacts to the lobbying task at hand. As one of the comparatively few Jewish corporate heads, as a lawyer, and as an active semi-public figure familiar with government, Shapiro had all the natural qualities to work out the boycott legislation.

From the vantage point of the Rosenthal aide, "in the whole process, they were very effective. They typically are multinational corporations, and their views in this area are accorded respect. On the other hand, everyone knew what they wanted. They mostly wanted to keep sacrosanct the principle that American law should not reach activities in foreign countries . . . they were the principal opponents of extraterritoriality, and the bill bears their imprint."

While the aide opposed some of the positions taken by the Roundtable, he credited it with having made "none of the extravagant claims of potential lost trade and jobs in America" that he said were made by other organizations.

The Roundtable effort to influence the boycott legislation did not end with the signing of the bill into law on June 22. Another task force ramrodded by Shapiro produced a 164-page document that was sent to then Secretary of Commerce Juanita M. Kreps "for her department's guidance in formulating regulations to carry out the legislation on foreign boycotts."

Government Regulation

The Business Roundtable, like many other business organizations, has become increasingly concerned about government regulation and its impact on business. In March 1979 the Roundtable released the results of a study showing that the regulatory policies of six federal agencies cost 48 major corporations operating in more than 20 industries a total of $2.6 billion in directly measurable effects in 1977.

The study, managed by the accounting firm of Arthur Andersen & Co., was distinguished from other regulatory cost studies by its specificity. It not only identified incremental costs, but also provided a breakout of costs of specific regulations.

Commenting on the study Frank T. Cary, head of the Roundtable task force on Government Regulations and chairman of IBM said, "Analysis of the costs of regulations is important if we hope to balance the impact of regulatory costs against intended benefits. Many regulations are necessary for the well-being of society. In many instances they help business meet its obligations to society. Yet, the findings of the study show that expenditures for regulations may often be wasteful and non-productive." The Roundtable favors legislation requiring economic impact analyses, congressional and agency review of regulatory programs on a systematic basis and greater flexibility for companies in meeting regulatory goals.

The government regulation study is an example of the vast resources the Roundtable can summon to carry out its projects. Post pointed out that although the Roundtable paid the fee charged by Arthur Andersen, the companies involved in the study contributed thousands of hours of research and staff time. IBM Chairman Cary also provided substantial staff support. The ability to draw on such resources helps immeasurably in arguing business' case in Washington.

Energy

The Roundtable predictably is interested in energy legislation and President Carter's energy policy.

The problem of consensus among the corporate members has been particularly acute here, however, since the interests of oil companies, manufacturing companies, utilities and other corporations diverge on energy issues. According to Post, the Roundtable is adopting generally the position of the "industrial energy users."

Nonetheless, one of the chief tenets of the Roundtable position is quite compatible with that of the energy producers: "A major shortcoming of the [Carter] program is its inadequate stimulus for maximum production of oil and gas. The crude oil equalization tax would raise the price to most consumers to the replacement or world price — a desirable objective, but it would divert needed funds from industry to government and perpetuate a crippling bureaucratic control," as a Roundtable energy position paper stated.

Post said the Roundtable opposed the crude oil equalization tax because it solved the pricing problem but failed to generate the capital businesses claimed they needed to

"Business managers must learn how to hold their own in public debate and know their way around in Washington...."
Reginald H. Jones
Roundtable co-chairman

produce more energy. Likewise, natural gas deregulation was favored since it would funnel greater capital into corporate tills to facilitate production.

Continued federal regulation of natural gas and the crude oil equalization tax were included in energy legislation passed by the House Aug. 5, 1977. The Senate, however, after a long and sometimes bitter filibuster, voted to end all regulation of the price of new natural gas. In another move favored by business, the Senate Finance Committee voted 10-6 to kill the crude oil equalization tax.

The Roundtable comes down hard on environmental restrictions that have lessened access to fuel sources. "We're getting so involved with litigation and procedures in this country that we're slowing everything down," argues Post.

Assessment

Despite its many critics, the lobbying strength of the Business Roundtable is unlikely to diminish greatly. Its leaders are convinced that their active involvement in public affairs is good for both business and government. In a 1977 speech Roundtable co-chairman Reginald H. Jones of General Electric explained the view of many business leaders:

"The main problems of business these days are external to the company and are determined in the arena of public policy. Therefore business managers are obliged to become students of public affairs. They must learn how to hold their own in public debate and know their way around in Washington.... When business managers bring their experience to bear in the formation of policy and law, they speak for millions of affected people and deserve a hearing."

A hearing for the members of the Roundtable is likely to remain easy to arrange. Even though the novelty of being lobbied by a chief executive may wear off for what Mark Green calls "impressionable" members of Congress, it likely will remain true that most members will not refuse to see a top corporate executive.

That means their views will seldom be excluded from congressional deliberations. As members of Congress frequently point out, that basic access — the ability to have your voice heard — is the most crucial long-term component of any successful lobbying. ∎

The Foreign Interest Lobby

CQ

Foreign Agents: More Selling Than Intrigue

There is perhaps no nation on earth that does not have something to gain or lose from decisions of the U.S. Congress and executive branch concerning defense spending, arms sales, grain and other direct trade, development aid and multilateral economic interests.

Consequently, foreign governments and companies maintain a small army of representatives in Washington to look after their interests and help achieve their goals in the U.S. political system.

Usually the men and women who carry on this work attract no more attention than their counterparts who lobby for domestic interests. But from time to time the activities of foreign lobbies arouse particular public and congressional concern over the influence of overseas interests on the conduct of U.S. policy.

One such wave of apprehension led to enactment of the statute that still governs the activities of foreign agents in the United States — the Foreign Agents Registration Act of 1938. Originally the act was intended to provide a means of monitoring the Nazi propaganda distributed in this country by Hitler's Germany.

In later years other foreign pressure groups — including the China lobby, the sugar lobby and more recently the South Korean lobby — provoked similar concerns that led to congressional inquiries and legislation.

The Foreign Agents Registration Act was extensively revised in 1966 and the Senate in 1977 began a review of the statute, prompted by a desire to halt some of the abuses brought to light by the Korean lobbying scandal. However, no substantial action was taken and interest in reform efforts again cooled off, at least temporarily. *(Details on how the act works, p. 135; Korean lobbying scandal, p. 153)*

The Korean scandal implanted the image of a Washington full of trenchcoated, money-laden foreign agents, an image that government officials and foreign lobbyists are quick to dispute. What is seldom disputed, however, is that there is a substantial amount — how much no one can be certain — of lobbying of Congress and the executive branch by agents of foreign interests. While some of those efforts may be heavy-handed and graft-ridden, the great majority are not. In fact, most foreign lobbying strongly resembles its domestic counterpart — right down to the names of the people doing the lobbying, the methods the lobbyists use and the fees they garner for their services.

Foreign Lobbyists: A Profile

The typical foreign lobbyist is the ubiquitous Washington lawyer. Quite often, that lawyer once held a high government post. Former Cabinet members such as Dean Acheson, secretary of State under Truman; Clark M. Clifford, secretary of Defense under Johnson; Richard G. Kleindienst, attorney general under Nixon; and William P. Rogers, secretary of State under Nixon; are or were associated with the representation of foreign interests. Former members of Congress, including Sen. J. William Fulbright, D-Ark. (1945-74), Sen. Charles E. Goodell, R-N.Y. (1968-

71), and Rep. James V. Stanton, D-Ohio (1971-77), likewise have registered as foreign agents.

Those foreign lobbyists who are not former high officials are likely nonetheless to be veteran political hands, such as F. Clinton White, mastermind of the 1964 presidential nomination drive of Sen. Barry Goldwater, R-Ariz., and Ted Van Dyk Jr., long-time aide to a series of liberal Democratic senators and adviser in the latter stages of the Jimmy Carter campaign.

Still other foreign lobbyists are media and public relations advisers or counselors. This category includes prestigious public relations firms such as Hill & Knowlton

Inc. and the New York-based Ruder & Finn, for whom Marion Javits, wife of Sen. Jacob K. Javits, R-N.Y., worked for a time.

Clients

The clients these lawyers and consultants serve include the governments and businesses of nearly every nation and principality in the world, from the Soviet Union to Madagascar. *(See box, p. 137)*

Two types of foreign interests tend to be most strongly represented in Washington. The first is what some lobbyists call the U.S. "client states." Such governments as those of South Korea and Israel rely heavily on U.S. military, political and economic aid to help them exist in the face of strong opposition from other political groups or nations. "For these countries," says one foreign lobbyist, "it's a matter of life and death — they have a real survival mentality" in their lobbying. That instinct to survive, several foreign lobbyists agreed, lay behind the extraordinary lengths to which the South Koreans apparently went to protect their interests with the U.S. government. Other nations, such as the former Rhodesian regime of Ian Smith and the white South African government, while not historically client states of the United States, are nonetheless embattled governments that have sought U.S. good-will through active lobby operations in Washington. The March 15, 1977, action by Congress to abandon the six-year-old Byrd amendment and join the worldwide embargo on

Rhodesian chrome was an example of the importance of congressional actions to a foreign nation.

The second type of national stake heavily represented in Washington is foreign commercial activity. In many instances, the intertwining of national ambitions with economic aspirations is so complete that separating commercial from political objectives is a practical impossibility. One clear example of that problem was the lobbying furor over U.S. landing rights for the British-French supersonic transport Concorde. In the Concorde and in many other cases, the client corporation or business is either owned outright or controlled by its home government, so that the lobbyist in fact if not in name is working for the political interests of that nation when advancing the commercial objectives of the foreign corporation. *(Concorde box, p. 132)*

Those nations with the largest contingent of registered agents in addition to their diplomatic representatives are the chief U.S. trading partners, including Japan, Canada, France, West Germany and Mexico.

The South Korean lobby itself is a good example of that commercial bent. Leaving aside the allegations of bribery and favor-currying of members of Congress by Tongsun Park and others, the South Koreans have put in place an extensive network of trade promotion offices.

Nine such offices are now in operation, from Seattle and San Francisco to Atlanta and Miami. Five different Washington law firms represent specific Korean commercial groups such as the Korean Stainless Steel Flatware Manufacturers Association and the Korea National Housing Corporation. In all, 23 agents represent disparate, presumably legitimate South Korean clients. (Tongsun Park never registered as an agent.) Most of those interests are the normal commercial outgrowth of one of the fastest-growing economies in the world, and one that is increasingly export-oriented.

Compensation

The fees received by the lobbyists from these foreign interests, both political and commercial, are often staggering by average-man standards. The government of oil-rich Venezuela paid a group of associated individuals and public relations firms including F. Clifton White $1,369,000 in the year ending in October 1976, according to the agents' Nov. 6, 1976, report to the Justice Department. That sum was for a public relations program for the Venezuelan mission to the United Nations.

In 1977 various Argentinian interests paid five law firms and public relations consultants $1,537,601. The law firm of Hogan & Hartson received $50,000 from Japan during 1978. The six-month reports required of foreign agents showed that Hogan & Hartson also received fees of $25,000 from the United Arab Emirates in the first half of 1979 and $50,000 from Saudi Arabia in the first half of 1978.

Some law firms develop specialties that can be very profitable. Galland, Kharasch, Calkins & Short, for example, offers its clients expertise in the area of international transportation. For the six months ending July 1978 the firm received $118,683.95 from the Atlantic Container Line, $114,881.55 from Japan Airlines and $63,318 from Lufthansa. Other clients included Swissair, Qantas Airways, Caribbean Air Transport and Singapore Airlines.

Arnold & Porter, one of Washington's largest and most prestigious law firms, received $270,000 from six foreign principals in the first half of 1979. Clients included the London Commodity Exchange, the French Bankers' Association and the Swiss government.

Services

In return for their fees, foreign agents perform myriad legal, political and public relations chores for their client governments and businesses. The range of their work points out the difficulty of pinning down the nature of lobbying. Some foreign agents interviewed by Congressional Quarterly objected to the term "lobbyist." They emphasize, correctly in many instances, that they generally do not expend their time contacting members of Congress or their staffs on behalf of their clients. But that narrow definition of a lobbyist is not appropriate to the times, one government lawyer argues, since "a lot of these guys simply give advice to their principal, often the country's ambassador to the United States or another diplomat. They let the official diplomats do the talking to Congress."

Direct Lobbying. Nonetheless, in many cases, an integral part of the foreign lobbyist's job is talking to members of Congress or to officials of the executive branch. For example, many foreign clients are suppliers of goods, including armaments, to one of the world's biggest procurement entities — the U.S. government. Thus their agents frequently are in contact with the staffs of the congressional Armed Services Committee and others in efforts to persuade them of the virtues of their client's products. The law firm of Charles Goodell, which represented the Concorde, also represented the German-made tank, the Leopard. Likewise, congressional opposition to the Concorde made direct lobbying of members a necessity for the several agents of the Concorde backers.

The extensive governmental control over the U.S. economy, and particularly over trade relations with other nations, means that many foreign representatives lobby executive and legislative officials directly for their client's right to export more goods to the rich United States market. The now-dormant sugar lobby has been the most visible example of that version of foreign lobbying, but others exist. For example, the law firm of Clark Clifford and Paul C. Warnke, who headed the U.S. arms reduction negotiations with the Soviet Union, has represented the Australian Meat Board for years, seeking to increase the allowable quantity of U.S. meat imports from Australia.

International trade is an area where strong lobbies often clash. There was extensive lobbying in 1979 during congressional consideration of multilateral trade legislation. Domestic industry sought a variety of protectionist measures, such as revision of anti-dumping and countervailing duty laws and changes in customs valuation methods. Foreign interests worked to reduce non-tariff trade barriers and liberalize entry into the U.S. market, but their efforts were not entirely successful. There was a feeling among some foreign lobbyists that the strong protectionist sentiment in Congress could lead to narrow interpretations of some of the bill's provisions concerning non-tariff trade restrictions.

'Grass-Roots' Lobbying. Many foreign agents — particularly public relations and media consultants — are essentially indirect lobbyists. Their main job is to influence public opinion, with the long-term aim of affecting the way the U.S. government views and treats their clients' national interests. For example, Ruder & Finn, the New York public relations firm whose contract with Iran National Airlines received extensive unfavorable publicity in 1975 because of Marion Javits' involvement, also had a contract with the Spanish government. The stated obligation was that "Ruder & Finn would seek to establish in newspapers, magazines, and on television a greater understanding in the

Foreign Agents' Fees: Typically High

The representation of foreign interests — whether as an attorney, a public relations consultant, lobbyist, political adviser or an amalgam of those — can be a lucrative business. Contracts on file with the Justice Department show that fees for foreign agents typically are in the range of thousands of dollars a month for part-time representation on a retainer basis. Hourly fees frequently are in the $75-$100 orbit.

These illustrative examples of registered agents, their past offices or political contacts, their fees and the nature of their representation are taken from filings over the past few years:

● Cambridge Reports Inc., the polling firm of Pat Caddell, President Carter's pollster during his campaign, contracted in March 1976 to provide public opinion analyses to Saudi Arabia at $50,000 a year. The basic service acquired for that fee was a quarterly written report, along with additional specialized analysis and an oral presentation of polling data. Another $30,000 in fees were charged for the inclusion of 30 extra "proprietary" questions requested by the Saudis in the polling done by Cambridge Reports.

● Former Rep. James V. Stanton, D-Ohio (1971-77) represented the Republic of Korea in matters relating to the allegations of bribery of members of Congress. Stanton's contract called for about $2,000 a month, based on a projected amount of work at $75 an hour.

● Van Dyk Associates, the firm of Ted Van Dyk, former aide to Sens. Hubert H. Humphrey, D-Minn. (1949-64, 1971-78), and George McGovern, D-S.D., and adviser to Jimmy Carter during the 1976 campaign, received a $5,000-a-month retainer from the government of Greece and $7,000 monthly from that of Pakistan in

parts of 1975 and 1976, for political counseling and lobbying for each country. The total received from the two governments during the six-month period ending in June 1976 was $78,000.

● Retired Army Maj. Gen. Chester V. Clifton, a former military aide to President Kennedy, in turn received part of the retainer paid by the Greek government to Van Dyk Associates. Clifton was paid $2,000 a month during most of 1975 for public relations counseling to the Greek ambassador to the United States. According to his report of Sept. 4, 1975, Clifton received $18,000 for activities that he summarized as: "Except for advice and counsel and introducing [the ambassador] to one newspaperman, there has been no other activity on my part."

● Keith Clearwater, former deputy assistant attorney general in the Antitrust Division under the Ford administration, registered in February 1977 an agreement under which he would provide legal services and analysis of governmental policies for the benefit of Hitachi, the Japanese multinational corporation. Clearwater's fee was set at $100 an hour.

● Clark M. Clifford, former secretary of Defense under President Johnson, is the lead partner in the law firm that represents the government of Algeria and the Australian Meat Board. Paul C. Warnke, formerly chief U.S. arms control negotiator, is also a senior partner. The Clifford firm receives annual retainers of $160,000 plus expenses from the Australian Meat Board and $150,000 from the Algerian government.

● Ruder & Finn, a New York-based public relations firm, contracted on Aug. 4, 1975, to conduct a public relations campaign for the Iran National Airlines for up to $507,500 a year, payable in advance on a six-month basis. The contract included plans to set up "small, elite meetings, some of which would be held under the cosponsorship of the Aspen Institute or the Brookings Institution and others who would be willing to cooperate with us . . . for the purpose of encouraging intellectuals from the USA to visit Iran."

Marion Javits, wife of Sen. Jacob K. Javits, R-N.Y., contracted on Sept. 5, 1975, to work as an agent on the account for a fee of $67,500 plus secretarial salary ($200 a week) when needed. Press criticism of the arrangement resulted in Marion Javits' resignation from the account and termination as an agent on Jan. 28, 1976, after receiving fees and expenses of $16,517.

Clark M. Clifford

James V. Stanton

United States for the policies of the current Spanish government." The fee: $10,000 a month.

Another relatively new government in the world has shown its sensitivity to U.S. public opinion by hiring as agents public relations experts. The government of Greece hired a communications and marketing consultant to "coordinate media, cultural and commercial relations" with the United States. The contract called for $72,000 a year plus expenses.

The government of Chile, which has been the target of considerable criticism by liberal groups in the United States, employed three public relations firms during 1977, one in Washington and two in New York.

Pervasiveness

A problem for anyone attempting to examine foreign lobbying is trying to determine how much of it there is. The Korean scandal and the role of Tongsun Park raised the specter of cells of foreign lobbyists well hidden from public and governmental scrutiny. Since Park himself never openly registered as an agent of the South Korean government, his case stands as evidence that there may well be foreign lobbying unknown to the public and unregulated by the government.

The current Foreign Agents Registration Act (FARA) was intended to prevent that situation. Although it con-

The Fight to Bring in the Concorde...

On April 6, 1977, Rep. James H. Scheuer, D-N.Y., received a phone call from New York. The caller was his colleague, Rep. John W. Wydler, R-N.Y. Wydler was concerned; he was picking up vibrations that the Port Authority of New York was wavering in its refusal to allow the British-French supersonic passenger plane, the Concorde, to land at New York's Kennedy airport. The Port Authority decision had been postponed for months; there was a meeting scheduled for April 14 and the decision could be made then, so Wydler wanted to take some action.

The two members of Congress saw a chance that the Port Authority could shift because of a wave of intensive lobbying, in person and through the press, by French and British officials and their hired representatives. It had been reported that morning that French officials had been meeting privately with individual members of the Port Authority "to explain just what we are looking for." A Scheuer call to Carol Berman, a leader of the grass-roots Long Island lobby opposing the Concorde, elicited the information that a new television ad campaign had just begun in favor of the "fair trial" the French were seeking for the Concorde at Kennedy.

Press reports also indicated that the media in France had raised the prospect of some American business interests in France being retaliated against if the Concorde were denied; at least two of the authority commissioners had significant European business interests. The possibility of subtle personal pressures being brought against the Port Authority members disturbed Berman and Scheuer.

Secretary of State Cyrus R. Vance had just returned from Paris where French President Giscard d'Estaing had warned him of the importance the French attached to the landing rights decision. British Prime Minister James Callaghan carried the same message with him on the Concorde as he flew in for a state visit in March. Giscard had done the same in May 1976 when he flew the Concorde to Washington and to Texas.

Wydler and Scheuer decided to respond to the latest flurry of lobbying activity by drafting letters to the Port Authority, to Vance and to President Carter. Their basic pitch was that these leaders all had met or talked with the foreign respresentatives, so they ought now to talk to the affected House members on the other side of the question. The two representatives agreed on tentative language for the letter, and Scheuer agreed to have his staff circulate it April 7 for the signatures of the other affected members of the New York delegation in the remaining day before the Easter recess.

Public Opinion and Votes

That anecdote is illustrative of a number of aspects of foreign lobbying. First, much foreign lobbying is targeted to public opinion. News stories, advertisements and, in the Concorde case, even high-level diplomacy are employed to affect public opinion with the hope that the government leaders will follow their constituents.

Second, foreign lobbying necessarily goes beyond Capitol Hill. Besides members of Congress and the Port Authority, Concorde lobbyists talked with members of the Fairfax County (Va.) Board of Supervisors (location of Dulles International Airport, where landing rights were also being sought), and members of Virginia and New Jersey state legislatures.

Third, members of Congress often fight the battle where it is joined by opposing lobbyists: through efforts to shape public opinion and by direct lobbying of other federal and state officials.

Even for members of Congress, the political process involves more than House and Senate votes. But there were congressional votes on the Concorde. Once the United States decided against building its own supersonic transport (SST) due to environmental (noise and ozone) and commercial worries, the question of allowing the Anglo-French craft to land at U.S. airports was quickly raised. In the 94th Congress 27 bills were introduced that attempted in various ways to exclude the Concorde from one or both of the desired landing sites at Kennedy and at Dulles in the Northern Virginia suburbs of Washington. Again in the 95th Congress several bills aimed at exluding the Concorde from U.S. airports were introduced. However, supporters of the aircraft had remarkable success in preventing passage of any anti-Concorde legislation. When such bills came up on the floor of either house, opponents could seldom muster enough votes.

'Educating' Congress

One reason the Concorde supporters succeeded in those votes was the efforts of its lobbyists. John Martin Meek, a public relations adviser with Daniel J. Edelman Inc., worked on the Concorde account for several years. He and his associates felt that they "turned around" a bad situation for the Concorde by an intelligent, aggressive effort to "educate" members of Congress about the Concorde.

"Some members thought this vote concerned the U.S. building an SST, not simply the question of letting a foreign-made SST fly in," Meek said. Other members, he said, had not grasped the significance of the Concorde matter. The task of the lobbyists was to impress upon the members of Congress that Franco-American relations, and international treaty relations generally, could be damaged by a negative Concorde decision.

The most immediate threat to treaty relations was in the area of

Charles E. Goodell

. . .A Case Study in Foreign Lobbying

bilateral agreements for the landing of aircraft. The British and the French, the lobbyists told members of Congress, might be moved to retaliate against American-made aircraft, by far the most numerous in the skies, by abrogating or ending treaties allowing them into their nations. That was not an idle lobbyists' threat; in late March of 1977 members of the British House of Commons raised such a prospect in parliamentary debate. The existing U.S.-British treaty on landing rights was being renegotiated at the time, which added to the pressures.

The Edelman group also directly addressed the main criticism of the Concorde raised by its opponents — takeoff and landing noise. Congressional staffers were invited to go to Dulles, where the Concorde was landing during a 16-month trial period mandated by then-Secretary of Transportation William T. Coleman in February 1976. There they were taken through the plane and given the chance to stand by and "hear for themselves" what the Concorde sound was. The relevant committee staffs were given noise information that backed up the Concorde defenders' arguments, and they were informed of the diminishing number of complaints from the Virginia residents near Dulles.

Heavy Bankroll

Meek and his associates were not alone in working for the Concorde interests. One aspect of the Concorde lobbying effort that disturbed some congressional opponents was its sheer size and the money expended on it. No fewer than seven prominent law firms were involved in the representation of matters arising out of the Concorde landing rights fight.

Included among them were Covington & Burling and the firms of former Secretary of State William P. Rogers, former Sen. Charles E. Goodell, R-N.Y. (1968-71), and former Environmental Protection Agency Administrator William Ruckelshaus. Two public relations firms also worked on the case, and the overall efforts of the French half of the fight were orchestrated by a

third, DGA International Inc., headed by a former staffer to NATO and Transportation Department official, Donald G. Agger.

The Goodell law firm represented Aeropatiale, the French government-controlled corporation that collaborated in building the Concorde. Goodell's partner, Arthur K. Mason, said the perception that the

Concorde people "have hired a lot of clout," as Scheuer put it, was not entirely accurate. The person who actually had the contacts with the French, as they confirmed, was Agger. Goodell was involved with the law firm and with DGA because he and Agger were college classmates. Likewise, Rogers "never sat in on a conference," to the memory of Mason. Rogers' firm was drawn into the case simply because it was a quality litigating firm with Washington and New York offices.

Nonetheless, Goodell's membership in the House (1959-68) and Senate clubs and his familiarity with the workings of both chambers were doubtless of some value to his colleagues in working for the Concorde and the outside appearance that Ruckelshaus and the others were hired for their entree is difficult to combat. Scheuer said that "it is inherent in the system" that these individuals know their way around and can do the job better.

The money question also nagged Concorde opponents. In the period from October 1975 through October 1976, Aerospatiale paid DGA $1,321,118.98 in fees and expenses. That sum included the monies earned by DGA, the Goodell firm and the Edelman firm, but not that of the representatives of the other

interests in the Concorde fight. The basic rate of pay for the Goodell firm was $80 an hour. Expenses of the DGA firm reported to the Justice Department included monthly items for meals at top Washington restaurants, such as the June 1976 expense of $277.40 for meals at the Palm.

Both sides of the fight worked hard to advance their views. Rep. Scheuer and other New York delegation members campaigned on the issue at home during the Easter recess. New York Concorde opponents visited Washington for a demonstration on April 12, 1977.

The Concorde lobby pressed its case that any refusal of the landing rights would be a serious blow to French-American relations. Embassy officials in Washington pointed to the French elections held in 1977 and noted that all of France, the left as well as the right, was "passionately" behind the Concorde. Some French voters and politicians taunted Giscard d'Estaing for having been "more pro-American than any French President since 1958" and then receiving such poor treatment in return.

In the end a compromise was struck that did not fully satisfy either side. It was announced Sept. 24, 1977, that the Concorde would be given permission to land at 13 U.S. cities. The order allowed the 16 existing Concordes to land in the United States, but newer models were required to meet strict noise guidelines. In addition any of the 13 cities could adopt stringent noise rules that would have the effect of keeping the Concorde out, but such rules also had to apply to aircraft operated by other airlines.

tains some prohibitions, most of the law's requirements aim simply at the public disclosure of any activities on behalf of a foreign government, corporation or individual. Anyone representing the interests of any such foreign "principal" is required to register with the Justice Department and to disclose the nature of his activities on behalf of the client. *(FARA box, p. 135)*

Despite the likelihood that there is some noncompliance with the registration and disclosure requirements of the statute, the files it has generated remain the best available guide to the extent of foreign efforts to influence U.S. policy.

Active Agents

Examination of the registration files show that from July 1942, when the Justice Department was assigned supervision of the law, to the late 1970s, nearly 3,000 individuals, groups and firms have registered as foreign agents. Some of those registrants have represented more than one client, while some foreign entities have over the years been served by several groups, each of which had to register. More than two-thirds no longer are active.

For most of the years since 1942, the attorney general has compiled an annual report listing the active registrants in that year, with a short statistical summary. The most recent available report, for 1977, shows that 110 new registrations were filed, while 61 agency relationships were terminated, leaving at the end of the year 631 active agents registered in the United States. Figures compiled by Congressional Quarterly show that between the end of 1977 and mid-September 1979, 206 new registrants filed. With 34 terminations since 1977, there were 803 foreign agents actively registered in late 1979.

The 1977 annual report also states that during the year 469 short-form reports required by the 1938 act were filed, and that 15,000 pieces of correspondence were processed.

Exemptions

Those figures do not represent the total magnitude of the efforts expended in the United States for foreign interests. Many representatives of foreign clients are not required under the act to register, including the duly accredited diplomatic and consular officers of foreign powers. Beyond that, there is no way to determine accurately the extent of compliance with the registration requirement.

Russell Howe, a veteran journalist and co-author of a critical study of foreign policy lobbying, *The Power Peddlers,* said in an interview that despite poor enforcement of the act most foreign lobbying is at least minimally registered with Justice under FARA, partly because so much of it is done by lawyers and "lawyers don't like to break the law." But several lawyers and lobbyists stated flatly that many of their colleagues who do foreign lobbying are not registered under FARA, in some cases out of genuine ignorance of the provisions and the reach of the statute.

Finally, the registrations do not include many groups that lobby, and do so heavily, for legislative and executive action in the areas of foreign policy, arms sales, aid and trade. Groups that are entirely domestic-based — that is, whose money, manpower and direction come from within the United States — are not required to register. The ethnic lobbies are perhaps the most visible examples of foreign policy lobbies that are not foreign agents within the meaning of the statute.

Where the Justice Department has reason to believe that such a group is in fact supported or controlled by a foreign principal, it may try to investigate whether the group is accurately representing its structure. It is hampered, however, by the lack of administrative subpoena powers under FARA.

Prompted in part by articles in Congressional Quarterly and other publications, the Justice Department sought in 1976 to examine the records of the American Israel Public Affairs Committee (AIPAC). "They cooperated fully," said Joel Lisker, chief of Justice's registration unit within the Criminal Division's internal security section. "We went through there with a fine-tooth comb. We found not one shred of evidence that they should be registered." *(AIPAC profile, p. 141)*

However, some domestic groups that lobby on foreign issues register with the Clerk of the House of Representatives under the 1946 Federal Regulation of Lobbying Act. AIPAC was one such group that so registered in 1979. Others included the American Hellenic Institute Public Affairs Committee, a group interested in matters affecting trade and commerce between the United States and Greece, and the Washington Office on Africa, a religious-oriented group concerned primarily with southern Africa.

The registration unit has acted against one group that wrongly claimed to be domestic based. In its first civil fraud case in recent years, the FARA unit in July 1976 charged that the United States-Japan Trade Council was in fact directed by the Japanese government and received 90 percent of its funding from that source. The council agreed in September 1976 to a consent decree prohibiting any further violation of FARA and calling for public disclosure of the council's past activities.

Past Enforcement

One reason a foreign lobbyist could be unaware of the registration and disclosure requirements of FARA is that the law has been widely disregarded. Former Sen. Fulbright, who as chairman of the Foreign Relations Committee instigated important 1966 amendments to the Foreign Agents Act, has been quoted as conceding that "people ignore the act or get by it." In the early years, during World War II, some persons were convicted for their wartime propaganda activities. Nineteen indictments were brought and 18 convictions obtained to 1944. For nearly 20 years after that — years when the U.S. role in world affairs was at its zenith and when many foreign lobbies were notoriously active in influencing Congress, the executive and public opinion — there were only 10 indictments and five convictions under FARA.

During the 1962 Senate hearings on sugar quotas, the high-profile lobbying on behalf of countries that desired enlarged quotas for the exportation of their sugar to the United States so angered Fulbright that he set in motion a lengthy re-examination of the effectiveness of FARA. Hearings on FARA were held in 1963, and the eventual result was the 1966 amendments, the most significant amendments to the act to date.

The experience with the 1966 amendments proved the dangers of attempting to tighten control over foreign lobbying. Both the Senate Foreign Relations Committee staff and the Justice Department lawyers who enforce the act agree that while some gains were achieved by the amendments, the act was in fact weakened in several respects through the efforts of the lobbyists themselves. In particular, the prestigious law firms experienced in foreign lobbying were successful in limiting the registration and disclosure requirements applicable to attorneys; the definition of

How Foreign Agents Registration Act Works

The basic statute that regulates foreign political activities in the United States, including lobbying, is the 1938 Foreign Agents Registration Act (22 USC 611-621). The central requirement of the act is that "every person who becomes an agent of a foreign principal shall, within ten days thereafter, file with the Attorney General" disclosing the existence of that agency relationship, along with details of any contract entered into.

The policy behind that requirement parallels the purpose of many "sunshine" or open government statutes: "to protect the national defense, internal security, and foreign relations of the United States by requiring public disclosure by persons engaging in propaganda activities and other activities for or on behalf of foreign governments, foreign political parties, and other foreign principals so that the government and the people of the United States may be informed of the identity of such persons and may appraise their statements and actions in the light of their associations. . . ."

Fear of Propaganda

The original impetus for enactment of the statute was the fear of foreign, especially Nazi, propaganda efforts in the years just before World War II. Thus the disclosure requirements dominated the act. Less attention was paid to the question of lobbying aimed at influencing the course of legislation.

In 1966 the act received a major overhaul (S 693 — PL 89-486) and its focus was shifted to place greater emphasis on "the protection of the integrity of the decision-making process of our government." The amendments were the outgrowth of lengthy hearings on lobbying and other foreign agent activity; the hearings, in 1963, were spearheaded by J. William Fulbright, D-Ark. (1943-74), then chairman of the Senate Foreign Relations Committee.

The disclosure requirements of the amended act reflect these two divergent goals, lobbying and propaganda, even though the literal language of the statute has continued to focus on the dissemination of information, or propaganda, on behalf of a foreign interest.

The disclosure requirements are embodied in a set of forms that all foreign agents must fill out and file with the registration unit of the internal security section of the Justice Department's Criminal Division. The initial registration form is calculated to give the department a complete picture of who the agent is, who the foreign principal for whom the agent is working is, the nature of the activities to be pursued on behalf of the principal and the compensation to be received for the work.

If the registering agent is a corporation or organization, details of the ownership and management of the group must be spelled out and the other activities of the agent, aside from service to the foreign principal, must also be outlined. The same questions must be answered regarding the foreign principal; if a corporation or group, the actual ownership or control of the entity must be stated, and the involvement of a foreign government or political party must be specifically set forth. With regard to planned activities, the precise form of all political propaganda efforts must be indicated (radio broadcasts, newspaper ads, letters, speeches) and the targeted recipients must be noted (legislators, other public officials, or editors). As to compensation, the existence of any written contracts with the foreign principal must be disclosed and copies filed, and all oral agreements must be fully described. In addition, the registering agent must file "short forms" naming each individual who will work on the project for the agent.

Once registered, the agent is required to report every six months on his activities on behalf of his principal, again disclosing what was done and the compensation received for the work. The agent also is required to file copies of any written or broadcast "political propaganda" disseminated within 48 hours of such activity. All such propaganda must also be adequately labeled so that the ultimate reader or listener will be put on notice of the source of the information. For example, many full-page political ads in newspapers bear a fine-print disclosure stating that the ad has been placed by a registered foreign agent. When contacting members of Congress or other government officials and when appearing at hearings, foreign agents must disclose their agency relationship and the identity of their principal.

Finally, whenever a foreign agent relationship is ended, the agent is obliged to file a termination statement. In most cases, that is a formality, but a 1977 case proved its importance. Both Paul C. Warnke, nominated to be the Carter administration's chief arms control negotiator, and Sol Linowitz, named as one of the Panama Canal negotiators, had neglected to terminate their status as registered agents for various foreign interests. Rep. Larry P. McDonald, D-Ga., raised the issue in opposing their appointments, and both hastened to notify the Justice Department that they wished to terminate the agency status.

Exceptions, Penalties

There are exceptions to the stringent requirements of the act, however. First, "duly accredited diplomatic or consular officers" acting within the scope of their diplomatic duties are not required to register, even though it is expected that they will be pursuing the interests of their government. Anyone engaging in "bona fide trade or commerce" for a foreign principal, where that does not entail lobbying or other political activities, need not register. Likewise, strictly charitable solicitations (food or disaster relief, missionary work) are not encompassed by the statute. Nor are purely academic or scientific activities covered. Finally, lawyers engaged in legal representation of a foreign client before a court of law or an agency proceeding are exempted.

The penalties provided for willful violations of most of the registration and disclosure requirements of the act are "not more than $10,000" or "not more than five years" imprisonment, or both. Certain other violations under the statute call for only $5,000 fine or six months' imprisonment or both. The statute, since 1966, also has provided for an injunctive remedy to prevent any person from continuing to act as a foreign agent while in violation of the act.

an "agent" in the act was made more restrictive, so that some activities on behalf of foreign principals became harder to reach and regulate, and the "commercial" exemption was broadened.

Eight years later, a 1974 General Accounting Office (GAO) report on FARA, which had been requested by the Senate Foreign Relations Committee, concluded that enforcement of the act continued to be inadequate, and that the impact of the 1966 amendments on registrations under the act was inconclusive.

"Since the enactment of the 1966 amendments, the department has not adequately enforced the act and related regulations," the GAO report said. "The department has appeared reluctant to use available enforcement tools to insure compliance...."

Stepped-Up Efforts

Lisker of the Justice Department registration unit conceded that the act was only slackly enforced for years. "This was just a sleepy little unit that took whatever was filed," Lisker said. Hampered by a lack of manpower, the unit under Lisker's predecessors did not attempt to inspect the office records of registrants to corroborate information they had filed with the department. Nor did the unit try to flush out foreign agents who were outright ignoring the act. The unfavorable March 1974 GAO report on the enforcement of the act "built a fire" under Justice, Lisker recalls. Then-Attorney General William B. Saxbe added manpower to the unit, which began to use the inspection authority in the act in a systematic way to verify information filed by foreign agents.

In 1977 the registrations unit staff inspected the books and documents of 34 registrants. In a number of cases it was determined that disclosures were inadequate and registrants were required to file amendments to their statements. However, in several other cases there appeared to be violations of the act. The more careful inspection of filings by the registration unit has led to renewed legal activity under the 1938 act. In 1977 the Justice Department began proceedings in three cases under the act.

The registration unit also has stepped up its efforts to make congressional staffers aware of the existence of the act. In the past, widespread ignorance of the provisions has meant that even heavy foreign lobbying on Capitol Hill might have gone unreported to the Justice Department authorities. The unit now issues regular press releases listing the new agents, foreign principals, activities and "short-form" registrants that have been filed with Justice.

Increased staff also has allowed the unit to extend its monitoring of publications, particularly newspapers, to ensure that the labeling and registration requirements that apply to the dissemination of political propaganda are being respected. Lisker and his associates now lecture classes of new FBI agents to prepare them to work in enforcement of FARA. Liaison with the FBI is facilitated by the fact that Lisker, like several of his associates, is a former FBI agent with experience in investigation.

Most important of all, the registration unit has begun to pursue a litigation strategy aimed at clarifying the many sections of the act and confirming the unit's power to compel compliance with them, according to Lisker. One case was successfully brought (against Concorde lobbyists) under the 1966-added ban on contingent fees for foreign lobbying. Another successful case was the one brought against the United States-Japan Trade Council for misrepresentation of the sources of its funding. A suit also was

filed to test the dimensions of the attorney-client privilege. The firm that was sued, the old Acheson firm, Covington & Burling, asserted the privilege as a bar to the FARA unit's exercising its statutory claim to search the records of a registrant for indications of inadequate or misleading disclosure of lobbying and propaganda activities.

Issues in Reform

Justice Department officials feel they are on the road to effective enforcement of the current act after years of inadequate regulation, but they point out that some reforms are still needed.

As the 1966 reform effort demonstrated, few bills are more apt to be heavily lobbied than one regulating lobbying. Thus Justice Department officials are sensitive to the risks entailed in any effort to reopen the question of foreign lobbying. Lisker and his associates feel, as he puts it, that they have "a pretty good statute, with some teeth in it.... We'd rather stick with what we have than risk getting a weaker law." That risk may be particularly acute since the aggressive enforcement effort of Lisker's unit has begun to generate resistance among the foreign lobbyists who are covered by the statute.

Terminology

Among the changes desired by Justice would be civil subpoena power to facilitate its investigations. Second, Lisker and others feel the language of the statute should be altered to eliminate the pejorative connotations of working for foreign clients. Justice feels the language of the act is itself a deterrent to compliance.

The terminology of the act is an historical anomaly: The lobbying emphasis of the 1966 amendments was awkwardly grafted onto the 1938 language aimed at ideological propagandists. One Washington lawyer registered as a foreign agent told of a client who, as a former wartime ally of the United States, was so incensed at being termed a "foreign agent" that he had his lawyers spend considerable effort to restructure his activities and exempt him from registration. Lisker suggests that such terms as "propaganda" in the statute should be changed to "promotional material" or another more neutral formulation. Lisker also said that placement of the registration unit outside the ominously titled internal security section of the Criminal Division might render registration less onerous.

Commercial Activity

But the problem runs deeper than mere nomenclature. Some registered agents question whether it is fair to apply politically inspired reporting and disclosure requirements to fundamentally commercial activity. One Washington lawyer argues that the requirements of the act as they are being enforced are essentially "non-tariff trade barriers, just like import quotas, special border inspections or anything else. It's discriminatory against foreign economic interests. In a competitive situation, your opponent can look at your actions, see who you are talking with, see how much you're paid, and so on, but not vice versa — just because you're promoting a foreign product and his is domestic." Supporters of domestic lobbying disclosure legislation have retorted that the solution to that inequity is to impose similar reporting burdens on domestic lobbyists. *(Lobby disclosure, p. 61)*

Mason and other agents further argue that it is inappropriate to cast the activities of many representatives of

Registered Foreign Agents, 1977

The following list includes the names of all countries that had foreign agents registered on their behalf during 1977, and the number of agents registered. The names of the countries appear exactly as they do in the Attorney General's report on the administration of the Foreign Agents Registration Act of 1938. In some cases the same country is listed in two ways, for example Egypt is also listed as the Arab Republic of Egypt.

Albania	2
Algeria	4
Anguilla	1
Antigua and Barbuda	5
Arab Republic of Egypt[1]	10
Argentina	5
Aruba	3
Australia	24
Austria	15
Bahamas	6
Barbados	8
Belgium	5
Belize[2]	2
Bermuda	7
Bonaire	2
Brazil	9
British Honduras	1
British Virgin Islands	2
Bulgaria	5
Canada	32
Cayman Islands	6
Chile	5
China (People's Republic)	4
China (Taiwan)	19
Colombia	7
Costa Rica	3
Curacao	5
Cyprus	2
Czechoslovakia	8
Denmark	7
Dominica, W. I.	2
Dominican Republic	26
Ecuador	1
Egypt	2
El Salvador	4
Finland	7
France	38

Germany (East)	7
Germany (West)	26
Ghana	2
Great Britain	27
Greece	12
Grenada	2
Guadeloupe and Martinique	2
Guatemala	4
Guinea	1
Guyana	3
Haiti	5
Honduras	2
Hong Kong	7
Hungary	6
Iceland	5
India	12
Indonesia	9
International	27
Iran	9
Iraq	1
Ireland	8
Israel	21
Italy	15
Ivory Coast	1
Jamaica	16
Japan	71
Jordan	3
Kenya	5
Korea	23
Lebanon	4
Liberia	3
Libya	2
Liechtenstein	1
Madagascar	1
Malaysia	5
Malawi	2
Malta	1
Mauritania	1
Mauritius	2
Mexico	36
Monaco	2
Montserrat, W. I.	2
Morocco	2
Netherlands	10
Netherlands Antilles	5
New Guinea	1
New Zealand	13
Nicaragua	11
Nigeria	1
Northern Ireland	10

Norway	5
Oman	3
Pakistan	1
Palestine	3
Panama	11
Peru	2
Philippine Republic	8
Poland	13
Portugal	7
Qatar	1
Rhodesia	7
Romania	18
Saudi Arabia	17
Scotland	1
Senegal	1
Singapore	3
South Africa	15
South Moluccas	1
South West Africa	4
Spain	17
St. Barts	1
St. Kitts	2
St. Lucia	4
St. Maarten	4
St. Martin	1
St. Vincent, W. I.	2
Surinam	1
Swaziland	1
Sweden	10
Switzerland	15
Tahiti	2
Tanzania	1
Thailand	5
Tibet	1
Tonga	1
Transkei	3
Trinidad and Tobago	2
Tunisia	1
Turkey	9
Turks and Calicos Islands	1
Uganda	1
Union of Soviet Socialist Republics (USSR)	27
United Arab Emirates	1
Uruguay	2
Venezuela	8
Viet Nam	1
Windward Islands	1
Yugoslavia	9
Zaire	2
Zambia	1

[1] *Also listed as Egypt*
[2] *Also listed as British Honduras*

foreign commercial interests as "lobbying," since actual contact with government officials is often only a small part of the "stream" of activities entailed in that representation. But Justice Department lawyers respond that such contact is a crucial part of the agents' work, and one about which the public has a right to be informed; that direct contact with government officials is an unrealistically limited definition of lobbying; and that foreign political and economic objectives are generally intertwined. The FARA enforcers do agree that certain categories of commercial registrants could be considered for less burdensome registration requirements. For example, FARA attorneys concede there may be little point to the registration of groups legitimately restricted to an interest in tourism.

Two Major Foreign Lobbies of the Past

The sugar lobby and the China lobby, both more prominent in the past than they are today, together illustrate the potential power that can be lodged in a foreign lobby. Taken separately, they highlight the two central reasons that foreign regimes have for trying to influence the U.S. Congress: 1) economic and commercial interests and 2) political and military needs.

Sugar Lobby: Commercial Gain

One of the most visible and highly criticized of all foreign lobbies, the sugar lobby arose in response to a succession of sugar import quota acts, beginning in 1934. The last major act, the Sugar Act of 1948 (PL 80-388), was allowed to lapse at the end of 1974. These acts divided the total U.S. market among various domestic and foreign producers and set price supports well above prevailing world levels. *(Details on sugar lobby, see p. 193)*

The supported price meant that foreign producers scrambled to get and enlarge their quotas, worth millions of dollars to these nations. In each of the years when the quotas were up for reconsideration by the House Agriculture Committee and the Senate Finance Committee, that scramble was translated directly into an intensive lobbying effort by individuals and firms hired by each country hoping to share a bigger share of the sugar quotas.

Rep. Paul Findley, R-Ill., now the third-ranking minority member of the Agriculture Committee, recalled that "there was always an aroma that was quite unsavory about the lobby which put a cloud over the whole Congress."

The 1962 lobbying was so intensive that Sen. J. William Fulbright, D-Ark. (1945-74), prompted a special requirement that all lobbyists file details of their relationships with their employers, including fees, with the Senate Finance Committee. His 1962 request drew filings from 24 foreign lobbyists, some of whom were operating under contingent arrangements that graduated their fees according to the quotas received. The potential for venality moved President Kennedy in a July 5, 1962, press conference to declare the lobbying arrangements "not satisfactory" and "an unfortunate situation."

The congressional and White House pressure did not noticeably affect the size of the sugar lobby. During the 1971 extension consideration, 31 different agents registered to represent 36 nations desiring a sugar quota. In 1974, 26 agents served 31 countries in their pursuit of quotas.

The pattern of former members of Congress serving as sugar lobbyists was long standing. Among the 1971 registrants was former Senate GOP Whip Thomas H. Kuchel, R-Calif. (1953-69), representing Colombia at a reported $200 an hour. Thomas Hale Boggs Jr., son of then-Majority Leader Hale Boggs, D-La. (1947-72), also was registered in 1971, representing Central American nations for a reported $36,000 to $50,000. Harold D. Cooley, D-N.C. (1934-66), was for 16 years the chairman of the House Agriculture Committee. As Findley recalled, the lobbyists had considerable influence under Cooley, who ran the committee "like it was his own domain." After leaving the House, Cooley did sugar lobbying for Thailand and Liberia, the latter at a reported $10,000 a year.

The sugar lobby may not be altogether a creature of the past. The Carter administration is considering the imposition of sugar quotas. "If they do that," Findley said, "that will regenerate the lobbyists' role, either before the executive or the Congress."

China Lobby: Political Survival

The lobby that supported the claim of the Taiwan government of Chiang Kai-shek to be the legitimate ruler of China was active in the United States for 30 years, and many observers regarded it, in its time, as one of the most successful of all foreign lobbies. But changing political realities eventually became too strong for the China lobby to resist.

Already in the early 1950s, the lobby was the subject of controversy. Longtime Senate maverick Wayne L. Morse, D,I,R-Ore. (1945-69), charged in 1951 that the China lobby had spent some $654 million between 1946 and 1949 in efforts to influence the American government and people. Then-Rep. Mike Mansfield, D-Mont. (1943-53), had called in 1949 for an investigation of the powerful and well-financed lobby. Morse repeated the call in 1951 at the MacArthur hearings, saying, "It is widely alleged that the China lobby, or pro-Chiang group, in the United States has for several years been conducting a violent campaign against American policies in China. . . . It is believed by many that the China lobby has been especially active in pressuring Congress for financial, economic and military aid. . . ."

Such appeals as those of Morse did not dim the influence of the China lobby. Stanley Bachrack, author of a recent study entitled *The Committee of One Million: 'China Lobby' Politics, 1953-1971,* has written that "for all intents and purposes, the China lobby was a part of Congress itself." The Committee For One Million Against the Admission of Communist China to the United Nations, one of several groups that worked to prevent American and international recognition of the Mao Tse-tung regime, benefited from the participation of Sen. John Sparkman, D-Ala. (1946-74), a former chairman of the Foreign Relations Committee; Rep. John W. McCormack, D-Mass. (1928-71), who was Speaker from 1962 to 1971; and Rep. Walter H. Judd, R-Minn. (1943-63).

Other supporters of pro-Chiang groups included former Rep. Clare Boothe Luce, R-Conn. (1943-47), former Democratic National Chairman James J. Farley and Gen. William J. Donovan, who had been head of the wartime OSS, predecessor of the CIA.

Widespread support for Taiwan continued long after President Nixon took the first steps toward eventual recognition of the People's Republic of China. But, when the United States severed formal relations with Taiwan in 1979 the China lobby, ironically, found that it had little support from the government in Taipei and was unable to prevent normalization of relations with mainland China. *(Details, p. 165)*

Identity and Fees

Other touchy issues are those arising from the identity of the foreign lobbyists and the fees they are paid. The "revolving door" of government-service-to-private-lobbyist, which President Carter has complained about, is a standard element of the foreign lobbying picture. Rep. James G. Scheuer, D-N.Y., said in an interview that "I don't know how you tell a guy who's been in Congress or in government that he just can't lobby at all. After all, these guys know how the system works. But perhaps you could stop former members from lobbying before the particular committees on which they served. And you could also stop the very high executive officials from lobbying their previous subordinates — people whose careers they advanced while being their boss." New rules governing contacts between ex-staff members and the agencies that formerly employed them went into effect in 1979. *(Box, p. 64)*

The money paid to the lobbyists presents two contrasting issues. On the one hand, a lobbyist who worked on the Concorde campaign, John Martin Meek, noted, extremely large fees give the appearance of impropriety since they raise the possibility in the public mind that the sums are being passed around for illicit purposes. That was the charge raised by the press in the Marion Javits case.

On the other hand, the size of many fees and the difficulty of assessing the results raise the ironic possibility that it is the foreign interests who need protecting rather than the American governmental process. While not denying there may be charlatans in the business, most foreign lobbyists interviewed said the high prices they charge are justified by the "going rate" for such services even for domestic clients.

"Anybody who wants to seriously criticize this [the fees] should be informed across-the-board as to what's being charged," said James T. Stovall III, law partner of Clifford and Warnke. Some foreign principals accept this reasoning. French embassy transportation attache Lansalot-Basou said that he did not object to the size of the Concorde lobbying fees, so long as he was certain that they were not discriminatory.

Parallel With 'Foreign Bribery'

Most lobbyists and foreign agents defended the quality of the work done for their foreign clients. Still, Ted Van Dyk, a former agent for Pakistan and Greece, conceded that smaller countries especially "will often retain someone who's a complete faker, who knows absolutely nothing." One registration unit lawyer stated that while most agents give bona fide service to their clients, "some of these guys must just laugh all the way to the bank" over the minimal work they actually do for a client. He said there is a certain parallel between this and the various commissions and agent arrangements that U.S. corporations have adopted abroad. In each case, an outside interest seeks to gain influence over the local government by hiring as a representative apparently well-connected, influential individuals. The public and Congress have viewed such techniques abroad as "foreign bribery" and legislation is now pending to attach stiff penalties to those payments. Stovall admonished that "the more you fling around that kind of general accusation the more you're unfair to those who are trying to earn their fees."

Outlook

Given the complexity of the issues raised by foreign lobbying, why is it allowed? In interviews with registered agents and their foreign principals, three arguments consistently were raised to rebut any move to exclude foreigners from the American political process:

● Simple fairness. The United States does not have, and should not have, a history of discriminating against certain interests purely because they are foreign. Moreover, the United States frequently is involved in attempting to influence the policies of other nations, so reciprocity is called for.

● Resourcefulness. It is impractical to try to exclude foreign interests from decisions that affect them so greatly. "If you shut off one avenue, another will be found, because these decisions affect us," one foreign diplomat emphasized, adding that the Korean example was a prime instance of political need ignoring statutory prohibitions.

● Possible retaliation. Virtually every agent interviewed said that the U.S. requirements are exceptional. As agents abroad of a foremost trading and military power, employees of the U.S. government and businesses seldom have been subjected to anything like our Foreign Agents Registration Act. New moves to tighten the language and the enforcement of FARA could result in retaliatory restrictions from other countries, particularly in the trade area.

Thus it appears likely that no attempt will be made to ban foreign lobbying outright. Some formula of disclosure by those agents continues to be the favored regulatory solution. What sort of disclosure will depend on the play of forces around any new legislation as it wends through Congress.∎

A Potent, Effective Force on U.S. Policy

In May 1975, 76 members of the United States Senate sent President Ford a special letter. "We urge you to make it clear, as we do, that the United States, acting in its own national interests, stands firmly with Israel in the search for peace in future negotiations, and that this promise is the basis of the current reassessment of U.S. policy in the Middle East."

The letter was the result of a major campaign by the American Israel Public Affairs Committee (AIPAC) urging the Senate to make "a significant contribution to the reassessment of American policy in the Middle East," as AIPAC's influential newsletter, *Near East Report,* reported.

The policy "reassessment" resulted from a breakdown in Secretary of State Henry A. Kissinger's "shuttle diplomacy" earlier that year, for which Kissinger and Ford publicly blamed Israel. As journalist Edward R. F. Sheehan later reported, "Kissinger's much trumpeted 'reassessment' of American policy in the Middle East was his revenge on Israeli recalcitrance." The letter of the 76 senators, Sheehan noted, "was a stunning triumph for the lobby, a capital rebuke for Kissinger in Congress." "It was," wrote Sheehan, in his 1976 book, *The Arabs, Israelis and Kissinger,* "the Israeli lobby that dealt reassessment its *coup de grace.*"

Maximizing its Influence

What is popularly thought of as the "Israeli lobby" is, beyond doubt, one of the most powerful influences on U.S. Middle East policy in the nation's capital. Still, it is often credited with an undeserved omnipotence. It is doubtful if former Sen. James Abourezk's, D-S.D., assertion that the lobby has the "ability to accomplish virtually any legislative feat involving military or economic assistance to Israel" is true. More accurate is the understanding that AIPAC has the ability to maximize pro-Israeli sentiments while often promoting what many consider anti-Arab policies. The billions of dollars in aid that Israel receives from the United States is an example of this maximizing influence. The 1977 legislation restricting compliance with the Arab economic boycott of Israel is an excellent example of this latter power.

"What's good for American society is terribly important to the Jewish community."

—Hyman H. Bookbinder, Washington Representative, American Jewish Committee

Moreover, the "Israeli lobby" is not in reality a foreign agent required to register with the Justice Department and the Congress. It is a lobby financed and supported primarily by the American Jewish community. While AIPAC and the Israeli government are in close and constant contact, it would be an exaggeration to say that Israel controls AIPAC. There have been instances where AIPAC has promoted policies or used tactics not fully supported by the Israelis.

In short, AIPAC is a unique institution mirroring the unique relationship between the American Jewish community and the state of Israel.

Effectiveness

During the past few years, AIPAC, which serves as the coordinator for the efforts of nearly all Jewish organizations, has been very active on a number of issues including:

● Amendments to the 1974 Trade Reform Act linking trade benefits to Communist emigration policies and limiting U.S. loans and credits to those countries.

● Requiring stringent restrictions on the sale of Hawk surface-to-air missile batteries to Jordan.

● A resolution calling for re-examination of U.S. membership in the United Nations if Israel were expelled.

● A bar on future U.S. support for the United Nations Educational, Scientific and Cultural Organization (UNESCO) because of its anti-Israel actions.

● Financial assistance for refugees from the Soviet Union and other Eastern European countries, with Israel receiving 80 percent of the money.

● An agreement by the Ford administration not to supply weapons to Egypt during 1976 except for six C-130 transport planes.

● An amendment by Sen. Abraham Ribicoff, D-Conn., to the Tax Reform Act of 1976 penalizing those American firms that complied with the Arab boycott of Israel by denying certain tax benefits on foreign source income; along with other anti-boycott legislation passed by the 95th Congress in 1977.

● Passage of a fiscal 1979 foreign aid bill that included $1.785 billion in military and economic aid for Israel, the same as appropriated in fiscal 1978.

Congressional Anxiety

In a 1976 year-end summary, AIPAC reported that during the 94th Congress it had "vigorously countered" the "moves to 'reassess' America's relationship with Israel." "On the basis of this fine record of congressional support for closer U.S.-Israel cooperation, we are confident that the 95th Congress will demonstrate the same awareness of fundamental U.S. interests by supporting a secure, viable Israel," AIPAC noted in its Oct. 27, 1976, edition of *Near East Report.*

There has developed, however, a growing uneasiness in Congress regarding the Middle East predicament and it has been reflected in a level of criticism of AIPAC unheard of just a few years ago. Most of this criticism is quiet and almost always "off-the-record." However, journalists Russell Warren Howe and Sarah Hays Trott uncovered substantial criticism when researching their 1977 book, *The Power Peddlers, A Revealing Account of Foreign Lobbying in Washington.*

Assessments of the strength of the Jewish lobby depend largely on the perspective of the assessor. Few, however, would agree with the president of Hadassah, the Jewish women's organization, who termed the Jewish lobby a "myth" created by journalists.

Senator Abourezk, of Lebanese origin who had been one of the few members of Congress espousing Arab interests before his retirement in January 1979, has said he is "envious" of the Jewish lobby. Abourezk told a Denver audience in March 1977 that "The Israeli lobby is the most powerful and pervasive foreign influence that exists in American politics." Others disagree. "There is a lot of mythology about the Jewish lobby," said Richard Perle, an aide to Sen. Henry M. Jackson, D-Wash.

In any event, the lobby's effectiveness was tested by the Carter administration. President Carter, within a few months after entering office, outlined some clear differences between the United States and Israel concerning resolution of the Middle East stalemate.

Even before Carter outlined his views, columnist Joseph C. Harsch wrote in 1977 that there is "a desire and intention on Mr. Carter's part to regain the control over aid and support to Israel which President Eisenhower asserted and kept." "It will come down to a test of strength in Washington between the White House and the Israeli lobby," Harsch concluded. "The lobby has won most rounds since the days of Lyndon Johnson. Which will win this new round? It will be a fascinating test of Mr. Carter's political skill and strength."

Mideast Jet Sales

One of the first tangible indications of the Carter administration's desire to pursue a more "evenhanded" Middle East policy was its proposal to sell $4.8 billion worth of military aircraft to Saudi Arabia, Israel and Egypt. The proposed sale to Saudi Arabia set off a major lobbying effort by the large and influential community of Israel's supporters in the United States that ultimately proved unsuccessful when Congress in May 1978 approved the sale.

A victory for the Carter administration but a bitter defeat for Israel and U.S. Jewish organizations passionately opposed to the weapons package, the Senate's 44-54 decision May 15 to turn down a resolution (S Con Res 86) blocking the sales was preceded by 10 hours of emotional debate on the heavily-lobbied issue.

Sales critics objected to linking Israel's supplies to the Saudi contracts and asserted that the Carter policy would "sap the morale" of the Jewish state.

Contract supporters argued that the United States now must be "evenhanded" in relations with both Israel and Arab states because of the complex weave of U.S. economic and strategic interests in the Middle East.

"We must have the courage, we must have the guts to face a changing world," said Ribicoff, referring to Saudi influence on international economic policies and Middle East peace efforts resulting from its oil riches. Ribicoff has been a longtime supporter of Israel.

Although Ribicoff and other administration supporters stressed that their position did not imply any lessening of support for Israel — that "commitment is unshakable," said Muriel Humphrey, D-Minn., — sales opponent Jacob

K. Javits, R-N.Y., told the Senate the vote might not be read that way.

"The Israelis and Americans who feel as I do are likely to read the signal that is going to go out from this chamber quite differently. . . . The vote today may raise doubts now for the first time in 30 years respecting our commitment given the overtone and context of the debate," he said.

Administration Pressure

Pressure by the administration began to build May 12, the day after the deadlocked Foreign Relations Committee voted to send the resolution to the floor without a recommendation, when President Carter sent every member of the Senate a letter stating that a rejection of the aircraft for Egypt would be a "breach of trust" with Egyptian President Anwar Sadat who "has turned away from a relationship with the Soviet Union" to work with the United States in the search for peace.

The White House also disclosed that Carter was calling many in the Senate to argue his case. Members of the Cabinet and others in the administration also were reported to have contacted undecided senators before the vote.

On the opposite side, the American Jewish Committee and other pro-Israeli organizations were swamping Senate offices with telegrams, Mailgrams, letters and phone calls as the vote approached, according to aides. Outside the Senate chamber itself, the reception lobby was choked with lobbyists on both sides of the issue.

It was the pressure from Jewish organizations, however, that prompted Sen. Mike Gravel, D-Alaska, and others to state publicly that their votes had become a "litmus test" for future support from Jews, although they had supported Israel on every issue in the past.

"This vote, if it is not done properly, kisses away in the future all kinds of financial support that would inure to a candidate for office," said Gravel. More troublesome, he added, the vote "will cost me some very important personal friendships."

Earlier George McGovern, D-S.D., warned the U.S. Jewish community's members that if they "press the case for Israel to the point where America loses its capacity to influence the Arab leadership . . . that may set in motion a backlash both in the Middle East and in the United States that can only harm the Israeli cause."

Bob Packwood, R-Ore., defended the lobbying, insisting that Jews have an understandable interest in the homeland of their forefathers as do Poles, Greeks and blacks. "It is with sorrow and disgust, therefore, that I hear the State Department time and again refer to the Jewish lobby or the Israeli lobby in a tone suggestive of a group which puts the interests of another country ahead of the United States."

AIPAC

Organization

AIPAC's origins are in the American Zionist Council which originally promoted support for Israel's creation and welfare. The current name was adopted in 1954 and until 1975 the organization was headed by I. L. (Si) Kenen. By 1979, it functioned as an umbrella lobbying organization with a staff of more than 20, an annual budget of about $750,000 and four registered lobbyists — an executive director, Morris J. Amitay, who replaced Kenen, legislative director Kenneth Wollack, and legislative liaisons Richard Straus and Ira Forman.

AIPAC's money comes from individual donations ranging from $25 to $5,000, which are not tax-exempt. More than 15,000 members contribute to AIPAC. Presidents of most of the major Jewish organizations sit on its executive committee and the Washington representatives of more than a dozen of these organizations meet weekly at AIPAC's offices. AIPAC does not contribute to candidates or rate members of Congress.

Separately incorporated from AIPAC is Near East Research Inc., a non-profit organization supported by subscriptions to its weekly newsletter, *Near East Report,* and individual donations. It conducts research on the Middle East and the Arab-Israeli conflict. Si Kenen, who in 1979 remained as honorary chairman of AIPAC, was its initial editor in chief and he contributed a column to *Near East Report.*

The newsletter, quartered with AIPAC near Capitol Hill, has an estimated readership of 30,000 and is legally separate from AIPAC. But Amitay is a contributing editor and his organization pays for mailing about 4,000 copies to every member of Congress, embassies, executive branch officials and United Nations delegations. The popular perception of the newsletter throughout Washington is that *Near East Report* is AIPAC's newsletter.

Operations

"The basic axiom of our work," said Amitay, "is the basic support for Israel that already exists. There is a broad base of support that shapes congressional feeling and the administration's. It makes our job a lot easier."

More and more, AIPAC's job is to counter the lobbying of pro-Arab groups and what Wollack has called the "petro-diplomatic group," which have greater financial resources but less power, in the view of AIPAC. The organization basically is a one-issue lobby. "We are pro-Israel — I don't deny that," explained Amitay. "But we make our case on the basis of American interests. . . .Our point of strength is not that we're so highly organized, but that so many people are committed to Israel. We have a lot of non-Jewish support. I'm very glad we don't have to rely just on Jews; if we did, we would be an ineffective group."

Amitay said the organization does "what all lobbies do" — informing Congress and the executive branch on the issues of importance to it — U.S.-Israeli relations, peace negotiations and military and economic assistance. It testifies for itself and on behalf of other Jewish groups, as it did on the proposed arms sale to Jordan. It provides members of Congress with information and encourages its members to communicate their views. "We keep in touch with other Jewish organizations," Amitay said, "but we're not a button-pressing organization" when it comes to mobilizing their members.

Amitay, since taking over in 1975, has greatly expanded AIPAC's Capitol Hill operations. Jews, Amitay explained, were ". . .concerned that after the Yom Kippur war [in 1973] that the United States' effort to improve relations with Arab states not be at the expense of the security of Israel." Under Amitay AIPAC has moved into new, roomier headquarters a short distance from the Capitol.

Publicly, and for obvious reasons, AIPAC has kept its distance from the Israeli Embassy in Washington. Amitay asserted that "We maintain no formal relationship or substantive connection with the Israeli Embassy." Many in Washington take issue with the assertion of complete separation. However, the relationship appeared to be close and often intimate — Amitay visits Israel regularly.

Evaluation

Commenting on the lobby's impact, Amitay said, "I think we've had some effect." Capitol Hill staffers have been more generous in their appraisal. "AIPAC is very effective," said a former staffer in the Senate minority leader's office. "They have a good grass-roots operation, which is vital. It can deliver letters, calls to members from their home state. At any given moment, it can mobilize."

"It's effective with very little in the way of resources," said an aide to a Democratic senator.

A House source called AIPAC's involvement "helpful" in preventing the sale of anti-aircraft equipment to Jordan. Besides its Senate testimony, it mailed information to members of Congress on the possible impact on Israel of the sale. It also described this in mailings to Jewish groups across the country. One House aide estimated that it helped round up an additional 40 co-sponsors to a resolution (H Con Res 337) opposing the sale, which had more than 125 co-sponsors.

Though widely acclaimed, AIPAC also has its detractors. One Washington professor often consulted by the Israeli Embassy on political matters acknowledged, when questioned about AIPAC, that "in the past two years I've heard more anti-lobby sentiment than in all the years before." And a former Foreign Service officer who worked on Middle East matters for a Democratic senator felt "AIPAC often does with a sledgehammer what should be done with a stiletto."

Other Groups

Other major Jewish groups play a less direct political role than AIPAC, leaving much of the explicit lobbying to it and devoting more of their time to issues besides Israel. Beyond their relatively small Washington operations, they have influence as sources of information to their members and the public through mailings and publications and as forums for political figures.

American Jewish Committee

"I'm concerned that there could be an impression that the Jewish community is interested only in Israel," said Hyman H. Bookbinder of the New York-based American Jewish Committee. "If we have to list our priorities, it is my top priority, but we also pursue a variety of other issues." He listed the extension of the Voting Rights Act, voter registration by postcard, housing issues and civil rights as among those his two-person office follows. And they keep up with executive branch actions, and comment on regulations and proposals.

Behind that course is Bookbinder's belief that "we can't expect people to be interested in our issue and in the security of Israel unless we're interested in theirs. What's good for American society is terribly important to the Jewish community." A long history of scapegoating, he said, shows that "when there are social ills, Jews get it."

Additional Support

B'nai B'rith's Anti-Defamation League also has a Washington representative, David A. Brody, a registered

AIPAC's Tough Executive Director

Morris J. Amitay, known around Washington as Morrie, became in 1975 AIPAC's second executive director in its 23-year existence. Amitay brought to his job a Jewish heritage, foreign affairs experience in the State Department and five years as a legislative assistant in Congress.

He replaced I. L. (Si) Kenen, who retired at age 70. AIPAC's new and roomy office on North Capitol Street near Capitol Hill keeps its front door locked and scrutinizes visitors on a monitor for security reasons.

Kenen once told an interviewer that he rarely went to Capitol Hill to lobby, because support for Israeli causes already was so strong. Amitay conducts a different operation, although support in Congress remains firm. "I'm trying to change things here from essentially a one-man operation to having many qualified people," Amitay said in an interview when he first assumed his position. "We hope for a greater presence on the Hill." AIPAC by 1977 had expanded to four registered lobbyists and a budget in excess of half a million dollars. The budget had been increased to about $750,000 by 1979.

Morris J. Amitay

"Until a few years ago, this was a public affairs organization," Amitay continued. "Now it's a nuts-and-bolts operation, analyzing legislation, gathering information, keeping up with the issues." Though AIPAC has grown since Amitay assumed the directorship, the organization has remained tightly controlled. "I put a premium on working quickly, on a quick response. That's why I like being fairly small and un-bureaucratic," he has said.

Amitay is known as a tough, no-nonsense partisan. He is a highly efficient, though sometimes abrasive fighter who knows how to pull the right congressional levers.

He is considered a much more controversial personality than his predecessor.

Journalists Russell Howe and Sarah Trott in their study of Washington lobbyists have focused on the personality difference between Amitay and Kenen. "Kenen stands in contrast to Amitay, the New Yorker whom he chose as his successor and who enjoys boasting of AIPAC power and the facility with which it procures 'confidential' documents from senatorial offices," the two authors have written. "Amitay seems to detect Hitlerian tendencies in all who disagree with Israel. Kenen, in contrast, attended the 1975 convention of the National Association of Arab Americans.... When pointed out in the audience..., he drew some laughs but did not appear to mind. Few could imagine Amitay submitting to this experience."

lobbyist. The league, too, is particularly interested in domestic issues, not just Israel. Bookbinder and Brody, as well as individuals active in other major Jewish organizations, are on AIPAC's 70-member executive committee.

But the amount of lobbying that any of them do is limited by law because of their tax status; contributions are exempt. "We obviously work with each other, cooperate and share information," Bookbinder observed. "But every Jewish group bends over backwards to comply with the law. So we welcome an explicit operation like AIPAC."

An aide to a Republican senator insisted that Middle East issues are not lobbied only by Jewish groups, because broader questions than just Israel usually are involved. On the proposed arms sale to Jordan, for example, Americans for Democratic Action, the AFL-CIO and other unions worked against it, he said. Non-Jewish groups were active as well in barring U.S. payments to UNESCO in late 1974.

Among the other Jewish organizations which work closely with AIPAC in Washington are the American Jewish Congress, various religious groups, the Institute for Jewish Policy Planning and Research, the National Council of Jewish Women and Hadassah.

Since the 1973 Mideast war, debate about Israeli positions and about U.S. Middle East policy has caused serious tensions even within the American Jewish community. A new organization, "Breira" which in Hebrew means "alternative," has acted as a catalyst for debate on both Israeli and American policies. The Jewish establishment has vigorously challenged Breira which at times has voiced an opinion separate from AIPAC on Capitol Hill. For example, following Sadat's 1977 visit to Jerusalem, the Washington chapter of Breira issued a public statement urging that "all Israeli settlements set up outside Israel since Sadat's visit should be withdrawn at once, and Israel should announce that all post-1967 settlements are temporary and subject to negotiation."

Effectiveness

"When I have a question, I'll call one of those groups," said one aide who has worked for more than 10 years for several House members. "It's an educational situation, though, not overt lobbying like AIPAC, which keeps members constantly informed." An aide to a Democratic senator said he feels that these Jewish groups fill a need by being active in social programs, but, in his view, are "necessarily less effective" as an influence on Middle East policy because they are not one-issue-oriented.

Bookbinder believes the nationwide personal contacts the organizations' members have with influential members of Congress and executive branch officials are as important as any Washington operation.

Citizen Support

In the view both of people on Capitol Hill and of representatives of Jewish organizations, the so-called Jewish lobby gains much of its power from citizen activism — both Jewish and non-Jewish — and widespread public backing for the longstanding U.S. policy of support for an independent Israel.

Jewish Community

"The influence of the Jewish lobby is not a result of people walking the halls of Congress, but of people back home," said Perle. "What happens in Washington is really

The Jewish Community's Relations with Carter

Although there is no doubt that the security of Israel is the ultimate "consensus position" for American Jews, some questioned certain of the policies of Israeli Prime Minister Begin, particularly on the West Bank settlements issue. In 1977 and 1978, many were equally apprehensive about the Carter administration's policy of "evenhandedness." In response, Carter sought to reassure leaders of the Jewish community of the continued U.S. commitment to Israel's existence and security by meeting with 40 Jewish representatives on July 6, 1977. Three months later, however, the October 1977 joint U.S.-Soviet statement calling for a Geneva conference with some kind of role for the Palestine Liberation Organization provoked an angry outcry from many Jewish Americans, who deluged the White House with critical telegrams and letters. "The assurances with which we walked out of the [July 6] meeting have turned to new doubts and new fears," said Rabbi Alexander M. Schindler, then chairman of the Conference of Presidents of Major Jewish Organizations.

By late October, however, the possibility of a confrontation between the Carter administration and the Jewish lobby had lessened somewhat. Carter met with a largely Jewish congressional delegation and pointed to places where the U.S.-Soviet statement had made concessions in Israel's favor. Delegation members said afterward that they were convinced that Carter had not swerved from his commitment to Israel. Nonetheless, an Oct. 13, 1977, Harris poll indicated that 60 percent of Jews interviewed gave Carter a negative rating, with an overwhelming 69.4 percent expressing disapproval of his Middle East policies. "There is a tension in the community that is almost electric," said Mark A. Siegel, an administration aide appointed to serve as a liaison with the Jewish community. Particular criticism on the part of many Jews had been directed at Zbigniew Brzezinski, Carter's national security adviser, over what were considered his critical remarks about Israel.

In early March 1978, a new element was injected into the shaky relations between Carter and the Jewish community with the resignation of Siegel, who said he had withdrawn from defending and explaining the administration's Middle East policy to Jewish groups "because I couldn't articulate it any more." Close on the heels of Siegel's resignation came the revelation of the administration's proposed jet sale package, which deepened the confrontation.

In June, the administration took steps to mend fences by appointing Edward Sanders, a Los Angeles lawyer and past president of AIPAC, to serve as a principal adviser on matters affecting the American Jewish community.

The September Camp David summit and resulting accords went a long way toward quieting the growing anti-Carter sentiment in the U.S. Jewish community. The agreements represented "a magnificent achievement in the cause of peace, made possible by major concessions from both sides under the wise and determined leadership of President Carter," said Theodore R. Mann, who succeeded Schindler as chairman of the Conference.

Much of the praise and optimism was based on the assumption that Carter would continue to play an active role as mediator. That assumption, however, was questioned by some Jewish spokesmen in December 1978. They charged that the administration had abandoned its evenhanded position and had become an advocate of Egypt's position.

There was widespread praise from the Jewish community over Carter's role in obtaining the March 26, 1979, Egypt-Israel peace treaty — and equally strong support for the $4.8 billion aid package for the two nations. However, there was also apprehension about Carter's comment that the United States would "immediately start working directly" with the PLO, although he repeated the administration's previous position that such talks depended on PLO recognition of Israel's right to exist and endorsement of UN Security Council Resolution 242 as the basis for Middle East peace negotiations. There was also criticism of the administration's efforts to woo Saudi Arabia as a "moderating" influence. Nonetheless, an editorial in the March 28, 1979, *Near East Report* concluded, "Without Carter there would have been no treaty signing between Israel and Egypt, and whatever lay ahead for Israel and Egypt or for Carter, the American president earned his day in the sun. All Americans can be proud of his accomplishment."

modest compared to what happens in the district. A newspaper story or an event in the Mideast can trigger an immediate response." Still, those familiar with AIPAC know how quickly a telephone or telegram campaign can be mobilized if AIPAC gives the signal.

According to 1973 census statistics, there are about 5.7 million Jews in this country, 2.8 percent of the population. But with their higher political participation, they account for about 4 percent of the vote nationally, wrote Stephen D. Isaacs in his book, *Jews and American Politics.* The electoral college system serves to further multiply that power, especially since Jews are concentrated in states with the greatest electoral votes.

An aide to Rep. Stephen J. Solarz, D-N.Y., noted that the "American Jewish community is very active and very well informed, especially in foreign policy matters, and it will make its views known." While this community is generally considered more liberal than the public at large on most issues, it draws some support from conservatives who have anti-communist views and reservations about detente.

Bookbinder defined the Jewish lobby as "the totality of Jewish influence in America. If AIPAC went out of life tomorrow, it wouldn't mean the death of the Jewish lobby." He noted the influence of academics, the business community, professionals, and socially and politically active individuals, including contributors to cultural and social causes as well as political campaigns.

"The idea of Jewish giving in return for support for Israel is very, very unfair," Bookbinder continued. "Compared to giving of others, like labor, corporations, environmentalists, the anti-war movement, Jewish giving is relatively unstructured and untargeted."

Jews, Blacks, Carter and the PLO

Relations between some spokesmen in the American Jewish community and the Carter administration became strained in late summer 1979, with the administration's criticism of the Israeli government's West Bank settlements policy and continuing Israeli raids on Palestinian bases in Lebanon. In addition, Israel was disturbed by the announcement of additional U.S. arms sales to Jordan and by hints from some administration officials of a link between Palestinian autonomy and oil supplies.

The atmosphere was further clouded by Carter remarks that seemed to compare the Palestinian problem and the U.S. civil rights movement — a comparison some said had been misinterpreted.

U.S. policy toward the Palestine Liberation Organization (PLO) also provided a catalyst for a deterioration in relationships among Jewish leaders and blacks, who traditionally had worked closely together in such areas as civil rights and socio-economic issues. Matters came to a head with the revelation that the black U.S. ambassador to the United Nations, Andrew Young, had met with an official of the PLO in July. The meeting, which had not been approved by the State Department and administration, led to calls for Young's resignation by many members of Congress and the public. When Young did resign, on Aug. 15, a number of American black leaders charged that the Jewish-Israeli lobby had been the major force pressuring him to step down. Jewish spokesmen denied the charge but expressed anger and apprehension at subsequent visits by U.S. black leaders to the Middle East to meet with Yasir Arafat and other representatives of the PLO.

Responding to a meeting at which representatives of major black groups aired grievances against American Jews, leaders of 11 major Jewish organizations, reacting "with sorrow and anger" to the black leaders' criticism, issued a statement on Aug. 23 saying, "We cannot work with those who, in failing to differentiate between the Palestinian Arabs and the PLO, give support to terrorism by legitimizing the PLO. We cannot work with those who would succumb to crisis.

We will continue to cooperate with those in the black community who fight for peace and justice in the Middle East."

The black leaders had "escalated the Andrew Young affair into a needless and hurtful confrontation between blacks and Jews," said Rabbi Alexander M. Schindler, president of the Union of American Hebrew Congregations and former chairman of the Conference of Presidents of Major Jewish Organizations. "The stark reality," he said, was that "the administration which let Andrew Young go has also failed blacks and Jews and all who believe in economic justice and compassion for the poor. Instead, the black and Jewish communities have been entrapped into squaring off against each other — a result that can only delight our common enemies."

The events surrounding Young's resignation not only produced a rift in relations between blacks and Jews; they also produced a rift between those two groups, traditionally strong Democratic supporters, and President Carter. While blacks criticized the administration for what they considered Jewish pressure behind the resignation, Jews were critical of the fact that the administration's policy toward the PLO appeared unclear.

Carter, in a speech delivered Aug. 30, urged blacks and Jews to resolve their differences, pointing out that "black Americans and Jewish Americans have worked side by side for generations in the service of human rights, social justice and the general welfare." And on Sept. 23 the president declared that no "American Jewish leaders or anyone else" urged him to seek Young's resignation.

Although a number of black and Jewish leaders said that the rift was exaggerated and only short-term, any continuation of tensions in the relationship between the two groups was likely to have an adverse impact on support among blacks for Israel and other causes espoused by American Jews and, conversely, on support for black causes by Jewish groups. And the situation potentially had a negative impact on the prospects for Carter's re-election in 1980.

John Thorne, former press secretary to Senator Abourezk, indicated the Jewish lobby is "better organized and more effective than the oil lobby, because it's scattered all over the country. Its power is due to pressure from constituents."

Public Opinion

Coupled with Jewish activism is public support for the U.S. policy, in effect since before Israel's founding in 1948, that the existence of Israel is in the U.S. national interest. Opinion surveyor Louis Harris documented that support in a poll concluded in January 1975 and described in a *New York Times Magazine* article April 6. He found that 52 percent of the public sympathized with Israel, up from 39 percent in 1973 right after the Yom Kippur War, with only 7 percent expressing sympathy for the Arab side. Sixty-six percent of the public favored sending Israel whatever military hardware it needed, but no American troops. On what

Harris called the "pivotal" question — whether the United States should stop military aid to Israel if this were necessary to get Arab oil — 64 percent of the public was opposed.

In an April 1978 Gallup survey, 44 percent of Americans who had heard or read about the situation in the Middle East said their basic sympathies were with Israel and 10 percent with the Arab nations. Nearly half, however, were not aligned with either side (33 percent) or had no opinion on the situation (13 percent).

Congressional Support

"Traditionally, the bastion of pro-Israel sentiment has been the Congress," wrote Mary A. Barberis, in an article on "The Arab-Israeli Battle on Capitol Hill," appearing in the Spring 1976 *Virginia Quarterly Review*.

The *Jerusalem Post's* Washington correspondent, commenting on the new faces in the 95th Congress, agreed.

"Pro-Israel support in Congress," Wolf Blitzer wrote in the Dec. 21, 1976, *Jerusalem Post Weekly*, "has traditionally been a crucial factor in balancing the more 'even-handed' slant in the administration, influenced by Arabists in the State Department."

Blitzer, a longtime pro-Israeli observer, further noted that "Had it not been for Israel's support in Congress, things would have been quite gloomy."

Si Kenen was quoted in Howe's and Trott's book, *The Power Peddlers*, as saying that "without the lobby, Israel would have gone down the drain," dramatizing the importance of AIPAC in influencing Congress.

A combination of local activism and public opinion, as well as the deep feeling that U.S. interests in the Middle East are served by support for Israel, is reflected in Congress, whose membership matches closely the Jewish population at large.

The number of Jewish members increased to 27 in the 95th Congress from 23 in the 94th and only 14 in the 93rd. That was 5 percent, just a little more than the voting strength of Jewish citizens. The 96th Congress had seven Jewish senators: Rudy Boschwitz, R-Minn., Jacob K. Javits, R-N.Y., Carl Levin, D-Mich., Howard M. Metzenbaum, D-Ohio, Abraham Ribicoff, D-Conn., Richard Stone, D-Fla., and Edward Zorinsky, D-Neb. There were 23 Jews in the House.

Aides to key members of Congress argue that Jewish lobbying is not solely responsible for the support on Capitol Hill. A Senate aide who has worked on Jewish issues has said, "It is fundamentally misleading to talk about attitudes up here toward the Mideast and Israel in terms of Jewish lobbying. Seventy-five percent of the Senate is pro-Israel for a whole lot of reasons."

An aide to a Republican senator said that the "interest and support on the Hill for Israel comes from the belief that it is vital to the U.S. national interest. American interests lie in the Middle East; extract Israel from the picture and things are not changed."

Staff Network

Augmenting the support for Israel is what has been called a "network" of staff aides who are interested in Jewish matters, particularly Israel.

They have included such people as Richard Perle in Senator Jackson's office, Albert Lakeland in Javits' office and aides to other senators, among them Birch Bayh, D-Ind., Ribicoff, Metzenbaum and Frank Church, D-Idaho, chairman of the Foreign Relations Committee. Senator Stone, one of Israel's strongest supporters, has assumed the chairmanship of the Subcommittee on Near Eastern and South Asian Affairs of the Senate Foreign Relations Committee.

In the House, a partial list of the staff "network" has included aides to Speaker Thomas P. O'Neill Jr., D-Mass., Sidney R. Yates, D-Ill., Charles A. Vanik, D-Ohio, and Stephen J. Solarz, D-N.Y.

In his book, Isaacs quotes Amitay, a former aide to Ribicoff, as saying in 1973, "There are now a lot of guys at the working level up here who happen to be Jewish, who are willing to make a little bit of extra effort and to look at certain issues in terms of their Jewishness, and this is what has made this thing go very effectively in the last couple of years."

As head of AIPAC, Amitay took a somewhat different view of the importance of any Hill network. "The talk of a Hill network is highly over-rated," he said. "It doesn't exist as such. It's not a question of the staff getting members of Congress to do things; it is the bosses who get the staff people interested."

Staffers who made up to so-called network described it in terms of people knowing each other from working on common issues. They denied that they may constitute an "Israel lobby" in their own right. "Staff people are important, just because of the way senators operate," said one aide. "But they are important on any issue, not just Jewish ones. Strongly held views on Israel are due to constituents — no staff can create that kind of concern."

Assessments

The success of the Jewish lobby thus has been attributed to a combination of U.S. national interest, widespread public support, community activism and an effective Washington operation. Former Senate Majority Leader Mike Mansfield, D-Mont., has said, "It's a strong lobby, But there are other strong lobbies, too." A longtime House aide observed, "Compared to some pressures, the Jewish lobby palls in comparison."

Bookbinder stressed that legislative successes were not the result of heavy-handed lobbying. "In the areas where we don't have substantial non-Jewish support, we don't make our case," he says. "Most of the Jewish community would like to have a federal welfare program or a multi-billion-dollar food assistance program, but we don't have that power.

"I'm concerned about a feeling that the Jewish lobby uses strong-arm, pressure-type tactics. That's nonsense. . . . There is a very small staff of professionals; we don't wine and dine members of Congress; we have no former congressmen on our payrolls; we don't give parties or have a direct political operation funding or rating people. It's just a bunch of fairly good, devoted people."

An aide to an influential Republican senator said he believes the claims of a powerful Jewish lobby were "way overrated and blown up" by State Department officials and Arab interests to suggest that Congress is "blinded and myopic" toward Israel. "Lobbies will win when they have the facts to support them," he observed.

The Israel lobby has facts — sometimes slanted — at its fingertips. AIPAC has both a director of research and a director of information and the instant availability of concise, hard information can often be translated into power and influence. *Near East Report's* indexed pamphlet *Myths and Facts: A Concise Record of the Arab-Israeli Conflict* is often the source of information on Capitol Hill.

Nonetheless, criticism of AIPAC has apparently begun to hurt. Some of AIPAC's supporters have called for a more low-key style but have expressed doubts that Amitay would be able to conform.

The coming years would be ones of great challenge for this key Washington lobby, which was likely to be deeply enmeshed in the politics of American involvement in the Middle East. ∎

Opening Doors That Previously Were Closed

In the view of Middle East Arabs and their American kinfolk, they have spent a quarter century anguishing on the sidelines while the Zionist lobby has called the plays that have helped thrust the United States into the deadly game of Middle East politics—on Israel's team.

But, since the October 1973 Middle East war, American supporters of the Arab cause have felt that at last they are getting into the game. Richard C. Shadyac, an Arab-American trial lawyer from Annandale, Va., who is a past president of the National Association of Arab Americans (NAAA), put it tersely: "The day of the Arab-American is here. The reason is oil."

Thomas Ruffin, former executive director of the NAAA, summed up the goal of the newly emerging Arab lobby. "We are not asking the United States government to take a pro-Arab, anti-Israeli position. We are asking that it weigh all aspects of the Middle East, that it adopt a balanced, even-handed approach in foreign policy."

Whether they consider it a tilt toward the Arabs or a bending back from Israel, American supporters of the Arab cause believed they witnessed a shift in U.S. policy. The shift began in the aftermath of the 1973 war, with its oil embargo and its oil price hikes. Until then, Arabists had viewed American policy, in tandem with that of the Soviet Union, as maintaining the status quo in the Middle East, meaning to them that the United States was doing nothing to remove Israel from occupied Arab lands and to bring about a "just settlement" of the Palestinian question.

But then Secretary of State Kissinger mediated initial troop disengagement accords between Egypt and Israel, and Syria and Israel. In the spring of 1975, he tried for further agreements among the belligerents. That mission came to naught, and an obviously annoyed President Ford commented, "If they [the Israelis] had been a bit more flexible . . . I think in the longer run it would have been the best insurance for peace." The White House announced a total reassessment of Middle East policy, covering "all aspects and all countries."

All this was an unfamiliar tune to Arab lobbyists, but it was music to their ears. Many Arab-Americans supported Gerald Ford for the presidency in 1976 on the basis of the

"I hope we are becoming known as the Arab lobby . . . the Arab-American lobby that is."

—Joseph Baroody, former president, National Association of Arab-Americans

shift in U.S. Middle East policy, especially in view of Carter's clearly pro-Israeli stands designed to attract the more numerous Jewish vote. Yet, by mid-1977, Carter's Middle East views were being applauded by many Arab-Americans. Joseph Baroody, then president of NAAA, may have captured the consensus when he said that "right now we're prepared to give Carter the benefit of the doubt. Until he gives us good reason to think he's not being even-handed, we'll assume he is being even-handed."

Thus the stated objective of the Arab lobby is simple. Its leaders all speak of a "balanced, even-handed approach." But to carry that message beyond the White House to other American institutions, principally Congress, as well as the populace at large, presents a complex problem. Arab lobbyists must present their case effectively to the American establishment—its political, financial and communications power structure.

At any table where American sympathy and support are the stakes, Arabs hold that they sit down with a shorter stack of chips than do their Jewish counterparts. It has been estimated that there are two million Americans of Arab origin or heritage in the United States, compared with almost six million Jewish-Americans. And the Arabs claimed they spent far less on their cause in the United States than did their opponents, mainly because, they said, they had fewer sources of money.

But the real problem for the emerging Arab lobby has been mobilizing Arab-Americans to become active. Baroody said that "Arab-Americans have always been a group that quickly assimilated. There hasn't been an Arab-American consciousness, we never thought of ourselves as a group in that sense." But as with other ethnic affiliations, being Arab-American has come into style. The 1967 and 1973 Middle East wars stimulated Arab-American identification much the same as they did with American Jews. And the conflict of "dual loyalty" might have to be faced by Arab-Americans, just as by Jewish-Americans, should the Arab oil-producing states clamp another oil embargo on the United States.

The question has arisen as to how the Arabs can square away their pleading poverty with the piles of "petrodollars" Arab nations have amassed since the 1973 war. Hatem I. Hussaini, former assistant director of the Arab Information Center in Washington who became the first director of the Palestine Liberation Organization (PLO) Washington office in 1978, said, "Only recently have Arab nations begun to think about Arab information in this country. Arab governments think that diplomacy—visits by heads of states, prime ministers—is more important than publicity campaigns in the United States."

Dr. M. T. Mehdi, founder of the Action Committee on American Arab Relations, said that "The Arab governments are really not part of the 20th century. They have hundreds of problems of their own. . . . Hardly any of them have come to power as a result of elections and free campaigns. So they do not quite understand the need for spending money in America to change public opinion."

Lebanese editor Clovis Maksoud who came to the United States in 1975 as an Arab League emissary, recommended then that the Arab League information offices either be substantially revamped or closed down in view of their ineffectiveness.

"We can't represent Arabs the way the Jewish lobby can represent Israel," said Baroody. "The Israeli government has one policy to state, whereas we couldn't represent 'the Arabs' if we wanted to. They're as different as the Libyans and Saudis are different, or as divided as the Christian and Moslem Lebanese."

A similar observation was offered by John P. Richardson, public affairs director of NAAA, who commented that Arab-Americans tended to have more varied and less clear perceptions of their identity than American Jews who are at least united on their support for Israel's existence and security.

Ugliness and Finery

Many observers of and activists in the Arab lobby believe that one of the major hurdles it must clear is overcoming the derogatory image of the Arab in the American mind, which they attribute to a large extent to the American media. "One of our most serious problems is image," said NAAA's public relations director Richardson. The group has been working with the media to point out the negative stereotypes perpetuated in television, cartoons, movies and so forth.

Writing in the Dec. 13, 1978, issue of *The Christian Century,* mass media specialist Jack G. Shaheen, professor at Southern Illinois University, concluded: "Television entertainment programs suggest that the Arab world consists of several stock characters. One is the oil-rich desert sheik, possessor of camels, Cadillacs and retinues; he is rich, irresponsible, backward and sex-mad. . . . Another Arab type is the terrorist or participant in political intrigue. . . . The Arab woman is seldom shown. A chattel of little importance, always veiled, she apparently has no function but to secure food and serve as member of a harem.

"Viewers are never shown the positive contributions Arabs have made to Western culture in mathematics, astronomy, medicine, physics and literature."

The Arab caricature image, wrote columnist Meg Greenfield in the Dec. 5, 1977, issue of *Newsweek,* "is one of the very few 'ethnic jokes' still indulged by our cartoonists and stand-up comics. It is somehow considered permissible where comparable jokes are not, and I do not think this is wholly owing to the absence of a big enough Arab-American political constituency to raise hell. There is a dehumanizing, circular process at work here. The caricature dehumanizes. But it is inspired and made acceptable by an earlier dehumanizing influence, namely, an absence of feeling for who the Arabs are and where they have been."

Greenfield (and others) observed that the widely televised visit of Egyptian President Anwar Sadat to Jerusalem in late November 1977 "transformed more than the political landscape of the Middle East. He has surely also transformed, or at least substantially altered, the American perception of the Arab and his cause. Unlike the set pieces to which we have become accustomed—the oil-rich sheik, the terrorist, the ululating crowd—Sadat was neither alarming nor strange. . . . He spoke as a man of the twentieth century. He bore his national and religious heritage with pride and confidence, but without swagger or put-them-to-the-sword rhetoric and posturing. . . . [W]hen the plane touched down in Jerusalem, Sadat stepped into

". . .U.S. foreign policy toward the Middle East is . . . injurious to our national well being."
—Joanne McKenna, president, National Association of Arab-Americans

American political reality, just as surely as he stepped onto Israeli soil."

Signs of Change

But there have been indications of rising influence of Arab governments and Arab-Americans in Washington. Arab nations have begun to spend considerable sums to retain the services of public relations firms and top-level political and legal experts. In addition, many large U.S. corporations are sympathetic to the Arab cause because of their interest in investments and business activities in the Middle East.

"It's still tough to present the Arab view, but for the first time we see a glimmering of a real debate in Congress over Middle Eastern policy," said NAAA's Richardson. "We are gradually being heard here. Now ambassadors of Arab countries are making regular trips to the Hill to meet privately with members of Congress."

Richardson's observation was vividly borne out during the debate over the proposed sale of fighter jets to Egypt, Israel and Saudi Arabia in the spring of 1978. Lobbying on both sides of the issue was intense, with Cabinet ministers and members of the Saudi royal family appearing on Capitol Hill almost daily to present reasoned arguments on behalf of the sale. During Senate and House committee deliberations on the jet package, representatives of NAAA testified along with the American Israel Public Affairs Committee (AIPAC), a group long familiar on Capitol Hill.

"It's just amazing how things are changing here in town," said Richardson at the time of the jet sale debate. "When AIPAC is invited to testify on something on the Hill, the committees are pairing us with them. We may not be able to match Morrie [Amitay of AIPAC] on everything he does, but at least we're in there. People are looking for an Arab point of view."

And, too, with the shift in the United States' traditionally Israel oriented foreign policy in the Middle East to accommodate growing diplomatic and financial involvement with Arab nations, the Arab-American populace—though small—has assumed new importance. "Traditionally, they have not been involved much in social activism. They are more entrepreneurial," said Richardson. "Now they are beginning to take some interest in political activity."

In Congress, the number of Arab-Americans has grown from none in 1966 to five in 1979: Reps. Abraham Kazen Jr., D-Texas; Anthony (Toby) Moffet, D-Conn.; Nick Joe Rahall, D-W Va.; James Abdnor, R-S.D.; and Mary Rose Oakar, D-Ohio. Arab-American Sen. James G. Abourezk, D-S.D., retired in 1979.

More significant than the growing number of Arab-Americans in Congress, however, has been changing attitudes among other influential members not of Arab ancestry. For example, Sen. Abraham Ribicoff, D-Conn., has spoken out against the Israeli government's West Bank settlements policy and has sometimes been critical of Jewish lobbying efforts. Ribicoff also supported the administration's proposed jet sale to Saudi Arabia, although he said his position did not lessen his support for Israel.

Both Sens. Jacob K. Javits, R-N.Y., and Richard Stone, D-Fla., strong supporters of Israel, have visited Saudi Arabia and have said they were impressed by the Saudis. Numerous other members of Congress have also visited the Arab nations at their invitation, and although they have not been won over to the Arab point of view, many of them have urged a more even-handed U.S. Middle East policy. At least six senators have met with PLO leader Yasir Arafat in Beirut. One of them, Sen. Charles McC. Mathias Jr., R-Md., said he found Arafat "very well informed."

One indication of the Arab lobby's growing strength came in May 1978. The NAAA considered that a major victory had been won when the Senate voted to support the administration's proposal to sell a package of jet aircraft to Egypt, Saudi Arabia and Israel. During the spring, the organization had circulated a position paper on the sales; NAAA witnesses were also invited to testify, along with AIPAC, at congressional hearings. "The political conclusion to be drawn from the vote is that the Israel lobby lost its first major fight and its apparent veto over American policy toward the Arab world," NAAA stated jubilantly. "[T]he vote . . . confirmed that the Israel lobby is subject to political limits. This reality opens the door to a more constructive and balanced American approach to the Middle East."

The NAAA

A multiplicity of domestic organizations promotes the Arab cause in the United States, but it is clear that one has had mounting importance since the 1973 war — the National Association of Arab-Americans.

Established in 1972 "to fill the absence of an effective political action group" on the national level, the NAAA staked itself out as the umbrella group for Arab-Americans (most of whom are of Lebanese ancestry) unable to identify with pro-Arab activists who leaned "too much to the left." In 1979, there were 20 local chapters and numerous affiliated groups (mainly cultural).

NAAA has attempted to act as the major Arab lobby, according to its former president Joseph Baroody. "Our basic support is among affiliates. There are 1,100-1,200 Arab-American organizations in this country. Virtually all of them are cultural, religious, or charitable, but many of them have affiliated with us for political reasons."

Michael Saba, the NAAA executive director from August 1976 to July 1977, emphasized relations with what he termed "affinity groups" and grass-roots lobbying. Responding to some criticism that the organization's efforts had not been sufficiently political, Saba replied that "We look to AIPAC as an organization that's done incredible things in this country and has mounted programs very significant in terms of American foreign policy. As a potential counter we need first to get our members more involved. The Jews relate more to the issues of the Middle East. We have to show our people that we can represent their interests."

Until 1975, NAAA was a small and relatively weak organization. In 1979, it was still small, with a membership of about 2,000 individuals and groups and a paid staff of six, but its influence had grown. The group's lobbying effort received a boost in 1977 when it hired Richardson — a well-respected and articulate Middle East expert of British and Norwegian descent who had headed American Near East Refugee Aid Inc. — as its public affairs director. Richardson registered as the group's lobbyist in 1978.

All members of the NAAA are Americans. "We don't accept money from any Arab country, though, the good Lord knows, there have been times when we could have used it," a former executive director said. While Arab governments do not contribute directly to NAAA, it does appear they help out by sponsoring such things as sessions at the annual convention and by taking out advertisements in the annual journal.

The group's annual budget was about $250,000 in 1979. Dues ranged from $25 to $100; about 70 percent of the budget was funded by U.S. corporations. Dues and contributions are not tax deductible, nor is the organization tax exempt. Among NAAA publications are a biweekly political affairs newsletter, *Focus*, a series of issues papers called Counterpoint, and a quarterly cultural and educational newsletter. In addition to the membership, publications are sent to members of Congress, journalists and other interested organizations.

The group works closely with U.S.-Arab chambers of commerce; participates in U.S. trade missions to the Middle East; provides assistance concerning international and domestic legal issues; and has established a nationwide "hot line" to alert the membership to upcoming congressional votes on critical issues.

NAAA presidents serve for one-year terms without compensation. They are selected by a 50-member board which meets about four times a year to set policy. In 1978, Dr. Hisham Sharabi, a history professor at Georgetown University and a Palestinian by birth, succeeded Baroody as NAAA president. In 1979, Joanne McKenna, a native of Cleveland of Lebanese ancestry who had been active in NAAA affairs since the group was established became the organization's president.

Meeting with Ford

NAAA was little known in government circles until 1976, when, on June 26, in a session that Ruffin termed "very historic," 12 NAAA representatives met with President Ford at the White House. It was only the second time such a meeting with an American president had taken place. (A small group of Arab-Americans met with President Lyndon B. Johnson at the time of the 1967 Arab-Israeli war.) The NAAA arranged the Ford meeting through Kissinger, who, Ruffin said, was interested in the NAAA's presenting its views to the chief executive.

A four-page position paper was presented to Ford by the then-NAAA president, Edmond N. Howar of Washington, D.C. He told Ford that the NAAA supported the president's initiatives in the Middle East, especially the administration's total reassessment of foreign policy in the region. However, Howar said the organization was concerned that certain fundamental problems not be overlooked. Ford was presented with these six points: a demand for Israeli withdrawal from territories occupied in the June 1967 war; protection of the rights of Palestinians; U.S. recognition of the Palestine Liberation Organization; special status for Jerusalem; a complaint about Israeli military incursions into Lebanon; and an expression of concern that congressional attitudes "are keeping more petrodollars from being invested in the United States."

Emphasis on "Americanism"

In speaking to Ford, as it did elsewhere, the NAAA stressed its American roots and its claim that its lobbying efforts were for objectives in the best interests of the United States. Ruffin said, "We don't speak on behalf of any Arab country or any Arab leader. In relation to U.S. policy, first and foremost we are Americans. We would not be pro-Arab if that hurt the United States. The reason why we are against the pro-Israel policy is that it hurts the economic and social well-being of the United States."

Said president McKenna at the annual NAAA convention in May 1979: "The fact is that we, the two million Americans of Arabic descent, are indeed Americans. When we talk about the United States of America, we are not talking about somebody else's country, we are talking about *our* country.... We have a constitutional mandate to utilize our freedom of speech to inform and enlighten our fellow Americans.... The condition of U.S. foreign policy toward the Middle East is ... injurious to our national well being."

The NAAA is "an organization of Americans, acting in the interest of the United States," said Abourezk, who added that he supported the association as long as it maintained an American posture and did not become a tool of Arab nations. "We try assiduously to stay out of inter-Arab politics," commented public affairs director Richardson. "It's not our job to tell the Arabs what to do. Our principal job is to influence *American* Middle East policy."

"We will not be involving ourselves in any inter-Arab or intra-Arab politics," said McKenna. "Our business is the United States government."

Obstacles to Action

NAAA has set for itself the goal of awakening the sense of Arabic heritage in two million Arab-Americans beyond the confines of Middle East food and music. There has been considerable success so far, but even NAAA's leaders freely admit there's a long, long way to go before there is an effective Arab lobby in Washington that can match the efforts of American Jews.

"Arab-Americans are more difficult to mobilize politically than are Jews," said Richardson, noting a number of reasons for this, among them the fact that much of the Jewish population is concentrated in large urban centers with electoral clout and the fact that many Arab-Americans take a somewhat conservative position on political issues, not wishing to "rock the boat." And, too, he said, due to the negative streotype, some Arab-Americans view their ethnic identity as a political liability. The NAAA has tried to overcome the tendency of its members to avoid political activity by encouraging Arab-American participation on local boards and governments as well as to increase the federal government's awareness of the needs and interests of the U.S. Arab community.

Pushing the Cause

Championing the Palestinian cause has become one of NAAA's important priorities. "I don't think there's any way to come up with a settlement in the Middle East without dealing face-to-face with the Palestinians," Baroody has said. In April 1977, representatives of NAAA visited the Middle East, meeting with various Arab officials

Other Domestic Lobby Groups

Additional facets of Arab lobby activity in the United States include educational and cultural organizations. The Chicago-based Federation of Arab Organizations encompasses small social and cultural Arab clubs throughout the nation. The American Friends of the Middle East, headquartered in Washington, D.C. provides education counseling to help place students from the Middle East in U.S. universities. Also in Washington, the Middle East Resource Center and the Middle East Research and Information Project (MERIP) provide information generally considered pro-Arab.

Another organization, the Association of Arab-American University Graduates (AAUG), has become more visible during the past few years in addition to NAAA. Not especially active in Washington, AAUG has not attracted the attention of journalists and politicians. But it has become an influence. "AAUG — they're more the academics and intellectuals," Baroody noted. "They identify more with internal Arab politics," Saba said.

Another component of pro-Arab activity in the United States encompasses organizations working to provide assistance to Palestinian refugees. Prominent among them is American Near East Refugee Aid Inc. (ANERA), a nonprofit organization funded by the Agency for International Development, corporations, foundations and individuals interested in aiding Palestinian refugees and other persons in the Middle East.

ANERA came into existence after the June 1967 war. Among the activities the organization has supported were the Industrial Islamic Orphanage in Jerusalem, the Palestine Hospital, Gaza College, the YWCA of East Jerusalem, Arab Women's Society of Jerusalem and the Association for the Resurgence of Palestinian Camps.

Over the past few years, ANERA has raised a few million dollars in the United States, of which 82 percent, mostly in cash grants but a small part in pharmaceuticals, has gone to the Palestinian organizations. The other 18 percent has been spent on administration and travel.

including Yasir Arafat of the PLO. Since then, NAAA board members have traveled frequently throughout the Arab world.

At its sixth annual convention in May 1978, NAAA delegates adopted a package of resolutions strongly denouncing what was characterized as an Israeli policy of military expansion in the Middle East. The resolutions called on President Carter to recognize the PLO as the sole voice of the Palestinian people; to halt the arms trade with Israel until Israel guaranteed the human rights of Palestinians and all other minorities living in Israel; and to renew negotiations for a "just and lasting peace." Speaking at the convention, Najeeb A. Halaby, a former administrator of the Federal Aviation Administration, past president of Pan American Airways and international businessman, portrayed the NAAA as an American moderator to help solve the Middle East crisis. "First, I believe that the best thing we can all do is to try to isolate the zealots on both sides who have made such a mess for themselves and for us in that part of the world," he said.

In the wake of the September 1978 Camp David summit, a group of five NAAA members headed by Dr. Sharabi in December visited eight Arab states and talked with six Arab heads of state and PLO leader Yasir Arafat. The Arab leaders, the NAAA group said on its return to the United States, "were eager to have their perspective understood in Washington and welcomed the visit of the NAAA delegation, whom they looked upon as unofficial American interlocutors with the White House and the administration."

On their return, the group immediately requested meetings with administration officials, including President Carter. They saw Harold Saunders, assistant secretary for Near East and South Asian Affairs, and William Quandt, head of the Middle East desk at the National Security Council. "We are not carrying messages between the two sides," Dr. Sharabi maintained. "We are citizens of Arab ancestry with privileged access in the Arab world and we feel that we have a role to play." Sharabi also expressed disappointment that Carter had declined to meet with the group.

That it was still an uphill fight for Arab-Americans to be heard in Washington was demonstrated by the seventh annual NAAA convention in May 1979. Both Carter and Secretary of State Cyrus R. Vance declined invitations to address the convention. Although the theme of the meeting was "Arab-American Awakening," a number of speakers emphasized the need for keeping Arab lines to Washington open. "From the Arab point of view." said Dr. Sharabi, "it would be a strategic mistake to allow a wedge to be driven between the U.S. and the Arab countries. . . ."

U.S. Middle East policy, particularly the Egyptian-Israeli peace treaty, was castigated by the majority of the speakers, who urged the Carter administration to start a dialogue with the PLO or "efforts toward peace in the Middle East may soon reach an impasse," in the words of Rep. Paul Findley, R-Ill.

Arab Governments

In addition to the NAAA — the major domestic lobby group — Arab governments themselves have developed substantial influence in Washington, spurred largely by the influx of petrodollars into the country. (In 1979 it was reported that Saudi Arabia alone had invested between $40 and $60 billion in the United States, most of it in U.S. Treasury securities.)

Lobbying on behalf of the Arab countries has been carried on by the Arab Information Centers, an arm of the Arab League, which provided at least $500,000 a year for AIC operations. The main Arab Information Center is in New York City; there are offices in Washington, Chicago, Dallas and San Francisco. Speakers and films are provided by the AIC for interested American university, church and civic groups. In 1975, the AIC began publication of a biweekly newsletter, *The Arab Report*, which it sends to members of Congress, journalists, television commentators and public opinion-makers. Also published is *The Palestine Digest,* principally a collection of news articles, editorials and speeches sympathetic to the Arab cause.

More effective than the AIC, however, have been the individual Arab governments and their representatives. There was little doubt that, following the 1973 oil embargo, officials and businessmen from Arab nations had begun to carve out a comfortable niche for themselves in U.S. government circles. By the mid-1970s, there was a growing awareness both within this country and in the Arab nations that their economic interdependence had necessitated cultivation of closer political relationships. In 1977, Saudi Arabia sent an information team to the United States; and others, particularly the Egyptian press office under the lead of press minister Mohamed Hakki and Egyptian ambassador Ashraf Ghorbal, were making impressive efforts to gain the ear of members of Congress and the administration.

A key figure in the new Arab prominence was Saudi Ambassador Ali Abdallah Alireza, who, according to Nick Thimmesch, in a May/June 1979 *Saturday Evening Post* article on Arabs in Washington, "has a reputation for being effective, energetic and savvy." Unlike his predecessors, Alireza has traveled around the country to make speeches and persuade businesses to invest in Saudia Arabia's massive development effort.

"The Arab nations have mobilized a vast network of influential lawyers, Washington lobbyists, public relations experts, political consultants and a host of other highly paid specialists" on behalf of their cause, commented a June 20, 1976, article in *Parade* magazine. Among them was Frederick Dutton, a well-known liberal Democrat who served in the Kennedy administration, hired by Alireza to serve as counsel and lobbyist for the Saudi embassy, reportedly at a $270,000 annual salary. The law firm of Clark Clifford, former Secretary of Defense, was paid $150,000 a year to represent the commercial interests of Algeria; and the law firm of former Senator J. William Fulbright, D-Ark., was receiving annual compensation of $25,000 for representing the interests of the United Arab Emirates as well as $50,000 annually from Saudi Arabia.

Another group mentioned in a June 24, 1979, *New York Times Magazine* article by Judith Miller ("The Arab Stake in America") was the U.S. Arab Chamber of Commerce, a private organization that has sponsored lobbying sessions — attended by Commerce Secretary Juanita M. Kreps and Treasury Secretary W. Michael Blumenthal — in several cities across the nation to promote U.S.-Arab trade.

Indeed, by 1979, it appeared that the Middle East lobbying scene in Washington had been substantially transformed, despite the small number of Arab-Americans and the rather late start of the Arab governments. "Until lately, the Arabs didn't even know where the Hill was," said Dutton. Now there seems to be an openness on the Hill. That is encouraging the development of an Arab lobby."

Commented Seth P. Tillman, former aide to Fulbright and a resident fellow at the American Enterprise Institute in Washington, "We have had a politically powerful pro-Israeli lobby in the United States for some 20 years, which has asserted that U.S. and Israeli interests are totally synonymous. Now, a pro-Arab lobby is beginning to emerge, and I believe that the interplay of lobbying by special interests, rather than merely by one side, may neutralize those interests and enable our national interests in the area to emerge."

"We have a lot of catching up to do," said NAAA's Richardson in June 1979. "The potential is there, but there's no product in political institutional terms. Our people and resources are strained, and we're still mainly reacting to events instead of initiating action. But our efforts will be helped when Congress sees us as a useful source of information. And that's beginning to happen." ∎

Congress Ends Korean Lobby Probe

A year and a half after they began their investigations, ethics committees in the House and Senate in the fall of 1978 wound up their probes into alleged South Korean influence peddling on Capitol Hill without recommending any severe disciplinary action against colleagues linked to the scandal. And one year later, in August 1979, the government ended its two-and-one-half year "Koreagate" investigation by moving to dismiss federal charges against Tongsun Park, the South Korean rice dealer and one-time Washington social figure who had been accused of orchestrating the influence-buying operation.

The investigation by the House Committee on Standards of Official Conduct, which began some 18 months earlier with reports that as many as 115 members of Congress had taken illegal gifts from South Korean agents, ended Friday, Oct. 13, 1978, with the House voting its mildest form of punishment, a "reprimand," for three California Democrats: John J. McFall, Edward R. Roybal and Charles H. Wilson.

Similarly, the Senate Ethics Committee, concluding its 17-month Korean investigation, issued a report Oct. 16 that recommended no disciplinary action against any incumbent or former senator.

A third committee investigating U.S.-Korean relations concluded that the South Korean government sought to bribe U.S. officials, buy influence among journalists and professors, extort money from American companies and rig military procurement contracts to win support for what the panel called the "authoritarian" government of President Park Chung Hee. In its final report, released Nov. 1, the House International Relations Subcommittee on International Organizations said that the South Korean government's illegal activities went beyond its legal and extralegal lobbying efforts. The 450-page report, which outlined the history of U.S.-Korean relations, indicated that the South Koreans frequently pursued policies antithetical to U.S. interests. The most notable of these incidents involved South Korean efforts to develop nuclear weapons, a project the subcommittee said was abandoned by 1975.

House Investigation

Completing its "Koreagate" investigation Oct. 13, the House Committee on Standards of Official Conduct issued reports (H Repts 95-1741, 1742, 1743) charging McFall, Roybal and Wilson with official misconduct involving cash contributions from Korean rice dealer Tongsun Park and statements made to the House standards committee concerning those payments.

In the closing arguments on the House floor, heard by fewer than a third of the members, questions about the ability and willingness of the House to discipline its members were raised anew. The Standards Committee was criticized both for being too harsh in its findings and for its inability to make the toughest of its charges stick.

Presented with reports on the committee's findings only hours before being asked to vote on them, few members evidenced any reluctance to uphold the committee's suggested reprimands of McFall and Wilson (H Res 1415 and H Res 1414). But confronted with the choice of voting to uphold the panel's recommended "censure" of Roybal (H Res 1416), who was of Hispanic descent, and suggestions that such a vote would be perceived as racist, a majority of the House backed off from the tougher recommendation.

The House rejected the resolution to censure Roybal 219-170 and then adopted a reprimand on a voice vote. Wilson's reprimand was voted 329-41 and McFall's was approved on a voice vote.

Censure is the harshest form of punishment the House can mete out short of expulsion, a course of action ethics Chairman John J. Flynt Jr., D-Ga., said was considered in committee for Roybal but rejected.

Background

On Oct. 24, 1976, *The Washington Post* had broken the story that the Justice Department was probing "the most sweeping allegations of congressional corruption ever investigated by the federal government."

The *Post* said that South Korean agents dispensed between $500,000 and $1 million a year in cash and gifts to members of Congress to help maintain "a favorable legislative climate" for South Korea.

Park, named as the central operative, fled to London shortly after the story appeared. He stayed there until August 1977 when he returned to Korea.

After the *Post* disclosure appeared, the rest of the news media picked up the story. The reports said the plan had been hatched in the Blue House, the South Korean equivalent of the White House, at a meeting in late 1970 or early 1971 of President Park Chung Hee, Tongsun Park, high KCIA officials and Pak Bo Hi, later a chief aide to Korean evangelist Sun Myung Moon.

President Park reportedly was concerned about a Nixon administration plan to withdraw about a third of the U.S. troops in Korea. The growing opposition to the war in Vietnam also raised fears in Korea that a pullout would lessen American ability to protect it against another invasion from North Korea. Continued U.S. congressional support therefore became a high priority of the Park regime.

The stories also said that Suzi Park Thomson, a Korean-born clerk in the office of then-Speaker Carl Albert, D-Okla., was among the persons under investigation.

Tongsun Park

By the late 1960s, when the conspiracy allegedly began, Tongsun Park was a familiar figure in Washington business and social circles, although little was known about him. A former student at Georgetown University, he became increasingly active in real estate and international business ventures, in addition to his work as a rice dealer.

He organized the George Town Club in the city's fashionable section, Georgetown, purchasing the property for it on June 22, 1965. The club, which opened the following year, became a popular gathering place for members of Congress and other prominent persons. Park and then-Rep. Richard T. Hanna, D-Calif., held a birthday party there on Dec. 10, 1973, for Thomas P. O'Neill Jr., D-Mass., then House majority leader; Vice President Gerald R. Ford attended as a guest.

The source of Park's money was a mystery to his acquaintances. After the Justice Department investigation came to light, Park told reporters in London that he received $1 million a month from a family-owned Gulf Oil Co. business in Korea. Gulf denied that it paid him any such sum.

According to the 1977 federal indictment against Park, it was part of the conspiracy that he was designated the seller's agent for all Korean purchases of U.S. rice, and that some of the money generated by those sales was used to bribe members of Congress.

Return From Korea

The House Standards Committee investigation, begun in January 1977, was renewed in early 1978, when Tongsun Park returned to Washington to answer questions about his activities.

For months the Justice Department and subsequently the Standards Committee under Special Counsel Leon Jaworski had negotiated with the Seoul government to gain Park's testimony. On Dec. 30, 1977, the Justice Department announced an agreement with the South Korean government to obtain Park's testimony in exchange for a grant of immunity from prosecution. (Park had been indicted on 36 charges, including bribery, conspiracy, mail fraud, making illegal political contributions and failing to register as a foreign agent. He pleaded innocent to all charges.) The agreement, which stipulated that Park testify only in Justice Department cases, was immediately denounced by Jaworski and Standards Committee Chairman Flynt.

Flynt labeled the deal a "facade" that would allow Park to refuse to testify on Capitol Hill. "Congress will not sit idly by and accept this insult," he said.

On Jan. 4 Flynt issued a statement saying that the committee would subpoena Park to appear before his panel immediately upon the South Korean's return to the United States. It was the first of a series of pressure tactics used by Flynt and Jaworski that led to an announcement Jan. 31 of agreement with South Korea for Park's testimony.

Flynt's Jan. 4 threat to subpoena Park was followed up two days later by an announcement from Jaworski that "we have requested that the South Korean government make Mr. Park available for testimony in proceedings of the committee at such time as the committee may schedule them." In making that announcement Jaworski separated the House investigation from the Justice Department probe, making it clear the House was ready to go its own way to obtain Park's testimony.

On Jan. 20 Jaworski asked the House for a resolution calling on the South Korean government to give unlimited cooperation to the committee's investigation. Three days later, on Jan. 23, a resolution was introduced in the House insisting that the South Korean government make Park, former Ambassador Kim Dong Jo and other officials available for questioning before the Standards Committee. The resolution, backed by Speaker Thomas P. O'Neill Jr., D-Mass., and Republican Minority Leader John J. Rhodes of Arizona, warned that the U.S. alliance with South Korea and American military and economic aid would be jeopar-

dized if the Koreans continued to resist congressional requests for information.

On Jan. 31, Ambassador Yong Shik Kim presented his government's agreement on Park's "voluntary" testimony to O'Neill and the Speaker indicated that a vote on the House resolution had been shelved — at least temporarily.

Park began testifying before the Standards Committee Feb. 28. But even before he returned to the United States, his credibility had been called into question. In 17 days of Justice Department interrogation in Seoul in January, he had denied that he was an agent of the South Korean Central Intelligence Agency, a statement that ran counter to a substantial body of evidence developed by House committees.

By the end of his first week of testimony before the House Standards Committee, Park's credibility was even weaker. Members in attendance described his responses to questions as "incomplete" and "evasive." Several members said they did not believe his answers.

Park House Testimony, Passman Indictment

Park completed his public testimony before the House Standards Commitee April 4, denying to the end that he was a Korean government agent.

Park also denied that he had conspired with former Rep. Otto E. Passman, D-La. (1947-77), to buy influence for South Korea.

Passman was indicted March 31 by a federal grand jury in the District of Columbia on charges of bribery and conspiracy to defraud the United States in connection with rice sales to the South Korean government. The indictment named Passman as a recipient of $213,000 in illegal payments from Park. An April 28 indictment accused him of failing to report $143,000 on his income taxes and of evading taxes of $77,000. Park was named as an unindicted co-conspirator. Passman, who had been chairman of the House Appropriations subcommittee that dealt with rice and other Food for Peace commodity sales as well as foreign aid, had denied any illegal or improper conduct in the Korean influence-buying scandal. (Passman, who was defeated in a primary re-election bid in 1976, was acquitted of the charges in April 1979.)

During his testimony, Park said that most of his payments went to three former House members — Passman, who Park testified received cash and gifts of between $367,000 and $407,000; former Rep. Hanna, who allegedly received $262,000; and former Rep Cornelius Gallagher, D-N.J., who Park said got $211,000.

Hanna pleaded guilty March 17 to one charge of conspiracy to defraud the government.

Park said he paid the three men because they helped him retain his lucrative job as the exclusive agent for U.S. rice sales to Korea. Park received $9 million in commission from that job between 1970 and 1975.

O'Neill Disputes Report

Park denied to the Standards Committee that he reported his payments to U.S. congressmen back to South Korean officials. He said he did not know how four purported reports got into his house.

One of the reports said that House Speaker Thomas P. O'Neill Jr., D-Mass., during a 1974 trip to Korea, asked Park to make contributions to House members and their wives. O'Neill branded the report "self-serving and a total fabrication," and denied that he had ever done anything more for Park than get him tickets to the 1969 World Series.

Members of Congress Mentioned in Indictment

The allegations contained in the 1977 indictment of Tongsun Park touched members of Congress in different ways.

Most of those named were mentioned only as recipients of money from Park. A few were mentioned as having been requested by Park or by former Rep. Richard T. Hanna, D-Calif. (1963-74), to do something on behalf of Park or of South Korea. Those allegations included the following:

● **Rep. Walter Flowers,** D-Ala. (1969-74), in the summer of 1974 was given a "pro-Korean" statement by Hanna for presentation to the Foreign Affairs Subcommittee on International Organizations, which was then studying alleged repression in South Korea.

A Flowers aide confirmed that such a statement had been received by Flowers, and that Flowers did submit testimony to the subcommittee that could be characterized as "pro-Korean." But the aide stated that the Flowers statement was not based solely on the Hanna document, and was a reflection of Flowers' longstanding opinion regarding South Korea.

● **Rep. Thomas S. Foley,** D-Wash., in 1971 or 1972 was given the draft of a letter by Tongsun Park that Park wanted sent on Foley's stationery to South Korea President Park Chung Hee. Also during that time Foley was caused by Park to call an unspecified official of the executive branch of the U.S. government.

● **Former Rep. Albert W. Johnson,** R-Pa. (1963-77), in the summer of 1974 was given a pro-Korean statement by Park for submission to the International Organizations Subcommittee investigation.

● **Rep. John J. McFall,** D-Calif. (1957-79), in June 1971 and again in February 1973 was given draft letters to be sent to President Park on McFall's official stationery. McFall previously had disclosed his being one of several members of Congress who had written letters to President Park on behalf of Tongsun Park. An aide confirmed that the two letters sent by McFall dealt with the activities of Park as a rice salesman.

● **Former Rep. William E. Minshall Jr.,** R-Ohio (1955-75), in June 1973 co-hosted with Hanna a party for McFall at Park's George Town Club.

● **Former Rep. John W. McCormack,** D-Mass. (1928-71), in January 1969 received a letter from Hanna "expressing appreciation" for the then-Speaker's support for a proposed congressional trip to South Korea. Carl Albert (D Okla., 1947-77), who later succeeded McCormack as Speaker, was mentioned as having led that delegation, including Hanna, on a March 1969 visit.

● **Cole McMartin,** a 1970 Republican candidate for the House from Iowa (against Democrat John C. Culver), also was mentioned as receiving a $1,000 contribution in 1970. The indictment erroneously listed his name as Philip B. McMartin.

The following present and former members of Congress or their election campaigns were listed in the indictment as recipients of cash or other valuables from Park.

Member	Amount	Approximate Date
Rep. E. Ross Adair (R Ind. 1951-71)	$ 500	1970
Rep. William H. Ayres (R Ohio 1951-71)	500	1970
Rep. John Brademas (D Ind. 1959-)	500	Oct. 30, 1970
	1,700	May 17, 1972
	2,950	Sept. 23, 1974
Rep. William S. Broomfield (R Mich. 1957-)	1,000	1970
Sen. Harry F. Byrd Jr. (D Va. 1965-71; Ind Va. 1971-)	500	1970
Rep. E. (Kika) de la Garza (D Texas 1965-)	500	1970
Sen. Elaine S. Edwards (D La. Aug. 1, 1972-Nov. 13, 1972)	10,000	Nov. 1971
Rep. Edwin W. Edwards (D La. Oct. 2, 1965-May 9, 1972)	5,000	Dec. 18, 1971
	5,000	Jan. 28, 1972
Rep. Thomas S. Foley (D Wash. 1965-)	500	1970
Rep. Peter H. B. Frelinghuysen Jr. (R N.J. 1953-75)	500	1970
Rep. Nick Galifianakis (D N.C. 1967-73)	500	1970
Rep. Richard T. Hanna (D Calif. 1963-Dec. 31, 1974)	100,000	1967-1975

Member	Amount	Approximate Date
Rep. Lawrence J. Hogan (R Md. 1969-75)	$ 500	1970
Rep. Albert W. Johnson (R Pa. Nov. 5, 1963-77)	1,000	Oct. 1974
Rep. Thomas S. Kleppe (R N.D. 1967-71)	500	1970
Rep. Spark M. Matsunaga (D Hawaii 1963-77; Senate 1977-)	500	1970
Rep. John J. McFall (D Calif. 1957-79)	3,000	Oct. 1974
	1,000	Nov. 14, 1972
Sen. Jack R. Miller (R Iowa 1961-73)	3,000	April 1972
Rep. Chester L. Mize (R Kan. 1965-71)	500	1970
Sen. Joseph M. Montoya (D N.M. Nov. 4, 1964-77; House April 9, 1957-Nov. 3, 1964)	3,000	Oct. 29, 1970
Rep. John M. Murphy (D N.Y. 1963-)	500	1970
Rep. Melvin Price (D Ill. 1945-)	500	1970
Sen. Stuart Symington (D Mo. 1953-Dec. 27, 1976)	500	1970
Rep. Frank Thompson Jr. (D N.J. 1955-)	100	1970
Rep. Morris K. Udall (D Ariz. May 2, 1961-)	300	1970

Park testified that he had no idea who wrote the report, but that it was false.

On July 13, the Standards Committee issued a report clearing O'Neill and stating that the only thing the Speaker did of "questionable propriety" was to accept two parties in his honor paid for by Park.

The lengthy report said the committee found nothing to warrant action against other House members whose names had figured in Park-related allegations. Besides O'Neill, they were Reps. E. "Kika" de la Garza, D-Texas, Thomas S. Foley, D-Wash., John M. Murphy, D-N.Y., Frank Thompson Jr., D-N.J., Melvin Price, D-Ill., Morris K. Udall, D-Ariz., Edward P. Boland, D-Mass., John B. Breaux, D-La., and Majority Whip John Brademas, D-Ind.

Focus Shifts to Kim

Once the agreement to obtain Park's testimony had been settled, the brunt of the Standards Committee's pressure on South Korea shifted to obtaining an agreement on the testimony of former Ambassador Kim Dong Jo.

"Kim Dong Jo is immeasurably more important to us than Tongsun Park," Jaworski said Jan. 16. "This whole thing was run right out of the Korean embassy ... and the Korean government might as well stop kidding itself. We're not going to rest until we've got everything."

Several witnesses had told investigators that Kim or his wife delivered envelopes containing $100 bills to congressional offices. Kim reportedly had more contacts among senators than Tongsun Park.

On Feb. 5 Jaworski called on President Carter to order the State Department to help the committee obtain the testimony of Kim. Three days later, on Feb. 8, Secretary of State Cyrus R. Vance responded. Addressing a House International Relations subcommittee, Vance said that U.S. aid to South Korea should be based on military needs and not used as leverage to get testimony on alleged influence buying. It was the kind of encouragement Seoul was looking for. *(Aid cutoff threat box, p. 157)*

The administration position remained the same. Justice Department officials apparently never tried to question Kim or other Korean diplomats because they believed them to be protected by diplomatic immunity, which South Korea had invoked.

The problem was simple: There are more American diplomats who have been accused of making political payoffs abroad than foreign diplomats accused of making payoffs here. Graham Martin, former ambassador to Italy, was reported to have made $9 million in payoffs to Italian politicians in 1972.

Despite the pressure, congressional committees were unsuccessful in their efforts to obtain Kim's testimony.

Jaworski Withdraws from Probe

Leon Jaworski withdrew from active participation as special counsel to the House Korea lobbying investigation Aug. 2, raising in his departing comments the very questions that underlined the inquiry from its inception.

Jaworski criticized the House's ability to investigate its own members, questioned the commitment of the chairman of the investigating committee, and took several shots at the Justice Department for its part in the Korean influence peddling inquiry.

At the same time, Jaworski appeared to have little difficulty giving his own investigative efforts a gold star in a report to the House leadership and Standards Committee.

"It is my opinion that everything that could be done was done," Jaworski said, dismissing as "extreme demagoguery" suggestions that the House could have threatened South Korea with a cutoff of military aid to obtain the testimony of former ambassador Kim Dong Jo.

Jaworski, who said he would be available to the committee for consultation, said the investigation had successfully exposed South Korean influence efforts and possible misconduct by congressmen.

"[T]he major portion of the facts of Koreagate have been ferreted out and published," he said. "They cannot be ignored by public officials tempted in the future to yield to greed. They cannot be ignored by officials who have been careless in dealing with persons whose backgrounds and intentions are not clearly known. And they cannot be ignored by foreign governments."

Standards Committee Hearings

Public hearings by the Standards Committee on the charges against Roybal, McFall, Wilson and Patten began Sept. 14.

During the first day of hearings, Roybal confirmed testimony by Tongsun Park that he gave Roybal a $1,000 cash contribution, which the committee alleged Roybal failed to report. Roybal said his failure to report the contribution was "a mistake of judgment."

The Standards Committee had accused Roybal of violating House rules in failing to report the campaign contribution and of converting the cash to his own use. It also had accused Roybal of testifying falsely in statements to the committee that he never received the money and, later, that he received the money but gave it to his re-election campaign.

Park told the committee under oath that he gave Roybal $1,000 in cash after then-Rep. Passman told him he had "two dear friends" who needed campaign contributions. Park said Passman later arranged for him to meet Roybal in Passman's office, where he gave Roybal the money.

Roybal confirmed Park's recollection of the events, but said he did not catch Park's name when he received the money and never asked Passman who the man was who gave him $1,000. Roybal testified that he previously told committee investigators he never met Park and never received money from him "because I didn't know that the man was Tongsun Park."

He said he had previously denied receiving money from a Korean national because "I didn't know that Tongsun Park was a Korean national. It could have been a Korean who was a citizen of the United States."

In addition to Roybal, statements of alleged violations were released in July by the committee against McFall, Wilson and Patten. None of the four congressmen named by the committee faced federal charges.

McFall. The ethics committee lodged three charges against McFall: 1) that he received a $3,000 "contribution" from Park in October 1974 and failed to report it as required by federal law; 2) that he converted Park's 1974 contribution to his personal use and failed to keep his campaign funds separate from his personal funds, in violation of Rule 6 of the House Code of Official Conduct and; 3) that he received cash contributions and gifts from Park "under circumstances which might be construed by reasonable persons as influencing the performance of his govern-

Korean Aid Cutoff Threat Fails

On May 24, 1978, the House International Relations Committee unanimously approved a resolution (H Res 1194) warning South Korea that the House would consider cutting off economic aid if former Ambassador Kim Dong Jo did not cooperate in its investigation of alleged bribery attempts.

Leon Jaworski, special counsel to the House Korean investigation, had asked for a resolution threatening an aid cutoff in order to obtain Kim's testimony.

Jaworski announced May 10 that the South Korean government had refused to make Kim available for questioning. Later that day, in action on a bill setting budget targets, the House voted 146-254 against cutting off aid to South Korea.

The resolution approved by the International Relations Committee was a watered-down version of the one Jaworski had requested. That resolution would have required the House to cut off non-military aid unless South Korea made Kim available for sworn testimony.

Members of the committee and the State Department expressed concern that the stronger resolution would establish a bad precedent, inviting other countries to ignore diplomatic immunity and coerce testimony from diplomats.

The State Department said the Carter administration could not support the resolution because of its "overt pressure."

The State Department suggested Jaworski accept an offer from Seoul to allow Kim to be questioned by House Speaker Thomas P. O'Neill Jr., D-Mass., by telephone. Jaworski responded that the offer would make "a mockery of Congress."

"It is my opinion," Jaworski said, "that the people of this nation will not accept legal niceties as an explanation for the failure of Congress to complete its investigation of corruption in its own chambers."

The House approved the non-binding resolution by a vote of 321-46 on May 31.

In action on another bill — agriculture appropriations (HR 13125) — the House June 22 voted 273-125 to cut $56 million in economic aid to Korea. The vote came on an amendment by Majority Leader Jim Wright, D-Texas, to delete the Korea funds from the Food for Peace program.

Wright said the House had "no other alternative" than to approve the amendment if it was to preserve its honor. "A cloud of suspicion has hung over the House; that cloud must be dispelled," he said.

Kim resigned his post as foreign affairs assistant to South Korean President Park Chung Hee the day after the House vote. Kim said he was "indignant at the coercive American action" but quit because he was "sorry for causing trouble" for his country.

Wright told the House that since its 321-46 vote May 31 in favor of a resolution threatening an aid cutoff,

the Republic of Korea had refused to make any concessions in making Kim available for interrogation.

Jaworski wrote House Speaker O'Neill that he had offered to accept written responses from Kim rather than sworn statements.

House Minority Leader John J. Rhodes, R-Ariz., who supported the resolution, charged that Jaworski "has given away the ballgame.... It seems to me that the counsel has already given away the possibility of obtaining meaningful testimony from Kim Dong Jo."

Rhodes and other members said an unsworn statement would be ineffectual and unacceptable to them. "I would rather have nothing from Kim Dong Jo than to have a statement not under oath," Rhodes said.

Members who opposed the Wright amendment said it was a "hollow gesture" that stood little chance of evoking Kim's testimony and that even if it worked charges against members could not be brought unless Kim testified under oath in U.S. court proceedings.

Rep. Neal Smith, D-Iowa, said the Wright amendment was the "weakest possible tool" that could be used to gain Kim's testimony and that it would hurt U.S. farmers because a glut of agricultural commodities on the world market would lead Korea to buy products from non-U.S. firms.

On Aug. 10, the Senate refused to go along with the House's action. Before voting to pass HR 13125, the Senate agreed 71-24 to table — and thus kill — an amendment by Lowell P. Weicker Jr., R-Conn., to keep South Korea out of the food program.

Opponents of the Weicker amendment argued that the Korean government had agreed to secure from Kim answers to written questions, and that more pressure would block further cooperation. But Weicker called "written interrogatories ... worthless" and told members that if they rejected his amendment, "it adds up to what so far has been called a resounding cover-up."

Weicker said he had quit the Senate ethics panel investigating the payoff allegations because his efforts to get witnesses had been thwarted. His amendment, he said, was an attempt to "bring back into focus what has been to date a shamefully inadequate investigation."

Ethics Committee Chairman Stevenson said that Weicker's comments on the uncompleted investigation were "premature."

"If the distinguished senator from Connecticut knew anything about these investigations, he would not make such silly charges," Stevenson said.

Majority Leader Robert C. Byrd, W.Va., backed Stevenson, calling the Weicker amendment "counterproductive." If Weicker "has anything other than innuendos, let him ... bring it to the Senate floor," Byrd said.

House and Senate conferees upheld the Senate position on lifting the ban.

ment duties, in violation of Rule 5 of the Code of Ethics of Government Service." McFall responded in writing, seeking a dismissal of the charges. He said that each count failed to "state facts constituting a violation of the Code of Official Conduct or any other applicable law, rule, regulation, or standard of conduct."

In his 19-page response, McFall conceded that he received $3,000 from Park in 1974, that he never returned it and never reported it. But he said he was not required to report it because he never unconditionally "accepted" the contribution and because he never "received" it as a contribution. The ethics committee staff response to McFall's explanation said that "the argument is completely without merit."

McFall also argued that his purpose in receiving the contribution, rather than Park's purpose in giving it, determined whether he had to report it.

The staff recommendation stated: "The statute unambiguously requires reporting of gifts *'made'* 'for the purpose' of influencing an election. Moreover, it is shocking to suggest that a candidate could unilaterally decide to use for some purpose of his own, money which was given to him solely to help elect him to office."

Wilson. The ethics committee alleged that Wilson deliberately withheld information when he answered a questionnaire from the committee concerning contributions from Park.

Wilson told the committee in July 1977 that he received no money from Park. But in a letter dated Feb. 7, 1978, he informed the committee that he and his wife had received wedding gifts from Park including $600 in U.S. currency. A staff memorandum on the case stated that "it is plainly unethical for a congressman to lie to a committee of Congress even if he later admits that he lied."

Patten. The ethics committee charged Patten with violating a New Jersey law by identifying as his own contributions from Park that Patten passed on to a county political organization. Patten denied the charge in a written response asking that the charges be dismissed. A staff response to Patten's motion said, "The respondent's papers ignore all the evidence except that which the respondent views as supportive of his position."

Final Arguments, Committee Action

On Sept. 27, the House Standards Committee voted to recommend that the House censure Roybal on three counts of failing to report a $1,000 campaign contribution from Park and lying to the committee.

The committee also recommended that the House "reprimand" Wilson for lying to the committee about money he took from Park in 1975 as a wedding present.

The 9-0 vote to recommend censure of Roybal was the strongest action the committee had ever taken against a member of the House. Censure required that the accused congressman stand before the House to hear the charges against him. The recommended reprimand of Wilson, which came on an 8-1 vote, is a weaker form of punishment than censure. Wilson would not have to be present when the House read its findings against him.

In final arguments before the ethics committee, committee counsel John Nields said, "Congressman Roybal has lied to this committee, lied to this institution repeatedly, and his latest version of the facts is also untrue."

Roybal's attorney, Richard Hibey, said Roybal received the cash but did not intentionally lie about it and that his earlier conflicting statements to the committee were the result of a faulty memory. "What you have before you is not a liar but an honest man who has made an honest mistake, an error in judgment, and is not the perjurer he is being painted by the staff."

In his testimony, Wilson said he forgot about the envelope of cash Park had given him at his wedding in South Korea in 1975. He said that when he responded to the committee's questionnaire, he thought the panel was looking for gifts intended to influence his congressional work, not gifts given "as a courtesy at the time of a wedding." Wilson said in a statement following the committee action:

"I'm deeply disappointed that the committee was unwilling to accept the fact, which I swear is absolutely true, that I had completely forgotten about the wedding present when I responded to the questionnaire."

In earlier action, the committee heard final arguments in its cases against McFall and Patten.

McFall said his efforts on behalf of Park were aimed only at assuring that California rice would be sold to South Korea. McFall said he did not "see any connection" between his gifts from Park and his efforts to sell the rice.

McFall said he wrote two letters on behalf of Park to South Korean President Park Chung Hee and that with Park's permission he put cash contributions intended for his campaign into his office account instead of reporting them as campaign contributions. He said he did not put them into his campaign account because he misunderstood federal law and believed he could not accept a campaign contribution from a foreign national in 1972 and 1974.

But under cross examination by Nields, McFall acknowledged that he had taken a contribution in 1972 from a Chinese national. He also said that only cash contributions went into the office account. Asked why, he said, "I don't know," but denied that it was an effort to prevent the contributions from being traced. McFall also acknowledged that after the House adopted a July 1974 rule requiring members to report the name of contributors to office accounts, he never put another cash contribution into the account.

In an emotional table-pounding defense before the committee Sept. 26, Patten denied ever receiving "a penny" from Tongsun Park.

"I have never in my life been accused of unethical or illegal conduct, let alone engaged in such activities," the 73-year-old New Jersey Democrat told the committee.

On Oct. 4, the Standards Committee voted to recommend that the full House reprimand McFall for failure to report a $3,000 campaign contribution he received in cash from Park. However, the committee rejected the two other, more serious, charges against McFall.

On the same day, the committee found Patten not guilty of the charges against him.

House Floor Action

In floor action Oct. 13, the House accepted the committee's recommendation of a reprimand for McFall and Wilson, but killed 219-170 the resolution to censure Roybal, reducing his punishment to a reprimand. Wilson's reprimand was voted 329-41 and McFall's was approved on a voice vote.

Throughout the Standards Committee hearings and the floor debate, none of the three congressmen acknowledged any illegality or wrongdoing.

On the House floor, Roybal contested the recommended punishment. Both McFall and Wilson said they accepted the committee's judgment. And the ensuing debate said as much about their culpability or innocence as about how members perceive their own ethical responsibilities and the House system of ethics.

The debate was viewed by Flynt as the conclusion of the House mandate to determine whether members accepted anything of value from the government of South Korea.

But it was also a debate, as Walter Flowers, D-Ala., defined it, on "whether we are going to continue to operate with a Committee on Standards of Official Conduct...."

The strength of the House ethics system was called into question from the beginning, on the resolution to reprimand Wilson. Wilson accepted the reprimand but insisted he was "innocent," had "very little to apologize for," and that the reprimand was "harsh," "cruel," "unjust and unfair."

He said he chose not to contest it because it would teach that "we in the House of Representatives are prepared to accept ethical standards for ourselves which are higher than those imposed upon any other citizen."

But he also said he believed the judgment "essentially exonerates me of serious wrongdoing," and that the committee had merely recommended that he be "chided" for a "careless mistake."

System Criticized

If Wilson's remarks could be construed as a defense of the system, his defenders' remarks could not.

"The entire thing to me stinks to high heaven," said Ronald V. Dellums, D-Calif. "I challenge not the personalities who serve here but the process itself, the structure of the institution." Dellums said the committee held no "judicial proceedings" and that it was not representative of Congress.

William "Bill" Clay, D-Mo., called the proceedings an "inquisition to suppress the heresy" of three "relatively inconspicuous" members "marched into this coliseum to face the lions and cheering mobs while bloodthirsty scribes sit perched high in the press gallery awaiting the carnage."

But by the time the House got around to the most serious charge — the censuring of Roybal — the lions' den had turned into a den of pussycats and the credibility of the ethics process had been challenged.

But defenders of the system also contributed to pointing up its weaknesses. While critics said it was harsh and arbitrary, others such as Flowers, said it deliberately had delivered a "light stroke" to the miscreants because the House could not conduct full judicial proceedings. "We are not looking for anybody's blood, "Flowers said. "We are trying to present a fair, moderate, middle-of-the-road case which we think represents a reasonable approach by reasonable people on the committee...."

While critics blasted the lack of "evidence" and the failure of the committee to issue reports in time for members to read them, other members openly acknowledged that they were voting purely on the basis of the committee's recommendations.

John W. Nields Jr., chief counsel to the committee, said the reduction of Roybal's punishment to a reprimand "arose out of the hostility expressed towards the committee by members on the floor."

"It looked as though the ethics committee had no taste for bringing this kind of report to the floor...," Nields said. "It will be painful for the next ethics committee to bring a similar thing to the floor unless there are indications the House will view such actions favorably."

Related House Probe

In tandem with the House Standards Committee, the House International Relations Subcommittee on International Organizations had been investigating the lobbying scandal since early 1977.

Unlike the ethics panel, however, its main concern was the impact on U.S.-Korean relations, not the wrongdoing of individuals.

At a hearing March 15, the subcommittee released documents backing up previous reports that President Park Chung Hee personally directed the Korean lobbying campaign.

Chairman Donald M. Fraser, D-Minn., said the summaries of U.S. intelligence reports showed that President Park was involved in discussions at his Blue House executive mansion that resulted in the lobbying effort.

Fraser stopped short of giving any indication that the South Korean president knew of or approved the disbursing of money to members of Congress. Nor did he disclose how the intelligence agencies were able to obtain reports on discussions within the Blue House.

William Porter, who was U.S. ambassador to Korea at the time, testified that he was skeptical about the authenticity of the report, although he conceded he had no evidence it was inaccurate.

"They knew how to keep secrets from us," Porter said. "I would not bet on that, necessarily, as a useful report on what went on at those meetings."

The Washington Post had reported in October 1976 that President Park had initiated the Korean lobbying effort and that U.S. intelligence reports "apparently" included tape recordings of the conversations obtained through electronic eavesdropping.

Korea Election Gifts

Sanitized summaries of U.S. Central Intelligence Agency documents released by the International Organizations Subcommittee March 22 revealed evidence that high-level officials in the Nixon administration were aware of illegal South Korean government influence-buying activities on Capitol Hill but did nothing to stop it.

The summaries stated that Korean President Park "was directly involved in directing the contribution of several hundred thousand dollars to the Democratic Party" in 1968.

A Nov. 24, 1971, memo from then-FBI Director J. Edgar Hoover said the Korean presidential mansion was directly involved in the contribution to the Democrats.

The intelligence summaries were based on secret National Security Agency (NSA) interceptions of cable traffic between the South Korean government and its embassy in Washington. The information was transmitted to the FBI and, according to the memoranda, to Attorney General John N. Mitchell and Henry A. Kissinger, national security adviser to President Nixon.

Mitchell Testimony

In testimony before the subcommittee, Mitchell, who was on medical furlough from prison where he was serving sentences for Watergate crimes, said he remembered receiving only one of three memos about Korean lobbying from Hoover. Mitchell said he never saw the memo alleging contributions to the Democrats and that he was sure he would have remembered it because of "the reference to hundreds of thousands of dollars to an election I had just gotten through managing on the other side."

A spokesman for Kissinger said the former national security adviser had "no recollection" of seeing any of the memos.

News reports said the subcommittee had also received reports that the Republican Party got a smaller contribution from the Korean government in 1968. The amount was reported to be in "six figures."

The memoranda released by the subcommittee included severe limitations placed by the FBI on the use of information obtained from the secret wire interceptions "to preclude any investigation whatsoever," even though "criminal activities are strongly indicated."

Michael Hershman, deputy staff director of the subcommittee, said the NSA did not request the restrictions when it passed the top secret cables on to the FBI.

William McDonnell, the FBI agent who drafted the memos for Hoover, said the bureau did not initiate criminal investigations because an intelligence officer said doing so might compromise the "sensitive source" of the charges.

The credibility of the reported South Korean government contribution to the Democrats was called into question by Rep. Edward J. Derwinski of Illinois, the ranking Republican on the subcommittee, who suggested that some of the intercepted messages were deliberate distortions by KCIA agents in Washington to impress their bosses in Seoul.

The intelligence summaries also stated that the Korean government was spending "large sums" to "develop control over" American and Korean journalists, that two congressional staff aides were connected with the KCIA, that Tongsun Park had made payments to a member of Congress and was acting under KCIA direction, and that a second congressman had sought contributions from Tongsun Park.

Allegations that Park was "under Korean Central Intelligence Agency direction" weren't passed on to the FBI Washington field office by the FBI headquarters. At the time the field office was conducting an investigation of Park at the State Department's request to determine if Park was acting illegally at the behest of the South Korean government. The field office found no grounds on which to act against Park.

An "eyes only" memo to Mitchell and Kissinger dated Feb. 3, 1972, reported that a congressman who had sought contributions from President Park Chung Hee said that Tongsun Park should be made Korea's chief U.S. lobbyist.

The top officer on the Korean desk at the State Department between 1970 and 1974 provided additional testimony concerning Park's relation to the South Korean government. Donald Ranard testified that he believed Park was under the control of the Korean CIA. Ranard said he believed Park "had an integral role, a very important role" in the Korean government's effort to win influence illegally among U.S. officials. Park had testified that he never worked for the Korean government.

The subcommittee released a summary of intelligence messages from Seoul warning U.S. officials that Park was "receiving assistance from the KCIA . . . and was under the KCIA's control, but was not an 'agent' as such." The summary appeared to support Park's assertion that he contributed $750,000 to some 30 congressmen as a businessman and not to buy influence for Seoul.

Hancho Kim Trial

Former Korean CIA agent Sang Keun Kim, the government's key witness in the perjury and conspiracy trial of Maryland businessman Hancho Kim, said he was unsure the defendant gave any money to members of Congress. S. K. Kim testified March 22 that about $44,000 of the money he gave to Hancho Kim came from a $100,000 check provided the KCIA agent by Tongsun Park.

S. K. Kim defected to the United States in November 1976. He said he feared he would be imprisoned if he returned to South Korea. At the time he was the second-ranking KCIA agent attached to the Korean embassy in Washington.

S. K. Kim testified that although he delivered $600,-000 in cash from the KCIA to Hancho Kim, Hancho Kim never told him if any money had been paid to members of Congress. Hancho Kim had denied receiving any money from S. K. Kim. S. K. Kim said Hancho Kim told him he had gotten congressmen to speak on behalf of South Korea in Congress.

Asked if he believed payments were made to congressmen, S. K. Kim replied: "I had no confidence that he [Hancho Kim] gave the money. . . . He spent money entertaining congressmen in a festive way, but there was no accounting of how it was spent. I was too low-ranking a guy to question Kim." S. K. Kim underwent three days of questioning that ended March 23.

Hancho Kim was charged with conspiracy to defraud the United States by plotting to interfere with the workings of Congress and of making false statements to a federal grand jury. He allegedly conspired to pass $600,000 to members of Congress on behalf of the Korean government.

Hancho Kim became the first person to stand trial in connection with the Korean influence-buying case. His trial began March 15.

Rep. Tennyson Guyer, R-Ohio, became the first sitting congressman to testify publicly in any of the Korean investigations when he appeared March 28 at the trial of Hancho Kim. Guyer said he had done political favors for Kim but that they were no different from favors he did regularly for constituents. He said he received no money from Hancho Kim.

Guyer said he inserted three statements based on information from Kim into the *Congressional Record*. He said he shared Kim's concerns for the security of South Korea. Guyer also said he tried unsuccessfully to get Kim an appointment with President Ford.

On May 19, Hancho Kim was sentenced to six months in jail for conspiring to corrupt members of Congress in return for favors for Korea and of lying to a grand jury about receiving $600,000 for the plot. Kim was ordered to serve three years on each of two counts, but U.S. District Court Judge Thomas A. Flannery said the sentences would be suspended after Kim served six months. Kim was convicted April 8 for conspiring to defraud the United States. Kim's conviction was the second growing out of the Korean scandal. The first person convicted was former Rep. Hanna.

Rev. Moon Connection

A former Korean military intelligence officer who was a top aide to Rev. Sun Myung Moon said March 22 that he received $3,000 in $100 bills from the Korean CIA.

Bo Hi Pak, interpreter for the Korean evangelist, said he received the money from Sang Keun Kim, the former KCIA agent. But he insisted he took the cash only as a favor to Yang Doo Won, a high-ranking KCIA official in Seoul, and that he passed it on to a Unification Church member from Japan as reimbursement for expenses incurred on an anticommunist speaking tour of Korea.

Pak had no explanation for why the KCIA rather than another Korean agency handled the "reimbursement."

House International Relations subcommittee staffers were quoted as saying they did not find Pak's explanation convincing.

Pak's testimony before the Subcommittee on International Organizations March 22 was the first indicating that

Moon's church had received money from the KCIA.

In that session Pak attacked news reports based on Central Intelligence Agency documents released by the subcommittee which said the Unification Church was founded by a director of the Korean CIA in 1961. He said the Church was founded in 1954 and challenged the CIA to swear to its evidence before the subcommittee.

A CIA report dated Feb. 26, 1963, based on statements from an undisclosed source, said "Kim Chong Pil organized the Unification Church while he was director of the ROK [Republic of Korea] Central Intelligence Agency, and has been using the Church, which has a membership of 27,000, as a political tool."

The reports reinforced the subcommittee's principal hypothesis, that senior officials of the Nixon administration were aware of the South Korean lobbying effort but failed to act on evidence they had obtained.

Chairman Fraser contended that "initiative for action pursuant to the intelligence reports was sporadic, half-hearted and inconclusive, with the result that Korean activities, which were both improper and illegal, continued to expand and gain momentum for some five years."

Final Report

In its final report, released Nov. 1, the International Organizations Subcommittee traced the origins of the South Korean lobbying campaign to fears in the early 1970s that U.S. support was waning. The report indicated that high-level U.S. government officials allowed the Korean lobbying effort to continue without interference because of an "attitude of permissiveness" that placed a premium on keeping Korean troops engaged in the Vietnam War.

The same attitude, the report said, sought to "maintain credibility for the U.S. position in Korea as an unyielding commitment to resist the threat of Communist aggression."

The committee's case study of a foreign government's influence-buying efforts also detailed the often illegal operations of organizations controlled by South Korean evangelist Sun Myung Moon. The report produced new evidence showing what it called "the Moon organization's" involvement in the production and sale of armaments.

Origins of Lobbying Effort

The investigation of Korean-American relations, headed by Donald M. Fraser, D-Minn., found that the initial objectives were to ensure congressional approval of a $1.5 billion military aid package between 1971 and 1975 for South Korea and to prevent further withdrawal of U.S. troops.

From 1972 onward, the committee said, the Koreans had another objective: "to convince Americans that Park's authoritarian government was justified" for reasons of national security and economic development.

The committee said the lobbying effort, directed from South Korea, began in 1970 and involved South Koreans operating either out of motives of patriotism or profit. In Washington, Tongsun Park's George Town Club, established with Korean CIA (KCIA) assistance, became a lobbying center for the Korean government.

KCIA operations in the United States included: 1) recruitment of American businessmen, congressmen and academics to advocate South Korea's policies, 2) visits to Korea by influential Americans, 3) use of commissions from U.S.-financed rice sales for KCIA activities, 4) infil-

tration of the Korean community in the United States to counter criticism of the Park government, 5) obtaining classified U.S. government information by cultivating U.S. officials.

Executive Branch Awareness

The Fraser committee concluded that by 1971 "appropriate agencies of the executive branch" were sufficiently aware of "questionable" Korean government activities to "warrant taking action toward halting the activities and preventing recurrences."

Instead, the report stated, "the activities were allowed to continue until a major scandal erupted five years later."

The committee said that by late 1971:

● The State Department and U.S. embassy in Seoul regarded Tongsun Park as an unregistered South Korean agent, presumed to be connected with the KCIA, who was offering gifts of cash to congressmen.

● The State Department believed Radio of Free Asia, sponsors of which included prominent Americans, was controlled by the KCIA.

● The State Department had indications that Kim Kwang, an aide to then-Rep. Cornelius E. Gallagher, D-N.J. (1959-73), was a KCIA agent.

● State Department officials suspected that Suzi Park Thomson, an aide to then-Speaker Carl Albert, D-Okla. (1947-77), was working for the KCIA.

● The FBI had information that "convinced its own officials" that "criminal activities [by Korean agents] are strongly indicated," that a KCIA agent working as a congressman's aide had made a "payoff" to the congressman, that Park had made payments to congressmen using money received in rice deals and that a congressman had sought campaign contributions from President Park and recommended that Tongsun Park be put in charge of Korean lobbying in the United States and of Korean rice purchases.

The Fraser committee concluded that "no effective action was taken to deal with any of these reported activities." The report suggested that the Justice Department and FBI whitewashed an investigation of Radio of Free Asia. And the report concluded that despite information strongly indicating that Tongsun Park worked for the KCIA, the Department of Agriculture was told Park had no connection with the government of South Korea when it queried the "appropriate" agencies in connection with Park's becoming a rice agent.

The report also indicated that former Secretary of State Henry A. Kissinger knew of allegations of payoffs to Rep. Gallagher four years before the Justice Department began a full-scale investigation during the Ford administration. Kissinger, the report stated, brought evidence of bribery to Ford's attention in 1975 when it indicated involvement of several congressmen.

Gallagher, formerly chairman of a House Asian affairs subcommittee, served 17 months in jail after pleading guilty to a tax charge.

Armaments

While the Rev. Sun Myung Moon was best-known for his "Unification Church," the Fraser report indicated that Moon's involvement with the South Korean government extended to the arms business. In 1977, the report stated, a Moon-controlled business in Korea approached Colt Industries in Korea to get permission to export M-16 rifles being manufactured in Korea. The report said the Moon organization was "apparently acting on behalf of the Korean government."

The M-16 incident was cited as evidence of South Korea's repeated requests that the United States allow it to become an arms exporter. The committee recommended that a task force of federal agencies investigate whether Moon's effort to export M-16s violated the U.S. Arms Export Control act and other possible violations of tax, banking, currency and foreign agent laws by Moon and his followers.

A spokesman for the Unification Church condemned the report as "prejudiced and biased." A Korean embassy spokesman denied any ties between his government and the Moon organization.

Other Findings

Among the committee's other findings were the following:

● That the Moon organization provided at least $1.2 million to capitalize the Diplomat National Bank in Washington in apparent violation of federal banking laws, and that Tongsun Park purchased $250,000 of stock in the bank in apparent violation of securities law.

● At least $8.5 million of American corporate funds were diverted to the ruling party in South Korea in connection with the 1971 elections.

● The Korean government negated the competitive bidding practices of the U.S. government by keeping contracts for U.S. military procurement artificially high, at a cost of millions of dollars to the U.S. Treasury.

● In 1970, a Korean government official attempted to bribe an official of the Voice of America, the U.S. propaganda network, apparently for the purpose of limiting unfavorable news about the Korean government.

In minority views to the report, Reps. Edward J. Derwinski, R-Ill., and Bill Goodling, R-Pa., said that they did not endorse all the findings. However, they said that they supported the section on the Moon organization and agreed that it "may have violated U.S. laws" and should be investigated thoroughly.

Senate Investigation

The Senate Ethics Committee concluded its 17-month Korean investigation with an Oct. 16 report (S Rept 95-1314) that recommended no disciplinary action against any incumbent or former senator.

At the same time the committee referred to the Justice Department evidence of possible law violations involving Birch Bayh, D-Ind., former Sen. Jack Miller, R-Iowa (1961-73), and aides to Bayh, Miller and Sen. Hubert H. Humphrey, D-Minn. (1949-64, 1971-78).

The possible illegalities involved perjury in all cases and acceptance of a campaign contribution on federal property, as well as failure to report a campaign contribution in the Bayh case.

The committee also released a somewhat ambiguous finding that Bayh was in "neglect of his duties" as a senator in failing to tell the committee in his written statements about an offer of a sizable campaign contribution from Tongsun Park, who the committee said was a South Korean government agent.

Bayh denied that he intended to mislead the committee.

"Neglect of duty" apparently was an unprecedented finding that carried no disciplinary penalty and required no vote or other action by the full Senate.

Finally, the committee report cleared numerous current and former senators of wrongdoing in the "Koreagate" affair. Most of those findings had been disclosed in the committee's interim report released in June.

Interim Report

In its first report on its secret inquiry into Korean influence peddling in the Senate, the committee revealed that shortly before his death in November 1977, Sen. John L. McClellan, D-Ark., acknowledged accepting an illegal $1,000 campaign donation from Tongsun Park. The report, issued in June, indicated that McClellan had violated the law and that there was conflicting testimony on the activities of Bayh, Miller and Humphrey.

McClellan Case

Ethics Committee Counsel Victor Kramer said that in October 1977 McClellan, the chairman of the Senate Appropriations Committee, asked to speak with him. McClellan related that he had received a $1,000 cash contribution from Park a few days prior to the November 1972 general election.

McClellan said he did not recall what he did with the funds, but they were not listed in publicly filed campaign reports as was required by the 1971 federal election law. McClellan said he never discussed any legislative matter with Park.

Park testified that his gift to McClellan was "close to $2,000 or even more" but that a portion of the money was sent back "with the explanation that the senator wanted to keep only $1,000."

The Senate report produced no hard evidence of impropriety on the part of Sen. John G. Tower, R-Texas. A member of the Ethics Committee, Tower had disqualified himself from participating in the inquiry because his name had been associated with Park. Tower acknowledged receiving gifts of jewelry from Park, but said they were worth less than $25. Committee counsel Kramer said the committee had not had the jewelry appraised.

The committee report also noted previously reported contributions from Park to Harry F. Byrd Jr., Ind.-Va., Spark M. Matsunaga, D-Hawaii, and former Sens. Stuart Symington, D-Mo., and Joseph M. Montoya, D-N.M.

The Bayh Case

The central questions in the Bayh case turned on two issues: 1) conflicting statements Bayh gave the committee concerning a campaign contribution offered to him by Tongsun Park and, 2) the events surrounding a meeting that took place in an office in the Capitol on Oct. 8, 1974.

The first issue provided the basis for the committee's Oct. 16 finding that Bayh was in "neglect of his duties." The second was the basis of the committee's referral to the Justice Department.

'Neglect of Duty'

In a questionnaire sent all 100 sitting senators and 56 living former senators who served in the Senate from 1967, the Ethics Committee asked in several different ways whether senators ever had received or been offered anything of value in excess of $35 by Tongsun Park.

In his response to the committee in October 1977, Bayh answered that he had never accepted anything of value from Park, and twice said he had not been offered anything of value from Park or someone he "now suspected" was a representative of the South Korean government.

In addition, Bayh stated in a July 1977 letter to committee Chairman Adlai E. Stevenson III, D-Ill.: "At no time, did he [Park] offer me any money, honorary degrees, trips to Korea, or any of the other numerous items we've all read about in the newspapers."

But in his testimony before the committee in April 1978 Bayh acknowledged that Park offered him a sizable contribution at a meeting in October 1974. Bayh said he refused to accept the contribution: "I had reflected on it; had come to the conclusion that that was not the kind of thing I wanted any part of. . . . I did not feel that it was the thing to do so far as my campaign was concerned to take money from someone who was not an American."

(Park testified that he had no recollection of Bayh's commenting on the propriety of accepting contributions from foreigners and that Bayh accepted the money.)

Bayh acknowledged that there were "rather pointed inconsistencies" between his July 1977 letter and his sworn testimony concerning offers from Park.

Bayh said he did not recall Park's offer until some time after his July letter and after Park had testified that he gave Bayh's administrative aide Jason Berman $1,500 to $1,800 for the Bayh campaign. Bayh said he remembered the offer in trying to figure out "why or how it was possible" for Park to make such a statement.

Bayh also testified that in answering the question about offers of money, "what was going through my mind was the sizable dollar figures that had been related, the offer of bribes and payoffs had been the thread of all the notoriety, as opposed to the kinds of offers that were purely legal on their face. . . . I testified here that he did offer a campaign contribution to me, [but it was] not illegal."

The committee report noted that Bayh had acknowledged in his July letter and his later testimony that Park's contributions and gifts to members of Congress had made front-page news for a long time prior to July 1977 and that both the Justice Department and congressional committees had launched investigations.

The committee concluded: "This publicity should have jogged the memory of any senator, especially any senator who was a close social friend of Mr. Park [as Bayh was], so that he would recall an offer of a contribution made directly to the senator by Mr. Park. Thus there appears to be no reasonable justification for Senator Bayh's misleading statements to this committee that Mr. Park had not offered him any 'money' or 'anything of value in excess of $35.' "

The committee also found, however, that, "in view of significant conflicts in the evidence, there is insufficient proof to establish that Senator Birch Bayh, his family, staff or campaign committees accepted a campaign contribution from Tongsun Park." And the committee said there was no evidence Bayh took any official action at the suggestion or request of Park.

Criminal Evidence

The second and more serious aspect of the Bayh case concerned conflicting testimony about where a contribution the "Hoosiers for Birch Bayh" committee received and reported was made, and whether it was received by Bayh or his aide Berman.

The committee concluded that "there is substantial credible evidence that Senator Birch Bayh, or his aide Jason Berman, received a $1,000 campaign contribution from Edward Merrigan on Oct. 8, 1974, in the Capitol of the United States of America." (The report said Merrigan was a friend of Park's.)

Receipt of a campaign contribution on federal property is a crime carrying penalties of up to $5,000 and three years in jail. There are apparently few precedents for the statute having been enforced. Bayh denied that he received the contribution at the Oct. 8 meeting.

The committee's evidence against Bayh and Berman included the following:

● Merrigan's testimony that he "made a $1,000 contribution to Senator Bayh sitting at his desk," at a meeting Oct. 8, 1974, at which Park and Berman were also in attendance. Merrigan said he "didn't give it [the $1,000] to anyone else but Senator Bayh, I am convinced. I wasn't there to give it to anyone else."

● Park's testimony that Merrigan "actually pulled out his checkbook, out from his suit pocket. And I was somewhat bewildered that he took the checkbook out right then and there and wrote out the check." Park said he recalled that the check was for $1,000 and believed it was given to Berman but was unsure on the latter point. Park said, however, he believed the contribution was made *before* Bayh arrived at the meeting.

● Merrigan's check was dated Oct. 8, 1974.

● Bayh's campaign schedules and calendars showed that he and Berman were in Washington on only one day in October 1974 — the eighth.

● A letter dated Oct. 14, 1974, found in a box marked "Jay Berman," which was sent out over Bayh's name thanking Merrigan for coming by the Senate and making a $1,000 contribution, and stating that Berman would stay in touch with Merrigan and Park.

● A list of contributions compiled in Indiana on Oct. 9, 1974, listing Merrigan's $1,000 contribution.

● A record of deposit of the Merrigan check in an Indianapolis bank on Oct. 9, 1974. The committee report stated: "It is extremely unlikely that the check could have been mailed to the Washington, D.C., office after the 5 o'clock meeting held on October 8, 1974, and have been received in the Indiana office on October 9, 1974. Instead, the evidence confirms the testimony of Mr. Merrigan and Mr. Park that the check was given to Senator Bayh or Mr. Berman at the meeting on October 8, 1974, and indicates that the check was carried back on a return flight to Indiana."

Bayh acknowledged that Merrigan made a $1,000 contribution in October 1974 but testified: "I don't think the Merrigan contribution was even discussed in any way, shape or form at that meeting. In fact, in my mind, I don't know what he was doing there."

In his first appearance before the Ethics Committee, Bayh said he had a "very strong recollection" of the October meeting and that during it Park offered him a contribution. But in his second appearance Bayh testified that his "memory is not as sharp as I wish it were" and that he was no longer sure that Park's offer had been made at the meeting.

Bayh said it was "conceivable" he met Park before the meeting or some time earlier in the year, but that he was "absolutely positive" he rejected Park's offer of campaign assistance.

While Berman first testified that Merrigan "did not say that he was going to make a contribution" at the meeting and did not do so, he later said it was "entirely likely" the meeting occurred on Oct. 8, 1974, and "entirely possible" Merrigan offered a contribution at the meeting.

Bayh said he was not "dead certain" the meeting occurred the eighth, that he had "no recollection whatsoever of the theatrics of [Merrigan] whipping out the checkbook and then giving it to me" and that Merrigan "did not give me a campaign contribution in person." He testified he was certain the contribution was not made in his presence.

Assuming the conclusions of the committee were correct as to the time and place of the Merrigan contribution, the Justice Department still had to determine *who* received the contribution — Bayh or Berman. Without greater certainty on that point, prosecution appeared unlikely. If the recipient issue were resolved, the Justice Department would likely have an additional crime to deal with — perjury.

Perjury

While the committee report did not specifically state which testimony might be perjurous in the Bayh case, page references in a footnote to the report suggested several possibilities. These involved conflicting testimony on the Merrigan contribution, conflicting testimony on receipt of a Park contribution, and conflicts between Bayh's responses to the committee questionnaire and his oral testimony. If it could be established that Park gave a contribution to Bayh or Berman, an additional crime, failure to report the contribution, would have been committed.

Bayh and the committee also disagreed over whether his statement that he and his wife had been the guests of honor at a dinner hosted by Park and costing $3,800 was thorough enough. The disagreement appeared unlikely to provide a basis for a serious legal challenge.

The committee referred all evidence of potentially perjurous statements in the Bayh case to the Justice Department. It also referred similar evidence in the Miller and Humphrey cases.

Humphrey and Miller

The Ethics Committee concluded that Park made a contribution of at least $5,000 in cash in April or early May 1972 to the Humphrey presidential campaign and that it was not reported as required by the federal election law.

It found, however, that there was no evidence Humphrey was ever aware of the contribution. The committee concluded that Humphrey's deputy campaign manager, John Morrison, "personally accepted the contribution from Mr. Park under circumstances that were difficult to forget

and that it is highly unlikely that Mr. Morrison does not remember meeting Mr. Park and receiving the contribution."

Morrison testified that he did not believe he ever met Park, could not recall a contribution of $5,000 in cash made to the Washington office and that he did not know of any contributions by Park to the 1972 Humphrey campaign. "I am not saying that it didn't take place," Morrison testified, "but I do not believe that it did."

The committee also reported that Park made a contribution of $3,000 in cash to the Miller senatorial campaign but that there was insufficient evidence to determine who initially received the contribution. "The evidence demonstrates that Senator Jack Miller or some member of his staff, other than Stanley Browne, must have known about Tongsun Park's contribution in 1972; the evidence is not sufficient to establish which of these people had such knowledge." Browne was Miller's administrative assistant.

The committee further reported that "much of the testimony of Stanley Browne is not accurate; however, the evidence is not sufficient to establish that Mr. Browne testified falsely when he said that he returned Tongsun Park's contribution."

Government Drops Case

The closing chapter in the Koreagate investigation was written on Aug. 16, 1979, when the Justice Department moved to dismiss charges against Tongsun Park.

While the government probe brought embarrassment and worries to some representatives and senators, it produced only one conviction and one defeat at the polls. Only two congressmen, former Reps. Richard T. Hanna, D-Calif. (1963-74), and Otto E. Passman, D-La. (1947-77), were tried.

Hanna pleaded guilty March 17, 1978, to one count of conspiracy to defraud the government. He was sentenced to between six months and 30 months in prison and was released after serving a little more than one year.

Passman was acquitted April 1, 1979, of taking as much as $213,000 in bribes from Park, failing to report $143,000 on his income tax returns and evading $77,000 in income taxes on the alleged bribes.

Perjury charges against former Rep. Nick Galifianakis, D-N.C. (1967-73), were dismissed Aug. 3. He received an alleged $10,000 campaign contribution from Park.

The only member of Congress ousted from office as a probable consequence of the scandal was Rep. McFall, one of the three California Democrats reprimanded by the House for accepting money from Tongsun Park. McFall, who had served in Congress since 1957, was defeated in 1978. The other two reprimanded members, Roybal and Charles H. Wilson, easily won re-election. ∎

New China Policy: Defeat for Taiwan Lobby

The debate surrounding President Carter's new China policy was apparently put to rest on March 29, 1979, when Congress cleared and sent to the president legislation (HR 2479) establishing unofficial relations between the United States and Taiwan and providing security assurances to the island.

The bill was an outgrowth of Carter's December 1978 decision to recognize the People's Republic of China (PRC) and to derecognize the Republic of China on Taiwan (ROC), a policy that had been expected to instigate heavy lobbying by conservatives on behalf of Taiwan.

But the massive lobbying campaign promised by several conservative groups in December did not materialize, partly because Taiwan officials themselves did not vocally press their own cause.

Although a loosely knit coalition of conservative groups had formed to oppose Carter's policy, lobbying against the new China policy was conspicuously absent during subsequent debates in the Senate Foreign Relations Committee and House Foreign Affairs Committee. The debates concerned legislation defining the basis of future U.S.-Taiwan relations.

Pro-Taiwan forces in the United States also didn't exploit the confirmation hearings of Leonard Woodcock, former president of the United Auto Workers Union, as ambassador to mainland China to enunciate their disapproval of what they viewed as the "abandonment" of Taiwan.

"There is a strategic focus lacking" among the pro-Taiwan groups, said Howard Phillips, national director of the Conservative Caucus, one of the most active organizations in the coalition.

Taiwan chose a cautious course that accepted as a *fait accompli* President Carter's recognition of Peking. In seeking to minimize its losses, Taiwan did not want to antagonize the United States on which, for better or worse, it must continue to rely for military and economic support.

But American conservative groups thought Taiwan stood to gain more by fighting back and, in particular, by insisting on government-to-government relations with the United States and continuation of the 1954 mutual defense treaty. Although these groups did not oppose recognition of Peking, they opposed it if it meant derecognition of Taiwan.

Taiwan 'Capitulates'

If American groups had any intention of fighting Taiwan's battle, that country's agreement Feb. 13, 1979, to accept the administration-proposed American Institute in Taiwan (AIT) as the vehicle for continued relations, drew the final curtain on such plans.

"I think Taiwan chickened out and capitulated too early," said James Chieh Hsiung, a New York University professor of politics. "If Taiwan accepts the AIT, there's nothing we can do."

Other Washington-based pro-Taiwan groups echoed Hsiung's pessimism concerning their ability to be of much immediate help in changing the fundamental direction of U.S. policy:

● "One of the difficulties in developing a confrontation with Congress on the Taiwan issue has been the unfortunate timidity, the willingness of the Taiwanese to cave in to State Department demands," said Gary Jarmin, legislative director of the 350,000-member American Conservative Union.

● "The Taiwanese blew it," said Anne Martin, executive director of the Committee for a Free China. "Since they gave in on the demand for government-to-government relations, I don't see how anyone could do anything for them."

● "You can't be more Catholic than the Pope," said Edwin J. Feulner Jr., executive director of the Heritage Foundation. "You can't tell them to go for the whole loaf if they're willing to go for half."

● "It is difficult for [Taiwan] supporters in the United States to launch a campaign if the people on behalf of whom you're working aren't taking a strong position," said William F. Rhatican, whose public relations firm organized a congressional tour to Taiwan in January. The Taiwan issue, according to Rhatican, "had the potential to be a major confrontation, but it fizzled."

Only Rep. Robert E. Bauman, R-Md., chairman of the American Conservative Union (ACU), thought Taiwan had

> *"The Taiwanese blew it. Since they gave in on the demand for government-to-government relations, I don't see how anyone could do anything for them.*
>
> —Anne Martin, executive director, Committee for A Free China

"made its views forcefully" at the time of Carter's recognition of Peking and saw "no wavering" since then.

Although conservatives generally viewed Taiwan's limited challenge to Carter as the underlying cause of their own weak response on behalf of Taiwan, three other factors hampered a forceful lobbying effort.

First, President Carter's Dec. 15 announcement caught pro-Taiwan forces off guard. With March 1 set as the date of establishing formal relations with Peking, and a new Congress just coming into town, Taiwan's friends had little time to mobilize a significant grass-roots effort.

Second, the U.S. business community failed to take a strong pro-Taiwan position, apparently finding the prospect of trade with mainland China irresistible.

Third, the foreign relations committees framed their debate in terms of providing greater assurances to Taiwan than Carter proposed, rather than insisting on full diplomatic relations.

Conservative Coalition

Most of the pro-Taiwan groups generally took a dim view of the Carter administration's foreign policy, arguing that the derecognition of Taiwan was the latest in a series of sellouts of longtime U.S. allies.

In a Dec. 30, 1978, fund-raising appeal for the Washington Legal Foundation — a group representing Sen. Barry Goldwater, R-Ariz., in a suit challenging Carter's termination of the 1954 mutual defense treaty with Taiwan — Sen. Gordon J. Humphrey, R-N.H., lamented "the giveaway of the Panama Canal" and urged support for pro-Taiwan efforts. "[R]ight now I feel ashamed," Humphrey wrote. "First, we abandon the Vietnamese and the Cambodians. Then we tell the Koreans we're pulling out. And now we break our word to the people of Taiwan."

Humphrey's appeal was largely consistent with that of other groups working on behalf of Taiwan, a coalition that read like a Who's Who of Washington conservative lobbies. These groups included:

● The National Conservative Political Action Committee, best known for pouring millions of dollars into the campaigns of conservative congressional candidates.

● The American Conservative Union, the largest organization of conservatives in the country.

● The American Council for a Free Asia, described by its national director, Gary Jarmin of ACU, as a "conservative anticommunist public interest lobby."

● The Conservative Caucus, which was active in opposing abortion, busing, gun control and the Equal Rights Amendment, and had made Taiwan a major priority for 1979.

● The Washington Legal Foundation, which handled Goldwater's lawsuit, also represented congressmen suing the administration to stop the Panama Canal agreement in 1978.

● The Heritage Foundation, a conservative research organization founded and originally funded by Joseph Coors. Heritage Foundation public relations were handled by Hugh C. Newton, a registered foreign agent of the Taiwan government, and Herbert Berkowitz, a former employee of Newton's firm.

● Young Americans for Freedom, a student-oriented lobby that waged a "wall poster" and newspaper advertising campaign protesting the late January 1979 U.S. visit of PRC Deputy Premier Teng Hsiao-ping as "a tyrant who runs the dictatorship with the worst human rights record in the history of the world."

● The Committee for the Survival of a Free Congress, a political and legislative action group (headed by Paul Weyrich, a founder of the Heritage Foundation) that funds conservative candidates.

● The Committee for A Free China, the last organizational vestige of the "old China lobby," formed in 1953 as the Committee for One Million Against the Admission of Communist China to the United Nations, directed its efforts largely at generating grass-roots support for Taiwan. Its president was former Rep. Walter H. Judd, R-Minn. (1943-63). Its treasurer, Charles A. Moser, was also treasurer of the Committee for Survival of a Free Congress.

● Friends of Free China, headed by Jack Buttram, a board member of the Committee for A Free China. The organization's national chairman was Barry Goldwater. Its national advisory board included Ronald Reagan. The "Friends" were the owners of the Taiwan embassy, its chancery and military attache's office, all of which were transfered to it shortly after Carter recognized Peking.

Grass-roots Lobbying

The lack of direct lobbying on the Taiwan bill surprised members of the foreign affairs committees and State Department officials. But the pro-Taiwan groups were not totally inactive.

A four-part plan of action by the coalition was outlined by its organizer, John T. Dolan, executive director of NCPAC and a director of the Washington Legal Foundation: 1) grass-roots lobbying and mail campaigns, 2) support for the Washington Legal Foundation lawsuit, 3) lobbying on foreign aid and economic legislation and, 4) coordinating trips to Taiwan to encourage greater support for Taiwan.

The Committee for A Free China sent letters to more than 100,000 homes urging citizens to write members of Congress, and distributed an inch-thick background paper on "The Taiwan Question" to every congressional office.

The American Council for a Free Asia, according to Jarmin, sent 300,000 letters urging people to sign a petition saying the Taiwanese should not be "enslaved or murdered by the Communists." NCPAC mailed 50,000 personalized letters through the Richard A. Viguerie direct mail company, enclosing postcards to be sent to senators saying, "Please do not let President Carter abandon the 17 million free people of Taiwan."

The Washington Legal Foundation sent out more than 500,000 of the Gordon Humphrey fund-raising letters, which included postcards almost identical to those sent out by NCPAC. An aide to Sen. William S. Cohen, R-Maine, reported that 3,000 of the 4,000 pieces of mail it received were foundation postcards.

1980 Politics

Even if conservative groups were to fail in their efforts to save Taiwan, many nonetheless saw a silver lining in the situation. Many conservatives hoped to cash in on what they viewed as Carter's weakness in foreign policy.

Phillips of the Conservative Caucus said, "In the 1980 presidential race any serious Republican candidate will be brought to heel on this. . . . We will discover how strongly the rank and file feel about Taiwan." Taiwan "will be a live issue in the 1980 campaign," Phillips said.

Jarmin of ACU said his group hoped to "generate so much political pressure" on the Taiwan issue "that Carter won't be able to survive in 1980." And while he said defeating Carter was "not our sole objective," he added "to a large extent that is the objective of the American Council for a Free Asia."

In the meantime, the legislation that cleared Congress in March tied the United States closer to ensuring Taiwan's independence than the original legislation submitted by the administration in January. However, the White House said it was acceptable and would be signed into law. Under the legislation, the United States agreed to conduct its relations with Taiwan through the American Institute in Taiwan, a private corporation. Taiwan, in return, continued its ties with the United States through an unofficial Coordinating Council in North America. The legislation assured that all trade, transportation and cultural links between the United States and Taiwan would remain in effect.

In a victory for Taiwan's supporters, the bill contained stronger language than President Carter had wanted expressing American concern for the future security of Taiwan; it pledged continued arms sales to the Taiwan government and said the United States would take actions (not specified) in the event of an attack on Taiwan. ∎

Public Interest Lobbying

CQ

Public Interest Groups: Balancing the Scales

The House Ways and Means Committee is at work on a multibillion-dollar tax bill, and the ornate, cavernous hearing room is, a committee member observes, "filled with $300 suits" — corporate lobbyists. But they are not the only lobbyists present.

Standing off by one wall, a lobbyist for Ralph Nader's Public Citizen Tax Reform Group is conferring with a committee member. One of his associates is seated among the onlookers, keeping his eye on the proceedings and kibbitzing with a congressional staffer. And seated an aisle away is a tax specialist working with Common Cause, the self-acknowledged citizen's lobby.

To most this scene would seem unremarkable, and that is testimony to the acceptance that Public Citizen and Common Cause have gained since they were established less than 10 years ago. These two organizations are as widely known as almost any lobby group in the nation's capital, yet they are relative newcomers. Their emergence represents a change in the politics of lobbying in Washington, a change that in many ways they were responsible for creating.

The two groups can share much of the credit for opening up the procedures of Congress to public view, and for increasing citizen participation in the legislative process.

Emerging Public Interest Groups

Now, says Sen. Abraham Ribicoff, D-Conn., "instead of the big lobbyists of the major corporations dominating the hearings process, you have had practically every committee in Congress according 'equal time' to public interest people." And former Rep. Abner J. Mikva, D-Ill. (1969-73; 1975-79), called the emergence of public interest groups "the biggest change I've seen" in Congress. The groups "have really come into their own," he said. "Instead of anti-establishment groups handing out leaflets on a street corner we have people working very effectively in the halls of Congress."

Skillful use of publicity, shrewd legislative and political tactics and recognized expertise on previously undeveloped issues were key ingredients in the groups' success. They also profited from good timing.

Common Cause and the Nader Public Citizen groups are not the only organizations claiming the "public interest" label.

"We are *a* citizens' lobby, *a* public interest group," said Common Cause President David Cohen. "The difference between 'a' and 'the' is very important. We don't define 'the public interest' in the sense that one group represents it while others don't."

Cohen's predecessor, Jack T. Conway, adds that "no one has a monopoly on the public interest, on virtue or on anything else."

Few other public interest groups, though, have been as publicized and, say Capitol Hill sources, as effective as Common Cause and the Nader operation. Sen. Edward M. Kennedy, D-Mass., who has worked closely with both, feels

they have become "almost an extension of Congress" and have been an important asset to lawmakers.

Achievements

Both groups can claim some notable successes. Common Cause, for example, is credited with a major role in enactment of the 1974 campaign finance law (PL 93-443), with helping to develop public pressure for House and Senate reforms and with aiding in the 1977 passage of "government in the sunshine" legislation. In 1979 the groups supported a resolution introduced by Senate Majority Leader Robert C. Byrd, D-W.Va., that imposed limits on delaying tactics often used to prevent a vote on a bill after cloture (cut-off of debate) had been invoked. The resolution, which passed the Senate 78-16 in February 1979, required that a final vote on a bill must be taken after 100 hours of debate, including roll-calls, if cloture has been voted.

The new procedure curtails tactics — used by liberals and conservatives alike to delay bills after cloture has been invoked — by offering hundreds of amendments and asking for a roll-call vote on each one.

Common Cause Vice-President Fred Wertheimer said that the action "takes away a chunk of the psychology of obstructionism" and could have a far-reaching effect on controversial legislation.

Nader's groups have won lawsuits against corporations, professional organizations and the federal government. Nader lobbyists helped shape congressional energy and tax legislation, including repeal of the oil depletion allowance, and won approval for a fund to help consumers petition the Federal Trade Commission.

After some of their past successes the Public Citizen groups were disappointed with the performance of the 95th Congress. Congress Watch, the Public Citizen group that specialized in energy and consumer issues, assailed it as "the corporate Congress." Indications were that lobbying on consumer issues would be just as difficult in the 96th Congress.

To solidify their position consumer interests, led by the Nader organizations, attempted to portray consumerism as

a vital component of the Carter administration's war on inflation and big government.

Mark Green, director of Congress Watch, said that his group had formulated three distinct legislative agendas to 1) fight inflation, 2) facilitate citizen accessibility to government, and 3) increase corporate accountability.

To advance their unique brand of inflation fighting, a number of consumer and labor groups banded together to form a coalition called Consumers Opposed to Inflation in the Necessities (COIN). Coordinated by Public Citizen and the Exploratory Project for Economic Alternatives, the group promoted the view that inflation should be attacked separately in each sector of the economy. The greatest inflationary pressures come from the housing, energy, health and food sectors of the economy, the group argued, and this is where the most vigorous anti-inflationary battles should be mounted.

"The conservatives have everybody else on the defensive on inflation," commented COIN spokesman Roger Hickey. "Their program is to cut back on health and safety regulation, raise interest rates and cut the budget. But this won't cut inflation. It will cause a mild recession and put people out of work. Our group's goal is to go after the real causes of inflation, which are the result of industry structures and bad government policy in energy, food, housing and health."

Citizen Involvement

Both groups have succeeded in involving the public in their work. Common Cause has approximately 220,000 members. Public Citizen, though not a membership organization, is supported by an estimated 196,000 contributors annually. By way of comparison, Consumers Union has about 200,000 members, the League of Women Voters 123,000 and Americans for Democratic Action 55,000.

Common Cause has been charged with having a liberal-Democratic bias and a membership top-heavy with upper-income professionals. In defense of his group, President David Cohen cited a survey showing that nearly half the Common Cause membership considered itself "independent" while only 38 percent were Democrats. Sixteen percent of the members were Republicans.

Cohen also pointed out that 75 percent of the $5.3 million budget for 1979 came from contributions of less than $25.

Public Citizen encourages its supporters to become active in local citizen action groups. It distributes free publications telling people how to become involved in the consumer movement and how to conduct grass-roots pressure campaigns on Congress.

Constituency

Congressional support for the Nader groups' and Common Cause's proposals most often has come from liberal Democrats and Republicans. The groups "have greater acceptance on the Democratic side," said Rep. Benjamin S. Rosenthal, D-N.Y., a Nader ally.

Common Cause apparently has been more successful than Nader in attaining bipartisan support. It has worked with Republican moderates, such as Rep. John B. Anderson, Ill., chairman of the House Republican Conference; Sen. Robert T. Stafford, Vt., and Rep. Tom Railsback, Ill.

The public interest groups are especially influential among younger members of Congress. An aide to one House freshman said that "I sometimes think he waits to see what Common Cause's position is before he decides how to vote."

Rep. Toby Moffett, D-Conn., himself a former Nader worker, adds that many of the younger political leaders come out of public interest group backgrounds and think accordingly.

Members who are sympathetic to Common Cause and Nader praise them strongly. Railsback credits them with "seeking to represent people who might not otherwise be represented." Sen. Kennedy calls them "invaluable."

But the groups are not without their critics, especially among more conservative members. Rep. Clarence J. Brown, R-Ohio, dismisses Nader as "increasingly partisan" and "predictable." Rep. Philip M. Crane, R-Ill., contends that both groups are hostile to the free enterprise system and have done "more harm than good."

At times relations with Congress have been strained, even when the same goals are being sought. Common Cause angered House leaders during consideration of legislation to provide public financing for House elections. They accused Frank Thompson Jr., D-N.J., chairman of the House Administration Committee that considered the bill, and John Brademas, D-Ind., majority whip, of "poisoning the well" for public financing by pushing enactment of overall spending limits for each party. The spending limits were vehemently opposed by the Republicans on the committee.

But according to Bob Moss, House Administration Committee counsel, Common Cause and some of the newer members of Congress pushed for quick action on the issue in 1978 when the votes needed were not there.

When the subject came up again in 1979, Common Cause was asked not to work in Congress on behalf of the bill, although it was encouraged to carry on a lobbying effort outside Congress. In May 1979 the committee voted 8-17 not to report the public financing bill, which killed the issue for the 96th Congress. Commenting on the defeat Mike Cole, legislative director of Common Cause, said, "It would have been a coup to get the bill out of committee. It's a legacy of the Wayne Hays era — a group of people who have resisted reform." *(Public financing, p. 67)*

Agendas

While Common Cause and Public Citizen share the general goal of giving the average citizen more influence in political, economic and social matters, the two organizations have evolved their own areas of specialty.

Nader's Public Citizen groups pursue a broad agenda of substantive economic, consumer, environmental, legal and social policy issues while Common Cause has focused on issues of political structure and procedure.

John Gardner   **Ralph Nader**
Founders of Common Cause, Public Citizen

John Gardner on Common Cause and Its Impact

As an organization Common Cause reflects the philosophy and beliefs of John Gardner, the group's founder and former chairman. Much of the press attention Common Cause generated in its early years was due to the reputation and public stature he commanded, and the principles he laid down still guide the organization. Following are excerpts from an interview with Gardner that took place shortly before he left the chairman's post in 1977.

Q: What do you see as your top accomplishments?

A: I think the most important accomplishment is the reform of campaign financing. Americans will never go back to the old secret, corrupt, pre-Watergate system. There's a lot of confusion in reaction to the Supreme Court decision, but they ruled affirmatively on three historic principles that will drastically alter campaign financing. One is disclosure, another is limits on individual contributions and the third is public financing.

They left the door open for a fourth historic change, and that is independent enforcement, when they said that Congress could reconstitute the Federal Election Commission to bring it into a constitutional posture. Now, their ruling on independent expenditures is a very serious problem. I don't think it's an unsolvable one. And, in my view of these battles is that they are never neat. You never solve anything all at once. Social change is a learning process in which you stumble, you try; it's like a baby learning to walk. You fall down, you get up, bump your nose, you finally learn. And I would guess that for several more years we're going to be learning how to bring campaign finances under control. But we've made major, major gains, really astonishing gains.

...All through the 1960s it was apparent that the old system of campaign finance was headed for disaster. And there is no doubt that had it not hit the disaster of Watergate, it would have hit some other kind of disaster. Soaring costs of campaigning, making it virtually impossible for individuals to run unless they were willing to make themselves beholden to sources of wealth, sources of money.

Open government, in which we have made astonishing gains, was pioneered in 1967 in Florida. The whole set of principles was laid out in Florida when they threw out the "Pork Chop Gang" in 1967, and that has swept the country. Most other states now have taken action towards some form of open government. We've opened up the bill-drafting sessions of the House of Representatives, which is just a profound change in way of operating. You can walk in and out of that Ways and Means Committee while they're drafting your tax laws. And now that you can, it seems insane that they ever thought they could do the public business secretly. But it works. It's been working for two years now, and working very well. So that's a major change because Common Cause forced that change.

Now we've had the biggest reform in Congress since 1910. I do not think it would be proper to credit Common Cause with that achievement, although I certainly think we've played a role, and everybody up there would say that we've played our role. But the Democratic Study Group and some very good people up there pulled it off.

We have had the biggest wave of state legislature reform since the nation began. The only thing comparable to it was the wave of reform in the 1920s. Again, I would not give Common Cause credit for all of it, but I think most state legislatures would tell you that Common Cause was very active in this move. Those are big things, big changes.

So I feel we've played our part. It isn't unique, I mean, we're part of a public interest movement that rose in the late 1960s, and there's something bigger afoot from which we're gaining strength. And so I don't want to leave the impression that we're here alone defying the laws of gravity and doing something that nobody else could do. Public interest law, Ralph Nader, the environmentalist movement, these are all parts of it.

Q: What is this something bigger afoot?

A: I think that it became apparent slowly that citizens were losing command of their own institutions. I think for a long time they even collaborated in the situation that produced that, in the sense that for a long time Americans were in love with bigness and large organization and the swift changes were occurring in our national life. And somewhere along in the middle of this century it began to become apparent to us that it was so big and complicated we couldn't really get a grip on it anymore. And there was a lot of kind of apathy and feeling you couldn't do anything. I think this movement is the beginning of an assertion by citizens that they can do something. If they're tough enough about it, tough-minded enough, professional enough, willing to organize in an effective way, they can regain command of some of these problems.

Q: At Common Cause, the concentration is on making the system work better. Shouldn't one element of that be to try and make it possible for legislation to be enacted in some sense of balance, without there being excesses, without having to go too far, lean too much?

A: I don't see how you can do it in a democracy. In a democracy, whatever you want to do has to be accompanied by a lot of enthusiasm, drum-beating, education. I don't see how the environmentalists could have made it to where they are if they had not pressed very, very hard with great enthusiasm, often excesses of zeal to make their point. . . .

I think that social change is a messy thing. It's untidy, it's a learning process. You don't sit down and blueprint something and say here's a problem, here's a solution, and we've proven it's the solution. Now we'll get it into legislation. It'll work! Go!

What you do if you're trying to get some change is you try the best you can. You discover that you haven't foreseen all the consequences, and you move ahead and try to correct it. This is true of social legislation as in the 1960s. It's true of reform legislation, and I think a lot of trouble comes from the people who really [are] kind of utopians. They have to need a picture of social change. They think, well, you know, we should just figure out the answer and then we put it in, it'll work.

Common Cause

Common Cause has pressed for enactment of "accountability" laws — such as revision and expansion of the lobby registration act, increased financial disclosure by members of Congress, restrictions on incumbents' use of congressional staff and resources in re-election campaigns and reform of the confirmation process in the Senate.

One of the organization's major long-term goals is a complete overhaul of the methods used to determine new state legislative districts after the 1980 census. The group predicted that unless changes were made before legislatures meet in 1981 to begin redistricting, "the political 'ins' will do all they can to clobber the 'outs' " by drawing district lines to ensure the election of incumbents.

A proposed model plan was drafted that would "bypass the self-interest of incumbent legislators and set objective standards for reapportionment." The plan had three major components: 1) strict anti-gerrymandering standards for new districts, 2) independent five-member commissions in each state to draw new lines and 3) prompt judicial review of the commissions' work.

In 1979 legislation was introduced in both the House and the Senate that generally conformed to the Common Cause plan. The supporters hoped that action in Congress would focus attention on the issue and encourage the states to act. Part of the strategy for pressing state action was to generate press coverage. Although there was some difficulty in getting people excited about redistricting before the 1980 census was completed, a Common Cause staff member pointed out that by the time the census was finished, it would be too late for many states to act. So the organization planned to devote much of its effort to publicizing the problem.

In 1978 Common Cause joined former Federal Election Commission member Neil Staebler in a lawsuit challenging the legality of the recess appointment of Staebler's successor, John W. McGarry. The suit maintained that since President Carter's appointment of McGarry was made after Congress adjourned, he should not take office until the Senate had confirmed him.

McGarry also was opposed because of his past employment on Capitol Hill and close friendship with House Speaker Thomas P. O'Neill Jr., D-Mass. Common Cause argued that McGarry would be ruling on cases that involved friends and former associates. But the Senate, nevertheless, confirmed McGarry by voice vote Feb. 21, 1979.

Another fight ultimately lost concerned a 15 percent limitation on outside earned income that was scheduled to become effective in the Senate on Jan. 1, 1979. Common Cause had worked hard to get the limit adopted initially in 1977. On May 8, 1979, by voice vote and with only six senators present the effective date was postponed for four years. Cohen called the delay the "Senate's version of 'take the money and run and the public be damned.' "

Three weeks later Sen. Gary Hart, D-Colo., introduced legislation to reimpose the limit. That bill was rejected on a roll-call vote, 44-54.

Hart later said that he was trying to force members to take a position because "the primary issue was that nobody knew where we stood on this."

Cohen said after the vote on the Hart proposal that "we're not satisfied with the result, but we're satisfied that they no longer can escape accountability. . . . Senators' first priority, their immediate priority, is their own financial well-being and not the concerns of their constituents."

In 1979 Common Cause also pushed for legislation to require direct election of the president and to control the activities of political action committees (PACs). "Unless there are some new controls on the PAC movement," commented Wertheimer, "we will see no controls for some time, if at all." *(PAC spending, p. 73)*

Common Cause also is one of the few non-congressional groups that have made major efforts to combat what they consider significant abuses of incumbent advantages through use of computers and the congressional frank (the free mailing privilege members are allowed for official business).

Evidence of abuses found by Common Cause led to both the House and Senate adopting a series of restrictions on the mailing privilege in their 1977 ethics codes. However, subsequent changes eroded the 1977 restrictions and Common Cause indicated that it might file lawsuits if it discovered blatant misuse of the frank in congressional re-election campaigns.

The organization's determined focus on procedural and political "reform" has been criticized by other groups and by some members of Congress. AFL-CIO lobbyist Kenneth Young, for example, says Common Cause's inattention to economic issues diminishes its claim to representing the public interest.

Cohen and John Gardner both respond that their past experience in organizations that sought substantive social and economic changes taught them that "process determines substance." Gardner also notes that the goal of reforming the political system has given Common Cause a unifying theme that has helped it find and maintain its constituency.

The organization's polls and referendums of its members' sentiments consistently have shown a greater degree of agreement on "accountability" issues than on substantive questions. And the polls' findings have been confirmed in the mailbags of congressional offices. Former Rep. Mikva said that the volume of mail from Common Cause members on tax reform was much smaller than the volume on reform issues.

To critics, though, the polls and the mail seem to confirm their suspicions that Common Cause's agenda reflects the biases of an upper-middle-class membership. Its former president, Jack Conway, said he does not dispute the nature of Common Cause's membership, "but what are we supposed to say about that? Certainly not apologize for it. It's a potent group." He dismissed some of the criticism as "carping" from people who wanted Common Cause to pursue their agendas rather than its own.

Public Citizen

While Nader's groups do try to select most of their projects in advance, their agendas are always subject to change. Joan Claybrook, former director of Congress Watch and currently head of the National Highway Traffic Safety Administration, said one of the organization's strengths was that it led the way on many key issues and did not merely react to issues stirred up by others.

A list of the projects Public Citizen was working on in 1979 indicated the breadth of its efforts:

● The organization set the fight against inflation as one of its top priorities. "People rightfully fear inflation and feel government is behind much of its growth," Mark Green acknowledged. "Inflation is making people financially insecure. But if there were a Proposition 13 against increasing utility rates or the cost of automobiles, that would pass too." Nader has coordinated the formation of Consumers Opposed to Inflation in Necessities (COIN) to apply pressure on Congress to reduce prices on essential items.

● Congress Watch aligned itself with Common Cause, the Consumer Federation of America and the AFL-CIO in support of lobby law revision, especially provisions calling for reporting of grass-roots lobbying expenses. *(Lobby disclosure bill, p. 61)*

● Congress Watch also joined with Common Cause to push legislation limiting the activities of political action committees. "Today corporate PACs outnumber labor PACs by about two to one," said Michael Rofsky of Congress Watch. "Yet of the nation's 1,000 largest industrial corporations, 80 percent did not have PACs as of March 1978."

● On energy issues, Nader would like to break up the major oil companies, retain controls on natural gas prices and halt expansion of the nuclear power industry. He also supports legislation to prevent the largest oil companies from acquiring any other corporations with assets in excess of $100 million.

● Public Citizen supports efforts to give individuals more opportunities to challenge governmental decisions in court. It also has worked on numerous health and safety issues.

● The organization's legislative efforts have been supported by dealings with executive branch agencies and by litigation in state and federal courts.

Just as the comparatively narrow "clean government" focus of Common Cause has been criticized as too narrow, the wide range of the Nader agenda has led to complaints that the Public Citizen agenda is too broad. One Senate aide said Nader's workers had diminished their effectiveness by spreading themselves too thin.

But in fact the Nader groups are selective on the issues they get involved with. The Health Research Group did not work with groups attempting to have warning labels added to liquor bottles "because our resources are spread so thin," according to one worker. Robert S. McIntyre, director of the Tax Reform Research Group, said in 1979, "We're not really thinking about tax reform because last year was such a bad year. We need a few years to bask in the luxury of doing nothing."

The Public Citizen groups turn down many requests from members of Congress and from other groups to help out on issues, so that they will have the resources to devote to currently active issues.

Nader's groups also try to avoid getting into areas where their allies already are working. Jack Sheehan, legislative director of the United Steelworkers, noted that Public Citizen does not try to duplicate the unions' agenda on economic issues. He credited Congress Watch and other Nader groups with having opened up entirely new areas for legislative action, such as energy policy.

Tactics

Common Cause and Public Citizen have adopted most of the normal pressure techniques used by interest groups with one major exception — neither group endorses candidates or makes campaign contributions. However, the groups do rate legislators on their voting record on selected issues.

"Given the fact that they don't make contributions or endorsements, the public interest groups have been very successful," said a Senate aide. But he noted, as did others, that the public interest groups did not have the sheer

Evolution of Two Groups

Public Citizen and Common Cause are the creations of two figures who are influential in their own right — Ralph Nader and John W. Gardner.

Nader first attracted public attention in November 1965 with the publication of his best-selling book, *Unsafe at Any Speed,* charging that the General Motors' Chevrolet Corvair was dangerous to drive.

The Connecticut lawyer testified at Senate hearings in 1966 on auto safety legislation, and on March 22 of that year GM President James M. Roche admitted to a Senate Government Operations subcommittee that the company had hired private detectives to spy on Nader. Roche apologized for it. Subcommittee Chairman Abraham Ribicoff, D-Conn., depicted the Nader-GM episode as "a David-Goliath confrontation, and David won."

Building on his personal triumph, Nader formed the Center for the Study of Responsive Law in 1969, staffing it with young lawyers. With the aid of student summer volunteers (dubbed "Nader's Raiders" by the press) they produced books criticizing, among other things, the Food and Drug Administration, the Federal Trade Commission, the Interstate Commerce Commission and antitrust policy.

Nader focused his attention on Congress in 1971 and 1972 with his mammoth "Congress Project," which was to profile every member of Congress running for re-election in 1972. He has since described the project as "my C-5A," a less-than-successful endeavor. But Joan Claybrook, currently head of the National Highway Traffic Safety Administration, who was one of the project's coordinators, defended it as "about 75 percent better than anything which had been done before."

One result of the project was Nader's decision to establish a permanent lobbying operation on Capitol Hill and to institutionalize his activities. Public Citizen was the name given the umbrella organization that raises and distributes money for Nader's activities. Its operating groups actually started in 1973.

Common Cause was established in 1970, an outgrowth of the Urban Coalition Action Council headed by Gardner, a former president of the Carnegie Foundation. He was secretary of Health, Education and Welfare from 1965 to 1968, resigning to head the Urban Coalition. Because of tax laws, the coalition established the Action Council as a separate lobbying arm.

Common Cause sources give two reasons for the decision to form an entirely new organization to replace the Action Council. First, Gardner and other council leaders wanted to work on a wider range of issues such as opposing the Vietnam War and advocating political reforms. Secondly, the group sought a wider base of support in terms of both citizen involvement and money.

From an initial membership of fewer than 100,000, Common Cause grew to more than 325,000 members, reaching its peak in 1974 at the height of the Watergate crisis. Its membership since has declined to about 220,000. Public Citizen does not have official "members," but the number of people who support it has reached nearly 200,000.

Nader Organization: A Group of Autonomous Units

There is more to Ralph Nader's organization than Ralph Nader.

Frank O'Brien, chief fund-raiser for Nader's umbrella group, Public Citizen, estimates that more than 100 people are employed by its operating groups — Health Research Group, the Litigation Group, Congress Watch, the Tax Reform Research Group, the Critical Mass Energy Project and the Public Citizen Visitors Center in Washington.

Public Citizen's operations often are preceived to be under Nader's tight control, but spokesmen for the groups say that view is incorrect.

"What people never understand" about Nader-sponsored projects, said Joan Claybrook, former director of Congress Watch, "is that the staff and volunteers do the work on their own." Nader hires the directors of the groups and sets their salaries, but his participation in day-to-day operations is fairly limited.

It is difficult to draw an organization chart for Public Citizen because there really is no bureaucratic structure or administrative hierarchy. However, here is a basic breakdown of the individual units within Public Citizen (budget figures given are from the *Public Citizen Report* for 1978 and refer to budget year 1977, the latest year for which figures were available):

● Public Citizen's fund-raising arm, headed by Frank O'Brien, spent $310,000 on direct-mail solicitation to raise $1,125,000. Additional revenue brought total income to $1,354,000; expenditures totaled $1,285,000.

● The Health Research Group works on a wide range of issues, but concentrates on monitoring the activities of health-related regulatory agencies. The staff is headed by an M.D. and includes four lawyers, a chemist, an economist and three support personnel. The operating budget is $155,000.

● The Litigation Group uses the judicial system to promote consumer interests. In addition to its own caseload the group works with the Freedom of Information Clearinghouse on public access issues. There are seven attorneys and three support staff working with a $200,000 budget.

● Congress Watch is the group that specializes in lobbying Congress, particularly on consumer issues. It prepares voting records and issues reports on various topics. Congress Watch Locals are being established in "swing districts" around the country, the eventual goal is to have three dozen such locals. Congress Watch has seven full-time lobbyists and an overall staff of 14. The budget is $197,000.

● The Tax Reform Group works to close tax loopholes and shift the tax burden to corporations from average and middle income taxpayers. The group has seven staff members, including five tax specialists, and operates on a $130,000 budget.

● Critical Mass Energy Project—Citizen Action Group concentrates on energy issues with special emphasis on nuclear power. It publishes *Critical Mass Journal* monthly. The four-member staff operates on a $95,000 budget.

● The Public Citizen Visitors Center in Washington has a $33,000 annual budget. Its purpose is to encourage Washington tourists to visit government proceedings as well as the monuments.

● The Aviation Consumer Action project receives only part of its funding from Public Citizen. It works to see that consumer views are represented before the Civil Aeronautics Board and the Federal Aviation Administration.

In addition to the Public Citizen structure, Nader has a number of aides who work in groups such as the Center for the Study of Responsive Law and the Public Interest Research Group/Corporate Accountability Research Project. These operations essentially comprise Nader's personal research staff. They are funded by Nader's speaking fees and book royalties and by similar income produced by the groups themselves.

Mark Green, director of Congress Watch, said that the Nader-funded groups "share the same offices and the same ridiculous salaries."

The Nader operation is known for its low salaries — "top of scale" is approximately $20,000 — and for its generally spartan style. But, in spite of the low pay, the Nader groups still seem able to attract talented people.

political muscle of organized labor or corporate political action committees.

Common Cause and Public Citizen agree that they are at a disadvantage when lobbying against groups that do make campaign contributions. Common Cause has been one of the leading proponents of public financing of U.S. elections because of its belief that the influence of "special interest money" on Congress must be curbed.

But both Common Cause and the Nader organization say they do not plan to become more directly involved in political campaigns. They say that a partisan role for the organizations would be inconsistent with their objective of trying to be a voice for the general public and would damage the organizations' credibility.

Publicity

Partisanship probably would threaten one of the public interest groups' biggest assets — favorable coverage in the press. The success of Nader and Common Cause in publicizing their views has led other interest groups to complain that they must pay for advertisements to publicize their views while Common Cause and Nader can reach the public free of charge.

Common Cause has used paid advertising, though. Paid newspaper ads were a key element of the group's lobbying campaign in support of campaign finance legislation.

But the greatest stress has been put on actively seeking news coverage by developing material to attract the media's attention. "One well-placed news story can change the outcome of a public issue," said one of Nader's former aides.

Both groups have tried to move beyond merely churning out press releases, although they do that, too. Their lobbyists have passed information along to the press as well as to members of Congress. Nader's tax group often has been cited in news reports on tax legislation. Common Cause also has developed a variation of the press release it calls an "editorial memorandum," presenting Common Cause's views for the use of editorial writers.

Another successful technique to gain news coverage has been Common Cause's annual survey of how well agencies are adhering to the government in the sunshine act. Its list of the agencies that have the worst records for closed meetings gets wide play in the press.

Nader has sought press coverage since the beginning of his Washington career, and in the early days of the Nader operation press releases and exposé-type reports were its mainstay. Nader also has sponsored gimmicky grass-roots lobby campaigns to attract media attention, such as urging consumers to send their representatives a nickel during consideration of the consumer protection agency. The idea was to dramatize Nader's claim that the new agency would cost each taxpayer only five cents a year. In a similar campaign in 1979 Nader urged people to send members of Congress a dollar bill with a string attached to symbolize influence buying. The dollars were to include messages supporting public financing of House elections. *(Box, p. 70)*

Litigation

Lawsuits have been a major activity of the Nader operation from the very beginning. Nader is a lawyer and so are most of his key aides. The organization believes in fighting its battles along several fronts if necessary — in Congress, in executive branch proceedings and in the courts.

The Public Citizen Litigation Group has filed over 100 lawsuits. It considers its biggest triumph to be the Supreme Court's ruling *(Goldfarb v. Virginia State Bar)* that lawyers and bar associations were subject to antitrust laws. The group also successfully contested the Nixon administration's appointment of Howard Phillips to head the Office of Economic Opportunity without Senate confirmation and participated in the court challenges to Nixon's impoundment policies. And Nader lawyers representing Carl Stern of NBC News won a major freedom of information case that forced the release of documents outlining FBI counterintelligence activities.

Common Cause's litigation effort is more modest, but also has played an important role in the organization's battles. In connection with the campaign finance issue, Common Cause obtained an out-of-court settlement from Nixon's Finance Committee for the Re-election of the President in 1973, under which the committee released a previously secret list of large contributors. Common Cause also filed a brief in defense of the 1974 campaign finance law when that measure was challenged in federal court *(Buckley v. Valeo)*. The U.S. Supreme Court sustained most of the law and threw out other segments.

Common Cause also filed a lawsuit in federal court seeking to bar the use of congressional franking privileges for political purposes. The group subpoenaed the administrative assistants of all 100 senators to supply information about the Senate's computerized mailing operation.

The Supreme Court in July 1979 ruled in *Hutchinson v. Proxmire* that the preparation and mailing of congressional newsletters are not activities related to a member's "speech or debate" and therefore are not protected from lawsuits by the Constitution. This meant that if lawmakers used official funds to print and mail newsletters they might be open to lawsuits if the material seemed to be designed to advance the member's chances of re-election.

Common Cause indicated that it might file such suits if it became necessary.

Grass-roots Effort

Both Public Citizen and Common Cause have done organizational work at the grass-roots level — but in different ways and with different objectives.

Common Cause has attempted to develop an indirect lobbying operation capable of producing letters and constituent contacts in response to important issues. Approximately 10 percent of the organization's membership participates in the lobbying work, organized by congressional district and linked with Washington through an elaborate telephone "chain" and newsletter "action alerts."

Over the last few years, Common Cause has permitted its district units to form statewide organizations to work on state issues, primarily "accountability" issues — lobbying disclosure, campaign finance, open meetings, conflict of interest and so on. Common Cause officials emphasize, however, that it remains primarily a national organization. The dues are paid to the national organization, the focus is on national issues and the local Common Cause units are responsible to the Washington office.

The Nader operation's grass-roots objective, in contrast, is to stimulate local action on local problems. One of Nader's main themes in his speeches is to urge his audience to become actively involved in public affairs.

Key vehicles for local action are the "public interest research groups" (PIRGs) that have been established in 30 states and the District of Columbia. However, the PIRGs are not under the control of either Public Citizen or Nader personally.

Rep. Moffett, who organized the Connecticut research group, said this arm's-length approach has caused disagreement within the Nader operation. Moffett said he felt that Nader would be more effective in Washington "if he had more clout back in the districts."

Some within the Nader organization have disagreed, however, noting that a firm organizational structure would be contrary to Nader's concept of citizen action.

Expertise

While Nader's lobbyists may be lacking direct grass-roots clout, members of Congress, aides and other lobbyists say they are impressed by their expertise.

Former Rep. Mikva gave "the highest of marks" to Nader's Tax Reform Research Group, calling it "almost the only source of expertise" available to Ways and Means Committee liberals. He said the group helped the liberals develop counter-arguments to the claims being made by corporate lobbyists. Sen. Kennedy gave a similar endorsement to Congress Watch and the health group as well as to the tax group.

Most legislators, their aides and even some lobbyists tend to be generalists. Richard Warden of the United Auto Workers' (UAW) legislative department saw this as a key reason why Nader's groups have been successful. Generalists always will warmly welcome someone who can supply facts and figures, he said.

Common Cause puts less emphasis on the facts and figures approach, although its lobbying staff does maintain regular contacts on the Hill. The organization's main tactic is what Cohen calls "inside-outside" lobbying — organizing a base of support for legislation among members of Congress and then attempting to build a public constituency for the measure through grass-roots and media pressure.

As with all lobbying groups, the Nader operation and Common Cause attempt to work with other groups to form as wide a coalition as possible in support of their positions. Both groups have been successful at this, but some Capitol Hill observers believe Nader has been more effective.

Common Cause, according to one of its lobbyists, does not try to forge firm, unchanging alliances. "We try to call 'em as we see 'em," he said. "If a guy is with us on one issue we will praise him in our newsletter. But that would not stop us from attacking him if he's against us on another issue."

In contrast, the Public Citizen groups are regarded as more concerned about maintaining firm alliances. Some members feel Nader has been pragmatic in selecting issues and has avoided some areas where his allies are in conflict.

Labor Relations

Common Cause's "call-'em-as-we-see-'em" philosophy is thought to have been especially damaging to its relations with organized labor. During the 1974 campaign finance battle, Common Cause ran a full-page advertisement in *The Washington Post* criticizing the Democrats' fund-raising practices, including big contributions from unions.

While labor did not lead the fight for the campaign bill, it did help the effort at criticial points. Participants in the drive for the law felt that labor was sufficiently displeased by being lumped with other special interest groups in the ad that the coalition for the bill was temporarily threatened.

Labor has disagreed with Nader's groups, too. The AFL-CIO, for example, thought that the tax group's drive to repeal the oil depletion allowance would jeopardize the 1974-75 tax cuts labor sought.

The AFL-CIO's Young said he works closely with Public Citizen on most issues. But he complained that Common Cause "spends an awful lot of time trying to convince the country and the press that they are *the* public interest group."

Differing Perceptions

The public interest groups also have clashed with each other, notably in 1975 when they publicly criticized each other's views on lobby disclosure legislation. Spokesmen for both sides said that they since have settled most differences and agreed to disagree on a few points. But the episode demonstrated that the two organizations can have differing perceptions of "the public interest."

The two groups have worked together on issues. They were in general agreement on tax reform, with Common Cause attempting to provide some grass-roots pressure for the issues developed by Nader's tax group. They agreed on open committee meetings, the Freedom of Information Act, the consumer protection agency and on keeping the Clean Air Act from being weakened. Both worked on passage of public financing of House elections and supported efforts to place restrictions on political action committees.

However, the groups have their own agendas and their own priorities. More often than not, they go their separate ways. The division of resources is born of necessity as much as choice. As one former Nader lobbyist pointed out, "there are so few public interest lobbyists we can't afford any duplication of effort." ∎

Public Charities: Clarifying Lobby Rules

Congress changed the rules of the lobbying game as played by nearly 390,000 tax exempt public charities when it cleared a sweeping revision of the nation's tax laws Sept. 16, 1976 (HR 10612 — PL 94-455).

The purpose of the section of the tax law revision on public charities, as House Ways and Means Committee Chairman Al Ullman, D-Ore., explained to the House June 8, was to provide "a new elective set of standards for determining whether a tax exempt charity has engaged in so much lobbying that it loses its exempt status and can no longer receive deductible contributions."

The revision allowed charities to decide whether they wished to be judged on a vague standard of assessing their lobbying activities, as under existing law, or on their specific lobbying expenditures, as stipulated in the revision.

Excluded from coverage under the revision were churches, church groups and private foundations. Many church groups had expressed alarm that the new terms, if applied to them, would infringe upon their constitutional rights by violating the First Amendment separation of church and state. Church spokesmen contended that the Internal Revenue Service had no authority to monitor church activities.

Charities' Lobbying Limits

Here is what tax-exempt charitable groups would be allowed to spend annually for lobbying at all levels of government under the formula in PL 94-455.

Group's Budget[1]	Allowable Lobbying Expenditures[2]
$500,000	$100,000 (20 percent)
$1 million	$175,000 ($100,000 plus 15 percent of expenditures over $500,000)
$1.5 million	$225,000 ($175,000 plus 10 percent of expenditures over $1 million)
$5 million	$400,000 ($225,000 plus 5 percent of expenditures over $1.5 million)
$10 million	$650,000 ($225,000 plus 5 percent of expenditures over $1.5 million)
$15 million	$900,000 ($225,000 plus 5 percent of expenditures over $1.5 million)
Over $17 million	$1 million maximum

1. Less expenditures for fund-raising.
2. Only 25 percent of this figure could be used for "grass-roots" campaigns to urge those other than a group's members to lobby.

Provisions

Charities electing to comply with the law would forfeit their tax exempt status if they exceeded their spending limits by more than 50 percent over four years. Specifically, Section 2503 of the tax revision:

● Set the basic level of allowable lobbying expenditures by a public charity at 20 percent of the first $500,000 of the organization's exempt purpose expenditures for a given year, plus 15 percent of the second $500,000, plus 10 percent of the third $500,000, plus 5 percent of any additional expenditures.

● Set a maximum annual expenditure limit of $1 million.

● Restricted "grass-roots lobbying," or attempts to influence general public opinion on legislation, to not more than one fourth of the total lobbying expenditure.

● Allowed eligible charities to choose for themselves whether to be subject to its terms, or to remain under the existing law.

● Set an excise tax of 25 percent of a charity's excess lobbying expenditures as the penalty for exceeding either the general spending limit or the grass-roots spending limit.

● Provided that a charity which exceeded the spending limits by more than 50 percent over four years would lose its exempt status.

● Provided that sanctions and penalties would operate automatically rather than at the discretion of the Internal Revenue Service.

● Defined "influencing legislation" broadly, and defined "legislation" as action by national, state or local legislative bodies, or by the public in initiatives, referenda or similar procedures.

● Excluded from its definition of lobbying: communications between an organization and its members; provision of information to legislative bodies at their request; provision of research or non-partisan studies; and instances of "self-defense" lobbying, when a legislative decision might directly affect an organization's existence, powers or tax status.

● Required charities electing to be governed by the bill's limits to disclose total lobbying expenditures.

● Excluded churches, church-related organizations and private foundations from the terms of the bill.

● Provided that the measure would take effect for taxable years beginning January 1, 1977.

Background

Section 501 (c) 3 of the Internal Revenue Code grants tax-exempt status to non-profit charitable, religious, scientific, cultural or educational groups and to groups engaged in "testing for public safety" or in preventing cruelty to children or animals. Tax experts use the term "public charities" to refer to these organizations. Such groups are eligible for tax-deductible contributions.

According to figures compiled by the IRS in 1978, nearly 390,000 local, state and national groups have this type of exemption.

Public charities judged by the IRS to be engaging in "substantial" lobbying lose their eligibility for tax-deductible contributions. Charities that have the eligibility do not want to lose it, because they fear they would then have trouble raising money.

Churches and church organizations are not required to file reports with the IRS. An IRS spokesman said the total charities figure included only those church organizations that voluntarily file reports. An IRS proposal to require religious groups to file the reports was withdrawn in the face of strong opposition.

Definition Difficulties

The tax code bars public charities covered by section 501 (c) 3 from engaging in partisan political activities and from devoting "substantial" effort to "carrying on propaganda, or otherwise attempting, to influence legislation." This applies to activities at all levels of government. Lobbying a county commission is subject to the same restrictions as lobbying Congress.

Despite the limitation, charitable organizations do lobby. The American Lung Association, for example, fought attempts to weaken the Clean Air Act. A number of hunger and nutrition research groups were involved in the Senate fight over the food stamp program. *(Clean air lobbying, p. 184)*

The public charities complain that the "substantial" test is so vague that even the IRS does not understand it. IRS regulations say decisions on whether a group has engaged in "substantial" lobbying will be made on the basis of the "facts and circumstances" of each case. The charities coalition that formed in 1976 to support changes in the law cited former IRS Commissioner Mortimer Caplan's observation that "revenue agents normally are experts in accounting, not ideology" and are not qualified to make such subjective determinations.

For most charities, according to some observers, the result is a "chilling effect" on their involvement in legislative issues. A legislative assistant familiar with the issue said that charities generally have taken a conservative course in this area and have avoided almost all participation in legislative affairs to avoid conflict with the IRS.

And Congress should want to hear from the charities, said Elvis J. Stahr, of the National Audubon Society and one of the leaders in the effort to have the law changed. He said the groups have considerable expertise on health, welfare, education and environmental issues.

But Stahr's viewpoint is not unanimously shared. Rep. Barber B. Conable Jr., R-N. Y., concedes that many members of Congress were "afraid this bill will unleash a torrent of zealous lobbyists upon Congress."

One member of Congress said the vagueness of the old law helped make the public charities "keep walking the straight line." He was opposed to any changes in the law that would "turn them [charitable groups] loose to lobby anyone on anything."

Maryland Case

Several proponents of a revised tax status for public charities cited the problems faced by the Maryland Mental Health Association as an example of the situation the bill sought to correct. The Maryland group's 501 (c) 3 tax status was challenged by the IRS in 1970 as a result of the association's 1968-69 dealings with the Maryland Legislature. The tax status was retained only after a long, expensive administrative appeal.

In 1974, the group was again audited, this time as a result of its 1972 legislative activities. IRS agents again recommended that the association lose its tax status. After another lengthy appeals process the IRS in October 1977 again determined that the association could retain its tax exempt status.

The Maryland case was attributed primarily to the restrictive definition of "substantial" adopted by the Baltimore regional IRS office. Spokesmen for several groups said their problems frequently came from such local situations.

But Jim Hamilton of the National Council of Churches charged that 501 (c) 3 groups that have become involved in causes such as civil rights or anti-war issues have become targets of politically motivated IRS audits. This has been a major problem for church groups, he said, which have been active on those issues.

The Nixon administration's attempts to use the IRS to harass political "enemies" were a major issue in the Watergate scandal and were one of the abuses of power cited in the second article of impeachment voted by the House Judiciary Committee in 1974.

The Fairness Issue

Another main point made by the public charities is that business groups are allowed to claim expenditures for direct lobbying and trade association dues as business deductions.

Against the opposition of the Kennedy administration, Congress, as part of a 1962 tax law (PL 87-834), overturned a 1959 Supreme Court decision *(Cammarano v. U.S.)* that had ruled such expenses were not deductible.

The restrictions on 501 (c) 3 groups, however, were maintained. The 1969 Tax Reform Act (PL 91-172), in fact, imposed additional burdens on the groups by requiring them to file "information" tax returns.

"It is almost inconceivable," said Stahr, "that Congress would wish to hear the views of business organizations but not those of charities."

The constitutionality of the restrictions on the charities has been challenged by Thomas A. Troyer, a District of Columbia tax lawyer. Troyer has chaired the American Bar Association's Committee on Exempt Organizations. He believes an argument can be made for even fewer restrictions than those current law imposes.

However some challenge the fairness argument and say the two situations cannot be compared. They point out that while corporations may deduct lobbying expenses from their gross income, they still must pay corporate income taxes, while the charities are exempt from taxation and receive contributions that donors may claim as deductions. This has been viewed as a double subsidy for the charities.

Muskie-Conable Bill

The 1962 tax law, however, led the American Bar Association (ABA) to issue a report in 1969 that said that "the former 'neutral posture of the tax law with respect to lobbying' has been upset in favor of the business interests as opposed to the charitable organizations." The ABA recommended corrective legislation, which was introduced in Congress that year but not acted upon.

Sen. Edmund S. Muskie, D-Maine, introduced another such bill in 1971. The problem had been called to his attention by Troyer, who was then one of Muskie's presidential campaign tax advisers. That bill also failed, as did a number of subsequent attempts.

The Coalition of Concerned Charities was formed in 1973 specifically to work for the enactment of corrective legislation. Muskie continued as the principal sponsor of the effort in the Senate. Rep. Conable led the cause in the House.

A public charities provision almost became part of the tax revision package that was before the Ways and Means Committee for most of 1974 but was not sent to the floor. Last-minute amendments to the public charities provisions were unacceptable to the coalition, and Conable had the provisions stricken from the bill.

'Weaving Webs'

Conable described the problem of winning support for the public charities bill as "like the weaving of a web . . . you can't even bring it into existence unless you are successful at tying a lot of otherwise unrelated things together."

One major problem to be tied together was simply attracting the attention of the Ways and Means and Finance committees and the staff of the Joint Committee on Internal Revenue Taxation, which provided the technical expertise for the tax-writing committees. "This is not considered a high-priority issue," said an aide to Rep. Ullman.

It was not until early 1976 that the joint committee staff began to work on the Conable-Muskie proposals. Conable and Muskie needed to obtain broad cosponsorship for their initial bills (HR 8021, S 2832) just to justify taking up the committee staff's time, according to a Conable staff member.

The joint committee staff worked with the Treasury Department, the charities and other concerned groups to develop the revised bills (HR 13500 and an amended S 2832).

Church Groups' Concern

One problem worked out in the redrafting was objections from religious groups. A U.S. Court of Appeals ruling (*Christian Echoes National Ministry Inc. v. U.S.*) took away the 501 (c) 3 status of a group headed by the Rev. Billy James Hargis because of Hargis' advocacy of right-wing political causes.

The churches contend that, because of the constitutional separation of church and state, their activities and tax status are not subject to IRS review. The National Council of Churches argued that the enactment of the original Conable-Muskie bills would have the legal effect of giving congressional sanction to the Christian Echoes decision. Language was added to HR 13500 that left the measure neutral on the decision, neither affirming it nor disapproving it.

Treasury Objection

Another problem throughout the seven-year effort was reversing the Treasury Department's objections to the bills, primarily to the formula for permitting lobbying expenditures. Until Conable's 1974 legislation, the proposals called for a flat 20 percent figure. The Treasury argued that the bigger charities could engage in multimillion-dollar lobbying efforts under such a plan.

Conable and the charity coalition resolved this problem in 1974 with a sliding scale and a $1 million ceiling, which were retained in the 1975-76 bills.

One concern of the Treasury about an earlier bill was its "affiliated organization" section. The Treasury wanted

language, later added to HR 13500, that would prevent a group from overcoming the spending limitation by splintering into numerous affiliated groups.

A 1975 report, *Giving in America,* issued by a private study group, recommended more leniency toward lobbying by charities than does the Conable-Muskie bill. The group found that "the increase in charitable contributions induced by the charitable deduction is greater than tax revenues lost."

Grass-roots Lobbying

Another revision was designed to deal with the amount of grass-roots lobbying the public charities would be permitted to do. Ways and Means Chairman Ullman objected to the idea of charitable groups being allowed to spend large sums to urge others to lobby Congress. HR 13500 permits charities to devote no more than 25 percent of their permitted lobbying expenditures to such lobbying.

Finally, a change was made to aid the charities. Under existing law, if an organization violates the tax code's "substantial" lobbying test, it loses its eligibility for tax-deductible contributions immediately, and its donors' deductions can be retroactively disallowed.

HR 13500 would establish a tax on charities of 25 percent of the excess expenditures — a public charity would have to pay a stiff penalty for violating the lobbying limits. However, it would not lose its 501 (c) 3 status unless, over a four-year period, its average lobbying expenditures exceeded 1-1/2 times its limit.

House Committee Action

The House Ways and Means Committee approved HR 13500 on May 26, 1976, and filed the report June 2 (H Rept 94-1210). In the report, the panel noted that existing law provided that public charities were to lose their tax exempt status and qualification to receive tax deductible contributions if the charity's efforts to influence legislation were a "substantial part of the activities" of the organization.

The "substantial part" provision was first enacted in 1934. The report declared that definition "unnecessarily vague," and noted that some people believed the vagueness tended "to encourage subjective and selective enforcement."

The panel's report estimated that HR 13500 "will not have any direct revenue effect," and noted that the Treasury Department concurred in that estimate.

Edmund S. Muskie   **Barber B. Conable Jr.**
Chief Sponsors of Charities Lobbying Act

"There is something here that's wrong and we should not allow it to go on."

—Rep. Millicent Fenwick, R-N.J.

House Floor Action

HR 13500 was brought to the floor under suspension of the rules and was not subject to amendment. Sponsor Conable termed the bill "an important opportunity to rationalize tax policy."

Rep. Joseph L. Fisher, D-Va., said "the act as it has been, simply does not give definition or form as to what a tax exempt organization may or may not do." Fisher said the existing law was confusing for charities, the government and prospective donors.

The only debate on the bill was initiated by Rep. Millicent Fenwick, R-N.J., who complained that the measure should have prohibited organizations from collecting tax deductible contributions in their own name and then transferring the funds to organizations not entitled to deductible donations.

"There is something here that's wrong and we should not allow it to go on," Rep. Fenwick said.

Conable explained that amending the bill would be "very difficult," and Rep. Fenwick withdrew her objections.

Senate and Final Action

The Senate Finance Committee voted June 4 to incorporate the terms of HR 13500 into the tax revision bill (HR 10612), with one minor exception. The exception specified that rules allowing deductions for out-of-pocket expenditures for lobbying did not apply to expenditures by organizations ineligible to elect the new expenditures test.

The Senate debated the sweeping tax revision bill for 25 days and held 209 votes on various aspects of it before passing it Aug. 6, 49-22, but the terms of the public charities lobbying section were not at issue.

The terms of Section 2503 were not altered by House and Senate conferees, and their compromise on the overall

Independent Sector

In late 1979 an organizing committee led by John Gardner, founder and former chairman of Common Cause, recommended the formation of a group to encourage development and expansion of voluntary giving to public charities. The new organization, tentatively named Independent Sector, emerged as a result of discussions carried on by the Coalition of National Voluntary Organizations and the National Council on Philanthropy.

The creation of a national agency to coordinate charitable activities had been recommended in 1975 by a private citizens' commission. At that time a government unit was envisioned, but no move in that direction ever was taken.

Independent Sector would have no government affiliation and thus would be able to devote some of its efforts to lobbying on issues affecting public giving.

Gardner said that the group would concentrate on public education and expanding awareness of the importance played by private charities in the American economy.

It has been estimated that the charitable and nonprofit sectors of the economy spend more than $80 billion a year and that they employ in excess of five million people.

The main goal of the organization would be to "provide a forum to encourage voluntary support and service for the public good," according to Gardner. The new group also would conduct research, carry out educational programs on the purposes and benefits of voluntary giving and engage in a limited amount of lobbying. One primary aim would be working to prevent any attempts by the federal government to institute central rule-making procedures over charitable organizations.

Among those involved in planning Independent Sector were the American Red Cross, the Mental Health Association, the National Urban League, the U.S. Olympic Committee and the United Ways of America—an association representing more than 37,000 local social services agencies and groups.

tax revision measure was approved by both chambers Sept. 16. The House approved the bill, 383-26, and the Senate did also, 82-2. ▋

Group Wants to Balance Nation's Checkbook

In April 1978 the National Taxpayers Union (NTU) issued its "Congressional Spending Scores" for the first session of the 95th Congress, a rating the group called "perhaps the most far-reaching congressional voting study ever produced."

Based on more than 100 votes, including those on every appropriations bill considered in 1977, the rating was designed to call attention to congressional "big spenders."

The results? Only seven senators and 42 representatives agreed with NTU more than half the time.

The reason became readily apparent.

"We didn't exactly take positions on the votes," explained NTU research director David Keating. "If it spent money, we considered it a negative vote. If it saved money, it was positive."

In other words, the less members voted to spend the better their scores — no matter what the issues. In effect, NTU opposed virtually the entire fiscal 1978 federal budget.

A similar broad-brush, "anything-can-go-from-the-budget" line of reasoning was underlying NTU's campaign for a constitutional convention to write an amendment that would require a balanced federal budget. And it was in part this very lack of definition that made NTU the largest and fastest growing organizational embodiment of the "tax revolt" in the country.

Broad Brush Approach

NTU has, from time to time, opposed specific government spending proposals such as those for Amtrak, the B-1 bomber, federal insurance for the nuclear industry and the supersonic transport (SST).

But the group's relatively recent strength and national prominence lay in the fact that it served as a national sounding board for a major grass-roots movement of taxpayers angered and frustrated over inflation and taxes.

A large measure of NTU's success appeared to lie in its opposition to all federal spending. That way it avoided attacking too many specific spending proposals, which could alienate one interest group or another. At the same time NTU subsumed the merits of all specific spending proposals to the taxpayer's lament over inflation and taxes. And in applying a principal of home economy — the balanced checkbook — to the federal budget it advanced a solution with which most Americans could identify.

Ironically, while NTU lost faith in Congress' ability to cut the federal budget — thus the need for a constitutional convention — it appeared willing to defer to Congress' judgment in making such cuts if a constitutional amendment were adopted requiring a balanced budget.

Background

The National Taxpayers Union and the "tax revolt" have done well by one another.

Founded in 1969, NTU was fighting "wasteful" government spending long before "Proposition 13" and its leader,

A portion of a National Taxpayers Union ad that appeared in *The Washington Post* in 1977 urging Congress to pass a constitutional amendment requiring a balanced budget.

Howard Jarvis, became household words. (Proposition 13, a state constitutional amendment approved in June 1978 by California voters, sharply reduced property taxes.) But as NTU's 24-year-old executive director Grover Norquist noted, the group never had a high profile. As recently as 1976, Norquist said, NTU had only 20,000 members. Since then it has doubled its membership annually with about 100,000 members enlisted.

NTU spent $1.1 million in 1978 for such activities as newspaper advertising, a monthly newsletter and other mailings. Norquist said he expected the group would spend more than $2 million in 1979. NTU treasurer William Bonner said most of NTU's funding came from its $15-a-year membership fees and that no more than 5 percent of its income came from wealthy individuals making large contributions.

Proposition 13 and other state and local taxpayer initiatives have contributed to NTU's growth. "Proposition 13 made a lot of local people much more confident. More people began seeing themselves as Howard Jarvises," said Bonner.

Bonner said it was only in late 1979 or so that NTU had "reached a turning point" in taking on the national leadership role it has always sought.

That role was explained by A. Ernest Fitzgerald, a celebrated whistleblower who exposed cost overruns on the C-5A cargo plane. Fitzgerald, who was one of NTU's first chairmen, said the group was set up as "an umbrella organization and listening post for local organizations." The problem with the tax revolt, Fitzgerald said, is that "a lot of these groups work well locally but they can't do anything about the feds."

Since 1975 the federal solution NTU has been pushing — through loose affiliations with more than 500 state and local groups — the constitutional convention to approve an amendment requiring a balanced budget.

Norquist and others at NTU insisted they would prefer that Congress pass a constitutional amendment and avoid the delay of a convention. And they acknowledged that the convention drive was an effort to force Congress' hand to approve such an amendment. "It's a vote of no confidence in Congress," said Norquist. "It says Congress is screwing up."

But neither Norquist nor Bonner expected Congress to approve such an amendment. And both said that the 34 states needed to call a constitutional convention would do so before Congress began taking the amendment seriously.

Conservative Alliances

NTU's case for a constitutional convention was based on an economic analysis that viewed deficit spending as the cause of inflation and the reduced real income — after taxes and inflation — of the average American family.

Reducing spending, NTU argued, would reduce the amount of money in circulation and reduce deficits. This in turn would reduce inflation, leaving more "real" money in the private sector for expanded production. Theoretically, this would also eliminate the need for higher taxes.

Speculating on the effect of the constitutional amendment in Congress, Bonner said the amendment would "make a tax increase very unlikely." With an amendment on the books, he said, "I don't think the clowns up the street would come in and raise taxes."

NTU concluded, in a *Wall Street Journal* advertisement, that a constitutional convention was necessary to force a balanced budget because Congress has been "unable to resist pressures to spend."

On Capitol Hill, NTU found the most receptive audience among conservatives, most of them Republicans. NTU literature has been replete with praise for such supporters of the convention drive as Sen. Harry F. Byrd Jr., Ind-Va., and Rep. Phillip Crane, R-Ill., both of whom scored high marks as penny pinchers in the NTU ratings. And NTU touted the economics of Sen. Malcolm Wallop, R-Wyo., a leading advocate of the balanced budget concept, and Sen. William Roth, R-Del., author of a plan to cut federal taxes to encourage people to save and invest.

While NTU and its budget-balancing allies rarely have said anything about where federal spending should be cut, they were not unaware of the issue. Its most fervent supporters have been those who have pushed for cutting social services.

Bill Burt, director of the California NTU office, noted that there "comes a point when the services people have come to depend on are called into question" by a balanced budget amendment.

NTU apparently was willing to wait to face such questions after it had won a constitutional amendment. NTU's critics were less patient.

The Critics

"NTU is very good at saying 'cut, cut, cut,' 'taxation is theft' and 'bureaucrats are a bunch of drones,'" said Tom Field, director of Taxation With Representation, a Washington, D.C.-area tax reform group. "I'd like to see some evidence of where those cuts are to come. If Amtrak is their idea of a big cut, it's not going to do much to reduce taxes."

Field's organization has worked to eliminate loopholes in tax laws and for more "equitable" taxation, an effort that was clearly distinguishable from NTU's mission. Bonner of the Taxpayers Union, said, for example, "We don't oppose loopholes. We think everyone should have one."

Field has characterized the balanced budget drive as "an exercise in political symbolism" and "nothing but pious wishes decked out in constitutional language." Field charged NTU with misleading the public into believing that a balanced budget would necessarily reduce spending and taxes. "The spectacle of a major national effort to amend the Constitution, followed by its failure to reduce spending and taxes will further promote public cynicism."

NTU had some even harsher critics. Several months before he announced his retirement, AFL-CIO President George Meany called on all state and local AFL-CIO affiliates to oppose a constitutional convention and to lobby for rescission where state legislatures had approved a convention resolution.

In a Jan. 24, 1979, letter to affiliates, Meany wrote that "an anti-government sentiment, inflation, increasing taxes and 'Proposition 13' fever continue to engender voter discontent which lends support" to the constitutional convention drive. Meany characterized that drive as a "very dangerous right-wing legislative effort." And the AFL-CIO's Committee on Political Education launched a campaign that sought to show the affiliation of NTU members with such organizations as the John Birch Society, the National Association of Manufacturers, and the Heritage Foundation, a conservative Washington, D.C., research organization, and Americans Against Union Control of Government.

NTU officials denied that their politics were "right wing," noting that the constitutional convention drive had won support from "liberals" such as California's Democratic Gov. Edmund G. Brown Jr. and Rep. Andy Jacobs Jr., D-Ind. They also noted that NTU had been aligned with liberals in opposing such projects as the B-1 bomber, the SST (supersonic transport plane) and legislation providing federally subsidized insurance to the nuclear industry. As Bonner saw NTU, "Our tradition is that of classic liberal politics where big government, big labor and big corporations are unable to dominate."

But if NTU was not boasting of them, its conservative affiliations were clearly identifiable in the records of its political action committee, the Taxpayer Action Fund.

Records of the fund on file with the Federal Election Commission showed that the group funded only conservative and ultra-conservative candidates. In 1978 the fund gave $500 to Sen. Jesse Helms, R-N.C.; $1,500 to Woody Jenkins, a New Hampshire Senate candidate who was a former supporter of former Alabama Gov. George C. Wallace, D, and $500 to Republican Sen. William L. Armstrong, who defeated liberal Floyd K. Haskell, D, in Colorado. The group also spent $3,600 on newspaper ads on behalf of Republican Larry Williams who ran against liberal Max Baucus, D-Mont., for a vacant Senate seat.

Fund records also showed that it received a $2,000 no-interest loan from the National Conservative Political Action Committee to get started in 1976. The political action committee and groups like it, such as the Committee for the Survival of a Free Congress, came to prominence at that time. Gerald Ford's moderate Republicanism had disillusioned many conservatives who sought to bypass the organized GOP and build a national conservative majority. Those efforts became known as the "new right."

NTU officials claimed responsibility for helping Malcolm Wallop unseat Sen. Gale McGee, D-Wyo. (1959-77), in 1976. NTU ran a newspaper campaign in Wyoming calling McGee "the bureaucrat's best friend." The ad said, in part, "we don't know anything about McGee's opponent. But he could hardly be worse than McGee."

Organization

NTU officials said they have worked with legislatures in at least 25 states that had either called for a constitutional convention or asked Congress to pass a constitutional amendment to require a balanced budget.

According to Bonner, NTU began to actively engage in building grass-roots coalitions in 1974. "For awhile we naively thought we could just spill the beans and tell the story of government waste, but it didn't work."

Consequently, NTU has sought instead to "find operatives and activists in various communities" who were willing to work with the national organization.

In a typical state, NTU would work with one of its stronger affiliates, picking one or two strong leaders to present the case for the convention to state legislators. At the same time, NTU might also encourage its members in the state to write letters, make phone calls or visit key members in the legislature. And the national organization might in addition run newspaper ads to generate public support for a local effort. In some states, such as California, the mail and lobbying efforts were targeted at key members of committees in the state legislature responsible for the constitutional convention measure.

NTU has rarely funded local organizations to any large extent, although it provided $2,400 to start a group in Oregon and has loaned money to other organizations to keep them afloat.

The California Campaign

One exception to NTU's standard approach has been California, where the organization had 20,000 members. NTU established an office there in July 1978 to lobby in the state legislature for the constitutional convention. That office was designed to work with the Santa Barbara-based Local Government Center, an NTU-funded research affiliate that made recommendations on how local governments could cut spending. Bonner estimated that NTU would spend $30,000 to $40,000 on its California effort. "California is where skateboards and Hula-Hoops come from. If California does something there's a good chance the rest of the country will follow."

California could indeed be a turning point. Both NTU and its opponents devoted considerable resources to the battle that was fought in the Ways and Means Committee of the California House over the issue.

Early in 1979, the legislature refused Brown's request that it call for a constitutional convention on a balanced federal budget. The proposal, which Brown unveiled in his second inaugural address, was to have been the cornerstone of his presidential campaign.

Brown's support for the convention route has been a key factor in focusing national attention on the issue. But Brown's support has been viewed as a mixed blessing by convention advocates who normally would welcome support from such a high visibility public figure.

"It would have been better to let a sleeping dog lie," said Bonner, acknowledging that NTU would like to have gotten closer to the required 34 states before the national media began examining the issue. "There was no point in heating things up. When Brown announced, we had to go more public."

Brown not only focused attention on the issue in the nation's most populous state, but generated the first wave of serious criticism of the proposal at the national level by economists, congressmen and other tax and spending limitation groups. And Brown may have made it more difficult for state legislators to support what until then had been a relatively easy vote. With serious questions being raised about the dangers of a constitutional convention, legislators might have become more reluctant to approve the proposal. In addition, Brown's failure to win approval of the proposal in his home state helped push that issue to the sidelines in the governor's own political campaign.

Countdown

As of September 1979, NTU counted 30 states that had called for a constitutional convention. Keating said the NTU had picked up three states since February 1979 — New Hampshire, Indiana and Iowa. Keating said he did not expect any other states to take up the issue until 1980. But he contended the NTU had "a reasonable shot" at getting at least four more state legislatures to call for a constitutional convention on the budget.

Despite the NTU's calculations, the Senate Judiciary Committee's Constitution Subcommittee had petitions from only 29 states on file. A spokesman said that while the NTU counted Nevada as a state calling for a convention, no petition had been sent to Congress as of September 1979. The governor vetoed the convention resolution after the state legislature passed it in 1977.

Along with Nevada's questionable action, several other state resolutions could be subject to challenge in Congress on matters of form. And at least three states said their applications would become void if Congress on its own proposed a balanced budget amendment.

Congress has never enacted formal procedures for calling a constitutional convention sought by the requisite number of states. Bills to establish ground rules for calling a convention were before Congress, but no action had been taken on any of them. ∎

Auto Fumes: Major Battle of Clean Air War

The opportunity to strengthen or weaken the Clean Air Act — especially its auto emissions standards — acted like a magnet for a wide variety of groups when the act came up for renewal in 1977.

Environmentalists, business groups, retailers, auto manufacturers, labor unions, governors, trade associations — these were among the many organizations and individuals that lined up to lobby for or against the amendments.

First enacted in 1970, the act was revised and extended seven years later when Congress, barely beating a deadline, gave final approval Aug. 4 to the Clean Air Act Amendments of 1977 (HR 6161 — PL 95-95).

Pressured by both the White House and the automobile industry, conferees negotiated for eight days before Congress began its summer recess. They finally reached agreement after a seven-hour session that ended at 2:20 a.m. Aug. 3. President Carter signed the bill Aug. 7.

The law amended and extended the 1970 Clean Air Act (PL 91-604). Its passage completed a major job left over from the 94th Congress. At the end of the 1976 session a Senate filibuster led by Jake Garn, R-Utah, killed a conference report produced after months of hearings, committee meetings and debate.

Taken together, the 1970 act and the 1977 amendments formed the nation's most comprehensive environmental law. It affected virtually all industrial and transportation activity, the production and use of energy, and real estate development. Its fundamental purpose was to protect public health by cleaning the air.

In its major provisions PL 95-95 did the following:

● Delayed existing standards for automobile emissions for two more years, but tightened standards for the 1980 models and again for 1981.

● Set new standards to protect clean-air areas, including national parks, but authorized variances and some development near such areas. (This was called the "non-deterioration" provision.)

● Extended the deadline for cities to meet national air quality standards until 1982, and in some cases until 1987. The previous deadline was 1977.

● Gave most industrial polluters up to three more years to comply before facing heavy fines.

● Directed the Environmental Protection Agency (EPA) to review criteria for ambient air quality standards before 1981 and required subsequent reviews every five years thereafter.

● Provided for continuing research into the effects of various substances and activities on the stratospheric ozone layer, and authorized EPA to regulate such substances.

● Established a National Commission on Air Quality.

● Required more than a dozen studies concerning air pollution.

Auto Emissions

The most difficult task in writing the 1977 amendments concerned new standards and deadlines for three pollutants from automobile exhausts — hydrocarbons (HC), carbon monoxide (CO) and nitrogen oxide (NOx). The lowest-level "statutory standards" under the 1970 act were to have been met by the 1975 model cars. But three postponements — two by EPA and one by Congress — delayed the standards until the 1978 model year.

The car manufacturers, who had insisted that they needed the three delays, said the standards still could not be met. As the 1978 cars were readied for production in August and September 1977, industry leaders threatened to shut down their assembly lines rather than produce "illegal" cars subject to fines of up to $10,000 each.

> *"What are you going to do when you have Henry Ford and Leonard Woodcock on the same side?"*
> —A supporter of tougher auto emissions standards

President Carter then urged Congress to act to avoid potential damage to the nation's economy. Congressional leaders took steps to delay the recess, scheduled to begin Aug. 5, until conferees agreed on a bill.

Background

In January 1975 President Ford submitted a series of amendments to the 1970 act that included postponing the final auto emission standards for five years. After nearly a year of hearings by the Senate Public Works Subcommittee on Environmental Pollution, chaired by Edmund S. Muskie, D-Maine, the full committee reported its version of the legislation (S 3219) on March 29, 1976.

On the House side, the Interstate and Foreign Commerce Subcommittee on Health and the Environment, chaired by Paul G. Rogers, D-Fla., began drafting its own clean air bill in the spring of 1975. The full committee reported the bill May 15, 1976. However, the bill was not brought up on the floor until early August, whereupon it was set aside for more than a month and finally was passed 324-68 on Sept. 15.

The biggest floor defeat for Rogers and the House committee majority came on the 224-169 vote adopting the less stringent, industry-backed auto emission timetable proposed by John D. Dingell, D-Mich., and James T. Broyhill, R-N. C. Their amendment would have postponed the final tailpipe standards for hydrocarbons (HC) and carbon monoxide (CO) from 1978 to 1982 and relaxed the final standard for nitrogen oxides (NOx) — which the automobile manufacturers had considered the most difficult to achieve.

Conference negotiations to compromise the two bills began Sept. 22 and ended after midnight of Sept. 29. The sessions were often tense, with members interrupted constantly for floor votes and repeated suggestions from some to abandon the bill in favor of a simple one-year extension of auto controls.

The auto emission provision finally agreed on by conferees was closer to the Senate's tighter schedule and would have imposed the final standards in 1979, except for a less stringent NOx standard to take effect in 1981.

Because the bill was defeated by a Senate filibuster — and never went to the House floor — the auto industry was left with the timetable imposed by the existing law, setting strict emission limits for all three pollutants on model 1978 cars.

1977 Action

Muskie and Rogers, the two principal sponsors of the legislation, began working on the Clean Air Act amendments early in 1977. Thorough hearings, though shorter than in the 94th Congress, were held by Muskie's and Rogers' subcommittees.

The House acted first. The Commerce Committee reported its bill (HR 6161) by voice vote May 12. The bill included the Carter administration's recommended schedule for auto emissions, announced April 18. Backed by Rogers, the committee wrote them into the bill despite protests from Dingell and Broyhill, who supported the automobile industry's demands for more relaxed standards and longer delays.

The House approved HR 6161 May 26 by a 326-49 vote. In three days of debate the House approved a Dingell-Broyhill substitute amendment for the car emissions schedule in the committee bill.

The Senate committee unanimously reported its bill (S 252) May 4. But debate did not take place for more than a month. The Senate approved the bill, 73-7, on June 10. Although its provisions on automobile emissions were somewhat weakened on the floor, S 252 under Muskie's guidance remained considerably tougher on the car industry than the House bill.

The conference was slow to get started. There was dispute over appointing House conferees and Senate conferees were in no hurry to meet, figuring time pressures were on the side of the adherents of stronger auto emissions provisions. But once it began, and as pressure for an agreement increased, the conference moved steadily toward conclusion at the late session Aug. 2-3. Disappointed in the final auto standards, Dingell refused to sign the conference report.

The conference report was published almost at once. Both chambers approved HR 6161 by voice vote Aug. 4.

The 1977 Lobbying Effort

As had occurred the previous year, the clean air legislation attracted lobbyists from almost every sector of the economy again in 1977. Their attention initially focused on the House, rather than the Senate, since the bill reached the floor of the former chamber first.

Walter Hasty, then a lobbyist for the Business Roundtable, composed of chief executives of many major corporations, said his group had won on two of three key amendments it sought — weakening auto emission controls (the Dingell-Broyhill amendment) and non-deterioration standards for air quality in certain parts of the nation — and was very pleased.

The Carter administration was on the losing side on the key auto emissions deadline issue. But its lobbyists sought to put the best face on the defeat by noting the closeness — 12 votes — of their loss and arguing that they would do better in the Senate as a result.

UAW Role

Virtually all observers of the battle agreed that a union — the United Auto Workers — was the key group in the clean air lobbying fight.

The union's success in winning a major weakening of auto emission controls was aided by its unusual alliance with the major auto manufacturers.

"What are you going to do," shrugged one supporter of tough emission controls, "when you have Henry Ford and Leonard Woodcock on the same side?"

Woodcock had recently retired as president of the UAW. The intensity of his union's commitment to weaker emission controls than those the clean air bill carried as it went to the floor was underlined in a letter to the White House Feb. 3. In it, Woodcock listed the emission standards the UAW was backing, based in large part on new information from studies done at the University of Michigan. The letter emphasized that those numbers were "*not* put forth as a bargaining position intended to achieve some other objective."

Woodcock personally underscored his commitment to the UAW position during discussions over making him an envoy to the People's Republic of China. Woodcock told Congressional Quarterly May 25, "I sent word to the White House that if this position was a problem for them, then to forget about my being an envoy . . . there was no question of my changing my position."

Howard Paster, the UAW legislative liaison in Washington, said he contacted "large numbers of people on the Commerce Committee" when the bill was before it. The UAW early in the week of May 23 brought to Washington 10 union officials from around the country to spend two days lobbying on Capitol Hill.

Several members also singled out the National Automobile Dealers Association as being aggressive and effective allies of the UAW, particularly because association members often have strong connections in representatives' districts.

Clean Air Coalition

That same technique of bringing local constituents to Washington also was employed by the National Clean Air Coalition, the major environmental group working against all three of the floor amendments favored by the Business Roundtable.

Operating with a special grant of several thousand dollars from the Sierra Club, one of their regular supporters, the coalition flew in constituents from more than a dozen states with delegations the coalition felt were important to the outcome. The Clean Air Coalition also relied on its network of phone contacts, calling key constituents in various states who then urged local citizens and groups to lobby their representatives.

Employment

One issue used extensively by backers of weaker emission controls was the threat of unemployment. A co-sponsor of the emission amendment approved by the House, Broyhill put the argument this way in a speech to the North Carolina Auto Dealers Association: "Decreased auto sales due to overly strict standards would have resulted in shutting down a large segment of the auto industry . . . progress towards cleaner air must continue, but the goal of protection of public health must include adequate employment. . . ."

That theme of the trade-off between environment and employment was seen as a significant factor in the outcome of the other loss suffered by the environmental groups — an amendment to ease the non-deterioration restrictions on areas with comparatively clean air.

Shortly after the vote on that amendment, one representative privately told some surprised and disappointed environmental lobbyists: "The mood of the House is ugly. Everyone is talking about the Washington election and worrying about jobs." The reference was to the May 17 upset Republican win in the race to fill the House seat of Brock Adams, D-Wash., who had joined the Carter administration as secretary of Transportation. That race was characterized as a "jobs" versus "environment" fight, and some members of the House were apparently affected by the anti-environmentalist outcome.

The UAW's Paster emphasized that the union believed the environment and public health were adequately safeguarded under the weaker emission standards. Thus there was no trade-off, just an effort to eliminate "unnecessary margins of safety" that might cost jobs, Paster said.

Divided Business

Despite the visible presence of the Business Roundtable, the Chamber of Commerce, the automobile majors, and other big business interests in fighting for the diluting amendments to the clean air bill, business was not united against the committee version.

Rogers, floor manager for the bill, issued a list of 58 business associations, corporations, and public interest groups supporting the committee version. On that list were the American Retail Federation, the Building Owners and Managers Association, the Independent Gasoline Marketers, the International Council of Shopping Centers, J. C. Penney, Montgomery Ward, and Sears, Roebuck and Co. The diversity of that list reflected the complexity of the bill. Congressional aides explained that the retailers, shopping center interests and realtors were concerned that relaxation of the emissions limits for automobiles would shift the burden of cleaning the nation's air to local developers and would curb local growth. Other groups, such as auto parts people, were concerned over comparatively obscure, but to them vital, provisions such as those on the warranties on clean air auto equipment and who would be allowed to do warranty repair work.

Administration Effort

Long before the House's rejection of stiff auto emission controls, administration lobbyists knew they did not have the votes to block adoption of the UAW-backed proposal in place of the Commerce Committee's stiffer standards.

But they thought the House might accept a compromise proposal midway between the two. That compromise was hastily put together May 25. The timing may have been costly. A House Democratic leader told reporters the compromise amendment might have been approved if it had been made public a day earlier. As it was, the compromise lost by only 12 votes.

President Carter had spoken out emphatically for a stronger clean air bill. His administration had concentrated its lobbying on the emissions section, the bill's most vulnerable point. Despite the low hopes for the more stringent emissions requirements in the committee bill, the administration believed it was vital to make a better showing than

in 1976, when the weaker emission controls carried by a 55-vote margin even though the bill itself later was killed.

A respected southerner, Richardson Preyer, D-N.C., was chosen to sponsor the compromise, which consisted chiefly of a one-year delay in the tighter standards in the bill.

The morning before the vote was taken, Charles S. Warren, who became director of the Environmental Protection Agency's (EPA) Office of Legislation on June 1, and White House liaison Jim Free contacted several governors and had them phone some members they thought might be open to persuasion to urge support of the Preyer amendment. This was the administration's final attempt to collect votes. But not the only one.

President Carter made some calls to Commerce Committee members. According to Free, he emphasized his interest in the legislation at regional meetings of members of Congress at the White House.

Carter gave the clean air bill a boost May 23, the day before it went to the House floor, by sending Congress his long-promised environmental message urging tough air quality controls. The same day, a May 19 analysis of automobile emission standards was made public. The analysis, prepared by the Transportation Department, the EPA and the Federal Energy Administration, was quoted often during House clean air debate. Its chief message: Stringent emission standards are needed if public health is not to suffer.

But doubts about the administration's effort remained after the fight was over. A senior House Democratic leader told reporters the White House did not go all out to block the weaker emission controls proposal. Some environmental

---

"At least it lets the Senate know we put up a pretty damn good fight. It's not a bad showing."

—White House lobbyist Valerie Pinson

---

groups were displeased also. Their lobbyists said the administration remained disorganized throughout the fight and never committed adequate manpower. One environmental lobbyist questioned the impact of personal phone calls from Carter, noting that the president had called three Commerce Committee members who then proceeded to support the Dingell-Broyhill amendment in committee.

Other environmentalists were critical of the slowness in naming Warren to the EPA. They said the agency's congressional liaison staff had been seriously short-handed and Warren's full-time efforts were needed sooner. But another environmentalist, Carl Pope of the Sierra Club, was less critical. "It took them a while to get going, but once they got going, they were very effective," he told a reporter.

Administration lobbyists were of two minds after losing on the Dingell-Broyhill amendment. They were anxious to put a good face on the outcome. "At least it lets the Senate know we put up a pretty damn good fight," said Valerie Pinson of the White House congressional liaison staff. "It's not a bad showing."

The lobbyists hoped the closeness of the Preyer amendment vote would give them more leverage in the Senate and the Senate-House conference on the bill. "It's okay," said the EPA's Warren. "It shows substantial support for a position that's stronger than Dingell's."

Administration lobbyists and bill-supporters for a time considered making a second try on the Preyer amendment through a recommittal motion just before the bill passed. Their strategy was to delay action on the bill over the Memorial Day weekend while they attempted to turn around a few votes. Business lobbyists appreciated the potential of the strategy. Roundtable lobbyist Hasty opposed a delay, noting "those guys have Jimmy Carter, and he'll be getting on the phone all weekend" if the bill is delayed.

But the strategy would have required the cooperation of House Republican leaders who controlled the recommittal motion. They would have had to agree to offer the Preyer amendment in the motion and it was widely known that they would not do so. One House Democratic leader flatly told reporters that House GOP leader John J. Rhodes, Ariz., would not cooperate.

The strategy was abandoned, largely because Speaker Thomas P. O'Neill Jr., D-Mass., told party members that the House had voted on the issue and he wanted the bill passed before Congress left for the holiday.

But even Preyer amendment supporters would not guarantee that a delay would have worked. Even though the amendment involved a major national issue, parochial

John D. Dingell   **Paul G. Rogers**

Antagonists in Auto Emissions Battle

interests typical of the House still were present. White House lobbyist Free approached one House member after the Dingell vote and asked if he would change his vote to support the Preyer proposal if a reconsideration occurred. The member responded: "If [Carter] will agree not to veto my water project." ∎

Environmental Lobby Won Bout on Alaska Bill

One of the most highly organized environmental lobbying efforts ever waged on Capitol Hill was behind a surprising 1979 House vote that backed a strong Alaska lands conservation bill by the wider-than-expected margin of 268 to 257.

The Alaska Coalition, representing every major national environmental organization, joined with the Carter administration to push what the coalition called the "conservation bill of the century."

House action came in the midst of continuing news stories about long gas lines and likely gas shortages all summer. As a result, coalition members knew their opponents would capitalize on the growing anger of car owners by arguing that energy shortages required exploration and development in Alaska.

But supporters of the bill (HR 3651) sponsored by Reps. Morris K. Udall, D-Ariz., and John B. Anderson, R-Ill., convinced an overwhelming House majority — including 66 Republicans — that their Alaska bill would leave 95 percent of the state open to development.

Administration lobbyists expected victory more than a week before the vote, with tallies steadily increasing from 221 commitments on May 10 to 232 on the 11th to 243 on the 14th. But until the last minute, Udall-Anderson supporters were cautiously predicting a close vote in what was by no means a one-sided contest.

Although the Alaska Coalition had organized a classic grass-roots effort, its basic appeal was primarily for a concept: preserving the country's last great wilderness.

On the other side was a powerful and well-financed organization representing the State of Alaska and its business interests as well as many of the country's leading corporations. This group appealed to the more tangible dollars-and-cents concerns of members.

Big Guns on Both Sides

Citizens for Management of Alaska Lands (CMAL) brought together the oil, timber and mineral company lobbyists in support of legislation sponsored by Reps. John B. Breaux, D-La., and John D. Dingell, D-Mich., and a second bill sponsored by Rep. Jerry Huckaby, D-La.

In addition to hiring five lobbyists, the state brought Gov. Jay S. Hammond, R, and Lt. Gov. Terry Miller to Capitol Hill for a week to lobby against the Udall bill. With them were members of the state department of natural resources and the attorney general's office.

The state also sent down the head of the Alaska Black Caucus, E. Louis Overstreet, to convince members of the Congressional Black Caucus that Udall's legislation would cause job losses in a state with a 20 percent minority population.

It was not clear whether state officials threatened to oppose ratification of a constitutional amendment giving the District of Columbia new representation in Congress. But Alaska State Rep. Mike Miller sent a telegram to Black Caucus members saying he would push D.C. representation in Alaska despite suggestions that a vote for Udall-Ander-

son "could result in adverse votes [on D.C. representation] in Alaska."

Meanwhile, industries with a financial stake in Alaska development, most notably U.S. Borax, engaged in a massive lobbying effort of their own. Virtually every congressional office surveyed by Congressional Quarterly reported contacts from U.S. Borax, which found itself in the unenviable position of lobbying for development of molybdenum, a mineral that may be as difficult to get members excited about as it is to pronounce.

The Alaska Coalition brought to town its biggest-name environmentalists: Russell W. Peterson, former Delaware governor who then headed the National Audubon Society, and the heads of the Sierra Club, the Wilderness Society, the League of Conservation Voters and the National Wildlife Federation.

In addition, the coalition was aided by Jacques Cousteau, the renowned marine biologist and explorer, who visited numerous congressional offices.

The coalition also worked with Americans for Alaska, which brought together well-known personalities to support the Udall bill. Among them were Henry Cabot Lodge, Cathleen Douglas, wife of the retired Supreme Court justice, former Sen. James L. Buckley, Cons.-R-N.Y., Mrs. Lyndon B. Johnson, Paul H. Nitze and Admiral Elmo Zumwalt.

White House Lobbying

Working with the Alaska Coalition, the Carter administration put together one of its more impressive lobbying efforts.

White House lobbyists said phone calls to House members were made by President Carter and top agency officials. Undecided members who seemed most concerned about oil and gas issues received calls from James R. Schlesinger, then Energy secretary, and John F. O'Leary, then deputy secretary. Calls also were made by Interior Secretary Cecil D. Andrus and Agriculture Secretary Bob Bergland.

White House tally sheets showed that some House members were contacted as many as four or more times. One member was said to have been contacted by Carter lobbyist William H. Cable; Brock Adams, then Transportation secretary; Kennedy Center Chairman Roger Stevens and the unidentified wife of a *New York Times* editor.

State of Confusion

A House member trying to figure out from the floor debate which Alaska bill to vote for might have had a hard time making a decision.

"I would just call to the attention of [Rep. Udall] the fact that he has just made another of the misstatements in connection with his legislation of which the record here has been so rich today." That charge by Dingell came less than 30 minutes into the debate on amendments.

Within the first hour of debate, members heard Udall charge the National Rifle Association (NRA) with "deliberate distortions" of his bill, an allegation that "extremist environmental groups ... have deluged well-intentioned citizens with misinformation and overkill rhetoric," charges from both sides that the other side was raising "red herring" issues, and the suggestion by one lawmaker that delays in passing a bill had led to an increase in suicides due to "uncertainties" among Alaskans.

But the confusion on the floor was perhaps best illustrated by an amendment from Peter H. Kostmayer, D-Pa., stating that the Udall measure applied only to Alaska, not to any state or territory outside Alaska.

That the Alaska lands bill applied to Alaska might have been assumed by a congressman listening to the debate. But it was by no means obvious to the NRA or its supporters. For example, Alaska Sen. Ted Stevens, R, in a press release, insisted "the issue is not only hunting and gun ownership in Alaska, but the future of hunting and gun ownership on federal lands across the nation."

The Gun Issue

In an April 26 Mailgram to NRA members, NRA Executive Director Neal Knox said, "The anti-gun, anti-hunting Carter administration and Congressman Udall are attempting to ramrod the Udall version of the Alaska lands bill through Congress, which will severely restrict hunting on all public lands."

In a May 3 Mailgram to representatives, Knox wrote: "Hunting on all public lands in U.S. at stake in Alaska lands bill now on floor. Breaux-Dingell bill allows hunting and state management fish & game; Udall bill doesn't."

Although members were looking for ways to distinguish the complex bills, some — including a key supporter of Breaux-Dingell who didn't want to be identified — said the NRA's rhetoric was counterproductive.

Another member, Pat Williams, D-Mont., said supporters of the Breaux-Dingell bill "owe my people in Montana an apology, not for educating them but rather for propagandizing in a misleading manner."

Udall responded to the NRA early in the debate.

"If anybody can find anything in our bill that has any restriction on hunters or on the owners of guns or on carrying guns in any states of the union ... I will eat a copy of my bill page by page without catsup or mustard.... The National Rifle Association's legendary lobbying machine notwithstanding ... Udall-Anderson is neutral on gun control, as it is on abortion, prayer in schools, busing, access to the notes of reporters, and ethical standards for lobbying organizations which spread deliberate distortions — as has the National Rifle Association."

The NRA effort was ultimately defused when an amendment to the Breaux-Dingell bill narrowed the difference with Udall-Anderson in terms of land open to sport hunting to less than 1 percent. But the NRA's lobbying nevertheless generated thousands of letters and phone calls to Capitol Hill and made the gun and hunting issue one of the most prominent issues in the debate.

Wildlife Federation Fiasco

Both sides in the Alaska debate sought to obtain endorsements from unions, trade associations, environmental and citizens groups.

Some endorsements claimed by Breaux-Dingell backers, such as that of the National Association of Home Builders, were denied by the associations. A Home Builder spokesman asked why his organization supported Breaux-Dingell, said, "We have no position on Alaska lands.... I

can't say the Alaska bill would lock up timber for homebuilding and frankly I don't think the Udall bill is that bad. It's not an anti-development bill."

But the fight for National Wildlife Federation affiliates was taken seriously by both sides. With its approximately four million members, the federation is the largest sport hunting group in the country. Its national office endorsed Udall-Anderson.

But Dingell, an NRA board member, and various NRA officials succeeded in persuading numerous state affiliates of the Wildlife Federation to break with their national office. A Dingell aide, Walter A. Sanders, said the congressman made a conference call to 20 board members of the Pennsylvania Federation of Sportsmen's Clubs, the state's Wildlife Federation affiliate. The board members then voted to support his bill. Sanders insisted there was a good correlation between the position of state affiliates and their support for Breaux-Dingell.

Sanders also claimed the federation's Washington office had pressured one federation affiliate in Georgia to

---

"The NRA's legendary lobbying machine notwithstanding ... Udall-Anderson is neutral on gun control, as it is on abortion, prayer in schools, busing, access to the notes of reporters, and ethical standards for lobbying organizations which spread deliberate distortions — as has the National Rifle Association."

—Rep. Morris K. Udall, D-Ariz.

---

endorse Udall-Anderson by threatening to make a $6,000 loan payable immediately if the affiliate didn't comply. Sanders further charged that an endorsement of Udall-Anderson from Georgia federation president Earl Wilkes had been sent without Wilkes' knowledge.

Those allegations were denied by both the federation's executive vice president, Thomas L. Kimball, and the Georgia affiliate's executive director, James Morrison. Morrison said he had been personally directed by Wilkes to send the telegram and that threats concerning a loan were "absolutely totally not true." The national office, Morrison said, "has never once insisted that we pay that loan back. Kimball made no threats to me at all."

In a statement in the May 10 *Congressional Record* Dingell claimed a resolution passed by the Georgia group and included in the Record showed it was "not in support of the Udall-Anderson bill." But that statement did not mention the Udall bill, Alaska or any Alaska bill.

Gearing for Senate Fight

Supporters of Udall-Anderson (which as passed became HR 39) were hoping to score a similar victory in the Senate. However, the Senate Energy Committee approved a version of HR 39 that was less conservation-oriented than the House bill.

Although Alaska Sen. Mike Gravel, D, said the bill was "terrible," he and Stevens agreed to try to bring it to the floor in late 1979 in hopes of averting passage of the House bill in 1980. A blue-ribbon advisory panel to Alaska Gov. Jay Hammond, R, said the Senate version was "livable." ∎

Lobbies At Work

CQ

Changed Times Challenge Sugar Lobby

The once-powerful sugar lobby has come on hard times in recent years as Congress, the consumer movement and the industry itself have changed. This was borne out on Oct. 23, 1979, when a broad coalition of consumer and labor groups combined to kill a House sugar price support bill.

The sugar industry was deeply involved in the 1979 congressional battle over industry subsidies, even to the point of drafting much of the language for the rejected House bill. But whereas the lobby once had only to call up a friendly chairman — the nearly legendary Harold D. Cooley of North Carolina — in 1979 it had to battle angry consumers and labor lobbyists, wrestle with a totally different House and look over its shoulder at encroaching competition from the corn sweetener industry.

"Everything's changed," said Horace Godfrey, the dean of Washington sugar lobbyists who in 1979 represented Florida sugar interests. "The approaches are different, the makeup of Congress is different, and you don't have the powerful chairmen that you used to have."

Godfrey is a man who should know. He and other lobbyists for sugar producers have found passage of a sugar bill to be a frustrating and increasingly difficult task. In 1978 a sugar bill went down to defeat, and consumer groups were fighting hard again in 1979 against legislation (HR 2172) approved by the House Agriculture Committee April 26. Three months later, on July 19, the House Ways and Means Committee voted 16-13 to approve HR 2172 after rejecting an attempt to drop the bill's direct federal payment provisions. The close vote indicated the bill faced a precarious future on the House floor. Opponents said the bill was inflationary and would hurt consumers.

Although the bill would not add much to the price of a bag of sugar — probably only pennies — the total impact would be huge. It would add an estimated $350 million a year to Americans' bills for sugar and products that use sugar, such as soft drinks, candy and baked goods.

With skyrocketing food prices helping push inflation to double-digit figures, many legislators were less than enthusiastic about the proposed sugar bill.

The task of Godfrey and his allies was made all the tougher because sugar refiners, big industrial sugar users and even a part of the sugar industry itself were opposed to parts of the bill. Unified industry support was considered essential for the bill to pass.

Sugar lobbyists played an active role in drafting HR 2172. Agriculture Committee action was put off several times during markup so the industry could agree on what it wanted in the bill. But it couldn't agree. The bill was reported anyway; differences would be fought out on the House floor.

Industry Protection

Basically, the sugar bill was designed to protect the domestic sugar industry in several ways. First, the bill would set a minimum price for sugar that is roughly comparable to the cost of U.S. production.

The minimum price is achieved by imposing fees — and, if necessary, quotas — on cheap foreign sugar brought into the United States. The fees ensure that the price of imported sugar is comparable to sugar produced within U.S. borders. At about 7.5 cents a pound in 1979, the world price of sugar was approximately half the U.S. price.

Second, the bill would provide U.S. growers a federal payment of up to half a cent a pound, with a limit of $50,000 for a single grower. Supporters of the system said it was necessary to keep the domestic sugar industry alive in the face of foreign competitors who often paid low wages to their workers and received subsidies from their governments. The United States should avoid dependence on foreign sugar supplies, they said.

Administration support was expected because the measure fell within its proposed spending guidelines. In 1978 President Carter threatened to veto any sugar bill with a minimum price of more than 15 cents a pound, but in 1979, against the advice of his anti-inflation advisers, he agreed to accept the 15.8-cent level in the Agriculture and Ways and Means Committees' bill. He reportedly was anxious to win congressional approval of an International Sugar Agreement (ISA), which was near collapse because of Congress' failure to implement it, and other important

Harvesting sugar beets

trade legislation. (As reported by the Ways and Means Committee, HR 2172 would implement the ISA.)

Sugar Lobby Split

Lobbyists opposing the bill had an unexpected ally in 1979 — sugar producers from the nation's largest sugar-producing state, Hawaii.

Hawaii's 15 major sugar plantations stood to lose millions because of the bill's provision limiting payments to a single producer to $50,000. The defection of the Hawaiians symbolized an important change: Sugar lobbyists found it increasingly difficult to live up to their reputation as one of the most powerful groups in Washington.

Though still regarded as an effective and talented lobby — especially in the Senate, where a few key senators from sugar states had helped their cause — sugar producers were finding it increasingly difficult to agree among themselves and get their message across to Congress.

Their problems were particularly serious in the House, where most observers agreed that the industry had to be unified to carry the day against the potential opposition of major industrial users, consumer groups and organized labor.

New Forces at Work

Much of the change has occurred since 1974, when Congress rejected the quota system on imported sugar that had shaped the politics of sugar for 40 years.

Since then:

● Sugar lobbyists for foreign nations have stayed in the background.

● Changes in the rules of Congress have diminished the power of committee chairmen and practically ended the days of back-room deals.

● Turnover in membership has lessened interest and commitment among members of Congress in sugar legislation.

● The rapid growth of the corn sweetener industry has added a new dimension to a highly competitive industry.

● Different regional interests among cane and sugar beet growers have caused a split in the industry itself.

"Up until 1974 everybody involved worked on the assumption that the Sugar Act was going to be renewed in some fashion or other," said Roger Sullivan of the Hawaiian Sugar Planters Association. "It was a question of making adjustments you wanted in an existing piece of legislation that had an institutional character of its own. Starting from scratch is much more difficult."

"Everything's changed. The approaches are different, the makeup of Congress is different, and you don't have the powerful chairmen that you used to have."

—Horace Godfrey, Washington sugar lobbyist

Background

For 40 years, lobbying on sugar bills was a balancing act between domestic producers seeking high price supports and growers of cheap foreign sugar scrambling to get into the U.S. market.

Beginning in 1934 with the passage of the Jones-Costigan Act, the U.S. government used a quota system to prevent oversupply and guarantee domestic producers a share of the market. The system placed limits on total sugar production and allowed domestic producers to provide about half of the nation's sugar needs. The remaining quotas were divided up among foreign producers. With the quota system helping to keep the U.S. price well above the world price, foreign competition for quotas became fierce.

In the scramble for sugar quotas that ensued during consideration of amendments to the Sugar Act in 1965, a major controversy developed over the efforts by lobbyists for foreign nations to influence the quotas proposed — and ultimately accepted — by the House Agriculture Committee. Critics focused particularly on the committee chairman, Harold D. Cooley, D-N.C. (1934-66), whose secretive dealings with foreign lobbyists vying for quotas earned him the title "sugar king" during the period. Suspicions of illegal behavior were so great that the Kennedy administration ordered Cooley's phone tapped, though criminal charges were never filed.

In 1965 the committee — reportedly as a favor to Massachusetts political leaders such as House Speaker John W. McCormack (D, 1928-71) — even granted Ireland a 5,000-ton quota. Though the Irish sugar crop was normally small and consumed entirely at home, Ireland sold the United States sugar at 6 cents a pound and replaced it with sugar from Poland at the world price of 2 cents a pound.

Shortly after his defeat in 1966, Cooley registered as a lobbyist for Thailand and Liberia at $25,000 a year. He was only one of many well-connected Washington figures speaking on behalf of foreign sugar interests. Others included former Senate Whip Thomas Kuchel, R-Calif. (1953-69), who represented Colombia at $200 an hour; Charles H. Brown, D-Mo. (1957-61), lobbyist for the Fiji Islands at $2,000 a month, and Thomas H. Boggs Jr., son of the late House Majority Leader Hale Boggs, D-La. (1941-43, 1947-73), who was employed by the Central American Sugar Council.

Committee members occasionally were tempted by the lure of foreign travel. A 1977 Justice Department suit charged that for at least six years the South African sugar lobby, fighting for its quota, used a front organization — the South Africa Foundation — to provide free trips and campaign contributions to members of the House Agriculture Committee. Among the beneficiaries were W.R. Poage, D-Texas (1937-1979), then committee chairman, and William C. Wampler, R-Va., the ranking minority member. The members who accepted money from the foundation said they were unaware the favors came from sugar interests. *(Box, p. 195)*

End of Quota System

Bad weather and shrinking world supplies caused world sugar prices to climb to over 40 cents a pound by the spring of 1974.

That was far higher than the supported domestic price, and the House by a vote of 175-209 rejected a bill to extend the foreign and domestic sugar quota system. Opponents of

South Africa Sugar Lobby Admits Gifts to Members

For at least six years, the South Africa sugar lobby provided free trips, campaign contributions and even a job offer to members of the House Agriculture Committee, according to documents filed in a federal court suit.

The principal beneficiary of the sugar lobby generosity was former committee Chairman Rep. W. R. Poage, D-Texas (1937-79), who supported South African sugar quotas in 1971 and 1974. Poage denied any wrongdoing and said he was unaware that the favors came from sugar interests.

The Justice Department charged in June 1977 that several South African lobbyists failed to disclose the trips and other favors, as required by law, in reports to the U.S. government. The suit was settled in August when the lobbyists made the belated disclosures but admitted to no illegalities.

Documents filed in the case showed that the South Africa Foundation, ostensibly an independent group that promoted the country, was used as a front to pay for trips to South Africa by members of Congress. In many cases, the money actually came from the South Africa Sugar Association, through the New York law firm of Casey, Lane and Mittendorf.

Until 1978, the law firm was a registered agent for both the sugar association and the foundation. The Justice Department said the sugar association was the biggest single financial contributor to the foundation.

Thought Recipients Knew Source

John R. Mahoney, former lobbyist for the sugar association, said in a court statement he believed the members of Congress were aware that the sugar group was the real source of the money.

The favors provided to the members of Congress were:

● In November 1970, the sugar association, using the foundation's name, paid $3,000 to rent an executive jet to fly Reps. Poage, E. (Kika) de la Garza, D-Texas, and George Goodling, R-Pa. (1961-65; 1967-75), from South Africa to Rhodesia and back. The three members were touring several African countries at U.S. government expense.

● In November 1971, the sugar association, through an intermediary, gave Poage $1,800 worth of airline tickets to use for trips to his home district.

● Lobbyist Mahoney donated $1,000 to Poage's re-election campaign in December 1971, through the Democratic Congressional Campaign Committee.

● In May 1972, lobbyist Mahoney offered a job as a consultant to retiring Rep. Thomas G. Abernethy, D-Miss., (1943-73), then a member of the Agriculture Committee. Mahoney said the offer "did not advance beyond the preliminary stage."

● During 1972, Rep. John J. Flynt Jr., D-Ga. (1954-79), and his wife traveled to South Africa. The South Africa Foundation paid $3,100 for Mrs. Flynt's expenses, including air fare and hotels. Flynt has said he later reimbursed the foundation.

● In May 1972, Poage and his then administrative assistant Dayle Hennington were flown on a private jet from South Africa to Rhodesia and back. The sugar association picked up the $3,000 tab, using the name of the foundation.

● In August 1973, Rep. William C. Wampler, R-Va., and John F. O'Neal, then chief counsel to the Agriculture Committee, were given a 10-day trip to South Africa, paid for by the sugar association through the foundation. The trip cost $6,500.

● Rep. David R. Bowen, D-Miss., visited South Africa in January 1976 as a guest of the foundation. The $3,100 tab was paid by the foundation, which was then reimbursed by the sugar association. At an unknown later date, however, the foundation reimbursed the sugar association.

Funneled Through Foundation

In their court statements, both the sugar lobbyists and the foundation admitted that payments were funneled through the foundation to conceal their true source. Mahoney said the payments were obscured "in order to avoid the appearance of a conflict of interest on the part of these Congressmen" who were helping draft legislation that provided sugar quotas for South Africa.

Poage told Congressional Quarterly he did not learn of the sugar association's role in this payment scheme until the court papers were filed. Asked about Mahoney's claim that the members of Congress knew the real source of the favors, Poage said: "I don't know on what basis he makes that statement . . . Mr. Mahoney was a foreign agent, and I had no right to accept any money from foreign agents. He knew that, I knew that, we all knew that."

Poage said the $1,000 campaign contribution came to him from the Democratic Party, not the sugar lobby. Mahoney, however, said Poage sent him a note thanking him for his contribution.

Under the revised Foreign Agents Registration Act (PL 89-486) it is illegal for foreign agents to make campaign contributions on behalf of foreigners, and for candidates to knowingly accept such contributions.

Mahoney said he made the contribution — from law firm funds — at the request of John F. O'Neal, "a fund raiser for Congressman Poage." O'Neal had been Poage's administrative assistant, and in 1971 was lobbyist for a shipping company and for W. R. Grace & Co., a food, chemicals and shipping conglomerate. In 1973 he became Agriculture Committee counsel. Poage was deposed as committee chairman in January 1975.

Justice Department reports showed a close relationship between South African lobbyists and committee members, especially Poage.

In late 1974, for example, South Africa Foundation lobbyists reported meeting with Poage to discuss sugar quota legislation. And in 1975 both Poage and Wampler reportedly hosted luncheons for the foundation.

From 1969 to 1977, the House ethics code prohibited members from accepting "gifts of substantial value" from lobbyists. The new House ethics code prohibits members from accepting gifts worth more than $100 from lobbyists, foreign nationals or agents.

the measure, including both consumer-oriented liberals and free-market conservatives, argued that the program was obsolete at a time when market prices were the highest since 1920. The bill's defeat was also attributed to the addition of amendments strengthening its labor protection provisions, which cost some Republican support.

But by 1976 the world price had returned to historically low levels of 7 to 9 cents a pound, while rising domestic production costs — estimated at 13 to 14 cents a pound — made it increasingly difficult for domestic beet and cane producers to make a profit. Sugar beet production declined from 29.4 million tons in 1976 to 21 million tons in 1977, reflecting a decision by many farmers to switch to other crops. In 1978 U and I Inc., one of the oldest sugar beet processing companies in the nation, said it would close its four plants in Washington, Idaho and Utah.

With cheap imports again posing a threat to domestic producers, lobbyists for domestic producers began to press for added protection for the domestic industry. An interim program set up by the Carter administration in 1977 was superseded by provisions of the 1977 farm bill that authorized sugar purchases and loans to support the commodity at not less than 13.5 cents a pound through the 1978 crop year.

Since 1978, attention has focused on using a system of fees and quotas on foreign sugar to achieve a minimum price that would approximate the average cost of production of domestic sugar. When the House rejected the conference report on the sugar bill at the end of the 1978 session, the matter was left for the 96th Congress.

An important related issue for the administration was ratification of the ISA, which would use quotas and stockpiling to maintain world sugar prices within an 11 to 21 cent range. Sen. Frank Church, D-Idaho, had held up ratification of the ISA in the Foreign Relations Committee until passage of a sugar bill that would satisfy sugar beet growers in his state.

A New Era

Changes in the sugar industry and in Congress have made a big difference in sugar lobbying since the days of the quota system.

For one thing, lobbyists for foreign nations have been much less visible. "There is not a great deal for the foreign lobbyist to lobby for," said Arthur Quinn, who represented the Caribbean and Panama. "The foreign supplier to a great extent sits on the sidelines and watches the battle."

"The [foreign] lobbying effort at this point is directed toward coming out with as little damage as possible and as little restriction on the entry of sugar as is feasible," said David Todd of Patton, Boggs and Blow, which represented the Central American Sugar Council.

Part of the change in lobbying for sugar legislation was attributable to new rules governing the legislative process. "It's a different kind of Congress," said House Agriculture Committee staffer Gene Moos. "You don't have that old entrenched southern domination in the committees that dealt with sugar, when Cooley and a couple of sugar lobbyists could sit down and write a sugar bill and that was the end of it."

"Seniority is no longer a compelling factor," he said. Election of committee chairmen by the Democratic Caucus "means they can't afford to be arbitrary, and that undermines the power of the committee chairman compared to what it used to be."

Open Meetings, New Leadership

Opening committee meetings to the public also has had an important impact.

"I remember the days when we had closed markup sessions," said Dale Sherwin, formerly a Senate Agriculture Committee staff aide who became a lobbyist for A.E. Staley Manufacturing Co., a major corn sweetener producer. "In the open it complicates things a lot. People have to take public postures."

The 1976 decision to assign sugar legislation jointly to the Agriculture Committee and the Ways and Means Committee also had a significant effect on the process. Ways and Means had waived jurisdiction in 1934 as a result of an informal agreement, but the agreement lapsed after the Sugar Act was rejected in 1974, and the joint assignment was made after the House adopted new rules in 1974.

Heavier urban and suburban representation on Ways and Means has provided a new opening for labor and consumer groups to get their message across.

Cooley's leadership is also a thing of the past. "Cooley would bring the sugar bill to the floor in the closing days of the Congress," recalled Joe Creed, chairman of the Sugar Users Group, a coalition of industrial users. "He'd tell the members this is much too complicated to explain, just take it on faith, and invariably it went by that way."

"You have a more sophisticated Congress now, more inclined to question, and there is more interest from other groups, such as consumers," Creed said.

By all accounts there also has been a change in leadership style under the 1979 committee chairman, Thomas S. Foley, D-Wash. "Foley is a consensus kind of guy," said David C. Carter of the U.S. Beet Sugar Association. "He doesn't knock heads."

Though Foley generally has been admired, there has been some feeling that he might sometimes carry his conciliation approach too far. "We've never had a better chairman than Tom Foley," Godfrey said. "He has more patience and knowledge — though I sometimes think he has too much patience."

The lobbyists' job also has been complicated by the fact that few members of the Agriculture Committee in 1979 seemed interested in taking major responsibility for sugar legislation. Bob Bergland, D-Minn. (1971-77), who became secretary of Agriculture in 1978, played this lieutenant's role in his days on the Agriculture Committee. "When Bergland was a member, he was able to bring the forces together," said Carter. "Foley is unable to do that simply because he's chairman."

Turnover in committee membership has been another factor affecting sugar legislation. Half or more of the members of the House in the 96th Congress were not there when the 1974 bill expired.

"You have to work with more members. Formerly you could work with the chairman more," Godfrey observed. "It's a much greater educational job now. You don't have sugar members, members that have a strong sugar constituency, that you once had," Godfrey said. "The Agriculture Committee has been a sought-after seat, and sugar is not a major commodity."

New members also have tended to be more skeptical about any sugar bill because of its past notoriety. "Sugar got a rather bad name when there was tremendous competition for foreign quotas under the old Sugar Act," Godfrey said. "The buying of quotas, as far as I'm concerned, was just a bunch of malarkey, but it did give sugar a bad name. There is still a carryover."

The Senate

Sugar lobbyists always have had more success in the Senate than in the House. As one veteran aide put it, "The power is always in the Senate, and the trouble is always in the House."

Geography is one factor. While only a few members of the House Agriculture Committee had a large number of sugar constituents, 10 states have major sugar beet industries and another four are major cane growers. Two senior senators from sugar states — Russell B. Long, D-La., and Frank Church, D-Idaho — have been particularly stalwart in supporting sugar producers.

Long usually has been regarded as the strongest spokesman for sugar legislation in the Senate — both in his role as chairman of the Finance Committee and as protector of Louisiana sugar interests. But his decision to back an administration compromise on sugar in the final hours of the 95th Congress shocked some observers and led to speculation that he might be taking a more pragmatic approach to sugar legislation than in the past. Others defended Long's role, and pointed out that his support for the administration bill was contingent on passing new legislation in 1979. "He's a negotiator, a compromiser," Godfrey observed. "I have no fault with Russell Long's leadership."

Church has been the greatest foe of the administration's effort to ratify the International Sugar Agreement. In 1978 he kept the treaty bottled up in his Foreign Relations subcommittee while proposing legislation that would have set the sugar target price at 17 cents a pound. If passed, his bill would have cost American consumers about half a billion dollars more per year than the administration proposal.

Change in the Industry

Dramatic changes also have occurred in the structure of the sweetener industry. The most significant change has been the rapid growth of the high fructose corn syrup market; U.S. consumption increased from 246 million pounds in 1972 to an estimated 2.1 billion pounds in 1977. Corn sweetener production costs generally have been several cents lower than sugar.

To gain new markets for their product, corn sweetener lobbyists have supported legislation that would raise domestic sugar prices, and thus make their own product even less expensive by comparison. They have opposed any direct federal payment to sugar growers that would not also go to corn sweetener manufacturers.

The rapid growth of corn sweeteners has unsettled the sugar industry and added a new dimension to the politics of sugar legislation. "There is really no commonly accepted benchmark on how much high fructose will expand into the market over the next three to five years," said Roger Sullivan of the Hawaiian Sugar Planters' Association in 1979. "It's a situation similar to cotton and imitation fibers in the 1950s, or butter and margarine," said Leo Mayer, an agricultural expert who in 1979 was working in the office of the special trade representative. "At some point sugar will reach a new balance, but today we're still in a painful adjustment period."

Regional Differences

Different regional interests among cane and sugar beet growers have made it more difficult for producers to agree on sugar policy.

<hr>

Writing a Bill

Though their overall influence may have diminished, producer lobbyists have continued to play an active role in the drafting of sugar legislation.

But most observers felt their ability to control the drafting of a bill was considerably less than it was in the days of the old Sugar Act.

"The days of somebody coming in and being able to write their ticket are gone," said Jim Culver of the House Agriculture Committee staff. "That was always done behind closed doors; new openness has made that impossible."

"I don't think sugar is any more different than other commodities," said House Agriculture Committee staffer Gene Moos. "When you're trying to put together legislation, you have to depend on the Agriculture Department and on industry specialists to help," he said. "The old sugar hands in that professional group are helpful because so many of us were not involved in sugar legislation when they did have a sugar program."

"They [the sugar lobbyists] understand the full range of considerations," added Bill Motes, an Agriculture Department specialist. "None of those guys get livid at the mention of a labor provision. They're not ideologues, and they know their trade very well."

<hr>

For example, Hawaiian cane sugar is generally produced on large plantations with unionized labor, while small growers in Louisiana use non-union labor. In Hawaii producers and refiners are the same organization; in Lousiana they are separate. Other factors, such as the opportunity to grow alternative crops, the relative importance of sugar in a given area, and differences in the cost of production, also contribute to different points of view.

Even differences in the size of sugar operations can cause disagreements among sugar producers. Limiting direct payments to individual producers to $50,000, for instance, has been opposed by Hawaiian interests, which have a few large plantations that would stand to lose millions of dollars under the limitation. They said the limitation would have little or no effect on the average small western sugar beet producer, and so "it would put us at a perhaps fatal disadvantage in competing with beet sugar in the West," said Sullivan.

Other issues such as minimum wage provisions have proved difficult for producers to resolve among themselves. Coalitions were built and fell apart almost weekly during consideration of the 1979 bill; one Senate aide described it as a political "kaleidescope." "Since we haven't had [existing] legislation to work with, we've become more segmented, looking more at our own positions," said Richard Blake, who represented western beet sugar interests. "We're not as cohesive as we used to be."

The Opposition

The power of sugar producer groups has been reduced by the increasingly visible presence of groups favoring a cheap sugar policy.

"We are most interested in countervailing power," said Gregg R. Potvin of the U.S. Cane Sugar Refiners' Association, a group of small independent refineries that has favored low tariffs on foreign sugar. "We go to our natural allies — consumers and firms that have to use sugar in manufacturing."

While other opponents of high sugar prices — major sugar users, labor unions, consumer groups — were less visible in the Agriculture Committee, they commanded more attention in Ways and Means and on the House floor.

Consumer groups, including the Consumer Federation of America, Congress Watch and Common Cause, formed a coalition called Citizens Against Sugar Hikes (CASH), and were working to defeat sugar legislation.

"I think the chances are good — it's been beaten before," said Maureen Shea of Common Cause, the public affairs lobby.

One indication of the influence of sugar users could be found in campaign contribution data. Federal Election Commission (FEC) records indicated that while producer groups gave substantial sums to members of Congress, major users were more numerous and also contributed heavily through their political action committees (PACs).

Producer groups such as the American Sugar Cane League gave $69,245 during 1977-78, including a $1,500 contribution to Foley, according to the FEC.

FEC records indicated the political action committee of the U.S. Sugar Corporation — a major Florida producer — gave a total of $43,718 in 1977-78, including a $1,000 contribution to Foley. But users also were heavy contributors in the same period. PACs of the Coca-Cola Co., gave $61,459, for example; PepsiCo contributed $31,135, and the U.S. National Confectioners Association contributed $13,800, including a $1,000 contribution to Foley.

House Defeats HR 2172

On Oct. 23, the House defeated HR 2172 by a vote of 158-249. The bill's defeat was attributed mainly to consumer attacks against its inflationary impact and labor dissatisfaction with the measure's minimum wage provisions. With both groups fighting the proposal, members from the industrial Northeast and urban areas lined up in nearly unanimous opposition. A Congressional Quarterly vote analysis found that members from urban and suburban districts rejected the bill by an overwhelming 29-126 margin.

Though supporters said the bill's inflationary impact would be negligible since sugar prices had risen above the support level in recent months, many members were apparently wary of casting a vote that could be construed as inflationary.

"The vote looked to the House like a vote against inflation, and many members were eager to cast one of those," said Bill Frenzel, R-Minn.

The 91-vote margin was deceptive, supporters and opponents agreed. The bill would have won another 20 or 30 votes if the House had adopted a key Frenzel amendment, which was defeated by 10 votes. The amendment would have barred direct federal payments to sugar producers as part of a sugar price support program. Other members were prepared to vote for the bill as a favor to colleagues, but switched at the last minute when it was apparent HR 2172 would be rejected anyway.

"When you look at the final vote, you must conclude that the votes were never there for a sugar program," Frenzel said.

Direct Payments Amendment

Frenzel argued that direct payments would create a government handout that would be impossible to stop once it was started, and that price supports should be achieved in the marketplace — where consumers can shop for substitutes — rather than indirectly through taxes.

Supporters, including Agriculture Committee Chairman Foley, said the assured return of 16.3 cents a pound in fees and payments was probably less than average sugar production costs and therefore necessary to help the industry survive, and that payments were used in many other farm programs.

Two opposition leaders — Peter A. Peyser, D-N.Y., and Margaret M. Heckler, R-Mass. — both urged members who opposed the bill to reject the amendment even though it would have made the bill more palatable to them.

'Tactical Decision'

"I had to make a tactical decision, and then convince my friends following my lead on this that this was the way to go," Peyser said. "If we had then lost the bill, it would have been a difficult vote to explain."

The tactic apparently was effective: 73 members voted against the weakening amendment, and then voted against the bill. The amendment was rejected, 200-212.

The outcome might also have been reversed if sugar producers had been willing to compromise and drop the direct payments, Frenzel said. In hindsight, a Foley aide said, "we should have accepted the Frenzel amendment" in an effort to defuse the opposition.

A second Frenzel amendment, to prevent direct payments from ever giving producers an assured return above 16.3 cents a pound, was rejected by a standing vote of 18-62. Foley argued that the proposal would be an administrative nightmare that would cost more to administer than it saved in lower payments.

International Sugar Agreement

The death of the sugar bill in the House raised hopes that the International Sugar Agreement could be considered as a separate issue. Senate approval of the 1977 agreement had been delayed by Church, pending action on the price support bill.

Speculation centered on the possibility that the administration might agree to administratively support the price at 15.8 cents in return for action by Church on the ISA.

"We'd be willing to consider supporting the price at 15.8 cents," said White House agriculture adviser Lynn Daft.

Ways and Means Trade Subcommittee Chairman Charles A. Vanik, D-Ohio, indicated his willingness to consider separate ISA implementing legislation if the Senate proceeded with the ISA. ∎

Business Wants Congress to Limit FTC

The problems of used car dealers and funeral home directors typically do not evoke a great deal of sympathy among consumers or their elected representatives in Congress.

But a sizable number of House and Senate members sided with these stereotypical wolves of the marketplace as they battled the Federal Trade Commission in 1979.

The car dealers, undertakers and others were among a growing number of businessmen seeking help from Congress in thwarting FTC-proposed  rules designed to give consumers more information about the products or services they buy. And the warm reception the objectors received was symptomatic of Congress' waning interest in defending FTC actions among disgruntled constituents.

Under Chairman Michael Pertschuk, many observers said, the FTC had become more aggressive in confronting powerful corporate interests than at any time in its 65-year history. Using its broad mandate to ferret out "unfair or deceptive acts or practices," it had antagonized, among others, the organized bar, the American Medical Association and the insurance, television, advertising, automobile and drug industries.

In retaliation, the business community seized on public disdain for government regulation to launch a massive — if somewhat scattershot — campaign to curtail the powers of the FTC.

Three-Pronged Attack

Lobbies for businesses affected by commission actions joined the U.S. Chamber of Commerce and the National Association of Manufacturers in a three-pronged attack that would:

● Give Congress the power to veto all FTC regulatory actions.

● Eliminate or cut FTC funding for public participation — a program that helped pay for private citizens and small businesses to participate in rulemaking sessions when they otherwise could not afford to do so.

● Stop the commission from proceeding with regulatory actions, rulemakings, investigations and lawsuits against specific business interests.

Most of the lobbying was directed at the FTC authorization bills pending in the House and Senate. The Senate bill (S 1020), reported May 15, 1979, by the Senate Commerce Committee, simply authorized funds for the agency for fiscal years 1980-82. The House bill (HR 2313), reported the same day by the House Commerce Committee, authorized funds for the agency for the three fiscal years but it also contained several provisions the business lobby had requested. These included a congressional veto, a reduction of funds available for the public participation program and

a prohibition on agency petitions for trademark cancellations.

But the annual appropriation for the commission also came under attack. Both the Senate and House Appropriations committees said they were unwilling to fund the FTC until disputes over the authorization bill were worked out.

No fewer than a dozen amendments had been introduced to the Senate and House authorization bills in anticipation of the floor debate. And several conservative senators who called themselves the Senate Steering Committee set up what amounted to an amendment factory. They in effect invited those with grievances against the FTC to suggest additional amendments.

Supporters said the commission had become the whipping boy for any group encumbered by federal regulations. Many of the lobby groups "would like to abolish the FTC, there's no secret about that," said Wendell H. Ford, D-Ky., one of the FTC's defenders and the chairman of the Senate Commerce subcommittee that oversees the agency.

And several consumer lobbyists suggested that big business decided to take on the agency after defeating the proposed Consumer Protection Agency (CPA) in the 95th Congress — a scenario that was characterized as "paranoid" by Jeffrey H. Joseph, a lobbyist for the Chamber of Commerce of the United States.

But Orrin G. Hatch, R-Utah, said, "The FTC has been captive of one philosophy for too long and, if it continues, I'd just as soon do away with it."

Source of Complaints

Many of the complaints about the FTC could be traced to two factors — 1) the increased authority Congress gave the agency in 1975 to make rules that affect broad economic interest groups rather than individual businesses, and 2) Chairman Pertschuk.

Weight of Law

The FTC's authority is in many respects tantamount to legislating because the commission's rules have the weight of law. During its rulemaking process, the FTC hears arguments from the business groups to be regulated, but commission rules are final, subject only to court challenges.

Some critics contend that through these proceedings the FTC is doing more legislating than Congress, that it has overstepped its authority and, in short, does whatever it pleases.

The broad discretion the FTC maintains in selecting its targets, without explicit direction from Congress, makes its rulings more vulnerable to attack than those of other regulatory agencies. In addition to affecting virtually every consumer in the country, FTC actions more immediately affect thousands of businessmen and professionals.

Since 1975, the agency has initiated about 20 proceedings to regulate industries ranging from children's advertis-

The FTC is "one of the most obstreperous and politically motivated agencies in the government."

—Sen. Orrin G. Hatch, R-Utah

ing to funeral homes. While most were initiated before Pertschuk became chairman, most are being completed under his leadership.

The FTC has become an "activist agency in the last few years," said Sen. James A. McClure, R-Idaho. "The FTC doesn't think there's anything too far afield for it to investigate."

Hatch characterized the FTC as "one of the most obstreperous and politically motivated agencies in the government. It uses [its rulemakings] to badger, bludgeon and extort" concessions from business.

Business lobbies view the FTC as a different kind of beast from other regulatory agencies.

"The FTC is an unusual agency in that it is bucking the trend of less intervention in the private sector," said James P. Carty, a lobbyist for the National Association of Manufacturers.

Chamber lobbyist Joseph described it as a "frustrating kind of agency. With EPA [Environmental Protection Agency] or OSHA [Occupational Safety and Health Administration] you can see what you're fighting. With the FTC, it's like shadow-boxing with a ghost. You never know where it'll hit you."

The FTC has "700 lawyers looking for things to get into," based on its mandate to act against unfair practices, he continued. The problem is that "unfairness is in the eye of the beholder."

Activist Pertschuk

Pertschuk, appointed by President Carter in early 1977 to serve until 1984, is regarded by conservatives in the Senate as a "radical" and an "activist," although he's been called worse.

The Washington Star in mid-1979 quoted a memo by Jack P. Alexander, public relations director for the Formica Corp., which was tangling with the FTC over use of its trademark. Alexander called Pertschuk "one of the most dangerous men in America" and a "complete socialist" who "is personally committed to the dissection of large corporations and the reorganization of business and industry, and, in effect, the redistribution of wealth."

Pertschuk responded by saying the FTC's effort to "strengthen the role of competition" is "the absolute antithesis of socialism."

Pertschuk defends the FTC's new direction and its accomplishments.

"Because we're an active agency and doing the job we ought to be doing, there are more groups into which the teeth of the commission are sinking now and more groups attacking [rules] as they come to fruition," he said.

Pertschuk characterized the business lobbying efforts as "last ditch stands" to stop the agency from making rules. "In years past [lobbyists] could make peace with the commissioners and administrators directly, or the White House would put an arm on the commissioners. That's no longer possible, so now they're going to the Hill."

He said big business is simply "feeling its oats," from its victories on the Consumer Protection Agency and labor law reform but has had no success impeding commission programs.

"Obviously the commission is sensitive to the will of Congress. But as of this moment nothing that's happened on the Hill has stopped the commission from continuing with any of its proceedings," he said.

'Tendency to Overstate'

Nevertheless, the growing interest in the legislative veto and the increasing complaints about FTC actions has had an effect.

That became apparent when the FTC came under attack at a Senate Small Business Committee meeting because of a ruling on franchises. At one point, Committee Chairman Gaylord Nelson, D-Wis., who is generally supportive of the FTC, became so exasperated he suggested he might be convinced to support a legislative veto to deal with irresponsible rulings.

The FTC's rulemaking procedures and its public participation funding program also were sharply criticized in a lengthy report by the Administrative Conference of the United States, an independent federal agency designed to promote efficiency and fairness in regulatory proceedings.

Even the commission's allies concede that it has brought on some of the criticism itself. The agency, according to one Senate aide, "has a tendency to overstate the issue" in its rulings. "It usually ends up cutting back on its rules rather than adding to them."

Said a House aide: "FTC rulemakings throw in everything but the kitchen sink to take attention away from things it really cares about. . . . And a stigma remains from such FTC proposals as one that said the funeral home guys couldn't make a profit on flowers."

But if business sharks appeared to be circling more closely around the FTC, it was also because they viewed the commission as more vulnerable. As one Senate aide put it: "The House right now smells blood whenever it hears the word FTC."

Legislative Veto

Those sharks have a raft of amendments ready for the FTC authorization bills when they reach the floor.

Most attention will be focused on attaching a legislative veto provision to the Senate bill. An amendment that would make all of the FTC's proposed regulations subject to a congressional veto was attached to the House authorization bill in committee.

Because of its vulnerability, the FTC is viewed as the ideal agency on which to try out a legislative veto. If proponents win there, they would like to see the veto applied to all agencies. A bill (HR 1776), sponsored by Rep. Elliott H. Levitas, D-Ga., which would permit congressional veto of all regulations proposed by all federal agencies, had more than 200 co-sponsors by late 1979.

While Congress has passed more than 200 legislative vetoes on individual bills, it has never approved a veto that would apply to all regulations issued by a single agency.

The last time it attempted such a veto — on the fiscal 1979 Department of Housing and Urban Development authorization — it was defeated in the Senate, 65-29.

The dispute over the congressional veto prevented passage of the FTC authorization bills since the beginning of fiscal 1977. In 1978 the House voted overwhelmingly to attach a veto provision to the authorization, but the Senate rejected it. A conference committee dropped the veto and the House refused to accept the measure.

Regulatory Reform Campaign

For organized business lobbies, such as the Chamber of Commerce, the veto idea has become the principal focus of their lobbying effort for broader regulatory reform as well as their campaign against the FTC.

Veto advocates deny that the legislative veto is the answer to all their regulatory problems, but many view it as providing partial relief. Joseph said the Chamber's board came out for the veto in 1979 because, "nothing else was moving" in the regulatory reform arena. "They bet the best horse that was running at the time."

He acknowledged that the Chamber had no comprehensive proposal for solving business' regulatory dilemma. "There are bits and pieces of regulatory reform all over the map, but what's best has yet to surface in any one package. I don't think anyone really knows the answer."

Veto critics regard the proposal as a desperate and simplistic solution to the regulatory problem. "The business lobbies "are riding the crest of an anti-government, anti-bureaucracy, anti-regulatory wave without any clear idea of what they want," said one Senate aide.

"The legislative veto," concluded another, "has become a catchall phrase for curing the ills of government in much the same way as balancing the budget has become the cure-all for inflation."

In response, Sen. McClure argued, "the legislative veto is not a cure-all, but where congressional oversight has not been successful it is necessary. We don't have a conceptual answer to the problem of regulatory reform yet, and if we can't get the broad general reforms we can at least begin to chip away at it with various agencies."

The efforts to amend the FTC authorization bills suggest what might happen if a legislative veto were enacted. Now, almost all of the FTC's rulings are appealed in court. If a legislative veto were enacted, business groups targeted by an FTC ruling would try to quash it on Capitol Hill before undertaking costly and prolonged litigation.

The FTC provision attached to the House authorization, which would expire after three years, would prevent an agency rule or regulation from becoming effective if: 1) the House and Senate vetoed it within 90 days after it was issued or 2) if one chamber vetoed it within 60 days after it was issued and the other chamber did not reject that veto within 30 days.

In effect, the second situation would allow for a one-house veto. Under both, the president would be removed from the process entirely, with no authority to veto congressional action.

Supporters argue that the veto proposal would take lawmaking out of the hands of unelected bureaucrats and return it to Congress.

But veto critics say it is unconstitutional, would impose new responsibility on an already overburdened Congress and that special interests could easily force Congress to kill unpopular rules. These critics foresee one-house veto situations in which one chamber would veto a rule and the

"Because we're . . . doing the job we ought to be doing, there are more groups into which — [FTC] teeth . . . are sinking now . . . ."
—FTC Chairman
Michael Pertschuk

other might not act in order to avoid debate on a controversial proposal.

"If there was a legislative veto," said Frances Zwenig, a lobbyist for Ralph Nader's Congress Watch, "you might see quid pro quo's with members saying 'I'll vote for your veto if you vote for mine.' "

Rick Neustadt, a White House domestic policy aide, said business sees the legislative veto "as a way to hobble the FTC. It would build in delay and politicize the [rulemaking] process."

Public Participation

The FTC is one of seven agencies providing funds for private citizens to participate in rulemaking proceedings. The idea is to include all interested parties in the proceedings, not just large manufacturers or business associations that can afford expensive legal representation.

The House Commerce Committee voted to set a $75,000 limit on grants to one participant in a rulemaking proceeding and reduced FTC's public participation authorization from $1 million a year to $750,000.

Critics of FTC's program insist that it has provided too much money to groups that support commission positions and has funded groups that should not qualify or that could afford to appear at their own expense.

But behind the criticism is the fact that public participation funding has made it more difficult for businesses to get their way in agency proceedings, FTC officials say.

In the Senate, Alan Simpson, R-Wyo., was expected to offer amendments to the FTC authorization bill that would kill the public participation funding program and prohibit other agencies from having similar programs without Congressional approval.

Simpson aide Joel Mandleman said FTC expenditures for public participants were "a flagrant abuse of the intent of the sponsors. . . . There is no longer any middle ground but to dismantle the program, particularly because of the way Pertschuk has used it."

'Hired Gunslingers'

Kendall Fleeharty, a regulatory affairs attorney with the Chamber of Commerce, said the Chamber would support the Simpson amendments.

Fleeharty charged that the FTC has tried "to pepper the record [of its rulemakings] with its own point of view and has hired gunslingers to come in and present those views. Intervenor funding should broaden the record, but instead we see an abuse of that objective to convert intervenor testimony to an alter ego of the FTC."

Mandleman charged that in the children's advertising rulemaking no money went to opponents of the rule, which he referred to as "Pertschuk's pet project." Commission records indicate the charge is substantially accurate.

Linda Larson, a Senate Appropriations Committee aide, speculated that opposition to the program came to a head because of its extensive use in the children's advertising debate.

During Senate Appropriations Committee hearings, considerable attention focused on the agency's public participation program. But a study put together by the majority and minority staff found that the program was basically well-administered.

FTC attorney Terry Latanick said rulemakings would "lose something very, very important" if public participation funding was abolished. "You can't assume that the consumer's viewpoint is the same as the commission's," he said.

The White House consumer affairs office headed by Esther Peterson has encouraged senators to hold firm on the funding program. An aide to Peterson said her office "has a major commitment to intervenor funding to insure that the consumer's viewpoint is represented in agency proceedings. . . . The FTC has been the pilot in developing what we think is a successful program."

Other Issues

In addition to the effort to give Congress a veto over FTC actions and to suspend the commission's public participation program, amendments expected to be offered would:

● Kill the highly publicized FTC rule that could ban some television advertising aimed at children and put limits on other ads.

● Kill the FTC rule on product "standards and certification," which deals with trade groups that voluntarily set uniform product standards for their industries. An example of such a group is Underwriters Laboratory, which sets standards for electrical appliances. The FTC regards some of these practices as non-competitive and argues that some standard-setting groups have failed to solicit views from all affected businesses.

● Prohibit the FTC from canceling the Formica trademark. The agency maintains that Formica has become the generic name for plastic laminate materials and that many consumers are inadvertently spending more money for Formica because they are unaware they are asking for a specific brand name.

● Kill the FTC rule designed to give consumers information about major mechanical and safety defects in second-hand cars.

● Kill the FTC's proposed rule to provide bereaved consumers itemized price information detailing costs of a funeral.

● Limit the FTC's authority to investigate professional organizations such as the American Medical Association, the American Bar Association and the American Dental Association.

The 'Kid-Vid' Controversy

The campaign to limit the FTC's authority started in 1978 with an organized attack on its children's advertising rule — the so-called "kid-vid" proceeding — which could affect $600 million in television advertising directed at children.

The FTC is considering banning advertising on programs where young children compose a significant proportion of the audience and/or banning advertisements of highly sugared products when children form a large proportion of an audience. The FTC argues that such advertising encourages children to consume sugared products that are harmful to their health.

A coalition spearheaded by the National Association of Manufacturers, the Grocery Manufacturers Association and Thomas Boggs Jr., an attorney with Patton, Boggs and Blow, is seeking language in the FTC appropriations bill report that would prevent the agency from issuing its children's advertising regulations.

A broader "kid-vid" alliance — including sugar, chocolate, cereal and toy manufacturers — plus broadcasting and advertising interests pulled together high-priced lawyers and consultants to fight the rule at the agency and to generate a grass-roots mail effort aimed at Capitol Hill.

Sen. Roger W. Jepsen, R-Iowa, at the urging of opponents, agreed to offer an amendment to the FTC authorization that would kill the proposed rule.

But the lobbying effort has expanded to reach other complaints as well. The Chamber of Commerce has put together what lobbyist Joseph called an "FTC victims' alumni," a broad group of businesses affected by FTC proceedings.

"These groups can become instant converts on congressional veto," a top Chamber priority, Joseph said.

In a special mailing to members from districts represented by congressmen on the Commerce committees, the Chamber urged them to contact their lawmakers on legislative veto, intervenor funding and the standards and certification rule. The Chamber made a similar appeal to 100,000 of its members, and the National Association of Manufacturers asked 14,000 members to do the same.

And for the first time, the American National Standards Institute (ANSI), the principal standards-setting group in the country, asked its 1,200 members — representing about 400 industries — to contact their representatives and senators opposing that rule. Several ANSI member groups, such as the Recreational Vehicle Industry Association, initiated their own letter-writing campaigns.

The Formica Controversy

In taking on the Formica Corp., the commission sent a chill through the ranks of other powerful corporations concerned about losing their brand names. The FTC insists it has clear legal authority under the 1946 Lanham Act to seek cancellation of a trademark that has become "generic," or a common descriptive name.

But a number of companies are seeking congressional assistance to abort this effort. Among them are the 3M Corp., Westinghouse Electric Corp., Procter & Gamble, General Foods, Eastman Kodak Co., Owens Corning Fiberglas Corp., United States Gypsum Co., Corning Glass Works, Pfizer Inc., Johnson & Johnson and Dow Chemical Co.

"Obviously, the business community is viewing a Formica petition as much more than an isolated incident," notes an FTC memo.

The effort on behalf of Formica paid off in the House Commerce Committee where Thomas A. Luken, D-Ohio, attached an amendment to the FTC authorization that would prevent the commission from challenging for three years any company's trademark that had become the common name for all products of its type.

Also successful in the House were lobbyists opposing the commission's used car rule. The Commerce Committee report on the authorization bill contained a statement signed by 20 of the panel's 42 members raising questions about the legality of the rule. The statement was added by Richardson Preyer, D-N.C.

The National Independent Auto Dealers Association, an 8,500-member used car trade association based in North Carolina, contacted Sen. Jesse Helms, R-N.C., who agreed to sponsor a Senate floor amendment to kill the rule. The group is represented in Washington by Michael R. Lemov, former chief counsel to the Commerce subcommittee with FTC oversight.

An FTC attorney handling the used car rule said 120 congressional offices had contacted him with questions about it.

Outlook

The House was considered likely to approve an FTC authorization with a strong legislative veto provision and several amendments limiting FTC rulemaking authority.

The key to the fight was the Senate. It had traditionally been a staunch foe of congressional veto, but because of the concerted lobby efforts by business interests and the growing anti-government regulation fever, the Senate's opposition was no longer certain.

Harrison "Jack" Schmitt, R-N.M., had 35 co-sponsors to a veto amendment for the FTC authorization bill. Normally that was not enough to predict passage, but aides to senators opposed to congressional veto believed Schmitt was within striking distance.

Senatorial aides working on the legislation and other congressional observers said some senators who had been counted on to oppose congressional veto of FTC regulations were switching sides because of pressure from the national and local Chambers of Commerce and other business interests. The one they named was George McGovern, D-S.D., who was lobbied when he went home for the August recess. A McGovern aide said the senator likely would vote for the congressional veto provision.

"There was a very strong and effective lobby effort on the part of small business. They [opponents] don't know how difficult it is to go to a small state where 20-30 personal visits are arranged," the aide explained.

Senate floor action was delayed until after the Senate Commerce Consumer Subcommittee completed oversight hearings on the FTC and several of the proposed amendments to the authorization bill. Those hearings began Sept. 18.

Funding Pressure

In fall 1979, the House and Senate sought to step up pressures to resolve the disputes over the FTC amendments by refusing to make fiscal 1980 appropriations for the agency until the authorization bill had been enacted. But that strategy quickly became entangled in an unrelated dispute over a congressional pay raise.

The House Appropriations Committee Sept. 17 reported an interim appropriations bill for the agency (HJ Res 402) that provided fiscal 1980 funds at the fiscal 1979 level until Nov. 15. The 1980 fiscal year began Oct. 1. The resolution also prohibited new FTC activities or promulgation of final regulations during that period. This continuing appropriations resolution was kept separate from one (HJ

> *"The House right now smells blood whenever it hears the word FTC."*
>
> —Senate committee aide

Res 404) providing temporary funding for several departments and agencies for which regular fiscal 1980 appropriations bill had not yet been enacted. The committee did not want any controversy over the FTC to delay approval of funds for other federal agencies.

Compromise Reached

The full House passed the FTC interim funding resolution by voice vote Sept. 20. But the Senate Appropriations Committee decided to combine the FTC resolution with the broader continuing resolution. That resolution continued funding for the FTC at the fiscal 1979 level only until Oct. 31 and placed no restrictions on agency operations during that period. The Senate passed the resolution by a vote of 76-11 on Sept. 27.

On Oct. 12 the House and Senate reached a compromise on the pay raise and other issues, and a new version of the interim funding resolution (H J Res 412) was cleared for the president. To keep up the pressure to resolve the congressional veto dispute, the resolution set a Nov. 20 deadline for passing FTC authorization legislation. ∎

The Broadcast Lobby: Resistant to Change

The broadcast industry lobby has been called one of the most powerful in Washington. To the casual observer it operates like most other Washington lobbies, but in one very important respect it differs. The broadcasters have a unique relationship with elected public officials: Members of Congress rely on broadcast news coverage to remain in the public eye and thus promote their re-election.

A politician's need for broadcast exposure in his home district is seldom discussed, but widely recognized by broadcaster and politician alike. Broadcast lobbyists, especially, are aware that it can be a potent lobbying tool even if never brought up.

"They are awfully powerful," Sen. Ernest F. Hollings, D-S.C., said of broadcasters during a television interview in Miami, Fla., in August 1977.

Hollings, chairman of the Senate subcommittee with jurisdiction over the broadcasting industry, ought to know. After he became chairman of the Commerce Subcommittee on Communications in January 1977, his first attempt to legislate in the broadcasting field crumbled under pressure from the broadcast media.

Saccharin Ban Delay

The attempt involved a proposal by Health Subcommittee Chairman Edward M. Kennedy, D-Mass., in 1977 to delay for 18 months a proposed federal ban on the sale of

---

"The average senator [would] vote anything that the local broadcasters want. . . . He's very interested in satisfying that local broadcaster because it's instrumental in his re-election."

—Sen. Ernest F. Hollings, D-S.C.

---

saccharin products. As part of the delay, Kennedy sought restrictions on television and radio advertising of saccharin products during the 18-month period.

The National Association of Broadcasters (NAB) called such restrictions "discriminatory" and mounted an extensive lobbying campaign to oppose them.

First the broadcasters went to Hollings asking him to have the bill referred to his Communications Subcommittee for the purpose of trying to weaken the restrictions. Hollings did so.

Then the broadcasters lobbied to stop the proposal from coming to a vote. The subcommittee ended up voting 7-1 to adopt a broadcast industry-inspired substitute measure deleting the restrictions altogether. Hollings was the sole dissenter.

"The average senator," Hollings later explained during the Miami television appearance, would "vote anything that the local broadcasters want."

"The local broadcaster calls a senator," Hollings said, "and the average senator doesn't keep up with communications, and he's very interested in satisfying that local broadcaster because it's instrumental in his re-election. . . . He's got a decent, fine broadcasting official in his home town . . . and he's asked to vote so-and-so, and why bother him with the facts?"

Hollings said that when he tried to amend the saccharin legislation, "we couldn't get a vote in the Communications Subcommittee. They had already been fixed. Rather than a chairman of a subcommittee, I felt like a foreman of a fixed jury."

"All politicians are convinced that their TV stations either favor them or don't favor them by clipping the candidate they don't like out of the evening news," commented a former Ford administration official involved in broadcast regulation. "The source of their power lies in their ability to control news coverage."

The official, who asked not to be identified, was a member of the Ford task force on regulatory reform, and in 1975 and 1976 he was involved in the drafting of legislation to deregulate the cable television industry.

Regulations on Cable TV

Conventional television broadcasting is protected from cable television competition by extensive federal regulations on cable, and broadcasters opposed the deregulation legislation even before it was drafted.

"The broadcasters never attempted to convince us of their case by citing facts and figures or making economic arguments," the official said. "Instead, they relied on the widely held belief that broadcasters, through their news programs, have the power to influence the opinions of the American people."

Referring to former President Ford's highly publicized clumsiness, he said: "They would approach Seidman [Ford adviser L. William Seidman] and joke, 'Well, you just keep this up and you'll see Ford falling down more on television.' It would be in a joking manner, of course, but it was believed that the broadcasters had that kind of power."

The official's account was confirmed by another member of Ford's regulatory reform group, but Seidman said he couldn't recall any such incidents.

Several months before the 1976 presidential election, the cable deregulation proposal went back to the drawing boards for "further study."

"In the end," the official went on, "Ford's top staffers may never even have shown him the decision memo we drafted. It just died of its own weight. They [Ford's top aides] just told us to stop it. The broadcasters kept telling them that all the task force was doing was making 800 broadcasters mad at the administration."

Influence in Washington

Broadcasters act surprised when told about their lobby's influence in Washington.

"The broadcasters have a good story to tell in Washington, but they tell it poorly," network lobbyist Eugene Cowan commented in an interview. Cowan, Washington vice president of the American Broadcasting Companies Inc., is also on the television board of directors of the National Association of Broadcasters and chairman of its congressional liaison committee.

A broadcaster, Cowan said, "is no different than any other constituent. What can a broadcaster do to a congressman? Nothing. And he won't try to do anything either. It just comes down to the congressman not wanting to get many prominent residents of his district mad at him."

Are broadcasters, then, no more powerful than any other prominent constituent?

"Gene Cowan knows better than that," commented House Communications Subcommittee Chairman Lionel Van Deerlin, D-Calif., "It's not true and no one knows it better than Gene Cowan."

As lobbies go, the broadcast industry's is neither the largest nor the smallest, the most powerful nor the least.

"They're rich and have a lot of clout, obviously," Ford adviser Seidman commented. "But they're nowhere as good as the oil boys or the specialty steel industry."

The NAB, representing 590 television stations and more than 4,700 radio stations, has an annual budget of

---

"Grass-roots support — broadcasters working at the local level with their own members of Congress — is more effective than relying on the Washington lobbyists."

—American Broadcasting Companies Inc.
Vice President Eugene Cowan

---

about $6 million and a legislative staff of five registered lobbyists. Members pay dues on a sliding scale, depending on their annual revenues, to support the association. Broadcast industry revenues totaled about $10 billion in 1978.

Many of the major broadcasting firms have their own lobbyists, but several of these represent their companies' other corporate interests in addition to broadcasting.

Because broadcasting is a regulated industry, practically every television and radio station also retains a lawyer or law firm as its "Washington representative," but few of these representatives do significant amounts of lobbying.

Local Broadcasters' Impact

The sole campaign fund representing broadcasters' interests is the NAB's Television and Radio Political Action Committee. The committee gave 109 congressional candidates about $70,000 in 1976 and an estimated $80,000 to 125 candidates in 1978.

"We're a modest PAC [political action committee] by most standards," commented Spencer Denison, the committee's executive director. "There are lots of trade association PACs that are bigger than ours, and lots that are smaller."

The most effective lobbying done on the industry's behalf, broadcasters agree, is that done by the local broadcasters rather than by their Washington representatives.

"Grass-roots support — broadcasters working at the local level with their own members of Congress — is more effective than relying on the Washington lobbyists" because the Washington lobbyists don't vote in the members' home districts, ABC's Cowan stated.

And television news plays a role in their power, Cowan admitted, though he denied the power emanated from a broadcaster's ability to control news coverage of members of Congress.

"People depend more on television news than any other medium for their information about what goes on in the government," Cowan said. "It's very important that this kind of information be available to the people."

"So when a broadcaster wants to tell his congressman about something that's hurting him, he should explain it in these terms: 'If we weren't here providing this type of service, who else would?' "

Communications Policy

Broadcasters, however, represent only part of the communications lobbying in Washington. The telecommunications industry representing computers, satellites, telephone and telegraph services, microwave radio and fiber optics has become an increasingly important segment of the industry. Broadcasters and the telecommunications interests are vitally concerned with national communications policy. That policy is based on the Communications Act of 1934. Its main purpose was to provide an organized system to be used by broadcasters and to help develop a nationwide telephone system through the American Telephone and Telegraph Co. (AT&T) monopoly. The act has been amended numerous times but never thoroughly overhauled.

Recently the inherent problems of regulating what have developed into two separate industries with one piece of legislation have become obvious, but attempts to make substantive changes have not gotten very far.

Attempted Revision

In March 1979 Communications Subcommittee Chairman Van Deerlin introduced an ambitious and a highly controversial plan (HR 3333) to rewrite the Communications Act of 1934. He had held 33 days of hearing on a similar bill in 1978.

The subcommittee had hoped the earlier hearings plus 24 days of hearings in 1979 on HR 3333 would spur action in the 96th Congress.

Van Deerlin's bill got as far as the markup stage on July 11. The subcommittee met briefly on a couple of provisions. But after meeting informally with some subcommittee members that afternoon, he canceled the scheduled markup session on July 12 and met with the subcommittee in private.

After that meeting, Van Deerlin decided to abandon his effort to rewrite the entire 1934 act.

Dropped were plans to deregulate the broadcasting industry and charge broadcasters for use of the airwaves. Van Deerlin's bill faced concerted opposition from the broadcast industry, citizen groups and labor, with no one group giving unqualified support of the rewrite effort.

"With the ABC [American Broadcasting Co.] Network coming down on the same side as Ralph Nader, it was hard [for members] to buck," Van Deerlin said in an interview. But the California Democrat said he would continue to push legislation dealing with government regulation of the telecommunications industry. He has always considered those provisions the most important part of the bill.

Those provisions were to be introduced as amendments to the 1934 act.

"It's not to be sneezed at that we're going to be moving on some very important legislation," Van Deerlin said.

A letter on July 13 to subcommittee members from Van Deerlin, ex officio member James T. Broyhill, R-N.C., and ranking minority member James M. Collins, R-Texas, said: "During yesterday's meeting, we were encouraged by

---

"With the ABC [American Broadcasting Co.] Network coming down on the same side as Ralph Nader, it was hard [for members] to buck."

—Rep. Lionel Van Deerlin, D-Calif.

---

the members' willingness to commit the time and effort necessary to resolve the telecommunications issues. This is a sign that passage of new common carrier legislation, after nearly three years of work, need not be delayed."

Despite the months of hearings, Van Deerlin and others close to the legislation said no consensus had been reached by members, the industry and citizen groups on the broadcasting provisions.

Some members also felt the task was too ambitious. A total rewrite was viewed as too radical.

Broadcast Provisions

HR 3333 would have deregulated radio immediately and allowed stations to hold licenses for indefinite periods.

The fairness doctrine and equal time regulations that help govern programming of controversial subjects and political campaigns would have been repealed. Television would have been deregulated after 10 years.

Under Van Deerlin's plan, radio and television stations would have had to pay fees for use of the spectrum, the range of sound wave frequencies available for broadcasting. Radio broadcasters wanted the deregulation legislation, but they were united with the television industry in their opposition to the spectrum fees.

Although officials of the National Association of Broadcasters generally supported HR 3333, influential television broadcasters opposed it.

Labor and private groups opposed repeal of the fairness doctrine and equal time regulations as well as limitations on broadcast license renewals. They maintained the regulations and limitations helped assure citizens they would have some check on the powerful broadcast media.

In the face of such opposition Van Deerlin had little choice but to withdraw his bill. ∎

Backers Score Victory on Education Agency

A well-organized lobbying effort on the part of the Carter administration, the National Education Association (NEA) and several other education groups played a crucial role in passage of legislation creating a separate Department of Education. They faced equally formidable opposition from an unusual alliance of liberals and conservatives.

The strongest supporters of the new department were involved in elementary and secondary education. NEA, the 1.47 million strong teachers' association, and other organizations of local education agencies felt their interests would receive a more sympathetic hearing from an education department than they had from the Department of Health, Education and Welfare (HEW).

After losing in 1978 when House opponents delayed the legislation, these supporters renewed their activity in 1979 with increased vigor. About 100 education interest groups formed a loosely knit coalition to push for the department. The coalition was modeled on the successful National Coalition to Save Public Education, set up in 1978 to block tuition tax credits for private school students.

A major reason for the increased effort in 1979 was that in 1978 the education department bill became too closely identified with the NEA. Critics claimed the department was certain to be dominated by that powerful organization. "Last year the NEA took all the criticism because they were in the lead. It was labeled an NEA bill. If there's one thing we can get across, we will get across that it's not an NEA bill alone," said Illinois education lobbyist Allan Cohen, a leader in formation of the coalition.

These supporters won powerful support from the White House. President Carter had promised to push for creation of an education department during his 1976 presidential election campaign; in return he received NEA's endorsement. But the administration's support was not designed solely to pay back a political debt. The president also badly needed a major legislative victory to offset several losses he had encountered on Capitol Hill.

The administration set up a task force of White House and agency lobbyists to coordinate action on the bill. Reflecting the administration's increased emphasis on the issue, the task force was one of about half a dozen such groups supporting major administration goals such as approval of the SALT II treaty and hospital cost containment.

In 1978 HEW lobbyists had virtually ignored the department legislation, in part because they had their hands full with elementary and secondary education authorizations and tuition tax credit legislation. Former HEW Secretary Joseph A. Califano had opposed creation of the department until it became explicit presidential policy. But in early 1979 an HEW education lobbyist said creation of the department was "a heightened priority for the president and we're all going to be working on it."

President Carter personally worked on it, contacting individuals members of Congress on at least two occasions, once while the bill was pending in the House Government Operations Committee and again when the House was considering the conference report.

Coalition of Opponents

Countering the well-organized tactics of department supporters was an unusual assortment of conservative members of Congress who feared the new department would interfere with the traditionally local nature of public schools and a variety of more liberal organizations who feared their influence would be reduced in a department run by professional educators.

The most active opponent may have been the American Federation of Teachers (AFT), an AFL-CIO affiliate and arch rival of the NEA for the allegiance of the nation's teachers. It was widely thought that AFT opposition to the department stemmed from fears that NEA would dominate it.

The AFL-CIO itself opposed the department, in part because of concern that it would lead to a sundering of labor's coalition with education interests in dealing with Congress.

Civil rights groups opposing the department worried that its leadership would not be so responsive to civil rights efforts as was the existing leadership in HEW. They also complained that the Office for Civil Rights within the new department would not have enough institutional support.

With AFT help, labor and civil rights opponents in April announced formation of a Committee Against a Separate Department of Education. This coalition was joined by the presidents of more than 50 colleges and universities.

Included were the heads of some of the most prestigious academic institutions in the country, such as Harvard, Columbia and Stanford, and the massive state universities of Illinois, California and Michigan.

The expression of opposition from individual schools was in marked contrast to the generally neutral attitude of most higher education organizations toward creation of the department. Many colleges had not been terribly concerned with the issue because they felt most of their interests would not be directly affected by the change. The Association of American Colleges, an organization of liberal arts schools, was one of the few higher education associations that opposed creation of the department.

New Opposition Stirred

A key strategy of the department's conservative opponents in the House was to offer conservatively oriented amendments on such matters as school busing. If these amendments were adopted by the full House, opponents reasoned that liberals might vote to kill the bill in order to kill the offending amendments.

The strategy worked — to a degree. The full House adopted amendments regarding school busing, school prayer, abortion and racial quotas in school admissions. These additions prompted the AFL-CIO to step up its lobbying effort against the department. The United Auto Workers (UAW), which formerly backed the measure, decided to remain neutral. The American Civil Liberties

Lobbying Blitz Blocks Transfer of Head Start Program

Some of the nation's poorest citizens blocked the shift of the Head Start program, which they considered uniquely their own, to the new Department of Education (DOE).

In one of the early skirmishes on President Carter's proposal for the department, an intense grass-roots campaign mobilized parents of children in the preschool program into a successful campaign to keep Head Start in the Department of Health, Education and Welfare (HEW), which lost most of its other education functions to DOE. (HEW was renamed the Department of Health and Human Services.)

Senate Governmental Affairs Committee Chairman Abraham Ribicoff, D-Conn., conceding "overwhelming opposition" to the move, agreed during a July 1977 markup of the DOE bill to delete Head Start and leave it in HEW.

Established in 1965 by the Office of Economic Opportunity (OEO) to help prepare children from low-income families to enter school, Project Head Start quickly became one of the most popular programs in President Lyndon B. Johnson's "war on poverty." It was given statutory authorization in 1966 (PL 89-794) and was expanded frequently, offering a wide variety of health and social services in addition to "pre-learning" experiences. Head Start has served more than 6 million children over the years.

President Nixon "delegated" the program to HEW in 1969 and it was officially transferred to that department in 1974 when OEO was dismantled. It was placed in HEW's Office of Child Development rather than in the Office of Education.

The special character of Head Start helped it to grow deep roots in poor and minority communities. Former Sen. Edward W. Brooke, R-Mass. (1967-79), observed that "this is one program which minorities have regarded more than any other as their own."

Head Start groups worried that control of the program by public educators would lead to the loss of its special characteristics. "They're paranoid about the educational establishment," remarked one Senate aide. Marian Wright Edelman, director of the Children's Defense Fund, told Ribicoff's committee that the education structure has "consistently resisted the kind of parental involvement and diversity that have been at the heart of the Head Start approach."

Backers of the transfer argued that the success of the Head Start groups in winning over the Governmental Affairs Committee disproved their contention that they were no match for the powerful education lobbies.

"They've got one of the most effective and articulate lobbies in the country," said Harrison Wellford, director of the Carter administration reorganization project.

Union and the Children's Defense Fund, which opposed the amendments, said they would work against the bill.

The amendments also drew the opposition of many members of the Congressional Black Caucus. The caucus decided not to formally oppose the bill but members threatened to vote against the legislation if it returned from conference with the amendments intact. House conferees agreed to compromise language on busing and racial quotas and dropped the amendments on prayer and abortion. This dissipated much of the liberal opposition to the bill in the House and the legislation won final approval with relative ease. ∎

Farmers Lobby for Higher Crop Prices

On tractors festooned with flags and slogans such as "Tractors Run on Gas, Not Red Ink," the American Agriculture Movement (AAM) crawled into Washington one winter morning with a legislative goal that most congressional observers predicted had virtually no chance of passage.

The militant farmers succeeded spectacularly in getting everybody's attention. An estimated 2,000 tractors and trucks blocked traffic and snarled commuter traffic on Feb. 5, 1979. Police efforts to unsnarl the tie-up led to sporadic violence that resulted in about 20 arrests.

The farmers also got attention on Capitol Hill, where they began a round of rallies and meetings with legislators to promote their goal: setting the loan rate for commodities like wheat and corn at 90 percent of parity.

But there was only a modest rush to champion the AAM proposal, which many believed was both inflationary and unnecessary.

Joint resolutions that would require Agriculture Secretary Bob Bergland to boost commodity loan rates to 90 percent of parity were introduced in the House by Richard Nolan, D-Minn., and Keith G. Sebelius, R-Kan. (H J Res 144, 148), and in the Senate (S J Res 20) by Edward Zorinsky, D-Neb. Even though the bills attracted a number of co-sponsors in both the House and Senate, the supporters admitted that chances of passage were slim.

Parity is an index relating prices and costs of production using the relatively prosperous period from 1910 to 1914 as a base. Since government loan rates serve to set a floor for farm prices, the effect of the AAM proposal would be to raise the minimum price for wheat to over $5 a bushel, from $2.35, while the minimum for corn would jump to $3.50, from $2.

In 1979, wheat was selling for $3.02 a bushel, while corn was selling for $2.10.

Administration Opposition

While the farmers won a few supporters in the House and Senate, the administration was unpersuaded.

Bergland withstood both a snowstorm and a hearing room packed with about 300 AAM members when he reported on the state of American agriculture to the House Agriculture Committee Feb. 7.

Seemingly unaffected by the outbursts of booing and applause that punctuated his testimony and committee members' questions and statements, Bergland took a hard line against any increase in loan rates in 1979, and repeated the generally upbeat report he had given the Senate Agriculture Committee Jan. 24.

Though "keeping in mind that 1977 was for many farmers a total disaster," he said 1978 was "substantially better" and that "most farms shared in the improved prosperity."

Farm prices at the end of January were 25 percent above a year earlier, and net farm income had increased an estimated $8 billion, to $28.1 billion.

The few paragraphs that differed from his Senate statement conceded that there were exceptions to the generally improved picture.

"It is true, of course," Bergland said, "that we measure the economic status of the farm community in comprehensive statistics — totals, averages, year-to-year comparisons, for example — and it should go without saying that despite general and widespread economic progress in agriculture, there remained individual farm operators in every region of the country who did not fare well in 1978."

The AAM contended that national figures were misleading and failed to show the plight of the "average farmer," who they said was often deeply in debt and struggling to meet higher production costs.

A few AAM members could not resist letting Bergland know how they felt about his comments the day before on national television that some of the protesters had made bad business judgments or paid too much for land and that others were "driven by old-fashioned greed."

When Nolan said he thought the secretary owed the farmers an apology, the audience applauded loudly and there was a yell from the rear: "Have him stand up and do it now."

Committee Chairman Thomas S. Foley, D-Wash., gaveled the crowd to order.

Bergland didn't back down. He said he knew neighbors who had paid too much for land, others who had bought farm machinery they couldn't afford and didn't need, and "of course, there's a little greed in all of us."

Responding to a statement from Sebelius, Bergland admitted there were some serious local problems in areas like western Kansas and eastern Colorado. Rising costs had been a particularly acute problem for farmers using irrigation in those areas, he said, and the department planned to hold hearings to see what it could do to help.

Impact of Higher Loan Rates

Administration objections to the AAM proposal to raise farm loan rates centered on three factors: the inflationary impact on consumer prices, the increase in production costs for livestock, and reductions in agricultural exports.

A 1978 Agriculture Department analysis said retail food prices would jump about 20 percent in the first year if farm prices were set at 100 percent of parity. Department analysts said the inflationary impact would be about the same with prices set at 90 percent of parity.

A second concern was the effect on livestock producers, who would be seriously affected by the jump in feed grain prices. "The sharp rise in production costs for livestock would put [herd] expansion plans on the shelf," Agriculture Department planning and budget director Howard Hjort said in an interview. "Both sooner and later you would have food price inflation."

"On the international side, U.S. prices would be well above world prices, and every buyer would look for alternatives before coming to us," Hjort added. "Consuming nations would minimize their imports, and producing nations would maximize their exports."

Background

AAM farmers first arrived in Washington in December 1977. Their goal then was a major new farm bill with prices raised to 100 percent of parity. To the surprise of many, the Senate passed a modified version of the proposal, but the conference report was defeated by the House, which historically has tended to be tougher than the Senate on generous farm price legislation.

AAM stayed on, however, and won enactment of a scaled-down "emergency farm bill" that gave the Agriculture secretary the discretion to raise target prices for wheat, feed grains or cotton whenever a set-aside (voluntary land diversion program) was established for those crops. AAM pressure was also instrumental in winning enactment of a farm credit revision bill that included a new $4 billion "economic emergency" loan program.

Improved Situation

Observers noted that there were important differences between the difficulties that provoked the rise of the AAM movement in late 1977 and the situation existing in 1979.

"There's a world of difference between a year ago and now," said Hjort. Then prices were reaching a low point, there had been a severe drought in the South, and the provisions of the 1977 farm bill hadn't yet had an effect on the problems.

Market prices have improved significantly since then, according to Hjort. Wheat has risen from $2.03 a bushel in August 1977 to $3.02; beef prices have risen 60 percent, and corn prices have held steady despite huge increases in yield that have tended to moderate net production costs.

The provisions of the 1977 farm bill also have begun to improve farm income, Hjort noted. Participation in a set-aside program helped cut overall production, while participation in the new farmer-held reserve program helped keep grain prices up.

Production expenses rose 9 percent in 1978, however, and the increases were felt particularly hard in certain regions of the country. One such region was the Southwest, where many farmers drilled wells and installed irrigation equipment in the 1973-74 period, when prices were high and the outlook for continued strong demand appeared good.

"When they were first installed, the water table was high and gas was cheap," Hjort said. "But since then costs have risen as the water table has sunk and the price of gas has gone up." The result, he said, was that corn growers in the Southwest had production costs that were about $1 a bushel higher than those that farmers in the "corn belt" had to pay.

John Bailey, an aide to Sebelius, told a similar story about farmers in western Kansas. Rainfall there is meager (14-16 inches a year), irrigation equipment costs $60,000 to $100,000 and is increasingly expensive to operate, and as a result many farmers are in a "real bind," Bailey said.

Outlook for Legislation

Although many members of Congress expressed sympathy for the financial problems of the AAM demonstrators, there was no apparent rush to try to legislate a solution. Even backers of the resolutions indicated they felt there wasn't much support for new farm aid in 1979.

Sebelius said he thought the chances of the 90 percent parity resolution being passed by the House were "frankly, very, very, very slim."

Bergland's adamant response to the committee plus the fact that it was not an election year did not bode well for the measure, he said. And unlike 1978, Sebelius said it was his impression that the basic reaction of House members to the farmers was "quite negative."

Paul Findley, R-Ill., also said he thought the bill's chances were "about as close to zero as any farm bill gets. But then, last year [in 1978] I really didn't think we would react to the farmer's movement with a farm bill, yet we did."

Findley cited the anti-inflation, anti-spending mood of the country and an "urban-oriented Congress" as important factors working against legislation.

Another factor was that other farm organizations did not necessarily support the AAM's effort. American Farm Bureau Federation president Allen Grant said 90 percent of parity was a reasonable goal but "it ought to be a market goal, not a legislative goal."

Grant said the best way to raise prices was to increase farm exports, which reached a record $27.3 billion in 1978.

Farm Bureau opposition to the AAM proposal in 1978 was credited with helping to kill that bill.

The 1979 AAM proposal was promised a hearing, however. Foley announced Feb. 7 that the committee would hold five days of public hearings beginning Feb. 13 for a general review of government farm programs, with two days of testimony reserved for AAM members. ∎

American Agriculture Movement Tractors Block Washington, D.C., Street in Demonstration for Higher Farm Prices.

OCS Bill: Effective Lobbying on Both Sides

The red capital letters in the full-page newspaper advertisement were two inches high: "If dependence on foreign oil is what you want, HR 1614 will get it for you."

The National Ocean Industries Association (NOIA) wanted to be sure the House knew that NOIA's 345 members opposed pending Outer Continental Shelf (OCS) legislation, even if it cost them more than $11,000.

"Propaganda," bill supporter Rep. Gerry E. Studds, D-Mass., called the various ads. "Red herrings," he labeled their claims that the bill would lead to an imaginery outfit dubbed FOGCO, a federally operated oil and gas company.

To a House aide trying to garner support for the very complicated bill, the ads were one more headache. "You've got full-page ads, with screaming headlines, saying, 'We're industry, we know this bill is going to be an unmitigated disaster,'" said the aide. "It's got to have an effect. How do you counter that sort of rhetoric?"

The members of the House Ad Hoc Select Committee on the Outer Continental Shelf eventually countered it by agreeing to take out offending sections on dual leasing and federal exploratory drilling. This defensive effort by the bill's supporters was evidence that their opponents were having some effect.

"It was a full-court press," said James Flug of Energy Action, a consumer and environmental organization, when asked about the oil and gas industry efforts against the committee bill.

But despite the industry's effort, Congress in August 1978 cleared and sent to the president legislation (S 9 — PL 95-372) providing the first overhaul of offshore oil and gas leasing laws in 25 years.

Background

The long-sought changes were given final approval by the House Aug. 17 on a 338-18 vote, and by the Senate Aug. 22, on an 82-7 vote.

The bill was designed to foster competition for leases and increase state participation in federal leasing decisions. Restrictions on drilling and production were tightened to protect the environment.

Congress had been struggling for almost four years to reach agreement on the controversial legislation, which had been bitterly opposed by the oil industry. However, the final compromise was generally accepted by most major oil companies, environmentalists and the Carter administration.

The congressional action came within days of the first commercial discovery of oil and gas deposits off the Atlantic coast. Texaco Inc. announced Aug. 14 it had struck gas about 100 miles from Atlantic City, N. J.

It was this coming expansion of offshore drilling to the Atlantic from the Gulf of Mexico that prompted the push for reform of the Outer Continental Shelf Lands Act of 1953.

The East Coast states, protective of their resort and fishing industries, sought, and won in the new law, more control over potentially harmful offshore activities.

Enactment of the new rules governing OCS exploration was expected to spur development on the Atlantic shelf, which was an extension of the continent that stretches up to 200 miles from the shore. In particular, leasing of tracts off the coast of New England, in an area known as Georges Bank, was likely to go forward. The state of Massachusetts and a conservation group had held up scheduled 1978 leasing with successful court suits, arguing that the new law should be in place before additional drilling was allowed.

The U.S. Geological Survey had estimated that potential recoverable resources of from 10 to 49 billion barrels of crude oil and from 42 to 81 trillion cubic feet of natural gas were located on the OCS of the United States.

OCS lands began three miles from the shoreline, where state jurisdiction ended. The federally held lands had been under the jurisdiction of the Department of the Interior. However, some authority for offshore energy development was transferred by the new law to the Department of Energy. The Energy secretary was to write many of the rules the Interior secretary would have to follow in administering the law.

Industry Letter Writing Campaign

In addition to the dramatic, full-page newspaper ads, individual companies and associations that represented them used some fairly sophisticated techniques to generate interest in the bill in districts far removed from the coast.

For example, Exxon Corporation, which refused to support even a watered-down substitute proposal endorsed by most companies, sent letters to each of its stockholders explaining its opposition to the House committee bill and suggesting that letters be written to Congress. Many responded.

NOIA, with a membership that included producing companies, diving contractors, caterers, makers of drilling rigs and other support services for OCS activity, tried to capitalize on its diversity with the same sort of "grass-roots" lobbying.

"This bill is so complicated," said Charlie Matthews, NOIA president. "The average member of Congress...who's not associated with the coast, not associated with this issue, well, he has so many demands, he can't know the details. I have tried to get my [member] companies to write and say, 'I'm in Oshkosh and I manufacture widgets that they use in Houston on drilling rigs. I oppose this bill.'"

Matthews also coordinated the placement of ads in a Washington newspaper by other groups, such as the Association of Diving Contractors, which also belonged to NOIA. The divers wanted to keep the Occupational Safety and Health Administration from getting jurisdiction over OCS activity, and they succeeded.

United Business Community

When the South Carolina banking community started calling Rep. John W. Jenrette Jr., D-S.C., about the House version of the bill, he was a little confused about why they should be interested.

"I started asking questions about dual leasing and revenue sharing, and the guy finally had to admit he was returning a favor for a fellow in Texas," said Jenrette, who voted against the position of the banking community and oil and gas interests.

"They're trying to work some trades" with votes on other bills, such as labor law, said another southern Democrat who had been contacted by local members of a national business community that was apparently united against the OCS bill.

Various segments of the energy industry already had been working together on the energy legislation before Congress. "There's a real need to be together," said Talbott Smith, associate manager of the resources and environment division of the Chamber of Commerce of the United States.

The old coalition of Republicans and southern Democrats, boosted by the solidarity of the Louisiana and Texas delegations, was operating on the OCS issue.

One of the reasons the coalition hung together on most votes was Rep. John B. Breaux, D-La. "When the issue is this complex, many members take their cues from the neighboring delegation," explained one committee aide.

"Breaux has been very effective," admitted a Carter administration lobbyist.

Administration Efforts

With the rash of votes on amendments and substitutes, both sides could claim some victories, and the administra-

tion was credited with the initial defeat of the weaker substitute bill offered by Breaux, as well as with getting the bill through the reluctant House Rules Committee.

"They made the difference," said a House aide, and Breaux agreed.

In 1976, when the conference report on similar OCS legislation was recommitted in the waning days of the 94th Congress, the Ford administration had been working hard against passage.

The Carter administration came through quickly with separate letters from Energy Secretary James R. Schlesinger and Interior Secretary Cecil D. Andrus renewing their endorsement of the committee bill after Republicans on the House floor raised the specter of a divided administration.

Deputy Under Secretary of Interior Barbara Heller, who formerly lobbied for the Environmental Policy Center on the same issue, spent hours nursing the legislation through the House. Liaison staff from Interior and Energy, operating out of a room near the House chamber, kept a close watch on the bill's progress.

The major criticism of the administration effort was the arrival on the Hill just before Rules action of some 50 primarily technical amendments that the administration wanted in the bill.

Members of the Rules Committee who sought to delay floor action seized on the amendments as another reason for postponing debate. ∎

Selected Bibliography on Lobbying

Books

Backrack, Stanley. *The Committee of One Million: The China Lobby and U.S. Policy, 1953-1971.* New York: Columbia Univeristy Press, 1976.

Bauer, Raymond A. et al. *American Business and Public Policy: The Politics of Foreign Trade.* Chicago: Aldine, 1972.

Berry, Jeffrey M. *Lobbying for the People: The Political Behavior of Public Interest Groups.* New Jersey: Princeton University Press, 1977.

Crawford, Kenneth G. *The Pressure Boys: The Inside Story of Lobbying in America.* New York: Arno Press, 1974.

Deakin, James. *The Lobbyists.* Washington, D.C.: Public Affairs Press, 1966.

Eastman, Hope. *Lobbying: A Constitutionally Protected Right.* Washington, D.C.: American Enterprise Institute for Public Policy Research, 1977.

Foster, James C. *The Union Politics: The CIO Political Action Committee.* St. Louis: University of Missouri Press, 1975.

Goulden, Joseph C. *The Super-Lawyers: The Small and Powerful World of Great Washington Law Firms.* New York: Weybright and Talley, 1972.

Green, Mark J. *The Other Government: The Unseen Power of Washington Lawyers.* New York: Norton, 1978.

Greenstone, J. David. *Labor in American Politics.* Chicago: University of Chicago Press, 1977.

Greenwald, Carol S. *Group Power: Lobbying and Public Policy.* New York: Praeger, 1977.

Grupenhoff, John T. and Murphy, James J. *Nonprofits' Handbook on Lobbying: The History and Impact of the New 1976 Lobbying Regulations on the Activities of Non-Profit Organizations.* Washington, D.C.: Taft Corporation, 1977.

Hall, Donald R. *Cooperative Lobbying: The Power of Pressure.* Tucson: University of Arizona Press, 1969.

Howe, Russell W. and Trott, Sarah H. *The Power Peddlers: How Lobbyists Mold America's Foreign Policy.* Garden City, N.Y.: Doubleday, 1977.

Isaacs, Stephen D. *Jews and American Politics.* Garden City, Doubleday, 1974.

Key, V. O. *Politics, Parties and Pressure Groups.* New York: Thomas Crowell, 1964.

Koen, Ross Y. *The China Lobby in American Politics.* New York: Harper & Row, 1974.

Lipsen, Charles B. and Lesher, Stefan. *Vested Interest.* Garden City, N.Y.: Doubleday, 1977.

McFarland, Andrew S. *Public Interest Lobbies: Decision-Making on Energy.* Washington, D.C.: American Enterprise Institute for Public Policy Research, 1976.

Mahood, H. R. *Pressure Groups in American Politics.* New York: Charles Scribner, 1967.

Mahood, H. R. and Maleck, E. S. *Group Politics.* New York: Charles Scribner, 1972.

Mazmanian, Daniel A. and Nienaber, Jeanne. *Can Organizations Change? Environmental Protection, Citizen Participation and the Corps of Engineers.* Washington, D.C.: Brookings Institution, 1979.

Milbrath, Lester W. *The Washington Lobbyists.* Chicago: Rand McNally, 1963.

Murphy, Thomas P. *Pressures Upon Congress: Legislation by Lobby.* Woodbury, N.Y.: Barrons Educational Series, 1973.

Oppenheimer, Bruce I. *Oil and the Congressional Process.* Lexington, Mass.: Lexington Books, 1974.

Ornstein, Norman J. and Elder, Shirley. *Interest Groups, Lobbying and Policymaking.* Washington, D.C.: Congressional Quarterly Press, 1978.

Platt, Alan and Weiler, Lawrence D. *Congress and Arms Control.* Boulder, Colo.: Westview Press, 1978.

Pratt, Henry J. *The Gray Lobby.* Chicago: University of Chicago Press, 1976.

Schriftgiesser, Karl. *The Lobbyists: The Art and Business of Influencing Lawmakers.* New York: Little, Brown, 1951.

Vogel, David. *Lobbying the Corporation: Citizen Challenges to Business Authority.* New York: Basic Books, 1978.

Trice, Robert H. *Interest Groups and the Foreign Policy Process: U.S. Policy in the Middle East.* Beverly Hills, Calif.: Sage Publications, 1977.

Wilson, James Q. *Political Organizations.* New York: Basic Books, 1973.

Truman, David B. *The Governmental Process.* New York: Alfred A. Knopf, 1964.

Ziegler, L. Harmon and Peak, Wayne G. *Interest Groups in American Politics.* 2nd ed. Englewood Cliffs, N.J.: Prentice-Hall, 1972.

Articles

Asbell, B. "Outlawing Next Year's Cars: Defeat of the 1976 Clean Air Act." *New York Times Magazine,* November 21, 1976, pp. 41, 43.

Baldwin, Frank. "The Korea Lobby." *Christianity and Crisis,* July 19, 1976, pp. 162-168.

Balz, Daniel J. "Attorneys Perform Dual Role as Lobbyists, Policy Makers." *National Journal,* October 4, 1975, pp. 1379-1386.

Barbash, Jack. "The Politics of American Labor." *Challenge,* May/June 1976, pp. 30-35.

Baron, A. "Jewish Clout." *Politics Today,* July 1978, pp. 8-9.

Branagan, Jacquelyn. "Nondegradation and the Clean Air Act Amendments of 1977." *Urban Law Annual,* 1977. pp. 203-232.

"Business Lobbying: Threat to the Consumer Interest." *Consumer Report,* September 1978, pp. 526-531.

"Business' Most Powerful Lobby in Washington: Business Roundtable." *Business Week,* December 20, 1976, pp. 60-63.

Cameron, Juan. "Small Business Trips Big Labor: Grass-Roots Organizations by the Hundreds Were Organized to Stop George Meany's Favorite Bill." *Fortune,* July 31, 1978, pp. 80-82.

Chapman, S. "Welfare Tractors: Farmers' Subsidies and Protest in Washington, D.C." *The New Republic,* March 3, 1979, pp. 16-19.

Cohen, Richard E. "New Lobbying Rules May Influence Grass-Roots Political Action." *National Journal,* May 27, 1978, pp. 832-836.

DeWitt, Karen. "Lobbying: Key to Lasting Political Influence." *Black Enterprise,* September 1976, pp. 43-45.

Ehrbar, A. F. "Backlash Against Business Advocacy." *Fortune,* August 28, 1978, pp. 62-64.

Elder, Shirley. "The Cabinet's Ambassadors to Capitol Hill," *National Journal,* June 29, 1978, pp. 1196-1200.

Evans, B. "Lobbying: A Question of Resources." *Sierra,* October 1978, pp. 54-55.

Fisher, John M. "The Disarmament Lobby." *American Legion Magazine,* November 1978, pp. 6-7.

"For Trade Organizations: Politics is the New Focus." *Business Week,* April 17, 1978, pp. 107-115.

Freitag, Peter J. "The Cabinet and Big Business: A Study of Interlocks." *Social Problems,* December 1975, pp. 137-152.

Friedman, Mel. "A New Communications Act: The Debate Begins." *Columbia Journalism Review,* September/October 1978, pp. 40-43.

Gall, Peter and Hoerr, John. "The Growing Schism Between Business and Labor." *Business Week,* August 14, 1978, pp. 78-80.

Golden, L. L. L. "Dangerous Rush to Political Action: Corporate Political Action Committees." *Business Week,* September 25, 1978, p. 14.

Guzzardi, Walter. "Business is Learning How to Win in Washington." *Fortune,* March 27, 1978, pp. 52-58.

"How the Weapons Lobby Works in Washington." *Business Week,* February 12, 1979, pp. 128, 130, 135.

Hudson, Richard. "Storm Over the Canal." *New York Times Magazine,* May 16, 1976, pp. 18-26.

Hunt, Albert R. "The Persuaders: How Rival Lobbyists Battled to Win Vote on Gas Deregulation." *Wall Street Journal,* July 15, 1977, p. 1.

Ignatius, D. "Stages of Nader: Public Citizen Congress Watch." *New York Times Magazine,* January 18, 1976, pp. 8-9.

Krebs, Frederick J. "Grassroots Lobbying Defined: The Scope of IRC Section 162(e)(2)(B)." *Taxes,* September 1978, pp. 16-20.

Lanouette, William J. "The Battle to Shape and Sell the New Arms Control Treaty: Supporter and Opponents of SALT II." *National Journal,* December 31, 1977, pp. 1984-1993.

Lanouette, William J. "The Many Faces of the Jewish Lobby in America." *National Journal,* May 13, 1978, pp. 748-752.

Levitt, Theodore. "Corporate Responsibility: Taking Care of Business." *American Spectator,* November 1977, pp. 21-25.

Lewin, T. "Navigating the Loopholes: The Invisible Lobbyists." *The Nation,* June 10, 1978, pp. 659-698.

McGovern, George. "Pluralist Structures or Interest Groups?" *Society,* January 1977, pp. 13-15.

Maize, Kennedy P. "Broadcasting's Deregulated Future." *Editorial Research Reports,* March 9, 1979, pp. 167-184.

Marshall, E. "New Feudalism: Economic Lobbies." *The New Republic,* January 20, 1979, pp. 13-14.

Meier, Kenneth J. and Van Lohuizen, J. R. "Bureaus, Clients, and Congress: The Impact of Interest Group Support on Budgeting." *Administration and Society,* February 1978, pp. 447-466.

Montgomery, Alan L. "Lobbying by Public Charities Under the Tax Reform Act of 1976: The New Elective Provisions of Section 501(h), Safe Harbor or Trap for the Unwary?" *Taxes,* August 1978, pp. 449-461.

Nord, David P. "The FCC, Educational Broadcasting, and Political Interest Group Activity." *Journal of Broadcasting,* Summer 1978, pp. 321-338.

North, James. "The Politics of Selfishness: The Effect, the Growth of Special Interests." *Washington Monthly,* October 1978, pp. 32-36.

O'Keefe, Brian T. "Corporate Tax Operation and Legislative Activity." *Tax Executive,* October 1977, pp. 49-57.

Osbourne, D. K. "Natural Gas: The Case for Deregulation." *Federal Reserve Dallas,* October 1977, pp. 4-12.

Peters, B. Guy. "Insiders and Outsiders: The Politics of Pressure Group Influence on Bureaucracy." *Administration and Society,* August 1977, pp. 191-218.

Prior, James T. "PACs: The Quiet Revolution." *National Journal of Business,* June 1976, pp. 14-17.

Quinn, Tony. "Political Action Committees: The New Campaign Bankrollers." *California Journal,* March 1979, pp. 96-98.

Riedel, James A. "Citizen Participation: Myths and Realities." *Public Administration Review,* May/June 1972, pp. 211-220.

Rieselbach, Leroy N. "The Lobbyist and Congress." *Congressional Politics,* pp. 194, 213. New York: McGraw-Hill, 1973.

Schneyer, Theodore J. "An Overview of Public Interest Law Activity in the Communications Field." *Wisconsin Law Review,* No. 3, 1977, pp. 619-683.

Singer, James W. "Labor and Business Heat Up the Senate Labor Law Reform Battle." *National Journal,* June 3, 1978, pp. 884-885.

Stratton, Debra. "Battle Looms Over Lobbying Reform." *Association Management,* October 1977, pp. 44-47.

"Sugar's Anguished Plea for More Federal Aid." *Business Week,* August 8, 1977, pp. 60-61.

Wall, J. M. "SALT and Special-Interest Politics." *Christian Century,* July 4, 1979, pp. 691-692.

Walsh, J. "Lobbying Rules for Nonprofits: New Option Sets Specific Limits." *Science,* April 1, 1977, pp. 40-41.

Wertheimer, Fred. "Has Congress Made it Legal to Buy Congressmen?" *Business and Society Review,* Fall 1978, pp. 29-32.

Wise, S. "Regulating Lobbies: Easier Said Than Done." *USA Today,* July 1978, pp. 10-12.

Wirth, Timothy E. "Congressional Policy Making and the Politics of Energy." *Journal of Energy and Development,* Autumn 1975, pp. 93-104.

Witt, M. "Coalesce Is More: Coalitions Between Labor and Other Interest Groups." *The New Republic,* April 14, 1979, pp. 12-15.

Documents

Mulhollan, Daniel P. *Overview of Lobbying by Organizations.* Prepared for the Commission on the Operation of the Senate. 95th Cong., 1st sess. Washington, D.C.: Library of Congress, Congressional Research Service, 1977.

U.S. Congress. House Committee on Agriculture. *Sugar Stabilization Act of 1978: Hearings, May 23-25, 31; June 1, 1978.* 95th Cong., 2nd sess. Washington, D.C.: Government Printing Office, 1978.

_____. House Committee on Government Operations. Subcommittee on Commerce, Consumer, and Monetary Affairs. *IRS Administration of Tax Laws Relating to Lobbying: Hearings May 22, 23, 25; July 18, 1978, part I.* 95th Cong., 2nd sess. Washington, D.C.: Government Printing Office, 1978.

_____. House Committee on Government Operations. Subcommittee on Commerce, Consumer, and Monetary Affairs. *IRS Administration of Tax Laws Relating to Lobbying: Hearings July 20, 21, 1978, part 2.* 95th Cong., 2nd sess. Washington, D.C.: Government Printing Office, 1978.

_____. House Committee on International Relations. Subcommittee on International Organizations. *Activities of the Korean Central Intelligence Agency in the United States: Hearings, March 17-September 30, 1976, parts 1-2.* 94th Cong., 2nd sess. Washington, D.C.: Government Printing Office, 1976.

_____. House Committee on International Relations. Subcommittee on International Organizations. *Investigation of Korean-American Relations: Hearings, June 22, 1977—June 20, 1978, 5 pts.* 95th Cong., 2nd sess. Washington, D.C.: Government Printing Office, 1978.

_____. House Committee on International Relations. Subcommittee on International Organizations. *Investigation of Korean-American Relations; Report, October 31, 1978.* 95th Cong., 2nd sess. Washington, D.C.: Government Printing Office, 1978.

_____. House Committee on Standards of Official Conduct. *Korean Influence Investigation: Hearings, October 19-21, 1977; April 11, 1978, Pursuant to H. Res. 252.* 2 vols. 95th Cong., 1st and 2nd sess. Washington, D.C.: Government Printing Office, 1978.

_____. House Committee on Standards of Official Conduct. *Lobbying: Efforts to Influence Governmnental Action: Hearings, December 2-4, 1975 on H.R. 15 and Related Bills.* 94th Cong., 1st sess. Washington, D.C.: Government Printing Office, 1976.

_____. House Committee on Standards of Official Conduct. *Report of the Committee on Standards of Official Conduct.* H. Rept. 95-21. 95th Cong., 1st sess. Washington, D.C.: Government Printing Office, 1977.

_____. House Committee on the Judiciary. Subcommittee on Administrative Law and Governmental Relations. *Lobbying and Related Activities: Hearings, April 4, 6, 21, 29, 1977.* 95th Cong., 1st sess. Washington, D.C.: Government Printing Office, 1977.

_____. House Committee on the Judiciary. Subcommittee on Administrative Law and Governmental Relations. *Public Disclosure of Lobbying Act: Hearings, September 11-23, 1975, on H.R. 15.* 94th Cong., 1st sess. Washington, D.C.: Government Printing Office, 1975.

_____. House Committee on Ways and Means. *Influencing Legislation by Public Charities: Hearings, May 12, 1976 on H.R. 13500.* 94th Cong., 2nd sess. Washington, D.C.: Government Printing Office, 1976.

_____. Joint Committee on Internal Revenue Taxation. *Summary of Issues: H.R. 13500, "Lobbying" by Charities.* Committee

Print, May 18, 1976. 94th Cong., 2nd sess. Washington, D.C.: Government Printing Office, 1976.

———. Senate Committee on Finance. Subcommittee on Tourism and Sugar. *Staff Data and Materials Relating to the International Sugar Stabilization Act of 1979.* 96th Cong., 1st sess. Washington, D.C.: Government Printing Office, 1979.

———. Senate Committee on Foreign Relations. *Senate Debate on the Panama Canal Treaties: A Compendium of Major Statements, Documents, and Record Votes and Relevant Events.* Prepared by the Congressional Research Service, Library of Congress, 96th Cong., 1st sess. Washington, D.C.: Government Printing Office, 1979.

———. Senate Committee on Governmental Affairs. *Lobbying Reform Act of 1977: Hearings August 2, 1977; February 6, 7, 1978.* 95th Cong., 1st sess. Washington, D.C.: Government Printing Office, 1978.

———. Senate Committee on the Judiciary. Subcommittee on Antitrust and Monopoly. *Public Impact of Natural Gas Price Deregulation: Hearings, October 3, 1977 on S. 2104.* 95th Cong., 1st sess. Washington, D.C.: Government Printing Office, 1977.

———. Senate Committee on the Judiciary. Subcommittee on Separation of Powers. *Panama Canal Treaty: Hearings, July 22, 1977—March 11, 1978, pts. 1-4.* Washington, D.C.: Government Printing Office, 1978.

———. Senate Select Committee on Ethics. *Korean Influence Inquiry: Interim Status Report as of May 22, 1978.* 95th Cong., 2nd sess. Washington, D.C.: Government Printing Office, 1978.

Index

The Washington Lobby

THIRD EDITION